THE
INSIDERS'®
GUIDE
TO
LOUISVILLE
AND SOUTHERN INDIANA

THE
INSIDERS'®
GUIDE
TO
LOUISVILLE
AND SOUTHERN INDIANA

James Nold, Jr.
and
Bob Bahr

Insiders' Publishing Inc.

Published and distributed by:
Insiders' Publishing Inc.
105 Budleigh St.
P.O. Box 2057
Manteo, NC 27954
(919) 473-6100
www.insiders.com

•

2ND EDITION
1st printing

•

Copyright ©1997
by Insiders' Publishing Inc.

•

Printed in the United States
of America

•

Publications from The Insiders' Guide®
series are available at special discounts
for bulk purchases for sales promotions,
premiums or fundraisings. Special
editions, including personalized covers,
can be created in large quantities for
special needs. For more information,
please write to Insiders' Publishing Inc.,
P.O. Box 2057, Manteo, NC 27954 or
call (919) 473-6100 x 233.

ISBN 1-57380-043-0

Insiders' Publishing Inc.

Publisher/Editor-in-Chief
Beth P. Storie

President/General Manager
Michael McOwen

Director of Advertising
Rosanne Cheeseman

Creative Services Director
Giles MacMillan

Sales and Marketing Director
Jennifer Risko

Director of New Product
Development
David Haynes

Managing Editor
Theresa Shea Chavez

Fulfillment Director
Gina Twiford

Regional Advertising Sales Manager
Nelson Outler

Local Advertising Sales Manager
Barry Warren

Project Editor
Amy Baynard

Project Artist
Carolyn Coon

Cover photos courtesy of
Dan Dry and Associates.

Preface

Louisville is not the showiest of places — Derby Week excepted — and as a result, it can seem rather opaque to an outsider.

If you drive down Bardstown Road, you might wonder why this narrow, wire-strung strip is anything other than something to hurry through. You have to get on the sidewalk, look at the menus in the windows, check out the hairdos and the babies and the fliers in the storefront windows, and then walk a block or so off the strip to realize that the city's hippest strip is smack in the middle of a neighborhood that looks like a park.

To get the proper flavor of Louisville, you have to travel a bit off the paths laid down by more official guides — eat fish sandwiches in the sprawling riverside confines of Mike Linnig's Place; watch a game of future and shoulda-been stars at Shawnee Park's Dirt Bowl basketball tournament; go down a Germantown alley after a Check's Cafe meal of rolled oysters and the world's most irrationally compelling burgers, only to discover a city dump's worth of colored plastic toys and Wisk bottles tacked onto Gus Ballard's backyard shed. You have to walk the neighborhoods, sit on the river bank, hit the church picnics. To use an ancient phrase — get with the people.

And to understand the town, you have to know that Louisville quietly walks away from stereotypes. The world knows us for the greatest of all horse races, but the percentage of the population that can talk knowledgeably about horses is about the same as voted enthusiastically for Bill Clinton. And even on Derby Day, the biggest sports story in town is likely to be something connected with basketball (as in 1997, when the state held its breath for Rick Pitino to decide between the University of Kentucky and the Boston Celtics).

It's a trickier place than it looks. That's why we took such great pleasure in putting together a second edition of the most comprehensive and pointed guide this city has ever known. (Sorry, WPA, but as Muhammad Ali, one of Louisville's native sons once said, It ain't bragging if you can back it up.)

We trust that we've given both visitors and newcomers to the community some sense of what we talk about when we talk about Louisville: our quaint native folkways (defense, Cardinals, defense!) and some of the signal achievements in Louisville history, along with a few of the dubious ones. We've tried to give you Louisville straight. We love the place, well enough we don't feel any need to gloss over its failings.

Anyway, Louisville's advantages far outweigh its faults. The excellence of its arts, from the highest to the lowest, is a byword. The parks, the restaurants, the architecture in the city's neighborhoods, the ease of getting around — these are the features of an eminently livable city. And what we like is that so much of what's best in Louisville is available to everyone (for example, that magnificent parks system).

We've been selective in what we've included, favoring the distinctive, characteristic and unique, although we haven't gotten snobby about it. A city where fried fish sandwiches are a native enthusiasm is not a place to be putting on airs.

But it *is* a place worth digging into with a healthy appetite.

About the Authors

James Nold Jr.

Early in his freelance career, James Nold, Jr., wrote an article on the Derby Festival Chow Wagon that a senior editor at *The Louisville Times* told him was the weirdest thing that ever appeared in one of the Bingham publications. He took that as a compliment and saw a life's mission in it.

In the succeeding years writing for the *Times*, *The Courier-Journal* and for *Louisville* magazine, Nold constructed a world tour using nothing but Kentuckiana business names, from the Kon-Tiki Apartments in Buechel to the Swedish Swish laundry in Jeffersonville, Indiana; had everything from a sheet cake to a pair of undershorts emblazoned with a silly picture of himself; and chronicled the steps that caused comic-book character Scrooge McDuck to make American landfall in Louisville. He has profiled noted Louisvillians from Tattoo Charlie Wheeler to Mayor Jerry Abramson. His more serious articles have looked at questions of Louisville identity, the state of civility in contemporary America and the tragic death of a Louisvillian in the Seattle music scene.

He has also written for *The Village Voice*, *The Atlanta Constitution*, *Saveur*, *Continental*, *Channels of Communication* and a number of state and local publications. He is restaurant writer for *Louisville* magazine and an adjunct lecturer in journalism at Indiana University Southeast. His video script for Donna Lawrence Productions, *African-Americans in Thoroughbred Racing*, shows daily in the Kentucky Derby Museum. He has won numerous Louisville Metro Journalism Awards for magazine writing and for his music and theater reviews in *The Courier-Journal*.

Nold is also the lead singer of Louisville's ground-breaking punk group, the Babylon Dance Band. *ArtForum* magazine called their 1994 Matador Records album *Four On One* one of the year's best records.

As a Louisville native, he knows that the answer to the question, "Where did you go to school?" is Waggener High School if he's talking to another Louisvillian, Princeton University (B.A., history) to the rest of the world. He and his wife, Cindy Read, live near Tyler Park with their sons, Max and Charley.

Bob Bahr

Writing a guide to Louisville was a natural for Bob Bahr, who is the first person his friends call when they need ideas for entertaining out-of-town guests. He'll enthusiastically recommend the city's best $20 entrée or 20¢ wing, its premier punk-rock haven or cocktail jazz hideaway or his pick in the fourth race at Churchill Downs.

A lifelong resident of the river city and an honors graduate of Bellarmine College, he has made a career out of celebrating in print Louisville's people, places and music. In seven years of freelance work, Bahr has written for Louisville's daily newspaper, *The Courier-Journal*, on diverse topics ranging from earplugs to Civil War re-enactments. *Hard Times*, the town's now defunct attitude-laden underground monthly, printed his stories on prescription drug abuse, FCC regulations and independent record stores. He is a regular contributor to *Louisville* magazine.

One great benefit of freelance writing, according to Bahr, is that it allows one to work next to a kitchen. Reach him at his home office and chances are good you'll hear something simmering, sautéeing or stir-frying in the background. This passion for food translates into culinary writing and restaurant reviews.

Food, the arts, movie reviews and personality profiles round out his work, but Bahr's forte is music coverage. He has written over a thousand articles on musicians from both the Louisville area and the national arena, and his critiques and commentaries on rock, pop, jazz, bluegrass, rap and funk have appeared on World Wide Web sites run by the San Francisco Bay Guardian and Turner Broadcasting. He has served as music editor and record reviews editor for a number of Louisville publications, and he acted as co-manager of a successful rock 'n' soul band, lovesauce & soulbones, for two years.

Bahr lives in the Belknap neighborhood, and readily interrupts his schedule to play basketball or watch the University of Kentucky Wildcats win yet another game.

Acknowledgments

Chip . . .

As I said in the first edition, my full list of thanks would probably begin with George Rogers Clark for his skill in city-siting and end somewhere with the young guys and gals who've kept the quality of Louisville music at a properly high level.

Everyone I thanked before deserves thanks again — this is an update, not a total revision. But since I don't want the thank-yous to extend to rap-album length, I'll just say, Thanks again, y'all, and refer scholars to the original book to see who I'm talking about.

For this edition, I'd mainly like to thank everyone who didn't hang up after I said, "Hi, this is Chip Nold. I'm a local writer and I'm updating a book called The Insider's Guide® to Greater Louisville and I wanted to check the information we listed about . . . ." But particular thanks for contributions to this edition go to Ken Neuhauser; Ronni Lundy; David Bell; Linda English; Randi Means; Dianne Holland; Fred Hines; Barbara Popp; John Peterson; Debbie Hassman; Tony Terry; Rob Kowalski; Frank Clay; Larry Rogers; and Susan Vessels.

On the professional front, Amy Baynard was both pleasant and rigorous, Beth Storie was as responsive as you'd want an editor-in-chief to be, and Bob Bahr not only wrote a set of distinguished chapters I'm glad to set mine next to, he also provided valuable insights for my own work.

As always, James Nold Sr. and Mary Ellen Nold gave helpful advice (and also had a great deal to do with forming my perceptions of Louisville in the first place — I'll leave it to them to decide whether that's credit or blame).

My work on this book is dedicated to my three favorite Louisvillians — Cindy Read and Max and Charley Nold.

Bob . . .

My work on this book could not have been completed without the gracious help and unfailing support of my co-author, Chip Nold. Thanks, Chip. I must also acknowledge the patience and good humor of Amy Baynard, the book's editor at Insiders' Publishing, Inc.

Just as important was the love and support I received from my parents, Charlotte Bahr and Louis A. Bahr Jr., and the inspiration and love given to me by Kelly Chinen. Thanks also to my friends Danny Kiely, Ray Rizzo, Bill Poynter and Jon Spalding — who listened to me cry and moan at various times; Fr. Clyde Crews — who unwittingly helped me much on the Worship chapter; Hannah Holler — who still hasn't seen the inside of Joe's Place; Kevin, Mark, Scott, Ai, Rick, Ardyle, Nick and Mike — for the essential weekly basketball games/ stress therapy; Dr. Gail Henson — my first and most important mentor; Jean Metcalfe — who started something by publishing a piece about a homegrown Kentucky opera; Ronni Lundy — who ceaselessly shows the enthusiasm good writing requires; and Jeffrey Lee Puckett — for the choice assignments.

Also, I thank Al Allen and Nancy Lacewell for help with the Retirement chapter and Jim Laval for sharing his knowledge of Louisville golf courses.

And to the makers of Surge soda — couldn'ta done it without you.

Table of Contents

Directory of Maps

Greater
Louisville

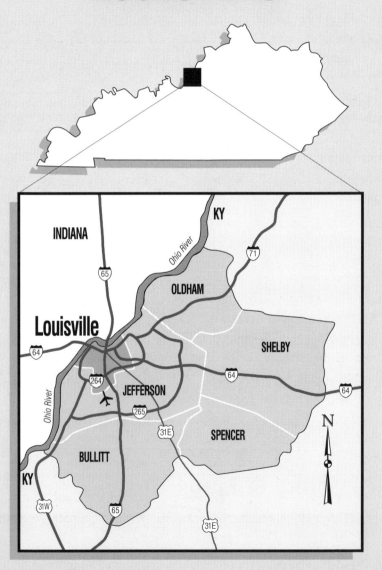

City of Louisville

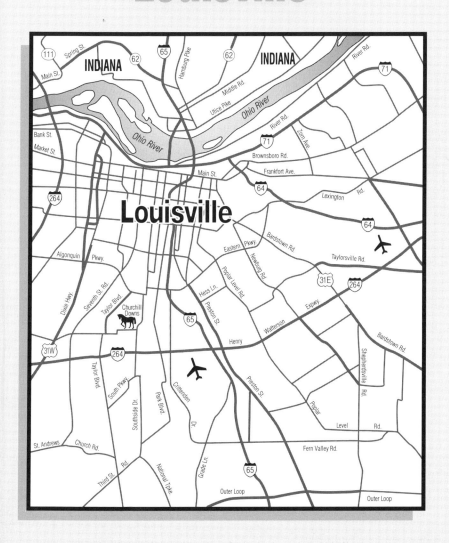

How to use this book

Somewhere in these pages is a paragraph about a place in Louisville that will absolutely captivate you.

We don't know where or what it is. You may find a Korean restaurant that serves the perfect buckwheat noodle dish. You may discover the perfect neighborhood for your family. You might decide that the line dancing at one particular nightclub is the absolute best this side of Nashville. Whatever it is, we're sure it's in here. Just read the book!

This guide is written both for linear reading — right through from preface to index — and for quick reference reading to discover where to go for tonight's supper. Our goal is to let the newcomer in on Louisville's secret treasures, while equitably pointing out the tried-and-true virtues of the town and presenting a wide spectrum of offerings to suit various tastes and predilections.

As in most cities, a visitor can get a horribly skewed idea of Louisville if the only area explored is what lies between the hotel and the restaurant where the evening meal is consumed. This book will enable a visitor to dig out some of the city's secrets even on the first visit, it will allow the newly relocated to grasp the breadth of recreational and housing opportunities of Louisville, and it will give the casual reader a feel for what it means to live life in this friendly city — a rather quirky place that isn't quite ready to trade in its small-town familiarity for full-fledged cosmopolitan glitter.

You'll notice that the book is structured so that the front chapters function as a visitors' guide, detailing attractions, nightlife and such, while the later chapters provide essential information for the person planning to move here. Information overlaps in some chapters, such as History, Worship and Attractions for interesting places to visit; or Shopping and The Arts for gifts; or Kidstuff and Parks and Recreation for things to do. We recommend that you read through the entire book, because you may find gold nuggets in chapters where you didn't expect them.

All phone numbers listed without an area code are local calls from Louisville (including Indiana numbers). If you're dialing from out of town, preface numbers with the 502 area code for Louisville numbers, 812 for Southern Indiana. Many Kentucky numbers inside the 502 area code are toll calls from here; if you see a 502 before a listing, it means you must dial the area code when dialing from Louisville.

There are no widely accepted geographic divisions for Louisville. In the heart of the city and to the west of downtown, residents describe where they live by naming their particular neighborhood, which is sometimes merely a nickname. That's certainly not good enough for newcomers to the area, and it actually won't fly with some of the cab drivers in this town. Most Louisvillians can steer you to the Portland, Smoketown or Old Louisville neighborhoods, and in the county, they would know St. Matthews, Crescent Hill, Fern Creek and Fairdale, but it doesn't go much further. In a more general sense, people speak of the East End, the South End, the West End and downtown. (A caveat: If you ask someone who lives near 42nd and Broadway where the East End is, he'll probably say something like "Clay and Broadway" — a mere four miles away and safely within the downtown area! To some city dwellers, if it isn't in the city, it doesn't matter.)

For this book, we've utilized these four general geographic areas that divide Jefferson County, and we've described places in terms of neighborhood only if the label is widely known and understood.

Neighborhoods are important, but Louisvillians are Louisvillians first and foremost. It's not discussed much, but there's a fair amount of pride in this town. A city-county merger proposal was voted down by the populace, but it was for economic reasons, not for stuffiness or provincialism. People LIKE to say they're from Louisville. For a concrete example, consider this: Although the Fern Creek area is a half-hour, 15-mile drive from downtown Louisville, few Creekers fail to put "Louisville, KY" on the return address of their mail, even though the postage cancellation will say "Fern Creek." They don't even think about it. All of Jefferson County effectively is Louisville, despite what the maps and markers say.

Three bridges span the half-mile or so of water that separates Kentucky from Indiana, Louisville from what our neighbors on the other side of the Ohio River call "the sunny side of Louisville." Hoosiers and Kentuckians freely partake of the amenities available on the opposite side of the bridges, but you will never catch a resident of Southern Indiana saying she's from Louisville. Never. The same is true of residents from Shelby, Oldham and Bullitt counties, and we include selected attractions from all these areas in this book. But our emphasis is on Jefferson County, its establishments and attributes, and the roughly one million people who live, work and play there.

Did we miss something? After you read all about Louisville, write to us with ideas, comments, praise or remedies at

The Insiders' Guide® to Louisville
P.O. Box 2057
Manteo, NC 27954
or visit us on the Internet at
www.insiders.com

This is our first update of this book. We'll be updating this guide again, and we welcome your thoughts on the book's coverage of our hometown.

In the meantime, this is what we like about where we live.

Louisville's a simple place, basically, but there's a lot you have to know to truly understand it.

Area Overview

Not long ago, the *Courier-Journal* wrote about a couple that had conducted an exhaustive search for a new place to live. They started with 150 possible locations, in all 50 states, and finally chose Louisville as their new home. The wife told the *Courier's* Bob Deitel, "Anybody who's never been to Louisville said 'Louisville?' But anybody who's been here, even passing through, said 'Oh, it's wonderful!'"

That's Louisville — to know us is to love us.

But the other point might be that you have to *come* to know us, because there aren't as many opportunities as there might be. We're a little modest, a little unsure of ourselves and less confident than we should be about our virtues.

The size of the city is essential to understanding its character. The city's finest corps of athletes, the University of Louisville's men's basketball team, is comprised primarily of what hoops junkies call "tweeners" — players who are big guards or small forwards, who fall roughly between 6-foot-3 and 6-foot-7.

Louisville is a tweener every bit as much as Dwayne Morton or the late Derek Smith. It's big enough to be a city, too small to be a major one. It's caught culturally between the North — the Midwest, really — and the South. It combines a forward-looking, hard-working spirit with a fundamental civic conservatism. It commands the world's attention one day a year — the first Saturday in May — and otherwise seems to stand outside the media stream, waiting to be noticed. It's a simple place, basically, but there's a lot you have to know to truly understand it.

Excellent!

One of Louisville's very real but intangible resources is that it has some real experience of excellence — most recently from Actors Theatre and the Cards, but also from Olympic gold medalists and heavyweight champions and for decades from *The Courier-Journal*, regularly listed as one of the country's best newspapers under the ownership of the Bingham family. Harping about the declining *Courier* has been a regular feature of Louisville life since Gannet bought the paper in 1986. But reading the newspaper in another community of Louisville's size brings home the fact that even in a diminished state, *The Courier-Journal* remains unusually literate and journalistically sound.

Louisville is one of the few cities its size to have a full complement of arts organizations: an orchestra (and a significant orchestra, too, in its recordings of works by modern American composers); the 12th-oldest opera company in the United States; a ballet; chamber music groups; a regular series of Broadway road shows; free summer Shakespeare. In Actors Theatre, Louisville has one of the best-known repertory groups in the country; 10 or more other companies stage everything from David Mamet to *The Three Little Pigs*. (See our chapter on The Arts.)

But the real excellence in Louisville takes place on the everyday level. By some lifestyle measurements, it ranks among the nation's most desirable cities: *The Places Rated Almanac* has ranked the city among the country's 10 best places to live three times running. ("Louisville forever!" inscribed a Rand-McNally researcher in a copy on the shelves at the Louisville Free Public Library.) We do less well in the *Money* magazine poll, which uses reader-selected criteria such as proximity to ski resorts.

The housing stock is exceptional — architects from New York exclaim over the quality of buildings for all economic classes and in all parts of the city — and also well-preserved and inexpensive. And new construction adheres to a high level of craftsmanship. Few cities have as much park space for their citizens, and even fewer have such a magnificent parks system, designed by the great landscape architect Frederick Law Olmsted. (See our chapter on Parks and Recreation.)

The cost of living is relatively low, especially for housing. The city is convenient to get around, so long as you own a car. The mean commute to work has been clocked at 21 minutes, and the Louisville definition of a traffic jam brings a sarcastic bark to the lips of people who've moved here from Los Angeles or Chicago.

"Our size is such you can get your hands around the city," says demographer Ron Crouch.

People here say — showing a certain amazement at discovering they feel so strongly about the matter — that Louisville is an absolutely great place to live. It's another Louisville paradox: They feel passionately about its very comfortableness.

"I think Louisville is a wonderful city to keep your balance in," said the late Wilson Wyatt, a former mayor, lieutenant governor and one of the city — if not the nation's — leading citizens for six decades.

Wyatt told a perfect story to illustrate what he meant: When he was managing Adlai Stevenson's 1952 presidential race, the heat of the campaign trail could sometimes persuade him that Stevenson was gaining on Eisenhower. When he returned to Louisville, his friends' concern for how he was doing convinced him, "better than any Gallup poll," of what bad shape Stevenson's candidacy was in.

Louisville is also comfortable in the untucked-shirttail sense. Despite the sophistication suggested by the high profile of our arts groups, this is not a very formal community. The Louisville Palace, a grand old movie house (formerly Loew's Theater) on Fourth Street, reopened in 1994. The city had been waiting for nearly a decade for the project to get off the ground. The black-tie gala for opening night featured a concert by New Age keyboardist Yanni and his 39-piece orchestra. As one of Yanni's self-serious compositions thundered to an end, someone in the audience shouted "Yee-haw!"

One reason Louisville is easy to get your hands around is that it doesn't move very fast. Area builders find that it's hard to go wrong with a two-story brick Colonial; you have to plead with local ethnic restaurants to turn up the heat in their cuisine. The city takes forever to catch onto a trend: It opened its first microbrewery in 1992, although, typically, when it did, the beer was great and the place was mobbed. A thriving coffeehouse scene started around the same late date.

It can be an excruciating city for people in their teens and early '20s, the age when being stylistically up-to-the-minute seems most essential. When the art movie you've been reading about for six months finally arrives in the theaters, it's usually a few weeks away from being available on video. A 1994 demographic mapping of the city found "What's Hot" to include Tupperware, *Southern Living* magazine, Sally Jesse Raphael's show, country music and power tools, while wine, *Rolling Stone* magazine, rap and — this really hurts to say — *The Simpsons* were not. Before the news-oriented A.H. Belo Corp. bought WHAS-TV, the station postponed *Nightline* for a half-hour to run reruns of — this really hurts to say — *Coach*, which justified their decision by beating both David Letterman and Jay Leno in the local Nielsens.

But while this can be a lonely community for someone who wants to run his or her finger along the cutting edge of culture, it offers a commendable sense of freedom and the space to develop by your own lights. A hip young band doesn't find itself wondering if it should go ska or grunge or techno; it finds its own way. Consequently, the Louisville rock scene — which has varying degrees of fan and club support — attracts national attention for the quality of groups such as Slint, Rodan, Rachel's and King Kong. The idea of Louisville being another Seattle, which gets floated from time to time, is laughable (and wasn't that supposed to be Chapel Hill, anyway? Or San Diego?), mainly because it's already Louisville, and when all is said and done, most people here are fairly pleased with that.

Louisville may be more like a town than a city in the way it spends its energies, first on family, friends and neighborhood and only then on larger civic matters. Native Morgan Atkinson's wonderful film *Falls City* captures in an affectionately ironic tone just what a muddle Louisville gets into when it tries to think about issues of identity: An interesting river

Photo: Daniel Dempster

Louisville sits at a bend in the Ohio River.

fountain ends up being a disappointment because it was sold as an attraction to rival the St. Louis' Gateway Arch. We're overly moved by boosterism. While present mayor Jerry Abramson has a host of accomplishments to his credit, it's his almost monolithically optimistic tone that creates his profile in the Louisville mind. To use an old-fashioned term, he's a go-getter.

But we're so susceptible to optimism that we can end up feeling like suckers. There's a standard dynamic in Louisville life: Someone proposes a large-scale project; it's criticized; those who proposed it complain about the "negativity" of people who would dare question what they do; the project proceeds or dies based on other criteria that have nothing to do with the debate. This process is starting to unfold in connection with a proposed downtown arena that proponents hope will attract the one major league sports franchise that would make sense for Louisville, an NBA team. Judge for yourself: Bold vision, or unrealistic boondoggle? Is the arena half-empty or half-full? Welcome to Louisville.

But such disputes don't eliminate certain very important baselines to the civic character. Our public life shows a strong tradition of generosity. You can start with the friendliness and courtesy of the average person on the street (one of the most Southern things about the city is its attachment to the idea of hospitality, although we modulate it into a lower, less ostentatious key). But it's also evident in some remarkable civic enterprises: the Fund for the Arts, an umbrella organization for the city's major arts groups that enjoys unusually broad-based support; the Crusade for Children, a telethon for special-needs children, created by the Bingham media companies and supported by the efforts of volunteer fire companies and others throughout the area; Kentucky Harvest, an innovative program of distributing excess prepared food from restaurants and other institutions to homeless shelters (it's collected over 17 million pounds of food over the last decade); and a vital and growing United Way. The National Center for Family Literacy is a national model for its method of simultaneously educating impoverished children and their parents.

And yet, while Louisville works best on a person-to-person basis, the reverse of the old cliché about New York doesn't hold — this isn't just a great place to live, it's a great place to visit as well. Churchill Downs and the Derby

Museum; a good zoo and a spanking new amusement park, which has been adding thrill rides that compare to those anywhere; historic districts to rival any in the country; arts and sports at a high level; great restaurants — if there isn't something that interests you here, well, there's no pleasing some people.

The Land and People

Louisville the city, founded in 1778, sits at a bend in the Ohio River above the only interruption in navigation along the whole length of the Mississippi-Ohio River system. It's a series of rapids known — a touch grandly — as the Falls of the Ohio, descending 26 feet over the course of 3 miles. Before they were dammed, the waters made an extraordinary rushing sound. When the river is low, the rock over which they pass is visible as an extraordinary Devonian fossil bed, remnants of the coral reef that was here when the area was covered by a tropical sea and more reminiscent of Bermuda than Muncie.

Once the 10th largest city in the country, now 60th, Louisville is the center of a metropolitan area that's usually considered to comprise all of Jefferson County; Oldham and Shelby counties to the east; Bullitt County to the south; and Clark, Floyd and Harrison counties in Indiana. Taken all together, the metropolitan area contains not quite a million people living in just fewer than 2,300 square miles. It's larger than Nashville, not much smaller than Indianapolis.

For many years, the area was losing people, but within the last decade, the trend has reversed. Between 1990 and 1995 the population grew by about 3.9 percent — modest growth, but that's the way we do things around here.

The climate is temperate but quixotic. Take 1994 for example. That year saw record-setting snowfalls (almost 16 inches) compounded by record cold. There were floods in February. The temperature exceeded 100 degrees for the first time in June, yet there was a spell of weather in mid-August that felt as mild as May. Only the June temperatures were typical, compounded by major-league humidity: You have to go to the likes of Charleston or New Orleans to find weather that is more consistently sticky in the summer.

Louisville sees periodic natural disasters: The 1937 flood (when the Ohio crested at 41 feet above flood stage, and you could row a boat up Fourth Street) and the 1974 tornado continue to have a powerful presence in the local memory. (The 1890 tornado, in which 100 people died, has been largely forgotten.) Recent years have seen devastating tornadoes and in the spring of 1997, the worst flood in decades.

Louisvillians have been inclined to believe in global warming less from drought than from the rude recent custom of going without spring — slamming straight from raw, windy 40s and 50s into air-conditioner weather, with only a rainy spell or two as transitions. It's a great loss. One reason the Kentucky Derby became such a major sporting event is that there are few things prettier than a Kentucky May, with the dogwoods blooming, the skies a deep, unambiguous blue and the air like a kiss. All year, the sudden appearance of pretty weather will draw the community outside as if we're so many kids daydreaming out a classroom window.

Being located almost exactly at the center of the eastern half of the United States has made Louisville a transportation center in nearly every era: flatboats coming downstream from Pittsburgh; steamboats going up from New Orleans; the L&N (as in Louisville and Nashville) railroad moving goods north and south; three interstate highways knotting together at Spaghetti Junction (which bring Nashville, St. Louis, Chicago, Indianapolis,

INSIDERS' TIP

One great advantage to Louisville — a study of 63 IRS districts showed taxpayers in Louisville were the least likely to have their tax returns audited. (The bad news: That may be because incomes are lower here.)

Memphis and Atlanta within a day's drive); the 1981 arrival of the UPS air hub, making Louisville in the middle of the night one of the busiest cargo points in the world.

Louisville no longer feels very much like a river city. Interstate 64 and a series of gravel and scrap-material companies have cut off much of the city from visual contact with the river. (It's one of Southern Indiana's most powerful claims to sanity that it has obstructed its riverfront less.) While many people still work the river, it's a diminished presence in the economy. Ironically, the Jefferson County Riverport, long a nearly vacant white elephant, has filled up with distribution companies less interested in proximity to the water than proximity to UPS.

If you're not lucky enough to live close to the Ohio, you can come to feel landlocked until a drive over one of the bridges brings you into contact with the magnificent spread of the Ohio, almost a half-mile wide between Louisville and Jeffersonville, Indiana.

More recently, the community has been making attempts to mend its relationship with the water and create a public attraction similar to Baltimore's harbor. The Waterfront Development Corporation has begun construction on a waterfront park that should be finished by late 1998. Its first completed section, the wharf area, was the site for 1997's hottest new festival, Rockin' at Riverpoints, a series of 10 outdoor concerts that drew large and enthusiastic crowds (see our Annual Events and Festivals chapter). The new RiverWalk provides an uninterrupted stroll (or pedal, or roll) along the river and the Portland Canal, which extends from downtown to Chickasaw Park in the West End.

Louisville's past as a river city has left its mark on her economy and character. Louisville has a more-than-nodding acquaintance-ship with vice. The liquor industry has always had a major presence in the city, and the bars may stay open until 4 AM. Poor, skulking tobacco remains a significant industry (during the national war on smoking, the state legislature passed an against-the-tide law that all public buildings in the state must include a smoking area, and Kentucky has yet to join most other states in filing suit for health costs against the tobacco companies). Legal gam-bling — at Churchill Downs and its off-track partner Sports Spectrum and through the Kentucky Lottery — is a major revenue producer, and bookies aren't that hard to find, either.

The city has periodic bursts of conviction that it should clean up the sex industry: the most recent attempting, with mixed success, to remove adults-only bookstores, movie theaters and strip clubs from the central business district. But it never takes the prim approach of a Cincinnati and shoves all vice across the river. It's also been tolerant of eccentrics passing through, from the legendary boatman Mike Fink to the denizens of the Churchill Downs infield on Derby Day.

The Jobs and the Money

Louisville's economy is stable, diverse and not given to booms and busts, although it has some crucial weaknesses, especially in high-tech sectors. And the decline in manufacturing jobs (down from a peak of 124,000 in 1974 to 92,000 today) has made it more difficult for folks with a high school education or less to find employment. These trends help explain why local corporations have been such solid supporters of education reform.

The Ford Louisville Assembly Plant, in danger of closing in the late '70s, turned around its labor-management difficulties and now produces the hugely popular Explorer and Ranger vehicles. Although its labor force is less than half what it once was, General Electric's Appliance Park — despite the name, it isn't a place to take a picnic and throw a Frisbee with the kids — is one of the world's largest manufacturers of home appliances such as washers, dryers, ranges, dishwashers and refrigerators. Brown-Forman not only distills Early Times and Old Forester bourbons but also owns Bolla Wines, Lenox China and our cross-border rival for sour mash supremacy, Jack Daniel's Tennessee Sour Mash Whiskey. Porter Paints is one of the country's leading paint manufacturers, while Devoe & Raynolds has one of the best endorsements in the paint business — Devoe enamel was Jackson Pollack's house paint of choice for dripping onto canvas.

And over the past decade and a half, the city has become home to several high-profile medical corporations: Humana, the former

On Pronunciation

A local beer commercial asks: "How do you pronounce Louisville?"

Someone says "Looey-ville," and a scornful guy appears on screen to sneer, "Out-of-towners."

But who's the out-of-towner?

"Loo-a-vull" — "LOO-uh-vull" might be a more accurate transliteration — seems to be the majority pronunciation these days. Certainly it's the one that's put on bumper stickers, T-shirts and taught to sportscasters when they come to town for a game ("You know how they pronounce it here, Dick? 'LOO-uh-vull.'" "Is that right, Al?") We have a somewhat lazy, slurring way with words in these parts, and that may have something to do with the way the initial L broadens, discombobulating the entire word until you swallow it from a lack of anything better to do. LOO-uh-vull is the way this writer, who's lived in the city for nearly four decades and was born to a pair of Louisville natives, has always pronounced the city's name.

But there is a staunch group of people who hear that pronunciation and grit their teeth. George Yater, author of *200 Years at the Falls of the Ohio*, the best civic history, says he never heard "LOO-uh-vull" until the '70s, when it popped up on bumper stickers; he had spent more than six decades as a Looey-villian. To his ears, folks who say "LOO-uh-vull" are the ones who sound like outlanders.

If you want to get huffy about it, neither pronunciation is the original one. George Rogers Clark, who only founded the city, wrote (and presumably pronounced) the city's name "Lewis-ville," a spelling that Yater says persists in city deed books up to the 1840s. Yater assumes that Looey-ville came from a more sophisticated understanding of French pronunciation (although we didn't take it all the way to Looey-veal). After all, as the joke goes, the city isn't named after King Loua.

Where'd we get "LOO-uh-vull"? Yater believes that it may have come from rural Kentucky, where towns such as Eddyville and Perryville are pronounced "Edda-vull" and "Para-vull." *Louisville* magazine editor Ronni Lundy, who grew up in the South End saying "vull," notes that the pronunciation is "vull-driven" — "Looey-vull" doesn't sound right.

My aunt once was talking about her mother, my grandmother, and how she'd managed to get a good education growing up in a small Hart County town (they moved to Louisville when my aunt was young). Mama was a stickler for proper grammar, Aunt Edith said — and then without a transition she said, "She couldn't stand 'LOO-uh-vull' — she always said 'Looey-ville,' and she'd correct us if we didn't."

As my aunt's story suggests, there may be a class aspect to the difference (and the prickly correctness on both sides) — I note that many who pronounce it Looey-ville tend to be educated East Enders, the type of persons who are most moved by the Edwin Newmans and William Safires to think that changes in language are inevitably declines (even the equable Yater uses the term "vowel decay" and said in a letter to the local paper *LEO* that the pronunciation results from rural Kentuckians' "bad speech habits").

Bellarmine English professor Wade Hall told Yater "LOO-uh-vull" was similar to the Biblical "shibboleth" — a way to tell which people are outsiders (although, unlike the Gileadites and Ephraimites of Judges 12, comparatively few people are slaughtered over our city's pronunciation). If you haven't grown up saying it, LOO-uh-vull requires

— continued on next page

practice, just like the French "r." (Most staunch LOO-uh-vullians make some accommodation to outside ears when they're giving an address, usually by reverting to "Looey-ville.")

That final "vull" renders the name unrhymable: Even the city's promotional song of the early '80s was "Look what we can do/Looey-ville!" (The way it's pronounced, it doesn't even rhyme with "dull" or "null," really). But it has its own provincial aesthetic — so backwater-ugly it's kind of attractive.

A few other notes on local speech:

Words are often compressed into a kind of silly poetry: If you hear someone talking about "Nobanny," they mean New Albany, Indiana. The people who answer the phone at the Shelby County Public Schools pronounce the county's name as if the letter "L" doesn't exist. Louisville stand-up comic Bob Batch has developed an entire routine based on transliterating the strung-together phrases we seem to use as single words — for example, "preshazdit" for "appreciate it." One of the best (also produced by *Louisville Times* writer Mary Caldwell): "Mominem," meaning your mother and her associates.

There's also a strong civic tendency to mangle certain words consistently — the same sort of thing that David Letterman will joke about on his show ("statistics . . . or as we say in Indiana, suh-tistics").

Something else you'll notice is that almost every business or institutional name in the area is turned in to a plural or possessive. I have never heard a Louisvillian call Big Spring Golf Course anything other than Big Springs; the defunct Italian restaurant Casa Grisanti, already possessive in Italian, was universally known as Casa Grisanti's; every Kroger grocery store is called Kroger's. This tendency has even been recognized in official usage: While longtime residents of the Floyd County hills call the area Floyd

— continued on next page

Photo: Dan Dry and Associates

Knobs, the U.S. Post Office proclaims it Floyds Knobs (although the employees there pronounce it with a silent "s").

A few other verbal and lexical idiosyncrasies follow.

Kentuckiana — The unesthetic but inclusive designation for the region on either side of the Ohio. Its poetry will come. (Jim Dandy: A Tale of Old Kentuckiana; My Heart Belongs to My Kentuckiana Home; When it's Harvest Time in Kentuckiana.)

Hoosier — A male resident of Indiana; also used as collective noun and adjective. In Kentucky, a pejorative that calls up images of Orville Redenbacker, not Cole Porter (who was born in Peru, Indiana — pronounced PEE-roo).

Hoosierina, obs. — Female Hoosier.

Jeff — Short for Jeffersonville, Indiana.

J-town — Short for Jeffersontown, Kentucky, but many people who live there hate the abbreviation.

Humana — Pronounced so the middle syllable rhymes with "can." (Humana Building architect Michael Graves pronounced the name with a broad, almost British "a" nobody would use here — or in his native Indianapolis).

Fontaine Ferry — Defunct, much-missed West End amusement park pronounced "Fountain Ferry."

Versailles — Town near Lexington pronounced "Ver-SALES."

Coke — Not a brand name but a generic term for carbonated drinks ("Would you like a coke?" "Yeah, gimme a 7-Up.") "Soft drink" is also used widely; "soda" and "pop" are terms from Mars.

Benedictine — A sandwich spread of cucumber, cream cheese and onion invented by Louisville cook Jennie Benedict; it has no relationship to the religious order.

Rees-ey Cup — Local pronunciation of Reese's Peanut Butter Cups.

Ate up — Obsessed with. ("He gets all ate up with the Wildcats.")

Later — See you later.

Say what? — Come again?

Do what? — Say what?

Just — Used to suggest one should not think too deeply about a matter: "It's just a name." Louisville's way of saying, "Forget it, Jake, it's Chinatown."

---

hospital corporation now evolved into a large medical insurance company; Vencor, the world's largest owner and operator of long-term hospitals (and a company that has grown so fast it didn't have a full-time spokesman until 1996). While "the Mayo Clinic of the South" Humana once pledged to create here has not materialized, the city is known for a number of medical specialties, such as Hand Surgery Associates and the Heart and Lung Institute at Jewish Hospital. And Audubon Hospital, formerly owned by Humana, was the site of the since-abandoned artificial heart program. Columbia/HCA, the world's largest hospital corporation, moved its headquarters here in 1994 shortly after acquiring Galen, the hospital corporation spun off from Humana. But in one of the defining moments in recent Lou-isville history, Columbia/HCA left for Nashville 10 months later, with its CEO Rick Scott citing Tennessee's "pro-business environment" (translation: lower taxes on the company) as a reason for the move. The decampment led to a great civic gnashing of teeth (especially from those who'd like their own taxes revised in a more pro-business fashion), but the city is still standing. Louisvillians have viewed Columbia/HCA's subsequent troubles with the law with understandable glee.

UPS grew quietly, until in the early '90s the city realized the company's international air hub made it the city's (and now the state's) largest private employer. The company's presence has attracted a number of businesses that depend on quick shipment (for example, computer repair firms — one of Louisville's few high-tech presences). It was also a major force behind the decision to expand the airport. What impact the 1997 teamster's strike will have on the city's relationship with UPS — especially in light of the Board of Aldermen's resolution supporting the strikers — remains to be seen.

Another area in which the local economy has made a national impact is fast food. Louisville has launched Chi-Chi's, Tumbleweed and Rally's (perpetrator of the grossest television commercials in recent memory). Papa John's is the country's fourth largest pizza chain (behind Pizza Hut, Domino's and Little Caesar's) and the fastest-growing; it's also the one that put its name on the new U of L football stadium. (When people praise Louisville's restaurant scene, by the way, these aren't the places they have in mind.) Louisville now has divided rooting interest in the pizza wars: In summer 1997 it won the contest to become headquarters of Tricon, the restaurant business spun off from PepsiCo that includes Kentucky Fried Chicken, long based in Louisville, Taco Bell and . . . Pizza Hut. Tricon's arrival keeps the city's count of Fortune 500 companies even. Insurance giant Providian was purchased in 1997 by Aegon, a Dutch company whose US operations are based in Baltimore. (Others on the list: Humana, LG&E Energy Corp. and Vencor, which just made the roll at number 500.)

The most controversial change in the local economy is on the horizon — Bridgeport in Harrison County, Indiana, across the river from southwest Jefferson County, is the proposed site for what would be the country's largest riverboat casino.

So, Are We Southern, Or What?

People come to Louisville knowing mainly the mint-julepy image of the Derby, thinking of Kentucky as part of the South, and express a certain shock at discovering Louisville isn't as Southern as they thought: "It's just like Cincinnati!" cried a disappointed visitor from Oklahoma.

But it makes sense that it would be like Cincinnati. Louisville was marked profoundly by the same wave of German immigration in the 1840s and '50s; nearly a quarter of the metropolitan population says it's of German descent. And, as alderman and archivist Tom Owen points out, that wave of immigration helped give Louisville a rather unusual religious configuration: The two largest denominations are Catholic (Irish and Italian as well as German) and Baptist — not a typical mix for a Southern city.

Until the Civil War, Louisville called itself neither Northern nor Southern. It was a Western town, a frontier place, a little rough and rude. Charles Dickens, visiting on the tour he described in *American Notes*, had some fun with the pigs who roamed the street of Portland as a freelance sanitation squad (other than the pigs and 7-foot-9 giant Jim Porter, Dickens found "no objects of sufficient interest to detain us on our way" and left after a night's rest at the Galt House). The city was plagued by the "ague" — a fever that was probably the result of malaria-bearing mosquitoes so prevalent in the swampy city. Its presence, along with other epidemics such as smallpox, earned Louisville its nickname as "The Graveyard of the West."

Kentucky was a slave-holding state, but it didn't secede from the Union. Louisville served as headquarters for the Union army during the war. Then Louisville did something extraordinary. It decided, after hostilities ended, to side with the South. There was opportunism in the stance, a chance for an unscarred town to open up trade with Southern markets. There was also a racial component: Many whites resented that a war to preserve the Union changed into a war to free the slaves. Louisville saw itself as a leader of a new, more progressive South — a position put most articulately by former Confederate Henry Watterson, nationally known for his editorials in *The Courier-Journal*.

But at the same time, Louisville looked for models of behavior to the East, and beyond them to England — St. James Court was named to recall London, not New Orleans or Chicago. And as time wore on, the advent of smokestack industries gave Louisville some of the characteristics of the rest of the Midwestern Rustbelt.

And yet much of what was written about Louisville in the mid-20th century portrayed it as a quaint, sleepy town, including the WPA guidebook to Kentucky and *Harper's* stinging 1937 article calling the city "an American museum piece . . . the land of let-well-enough-alone." The city retained a certain insular formality. Up until World War II, everybody dressed up to go downtown on Saturday; a visitor from Evansville, Indiana, said that every girl in Louisville must own a dozen pair of white gloves.

While the Southern accent may not be thick — if it is, you have a right to be suspicious — it definitely flavors the regional speech, softening and slurring the words. But, as one 78-year-old native put it, "Louisville never worked at being Southern the way Lexington did." And the coming of out-of-town corporations such as GE in the 1950s and UPS in the '80s has brought in a number of folks from less drawling climes.

One of the most Southern-seeming aspects of the city is its distrust of public debate. We don't like to criticize, and we don't take it very well. It was entirely characteristic that, as Lexington-born historian George C. Wright shows in his book *Life Behind a Veil*, both black and white Louisville considered the more polite form of racism practiced here as a great improvement on race relations in the rest of the country — even though this "enlightened" paternalism was every bit as effective at keeping blacks subordinate as a harsher regime would have been.

The city's desegregation of its public schools in 1956 won national attention as one of the first successful implementations of the law created by *Brown vs. Board of Education*. Books and articles told *The Louisville Story*. But the real story in Louisville, still not finished, was the movement to the suburbs, which created a predominantly white county school system. By 1975 the city school system had collapsed into the county system, the racial imbalance caused by residential patterns was challenged in court, and a federal court ordered busing to remedy the disparity. This time, desegregation wasn't accomplished peacefully — some protests turned into riots, and busing helped spur white flight into the surrounding counties, which have, on the whole, much more homogeneous populations than Jefferson's.

But the Louisville story didn't end in 1975, either. In the '80s, Jefferson County schools received national attention for turning a troubled system around, in particular, for an innovative program that put computers into every school. Kentucky adopted the country's most sweeping educational reform act in 1990 — a bold experiment the results of which won't be known for better than a decade.

In addition to the Jefferson County schools, the city has the state's third-largest school system, the Archdiocese of Louisville's parochial schools. The city also contains the oldest municipal university in the country, the University of Louisville (now a part of the University of Kentucky), Jefferson Community College (which has two campuses), Presbyterian and Southern Baptist seminaries and two distinguished Catholic institutions, Bellarmine College and Spalding University. Across the river is Indiana University Southeast, a community college campus in the Indiana University system.

What the Ends Mean

When people in Louisville talk about the various ends of town, they're talking about something more (and less) than geography: a set of economic and demographic stereotypes with a rough — but only a rough — congruence to reality and no clear definition.

INSIDERS' TIP

Louisville, like Kentucky as a whole, has voted Democratic since the Civil War. That may be changing at both levels: In 1996 Louisville elected its first republican member of Congress in forever, Anne Northup. Only one of Kentucky's six seats in the House of Representatives is held by a Democrat, and Gov. Paul Patton beat Republican Larry Forgy by the slimmest of margins.

The East End, a slice of pie with a south-western edge described by Baxter Avenue and Newburg Road that sweeps north and east from there to the river and the county line, is supposed to be home to the upper-middle class and the wealthy. The South End, from Preston Highway on the east to the river on the west and south from the University of Louisville to the Bullitt County line, is supposed to consist of lower-middle and working-class whites. The West End, roughly from Ninth Street west to Shawnee Park and from Algonquin Parkway to the Ohio, is supposed to be mostly black residents.

It's as if the city were a clock face pivoted around downtown, with the distribution of class and income decreasing as you approach midnight (which would be in Southern Indiana, whatever that means). U of L geographer Bill Dakan, who's lived in other cities such as Denver, Los Angeles and Milwaukee, says he's never known a city where sectional differences were so clearly articulated or where they were viewed as such pejorative terms. At its grossest, the stereotype suggests that no one with a college degree lives west of Bardstown Road, and that no African American lives anywhere other than west of Ninth Street.

But the West End has the greatest extremes of income and surroundings in the entire metro area: pockets of dire poverty and beautiful homes across from the park. While the area's population has been predominantly African American since the 1960s, Portland at its far north corner remains a mostly white enclave. The South End, experiencing robust growth since the 1987 completion of the Gene Snyder Freeway, contains a wide variety of neighborhoods and people, from tattoo artists to former White House Fellows. It's beginning to see the kind of $200,000-and-up new homes that successful professionals used to have to leave the neighborhood to buy. The East End, which sprawls unchecked toward and into Oldham County, has its share of modest-income households.

Downtown continues to have the largest concentration of jobs in the area; it's where the city's performing arts groups put on their shows; it's the site of any citywide celebration. But Louisville has lost downtown as a shopping district, and it's hard to determine if it can ever win shoppers back from the putative at-tractions of suburban malls. Except for some apartments and a precious few lofts, there's little housing downtown. The closest neighborhood is Old Louisville, between downtown and the university.

There is a new round of downtown projects — the Waterfront project, Vencor's new riverfront skyscraper, a new luxury hotel in the long-vacant YWCA, the proposed arena, a proposed but likely baseball park on east Main Street, a possible museum honoring Muhammad Ali (which may be located elsewhere in town). These may revive downtown. And Hillerich & Bradsby's Main Street complex, with its headquarters, factory and Louisville Slugger Museum, has already brought new life to West Main Street. But there have been a number of projects with the same intention already, and at best downtown has held its ground.

The East End is, for many of its residents, virtually self-sufficient. Some people are beginning to call Hurstbourne Lane a second city — a center of gravity to rival downtown. (Like most edge cities, it lacks the traditional institutions that mark older urban areas: a city hall, legitimate theaters, mass transit. There is, however, a Denny's.)

Suspicion of the East End is based in the belief that Louisville is a city controlled by a small group of rich and powerful men who live in the eastern part of the county. The power of the East End is a local version of the myth of an omnipotent Trilateral Commission — although at one time, it was apparently true that epochal decisions were reached at the exclusive Pendennis Club (the club is downtown, but most of its members have to travel in a westward direction to get there).

People still tell you, in a significant (and amusingly hushed) tone, that so-and-so belongs to a particular family. Old ways die hard. But few of the movers and shakers of recent years have moved and shaken because of any privileges of birth or class. Race and sex may be another matter, but those boundaries are slowly coming down as well.

Humana, the signal business success of the 1970s and '80s, was the product of a man who grew up in the West End neighborhood of Parkland (David Jones) and a fellow from Horse Cave, Kentucky (the late Wendell

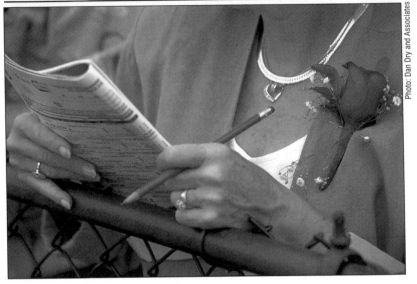

Photo: Dan Dry and Associates

Legal gambling is a major revenue producer for the city.

Cherry). Banker Malcolm Chancey, generally considered to be one of the city's most powerful men, grew up in Fairdale, on the other side of the county from the Brownsboro/River Road corridor. And the shift in who wields influence isn't just a question of new recruits for the available slots in the power class. Civic groups such as Goals for Greater Louisville have worked to expand the range and number of people who sit down at the table. And because so many locally-owned companies — the banks, the *Courier-Journal* and now Providian — have been purchased by out-of-town concerns, the heads of those companies aren't autocratic owners but managers who have to check with the home office before making major moves.

The schema of the Ends suggests one of the area's most fundamental problems: A division into different factions that keeps the community from acting coherently. In fact, Louisville often seems like a collection of villages. The Highlands Kroger store is like a hurried version of the courthouse square. If you go there and don't see a half-dozen people you know, you must be friendless or shopping at 3 AM. But it's rarer for people to travel between different parts of town.

Louisville and Jefferson County tried twice in 1982 and 1983 to merge their governments into a single countywide entity (at present population levels, a merged government would make us about the 16th-largest city in the country). The ballot initiative failed both times, defeated by an unlikely coalition between county residents and West End African Americans. The county didn't want to pay more taxes; the West End didn't want to lose the degree of representation it currently has in Louisville's city government. The most recent attempt at bringing the governments together failed without even coming to a popular vote. The city and county have compromised by forging an unprecedented compact to combine many city agencies. It comes up for renewal in mid-1998 and there's talk about taking it further, by merging the city and county police departments. (While this is usually seen as a good thing, as progressive as we can hope for under the circumstances, there's a line of analysis which argues the compact hurts the city by limiting its annexation powers.)

Jefferson County has more cities, per capita, than any county in the country. Merger already exists in the popular mind — if an outsider asks someone from St. Matthews or

Jeffersontown where they live, it's only a rare diehard who won't say "Louisville." The smaller city is used as a neighborhood name. Nevertheless, this is Kentucky, land of political fractions — 120 counties and no sign they'll ever consolidate. It's not clear whether the area's small cities are any more likely to relinquish power.

A lack of cohesion among neighbors doesn't prevail exclusively inside Jefferson County. Louisville and Indiana look at each other warily across the Ohio and the Mason-Dixon line. Barbs fly back and forth across the river (How do you keep a Hoosier happy in his old age? Tell him a joke when he's young), and there is a degree of true incomprehension behind them, as the issue of building a bridge over the Ohio has shown.

Indiana can't see why a span can't be built between the Gene Snyder Expressway in eastern Jefferson County and I-265 on the opposite side of the river. The path would come through some of the choicest real estate around (Harrods Creek, the most likely landfall, is one of the wealthiest zip codes in the nation). Kentuckians — or at least their governments — see the most crucial transportation issue as relieving the terrible traffic on the Kennedy Bridge carrying I-65 across the Ohio, which would be better accomplished by a new downtown bridge. The issue has been actively debated for a decade and had some history to it before that; there have been no end of studies (but not any practical surveying work on the river bed to see where construction of a bridge would make sense) and still no resolution as we go to press. The latest enlightened thinking seems to be that we should build both an eastern bridge and a new one downtown, although nobody knows where the money for either project will come from.

Both New Albany (once the largest city in Indiana) and Jeffersonville had ambitions of being the major city at the Falls; once Louisville built the Portland Canal on the Kentucky side of the river, the issue was essentially settled. Indiana is the larger, more prosperous state, but Louisville is the largest city in the region called by the less-than-euphonious name of Kentuckiana, and so it takes the protagonist's role in local affairs. Hoosiers cross the river for shopping and services and

the arts; Kentuckians go the other way somewhat less often. You can overstate the degree of the divergence: Derby Dinner Playhouse is in Clarksville, Indiana, Jeffersonville's Inn on Spring belongs in the first rank of local restaurants, and any Louisville workplace contains a sizable contingent of rabid IU basketball fans.

People in Southern Indiana sometimes feel estranged from the rest of the Hoosiers — in a different time zone, at a far end of the state, perceived to be in Louisville's ambit. And yet it's turned out to be a good ambit for Southern Indiana to be in — its counties comprise one of the fastest-growing parts of metropolitan Louisville.

Louisville, Kentucky

The relationship between Louisville and Indiana is simplicity itself compared to the relationship between Louisville and the rest of Kentucky.

Jefferson County is unique in the state. It's the largest urban center by far and the wealthiest and most ethnically diverse county (in the 1990 census, Jefferson County had 43 percent of the state's black population). But despite its size, it has seemed at times oddly peripheral to the rest of a state that historically has been rural and isolated. Only one resident of Jefferson County, Lawrence Wetherby, has ever been governor of the state, and he made a point of telling people he was from Middletown, not Louisville.

The relationship has been played out through the power of the L&N Railroad, which was widely seen as bullying the rest of the state and denying rival railroads routes through the state; on the basketball floor, with Louisville challenging the beloved UK Wildcats; and in the press, where the popularity of Louisville papers in the rest of the state may have painted an image of a place riddled with crime, corruption and sin.

In recent years, relations between Louisville and the rest of the state have been characterized as less prickly, thanks to modern advances in communication and transportation, and with the State Fair and the Kentucky Center for the Arts drawing folks from other parts of the state here. But the 1994 legislature voted down a list of Louisville projects (expanding the Commonwealth Convention Center, building a new courts complex, funding a new football stadium), and suddenly the papers were filled with new talk of a rift. The University of Louisville prepared a study for the Chamber of Commerce that proved a longtime contention: Louisville is a "cash cow" that contributes far more in taxes than it gets back from the state in services and spending. In fiscal 1990-91, Louisville paid $1.1 billion; the state's expenditures here were only $600 million.

The joke is that the only accurate answer to the question "Is Louisville a Southern city or a Midwestern city?" is "It's a Kentucky city." Nearly three-quarters of the metropolitan area's residents live in the state in which they were born.

A Place to Begin

Louisville has been a propitious place for beginnings. Although St. Louis is usually cited as the starting point for the Lewis and Clark Expedition, Merriwether Lewis and William Clark joined forces here and recruited many members of the expedition in the area. Zachary Taylor, the hero of the Mexican War and president for six months, grew up and is buried here (he was also exhumed here, to see if he was poisoned). John James Audubon and Thomas Edison lived here as young men; Audubon kept store, Edison was a telegraph operator. Edison returned in 1883 for the Southern Exposition, the first large-scale exhibition of his incandescent lamp.

Around the same time Edison was working for Western Union, Louis Brandeis and Abraham Flexner were growing up in the city's liberal Jewish community. Brandeis, the first Jewish justice of the Supreme Court, was perhaps the foremost proponent of "sociological jurisprudence," the idea that the law ought to reflect and transform the conditions of the society in which it is made. Flexner transformed American education, in particular the training of doctors, and served as the first director of Princeton's Institute for Advanced Study — making him, in essence, Einstein's boss.

The first great film director, the man who created much of the basic grammar of filmmaking, D.W. Griffith, grew up and is buried in Oldham County and honed his knowledge of the theater on the Louisville stage; he also worked at the Flexner family bookstore. Ironically, the Louisville NAACP had *Birth of a Nation* banned from Louisville showings after two days of a revival in 1918, making Louisville one of only eight cities where Griffith's tale of the Civil War and the birth of the Ku Klux Klan was banned. The city's other natives to become major film directors had less mainstream visions of cinema, but their contributions are striking nonetheless — Tod Browning, who directed *Freaks* and *Dracula*, and Gus Van Sant of *Drugstore Cowboy* and *My Own Private Idaho*. Movie stars Irene Dunne and Victor Mature and comedian Billy Gilbert were natives; so are Ned Beatty, the late William Conrad of *Jake and the Fatman* fame (he was also the narrator for *Rocky and Bullwinkle*) and the character actor Leo Burmeister. Tom Cruise went to high school here; Sean Young was born in Louisville but moved away early. Warren Oates used to act in Shakespeare in the Park.

Louisville gave birth (and musical training) to a number of jazz musicians: Lionel Hampton, Helen Humes, Jonah Jones and the late bebop guitarist Jimmy Raney, who played around town for a decade or more before his death. Two significant rock groups formed here and moved elsewhere to become famous: The Moonglows of "Ten Commandments of Love" (their tenor, Harvey Fuqua, later became the vice president in charge of Motown Records' famous artists development department and was the man who discovered Etta James and Marvin Gaye, among others) and NRBQ, formed by a pair of Shively boys, which headed off into widespread regard as the world's greatest live band (founder Steve Ferguson, now a

---

INSIDERS' TIP

When someone asks "Where'd you go to school?" he or she wants to know the Louisville high school you attended, not where you went to college.

solo act, is one of the city's great treats). Rock singer Joan Osborne grew up in Anchorage. Sometime-Louisvillian Pee Wee King co-wrote country music's best-selling song, "Tennessee Waltz"; current star Patty Loveless graduated from Fairdale High School.

But Louisville's most important contributions to musical history come from a pair of songs. In 1830 at Samuel Drake's City Theatre on Jefferson Street, the singer Thomas D. Rice introduced what was described in the evening's program as "the comic Negro song of 'Jim Crow,'" an imitation of an arthritic slave at a nearby livery stable that is generally considered to be the beginning of the American minstrel show. So, in a sense, Mick Jagger's career stems from something that happened in Louisville. (The term "Jim Crow" later became applied to the segregating laws of the Reconstruction period.) In 1893 a pair of Louisville sisters wrote a kindergarten greeting song, "Good Morning to You"; it later became the most-sung song in the world, "Happy Birthday to You."

Network television's blond symbol of class used to be our local weather girl, Diane Sawyer, whose father was county judge in the 1960s. The well-informed person's first morning voice, Bob Edwards of National Public Radio's *Morning Edition*, grew up in the South End and went to St. X and U of L. *The Courier-Journal* has brought scores of talented newspapermen through town, from "Marse Henry" Watterson to Arthur Krock, later a famous voice at *The New York Times*, to such contemporary journalists as William Greider, Howard Fineman and Joel Brinkley of *The New York Times*, who won a Pulitzer Prize at *The Courier-Journal*.

A very different type of journalistic excellence has been produced by native son Hunter S. Thompson, creator of a mixture of intoxication and self-expression he dubbed "gonzo journalism." Thompson's first published writing appeared in the literary magazine of the Athenaeum, a high school social club and carousing society that continues to this day. And some of Thompson's influence may be seen in *Wired*, one of the notable magazine successes of the decade, founded by Louisville native Jane Metcalfe and her husband Louis Rosetto.

Louisville is practical enough to be a cradle of journalism rather than more imaginative forms of literature, but it has produced its share of fiction writers as well — notably, in recent years, the late Michael Dorris, a St. Xavier grad who wrote *A Yellow Raft in Blue Water* and *The Broken Cord*, and Sue Grafton, whose alphabetically-titled adventures of female detective Kinsey Millhone are considered to be among the best-written of contemporary mysteries.

You want athletes? Pee Wee Reese, the Hall of Fame shortstop for the Brooklyn Dodgers, grew up here and played his minor league ball for the old Louisville Colonels. And Paul Hornung, the Golden Boy of football, a player so gifted he won the Heisman Trophy on a college team with a losing record, went on to lead the NFL in scoring (on and off the field, they say). And there are others: Wesley Unseld, the only player to win the NBA's Rookie of the Year and Most Valuable Player awards in the same season; Darrell Griffith, who led the University of Louisville to a national title, and, at one point in his career, would have been on his own the leading three-point-shooting team in the NBA; Phil Simms, who quarterbacked at Southern High School and Morehead State University in eastern Kentucky before he led the New York Giants to a Super Bowl victory; Danny Sullivan, winner of the Indy 500; and Olympic gold medalist and Wheaties cover girl Mary T. "Madame Butterfly" Meagher, who won her first medals at Lakeside Swim Club in The Highlands.

Not to mention the greatest fighter who ever lived (and one has to agree with his own assessment too: the prettiest, in several senses of the word), Muhammad Ali, born Cassius Marcellus Clay Jr. in Louisville General Hospital in 1942, who fought his first fights on a local television show called *Tomorrow's Champions*.

Nearly all of these folks had to leave Louisville to achieve greatness. But many others arrive here on a rising arc and end up staying, even when they could go anywhere else they wanted. Look at Jon Jory of Actors Theatre, or the man who coaches the team we began this discussion with, U of L's Denny Crum.

Here's hoping the rest of this book provides you with a guide for your own beginnings in this tweener town.

The early history of Louisville is in large part the gradual creation of institutions that we take for granted; reading the mileposts is a steady instruction in what makes up urban civilization.

History

Louisville was inevitable.

That is, it was all but certain that as the United States moved west there would have to be some settlement at the Falls of the Ohio, where the rapids forced all but the most daredevil pilots to dock their boats and portage around.

But this particular city began its recorded history as a military tactic — a ruse of sorts. George Rogers Clark brought down a small group of settlers in the spring of 1778 as camouflage for his real intentions: He planned to attack the British garrisons at the former French towns of Kaskaskia, Cahokia and Vincennes in what was then called the Illinois Territory. The Falls of the Ohio was his base of operations for the Northwest Campaign, which broke British control of the upper Midwest.

Clark left behind a small group of 60 or so settlers who built forts, raised the crop of corn that gave their first home the name Corn Island and scouted the mainland for a more permanent home. They moved to the Fort-On-Shore, at the present-day intersection of 12th and Rowan streets, by fall of 1778. (Corn Island is now entirely submerged.)

The Early Settlement

By 1779, there was a plan drawn for a city on the south side of the Falls, already named after French King Louis XVI, whose government's treaty with the American colonies gave Clark a valuable instrument in his bloodless capture of the former French settlements. But it was not the first city platted for the site. A plan had actually been laid out in 1774 by a pair of Pittsburgh speculators, and for several years title to the land was disputed in the courts and in the Virginia Assembly. (American Indians had been coming here for thousands of years, but we have only a few archaeological records to confirm their presence.)

The settlement was almost wiped out by cold weather and a lack of food in the hard winter of 1779-80; 300 boats arrived the following spring, bringing supplies and new families. But Indian raids were a more constant concern, and the town lived its first 15 years under their threat. In 1780, county lieutenant John Floyd wrote governor Thomas Jefferson, "We are all obliged to live in Forts in the Country, and notwithstanding all the Caution that we use, forty-seven of the Inhabitants have been killed and taken by the Savages."

The Indians were discouraged by the 1781 construction of Fort Nelson on Main Street, the strongest fort in the West after Fort Pitt. But the raids didn't stop. A horrible 1789 attack on Chenoweth's Station (near what's now Middletown) killed two soldiers and three children; Mrs. Chenoweth was scalped and left for dead. Louisvillians couldn't feel secure until 1794, when Gen. Anthony Wayne's victory at the Battle of Fallen Timbers in Ohio destroyed the Indians' power in the Northwest.

In the early years of settlement there were a number of stations (small forts) in the rural part of the county, almost all of them to the east along the various forks of Beargrass Creek. (Many survive in place names, such as Linn Station Road in Plainview, named after an early settlement established by William Linn.) Perhaps the most important spots in the area were the two salt-making operations to the south of Louisville, at Mann's Lick (now Fairdale) and Bullitt's Lick (in what's now Bullitt County). They were the West's primary source for salt, a vital food preservative; they also provided employment, working hundreds of men round the clock.

The growing town of Louisville was in an area of great natural abundance. There were large flocks of wild birds and plentiful game. A traveler coming down the Ohio in 1792 saw six different herds of bison along the bank the day before he reached the town. And it was beautifully situated. In one of Louisville's favorite blurbs for itself, John James Audubon wrote, "The prospect from the town is such that it would please even the eye of a Swiss." The view was soon lost when the city allowed construction on the north side of Main Street, preventing the city from showing its best face to the river — an error compounded by the construction of Interstate 64 and belatedly addressed more than 200 years later by the Waterfront Development Corporation.

Accounts of the human inhabitants sounded a less delighted note. Moses Austin, a traveler who came through in 1796, wrote, "Louis Ville by nature is beautifull but the handy work of Man has insted of improving destroy.d the works of Nature and made it a detestable place." (sic)

Pretty snooty for a guy who couldn't spell "instead," but the town was in a very rough infancy. The 1790 census found only 300 people here; 1800 showed only 59 more, which ranked Louisville fifth among Kentucky's cities, behind Lexington, Frankfort, Washington and Paris. (The entire population of Jefferson County was 8,754.)

As George Yater observes in *200 Years at the Falls of the Ohio*, Louisville was, from its very beginnings, separated from the Bluegrass region of Kentucky. It was too far removed to provide any protection to the area during the Revolutionary War. As soon as Virginia's gigantic Kentucky County was divided into three smaller counties in 1780, Lexington and Louisville were county seats of Fayette and Jefferson counties, respectively. (We were named after Thomas Jefferson, the governor of Virginia, not yet president, and comprised a territory that included all or parts of 28 present-day Kentucky counties.) The first settlers of Louisville were Scotch-Irish and the so-called Pennsylvania Dutch, descendants of German and Swiss immigrants to Pennsylvania — not the English-descended Virginians who settled Lexington, Danville and Harrodsburg.

Kentucky became the 15th state in 1792, after 10 constitutional conventions. Both Lexington and Louisville vied to become the state's capital (the imposing Jefferson County courthouse was built in the 1830s with an eye toward serving as Kentucky's capitol). Instead, the state chose — "virtually invented," historian Richard C. Wade has it — Frankfort, located more or less halfway between them.

The early history of Louisville is in large part the gradual creation of institutions that we take for granted; reading the mileposts is a steady instruction in what makes up urban civilization. The city's first brick house was built in 1789; its first hotel in 1793; a post office in 1795; a bank in 1800; a newspaper in 1801; a theater in 1808; a racetrack by 1815, if not earlier; a public school of 250 students crowded into a single room in 1829. Priorities weren't always what we might choose today: The city had its first dancing school in 1786, 37 years before it had a hospital.

In its early days, Louisville was every bit a frontier town. One traveler claimed that eye-gouging was a habitual way of settling differences; biting also was accepted as a fair way to fight. In 1786 one Richard Butler found the city's potential for improvement impeded by the population's laziness and poor character: "I see very little doing but card-playing, drinking and other vices among the common people, and am sorry too many of the better sort are too much engaged in the same manner." The only exceptions he noted were a few shopkeepers he found willing to "take the advantage of the ignorance or innocence of the stranger." People were too indolent even to catch the abundant wild fowl, "though in great need."

Others confirm the popularity of drinking, gambling and billiards. The ever-particular Moses Austin found no tavern in town "that deserves a better name than that of Grog Shop."

Worse than the vices of the inhabitants was the "ague" — a fever that was probably the result of malaria-bearing mosquitoes in the swampy city. Its presence, along with other epidemics such as smallpox, earned Louisville its nickname as "The Graveyard of the West." There was resistance in some quarters to draining and filling in the ponds, which served as fishing lakes, skating rinks and swimming holes; but after a smallpox epidemic in 1817 and an attack of bilious fever that killed at least 140 in 1822, the Pond Fund became the city's chief priority, bankrolled by a lottery and theater performances, among other means.

Growth and Prosperity

The main factor holding back Louisville's development in the 18th century may have been the protracted controversy about whether the United States could trade with Spanish territory downriver (Louisville's most promising outlet). In 1789 the governor of New Orleans removed barriers to navigation and lowered import duties, but it wouldn't be until 1795 and the Pinckney Treaty that trade downstream from Louisville was not contingent on the whim of the Spanish.

The opened river became the key to the city's development. That was already apparent during the era of flatboats and keelboats: The population increased 400 percent between 1800 and 1810. But the true dimensions of the future came clear at midnight on October 28, 1811, when the night was disturbed by an apocalyptic hissing and roaring on the river: the arrival of the *New Orleans*, the first steamboat to stop at our docks. It was followed by the first steamboat to come upriver (the *Enterprize*, in 1815) and the first to be built in Louisville (the *Governor Shelby*, 1816). By 1820, the population had nearly tripled from 1810's, to 4,012; 1,124 were blacks, only 93 of them free. Since Louisville lacked a plantation economy, many of the slaves were hired out as labor; others were sold or used as servants (Kentucky law made it difficult to free them).

Louisville was not the only community at the Falls. Shippingport, a largely French settlement on land since turned into an island by the Portland Canal (and finally cleared of residents in 1958), was founded in 1803; Portland, a little to the west, in 1814. On the north side of the river, in 1783, the Virginia Legislature had given George Rogers Clark and his soldiers 150,000 acres of land, known as Clark's Grant. Jeffersonville was organized in 1801, laid out according to a plan drawn up by Thomas Jefferson. New Albany, below the Falls, was founded in 1813.

Each of these cities (with the possible exception of Shippingport) had ambitions to be the predominant community at the Falls. Why did Louisville win?

In his classic study of the first Western cities, *The Urban Frontier*, Richard C. Wade suggests a number of reasons. Louisville was the first of the cities to be settled, so it had an early grasp on river trade. Louisville was surrounded by rich farm land, whereas the Indiana towns were hemmed in by the steep knobs above them, and Portland was somewhat circumscribed by the river's bend to its west. And perhaps most importantly, the city had a marvelous natural harbor where Beargrass Creek entered the river — a "commodious and sheltered inlet [that] kept barges, keels and flatboats from being sucked into the falling waters," Wade writes.

The deal was sealed with the completion of the Louisville-Portland Canal. A canal was chartered by the state in 1804, but never built. Indiana instituted a lottery to pay for constructing its own canal, but plans were scuttled by the Panic of 1819. Cincinnati, looking to assure its preeminence over Louisville, made attempts to sponsor a passageway on the Indiana side, although engineering difficulties made it three times more expensive to build there. Much of Louisville was dubious about the project (the city's business depended on the interruption of trade, not its smooth progress) but the prospect of a canal being built on the opposite shore pulled the city together, and the recent success of the Erie Canal also whipped up enthusiasm (especially when DeWitt Clinton, the New York governor behind the Erie Canal, visited and said the Kentucky side "had been pointed out by the finger of nature").

The Louisville-Portland Canal was begun in 1825 and opened at the end of 1830 (it was widened in 1872 to accommodate the increasing size of steamboats). Portland was eventually annexed to the city in 1852, although it later made a mocking attempt to secede and

Photo: Dan Dry and Associates

Louisville was so named for Louis XVI.

continues to have its own honorary "mayor" and a generally independent spirit.

Another civic rivalry brought Louisville what would eventually become the University of Louisville. The city attempted to attract away the disgruntled medical faculty of Transylvania University, Lexington's greatest point of pride. A promotional effort managed by James Guthrie, Louisville's leading citizen and eventual president of the University, resulted in the city chartering a complete university. The medical school was established by 1838, a law school by the next decade, but it was 1907 before a college of arts and sciences was firmly established, and the university lacked a full-time president until the Jazz Age.

Louisville was incorporated in 1828, the first city in the Commonwealth with its own judicial and taxing authority. It was a merchant town — one contemporary observer noted that its unique position meant "all the wealth of the Western country must pass through her hands" — and a prosperous one: In 1839, it became the first western city to light its streets with gas lamps. It was single-minded, however: Henry McMurtrie wrote in 1819 that the city's merchants disdained "literature, or the acquirement of those graceful nothings, which, of no value in themselves, still constitute the one great charm of polished society."

The Louisville and Nashville Railroad, chartered in 1850 and constructed with nearly $2 million of city money, began connecting Louisville to other markets with a new degree of directness and reliability (Nashville was 506 miles away by river, as opposed to only 186 rail miles, and rail lines didn't go dry in the summer or ice over in the winter).

Manufacturing lagged behind trade, but there were significant shipbuilding operations, foundries, distilleries and the Tarascon brothers' mill on Shippingport (which later became the Louisville Cement Company). By the 1850s, the city trailed only Cincinnati as a meat-packing center.

Louisville was the 10th-largest city in the country in 1850, and the population continued to swell with Germans fleeing persecution after the revolutions of 1848 and Irish escaping the potato famine. Many of them were Roman Catholics, whose faith gave Louisville an unusually Catholic face for a Southern city; there were also a fair number of Jews. The German liberals — urban, educated, antireligious and scornful of much of American culture — roused the ire of the American Party, the antiforeign, anti-Catholic Know-Nothings. Know-Nothings took control of both city and county government by 1855, and George D. Prentice of *The Louisville Journal* — seeing the Know-Nothing movement as a way to evade the complex agonies of the slavery issue — wrote fiery editorials against the newcomers.

They were fanned into actual flame on Election Day, August 6, 1855, when rioters attacked Germans and Irish, beating and shooting immigrants, burning houses, churches and breweries and killing anywhere from 19 to 22; there were literally pools of blood in the streets. "Bloody Monday" left the city shaken. In *200 Years at the Falls of the Ohio,* Yater says the riot was in part the result of Louisville's unique indecisiveness between North and South: It imbibed both the anti-immigrant resentments of Southern Know-Nothings and the anti-Catholicism of Northern Know-Nothings and found the mixture deadly. And yet the nativist movement declined rapidly in influence. In 1865, a city whose population was by then one-third German and Irish elected German Philip Tomppert mayor.

The Civil War Years

Kentucky began the Civil War as a neutral state. The city was predictably divided and in search of a middle ground that national politics were in the act of erasing. In the 1860 election, its favored candidate was John Bell of the Constitutional Unionists, whose platform of preserving the Union made no mention of the slavery issue. Abraham Lincoln, whose campaign song promoted his Kentucky heritage, won only 91 votes in the city, only slightly more than 1 percent of the total, and only 15 votes in the rest of Jefferson County; Kentuckian John C. Breckinridge, the candidate most identified with the South, did little better. While most of the city's sympathies were with the Union, Louisville sent five companies of volunteers to the Confederate army and continued trading with the Confederacy until the middle of 1861; some prominent citizens belonged to a secret secessionist group called the Knights of the Golden Circle, although one

historian dismisses them as being "about as potent and dangerous as a debating society."

The city even created its own Home Guard to defend against both North and South, headed by Brig. Gen. Lovell Rousseau — as Yater writes, perhaps the only municipally-appointed general in U.S. history. But Kentucky declared itself a Union state in September 1861, and Louisville's loyalties followed suit.

Both Louisville and Clarksville were major supply points for the Union Army. A Jefferson County native, Maj. Robert Anderson, had commanded Fort Sumter when the Confederates attacked it, thereby beginning the war. Anderson, promoted to brigadier general, established his headquarters in Louisville; he was succeeded in October 1861 by his second-in-command, William Tecumseh Sherman.

The city was twice threatened with capture by the Confederates. In the fall of 1861 some in the Union camp figured the fall of Louisville was a foregone conclusion, but Simon Bolivar Buckner's troops came no closer than Lebanon Junction. They held the L&N Railway south of Elizabethtown through the winter and also had the company of Walter Haldeman and his secessionist *Louisville Courier*, which retreated to Buckner's Bowling Green headquarters after the Union Army suppressed it in Louisville.

In September 1862 Confederates had already captured Lexington and Frankfort, and 500 cavalrymen raided Louisville near 18th and Oak streets; there were other skirmishes in Middletown and at Gilman's Point (now St. Matthews), but the Confederates' main force was turned back at the Battle of Perryville in central Kentucky, and the threat to Louisville effectively ended. Their safety assured, Louisvillians grew disenchanted with the war and estranged from the Lincoln administration.

After the war, as we noted in this book's Overview, former Confederates took on positions of power and respect in the community. Walter Haldeman returned from Confederate territory and his *Courier* soon became the city's dominant paper; in 1868 it joined with the *Journal*, edited by Henry Watterson, a reluctant Confederate officer from Tennessee who became the city's best-known journalist, an important spokesman for the idea of a progressive, industrialized New South.

In the postwar years, the city seemed to

declare on the side of the very people it had played a part in defeating as a Union base of operations. There was a large procession in honor of Robert E. Lee's funeral, with 250 businesses closing as a sign of respect; there was an extraordinary celebration in 1877 when the last federal troops were removed from South Carolina and Louisiana.

Some of this retrospective fondness for the Confederacy was the result of racial politics. Kentucky was the only Union state in which slavery was still a living institution at the end of the war. As historian George Wright observes in his book *Life Behind a Veil*, the Emancipation Proclamation freed only slaves in the Confederacy, while Kentucky's slaves had to wait for the passage of the 13th amendment in December 1865. So Kentucky was in a sense the last state to free its slaves. The state was so resistant to any actions to protect or assist the former slaves that the Federal government brought in the Freedmen's Bureau to work on the blacks' behalf, which compounded white resentment of the African Americans pouring into the city (Louisville's black population more than doubled between 1860 and 1870).

The city also viewed itself as the "Gateway to the South" — as the natural channel through which trade would move to the Southern states. While Yater argues against assuming that the city was universally sympathetic to the "lost cause" — a number of prominent Unionists settled in town as well, and men who had been on either side of the war worked together on a variety of enterprises — the image of the Southern planter held symbolic sway in the city for a long time afterwards, evoked by such disparate men as Watterson, liberal post-World War II mayor Charley Farnsley and Col. Harland Sanders.

A Move to Manufacturing

In the years after the war, the L&N lost its exclusive position as the only railroad passing through the state, but under Victor Newcomb it expanded to become the largest railroad in the South. It retained great power in Kentucky: There is a perhaps apocryphal story that a rural legislator once said in the General Assembly, "If the L&N Railroad has no other business to conduct, I move we adjourn." But that power ceased to be exclusively Louisville's to exercise; the city sold its stock in the railroad, fewer Louisvillians sat on the L&N board and Newcomb moved to New York.

Some in the city worried about the loss of the transshipment business that had created Louisville's economic position, fearing that bridges and railroad connections were making Louisville into a point to be passed through rather than stopped at. The first bridge across the Ohio was built in 1870, with two more following by 1895. But when the Louisville, Cincinnati & Lexington Railroad came into town, the city created a railway equivalent to the Falls of the Ohio: Its tracks had to be of a different gauge from the L&N's, so that goods still needed to be transferred from one train to another.

The real transportation problem for Louisville was that as the country grew westward, the important trade routes bypassed us entirely. As local historian Carl Kramer notes, Chicago beat out St. Louis for control of western trade, moving the patterns of shipping to latitudes well north of us. While the city actually did more business with the North in the late 19th century, trade with the South — the most economically depressed part of the nation — was seen to be Louisville's logical economic niche.

Little wonder that the city finally developed ambitions to become a manufacturing as well as a mercantile center. Woodworking, tanning and metalworking were the city's largest industries, but the Louisville economy's most striking feature, then as now, was its diversity in manufacturing. The city put on two large showcases of industry: the Louisville Industrial Exposition in 1872 and the mammoth Southern Exposition in 1883, which drew several million visitors and was the first large-scale demonstration of Edison's incandescent bulb.

Louisville's prosperity (or at least, that of its businesses and their owners) can be read in the extraordinary buildings that remain from the post-Civil War period, including the Carter Dry Goods building on Main Street, the mansions of the Southern Extension (now called Old Louisville) and the Cherokee Triangle. And in 1883 the city had one of its few moments as an avant-garde bastion: Henrik Ibsen's controversial *A Doll's House* (renamed *Thora*) had its American premiere at Macauley's Theatre. (A local candy maker dipped marshmallows in caramel in honor of the lead actress, Polish-born Helena Modjeska; modjeskas are still sold in Louisville candy stores.)

Although the city's position among American cities declined steadily (by 1880 it was only the 16th largest; the 1910 census showed a greatly slowing rate of population growth), Louisville's boundaries grew dramatically. It was after the Civil War that suburban expansion began in earnest, with mule-drawn street cars extending south of Broadway out to Cave Hill and eventually as far as the present site of Bowman Field.

The electric trolley extended the city farther. When the Louisville Jockey Club, since renamed Churchill Downs, opened in 1875, it was on the outskirts of town. When Mayor Charles Jacob purchased what's now known as Iroquois Park in 1889, it was called Jacob's Folly for being so much land, bought for so much money, so far from town (even farther south than the Downs). But the trolley brought the city's new park system, which included Cherokee in the east and Shawnee on the west, within easy range of city dwellers and made a booming success of such new suburbs as Beechmont (between the track and Iroquois Park) and the Cherokee Triangle. Louisville annexed all these areas, as well as Clifton, Crescent Hill, Parkland and the West End to 32nd Street (as well as a piece extending out to Shawnee Park). The Interurban Railway extended well past the city to Fern Creek, Prospect, Jeffersontown and other outlying communities.

Expansion in the '20s

World War I brought *The Courier-Journal* its first Pulitzer Prize — for Watterson's editorials urging entrance into the war — and brought Louisville Camp Zachary Taylor, a training base for new recruits whose young officers included Princeton dropout F. Scott Fitzgerald, who made Daisy Buchanan of *The Great Gatsby* "by far the most popular of all the young girls in Louisville." Camp Taylor was a boost to the local economy, but it was also the focus of the local outbreak of the deadly Spanish influenza. (Its presence also led to a cleanup of vice-ridden Green Street downtown; as part of the sanitation, Green was renamed Liberty.)

The '20s were prosperous in Louisville, inspiring a wave of building that included such imposing structures as the 700-room Brown Hotel and Loew's Theater, now the Louisville Palace. The spread of private automobiles, some of them built at the Ford Motor Company's assembly plant on South Western Parkway, once again extended the city limits. The decade saw the introduction of some of the city's chief institutions: Bowman Field, the city's first airport (1919); WHAS, the city's first radio station (1922); the University of Louisville's Belknap campus (1925); a hydroelectric plant at the Falls dam (1927); the first automobile bridge across the Ohio, at Second Street (1929).

The Depression hit Louisville hard because of the 1930 failure of BancoKentucky, the holding company that controlled both the National Bank of Kentucky and Louisville Trust. One of the largest bank failures of the period, it wiped out many Louisville families. The economic downturn could have been worse, however. The demand for cigarettes went up during the Depression, and local production tripled between 1931 and 1932. Although Prohibition put most of the city's brewers and distillers out of business, Brown-Forman Distillers had one of the 10 permits issued to sell existing stocks of whiskey for medicinal purposes and

INSIDERS' TIP

If you want to sound wise about Louisville history, talk about James Guthrie, who dominated Louisville affairs from the 1820s until after the Civil War. The man who was behind the Portland Canal and the University of Louisville was also Secretary of the Treasury (under Franklin Pierce), a U.S. Senator and president of the L&N Railroad. Local historians decry the fact that two-block Guthrie Street is his only memorial.

did so well at it that the company bought up what less-fortunate competitors had on hand.

In 1937, Louisville was starting to pull out of the Depression when the Ohio unleashed the worst flood in Louisville history: When it crested, the river was 40 feet above its normal level. Pictures from the time show rooftop rescues from the West End, men paddling boats down Fourth Street, houses toppled onto their sides or washed out into the street. All homes west of Fifteenth Street were ordered evacuated, 90 people died, and there was nearly $50 million in property damage. Downtown was cleaned up in time for Derby, but some observers believe the flood created a lasting perception of Western Louisville as an unsafe and undesirable place to live. After a 1945 flood that ranks second among Louisville deluges, the city built a flood wall.

A somewhat less slimy disaster was the 1938 Kentucky law making it all but impossible for first-class cities such as Louisville to annex incorporated areas — a law that has hampered Louisville ever since. It led to the immediate creation of Shively around a number of distilleries; after World War II it led to the county's present patchwork of small cities, with areas such as St. Matthews fighting tooth and nail to avoid being incorporated into Louisville.

War Brings New Industry

World War II brought an incredible expansion of local industry: an artillery powder plant in Charlestown; the Naval Ordnance Plant near the L&N railroad yard; several plants devoted to producing synthetic rubber and other plastic manufacturers in what became known as Rubbertown; and the Curtis-Wright airplane plant (later purchased by International Harvester) at the new airport, Standiford Field. The largest single addition came in 1951, when General Electric built Appliance Park near Buechel. Until very recently, GE was the city's largest employer.

Under wartime mayor Wilson Wyatt (who later became lieutenant governor and managed Adlai Stevenson's presidential campaign) the Louisville Area Development Association, forerunner of the Chamber of Commerce, did the first comprehensive planning the city had ever had. LADA laid out such postwar features as the Inner-Belt Highway (the present-day Watterson) and the North-South Expressway before the national interstate system existed. It made its share of erroneous assumptions, such as the idea that these highways would retard growth on the city's periphery by making downtown easily accessible, but LADA gave Louisville a blueprint for the postwar world.

The most interesting character of those postwar years was Charley Farnsley, a Louisville lawyer who became mayor all but by accident after the incumbent died in office. Farnsley's sartorial trademark was the string tie. His intellectual penchant was for archaic, outlandish analogies: He called himself a "physiocrat" — the first declared one since Benjamin Franklin, an observer noted — and believed World War II expressed the conflict between the "totalitarian" thought of Plato and the democratic thought of Confucius. But his hallmark as mayor (1948-1953) was a rejuvenation of the city that brought it new revenue from an occupational tax, better roads and parks, the first moves against racial segregation and a civic aliveness to new ideas.

It was under Farnsley that Louisville began to see itself as a community that loves and supports the arts. The Louisville Orchestra, which had its origins in an amateur orchestra organized by the Young Men's Hebrew Association, developed a worldwide reputation for commissioning and recording new works. And the Louisville Fund (now the Fund for the Arts) began fund raising for the city's arts groups. (Both the orchestra's commissions and the Fund for the Arts were Farnsley ideas; he also made the Louisville Free Public Library and the University of Louisville chief priorities.) In a 1955 Harper's article, William Manchester compared Louisville's civic comeback to golfer Ben Hogan's and wrote, "Here is the only American city which has ever used culture as an industrial asset."

It was about the same time that *The Courier-Journal*, under the guidance of Barry Bingham Sr. and Mark Ethridge, returned to the national reputation it had possessed in Watterson's time, being regularly named as one of the country's best papers — even, in some eyes, as the chief engine of progress in Kentucky. Bingham and his wife Mary, Farnsley, Wyatt, aldermanic president Dann C. Byck Sr.

Churchill Downs, formerly the Louisville Jockey Club, opened in 1875.

and others made up the most exceptional elite Louisville has ever possessed. The postwar years now look like Louisville's Golden Age.

Louisville had taken few steps toward integration before 1948, when Louisville schoolteacher Lyman T. Johnson filed suit to attend the graduate school of the University of Kentucky. The state's 1904 Day Law forbade integration in institutions of higher learning, but Johnson argued that the courses he wished to take were unavailable at the state's colleges for blacks. Johnson won the suit, a rare instance of the doctrine of separate but equal being used against segregation.

The main branch of the Louisville Free Public Library was integrated in 1948, all branches in 1952; public parks were integrated by a mayoral order in 1955.

In 1956, after the Supreme Court's decision in Brown vs. Board of Education, the city's schools were peacefully desegregated, but not integrated. The distinction is worth making because the school system included a safety valve, of sorts, in its plans: All students could ask to be transferred to a different school (an option taken by 85 percent of the white students). County-wide integration by forced busing in 1975 provoked rioting, but has come to

be accepted by a large part of the community (excepting those who took it as a cue for white flight into outlying counties).

The City's Changing Role

By 1960 Louisville's population reached its all-time high of 390,639, but Jefferson County was showing the really explosive growth, nearly doubling its population since 1950. In 1956 the first attempt at bringing the county suburbs into the city failed; later attempts in 1970, 1982 and 1983 failed as well. The '50s saw a drop in downtown retail sales that only worsened in the '60s. Shoppers went to suburban malls and shopping centers rather than downtown; even the Fourth Street movie theaters were eclipsed by the Showcase Cinemas on a stretch of Bardstown Road just outside the city limits.

In the 1960s the West End became predominantly African American. Real estate practices hastened residential segregation: "Blockbusting," in which real estate agents tried to drum up business by persuading whites to sell because blacks moving into the neighborhood would drive down real estate prices; and a combination of habit and public pressure which made Realtors and lenders keep blacks in certain sections of the city (some saw a "white plot," but there was no need for a conscious conspiracy). In 1967 the city was caught up in a series of protests against housing discrimination which included a visit by Martin Luther King, Jr. and threats to disrupt the Derby. In response the city passed a strong open-housing ordinance at the end of a year (after elections swept the opposing aldermen out of office).

White flight was also hurried along by the construction of I-264, Urban Renewal practices that displaced many blacks in traditionally African-American neighborhoods near downtown and a 1968 riot (small by standards of the time, but deeply disturbing to the city) in the heart of Parkland, which is just now starting to recover as an economic center. The open-housing ordinance now seems more of a symbolic victory than a harbinger of true change: The residential patterns established before it was passed continue to this day.

Attempts to revitalize the center city as a shopping district have never taken off. Fourth Street, the city's longtime commercial center, is like a burned-over district of different "solutions" to downtown's decline. It was paved over for a pedestrian mall; the city built a downtown shopping center called the Galleria which straddles Fourth between Liberty Street and Muhammad Ali Boulevard; it began running a trolley up what's been renamed Fourth Street; and most recently, the street was reopened to auto traffic for part of the day.

Downtown has held its own, however, as a center for government, arts and as an office location. A number of skyscrapers, such as the Citizens' Plaza and the First National Tower, which both went up in 1971, now define the city's skyline. More than $1 billion was invested in the central business district by private and government groups between 1968 and 1986, and the property-tax base more than tripled. The 1983 opening of the Kentucky Center for the Arts, home to all the city's major performing arts groups except Actors Theatre, reaffirmed the city's commitment to the arts and created a valuable link with the rest of the state.

The 1974 tornado was another devastating blow to the city — even more powerful than the 1890 twister that killed 100, although only a twentieth of that number died during the later storm. Neighborhoods in the Highlands and Crescent Hill suffered extensive damage.

But the greatest change to Louisville came with a drastic decline in blue-collar employment that began to be felt around the end of the 1970s. In 1963, 42 percent of the area's jobs were in manufacturing; today, it's around 18 percent. Service- and financial-sector jobs have made up the gap, but declining employment rolls at places such as Appliance Park, and the closing of such plants as International Harvester had a wrenching impact. A reputation as "Strike City" hurt efforts to attract businesses (although Louisville's Ford plants survived through an unprecedented cooperative effort by labor and management).

The 1980s brought Louisville the international headquarters of the Presbyterian Church U.S.A., accomplished with great ballyhoo that included a civic pep rally on the steps of the Arts Center. More quietly, in 1981, UPS chose Standiford Field as the hub for its air operations; UPS is now the largest private employer in Kentucky (and the eighth largest airline in the country).

INSIDERS' TIP

Louisville poet Madison Cawein (1865-1914) was known as "the Kentucky Keats" (although we already had a non-poetical one: John Keats' younger brother George lived in Louisville and is buried in Cave Hill Cemetery). In 1995 a scholar wrote the *Times Literary Supplement* remarking on the similarities between T.S. Eliot's *The Waste Land* and Cawein's poem *Waste Land*, published in a 1913 issue of *Poetry* Eliot would likely have read (although, if he was poaching, Eliot passed by Cawein's image of "the chipmunk's stony lair").

The great local success story was Humana, a for-profit hospital and insurance company that became most famous for Bill Schroeder's 20 months on the Jarvik-7 artificial heart. In 1985 Humana built a handsome headquarters on Main Street that was one of the signal pieces of post-modern architecture. A changing business climate eventually forced the company to split itself into two parts: an insurance company that retained the old name and a hospital company that started out life as Galen and was shortly merged into Columbia/HCA, the largest hospital corporation in the world. Columbia was briefly headquartered in Louisville, then moved to Nashville in 1995. The relocation was greeted in Louisville with a mixture of soul-searching and an attitude, directed at abrasive CEO Ric Scott, that could be summed up as "Don't let the door hit you as you leave."

The 1980s also saw many longtime Louisville companies bought by out-of-town owners: The L&N, bought in 1972 by Seaboard Coast Line, was merged into CSX and retired as a separate corporation. The trend continues into the '90s, with Bank of Louisville the only major bank still locally owned and giant insurance company Providian (formerly Capital Holding) being acquired by Aegon NV of Baltimore. The change in ownership that received the most attention was at the city's newspapers (see our Media chapter).

Jerry Abramson, elected mayor in 1986, was the city's most popular politician since Charley Farnsley, and its first Jewish mayor. His ability to inspire both civic and corporate enthusiasm gave the city the perfect opportunity to abandon one of its government's most profound structural flaws — the law forbidding mayors more than a single term. (Abramson, whose third and final term expires in 1998, is jokingly called Louisville's mayor-for-life.)

Whether it was Abramson's example or a business climate that was largely recession-proof in the early '90s, the city has had a good share of recent successes. Louisville is near the end of an ambitious plan to expand its airport (now called Louisville International, most of the overseas traffic consisting of UPS packages); while its parallel runways will fill a void that's kept the city from attracting many opportunities, it also caused bitterness when it required several modest neighborhoods near the airport to be condemned and cleared. Aggressive management transformed lagging Churchill Downs into one of the nation's premier racetracks (and not only on the first Saturday in May). Louisville-based Vencor became the nation's largest full-service provider of long-term care, squeaking into the Fortune 500 and planning a spectacular riverfront skyscraper as its new headquarters. Papa John's unseated Pizza Hut as the nation's best pizza chain, according to one industry publication, and contributed enough money to a new football stadium that it's now called Papa John's Cardinal Stadium. Proposals are circulating for a new downtown baseball park and maybe even a downtown arena, for purposes of attracting an NBA team to one of the nation's most basketball-crazy towns. The Kentucky Kingdom amusement parked turned around from a civic joke into a "thrill park" that challenges the Downs as the city's leading tourist attraction. And a new park on the riverfront may finally bring the city back into a close relationship with the Ohio.

But no changes in attitude could inure the city and its environs to natural disaster. In May 1996, tornadoes ripped through southern Jefferson County and into Bullitt County. Then in February 1997, the city suffered a two-stage flood that was its worst in over 30 years. First, after 10 inches of rain fell in 24 hours, creeks and sewers flooded low-lying areas, most disastrously in the southwestern Jefferson County flood plain; then, as that water fed into the Ohio, the river overflowed its banks with more authority than it had mustered since 1964.

Louisville in the 1990s bears a striking resemblance to the city it was in preceding decades — still ethnically and economically diverse; still divided politically between city and county governments, despite a new level of cooperation; still spreading out centrifugally from the center city; still intimately involved in the shipment of goods; still squabbling about bridges and such; at times, outside of national trends, at others, entirely at their mercy; still acquiring the appointments of a proper city, from roads to parallel airport runways to waterfront parks.

The past seems less like a prologue and more like a conversation we were having just the other day.

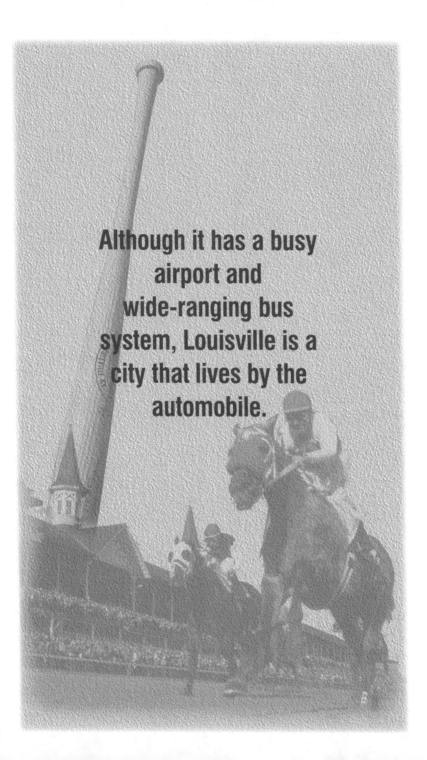

Although it has a busy airport and wide-ranging bus system, Louisville is a city that lives by the automobile.

Getting Around

Although it has a busy airport and wide-ranging bus system, Louisville is a city that lives by the automobile. And dies by it. Many of the main streets in the metropolitan area, such as Dixie Highway and Hurstbourne Parkway, are so indifferent to pedestrians they might as well be hostile. There is little car pooling, few accommodations for bicyclists, and although the bus system does a pretty good job, few Louisvillians who can afford their own cars choose to ride the bus.

Nevertheless, if you've ever driven in a city with really bad traffic, such as New York or Los Angeles or Chicago, you'll find Louisville's traffic is easy going — congested on the biggest roads in morning and afternoon rush hours, but only rarely resembling parking-lot conditions. Most of the time this is an easy city to get around in, and the powers that be have devoted effort and expense in recent years to making it even more convenient (for drivers, anyway).

As for getting here, driving's a snap — one favorite statistic of the Convention and Visitors Bureau is that Louisville is within a day's drive of half the country's population. Flying in and out has gotten easier in recent years, although Louisville has fewer direct flights than larger cities. Air travel should continue to get easier, with the approaching completion of an airport expansion that will give the city an aviatic amenity it's lacked — parallel runways.

The Big Picture

On the Kentucky side of the Ohio River, the city spreads like a fan, with downtown Lou-isville at the narrow end and the major arterial streets radiating like ribs, more or less.

Two beltways loop from near the Ohio on the northeast side of the county to near the Ohio on the southwest side — either one could be the fan's outer edge. And indeed, each marks what, at the time of construction, was perceived as the outer limit of Jefferson County development: the Watterson Expressway (Interstate 264), the frontier as imagined in the late '40s, and the Gene Snyder Freeway (Interstate 265, Ky. Highway 841), which still seems like the outskirts but probably won't be for long. (Called the Jefferson Freeway on some maps, the Snyder was renamed for the congressman who obtained many of the funds to build it.)

The three chief interstate highways — Interstates 65, 64 and 71 — converge just south of the Kennedy Bridge, in the area everyone calls Spaghetti Junction (a name you won't find on maps). We'll put off discussing that for a moment.

In the past, the Watterson — two lanes each way, with some ramps you might mistake for driveways — was the place you least wanted to be at rush hour. But in 1995 the state highway department finished a lengthy reconstruction of this artery, widening it to a minimum of three lanes in each direction and greatly improving the rampage. It now moves reasonably well, especially westbound, unless there's construction or an accident, with a single exception: the eastbound exit to Poplar Level Road.

The Snyder Freeway is still somewhat underused. The Snyder makes its loop so far from the center of town that it's impractical for many destinations, although the area between its interchanges with U.S. Highway 60 and I-64 often sees congestion.

The most heavily traveled interstate is I-65, the North-South Expressway, as it's sometimes called, a major trucking route that connects Chicago to Mobile, Alabama, (via Indianapolis; Nashville, Tennessee; and Birmingham, Alabama). It crosses the river from Jeffersonville, Indiana, on the densely traveled John F. Kennedy Bridge; it ties into the Watterson Expressway at the airport, then heads south into Bullitt County.

I-65's most frazzling segments are the bridge; the southbound portion between Liberty Street downtown and Arthur Street near the University of Louisville; and around its interchange with the Watterson Expressway — an area you'll sometimes hear traffic reporters refer to as "the horse barns," referring to the stables at the Kentucky Fair and Exposition Center north of the interchange with the Watterson.

Northbound traffic tends to move more smoothly, although a major accident near downtown can back up traffic for several miles, and the horse barns are sometimes a marker of morning congestion.

I-71 begins in downtown Louisville and heads north through Cincinnati to Cleveland; locally, it connects downtown with the eastern part of Jefferson County, and beyond it Oldham County, one of the fastest-growing counties in the state. It often backs up in the mornings near the Zorn Avenue exit.

I-64 comes from the east, through Louisville's intrastate rival, Lexington. From downtown it goes west along the river to the Sherman Minton Bridge, where it crosses into Indiana and heads for St. Louis. Its usual congestion points are Grinstead Drive, Cannons Lane, its intersection with the Watterson Expressway in east Jefferson County and Hurstbourne Parkway a little farther east.

All three interstates come together at the aptly named Spaghetti Junction, a tangle of roads and ramps between Butchertown and the Kennedy Bridge. There's no simple way to describe it — did you think they called it Spaghetti Junction because it was so straight and

narrow? Most maps don't portray it very well, either. It became a jumble of two-lane ramps, rather than a single megahighway, because when it was built the ramps had to go between the columns that supported the approach to the Big Four Railroad Bridge, which is now a rusting relic with its approaches torn down.

Spaghetti Junction was what Louisville had for thrill rides before Kentucky Kingdom was built. It has hairpin turns (the so-called "Dead Man's Curve" leading from I-71/I-64 to southbound I-65), spots where two expressways combine to become a single road, counter-intuitive lane assignments, a lack of what we writers call parallel construction — Spaghetti Junction's got it all. Finding and staying in the proper lane is crucial, and drivers don't tolerate fools gladly.

In the afternoons, Spaghetti Junction traffic can back up onto the southbound lanes of the Kennedy Bridge, creating a hazardous situation: Some motorists approaching the bridge on the expressway don't heed the signs to reduce speed and as a result meet fellow motorists with more intimacy than either would have chosen. Little wonder, then, that the Kennedy's congestion is a leading impetus behind the idea of building another bridge across the Ohio.

Any interstate route that passes through Louisville must pass through Spaghetti Junction. The best advice is to drive intelligently: Watch the road signs with extreme care as you begin to approach downtown, get into the proper lane and stay there. But between 3 and 6 PM, it's worth avoiding if you can. Coming from the west on I-64, you can get off on I-264 and loop around; same if you're coming from the east on I-71. If you're crossing the Ohio, you can take the George Rogers Clark Memorial Bridge, which connects Second Street in Louisville to the no-man's-land between Jeffersonville and Clarksville in Indiana (and eventually connects to Ind. Highway 62 and I-65). You'll need to find your way back to the Interstate if you're heading south, but on the Indiana side, that DMZ leads into ramps that will take you either to I-65 or Ind. 62.

On the Indiana side of the river, I-65 is

FYI

Unless otherwise noted, the area code for all phone numbers listed in this chapter is 502.

right at the boundary between Jeffersonville and its western neighbor, Clarksville. One of its hairiest spots is northbound, at the Eastern Boulevard exit in the afternoon — a driver can avoid that by getting off early to take the 10th Street/Ind. 62 exit (Exit 1) and taking Stansifer Avenue to Spring Street, which branches into Eastern Boulevard.

I-64 passes through New Albany and up into Floyds Knobs; it is most likely to back up at Ind. Highway 150 in Floyds Knobs in the morning. Indiana's portion of I-265 (as yet named for no politician) connects I-64 to I-65 and beyond it to the Clark Maritime Center on the river near Six Mile Island. It also serves as a convenient way to bypass 10th Street in Jeffersonville. There are times when I-65 backs up badly enough that I-265 becomes a useful detour to I-64 and across the river, even though it's 7 miles out of the way.

On the Surface . . .

Downtown Louisville, from Main to Chestnut streets and from Jackson to Eighth streets, is, with a few exceptions, a grid of one-way streets. Streets are numbered east and west from First Street (so 720 W. Muhammad Ali is at Seventh and Ali) and north and south from Main Street. Since Main is the major street closest to the river, there are precious few addresses such as 125 N. First Street.

The single-direction traffic moves well, although the arrangement often means you may have to go around the block to reach your destination. Most downtown corners are posted with black-and-white signs forbidding right turns on red. During rush hours, parking is prohibited in certain lanes and no left turns are allowed on Broadway between First and Seventh streets.

Fourth Street, the city's principal shopping street since the turn of the century, was closed to traffic from Broadway to Market Street in the '70s, turning into a pedestrian mall in (mostly vain) hopes of attracting shoppers back downtown; in the '80s, it added a trolley and a shopping mall. It's now come full circle: Since all attempts at revitalizing Fourth Street have failed, it has been reopened to local-access car traffic (although it's closed to auto traffic from 10 AM to 2 PM daily, so the city doesn't have to repay the federal government for the $2.2 million it spent to build trolley lanes).

Although downtown has lost some jobs to the suburbs, especially the Hurstbourne Parkway corridor in the eastern part of the county, it remains the greatest concentration of employment in the area and so has the densest rush hour (except perhaps for Hurstbourne Parkway, which is the major street in a heavily developed commercial and industrial area).

Right now, the quickest commute of any distance to downtown is from Floyds Knobs or Edwardsville in Indiana, taking I-64 across the Sherman Minton Bridge (unless construction on the bridge reduces the number of lanes). Folks who take a half-hour or more to come in from eastern Jefferson County hear their Hoosier neighbors brag about 15-minute commutes.

The quickest surface routes into downtown are Main and Jefferson streets from the east, Market Street from the west — all streets with four traffic lanes and parking lanes on each side. South of Broadway, Breckinridge and St. Catherine streets are the quickest routes from the east, Kentucky and Oak streets from the west. Second and Third streets are the best routes from and to the south.

The radial streets leading from central Louisville are the area's most important surface roads — major commuting routes, commercial spines for neighborhoods. In many cases, they follow the same path as historic turnpikes

---

INSIDERS' TIP

Every Monday in its Metro section, *The Courier-Journal* publishes "Road Show," a rundown of road construction in the area — a guide to highway headaches for the upcoming week. More up-to-the-moment information is available from the Kentucky Transportation Cabinet's Road Report phone line: (800) 459-7623.

Cruise down the river aboard *The Spirit of Jefferson.*

dating back to the 19th century (part of Preston Highway follows the Wilderness Trail that began where Daniel Boone came through the Cumberland Gap).

Moving clockwise from about 2 o'clock on an imaginary clock face, the major arteries are River Road (used by some commuters, but also noteworthy as one of the prettiest drives in the area); Brownsboro Road (U.S. Highway 42); Frankfort Avenue and Lexington Road, which converge to form Shelbyville Road (U.S. 60); Bardstown Road (U.S. Highway 31E-150), with Taylorsville Road (Ky. Highway 155) branching off at The Highlands; Preston Highway (Ky. Highway 61); and Dixie Highway (U.S. Highway 60-31W).

Shelbyville Road tends to be congested, especially in the afternoon, from Oxmoor Mall to Thierman Lane in St. Matthews. In the afternoon, Dixie is often bumper-to-bumper for the mile between the Watterson Expressway and Rockford Lane but otherwise experiences only minor hang-ups at some of the major intersections farther south.

Bardstown Road north of Douglass Boulevard (and its "feeder" from downtown, Baxter Avenue) is the only street in town with reversible lanes. At rush hour, parking is prohibited and flashing yellow Xs designate one of the center lanes for turning, providing two unobstructed lanes in the most heavily traveled direction. Since a new system of computer-controlled signals was installed in 1994 — harbinger of the system that will soon control all of Louisville's stop lights — Bardstown progresses well during rush hours. Its worst congestion actually comes during lunch, when folks flock to its restaurants, parking takes up a lane on either side of the street and three-phase lights at Broadway and at the junction of Bardstown, Baxter and Highland Avenue hang up traffic.

There are fewer cross-county routes than radial ones — one reason the Watterson gets so much traffic — although the magnificent set of parkways designed by Frederick Law Olmsted link together to traverse a good part of the city, and Hurstbourne Parkway traverses from Bardstown Road to U.S. Highway 22.

Southern Indiana's closest equivalent to the Watterson Expressway is more circuitous: Ind. 62, which, as it passes through the area, takes on more guises than Lon Chaney. It's Charlestown Road and 10th Street in Jeffersonville, then it runs alongside I-65 through Clarksville, becomes Spring Street in

New Albany and finally joins pavement with I-64 until Edwardsville, where it becomes plain Ind. 62 again and heads south.

It Fell from the Sky

In normal conditions, Louisville-area drivers are no better or worse than those anywhere else — although there's a lot of bickering back and forth across the river on how bad Kentuckians or Hoosiers drive. But Louisvillians are, with few exceptions, terrible drivers in snow and ice; even a comparatively light dusting turns the highways into a scary mixture of too-cautious and too-reckless motorists.

We only have to deal with winter storms a few times a year, so people never develop good skills for ice driving — and they don't seem to remember what they might have learned from the last storm. One local television newscast actually ran a feature on driving in snow with such didn't-you-take-Driver's-Ed? tips as "Reduce speed," "Don't follow other cars too closely," "Plan your trips to give yourself extra time" and "Steer into a skid, not out of it." A town where this advice qualifies as news is not very snow-savvy.

The winter storm of January 1994, which brought a triple whammy of freezing rain, more than 16 inches of snow and record low temperatures, paralyzed the city for nearly a week. Spaghetti Junction and other expressway ramps turned into truck camps; snow plow blades broke or skipped over the hard pan of ice and packed snow. It was a mess.

We haven't had a big snow since, although threats of one in early 1997 brought out a comic-opera level of preparedness on the part of city, county and state road crews and and all of the area's action news teams. But Louisvillians' snow-driving skills may be less quick to improve.

Car Pooling

Louisville's air quality is bad enough that reducing auto pollution is becoming, slowly, a greater community priority. To reduce the number of single-passenger vehicles on the road, the Kentuckiana Regional Planning and Development Agency (KIPDA — yeah, we know the letters don't match up) set up the Commuter Pool, a clearinghouse to match people with car and van pools. Call 267-5400 or (800) 826-7433 (VAN-RIDE). Riders registered with the Commuter Pool qualify for the Guaranteed Ride Home Program, which allows folks who miss their ride because of an emergency to get an 80 percent reimbursement of cab fare. (But don't use it too liberally — you're limited to four reimbursements a year.)

Bicycling

While biking for pleasure is popular in Louisville — the Louisville Bicycle Club, formerly the Louisville Wheelmen, is 100 years old, and one of the larger clubs in the country — bicycling for more practical purposes has yet to catch on.

When Cornerstone 2020, the county's new land-use plan, looked at patterns of bicycle use in the metro area, it concluded "Most of the existing system fails to provide direct and continuous routes to destination points for commuting or other utilitarian trips . . . . Routes are difficult to follow if you don't know where you're going."

They're even more difficult to follow because many of the green triangular signs that mark the bike paths have fallen down. And there are few dedicated bicycle paths, or even bike lanes — most bike routes are shared with automobiles. It's little wonder that a system of bike lockers installed downtown in the '70s was removed for lack of use.

The most extensive set of bike paths connect the city's three major Olmsted Parks — Shawnee, Iroquois and Cherokee — with downtown. (The Cornerstone 2020 study said the West End provided some of the most direct routes).

The best bike path — and the best place to walk, run or skate, for that matter — is the new RiverWalk, which travels around the city's northern perimeter, from downtown to Chickasaw Park in the West End.

A comprehensive map showing bicycle routes and describing points of interest along the way is available from the Louisville and Jefferson County Division of Planning and Development Services. Call 574-6230 or write them at 531 Court Place, Suite 803, Louisville KY 40202.

Parking

Parking is increasingly tight in downtown Louisville — the person without a reserved spot finds himself learning just how many stories they put into those parking garages, and "Full" signs are not uncommon, especially around the courts complex at Sixth and Jefferson streets. Rates vary from $18 to $100 a month (the average is almost $58) or from $1 to $10 a day (the average is $4.71).

There is also on-street parking at more than 3,500 parking meters, for periods ranging from 30 minutes to 10 hours, at rates ranging from 20¢ to 75¢ an hour. (The best long-term deal? On Roy Wilkins Avenue, a.k.a. 9th Street, from Broadway to Main Street, there are 10-hour meters at 20¢ an hour.)

A map of downtown parking lots and garages is available from Louisville Central Area, 555 Brown and Williamson Tower at 401 S. Fourth Street, 583-1671, or from the Downtown Management District Safety Team, a group of red-jacketed retired police officers who walk a beat in the Central Business District.

Finding parking prices takes some looking. Most downtown garages have a sandwich board outside advertising an "early bird" all-day rate, but their hourly rates usually aren't posted until you get to the ticket booth.

Another option is the Downtown F.L.I.E.R., which for $35 monthly provides parking in a lot on the fringe of downtown (it's located at Hancock and Madison streets) and a pass for free rides on a shuttle from the parking lot (or any other city bus serving the central business district).

Buses

Transit Authority of River City (TARC)
Union Station, 1000 W. Broadway
• **information 585-1234, offices 561-5100**

TARC, a bus line established in 1974, is the only mass transit system in the area. (Al-

though a light rail system is being studied and has passionate advocates.)

Ridership is higher and bus service more extensive in Louisville than in many comparably sized cities. In some locales, it provides great service (there is a bus every five minutes or so coming along Broadway and Bardstown Road); some areas far from the center of town only see a bus twice a day and others not at all. The buses are generally well-maintained and safe.

TARC is on the way to recovering from a grave fiscal crisis that came to a head in 1994, although its budget is still tight. TARC has made some recent moves toward expanding service — significantly increasing service in Southern Indiana (with a comfortable hub located in Clarksville's River Falls Mall) and offering "night owl" service that offers curb-to-curb rides ($1.50 each way) to late shift workers in the city's empowerment zone (parts of the West End and the Shelby Park and Smoketown neighborhoods just east of downtown).

Among the most pleasant sights on Louisville's streets are the illustrated buses, painted all over as a kind of rolling billboard. They look like giant cars or pickles or grocery sacks; they appear as if Ronald McDonald is behind the wheel or Bart Simpson is spray-painting the side.

Buses now run weekdays from 5 AM to midnight, 6 AM to 10 PM Saturday and 7 AM to 9 PM Sunday and holidays. Five core routes — Fourth Street, Market Street, Muhammad Ali Boulevard, Preston-to-18th Street and Broadway — operate 5 AM to midnight weekends.

Cash fares are $1 during peak hours (Monday through Friday, 6:30 to 8:30 AM and 3:30 to 5:30 PM), 75¢ all other times, exact change only. Children aged 5 and younger accompanied by an adult ride free.

Students and people with disabilities pay 50¢ at all times, if they have a TARC photo ID. Senior citizens with an ID pay 25¢ Monday to Friday, 10 AM - 3 PM; all other times they pay 50¢. Downtown circulators are 10¢; the Fourth Street trolley is free. (It's officially *Toonerville*

FYI

Unless otherwise noted, the area code for all phone numbers listed in this chapter is 502.

II, after Louisville native Fontaine Fox's Jazz Age comic strip "Toonerville Trolley.")

TARC also sells Fare $aver tickets, sold in strips of 10 for $5.00 ($4 for students, senior citizens and people with disabilities). They're available by mail, at most banks in the metro area and several other locations as well. There's also a monthly pass that costs $23 and is good for unlimited rides. And persons 100 years old and older receive honorary rider passes allowing them to ride free at any time.

The Stop 'N' Go Passport — a.k.a. a transfer — allows you to board any TARC route within two hours after it's issued. You can transfer to an intersecting route; stop, then re-board and continue your trip; even use it to go to and from the same destination. Crazy times, man. It's free, but you have to ask for it when you board the bus.

Bus stops are marked with TARC's red-and-white signs. Seats directly behind and across from the driver are reserved for elderly and disabled passengers.

Commuters can take advantage of a number of free "Park and TARC" parking lots throughout Jefferson County; there are also several in Southern Indiana and Oldham County.

TARC's information number is 585-1234 (the TTY phone for hearing-disabled customers is 587-8255). Tell the operators where you are, where you'd like to go and when you'd like to arrive, and they'll figure out which bus (or buses) you need to catch.

TARC offers TARC3: door-to-door paratransit transportation for customers unable to use its regular fixed-route buses due to a functional limitation and who are traveling to and from locations that are three-quarters of a mile or less from a bus route. Fare is twice the prevailing rate for the regular bus ($2 during peak hours, $1.50 all other times); service is scheduled no more than 14 days in advance, available on a first-come, first-served basis.

Greyhound Lines
720 W. Muhammad Ali Boulevard
• 561-2805

Interstate buses leave daily from the Greyhound Terminal. It's mostly a north-south travel point — more buses go to Nashville and points south or Cincinnati, Indianapolis and points north, and fewer through Lexington to the east or St. Louis to the west.

The terminal is open 24 hours a day. Tickets must be purchased in person. Passengers are advised to purchase their tickets in advance and to arrive at the terminal 45 minutes to an hour before departure time. For schedule and fare information, call (800) 231-2222.

Taxis

Louisville is not a city where passengers hail a roving taxicab. In fact, it's illegal to hail one other than at a marked cab stand. Cabs stand at only a few locations: Louisville International Airport; the Greyhound Terminal; in front of the Levy's Building, 235 W. Market; and at Churchill Downs during racing season. They may also be found in front of local hotels, especially the Galt House, Seelbach and Brown.

Otherwise, you have to call the dispatchers for the two companies that control the local cab fleet: **Star Community Cab Company**, 772-2503, and **Yellow Cab**, 636-5511. Fare is a maximum of $3.25 for the first mile and $1.50 for each additional mile. All cab drivers go through a training program on Louisville history and local attractions, although "Where do I go to get some action around here?" is not the way to find out more about George Rogers Clark and the historic homes in the area.

Limousines

The following companies provide the inimitable pleasure of wondering who last sat on this fine Corinthian leather. Was it Hank Williams Jr.? Lloyd Bridges? The King and Queen of the Ballard High prom?

Rates average around $40 or so an hour, ususally with a three-hour minimum; while it's easy to book a limo during the rest of the year, you need to book months in advance for Christmas, New Year's Eve, Prom season and Derby.

Accent Limousine • 222-0638.
Ambassador Capital Limousine • 964-7139
Aristocrat Limo Service • 361-8007
Aristocrat Limousine Service • 968-8818
Bee Line Limousine Service • 964-9969
Community Limousine Service • 778-1350
Cosmopolitan Limousine Co. • 966-5466.
Gray's Limousine • 367-1177
Limousines by Pierre • 775-5104
Prestige Limousine Service • 957-5073
R&R Limousine Service • 957-4254
Renn's Luxury Limousine • 239-2929
Royal Charters, Inc. • 454-7722
Supreme Limousine Service • 772-0200
Yellow Limousine Service • 636-5517

Air Travel

Commercial Airports

Louisville International Airport at Standiford Field
I-264 at Freedom Way • 368-6524, information booth 367-4636

Few things show off the mingled advantages and disadvantages of Louisville's middling size as well as its airport and the air service it provides.

No one would ever choose to have a major airport in the middle of his or her city, which is what's happened as Louisville grew to and beyond Standiford Field after it opened in 1947 on a tract of land between Crittenden Drive and Preston Highway. Then in the '80s, when the city fathers decided the airport needed to grow, whole neighborhoods were annexed for its new runways and accompanying development, creating a great deal of pain and ill will among the displaced.

But it's good luck for the traveler: When you fly into Louisville, your ultimate destination is probably 20 minutes or less away.

In the airlines' hub-and-spoke system, Louisville is a spoke, although the UPS air service makes it one of the largest cargo hubs in the world. And while the city would dearly love to pursue a passenger hub, it seems unlikely — airlines are leaning away from hubs and not looking to add new ones to their systems.

As a result, there are comparatively few nonstop flights to and from Louisville — the biggest complaint of Louisville travelers. The majority of nonstops are to hub cities, among them Atlanta, Charlotte, Chicago (the leading destination from Louisville), Cincinnati, Cleveland, Dallas/Fort Worth, Houston, Indianapolis, Memphis, Minneapolis, Pittsburgh, St. Louis and Washington, D.C. And there is an additional number of direct flights that involve a stop but not changing planes. But while connections are a hassle — and some Louisville flyers still drive to Cincinnati to avoid them — most U.S. destinations (except the West Coast) can be reached from Louisville within 4 hours.

But there are advantages to being a spoke, the main one being price — on average, flights from spoke airports are less expensive than those from hubs. More importantly, several "no frills" airlines — Continental, America West Express and Southwest, now the airport's leading carrier — came in 1993 and brought a new degree of price competition into the market. Southwest now rivals Delta as the city's leading air carrier.

The airport has grown dramatically in recent years. The new terminal was only completed in 1989, and the number of both passengers and flights increased dramatically in recent years. The presence of UPS, the construction of parallel runways (due to be completed in 1997) and an aggressive marketing campaign have raised the airport's profile in the industry and are good indications that the airport should continue to grow.

And in 1995 it received its grand new name, a subject of much local snickering — virtually all the international flights are UPS cargo planes. (The airport retains SDF as its three-letter identifier.)

The airport's size has other advantages. Baggage gets out quickly. The rental car area is conveniently located on the lower level of

Landside Terminal. And parking is easy: While there's a shuttle service from the farthest reaches of the long-term lot, most parking is an easy walk to the terminal, and a new parking garage directly across from the terminal has added over 4,000 new spaces.

And frequent travelers say they come to know the people who work at the airport — giving the experience of flying a friendly feeling that's impossible at larger airports.

The terminal building is divided into Landside Terminal, where tickets are sold, bags claimed and gifts purchased. It's next to the parking lots, with departures on the upper level and arrivals on the bottom. Airside Terminal, where passengers embark or deplane, is a long Y shape, with gates in the arms of the Y. (If there's one complaint about the terminal, it's that the walk from Landside Terminal to the gates is long, despite the moving sidewalk. There's no pleasing some people.)

The easiest way to reach Standiford Field is to take the airport exits from Interstates 65 and 264; or take Phillips Lane (which runs between Preston Highway and Crittenden Drive) and turn onto Freedom Way.

Several car rental companies have offices at the airport, including **Alamo**, (800) 327-9633; **Avis**, 368-5851; **Budget**, 363-4300; **Dollar**, 366-1600; **Hertz**, 361-0181; **National**, 361-2515; **Rent-A-Wreck**, 363-1639; and **Thrifty**, 367-2277

General Aviation Airports

Bowman Field
2815 Taylorsville Rd. • 368-6524

Bowman Field, the city's first air field, is centrally located on Taylorsville Road, near the Seneca Park golf course. It has three paved and lighted runways and a control tower; instrument landing is permitted. The Unicom frequency is 122.95. The terminal is a landmark for architecture — it's an attractive building, built by the WPA — and cuisine: It houses one of the city's best restaurants, Le Relais (see our Restaurants chapter). Ground service is provided by Central American Airways, 458-3211 and Triangle Flying Service, 452-1185.

Clark County Airport
7001 Airport Dr., Sellersburg, Ind.
• **246-7460**

Sixteen-year-old Clark County has a full Instrumental Landing System. Its two paved and lighted runways are 100 feet wide; one is 5,500 feet long, the other 3,900 feet. The Unicom frequency is 122.7. It's open 24 hours and there are no landing fees.

Ground service is provided by two fixed base operators. Hap's Aerial Enterprises, 246-5491 (ARINC frequency 129.275), supplies all grades of fuel (80, 100-LL and Jet A) and waives parking fees if you purchase fuel. Hangar space is available. Their mechanics perform major and minor repairs, maintenance and avionics. Haps offers flight instruction and charter flights.

Aircraft Specialists, 246-4696 or (800) PRO-JETS (ARINC frequency 128.90), is a Phillips 66 Partners-Into-Plane dealer. It supplies 100-LL and Jet A fuel, and waives parking fees if you purchase fuel. Hangar space is available. Their mechanics perform major and minor repairs, maintenance and avionics. Aircraft Specialists offers flight instruction, charter flights and rental planes.

American Car Rental, 581-1972, and **Whirlaway Helicopters**, 246-5454, serve the airport.

Trains

There is no passenger train service from Louisville, and the nearest stations see only a few trains daily. There is a daily Thruway bus departing at 6:35 AM from the local Greyhound station (see above) which connects to Amtrak in Chicago.

The closest Amtrak service is in Cincinnati (Union Terminal, 1301 Western Ave.), where the *Cardinal* connecting Chicago and Washington, D.C. makes stops in the early morning; there are also Thruway buses to Chicago and Cleveland. Indianapolis is also a stop on the *Cardinal*. Centralia, Ill. (209 miles west on I-64) is a stop on the *City of New Orleans*, connecting Chicago and the Crescent City.

Weary travelers looking for a clean, hospitable place to wash away the dust of the road, have a good meal and lay their heads at night will find fine choices in Louisville.

Accommodations

Weary travelers looking for a clean, hospitable place to wash away the dust of the road, have a good meal and lay their heads at night will find fine choices in Louisville: modern, luxury facilities with the latest amenities; bed and breakfast inns in Victorian mansions furnished with antiques; historic hotels with elegant detailing; and moderate- and budget-priced motels for cost-conscious business and family travelers. The city's hotels and motels are clustered in three areas: downtown, around the airport and the East End.

In this chapter, we've listed accommodations in a range of prices that apply to every week of the year except one — Derby Week. The first week in May, room prices are at least double, often triple and sometimes more. There are other considerations during Derby Week that you would do well to heed. Many hotels and bed and breakfast inns require reservations for the entire three-day weekend — Thursday, Friday and Saturday. Hotels and bed and breakfast inns send letters to their guests from the previous year, giving them first crack at renewing their reservations for the coming year. And it's the norm for people to reserve a room a year or more ahead when they're checking out. If you plan to visit Louisville during that time, call or write as early as you can and reserve your place. Some hotels keep a waiting list, and if there are rooms available after the regulars have responded, they'll let you know.

Some Derby visitors take the path of least resistance and stay in Lexington, Cincinnati or Indianapolis and drive in for the day. Bleak as it may seem, a word of optimism is probably in order: Last year, there were rooms available at the last minute in some of the smaller, less convenient hotels and motels. You may have to drive a distance to the Downs and do without some luxuries, but you will find a place to catch a few Zs in between races. Breeders Cup weekend is nearly as popular as Derby, so the same arrangements prevail.

Because of the frequency of large conventions, sporting events and conferences, reservations are recommended for all of Greater Louisville's large hotels and motels. For a listing of smaller accommodations, call the Convention and Visitor's Bureau at (800) 626-4656 and ask for a free copy of its Guide to Greater Louisville.

Hotels

Downtown

The Brown
$$$$ • 335 W. Broadway • 583-1234, (800) 866-ROOM

In 1922, J. Graham Brown, millionaire lumberman and capitalist, announced he would build a $4-million, 15-story hotel at the corner of Fourth and Broadway. David Lloyd George, former Prime Minister of Great Britain was the first person to sign the guest register. On the nights of October 25 and 26, 1923, people jammed the streets in front of The Brown for its official opening. Each night, capacity crowds of 1,200 people attended inaugural dinner dances inside. When the doors were opened to the public, 10,000 people trooped through the new building.

In 1925 Brown built an office building that included The Brown Theatre (now the Macauley). Lily Pons, while playing there, let her pet lion cub roam free in her suite. Al Jolson got into a fight in the hotel's English Grill, and Queen Marie of Romania visited in 1926 and was royally entertained in the Crystal Ballroom, complete with a red carpet and gold throne. Victor Mature had a brief career here as an elevator operator before earning fame in Hollywood.

In April 1980 the Broadway/Brown Corp. was formed to coordinate Louisville's Broadway Renaissance, and The Brown was renovated. The old rooms, small by modern standards, were opened to create 296 instead of the original 600. Maroon and green Bottocino marble, polished brass, crystal chandeliers, mahogany and oak were used to restore the charm of the hotel. The arches of the mezzanine, enclosed in 1971 when the hotel was forced to close, were reopened, the ballroom's five original crystal chandeliers refurbished and new color painstakingly applied to the ballroom and lobby's intricate plaster detailing. Its previous grandeur retrieved at an expenditure of $25 million, The Brown reopened January 11, 1985.

FYI

Unless otherwise noted, the area code for all phone numbers listed in this chapter is 502.

The Brown is a Camberley Hotel offering a full range of guest services that include the Camberley Club, airport shuttle, fitness center, free overnight shoe shine, fresh flowers in every suite, morning newspaper, ample parking and airport limousine service. All rooms have cable TV and HBO.

The Courier-Journal rated the hotel's English Grill the Best Restaurant in Louisville (see our Restaurants chapter). Casual dining is available in J. Graham's Cafe; the Thoroughbred Lounge and Lobby Lounge serve cocktails. Distinctive meetings and social events are accommodated in eight renovated rooms, including the Crystal Ballroom, for up to 700 people.

Days Inn Central
$ • 1620 Arthur St. • 636-3781, (800) DAYS INN

Days Inn Central has rooms with one or two double or king-size beds, HBO and basic cable TV, free local calls and complimentary continental breakfast daily. This is inexpensive housing, so don't expect the Ritz.

Galt House
Galt House East
$$$-$$$$ • On the river at Fourth Ave. • 589-5200

In the early 1800s, the original Galt House at the corner of Second and Main streets was the residence of Dr. W.C. Galt. In 1835 a 60-room hotel was opened as the Galt House on the opposite corner and was noted for its excellence in food and lodging.

The original hotel was destroyed by fire in 1865, and a second Galt House opened at First and Main in 1869. This hotel was considered the finest in the South and entertained presidents Teddy Roosevelt, Arthur, Fillmore and Taft and actresses Lillian Russell and Sarah Bernhardt. By the end of World War I, the Galt House was considered past its prime and was razed in 1921.

In 1972 the present Galt House was built, and in 1986 the Galt House East "all suite" tower was added, making the 1,300-room Galt House complex one of the 150 largest hotels in the United States. The Galt House has 700 guest rooms, including 45 suites with balconies. The decor is quite fascinating — some say that no two rooms at the Galt House even remotely look alike, and eras and styles of furniture are mixed in what could only have been madcap designing glee.

Revolving 25 stories above Louisville, the Flagship restaurant features continental cuisine, nightly entertainment and a view of Louisville and the Ohio River (see our Restaurants chapter). The Fountain Room features a luncheon buffet, and the River Grill offers casual dining (see our Restaurants chapter). Three lounges offer nightly entertainment.

The hotel has a large outdoor pool. Facilities for the handicapped are available. Enclosed free parking is provided in the adjoining garage. An in-house shopping complex includes specialty shops, a beauty salon and a portrait studio. The Belvedere Riverfront Plaza, Kentucky Center for the Arts and Actors Theatre of Louisville are nearby.

Holiday Inn Louisville Downtown
$$ • 120 W. Broadway • 582-2241, (800) HOLIDAY

The Holiday Inn Louisville Downtown has 287 guest rooms and eight deluxe suites, many offering views of Louisville. You can reside like a prince or live like a pauper at this hotel. Rooms for the handicapped are available, as are visual alert systems for the hearing impaired; in-house wheelchairs; special rooms for smokers, nonsmokers and female travelers; and same-day valet service. Irons and ironing boards, makeup mirrors, coffee makers and hair dryers are in all the rooms.

Bentley's Restaurant offers casual dining for breakfast, lunch and dinner. Bentley's Lounge serves cocktails with a complimentary hors d'oeuvre buffet and live entertainment. Meeting and banquet facilities can be set up to serve 10 to 600 people and include two rooms with panoramic views of the downtown skyline.

The hotel has a gift shop, exercise room, indoor heated pool with outdoor seasonal deck, free parking and basic cable TV with pay-per-view movies. Pets are allowed.

The Hyatt Regency Louisville
$$$ • 320 W. Jefferson St. • 587-3434, (800) 233-1234

The Hyatt Regency Louisville underwent a $5 million renovation in 1992. The hotel has an 18-story atrium lobby, 388 guest rooms, executive suites, a heated pool, whirlpool, health club, gift shop, art gallery, outdoor tennis court and a shoe shine stand in the lobby. The Regency Club provides deluxe accommodations for VIP guests. Nonsmoking rooms also are available.

A variety of dining and entertainment settings are available. The Spire, a revolving rooftop restaurant, offers a panoramic view of the city and the riverfront. A lunch buffet served Monday through Friday includes salad and pasta bars, a variety of entrées and freshly baked breads. Dinner and cocktails are served Monday through Saturday. The Trellis cafe in the atrium serves breakfast, lunch, dinner and Sunday brunch. Pepper's Sports Bar lounge features pool tables, a large-screen TV and drink specials.

The hotel is connected by covered pedestrian walkway to the Commonwealth Convention Center and the Galleria Shopping Mall and is within walking distance of the theater district, museums, galleries, the *Belle of Louisville* and historic landmarks.

Twenty-three meeting and conference rooms are available for gatherings of 10 to 1,000 people. Facilities for the handicapped are available. Parking in the garage is $8 per day for unlimited in and out privileges.

INSIDERS' TIP

If you're choosing your accommodations based on location, consider proximity to the restaurant rows (Frankfort Avenue and Bardstown Road), the shopping areas and the Watterson Expressway, which is your quick and easy path to the airport and the interstates.

The Seelbach
$$$$ • 500 Fourth Ave. • 585-3200,
(800) 333-3399

The Seelbach represents the life's work of two Bavarian immigrant brothers, Louis and Otto Seelbach. In 1869 at the age of 17, Louis came to Louisville, followed by his brother in 1878. They opened the Seelbach European Restaurant and, later, The Old Inn. By the turn of the century, the brothers began building what they envisioned to be one of the world's finest hotels; by 1905, the hotel was completed.

Italian and Swiss marble pillars decorate the entrance, and at the lobby's crown, original murals depict historical events from Kentucky's pioneer days (the murals are considered the greatest works of world-renowned painter Arthur Thomas of New York). The hotel's Rathskeller, a meeting room that's been the scene of important social events for nearly a century, is the world's only intact Rookwood pottery room.

The Seelbach has been the focus of articles in *Southern Living*, *Historic Preservation* and *Newsweek*, among others.

The Seelbach's 332 guest rooms have 18th-century furnishings — armoires, carved four-poster beds and marble baths. In the Oakroom restaurant, elegance is evident in the hand-carved oak paneling and in the presentation of exquisite American cuisine (see our Restaurants chapter). After dinner, jazz is featured in the Old Seelbach Bar, rated among the South's three best by *Esquire* magazine (see our chapter on Nightlife). For casual dining, the hotel has a cafe.

A one-bedroom suite, Seelbach Suite and Presidential Suite are available, among other rooms.

Meetings are held in private dining parlors, board rooms, the Rathskeller and a Grand Ballroom, a new $6.2 million addition that can accommodate from 10 to 1,400 people. The Seelbach is managed by New York-based Medallion Hotels Inc.

Expect all the amenities — valet parking (for a fee), room service, overnight shoe shine and courtesy vans to and from the airport. The hotel is adjacent to the Galleria shopping complex, a short walk from the Commonwealth Convention Center and convenient to the city's theater and arts centers. Facilities for the handicapped are available.

Airport Area

Executive Inn
$$$ • 978 Phillips Ln. (Watterson Expressway at the Fairgrounds) • 367-6161, (800) 626-2706

The Executive Inn features 465 guest rooms, including 16 one- and two-bedroom suites, 15 conference suites, seven executive suites and nonsmoking rooms. The hotel has a courtyard and a heated outdoor pool; inside, there is a heated Olympic-size pool and a fully equipped health club with sauna and tanning beds. Basic cable is supplied in all the rooms.

The Empire Grill serves dinner and late-night snacks; the Tudor Room serves breakfast and lunch. The Empire Bar has a relaxed atmosphere. Conference and banquet facilities accommodate up to 400 people. The hotel has a gift shop, beauty shop and barber shop and free parking with 24-hour security. Airport van transportation is available. Pets are permitted at an additional $100 nonrefundable charge. Handicapped-accessible facilities are provided.

The Executive Inn is close to the Kentucky Fair and Exposition Center, the airport, Churchill Downs, Kentucky Derby Museum, downtown Louisville, University of Louisville Sports Center and Kentucky Kingdom amusement park.

Executive West
$$-$$$$ • Freedom Way • 367-2251

Just across the expressway ramp from the Executive Inn is its sister hotel, the Executive West, with 611 rooms and suites. There's an indoor/outdoor pool, the Boozseller Lounge, the Golden Targe Tea Room and the Derbyshire Room (for dining, music and dancing). The hotel runs a courtesy car from the airport, 3 minutes away. From I-264 and I-65, you can drive to the downtown business district in 10 minutes.

For business sessions, Executive West has 19 meeting rooms encompassing more than 50,000 square feet of space. The large ballroom accommodates up to 1,800 people. Smaller rooms are available for break-out sessions, seminars or smaller meetings. Complete audiovisual and amplification systems are

Photo: Dan Dry and Associates

Water patterns at the Louisville Falls Fountain change twice every 15 minutes.

available at no charge. The catering department can serve breakfasts, luncheons, cocktail receptions and more.

Pets are permitted for an additional $100, and handicapped-accessible facilities are provided.

Holiday Inn Louisville-Southwest
$ • 4110 Dixie Hwy. • 448-2020, (800) HOLIDAY

Off I-264, this hotel is minutes from the airport, Churchill Downs, Kentucky Derby Museum, Fort Knox, the Kentucky Fair and Exposition Center and the University of Louisville. The high-rise hotel has 169 guest rooms and suites. The Monarch Dining Room is open daily for breakfast, lunch and dinner, or you may order room service. Reflections Lounge offers live entertainment Tuesday through Saturday.

Complimentary van service runs to and from the airport. Also available are free parking, valet service, coin-operated washer and dryer, basic cable TV and in-room pay movies. Indoor recreation includes a heated swimming pool, whirlpool and exercise equipment.

Meeting rooms can accommodate groups of 10 to 200.

Signature Inn
$$ • I-65, Exit 128 • 968-4100, (800) 822-5252

The Signature Inn is a two-floor, 123-room hotel with 68 Signature Rooms (each has a recliner and a 12-foot desk) for business travelers, six handicapped-accessible rooms and 87 rooms for nonsmokers. The following perks are provided free: breakfast (Danish, muffins, bagels, fresh fruit, cereal, beverages and juices) served from 6:30 to 9:30 AM, complimentary copies of *USA Today* and *The Wall Street Journal* delivered to your room each weekday, local telephone calls, cable TV with HBO, an outdoor pool, telephone centers and guest storage. Movie rental is available for a nominal charge, and discounts are offered at local restaurants.

Meeting rooms accommodate five to 85 people and include free TV and VCR services.

Hurstbourne Parkway Area

Courtyard by Marriott
$$$ • 9608 Blairwood Rd. • 429-0006, (800) 321-2211

Courtyard by Marriott advertises itself as a haven for the weary business traveler, and it also offers weekend discounts of 30 percent especially for pleasure travelers. Each guest room has double locks for security; a large work desk; remote-controlled TV with basic cable, HBO and pay-per-view movies; and in-room coffee and tea service. Each king suite and double-bed suite also has a parlor and refrigerator.

A restaurant and lounge, outdoor swimming pool and whirlpool and exercise room are available to guests. Two 25-person conference and meeting rooms are available.

Fairfield Inn Louisville/East
$ • 9400 Blairwood Rd. • 339-1900, (800) 228-2800

Fairfield Inn is Marriott's economy lodging. Guest rooms are equipped with a well-lit work desk and remote-controlled TV with basic cable and pay-per-view movies. Nonsmoking rooms are available, as are special facilities for handicapped travelers. A complimentary continental breakfast of coffee or tea, fresh fruit, Danish, muffins and juice is served. Local phone calls are free, and same-day dry cleaning and fax service are available, as is a guest laundry room. Meeting rooms that accommodate up to 10 people are for rent. No pets are allowed.

Holiday Inn Hurstbourne
$$ • I-64 E. at Hurstbourne Pkwy. • 426-2600, (800) HOLIDAY

Twenty minutes from the airport and 20 minutes from the downtown business district, the Holiday Inn Hurstbourne has 268 guest rooms and eight suites. Handicapped-accessible rooms are available, as is free transportation to and from the airport.

The Terrace Bistro serves breakfast, lunch and dinner; Filly's Lounge serves cocktails and has entertainment until midnight. The health club has a heated indoor pool and exercise center with Universal and Nautilus equipment, Jacuzzi, sauna, treadmill, stationary bicycle and sun deck.

There are eight meeting rooms, including the Executive Boardroom (with service bar and bathroom) that can accommodate up to 800 people. All the meeting rooms are on the first floor next to the atrium exhibit area. Rooms have teleconference and AV equipment for a nominal charge. Other services include express check-in and checkout, laundry facilities, complimentary morning coffee and paper and free parking.

Club Hotel by Doubletree East
$$$ • 9700 Bluegrass Pkwy. • 491-4830, (800) 444-CLUB

The Hurstbourne Hotel and Conference Center features 399 newly renovated guest rooms and 52 suites, among them five luxury Jacuzzi suites. The rooms have cable TV with free HBO and Showtime, and one package offers first-run pay movies. Another feature: You can order your room-service breakfast in advance by television.

FYI

Unless otherwise noted, the area code for all phone numbers listed in this chapter is 502.

The Grand Belle Hall can seat as many as 2,500 people theater-style or will house more than 100 8-foot-by-10-foot exhibit booths. Julia Belle Hall, which adjoins Grande Belle Hall, has elegant detailing and theater-style seating for more than 500; it's often used for dinners, weddings, social events and receptions. In addition, 12 break-out rooms that seat 18 to 200 people are available. A total of 14 column-free rooms provide meetings and conventions with an unobstructed view.

Two heated pools, a game arcade, dry sauna and Healthplex are available in the Tropidome. Facilities for the handicapped are available, and pets are permitted for a $25 fee. The hotel also has a locally known lounge named Legends, beauty and barber shops, a gift shop and rent-a-car service on-site. Au Bon Pain!, a French cafe that prides itself on its breads, is on the premises.

A separate but affiliated company will help hotel guests coordinate events at the meeting and convention facilities. There's an on-site convention manager, audiovisual presentation aides, an award-winning chef, a banquet and catering staff and a sound system in most meeting rooms.

Louisville Marriott Hotel
$$$ • 1903 Embassy Square Blvd. • 499-6220, (800) 228-9290

The 255-room Louisville Marriott Hotel is in eastern Jefferson County. The 10-story building has a glass-enclosed atrium featuring a pool, Jacuzzi, exercise room and game room. Casual dining is available at Zachary's Restaurant. Meeting facilities serve up to 500 people. You can choose from one of the suggested international menus, or the catering staff can customize a menu.

The guest rooms are spacious, with individual climate control, remote-controlled TV with radios and pay-per-view movies. Some rooms have balconies onto the atrium. Other amenities include complimentary parking, travel agency, pool tables and a video arcade. Facilities for the handicapped are available.

Red Carpet Inn of Louisville
$ • 1640 S. Hurstbourne Pkwy. • 491-7320, (800) 251-1962

There are three buildings at this inexpensive hotel, and two of them are new and nicely furnished. The third one is used for "party people," as the woman at the desk put it. You have been warned.

Red Carpet Inn has rooms with one king- or queen-size bed or two full-size beds (three rooms have king-size waterbeds). Cable TV with basic HBO and an adult channel and free coffee and doughnuts in the mornings are other amenities available to guests. A Wendy's restaurant is nearby. Handicapped-accessible facilities are provided.

Residence Inn by Marriott Louisville/Hurstbourne Forum
$$$ • 120 N. Hurstbourne Pkwy. • 425-1821, (800) 331-3131

Suites and studio rooms with a residential look and feel is the main feature of this hotel. Guests can make fresh coffee or tea in the fully equipped kitchen; fireplaces add a coziness to winter stays in some rooms. The work space includes multiple phone jacks for computer use. Daily complimentary breakfast is served in the Gatehouse. The inn has a weekly social hour and barbecue, a swimming pool, a heated spa and outdoor courts for racquetball, basketball and volleyball.

The Penthouse and two-bedroom suites accommodate two business people or a relocating family. The studio units are for singles. Conference facilities are set up for 20 to 30 people upon request and if available, and the staff will assist you with secretarial services and transportation. Rates vary with length of stay; special rates are available for extended stays. Pets are allowed, but there is a nonrefundable fee of $50.

Bardstown Road, Newburg Road and Taylorsville Road Areas

Breckinridge Inn Hotel
$-$$ • 2800 Breckenridge Ln. • 456-5050

Personal service is emphasized in this thoroughly remodeled Southern Colonial hotel, where full room service is offered for its 123 rooms. Handicapped-accessible facilities are available. Seven convention rooms with versatile seating arrangements can accommodate 25 to 350 people.

All convention and inn guests are extended free use of the Club Breckinridge, which has an outdoor junior Olympic-size pool, sun decks, chaises and a family recreation area in a landscaped courtyard. The heated indoor pool has swimming lanes and a lap clock. A lighted tennis court and fitness room with a variety of aerobic and strength training equipment are available, and the shower and locker areas include sauna and steam rooms. A licensed masseur is on the premises.

A full-service restaurant and lounge offer meals and beverages. The lounge features cocktails and darts, pinball, billiards, checkers or backgammon, while sports fans can catch the game of the week on a giant screen TV.

The hotel also has a barber and beauty salon, laundry and dry-cleaning services, free parking, security throughout and video surveillance in all public areas. Complimentary transportation to and from the airport is also provided. Pets are permitted for a $50 fee.

Holiday Inn Airport East
$-$$$$ • 1465 Gardiner Ln. • 452-6361, (800) HOLIDAY

This comfortable hotel is off I-264 at Gardiner Lane, convenient to the airport, Kentucky Fair and Exposition Center and Freedom Hall. The hotel offers 200 guest rooms, including 14 king executive suites, two one-bedroom suites and 60 nonsmoking rooms — accomodations fit for travelers of most any means. Five meeting rooms accommodate from 10 to 300 guests.

The Red Horse Grille and Bar is off the main lobby and serves lunch and dinner. The bar features theme buffets in a lounge atmosphere. Amenities include free parking, continental breakfast, airport transportation, coffee and wake-up service and express check-in and checkout. Many double occupancies cost no more than $70. The hotel has one handicapped-accessible room.

Guests may use the outdoor tennis court, swimming pool, basketball court, volleyball court (in summer) and workout and recreation equipment. The hotel has a handicapped-accessible room. Pets are permitted.

Holiday Inn Southeast
$$ • 3255 Bardstown Rd. • 454-0451, (800) HOLIDAY

This attractive hotel has 193 guest rooms, including deluxe double rooms or executive king rooms, all with remote-controlled TVs with HBO and other cable channels. When visitors have leisure time, they may use the Holidome Indoor Recreation Area, where equipment includes an indoor pool, a whirlpool, bumper pool and video games. The Fitness Center has a ClimbMax stair step machine and stationary bicycles. The hotel has a restaurant, and the Sports Page Lounge is open 4 PM to midnight.

The catering staff will handle arrangements for private parties and business events. Private rooms accommodate 10 to 225 people. Facilities are handicapped accessible, and pets are permitted.

Ramada Hotel Airport East
$$ • 1921 Bishop Ln. • 456-4411, (800) 2-RAMADA

The 150-room Ramada Hotel Airport East is off I-264 at the Newburg Road S. exit. Some rooms and suites have king-size beds. Nonsmoking and handicapped-accessible rooms are available. Children 18 and younger stay free with their parents, and senior citizens with

ID receive a 10 percent discount. Four meeting rooms accommodate 50 to 150 people in banquet, classroom, theater or conference seating arrangements. The hotel provides equipment for meetings, including lecterns, chalkboards, TVs, VCRs and portable bars, and special menus and custom buffets are available.

Guest amenities include courtesy airport transportation, room service, same-day laundry and dry cleaning and remote-controlled cable TV. The hotel has an outdoor swimming pool, and an 18-hole golf course and health facilities are nearby. Guests may dine at Maxwell's cafe or party at Horsefeathers lounge.

Eastern Jefferson County

Holiday Inn Rivermont
$$$ • 1041 Zorn Ave. • 897-5101, (800) HOLIDAY

The Holiday Inn Rivermont sits on a landscaped 5-acre site and is easily accessible from I-71, one exit from downtown and within 2 miles of all major interstate highways and arteries to the city. It features 120 guest rooms, including two luxury Board of Directors rooms for meetings; an outdoor pool; Anytimes Restaurant and Lounge for breakfast, lunch or dinner; an atrium; and patio dining. In 1990 the hotel won a Holiday Inn Superior Hotel Award.

Banquet and meeting facilities for up to 250 people are available for business and social events. The hotel is 10 minutes from downtown Louisville, 20 minutes from the airport, a half-block from the Ohio River and a half-mile from the Veteran's Hospital.

Ramada Inn Northeast
$ • 4805 Brownsboro Rd. • 893-2551, (800) 2-RAMADA

The Ramada Inn Northeast is 8 minutes from downtown and 10 minutes from the airport. The two-level courtyard-style inn surrounding outdoor and indoor swimming pools has 144 rooms (many of them recently remodeled), including 18 suites with Jacuzzis. King-size and double beds and four handicapped-accessible rooms are available.

The Brownsboro Cafe offers casual dining for breakfast and an upscale atmosphere for lunch and dinner. Meeting and banquet rooms that accommodate up to 550 people, with audiovisual equipment available, can be reserved for a nominal fee. Jerry Green and Friends lounge features live entertainment from one of Louisville's smoothest R&B vocalists (Mr. Green himself) and a complimentary hors d'oeuvre buffet (see our Nightlife chapter).

Guest amenities include free parking, free HBO, AM/FM radio, room service and laundry and valet service.

The hotel is 25 minutes from the airport and is readily accessible to the Kentucky Center for the Arts, shopping centers, hospitals and Louisville attractions.

Indiana

Days Inn
$ • 350 Eastern Blvd., Jeffersonville
• 288-9331, (800) DAYS INN

Choose a room with a king-size bed or two double beds from among Days Inn's 172 choices. Each has a shower and bath, and your stay includes a free continental breakfast daily. An outdoor pool is on the premises. The motel is within driving distance of restaurants — head toward New Albany.

Ramada Hotel Riverside
$$ • 700 Riverside Dr., Jeffersonville
• 284-6711, (800) 537-3612

One mile from downtown Louisville, this hotel is off I-65, overlooking the Ohio River and the Louisville skyline. Complimentary morning coffee is provided for guests in each of the 186 rooms and suites. Bridges Dining Room faces the Ohio River and serves breakfast, lunch and dinner and a large Sunday brunch. Bridges Lounge has dancing.

Other amenities include remote-controlled cable TV with Showtime, valet service, a game room, an outdoor pool, free parking and shuttle service. Handicapped-accessible facilities are available, and pets are permitted for a $5 per

night fee. Ample meeting space accommodates up to 600 people for business and other gatherings; catering service is available.

Corporate Apartments

Corporate Lodgings
7505 New La Grange Rd., Ste. 101
• 426-9501

Corporate Lodgings has fully furnished one- and two-bedroom apartments for people on extended stays (three nights or longer), including visitors, business people and those who are relocating to the area. Lodgings are available in Jeffersontown, Lyndon/St. Matthews, Brownsboro Road and downtown. Each apartment has a living room, a dining room, a private bath and a fully furnished kitchen (including microwave oven). Amenities include housekeeping service, linens, telephone, cable TV, laundry appliances and 24-hour maintenance service.

Rates vary according to length of stay. Pets are allowed at the Lyndon location only, and there is a $50 charge. All locations are handicapped accessible.

The Imperial House
3201 Leith Ln. • 451-4293

For an overnight stay or an extended visit, the Imperial House has one- or two-bedroom apartments, each with a kitchen. Guests may use the outdoor pool, fitness rooms and club room. Amenities include free telephone service, free utilities, TV and linens. Each floor has a laundry room, and the hotel provides maid service and a night doorman.

Rates vary according to length of stay, size of unit and whether or not you use the maid service. You'll pay a nonrefundable $100 fee to keep your pet (it must weigh less than 25 pounds).

Park Chateau
512 W. Ormsby Avenue • 636-5525

In Old Louisville, Park Chateau has one-bedroom apartments and efficiencies, free off-street parking, a laundromat, a private pool, a sauna and an exercise room and a party and game room; it's within walking distance of Central Park's tennis courts.

Sure, you pay more at a
bed and breakfast, but
it's like staying at a
friend of a friend's
house.

Bed and Breakfasts

Like other major cities, Louisville didn't have much of a bed and breakfast inn scene until the last decade. But the trend that started in Europe finally made its way into Kentucky's biggest city, and now business is good within the small Louisville bed and breakfast market.

It's no mystery why. Compare a bed and breakfast, furnished with antiques, housed in a beautiful Victorian mansion, to a drab, fluorescent-bulb-lit, square hallway and an equally boxy and generic hotel room. Think about the last "continental breakfast" you had at a hotel, and compare it to breakfast at one of these inns served on china and, more often than not, brought to your table by the same kindly owner with whom you made your reservation.

Sure, you pay more at a bed and breakfast, but it's like staying at a friend of a friend's house. It's a temporary home — even if you're just staying for one night. Louisville's bed and breakfasts are a delightful change from the hotel chain mentality, and they're one sure way to get a proper taste of what our city is about — the heart of the town's bed-and-breakfast market is in Old Louisville, a historic, quaint, but far from sterile section south of downtown. No, most Louisvillians' homes are not furnished like these inns. But we might wish they were.

Price Code

The following codes are listed in the information for each establishment. Bed and breakfasts almost always have different sized rooms, and that can mean a variance in rates. Thus, we present a range of prices when appropriate. We guess we don't need to tell you that the cost of the room includes breakfast the next morning.

$	$35 to $70
$$	$71 to $100
$$$	$101 to $140
$$$$	$141 and up

The following are all members of the Bed and Breakfasts of Old Louisville, an informal group established to promote the inns and their neighborhoods.

Inn at the Park
$$-$$$ • 1332 S. Fourth St. • 637-6930

Built in 1886, Inn at the Park was originally home to Russell Houston, a well-known attorney and cofounder of the L & N Railroad. The mansion was restored to elegance in 1985 and has once again become a queen of Old Louisville. Adjacent to Central Park, the inn showcases a splendid example of Richardsonian Romanesque architecture. Among its many period details are a grand, sweeping staircase, rich hardwood floors, 14-foot ceilings, marble fireplaces, crown moldings and second- and third-floor balconies. Six spacious guest rooms boast amenities such as private baths, fireplaces, cable television, fine linens, elegant period furniture and a beautiful view of the park through grand windows.

You will awake to the aroma of freshly brewed coffee and enjoy a full breakfast, prepared by innkeeper Theresa Carskie, served in the elegant central dining room or in the privacy of your room. Choose from fresh-baked muffins, croissants and breads; juice; French toast; banana-walnut pancakes; omelets; Belgian waffles; vanilla yogurt with granola, preserves and honey; bacon or sausage; and a banana-strawberry yogurt smoothie. Dietary restrictions and personal preferences can be accommodated, but be sure to let the innkeeper know in advance.

Inn at the Park is also available for special events including weddings, receptions, anniversaries, holiday parties and corporate meetings. Enjoy cocktails on any of the inn's five porches or an evening stroll in the park. Complimentary shuttle service to and from the airport and downtown locations is available. Forty-eight-hour notification is required for cancellations. Children are welcome, but pets are not. A smoking room is available on request, but the remainder of the house is nonsmoking. You can also smoke on the porches.

The Old Louisville Inn
$-$$$$ • 1359 S. Third St. • 635-1574

The Old Louisville Inn was built in 1901 as a private home for John Armstrong, president of the Louisville Home Telephone Co. The 10,000-square-foot mansion was office space before renovation in the early 1970s restored the home's residential grandeur. As you enter the lobby from Third Street, you will see massive, ornately carved mahogany columns. Twelve-foot-high ceilings have hand-painted murals. Soft music playing in the background, tempting aromas from the kitchen and peaceful colors in the rooms create a comfortable atmosphere for travel-weary patrons.

On the first floor of the inn, the breakfast room seats 20 guests and showcases a built-in, delicately carved buffet and original etched-glass chandelier. The parlor has a fireplace and books. The game room has an old version of Monopoly, television and VCR.

Each of the 10 guest rooms on the second and third floors is decorated with antiques and heirlooms purchased from local estate auctions and antique shops. Five of the rooms feature marble baths with original fixtures modernized to include showers. King-, queen-, full- or twin-size beds are available, each with an antique quilt. The third-floor honeymoon suite has a king-size, arched canopy bed, sitting area, fireplace and modern bath with whirlpool. All rooms have private baths. Other touches include a bouquet of fresh flowers and a cheese and fruit tray.

Breakfast features freshly baked breads, muffins and popovers. The innkeeper makes her own granola, and fresh fruit and yogurt are included with breakfast, as is freshly squeezed orange juice and fresh-ground coffee.

The inn is available for private parties, weddings, teas, business meetings and other occasions. Innkeeper Marianne Lesher can arrange a horse-and-carriage drive to a restaurant or through Old Louisville, or she will cater a candlelight dinner for two in your room.

A 50 percent deposit is required on all reservations. (The full amount is required for a one-night reservation.) Your deposit will be refunded if cancellation is made 48 hours prior to your arrival.

Cribs are available.

Rose Blossom Bed & Breakfast
$$, no credit cards • 1353 S. Fourth St.
• 636-0295 after 6 PM

Rose Blossom Bed & Breakfast is housed in an 18-room, three-story Victorian home built in 1884 and listed on the National Historic Register. It was constructed by Vernon D. Price, the vinegar manufacturer who later became president of *The Saturday Evening Post*.

In 1992 innkeeper Mary Ohlmann purchased the house and renovated it, retaining the original look as much as possible. The brass was cleaned and polished, and the leaded glass in the entrance hall and stairwell were enhanced by the addition of more windows and transoms of leaded glass. Architectural details, such as the hammered-brass hardware, oak paneling, 14-foot ceilings with crown molding and medallions, and crystal-and-brass light fixtures, are in keeping with the period of the house. Ten fireplaces are original, many with carved mantels and ornate tile and metal. A sun room and solarium were added to the rear of the house for quiet retreats, and a large breakfast room and Victorian porch provide views of the gardens.

Breakfast includes such hearty fare as country ham, pork chops, sausage, egg dishes, French toast, pastries, grits, potato dishes, juice, coffee and tea.

The house is in Old Louisville, across from Central Park, where you can play tennis or view Shakespeare in the Park in the summer. The St. James Art Show stretches for blocks one weekend in October (see our Annual Events and Festivals chapter). Restaurants, theaters and museums are nearby.

Reservations are required with a 50 percent deposit. A 48-hour notice is needed for cancellations with a refund. King-, queen- and twin-size beds are available on request.

FYI

Unless otherwise noted, the area code for all phone numbers listed in this chapter is 502.

Old Louisville has a number of bed and breakfasts.

Towne House Bed and Breakfast
$$ • 1460 St. James Ct. • 636-5673, 585-4456

The Towne House Bed and Breakfast is the restored turn-of-the-century home of a former Louisville mayor, and the surrounding Old Louisville neighborhood retains the look of that era.

Four guest rooms have been decorated and furnished with period antiques by the innkeeper, Shirley Romo, who also operates an antique shop in a restored 1866 town house in downtown Louisville. A bowl of fruit and decanter of sherry come with each room, and a bath is adjacent and a phone nearby.

The innkeepers serve a continental breakfast in the handsomely appointed candlelit dining room between 8 and 10 AM. Homemade sweet breads and croissants are presented on antique china. Guests may share a bathroom, depending on the occupancy.

A three-day cancellation notice is required. Neither pets nor children are permitted.

Ashton's Victorian Secret Bed & Breakfast
$-$$, no credit cards • 1132 S. First St. • 581-1914, evenings and weekends

Ashton's Victorian Secret Bed & Breakfast, housed in a 100-year-old, three-story Victorian mansion in Old Louisville, provides spa-cious accommodations with antiques and period furnishings. Queen- and king-size beds are available, and all rooms have wall-to-wall carpeting and in-room color TV.

The home has 14 rooms and 11 fireplaces. It's centrally air conditioned; a washer and dryer are available; and you may take advantage of a sun deck and workout room with benchpress, rowing machine, bicycle and other equipment.

Nan and Steve Roosa are the innkeepers. Children are welcome, smoking is permitted and first-floor accommodations are available for the elderly. No pets are permitted.

Reduced rates are available for weekly guests and employees of nonprofit organizations on business travel. A deposit is requested with advance registration. Only three guests rooms are available, so reservations are requested.

Towne House Annex
$$-$$$ • 105 W. Ormsby Ave. • 636-1705, 585-4456

This is a newly renovated turn-of-the-century brick house in Old Louisville, furnished with antiques. Lace curtains, brass chandeliers and an impressive entrance are notable features.

Two suites are available. One takes up the entire third floor, with a bedroom, living room, kitchen and bath. The second-floor suite has a bedroom, dressing room and bath. Innkeeper Kristine Crawford provides a carafe of white wine or lemonade and appetizers each day.

Guests may have breakfast in their suites or in the dining room. The meal includes coffee, fresh-squeezed orange juice, fruit and homemade sweetbreads such as muffins or banana-nut streusel loaf with toasted pecans. (Let Kristine know ahead of time if you have food allergies.)

At bedtime the traditional pillow mint has been replaced by Kentucky's popular confection, the bourbon ball.

For a small additional fee, the innkeeper will include flowers or champagne. A private Jacuzzi is available. Well-supervised children are welcome; pets will be considered on an individual basis (ask in advance). Rooms are not handicapped accessible. A 24-hour notice is required for cancellations.

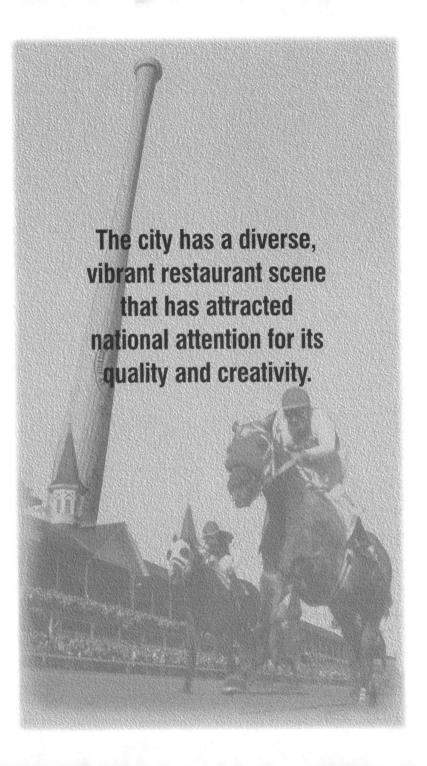

The city has a diverse, vibrant restaurant scene that has attracted national attention for its quality and creativity.

Restaurants

If you have a bad meal in Louisville, it's your own damn fault. The city has a diverse, vibrant restaurant scene that has attracted national attention for its quality and creativity.

That's not to exaggerate the quality here; every city has good restaurants anymore — even Indianapolis, we hear. But when you sit down, as we have in this chapter, to list the city's best restaurants, it's startling to see how many first-rate places there are here.

Louisville has three major restaurant strips, roads where you can cruise in search of just the right place to eat. Bardstown Road is generally given the title Restaurant Row. It's the land where the bistro was born — up and down the blocks between Highland and Douglass avenues are a number of restaurants that bring continental touches into varying degrees of informality.

Frankfort Avenue's restaurant boom began in the late '80s when Bim Deitrich moved from Formally Myra's in the Highlands into the old Crescent Theater and made the restaurant now called Brasserie Deitrich a sensation as the most dramatic dining space in the city. Other restaurants followed. Because it's newer, Frankfort Avenue has a bit more youthful panache and a few more inexpensive ethnic restaurants than Bardstown.

Hurstbourne Parkway has fewer distinguished restaurants, although Asian Pearl and Sichuan Garden rank among the city's finest Chinese places and Shalimar is a good Indian restaurant. The typical place along Hurstbourne is large, believes Texas is the place where American culture and cuisine reach their fullest flowering and is more admirable as a business operation than as a kitchen.

For many years, the city's greatest lack was good, cheap ethnic restaurants. While Louisville still lacks anything like a Chinatown or the Indian restaurants along East Sixth Street in Manhattan, a person with a car can travel around the world in culinary terms. Now there are four good Korean places, a load of

pita places and a Pacific Rim eatery that ranks among the city's best restaurants. There's no Tibetan food — yet.

A great amount of lip service is paid to the idea of regional cuisine, but the city and the area are without anything like the Creole and Cajun palaces of New Orleans. Often, the regional cuisine that is celebrated is someone else's. One of the most popular dishes on local menus is crab cakes, although you may already have noticed the lack of an ocean. Borrowing another region's cuisine has a long local tradition of its own: The 19th-century Galt House had a Creole restaurant. The best young local chefs are thinking about how to bring Bluegrass traits into the mix, and sooner or later someone will take the full plunge.

Price Code

We've put the restaurants into four dollar categories, based on what two adults could expect to pay for entrées, or dinner plates, or however else a restaurant cares to denominate the main part of the meal — in other words, *excluding appetizers, drinks (alcoholic or not) and desserts*. These are only intended as a general guide, a way of knowing the basic level of pricing — as any restaurant patron knows, you can eat cheaply at a generally expensive place, expensively at a cheap one. And the categories are:

$	Less than $15
$$	$16 to $25
$$$	$26 to $35
$$$$	More than $35

Except where noted otherwise, restaurants generally accept most, if not all, major credit cards. And unless noted, assume a restaurant allows smoking — this is tobacco country, after all.

This is a selective, subjective guide; we're more comfortable with saying that the places we've included are worth your time than we are with saying that the ones we've neglected aren't. In particular, we've avoided chains, because they're the same city to city — that's the point, isn't it? Exceptions are made in a few cases where the restaurant seemed to fill a niche or does an especially good job.

Fine Dining

Brasserie Deitrich
$$$$ • 2862 Frankfort Ave. • 897-6076

A showplace at least as much for the room as the food: a neighborhood movie theater converted into something right out of the movies, the sort of place you might expect to see Nick and Nora Charles, or the Katherine Hepburn and Cary Grant of *Bringing Up Baby*, out for an evening. The bar is where the concession stand used to be; the dining room slopes down, as the auditorium once did, underneath a ceiling kept as high as when the Crescent used to show midnight movies; and where the screen used to be, an open kitchen in which the chefs perform feats of showmanship. The menu changed this past year from an eclectic, contemporary American approach to a more classically French one (duck with armagnac and port sauce, sole poached in cider, steak au poivre with cognac sauce). There's also an assortment of Belgian ales, in addition to a consistently good wine list. The restaurant sells cigars but prefers for patrons to smoke them in the bar rather than the dining room. The restaurant is open for dinner seven days a week.

Buck's
$$$-$$$$ • 425 W. Ormsby Ave. • 637-5284

This eclectic spot in the Mayflower Apartments (formerly Hotel) is among the city's prettiest places for dining, inside or out. Al frescoing it on the wide, columned porch is one of the city's great fresh-air treats. The dining room has dark green walls, white tablecloths, artfully mismatched antique china and so many white flowers the monthly florists' bill approaches $1000. Customer-favorite dishes include spicy noodles (a Thai-style dish with a

FYI

Unless otherwise noted, the area code for all phone numbers listed in this chapter is 502.

choice of chicken, shrimp or pork) and soft-shell crab. Dinner is served Tuesday through Saturday.

Cafe Metro
$$$$ • 1700 Bardstown Rd. • 458-4830

The careful handwriting on the menu tells you that this is a place that takes pains; the smell of the grill perfumes its Deer Park neighborhood. Owner Nancy Shepherd is the sort of flamboyant presence who calls you "honey" in a way that seems to mean "co-conspirator of mine." The food is more likely to say "Mon cher ami" — continental without being rigorous, alive to the change of the seasons. It may not be quite as cutting-edge as it once was, but the Metro is still a place that knows what quality dining is about. Dinner is served Monday through Saturday.

The English Grill
$$$$ • The Camberley Brown Hotel, Fourth and Broadway • 583-1234

The room where the Hot Brown was born (see our close-up in this chapter), and for many years Louisville's place to see and be seen. In the past several years, it has taken on a new prestige as what many folks consider to be the city's best restaurant.

Much of that respect is due to chef Joe Castro, who's been profiled in *Gourmet* magazine as a rising young culinary star (and who also appears on WHAS-TV news to demonstrate recipes well worth following). Castro's food goes high and low — he's the sort of classically trained chef whose sauces are based on a stock that began cooking three days earlier, while at the same time he's talked about opening a cafeteria with great macaroni and cheese and green beans cooked into submission. The result is that the English Grill's food is adventurous, made from impeccable ingredients, and yet it touches familiar bases. So for example a wonderful lamb loin might be accompanied by garlic cheese grits, or quail breasts (sautéed in a cast iron skillet) may sit on a mess of greens. The results are usually spectacular. The restaurant is open seven days a week for dinner only.

The Equestrian Grille
$$$ • 1582 Bardstown Rd. • 454-7455

It's sort of the Cocktail Nation idea writ large, expensive and horsy: There are 101 different martinis, a Cigar Study, original equestrian artwork everywhere and a menu that calls itself "classic American grill" — contemporary, but heavy on the beef (although there's also seafood and nightly vegetarian specials). There's a choice of 18 different butters, relishes and what-all available with any grilled entrée (from corn relish to Bordelaise). The menu is à la carte. Dinner is served Monday through Saturday.

Equus
$$$$ • 122 Sears Ave. • 897-9721

Tucked away inside a St. Matthews office building, Equus feels a little bit like a private club, although if you know of a club with food like this, send me an application. The menu standbys that people swear by remain — the mushroom fumé, the crab cakes, the sea bass coated in Parmesan — and are joined by such interesting newcomers as saddle of rabbit (stuffed with sun-dried cherries and served with goat cheese and a guinea hen sauce) and a cigar-shaped roll of smoked salmon. But the real bet here is to put yourself into the capable hands of executive chef/owner Dean Corbett and chef de cuisine Dave Cuntz. The evening's specials are like a guided tour of the best food available in the market that day. The tasting menu brings together the specials and standbys for one of the city's special evenings (and an unhurried one — the table is yours for the evening). Equus serves dinner only Monday through Saturday; reservations are recommended.

The Flagship Room, the Galt House
$$$$ • Fourth and River Rd. • 589-5200

An amazing view of the Ohio River is the highlight of this rotating restaurant at the top of our riverside hotel. The food isn't bad, either — mostly consisting of six or more nightly specials. Fresh seafood is a particular specialty; the signature dish is Tournedos of Beef Flagship (a pair of tenderloin steaks, each in its own sauce, Cabernet Sauvignon and a crabmeat bearnaise). Dinner is served Monday through Saturday, brunch on Sunday.

The Inn on Spring
$$$$ • 415 Spring St., Jeffersonville, Ind. • (812) 284-5545

It's the best of Indiana, back from the dead: The original Inn on Spring, a storefront building in Jeffersonville's historic downtown, burned down in 1995, and it wasn't until April 1997 that it reopened just down the block from the old location. But the cuisine has changed even less than the neighborhood. Owner/chef Jonn Frey was trained at one of Louisville's legendary restaurants, 610 Magnolia, and he brings 610's sort of world-roving intelligence and sense of adventure to an eclectic menu that changes seasonally, sometimes weekly. The seafood tostada is back, and it's ba-aa-ad. The Inn serves lunch Tuesday through Friday, dinner Friday and Saturday. It's a smoke-free establishment.

Le Relais
$$$$ • Bowman Field • 451-9020

The art deco decor at this restaurant hits just the right note. The warm orange wood paneling and the airplane posters from early in the century fit with the aerodynamic heritage of the city's first airport. And you can imagine a dashing French aviator from between the world wars flying in just to eat some of this perfectly prepared, classically inclined French food. Recommended to everyone, but required for *The English Patient* fanatics. Reservations are suggested, as are jackets (the deck is casual). Lunch is served Tuesday through Friday, dinner Tuesday through Sunday.

The Oakroom in the Seelbach Hotel
$$$$ • 500 S. Fourth Ave. • 585-3200

This grand dining room — paneled in rich, dark-brown oak, with amazing arched windows that are taller than a non-NBA man, but so wide that they seem short at first glance — for years lagged behind its up the street rival, the Brown Hotel's English Grill. But it's made a strong run for the top with an approach chef Jim Gerhardt calls Kentucky Fine Dining. It involves making use of Kentucky ingredients in everything, from country ham in the ravioli to bread made with the spent grains from Brown-Forman's Early Times distillery to exceptionally fresh-tasting caviar from the spoonfish, a Kentucky sturgeon that dates to prehistoric times. The restaurant is attracting the attention of everyone from the *New York Times* to the *Wine Spectator* to the James Beard House (where Gerhardt has cooked twice); a fixed-price menu is based on Gerhardt's evening at the Beard House. Cigars are sold in the anteroom. Reservations are recommended; no casual sportswear allowed. A lunch buffet is available Thursday through Friday and Sunday. Dinner is served Monday through Saturday.

Shariat's
$$$$ • 2901 Brownsboro Rd. • 899-7878.

The decor in this elegant, intimate dining room echoes Matisse, but the cuisine is artistry of a more original stripe, beautiful to look at and better to eat. Owner and chef Anoosh Shariat has picked up culinary influences from around the world (he was born in Iran, trained in Germany by French chefs and has worked in Kentucky for about a decade). He brings them together like a host putting together the perfect party; each dish begins with a deep consideration of the ingredients' best qualities, then they're combined with a wicked sense of surprise.

Shariat's serves some of the city's best vegetarian entrées (Anoosh is a vegetarian himself), but no carnivore will ever feel slighted. The menu changes seasonally and has à la carte and fixed-price sides; either one offers large pleasures. There's a monthly kids' night with activities and dinner for children in the downstairs private dining room. Reservations are recommended; dinner is served Monday through Saturday.

211 Clover Lane
$$$$ • St. Matthews Colony Center • 896-9570

The atmosphere in this St. Matthews restaurant, tucked away just over the railroad tracks, could be called light-formal — despite the white tablecloths and the austerity of the white walls and dark wooden beams, it's a little Californian in ambiance, the cuisine makes frequent stops in vegetarian land (salads are especially good), and it's trendy but never merely so. The menu changes seasonally and features everything from corn cakes with corn relish and creme fraiche to some interesting sausage dishes. Reservations are suggested. It's open Tuesday through Saturday for lunch and dinner and Sunday for brunch. The restaurant is smoke-free.

Mr. and Mrs. B's The Veranda on Shagbark Hill
$$$-$$$$ • 15206 Shelbyville Rd. • 253-0580

This restored historic home, with seating on the namesake wraparound porch, is home to a new restaurant that is trying to combine Southern cooking with contemporary touches — so you get Kentucky Country Ham Cakes with Bourbon Sweet Potato Mash and Apple Cider Gravy on a menu that also employs chipolte peppers, tamarind and a chiffonade of basil to make its culinary points.

It's open for lunch and dinner Monday through Friday, dinner only on Saturday and brunch on Sunday. Reservations are recommended. There is a cigar room, but the main part of the restaurant is smoke-free.

Vincenzo's
$$$$ • 150 S. Fifth St. • 580-1350

In the late '70s and early '80s, the city's best restaurant was indisputably Casa Grisanti, an Italian establishment that would have classed up Florence. It's gone, but much of the same spirit survives at Vincenzo's, a spacious restaurant whose decor and service are in keeping with the mammoth scale of its next-door neighbor, the Humana Building.

A writer of our acquaintance says one of his favorite afternoons ever was spent in the kitchen of Vincenzo's, watching chef Agostino Gabriele turn out one marvelous dish after another, offering a little taste here and there, accepting a shipment of this, sending away a batch of that. Brother Vincenzo, a Grisanti alum, runs the front of the house the way the front of a house that serves the city's finest Italian and Continental cuisine should be run. There's a nightly theater menu. Jacket and tie are preferred for men. Lunch is served Monday through Friday, dinner Monday through Saturday.

Winston's Restaurant at Sullivan College
$$$$ • 3101 Bardstown Rd. • 456-0980

Rarely has it tasted so good to help in someone's education. The food at this small, pretty fine dining room is prepared and served by final quarter students in Sullivan College's highly-rated culinary arts program. The menu changes every 12 weeks (it's tested by the advanced culinary class), and it shows the enthusiastic virtuosity of young chefs: One menu had salmon encrusted in pan-fried potatoes, another roast breast of duck with blood orange-tarragon coulis. But the restaurant is supervised by experienced professionals (executive chef David Moeller, general manager Greg Fearing) who know how to temper that enthusiasm into consistent quality. The vegan wild mushroom risotto is a menu standby; so is the bourbon barrel-smoked sturgeon. There's a full service bar (finally, it's starting to resemble our college experience). Winston's serves lunch and dinner Friday and Saturday and brunch Sunday.

INSIDERS' TIP

It's got a good line in pub food and better, but the greatest attraction at Jk's Corner Pub (1800 Frankfort Avenue) may be the wisecracking menu. Here are a few samples:
- **Buffalo, New York Strip: "The best things in life are free. This is not the best thing in life, and it's not free, but it's good."**
- **Bullitt Catfish Sandwich: Farm-raised catfish done Southern-style. "Farm-raised means from an old pond down in Bullitt County, and Southern-style means we cook it."**
- **And the Homemade Mozzarella sticks inspired this gem of menu Zen: "Tastes like your other foot's asleep."**

Restaurant decor in Louisville ranges from the kitschy to the elegant.

Bistros

Bistros make up the present-day mainstream of Louisville dining. This category includes some of the best and most creative restaurants in the city — Lilly's and Jack Fry's make everyone's short list of the top places in town, with Bobby J's, Azalea and Club Grotto close behind — and some places that are a more contemporary version of the all-purpose diner, places to which you can take a crowd and be assured that everyone should find something satisfactory on the menu. The common ground is in that silly phrase, casual elegance — in other words, places a touch less formal than the fine dining scene but often serving up food that would fit in there.

Austin's

$$ • 4950 U.S. Hwy. 42 • 423-1990

This East End clone of the popular KT's is a perfect example of the Louisville mainstream as created by the Bristol (see below): a large, casual bistro with an extensive menu appealing to a wide variety of appetites. Pastas and seafood dishes are popular; burgers are, too. It's open daily for lunch and dinner.

Azalea

$$$ • 3612 Brownsboro Rd. • 895-5493

The large menu at this Melrose Place-ey (for Louisville) establishment is like a tour of current trends: Asian, Southwestern, Italian and fusions of all the above and more. (It's cloned from a restaurant in Atlanta.) But there are very few stops on its relentlessly trendy menu that don't justify the trendiness. There are pastas, gourmet pizzas and a variety of specials: The daily soup specials sometimes hit heaven, and the kitchen's touch with fish is celebrated. It's open daily for lunch and dinner (going until 11 PM weeknights, midnight on the weekend, 10 PM Sunday) and for a well-loved Sunday brunch. There is a special room for cigar and pipe smoking, which is also allowed on the large and attractive patio.

Baxter Station

$$ • 1201 Payne St. • 584-1635

A fun little place with a railroad motif that draws a youngish crowd, Baxter Station used to be a neighborhood bar called John and Jean's, where the unofficial motto was, "If they can grow it, Jean can fry it." But while some of the neighborhood feel has survived its upscaling, the fried vegetables these days are artichoke fritters served with cumin mayonnaise. The black bean cakes are incredibly good, the GBLT (G = guacamole) is a nice innovation at lunch, and dinner has a full complement of spicy dishes as well as Tequila lime chicken and grilled vegetable lasagna. Lunch and dinner are served Monday through Saturday; there's a Monday night tapas menu. (The food's not strictly Spanish, but tapas sounds a lot classier than Mega-Appetizer Platter Night, now doesn't it?)

Bluegrass Brewing Company

$$ • 3929 Shelbyville Rd. • 899-7070

This bustling, attractive brewpub is recommended to everyone who loves beer — brewmaster David Pierce is a young master, and the beers he makes are well-crafted, largely true to the city's German heritage and pleasing to both the average person and the most rigorous beer snob (the light beer is a kolsch, one of the few if not the only American version of this classic Cologne style). But it's recommended to teetotalers as well: BBC brews its own root beer and serves a varied menu of food from brick oven pizzas to pasta dishes.

The BBC is open daily for lunch and dinner.

Bobby J's

$$-$$$ • 1314 Bardstown Rd. • 452-2665

Hedonism's local headquarters. This swank new bistro and nightclub — a snugger, more cost-conscious version of an Astaire and Rogers hangout — serves martinis so good they gave their name to the house jazz band, the Flying you-guessed-its. The food is fairly airborne as well. We especially like the spinach and bleu cheese soup based in a chicken broth that's like a snazzed-up caldo verde and the calamari fritters: When you bite into these fist-sized things, rings of squid spill out like spring-loaded snakes from a Beer Nuts can. And the garlic potato flan is a classic. There's a cigar-smokers' balcony with its own bar. The restaurant serves dinner every night but Monday.

Bristol Bar & Grille
$$ • 1321 Bardstown Rd. • 456-1702
$$ • Kentucky Center for the Arts
• 583-33429
$$ • 300 N. Hurstbourne Pkwy. • 426-0627

The Bristol, the restaurant whose casual bistro approach launched the present generation of Louisville dining, is the city's great fallback option and (especially on Bardstown Road) a great people-watching spot (it's where Hunter S. Thompson and Johnny Depp had a late, pestered dinner after an event honoring the 25th anniversary of Fear and Loathing in Las Vegas). There are always new wrinkles on the menu, but we find ourselves invariably returning to the standbys: the green-chili won tons, the artichoke fritters, the steak sandwich, the California club salad, the Bristol burger and the pork Dijonnaise.

There are only slight differences in menu and atmosphere between the downtown Bristol, the Bardstown Road original and the one on Hurstbourne Parkway. Lunch and dinner are served daily, with a late-night menu from 10 PM to 2 AM at the Bardstown Road venue.

FYI

Unless otherwise noted, the area code for all phone numbers listed in this chapter is 502.

Club Grotto
$$$ • 2116 Bardstown Rd. • 459-5275

Few local restaurants have risen more in our estimation over the past several years than this "American Bistro," as it calls itself. The Grotto has an appealingly urban feel only a few other places in Louisville can match and a menu that swerves between innovation and tradition. Look for the Chef's Vegetable Orgy, which is clustrous enough to please Tiberius — more than a dozen different vegetables on the plate when we tried it out. The Club is open for dinner only, Monday through Saturday.

Corner Cafe
$$-$$$ • 9307 New La Grange Rd.
• 426-8119

A little more interesting than many of its bistro brethren, this successful East End restaurant is strung together from several strip-center storefronts. It was one of the first local places to make gourmet pizzas, and they remain a highlight; the rest of the menu hits Italian and Cajun bases and also offers seafood specials and New York baked subs. It's open for lunch and dinner Monday through Friday, dinner only on Saturday.

Ditto's
$$ • 1114 Bardstown Rd. • 581-9129

It's like one of those post-modern children's books that parents buy because the artist has a name and that kids love because it's got such vibrant colors. Founded by a pair of chefs who honed their chops at the revered Casa Grisanti, Ditto's is informal with a flair — the pizzas, the Chinese burritos (moo shu with a drawl), the calamari and the crab cakes are all worth a look-see from grown-ups, while the children's menu offers the kind of side dishes that might actually sneak some nutrition in unawares. It's open for lunch and dinner seven days a week (with morning hours on weekends.)

Ermin's French Bistro
$$ • 1538 Bardstown Rd.
• 485-9755

With its sleek, simple decor, Ermin's is one of the handful of Louisville restaurants truly reminiscent of European models, the sort of moderately-priced place you'll run across walking through an Italian city. It's not listed in your guidebook, but it's perfect for a quickly grabbed meal as you're out walking — and good enough to return for dinner later in the week. The cuisine isn't food worried over with tempestuous concentration. It's like the home cooking of a friend with a Continental palate, so much ease in the kitchen she sees no need to make anything fancy. Ermin's is open Tuesday through Sunday for lunch and dinner.

Harper's
$$-$$$ • 871 S. Hurstbourne Pkwy.
• 425-2900

Part of a chain that began in North Carolina, Harper's has had a runaway success in Louisville. It's clearly one of the most appealing broad-menu choices along the Hurstbourne corridor, for a good many reasons: The hickory grill, a good roster of gourmet pizza, an exemplary selection of beers, a portobella mushroom sandwich to die for (it's served with chipolte mustard, provolone cheese and coleslaw on the bun, like a Carolina barbecue sandwich) and chicken fingers you won't feel sick watching your kid eat (they're actually an adult appetizer, Chicken Supremes, fried in an herb-laced tempura batter that gave them a lightness and concentrated flavor well beyond the McNugget). Harper's is open for lunch and dinner daily.

Jack Fry's
$$$ • 1007 Bardstown Rd. • 452-9244

If Melville's, the white-tablecloth restaurant upstairs, joined forces with Cheers, the result might be something like this: a former old neighborhood bar that serves some of the best and most inventive food in town. Few restaurants manage to combine classic and adventurous dishes with such ease, or to achieve such heights of dining so casually, with the likes of the shrimp and grits with redeye gravy, the pepper-seared tuna or the simple and succulent grilled lamb chops.

Lunch is served Monday through Thursday; dinner Monday through Saturday.

KT's
$$ • 2300 Lexington Rd. • 458-8888

Any place that's popular with young singles AND with children has found out what "common denominator" means. For one thing, it means that at almost any hour of the day or night, there will be a lively crowd (although it's only at peak times that waits get bad). For another, it means burgers, salads, seafood and prime rib. It serves lunch and dinner every day, with brunches on Saturday and Sunday.

Lilly's
$$$$ • 1147 Bardstown Rd. • 451-0447

Owner Kathy Cary has been twice to cook at New York's James Beard House (the closest thing to a Kennedy Center for American cuisine) and is in a book called *Great Women Chefs of the United States*. She's been profiled in *The New York Times* and throughout the cooking magazines, appeared on the *Today* show and the Food Channel game show *Ready . . . Set . . . Cook!* (the foodie equivalent of *Beat the Clock*).

It's the kind of myth any writer would love to puncture, except for one thing — Lilly's delivers food that vindicates that reputation, maybe even makes you wonder why people don't give Cary a little more credit. The seasonally changing menu is freewheeling, with such elements as Thai, Vietnamese, French and Italian making surprise appearances with the crack timing of characters in a bedroom farce.

But Cary is also interested in the food of her home state — Kentucky lamb is always a menu highlight — and Lilly's loves organic, locally-grown vegetables. It ain't home cookin' — it's something better. A local classic that started here: roasted garlic with a hunk of bleu cheese. Reservations are recommended. Lunch and dinner are served Tuesday through Saturday.

Ramsi's Cafe
$-$$ • 1293 Bardstown Rd. • 451-0700

The cuisine globe-hops in a most untrendy

INSIDERS' TIP

Bill Bayersdorfer always wanted to own a down-home barbecue joint. While he waited, he honed his barbecue chops with a portable barbecue stand that found temporary homes downtown, in St. Matthews and in Irish Hill. He served superbly smoked pork, ribs, chicken and sausage with a fiery sauce (and special orders such as smoked salmon and beef tenderloin were revelatory). He finally has his plain little barbecue joint along Harrods Creek: Willy B's Smokehouse Barbecue (6313 Upper River Road, 228-5333), serving forth all of the above plus an array of excellent side dishes. He opens Tuesday through Sunday at 11:30 AM and serves til the food runs out.

fashion — there's very little "fusion" cuisine here, just dishes from different cuisines worth respect, from stir fry to pesto to felafel to jerk chicken (which, like most of Ramsi's sandwiches, is served on foccacia). The foccaccia appetizer could be titled Reasons to love Italy — the flat bread is topped with a simple basil pesto, a mixture of feta and Parmesan cheese, diced tomatoes and extra-virgin olive oil. Ramsi's is wildly popular — some folks hang a Generation X tag on it, but we don't see that: Older folks fit in just fine, and it's nice to see young people taking an interest in good food. Ramsi's is open for lunch and dinner Monday through Saturday and opens mid-afternoon on Sunday.

Sugar Doe Cafe
$ • 1605 Story Ave. • 584-8440

The Sugar Doe has a relaxed, Bohemian atmosphere and interesting, freshly made food. It's especially well-loved at breakfast, where the likes of the grilled polenta and the breakfast salad provide some interesting alternatives to the usual run. But pastas, vegetable entrées and other fare make lunch and dinner worthwhile as well. Some folks are intimidated by the young hipsters who seem to set the tone, especially on those occasional evenings when hot alternative bands play shows there. (It's guaranteed that Royal Trux won't be playing at KT's any time soon.) But last time I was there I saw a local businessman on the far side of the baby boom, a television news anchor and her lawyer husband and other full-time members of the middle class. In other words, the Sugar Doe attracts intelligent folks who look in and out of the mainstream for stuff of quality. The cafe is open for breakfast, lunch and dinner Wednesday through Saturday, breakfast and lunch Sunday and Monday and closed Tuesday. It's smoke-free.

Timothy's
$$$ • 826 E. Broadway • 561-0880

Timothy's original owner and namesake, the late Tim Barnes, had a panache that lives on in this East Broadway eatery. The dining room, with leopard-skin carpet and the paintings in the style of de Chirico, is the most playful formal room in town; the cafe, with black marble table tops, cloth napkins and fresh flowers on every table, is the most elegant of local bistros. The most famous dish is the trademarked (literally) white chili; there are also seafood and vegetarian specials and more traditional dishes prepared with flair. Reservations are requested. Lunch is served Monday through Friday, dinner Tuesday through Saturday.

The Train Station
$$$ • 1500 Evergreen Rd. • 245-7121

Anchorage could make you turn socialist out of envy. Not only is the wealthy suburban town beautiful, with one of the state's best schools within walking distance of all its kids, it also has this pretty, frequently excellent restaurant smack in the middle of town. You'll find a deck, overhung with plants, and an interior of blond wood that's bright and bosky (from the large windows showing the trees outside). The crab/lobster cakes with Wasabi honey butter are kickin', and the white chocolate mousse torte is one of the city's most impressive desserts. The Station serves dinner only and is closed Tuesday.

Uptown Cafe
$$-$$$ • 1624 Bardstown Rd. • 458-4212

A touch (but a very slight one) less upscale than its across-the-street progenitor, Cafe Metro, the Uptown lives up to its name by providing pastas and such "Good idea!" dishes as seafood pot pie, the duck ravioli or the veal pockets. Desserts begin in chocolate, then get more chocolate. It's open for lunch and dinner every day except Sunday.

Zephyr Cove
$$$ • 2330 Frankfort Ave. • 897-1030

One of the hottest new spots along Frankfort, Zephyr Cove is named for a town near Lake Tahoe whose laid-back ambiance owner John Richards and his wife Heidi wanted to emulate in their establishment. We don't know if they entirely succeeded in the laid-back part, because there's sure as shooting enough going on here: a lively menu with lots of wild game, and one which never met a dipping sauce it didn't like; a house band led by Richards (his band and club, both named City Lights, were a big hit in the early-to-mid '80s); scads of wine by the glass; and an intense interest in the latest culinary trends. They're open Monday through Saturday for dinner.

Only in Louisville

You could call them local institutions — the places that seem to carry the city's history in their floorboards. We've spiced up the category by adding a few places so idiosyncratic — or so entirely typical — that they define the city as well as anything we've written in the rest of this book.

Captain's Quarters
$$ (outside) to $$$ (inside) • 5700 Captain's Quarters Rd. • 228-1651

Here's a riverside location where you can eat anything from a burger to crab legs on a sprawling, multilevel deck that extends down to a dock where the boating class ties up. Inside, the building has sections that date back before the Civil War. Lunch and dinner are served seven days a week; hours vary seasonally.

Check's Cafe
$ • 1101 E. Burnett Ave. • 637-9515

Check's is the archetype for a particular kind of Louisville bar/cafe — a family-oriented tavern, with simple, unpretentious food — prevalent in the Germantown and Schnitzelburg neighborhoods. It's in one of the most tradition-bound parts of the city, as the menus prove: burgers, brats, bean soup, chili, fried chicken, fish sandwiches, rolled oysters, all of them for rock-bottom prices.

It has an idiosyncratic method of service, based in an oral tradition rather than a written one. You place your order with a bartender, who writes down the price of each item you mention, but no other identifying information, on a white scratch pad filled with sums, which represent the orders that preceded yours. He yells back to the kitchen ("I NEED A PAN FRY!"), gives you soup from a crockpot or a jelly glass full of beer. Then you retire to your table, waiting for a waitress to walk out crying your order.

Check's serves lunch and dinner daily.

Cunningham's
$ • 900 S. Fifth St. • 587-0526

Local legend has it that Cunningham's was once a bordello (all those small rooms upstairs, with the saloon doors); it's been a restaurant since 1870, and some of the waiters look to have been here since the kitchen fired up. The food wouldn't be too confusing to anyone who'd skipped forward a century from its opening: Corned beef and cabbage, turtle soup and pan-fried oysters are among the specialties; many people swear by the fish sandwich. Lunch and dinner are served Monday through Saturday.

Kunz's
$$ • 115 S. Fourth Ave. • 585-5555

You can tell this Louisville restaurant, owned and operated by the same family since 1892, must be venerable by the name it had until 1987, when the original location burned down: Wasn't nobody naming nothing "Kunz's the Dutchman" this century. The menu favors steaks, seafood, Old Dutchman Favorites (jaeger schnitzel and zweibel roastbraten), as well as a seafood raw bar. Lunch and dinner are served Monday through Saturday, dinner only on Sunday.

Lynn's Paradise Cafe
$$ • 984 Barret Ave. • 583-3447

Lynn's is like a cross between a country inn and one of those '40s California diners that's shaped like a bulldog. You can tell you're there when you see the giant plaster coffee pot and cups along the sidewalk (it's a fountain), or from the back, the giant Indian-corn mural. Lynn Winter loves kitsch in her decor but not in her kitchen. What it serves forth is a contemporary variation of home cooking that takes equally from Kentucky, California and familiar ethnic traditions (pesto lasagna, a breakfast burrito).

The meat loaf, made from Ma Winter's recipe, is superb; so is the breakfast burrito, the French toast, the big plate of home fries covered with onions and some melted cheese, the biscuits — hell, everything. The dinner menu has a lot of variety, but it includes such standbys as a walnut-encrusted chicken with a hot, almost-Chinese mustard sauce and a choice of wonderful side dishes that include mashed potatoes and lima beans that folks swear by.

It's open for breakfast and lunch every day

but Monday and for dinner Thursday, Friday and Saturday (prepare yourself for a wait those nights).

Masterson's
$$ • 1830 S. Third St. • 636-2511

Huge — it claims to be the state's largest full-service restaurant and serves as a food service option for students at nearby U of L; it also has a number of different rooms to suit almost every dining situation and an inspiringly massive bar room. The menu is pretty straightforward, featuring steaks, pastas, salads and the like. The best bets go against the grain of the Tudor architecture and toward the owners' ethnic background: Masterson comes from Mastoras, a Greek name, and the gyros and Greek salads are pretty fair. Lunch and dinner are served daily, with a 9 AM opening on the weekends.

FYI

Unless otherwise noted, the area code for all phone numbers listed in this chapter is 502.

Mazzoni's Oyster Cafe
$, no credit cards • 2804 Taylorsville Rd. • 451-4436

Oysters are the thing — pan fried, in oyster stew, on the half-shell, served in a "shooter" with tomato juice and hot sauce — but especially rolled (see our close-up in this chapter): Mazzoni's is where this distinctly Louisville dish was invented in 1884, and the barroom that continues the tradition retains that turn-of-the-century feel without being goofy about it. It's open for lunch and dinner Monday through Saturday, bar seating only.

Melrose Inn
$$ • 13306 U.S. Hwy. 42 • 228-1461

The restaurant in this charming hotel just across the line into dry Oldham County is a pretty good time capsule; if the menu of fried chicken, country ham, chicken livers and steaks has changed appreciably since Ike's day, it's hard to see how. Nice touches include the biscuits and a good relish tray that comes with each meal. Historical note: Derby Pie was invented in the Melrose kitchen, and it's still served here. Breakfast, lunch and dinner are served daily. The hotel may be turned into a quaint shopping center in the near fu-

ture, but it's a safe bet the restaurant will stay very much the same.

Old Spaghetti Factory
$ • 235 W. Market St. • 581-1070

Why's this chain listed with Louisville's distinctive haunts? Because it's in a magnificently renovated version of the Levy's Building, with its hundreds of lights that gave rise to a local expression for being drunk: "Lit up like Levy's." (Maybe a future generation will talk about dates that are "Fixed up like the Spaghetti Factory.") Inside, the food is inexpensive, reliable and nostalgic; if you're a baby boomer, its dishes will taste more like what you grew up calling spaghetti than any pasta you've had in 20 years. Nicest variation: the spaghetti with browned butter and mizithra cheese; there's also white clam sauce. Lunch and dinner are served daily.

Rudyard Kipling
$$ • 422 W. Oak St. • 636-1311

This restaurant is as eclectic as Old Louisville itself: a mixture of Kentucky, vegetarian, British Isles, Italian, French and a few other cuisines, pulled together with a loose funkiness that's (to use the restaurant's preferred term) "idiosyncratique." One of the city's best lunch spots — the pub plates always make a tasty, surprising and nutritious impression — it's also the only place in town that treats burgoo with proper seriousness. There are also Cornish pasties (pastry crusts stuffed with various fillings), curries and stews and a signature dish for the ages: Crepes Delbert — crepes filled with black beans and the incomparable Gatton Farms country ham, in a dijon-chablis veloute sauce. Late nights, it's one of the city's most interesting nightspots, with a booking policy as eclectic as the food. Lunch and dinner are served Monday through Friday; it's dinner only Saturday.

Towboat Annie's
$$ • 201 W. River Rd. • 589-2010

A shoreside restaurant in a towboat formerly called the *Choctaw*, the *Port of Houston* and the *Gregory J.*, Towboat, Annie's moved recently from Jeffersonville's waterfront to Louisville's. The restaurant combines seafood, specialties such as a fish sandwich and peel-and-eat shrimp with such landlubbers' fare as pork chops, steaks and veggie burgers. It's open seven days a week during its season, which runs March 1 through December 31.

Steaks

Del Frisco's
$$$$ • 4107 Oechsli Ave. • 897-7077

Del Frisco's has a simple and enviable reputation — the best place in town to have an aged prime, I say prime, steak. It's formal and dark, and the only thing anyone ever talks about other than the steaks is the Green Phunque, a cheesy spinach casserole (although fresh seafood is also on the bill of fare). It serves dinner daily.

Louisville Chophouse
$$$$ • 2224 Dundee Rd. • 454-0054

Formerly Gibs Smokehouse and Grill — famous for its still manufactured "Bottled Hell" hot pepper sauce — this restaurant seems meant for the guy (or gal, but it's usually a guy) who finds himself saying "To hell with it!" when he looks over a menu featuring Seychelles-Paducah cuisine with a Florida twist. A full two-thirds of the entrées are beef, if you count the three surf-n-turf — when was the last time you heard that expression? — combinations; there is also excellent pizza bread and crab cakes of distinction. The atmosphere is dark and classy, but the dress is casual. The Chophouse serves dinner Monday through Saturday.

Pat's Steak House
$$$, no credit cards • 2437 Brownsboro Rd. • 893-2062

They don't make them like this anymore, but some of them survive, relics of a way of life that looks odd and yet strangely familiar today: '60s suburbia. The waiters wear white jackets, the drinks keep coming, and the steaks (or chicken livers, or veal cutlets) serve as pre-text and summit of the whole occasion. It's open for dinner Monday through Saturday.

Home Cooking, Plate Lunches and Cafeterias

Folks attracted to this heading should also check out the fried fish places below and the local institutions grouped under Only in Louisville.

Andrew's
$, no credit cards • 2286 Bardstown Rd. • 458-9421

It's always fun to drop in on this modest steam-table place, where cabbage rolls' appearance on the daily menu is a cause for celebration, and the butterbeans, mashed potatoes and other side orders rule. Lunch and dinner are served Monday through Friday.

Colonnade Cafeteria
$, no credit cards downtown • Starks Building, Fourth Ave. and Muhammad Ali Blvd. • 584-6846
$ • 4040 Dutchman's Ln. • 896-0056

This cafeteria is a Louisville classic, as you can tell from watching the customers, who range from young whelps in the accounting department to folks who can tell you what they were doing on V-E Day. It serves up soups, sandwiches, plate lunches and a well-loved assortment of cakes and pies. The downtown location is open Monday through Friday for breakfast and lunch.

The Dutchman's Lane location has slightly different policies, befitting its suburban location. It's open Sunday through Friday for lunch and dinner, and it accepts credit cards.

Cottage Cafe
$$, no credit cards • 11609 Main St., Middletown • 244-9497

This cafe is a pleasant, slightly ramshackle yellow cottage that serves a sandwich-heavy lunch and weekend dinners with the likes of meat loaf, roast turkey, a Hot Brown that claims direct line of descent from the original and more variations on chicken salad than you might think possible. Desserts are rich and tend toward bars and cheesecakes. Hours include lunch and dinner Monday through Saturday.

A Taste of Louisville

"What is Louisville and Kentucky cuisine?" the traveler asks.

"Well . . ." the native answers.

There are a number of dishes that have originated in Louisville and are served here more than anywhere else.

• The most famous of them is probably the Hot Brown, an open-faced sandwich invented at the Brown Hotel. It's made with turkey, toast, a cheese sauce, bacon or ham and occasionally tomatoes. There is no better way of using up leftover turkey.

• Benedictine spread, an invention of Louisville caterer and restaurateur Jennie Benedict, is classic finger-sandwich fare: a light, satisfying combination of grated cucumber, grated onion, softened cream cheese and other seasonings. Many local sandwich shops make it a bit heartier by adding a slice of bacon or two.

• Henry Bain Sauce is a superior steak sauce invented by a former waiter at the Pendennis Club. It's a combination of several other bottled sauces that has a zip far beyond A-1 or Heinz 57.

• The rolled oyster, created at Mazzoni's in 1884, is made by rolling several raw oysters in pastinga, an Italian batter and frying the lot of them.

• We should also note that Kaelin's claims to have invented the cheeseburger in 1934, although anybody who thinks man never slapped yellow cheese on ground meat before the Roosevelt administration is more credulous than we are.

• Derby Pie, invented in the kitchen of Prospect's Melrose Inn, is a registered trademark of Kern's Kitchen (and they take it seriously — if a restaurant serves something by that name and doesn't buy from Kern's, it's in trouble; local waiters are trained not to describe a similar pie by saying "It's like Derby Pie"). It's a chocolate version of pecan pie (although the nuts are walnuts), and many return visitors to the city make sure they always leave with a pie or two in their suitcases (and another couple under their belts). The original, the recipe of which is guarded with great secrecy and the full force of the laws, is available frozen in many local food shops; near-cousins traveling under such monikers as Triple Crown Pie show up on local menus and many home cooks make unauthorized versions.

• And there is the modjeska, a sweet soft mouthful of a marshmallow dipped in caramel, named in honor of the Polish actress Helena Modjeska, who appeared here in the American premiere of *A Doll's House*.

But does this add up to a cuisine? I don't think so. These indigenous dishes are side alleys, not main streets. People travel to Louisiana for the sole purpose of eating barbecued shrimp or jambalaya; only a fanatic would go far out of his way for a spread of cucumber and cream cheese.

And yet Kentucky cookery is a very special thing. Trigg County native John Egerton wrote in his book *Southern Food*: "No Southern state except Louisiana has a more vibrant and ongoing food history than the Bluegrass state; its cookbooks, famous cooks, distinctive dishes and culinary lore combine to make a rich heritage that Kentuckians proudly claim as their own."

There are a few other foods that belong distinctly to Kentucky. Bibb lettuce, the most delicate of salad greens, was developed in a back yard in Frankfort. Beer cheese is a

— continued on next page

popular regional snack food — a combination of cheeses, beer and various heating-up agents (mustard, garlic, hot pepper, Worchestershire sauce) to make it appropriately snappy.

Western Kentucky has its own distinct barbecue style — its meat of choice isn't pork or beef, but mutton. Many people will drive the two hours to Owensboro's Moonlite to eat at the exceptional buffet (or Old Hickory Bar-B-Q, the city's other premier pit); there is an annual International Barbecue Festival. Mutton barbecue is served occasionally in Louisville, at Paul Clark's Owensboro-style establishment and the annual Pitt Academy barbecue in May, among others, but the best local 'cue is likely to be pork. One frequent (though not ubiquitous) local side dish: thick, spicy potato wedges.

Burgoo is a Kentucky stew, virtually identical to what's called Brunswick stew in North Carolina. It's made with several kinds of meat, ideally some of them shot off a tree (squirrel is classic) and cooked in a huge kettle, preferably outdoors, with a mess of vegetables (corn, green peppers, carrots, potatoes, lima beans, tomatoes, onions, garlic and, optionally, okra) and whatever flavoring agents will give it an appropriate snap and tang (the best recipe I know uses lemon juice, cider vinegar and red pepper).

But the essential ingredient in a good burgoo is time. It needs a long cooking, as long as a half-day, to break down its constituents — for the chicken to split into shreds, for the red meats to swap flavors, for the vegetables to lapse into spinelessness. Many of the local versions are not much more than motley vegetable soups, although the Rudyard Kipling serves an authentic one. (Speaking of squirrel, the squirrel-brains story — that folks in rural Kentucky eat them, risking Kreuzfeldt-Jacob syndrome — was as completely surprising to most of us as it was to you.)

The most famous Kentucky product is bourbon, our native sour mash whiskey, aged in charred oak barrels since about 1775 — the state's first corn crop. It's best appreciated unadorned or with a little water — although it's the foundation of the mint julep, the cloyingly sweet drink of the Derby that few Louisvillians taste any other time of the year. One of the most enduring things *Courier-Journal* editor Henry Watterson wrote was his julep recipe: "Pluck the mint gently from its bed, just as the dew of the evening is about to form upon it. Select the choicer sprigs only, but do not rinse them. Prepare the simple syrup and measure out a half-tumbler of whiskey. Pour the whiskey into a well-frosted silver cup, throw the other ingredients away and drink the whiskey."

The Twig and Leaf claims to have the best breakfast in town.

Bourbon also shows up in other dishes: as a flashy regional accent for creative

— continued on next page

young cooks; as a warm, fragrant note in sauces for bread and biscuit puddings; as the heart of the amazingly potent candy called bourbon balls.

The most fundamental food in Kentucky through the 19th century and into the 20th was corn, and not only in whiskey. For most people the staple was corn meal cooked into some kind of cornbread, from the standard fluffy yellow bread to the flat, golden-brown hoecakes to spoonbread, which Egerton rightly compares to a cornbread soufflé. When a Kentuckian eats any of these — especially the humbler ones — it feels like a small homecoming.

The state's other long-time staple has been pork, and as in Virginia and North Carolina, one of the great delicacies available is a properly cured country ham. And bacon, popular enough on its own, provides an essential by-product: the bacon grease that gives a long-cooked pot of pole beans the proper savor.

Needless to say, the other popular main dish is the one that has carried the state's name throughout the world (although Col. Sanders was a Hoosier). Fried chicken is a much-abused dish, but it's done right here as much as it is anywhere.

But the main dinner tradition has less to do with the main dish and more to do with what's on the side — a profuse choice of vegetables and other accompaniments that's summed up in the lunch-place formula "meat-and-three." The three may not always be healthy. Steve Lee, owner of the Cookbook Cottage cooking school, says one of the characteristics of local cooking is "three starches on every plate," and both Jell-O salad and macaroni and cheese are as often listed as vegetables as greens, fried apples, mashed potatoes, black-eyed peas and stewed tomatoes. But the wide choice of dishes harks back to our traditions of hospitality — wanting to give your guests a full table — and to a time when people worked hard and ate big, and when the season's produce came fast and thick and needed to be used quickly (while its canned and pickled remainder provided the chief source of variety in the winter).

When you get down to the baseline of Louisville eating, you find a great love of fried food, especially fried fish — hard not to figure how that might happen, in a very Catholic city on a major river (although meatless Fridays and Ohio River catch have faded, victims of different aspects of modernity). Churches and fraternal organizations keep alive the tradition of the Saturday night fish fry; the Kingfish and Moby Dick are local empires built on breading, cod and great vats of hot oil. (Moby Dick's reminder of freshness, a neon sign blinking NOW FRYING, is widely imitated, most notably by the upscale Timothy's, which flashes a satiric NOW SAUTEEING).

The local style of fried fish worth checking out is called Green River, a thin, peppery corn meal breading that interposes less grain between you and the fish. It's at its best at its Louisville fountainhead, the Suburban Social Club, at the corner of Third Street and Central Avenue, a Masonic Lodge that has hosted a Saturday fish fry since the Harding administration, April through November and on Good Friday; it's nearly as good and available six days of the week at the Fish House at the corner of Barret and Winter Avenues. The fried-fish experience worth checking out is Mike Linnig's, a sprawling church picnic carried out by other means in Pleasure Ridge Park, just over the earthen floodwall from the Ohio.

This being the South, to the extent that it is, Southern-style sweets are popular (although more often at home or to be read about, than in a restaurant) — jam cakes (the jam isn't a glaze or a frosting, it's mixed into the cake batter), caramel cakes, pies, cobblers and ice cream. A special treat, if you're unfamiliar, is the sweet butter-sugar-and-eggs pie called chess pie (although no restaurant in town serves its ultimate refinement, vinegar pie — a teaspoon of white vinegar to lighten the heavy sweetness). You will often find its cousins buttermilk pie, country pie, transparent pie and Jefferson Davis pie on local menus.

Joseph Huber Family Farm and Restaurant

$$ • 2421 Scottsville Rd., Starlight, Ind.
• (812) 923-5255

As much a dining experience as a culinary adventure, this is a large hall at Southern Indiana's most active U-pick farm (flocked to in strawberry, pumpkin and other applicable seasons) where you sit at long tables and enjoy country ham, catfish or the meal that sums up Huber's spirit: all-you-can-eat chicken and ham. The chicken is fried, of course, and the ham is baked in apple cider and honey on the premises. It's open daily.

Jay's Cafeteria

$ • 1812 W. Muhammad Ali Blvd.
• 583-2534

The city's foremost soul-food restaurant is one of the great crossroads of the community. It features fried chicken, barbecued rib tips, pigs' feet and a varied set of side dishes in spacious modern digs. The supreme treat: individual-size pies. Fruit is barely implicated in their making — these are sweet custard pies: chess, lemon meringue, sweet potato, egg custard, coconut, chocolate, transparent (a sweet amber custard that tastes something like chess pie, only lighter). Jay's is open daily for lunch and early supper (it's closed by 7 PM weekdays, 8 PM on Friday and Saturday).

McCulloch's Cafeteria

$, no credit cards • 1330 Ellison Ave.
• 454-5651

The sort of place that serves its Blue Plate Specials on blue plates, McCulloch's is known for honest, freshly made home cooking: sliced meats, fried chicken, spaghetti and meatballs, real mashed potatoes. It's also the sort of place where lunch specials are $3 for an entrée, two vegetables, bread and beverage. It's open Sunday through Friday, breakfast through dinner.

South Side Inn

$, no credit cards • 114 E. Main St., New Albany, Ind. • (812) 945-9645

Tour buses stop for lunch, lines form on the sidewalk — this Indiana cafeteria's home cooking is celebrated for the homemade pies,

the Friday fish, the fried chicken and the mashed potatoes, which are spooned into the steam table out of large pots and which the management will inform you are real and only real. It's open for lunch and dinner Monday through Saturday.

Sue's Touch of Country

$ • 2605 Rockford Ln. • 449-4086

A sensational success when it was transplanted from St. Matthews to Shively, Sue's offers simple home cooking, from catfish to country ham, with homemade cobblers and pies as a special treat. Sue's is open daily for breakfast, lunch and dinner.

Fish, Fried and Otherwise

Carolina Shrimp & Seafood

$ • 3922 Westport Rd. • 894-8947

Here's a new approach for this land of golden breading — steamed seafood, in particular shrimp (as many as 54) prepared in a Carolina style that doesn't eschew spice, but doesn't wallow in it either. It also serves cod sandwiches (steamed as well and Kingfish be damned), scallops, oysters and inexpensive lobster. They're open Monday through Saturday for lunch and dinner. No smoking, except for at the outdoor tables.

The Fishery

$, no credit cards • 3624 Lexington Rd.
• 895-1188
$, no credit cards • 2918 Hikes Ln.
• 451-2913

Where scrod is God — they fly it in daily, fry it, bake it and give it due homage. There are also noteworthy oysters, chicken dinners, shrimp and frog legs in this New England-styled fixture of local eating. The Fishery is open for lunch or dinner daily. The Lexington Road location is smoke-free.

The Fishhouse

$, no credit cards • 1310 Winter Ave.
• 568-2993

The best bet is the Green River-style fish sandwich (see the close-up in this chapter), but this place is more than just frozen cod and a vat of grease: These folks, former operators of a snazzy joint called David's Seafood, know their way around our gilled and finned friends. Other treats include chowders, salmon croquettes, Boston scrod and fried fish in the more common kind of golden breading. It's closed Sunday.

Joe's Crab Shack
$$$ • 131 E. River Rd. • 568-1171

Lots of folks weren't pleased when the concession for a riverfront restaurant went not to a Louisville firm but to the Landry's chain, but the truth is that few local restaurateurs have the money for such a large and risky venture, and who wants a giant Rally's on the riverfront? Joe's is the sort of place designed for tourists and for Louisvillians who want to feel as if they're on vacation (as well they might — if there were ever crabs here, that was in the Devonian era). It's loud and lively, with a wait staff that forms into a conga line and similar deviltry.

Whatever their provenance, Joe's has crabs in abundance — crab balls, crab legs, crab cakes, stone crabs, blue crabs, soft shell crabs, Dungeness; the surprise is that there isn't a crab tiramisu — along with coconut shrimp, fried oysters, fried catfish, gumbo and a lot more.

It's open daily for lunch and dinner.

Mike Linnig's Place
$ • 9308 Cane Run Rd. • 937-9888

Like a gigantic, nondenominational church picnic (six days a week since 1925), this place serves oversize portions of fried fish, onion rings, frog legs, fried chicken and other stuff (check out the scallops). There are indoor seats, but sitting outside at the concrete tables or inside the screened-in cabins is the only real way to appreciate Linnig's (although there are those who prefer the evening in January when the restaurant reopens with pristine oil). It's closed Mondays and (typically) from the first Sunday of November through the last Thursday of January. (A cartographical note: Cane Run Road is shown as Lower River Road on maps.)

FYI
Unless otherwise noted, the area code for all phone numbers listed in this chapter is 502.

New Orleans House
$$$$ • 9424 Shelbyville Rd. • 426-1577

Here's the average person's best opportunity to know what it might have been like to be Nero, although even a Roman emperor might goggle at the profusion of seafood available at the New Orleans' buffet: steamed shrimp, Blue Point oysters on the half shell, smoked salmon, herring in sour cream, cheeses, salads, shrimp and lobster chowder, clam broth, steamed clams . . . .

Those are just the preliminaries, you understand, to the choices of main dish: Alaskan king crab legs, shrimp Creole, broiled scallops, New Orleans chicken, mussels — unless, of course, you pay extra for a steak or a lobster. If you're still alive, there's also a dessert bar, with cheesecake and build-your-own hot fudge sundaes. Reservations are suggested; the owners recommend setting aside two hours for the feast. They're closed Sunday.

Rumors Restaurant & Raw Bar
$$ • 12339 Shelbyville Rd. • 245-0366

This relaxed place seems to have been transplanted via some tsunami from Fort Lauderdale to the concrete shores of Middletown. It serves some of the city's best Buffalo wings, sandwiches and other bar food, but its real raison d'être is the fresh shellfish: buckets of steamed clams, roasted oysters and peel-and-eat shrimp. It's open Monday through Saturday for lunch and dinner, Sunday for dinner only.

Stan's Fish Sandwich
$ • 3723 Lexington Rd. • 896-6600

Stan's sandwich deserves star billing; it's sweet, moist scrod, breaded with corn flour, fried in canola oil and served on a multigrain bun. You can also have broiled tilapia and swordfish, rolled oysters — with minced oysters in the batter, no less — a shrimpburger (the decapods spilling out of the slaw-dressed bun) and other clever ways to persuade you to sit down in the snug, attractive dining room and get to know our aquatic friends a little better. It's open Monday through Saturday for lunch and dinner.

Ethnic

Asian

Asiana
$$ • 2039 Frankfort Ave. • 893-0380

This proficient purveyor of excellent and authentic Korean food fits awfully well into the faux-'50s surroundings of the late Bobbie Soxer's diner (although it's a safe bet Potsie and Ralph Malph would be surprised to see the table-top grills). From bee bim bop to bulgogi, Asiana serves Korean food at a par with any that's been presented in a city that's had a full (if surprising) share of good restaurants serving this cuisine.

Asiana is smoke-free. It's open for lunch and dinner every day but Tuesday.

Asiatique
$$$ • 106 Sears Ave. • 899-3578

The city's first Pacific Rim restaurant woks and grills its way through the East, over to California, to mouth-dazzling effect. Seafood dishes are a special treat, especially the wok-seared salmon with roasted shallots and Szechuan hot oil, a dish that changes from hot to sweet to oceanic with each bite. But then there's the appetizer of stir-fryed lamb in a sweet potato basket, or the roasted quail (haunch-pickin', lip-smackin', finger-lickin' Henry VIII time). Asiatique offers some of the most unusual desserts in town, featuring grilled fruits, interesting ice creams and some of the most unusual juxtapositions since Little Richard sang that duet with Tanya Tucker. And the bibulous should take note of the martinis, shaken (not stirred) tableside and the list of premium sakes. The restaurant is open seven days a week for dinner only. The management asks patrons to refrain from smoking pipes and cigars.

August Moon
$$ • 2296 Lexington Rd. • 456-6569

Its weekend Pacific Rim specials were that style of cooking's first beachhead in Louisville, before it moved on to sister establishment Asiatique. But every day August Moon serves a Malaysianized version of Chinese cooking that brings a surprising twist to familiar dishes. Lunch and dinner are served daily.

Bonsai Japanese Restaurant
$$ • 916 Dupont Rd. • 897-3600

This new Japanese restaurant offers a full range of Japanese cuisine, from sushi to table grilling, in attractive suburban surroundings. They're open for lunch and dinner every day but Sunday.

Cafe Mimosa
$$ • 1216 Bardstown Rd. • 458-2233

The more elegant of the city's Vietnamese restaurants serves an exemplary version of the cool, delicate Vietnamese spring rolls and fine lemon-grass pork (or chicken, beef, shrimp or a combination) on noodles. Lunch and dinner are served daily; there's an intriguing Sunday brunch with a number of Vietnamese dishes.

Double Dragon
$, no credit cards • 1255 Goss Ave. • 635-5656
Double Dragon II
$, no credit cards • Cedar Springs Shopping Center, 6832 Bardstown Rd. • 231-3973

This small, mostly carry-out operation looks like many others of the hundred or so Chinese restaurants in town and even more like the sort of Chinese take-out place you find in Northeastern cities, where every customer faces the choice "Pints or quarts?" But it has a good reputation among folks who know Chinese food, because it gives good quality and impressive quantity — the fried dumplings are as big as a toddler's fist, and the eggplant in garlic sauce and the boneless barbecued pork are excellent. The same food is also available at the new Double Dragon II in Fern Creek. They're open for lunch and dinner daily.

Empress of China
$$$ • 2249 Hikes Ln. • 451-2500

When it opened in 1980, the Empress was probably the first Chinese restaurant in Louisville to place Oriental food on a more impressive footing than what used to be called "a chop-suey joint," and it gave Louisville its first fiery taste of Hunan-Szechuan cooking. But this pioneer is not grizzled or bedraggled. Despite the number of peers that have joined the field since it opened, at age 12 it remains one of the best Chinese restaurants in town, serving such wonderful dishes as the pork with Szechuan string beans, cold noodles with sesame sauce and Beggar's Chicken, in relaxed, spacious surroundings.

The Empress is open for lunch and dinner daily.

Emperor of China
$$$ • Holiday Manor Shopping Center, U.S. Hwy. 42 • 426-1717

It's identical in most important respects to its original, the Empress (see above). Lunch and dinner are served daily.

Jade Palace
$$ • 1109 Herr Ln. • 425-9878

A good Chinese restaurant that becomes a noteworthy spot for a four-day weekend, Friday through Monday from noon to 4 PM, when it's time for dim sum — the Chinese meal of "small dishes" that's one of the world's great culinary pleasures. It's open seven days a week.

Kim's Asian Grill
$-$$ • 2354 Frankfort Ave. • 893-3725.

Moved to Clifton from East Market Street (it made way for the Mayan Gypsy), Kim's is among the most attractive Oriental restaurants in town, with its hot pink exterior, yellow walls with lilac trim and its high-backed black Art Deco chairs. It's pretty but restrained, and there's a certain spareness to Kim's approach to Korean food — for example, the side dishes that come in such plenty at other restaurants are reduced to a telling one, two or three (watch out for the yellow slices of pickled daikon radish — they're irresistible). Appetizers include yaki mandoo, one of the best variations on the pot sticker theme we've ever had, and geem bop, a Korean style of sushi. And unless your dietary laws (Muslim or Weight Watchers) prohibit it, try the dae jee koki, thin, supple slices of pork in a fiery cayenne sauce. Kim's is open for dinner Monday through Friday, dinner nightly.

Lee's
$$ • 1941 Bishop Ln. • 456-9714

The city's first Korean restaurant has its share of hot stuff, but it also offers sweet and tangy flavors in such dishes as gal bee jim — like Irish stew made with marinated ribs. There's also a full selection of meal-in-a-bowl Korean soups, such as jam bong. It's open for lunch and dinner Monday through Saturday.

Sichuan Garden
$$ • 9850 Linn Station Rd. • 426-6767

There are no gimmicks, no daring new approaches — just some of the best Szechuan food you're likely to encounter, from hacked chicken to orange-flavored beef to Empress chicken. Among an embarrassment of choices, the seafood dishes stand out. It's open daily.

Shalimar Indian Restaurant
$$ • 1820 S. Hurstbourne Pkwy. (in the Hunnington Place Shopping Center) • 493-8899

One of the best Indian restaurants Louisville's ever seen, Shalimar draws its menu mostly from Moghul cuisine and other Northern Indian traditions. There are a lot of choices — more than 30 entrées, plus abundant appetizers, breads, vegetables, rice and side dishes — and it's reasonably authentic: No beef on the menu, only lamb, chicken and seafood. And while many of the same approaches pop up, Chinese-restaurant-style, to be applied to each kind of flesh in its turn, there's still a fair degree of variety — as opposed to the stair-step approach you sometimes see, in which Madras, Vindaloo, etc. are essentially each the same dish with increasing amounts of hot pepper.

And the restaurant makes slight but pleasing departures from the usual run of things throughout the meal, from the especially savory pappadums and mint relish that begin the meal, to the mango kulfi (India's chewy ice cream) that should end it. Shalimar's is open Tuesday through Sunday for lunch (a buffet) and dinner. The restaurant is smoke-free.

Thai Cafe
$$ • Holiday Manor off U.S. Hwy. 42 • 425-4815

This brightly-lit Thai place has a good

many vegetarian and seafood dishes on the menu, along with such specialties as spring rolls, tulip dumplings and Royal Thai curry. One of this book's authors tipped the other to tom kha gai, a symphony in sour made with chicken broth, coconut milk, lemon grass and galanga (ginger's sassy cousin). The tipee is eternally grateful. It's open for lunch and dinner Monday through Friday, dinner only Saturday.

Thai Siam
$$ • 3002 Bardstown Rd. • 458-6871
You'll find this an attractive place to sample Thailand's cuisines of clashing tastes. The best bets are almost always the coconut-milk curries (one of the lot is a daily lunch special). There are usual suspects in evidence: the crisp-fried noodles called mee krob, pla thod and our good buddy Singha beer. It's open for dinner Tuesday through Sunday, lunch Tuesday through Saturday.

Vietnam Kitchen
$ • 5100 S. Third St. (in the Iroquois Manor Shopping Center) • 363-5154
One of the city's most enjoyable places, hidden on the back row of a suburban shopping center, it's nothing to look at (the kind of space that could just as well be a laundromat). But Vietnam Kitchen serves dishes that imprint themselves on your mind, such as deep bowls of vermicelli noodles, char-grilled pork and vegetables that get more jumbled up together as you near the bottom of the bowl or seafood hot pots that cook on your table top. It's also a place for such cross-cultural experiences as hearing a Vietnamese-language version of "And I Love Her" or a bilingual rendition of "The Greatest Love." It's open for lunch and dinner seven days a week.

Cajun

Cajun Cafe
$ • 1616 Grinstead Dr. • 561-9551
$ • 716 E. 10th St., Jeffersonville, Ind.
• (812) 285-9219
Louisville never catches a wave soon enough for it to crash onto the beach. While there have been a number of attempts at a local restaurant specializing in Cajun stuff, it wasn't until the end of 1995 that the Cajun Cafe took off. But they got it right — the food is cheap, fiery and authentic (although they'll make adjustments for vegetarians), and they serve it speedily. Check out the crawfish etoufée, which has the well-balanced hedonism of Big Joe Turner singing "I'm like a one-eyed cat peeping in a seafood store," and the pecan pie. The cafe is smoke-free at both locations.

German

Gasthaus
$$-$$$ • 4812 Brownsboro Rd. • 899-7177
The city's largest ethnicity gets back to its roots in this small restaurant, run by a family from the vicinity of Dusseldorf. The decor is standard — Alpine and Black Forest murals — but the schnitzels sizzle, the rouladen rules and the spatzle sparkles. Gasthaus is open for dinner Tuesday through Saturday.

Irish

The Irish Rover
$-$$ • 2319 Frankfort Ave. • 899-3544
This pub's Irishness is not an affectation

INSIDERS' TIP

If you're still puzzling out the question of Louisville's regional identity, here's another bit of paradoxical evidence: While you find grits on Louisville menus, they're usually a sign not of Yankee-baiting obdurateness, but of quality — they're more likely to be on ambitious menus (see Lilly's, the English Grill) than on more modest ones, and as often in Carolinian shrimp and grits as in more local guise.

— it's owned and managed by Michael Reidy, a native of County Clare, and his wife Siobhain. The pub offers smoked salmon, colcannon, Dublin coddle, Limerick ham and the like. Not to be missed: the smoked salmon and potato gratin, a rich potato gratin, flecked with small pieces of smoky fish, that *Louisville* magazine called "comfort food, Ph.D." The bar is noteworthy for its draft Guinness and a wide selection of Irish whiskies. Kitchen hours are Monday through Saturday for lunch and dinner.

Italian

If you're hankering for Italian, remember that it makes up the baseline for most present-day bistros as much or more than French cooking. You should also check out the description of the city's premier Italian restaurant, Vincenzo's, under Fine Dining.

Allo Spiedo
$-$$ • 2309 Frankfort Ave. • 895-4878

Allo spiedo means "on the spit," and its rotisserie-cooked pizzas and skewered meats represent the hearty, straightforward side of Italian cooking as well as any Louisville restaurant, while its outdoor terrace is al fresco at its fresc-est. The antipasti are excellent, and specials frequently reach the best level of Italian cooking — perfect without being showy. It's open for lunch and dinner Monday through Saturday and dinner only on Sunday.

Ferd Grisanti's
$$$ • 10212 Taylorsville Rd. • 267-0050

The Grisanti name still is a guarantee of quality — this Jeffersontown hub is known for veal and for reliable versions of such classics as minestrone and veal Parmesan; our coauthor, a former employee, commends the marinara sauce. Dinner is served Monday through Saturday; reservations are preferred on the weekend.

Mamma Grisanti
$$ • 3938 Dupont Cr. • 893-0141

Decorated to look like an Italian farmhouse (with Grisanti family possessions in some of the rooms), Mamma's features a wide range of Italian food from across the boot such as lasagna, chicken pesto salad, a white pizza

with garlic-cream sauce replacing tomatoes. On Bambino Night, Monday and Tuesday, children 12 and younger eat for free from the children's menu and also get a sundae. Lunch is served Sunday through Friday, dinner daily.

Porcini
$$-$$$ • 2730 Frankfort Ave. • 894-8686

This stylish dinner spot features some of the suavest Northern Italian entrées in town, along with salads and pizzas that draw a more cost-conscious set. It's closed Sundays.

Romano's Macaroni Grill
$$ • 410 S. Hurstbourne Pkwy. • 423-9220

From the strolling opera-singing waiters (not all of them all the time, however) to the huge jugs of house wine, this Dallas-based chain provides some idiosyncratic touches, along with almost any ilk of Italian food — wood-fired pizzas, a rotisserie oven, a mesquite grill (huh?) and big bowls of satisfying pastas. It's large, but not sterile, and open daily.

Mexican, Southwestern, Spanish and South American

Alameda
$$$ • 1381 Bardstown Rd. • 459-6300

While most Louisville Mexican establishments serve a satisfying but stereotypical menu of burritos, enchiladas, tacos and these newfangled fajita things, the prettily-appointed Alameda takes a more serious look at Mexican and Southwestern cuisine. (Check out the Southwestern tapas menu.) It has luncheon hours Monday through Friday and dinner Monday through Saturday.

De la Torre's
$$$ • 1606 Bardstown Rd. • 456-4955

This is a wonderful, elegant Spanish restaurant in the heart of Restaurant Row, decorated with colorful tiles and pottery that give it a more authentically Castillian feel than most places in the Ohio Valley. In addition to superb tapas and paella, the lamb and seafood dishes are always worth checking out (there are people who swear by the scallops and the squid). Point of interest: It has an all-Spanish wine list. De la Torre's is open for dinner Tuesday through Saturday; there's a tapas-only menu available weeknights.

Frontera
$ • 10602 Shelbyville Rd. • 244-8889
$ • 7707 Preston Hwy. • 966- 2828

Located at a bend in the road just shy of Middletown, the former La Cazuela is popular with the Hurstbourne bunch for lunch and dinner alike. Ask for the tomatilla salsa with your chips, ponder the chef's specials such as pollo poblano, pop a Negra Modelo and relax. The Preston Highway location works the same set of tricks. It's open for lunch and dinner daily.

Judge Roy Bean's
$$ • 1801 Bardstown Rd. • 459-6398

Don't be misled by the chain-sounding name: Judge Roy serves Southwestern-and-beyond delights (such as stew with wild boar, venison and savory spices, or the crawfish bisque). The wine list has won awards, though it's reasonably priced, the assortment of microbrews is savvy, and there are monthly wine (and occasionally beer) tastings. It's open for lunch and dinner daily.

Mayan Gypsy
$$, no credit cards • 813 E. Market St. • 583-3300

The hottest new restaurant since Lynn's Paradise Cafe is one of the most unlikely — it developed from a roving truck serving a kind of food that conservative Louisville had never before tasted.

But the only objection you'll hear to the Mayan Gypsy is from the people who've had to wait to get in. The food, based on recipes from owner Rosendo Ucan's family in the Yucatan, is just extraordinary: We know people who went there for lunch, then came back for dinner the same night. And no wonder. The mole is already legendary; the various ways of cooking squash will get you eating your vegetables with a smile; and the salbute, a puffy, hand-rolled variation on the tortilla, is a wonderful staging ground for everything from black beans to pork. The atmosphere is casual and artily funky, the prices ungodly cheap.

This isn't a stuffy, reservations-are-recommended type of place, but they're a good idea, because there are only a dozen or so tables (there's also a large party room). It's open for lunch and dinner Monday through Saturday. A beer and wine license is pending, and when that's approved, the restaurant will begin accepting credit cards. The restaurant is smoke-free.

Picasso Restaurant
$$ • 1758 Frankfort Ave. • 893-1774

This place opened in 1995 as a deli, with a small, idiosyncratic space that looks as if it could be designed by (or in homage to) its namesake. It still serves soup, salad and sandwich with the best of them, but it's gotten much more interesting by taking a *nuevo latino* approach to its dinner menu. It's one of the city's best bargains: The food is excellent, plentiful and less expensive than most of its peers in quality. The long, narrow patio is an excellent outdoor dining spot; there's also an interesting selection of beer (no wine). It's open for lunch Monday through Saturday, dinner Wednesday to Saturday, and there's a well-loved Sunday brunch. The restaurant is smoke-free (except on the patio).

Thatsa Wrapp
$, no credit cards (checks accepted) • 3801 Willis Ave. • 896-1235

Coming soon to your town: This new restaurant, already sprouting in other cities and eying other neighborhoods besides its St. Matthews birthplace, makes the most of the current fad for wrapping stuff in some version of a tortilla. The fillings in what a manager describes as "international gourmet burritos" reach Thailand (peanut chicken), the Caribbean, Italy (pesto chicken) and the realms of sheer cornball (the Hail Caesar is a chicken Caesar salad). It's open Monday through Saturday for lunch and dinner.

Middle Eastern

Grape Leaf
$ • 2217 Frankfort Ave. • 897-1774

A step above the usual pita place — although the sandwiches are first-rate — this offspring of the popular Pita Palace has a variety of interesting kebabs, moussaka and vegetarian dishes, as well as the usual dessert pastries. It has lunch daily, dinner Monday through Saturday, breakfast Thursday through Sunday.

Pita Delight
$ • 1015 Barret Ave. • 583-2926

Pita Delight is a small place that does the usual Middle Eastern thing — felafel, hummus, wonderful pastries — with distinction. It's open Monday through Saturday for lunch and dinner.

Pita Pantry
$ • 1611 Eastern Pkwy. • 451-7482

This family-run pita place has good chicken gyros and one of the best felafels we or our friends have ever tasted, not to mention good, garlicky baba ghanouj, fine fool m'dammas and Middle Eastern tea that will take you to another continent, if not world. It's open Monday through Saturday.

Pan-African

Cafe Kilimanjaro
$ • 649 S. Fourth St. • 583-4332

Many foods that have a common origin in Africa, from Ethiopian doro wat to Jamaican curry and Southern-style barbecued chicken, are served in a colorful spot that also has some of the best vegetable dishes in town — like palawa, a spicy spinach dish that's about as good as greens get. A good bet is the sampler plate. They're open for lunch every day but Sunday and for dinner Wednesday through Saturday.

Barbecue

Mark's Feed Store
$$ • 11422 Shelbyville Rd. • 244-0140
$$ • 10316 Dixie Hwy. • 933-7707
$$ • 1514 Bardstown Rd. • 458-1570

Two exceptional things, a mustardy bar-

becue sauce and the buttermilk pie, distinguish this popular barbecue operation, although the pulled pork and baby-back ribs are fine, and the onion straws (thinly cut onion rings) are addictive (but you may regret it in the morning). The atmosphere lives up to the rural name; it's like eating in a big, bustling barn. It has lunch and dinner daily.

Paul Clark's Owensboro Bar B Q
$, no credit cards • 2912 Crittenden Dr. • 637-9532

This diner brings the best of the country into the city: There's western Kentucky's distinctive chopped mutton barbecue, meaty country-style ribs (as well as the more typical, close-to-the-bone rack) and country pie — a buttermilk pie, sweet and sugary, very similar to chess. It's open until 5 PM Monday through Wednesday and until 8 PM Thursday through Saturday.

Rib Tavern
$$ • 4157 Bardstown Rd. • 499-RIBS

The Rib Tavern is where Louisville comes together to jaw over ribs (duh) wreathed in sweet, smoky sauce, and take up yet again the age-old question: A loaf or half-loaf of onion rings? It has a long history as a post-game hangout for U of L fans and players. It's open for lunch and dinner daily.

Rich O's Barbecue's and Public House
$ • 3312 Plaza Dr., New Albany, Ind. • (812) 949-2804

The barbecue's good, the decor is quirky enough to draw a gander, but the real draw is the beer. Owner Roger Baylor is a longtime agitator for better brew who charges more for a mainstream American beer — Miller or Budweiser — than for many of the 100 or so excellent microbrews and imports his place stocks (which include our all-time favorite, Sierra Nevada Pale Ale).

Vince Staten's Old Time Barbecue
$ • 9219 U.S. Hwy. 42 • 228-7427

You've read the book, now eat the 'cue. All of the smokelore Vince Staten accumu-

FYI

Unless otherwise noted, the area code for all phone numbers listed in this chapter is 502.

lated researching his and Greg Johnson's book *Real Barbecue* is on display in this Prospect eatery. It has a sauce list and a wall with more different brands of barbecue sauce than are dreamt of in your philosophy, as well as great pork, beef, chicken, ribs, cole slaw, banana pudding — we'd go on, but that should be enough. It's open daily for lunch and dinner. Ironically enough for a barbecue place, the restaurant is smoke-free.

Burgers

Dizzy Whizz Drive-In
$, no credit cards • 217 W. St. Catherine • 583-3828

Dizzy Whizz is a classic drive-in from the late '40s, one of the few places in town to still offer curb service. The house specialty is the — why would we make this up? — Whizz Burger: a doubledecker with cheese, lettuce and special sauce; there are also especially good milk shakes. They're open for lunch Monday through Saturday, dinner and late nights daily.

Genny's Diner
$, no credit cards • 2223 Frankfort Ave. • 893-0923

Here's a landmark in gluttony, if nothing else. This plain Clifton diner is the home of the notorious Sweet Daddy Burger, a pound and a quarter of beef on a bun. (That's like five quarter-pounders!) The other house specialty is the frickled pickle — a deep fried slice of dill. Genny's is closed Sunday but open every other day from breakfast hours through late evening.

Kaelin's
$$ • 1801 Newburg Rd. • 451-1801

This spot is where the cheeseburger was born, they say, one frosty mornin' in 1934. And it's still having babies: One of the restaurant's appetizers is a plate of a dozen (or a half-dozen) mini-cheeseburgers. The fried chicken is also celebrated, and it comes accompanied by real mashed potatoes; the desserts are also homemade. It's hard to beat the friendliness of the sign outside too: "If you can't stop, please wave." Kaelin's is open seven days a week from lunch hours through late evening.

Ollie's Trolley
$, no credit cards • Third and Kentucky Sts. • 583-5214

Ollie's is yet another of John Y. Brown's failures to duplicate the success of Kentucky Fried Chicken. This remnant of the chain, a narrow mock trolley car, has lunchtime lines out the door for the Ollieburger, a well-done, well-spiced patty with a tangy special sauce, and french fries sprinkled with a fiery blend of herbs and chili pepper. It's closed Sunday.

White Castle
$ • 16 locations • main office 361-2317

Here's one piece of evidence in the "Is Louisville Southern?" debate: The local source of thin, square burgers with sweated onions isn't Nashville's choice, the Krystal, but New Jersey's. The city continues its love affair with the "slider" (when a longtime location at Bardstown Road and Eastern Parkway closed, local filmmaker Ron Schidlknecht made a elegiac film called *My Porcelain Past*). They're open every hour of the year except Christmas Day.

W.W. Cousins
$ • 900 Dupont Rd. • 897-9684

Burgers are taken with real seriousness here: They're freshly ground on the premises and served on homemade buns, with a condiment bar of more than 40 items — a virtual directory of the ways in which a hamburger can be transformed or desecrated: You may, God help you, top a burger with chopped peanuts, horseradish, sauerkraut and sweet 'n' sour sauce if you wish. The menu also includes soups, salads, charbroiled chicken sandwiches, grilled swordfish and homemade pies. It's open every day from lunch through late evening. Children 12 and younger eat free with parents after 4 PM Monday and Tuesday.

Pizza

Clifton's Pizza Co.
$ • 2230 Frankfort Ave. • 893-3730

This spiffily renovated Clifton joint has good

'za, sandwiches, pastas and calzones served in a large, open room decorated with a cool if confusing array of clocks. Hours start at lunch and go through late night; they're closed Monday.

Impellizzeri's
$, no credit cards • 2306 Bardstown Rd.
• 451-7177
$ • 12107 Shelbyville Rd. • 244-4697

These family-owned pizzerias serve an Italo-Louisvillian style of pie — big, loaded with lots of ingredients — that has been synonymous with good pizza for more than a decade. Other possibilities include spaghetti and meatballs, stuffed shells and ravioli. The buttery, doughy bread sticks are built along the lines of the pie. The Bardstown Road restaurant is closed on Monday; the other is open seven days a week.

Rocky's Sub Pub
$ • 1207 E. Market St., Jeffersonville, Ind.
• (812) 282-3844

Hoosier pizza rules — at least it does in this Jeffersonville success story that also serves a full menu of Italian dishes, sandwiches and other appropriate fare. It's closed on Monday.

Wick's Pizza
$ • 971 Baxter Ave. • 458-1828

Move over, Impellizeri's! Wicks has the most massive entrant into Louisville cuisine since the Sweet Daddy: the Big Wick, a supreme pizza with the works and more that weighs in at 10 pounds. Wick's is open seven days a week from lunch through late evening.

Delis and Lunch Places

The Cafe at the Louisville Antique Mall
$ • 900 Goss Ave. • 637-6869

This wonderful restaurant is on the top floor of an old warehouse that's now filled with stalls selling everything from chifforobes to Depression glass. The menu takes on some of the native setting: There's a sandwich called the Queen Anne, a superb bacon Benedictine; a turkey, roast beef and Swiss hoagie on a baguette is called the French Provincial. (Thankfully, there's nothing called Overpriced Crap We Bought Cheap in the Country.) Soups and daily specials are worth checking out, and if Italian cream cake is offered for dessert, get it. The smoke-free cafe is open daily for lunch.

The City Cafe
$ • 505 W. Broadway • 589-1797
$ • 1907 S. Fourth St. • 635-0222
$ • 500 N. Preston St. (in the University of Louisville Health Science Center)
• 852-7539

These wildly popular spots were founded by Jim Henry, who made a reputation as a "culinary outlaw" at the Winery in the early '80s, a time when that wasn't every other young chef's schtick. They're at their best at lunchtime, when the excellent soups, creative sandwiches and other inexpensive items they serve up make perfect midday fare. If chicken pot pie is the day's special, get it — it's served in a puff pastry, sitting in a pool of vegetables and cream sauce. The Broadway location, which virtually serves as a second cafeteria for the *Courier-Journal*, is open for lunch Monday through Friday; the Preston location is open from 7:30 AM to 3 PM weekdays; the original location on Fourth Street, near U of L, is open from 8 AM to 8 PM Monday through Friday and 11 AM to 4 PM Saturday.

La Peche
$-$$ • Holiday Manor Shopping Center, U.S. Hwy. 42 • 339-7593

The business which spawned Lilly's, which vies for the title of best Louisville restaurant, remains an essential source of distinctive gourmet-to-go items: the likes of sesame chicken and soy-honey salmon, along with a number of vegetarian dishes and amazing desserts, from lemon bars to tortes. There are also tables for eating in. It's open for lunch and dinner Tuesday through Saturday. It's smoke-free.

Stevens & Stevens
$ • 1114 Bardstown Rd. • 584-3354

This deli is a little pretty and a little cute. (Why is the corned beef sandwich named after Henny Youngman?) But somebody's put a lot of creativity into more than just the name of Me Turkey, You Jane (turkey, bacon and Benedictine on French bread). Soups, salads and baked goods are all good for eating in or carrying out. It's open Tuesday through Saturday, lunch through 7 PM.

Coffee and Dessert

Day's Expresso and Coffee Bar
$ • 1420 Bardstown Rd. • 456-1170

If your favorite part of cappuccino-style drinks is the frothed milk, I'm not sure anyone does it better than this mutedly attractive, smoke-free spot, which has a bit more sedate atmosphere than the more social coffee places do. The coffee itself is second only to Heine Brothers. They're open daily.

Heine Brothers Coffee
$ • 1295 Bardstown Rd. • 456-5108
$ • 2714 Frankfort Ave. • 899-5551
$ • 11800 Shelbyville Rd. • 244-2064

You know how people in less caffeinated climes bring home Starbucks coffee from a trip to a bigger city? Not after they visit Heine Brothers, they don't. The Heines' hot air roaster (which keeps the Middletown location fragrant as a coffee-fiend's dream) is set loose on some of the world's finest coffees, such as the authentic Yemeni mocha java and our favorite, the Tanzanian peaberry. The Frankfort Avenue and Middletown locations serve pannini made by Lotsa Pasta. It's open daily, early til late; all locations are smoke-free, although it's allowed outside (the outdoor seating is the most abundant at the Bardstown Road location).

Sweet Surrender
$, no credit cards • 2311 Frankfort Ave.
• 896-0519

This establishment in a historic tollkeeper's house has a rather schizophrenic identity: during the day, it serves healthy, vegetarian lunches such as a curried eggplant sandwich and vegetarian couscous; at night it offers the yang to that yin — desserts, such as its white chocolate mousse, that have no more truck with restraint than your Aunt Lurleen. It's closed Sunday and Monday.

Worth a Drive

We'll conclude with a few places that are a bit of a drive from Louisville, although none is more than an hour or so, and each has its own flavor to offer to the local dining scene — in other words, if they were in Louisville, you'd have read about them already in this chapter.

Blue River Cafe
$$ • 1 Main St., Miltown, Ind.
• (812) 633-7510

A customer told the *Courier-Journal*, "It's so nice to have a college-town-type restaurant in this rural part of Indiana." That captures it pretty well. Miltown is a small town west of Louisville that is most noted for its access to a pretty, and pretty easy, patch of the Blue River perfect for canoeing and tubing. The Blue River Cafe is inside a ramshackle old store, but the interior has been decorated with hanging plants, posters and a new paint job that make it seem like the sort of place where you'd break up with your poetry professor.

There's a standing menu of sandwiches and such, but the reason people come to Blue River from 40 miles away is for the six or so nightly specials listed on the chalkboard: orange roughy with roasted sweet peppers, spicy baked shrimp on basmati rice or prime rib. A must-get side dish is the ravioli nudi — three fat blobs of the kind of filling that you would find inside some especially good spinach ravioli. The bread pudding is one of the best, and most unusual, we've ever tasted — more

---

INSIDERS' TIP

The soufflé du jour at the Brown Hotel's English Grill is one of the best desserts in town, but be prepared — you have to order it 45 minutes in advance.

like French toast — and the yeasty homemade breads are a real treat. The Cafe is open for lunch and dinner Friday and Saturday and lunch on Sunday.

Claudia Sanders Dinner House
$$-$$$ • 3202 Shelbyville Rd., Shelbyville, Ky. • (502) 633-5600

Col. Harland Sanders built this restaurant, named after his wife, in 1964, after he had become a millionaire from the sale of Kentucky Fried Chicken. Of course you're gonna have the chicken — although there's also baked and country ham, chicken livers and other entrées. But the real attractions are to the side: The eight vegetable dishes, which range from fair to great, and come around in large bowls, to be served family-style; and the wonderful homemade breads — yeast rolls that we could make a meal out of by themselves, and biscuits and corn muffins nearly as good. It's open Tuesday through Sunday for lunch and dinner.

Photo: Courtesy of Steve Lee

Steve Lee, owner of the Cookbook Cottage cooking school, cites one hallmark of local eating: "Three starches on every plate."

Doe Run Inn
$$ • Route 3, Hwy. 448, Brandenburg, Ky. • (502) 422-2042

The view from the Doe Run Inn's screened-in porch, with the mist rising off the pretty little namesake creek, made its way into John Egerton's definitive book *Southern Food* as an image of the good life, and no wonder. The Doe Run is a historic inn about two centuries old (Abraham Lincoln's father is said to have helped build it) that makes a perfect weekend getaway; many more folks drive from Louisville to have dinner there. The biscuits are better than homemade, the green beans a perfect example of the cooked-into-submission Southern style, the signature lemon chess pie is an explanation of the simple superiority of Dixie desserts and such main dishes as fried chicken and country ham fit perfectly into the gestalt, y'all. They're open for breakfast, lunch and dinner daily (call to check about winter hours).

Marimba Mexican Restaurant
$ • 2059 Midland Tr. (U.S. Hwy. 60 W.), Shelbyville, Ky. • (502) 647-1990

Some friends from Texas hipped us to this Mexican place in Shelbyville — a combination of facts that often has us looking for the nearest exit. But this place, atop a little hill just outside downtown Shelbyville, has the goods, with chiles relleno, carnitas, superb guacamole and other Mexican specialties. It's open for lunch and dinner daily.

Science Hill Inn
$$$ • 525 Washington St., Shelbyville, Ky. • (502) 633-2825

Nobody has come closer to re-imagining traditional Kentucky cuisine for contemporary tastes than Science Hill. The menu makes it possible to eat a contemporary kind of eclectic high cooking — grilled chicken topped with a pineapple salsa, say — or food conservative enough for a country club. But Science Hill pays attention and respect to both sides of the menu. The traditional dishes aren't made with gotta-do-it doggedness; the newer and more foreign touches don't seem ill-conceived, like Grandpa in hot pants.

It reaches perfection with the best fried chicken you'll ever taste. The thin pan-fried crust is like a drawing out of the skin's hidden crispness; the meat inside is tender and juicy. The perfect accompaniment: Green beans cooked in a slightly sweet country ham stock.

Then there are the great breads (buttermilk biscuits and hot-water cornbread) and desserts such as the masterful biscuit pudding, a bread pudding with bourbon sauce that's about as good as dessert gets . . . . Are you still here? Get going already! They're open Tuesday through Sunday for lunch (Sunday is a buffet) and for dinner Friday and Saturday.

Upper Crust
$$ • 209 West Main St., Madison, Ind.
• (812) 265-6727

Nick Izamis, a former Louisville restaurateur, plays the host's role to perfection in this storefront dining room in the historic section of Madison, Indiana (see Daytrips). The dining room, tastefully decorated with copper utensils and black and white posters of European scenes, is a place that could feel either intimate or gregarious, depending who else showed up. But the food on the extensive menu is as unfailingly hospitable as Nick himself — the boldly garlicked hummus, the crisp and teasingly sour orange roughy, the skillets of browned vegetables that seem as if their best qualities have been drawn out and doted upon. It's open for dinner Tuesday through Saturday.

The most recent trend is toward the biggest bars — megabars, they're sometimes called — which have a number of different stages and rooms or incorporate some sort of sport.

Nightlife

Suppose one night you decided to drink as fully from Louisville's nightlife as one possibly could. Your night would probably be a little something like this:

At 5:30 PM, you leave your work clothes on and head straight to the Old Seelbach Bar, where the sophisticated jazz of vibraphonist Dick Sisto makes you forget about your boss, your big project at work and bothersome rush-hour traffic. Then it's over to Bank Shot Billiards, where the game of pool is given proper respect and the classy atmosphere is nearly as transporting as the one you just left at the Seelbach.

On the way home to change clothes and tackle the dinner issue, you stop at Kern's Korner to see if a golf scramble sponsored by the neighborhood bar still has some slots open for you and your friend. Everybody there knows your face, if not your name.

You leave home at about 9 PM to see one of your favorite rock bands crank out music at the Phoenix Hill Tavern. It's standing room only, and the Tavern's huge ceiling fans languidly circulate the excitement-laced air. Two hours and twenty songs later, you walk out of PHT happy and ready to dance. Lucky you — it's Friday, and that means salsa night at Utopia International Cafe. The eclectic crowd swallows you up and two hours pass.

The hour of 1 AM means one thing to many Louisvillians: Bloody Marys at the Outlook Inn. You're ready for something spicy, and you know that this is just the time of night when the Outlook starts hopping. The Bloody Mary tastes good. After visiting with the regulars there and listening to a fair share of the groovy rock they favor on their sound system, your stomach lets you know that dinner was hours ago; La Bamba calls with an avocado and bean burrito "as big as your head," as their sign promises. The tiny restaurant, which is open until 5 AM, is just down the street from the Outlook. Your night on the town has tapered off just perfectly. Now, what was the name of that person you met at Utopia?

This is just one possible scenario — there are comedy clubs, coffeehouses, cinemaplexes, country music nightspots and oodles of neighborhood bars out there crying for your attention. The best way to keep on top of things is to consult one of the local papers. *The Courier-Journal* publishes a weekly roundup of who's playing in its "Weekend" section on Friday (arranged by section of the city and type of club); *LEO's* "Plugged In" centerfold is a day-by-day account of what's happening at 40 or so local nightspots; and *Louisville Music News*, which covers the local music scene in great detail, publishes a monthly calendar.

In nightlife, as in so many other things, Louisville is a relatively affordable city: Cover charges range from $3 to $5, and the $5 usually buys an implicit guarantee that you're getting something worthwhile for the money (even if it's just admission to a really hot club).

The most recent trend is toward the biggest bars — megabars, they're sometimes called — which have a number of different stages and rooms or incorporate some sort of sport (as in The Brewery's hugely successful beer-and-volleyball combination). It's the malling of nightlife, combining several different choices under a single roof. But the megabars haven't run other options out of town yet.

We outline a few nightlife options below, but this is one area where empirical data far outstrips someone else's subjective recommendations. In other words, use this guide as a jumping off point, and explore the Louisville scene for yourself. These are merely our highlights.

Megabars

O'Malley's Corner
133 W. Liberty St. • 589-3866

It's vast, matey. From beginnings as a dueling-piano bar called Hurricane O'Malley's, this has grown into a complex that takes up a good part of the block at Second and Liberty streets. It's got a variety and changeability of atmosphere rare among bars; if Elmer Fudd were to chase Bugs Bunny through a nightclub, it might be one like this.

The main attraction is Coyote's (named after local country DJ Coyote Calhoun, a partner in the enterprise), which stretches the length of a block and has haute-Southwestern decorations, such as a desert-landscape wall mural in electric colors. It's got a dance floor full of line dancers and two-steppers (although they tend to be a bit more nouveau ranch than the habitués of less-glitzy country bars). It's also hosted concerts ranging from Emmylou Harris and the Nash Ramblers to George Clinton and the P-Funk All-Stars.

Once Elmer hurtles out of Coyote's, what does he find? Hurricane O'Malley's is still in the business of hectoring you to sing along with Beatles songs and other familiar tunes. The Rock-It Club is a dark spot for dancing to new rock and alternative sounds, while the Backstage Blues is the city's slickest blues venue.

Phoenix Hill Tavern
644 Baxter Ave. • 589-4957

The original Phoenix Hill was one of Louisville's wonders — a vast beer garden and amusement park that hosted rallies for the likes of William Jennings Bryan and Theodore Roosevelt.

This Phoenix Hill has made its own kind of history: the first Louisville club to prove that folks in this city love a rambling bar with more than one stage; with the Butchertown Pub, the most enduring nightlife presence on the local rock scene; the definition of Louisville's rock 'n' roll mainstream (when the Ramones played Phoenix Hill, it was a sign the world had changed).

Most nights, however, the music comes from local cover acts. Those in the Tap Room tend toward the acoustic and bluesy. The Saloon, as the largest room in the house, gets the most raucous acts. The glassed-in Roof Garden is the neatest room on the premises:

It feels as if you've gone to a concert in a greenhouse.

There's also a deck with a bar and DJ music (when the weather's warm enough to permit it). And Phoenix Hill holds a number of well-attended special events named according to the tavern's phanciphul orthography (the Phall Ball, the Spring Phling).

The Butchertown Pub
1335 Story Ave. • 583-2242

Butchertown (like its rival to the south, Phoenix Hill) began as a neighborhood folk club in the early '70s and grew incredibly. It now has three stages: the Dance Hall, which offers a mix of cover and original bands pegged to a collegiate and just-post taste; the Pub Stage, which has blues, bluegrass, jazz and R&B groups; and the Courtyard, where a different flavor is served, be it aggressive rock, classic rock or experimental rock. The Butchertown Pub is too big to feel homey, but sometimes it comes really, really close.

The Brewery
426 Baxter Ave. • 583-3420

A few years ago, this popular bar in Phoenix Hill set up a sand volleyball court in a vacant half-lot next door and found a side dish turning into an entrée. Next thing you knew, the corner across the street was transformed into Baxter Jack's, a large sandlot filled with volleyball courts; there was a pro shop on the premises; and more teams were spiking across the net than a horde of Microsoft programmers.

The Thunderdome is a large concrete shell attached to the original Brewery that can hold about 1,000 concert customers. Although many folks complain about the sound, the dome can sound good in the hands of a good sound man. Don't miss a show just because of the acoustics' horrible reputation. A late-night munchies menu has pleased many patrons over the years; the frozen margaritas have slaked many a thirst.

Jim Porter's
2345 Lexington Rd. • 452-9531

Jim Porter's is Phoenix Hill for the mortgage-bound. This large three-stage place, in a building that began life as an outsized restaurant called L'il Abner's, is for folks from their mid-30s and older to hang out and listen to pre-digital rock and country.

The Ballroom is one of the city's nicest places to see a band (unfortunately, it isn't booking many touring acts these days) and the snug Melody Bar features blues acts on one of the city's coolest stages, a little niche in the wall behind the bar.

Dance

Of course, dancing goes on in almost every bar at some time or another. But a few Louisville nightspots are devoted to the boogie. We hit the highlights below.

The Connection
120 S. Floyd St. • 585-5752

There are more than 20,000 square feet in this entertainment complex and convention center. The Connection attracts a primarily gay clientele (some of it drawn from other states by its reputation). If you're serious about getting some dancing done, this should be destination #1. It's one of the city's best places to go to shake it — and the weekend drag shows in the classy, red-curtained theater are a trip. The sprawling complex also includes several bars, a restaurant (The Missing Link Cafe and a gift shop.

Sparks
104 Main St. • 587-8566

Sparks is a Louisville success story — "a dirty rotten hellhole with clean bathrooms," in the words of a manager — which once found itself on *Details* magazine's list of the country's top nightspots.

Warehouse-bare, with a technologically psychedelic dance floor, various forms of underground dance music, from house to rave, flourish here. (Ironically enough, the club is next door to the local headquarters of Muzak.)

This is a loud, young club, but Sparks has a number of rooms that let a patron escape any noise, person or sight that displeases. A pool table in one room seems like an anachronism, but it's always in use. An outdoor garden is a good place to cool off from dancing or heat up a romantic conversation. Originally a gay bar, Sparks now considers itself "gay-friendly." It has a mostly straight crowd but an imperative posted at the door barring sexist, racist or homophobic language.

Cafe Kilimanjaro
649 S. Fourth St. • 583-4332

Dance to world beat music on Friday and Saturday nights until 3 AM at this restaurant/bar, located in the heart of downtown in Theater Square. In this one bar, for a few hours, Louisville seems a little less homogenous than it usually does — expatriates from a number of African and European countries have discovered the nice vibe at Kilimanjaro's. Come

---

INSIDERS' TIP

Ah, wings. Those labor-intensive, calorie-soaked, palate-singeing morsels seem to go with late-night munching like olives pair up with martinis. When an early-morning hankering for chicken wings hits Louisvillians, they are blessed with multiple options. Among the best: Open very late are Indi's (1033 W. Broadway) and King's (2101 W. Broadway) two West End joints that are infamous for serving particularly fattening and spicy fried wings. BW-3 (the corner of Shelbyville Road and Breckinridge Lane) and Wings Sports Cafe (2427 Bardstown Road) both serve wings post-midnight in a dozen flavors ranging from garlic to teriyaki — or blazin' hot. And to single out one pub in particular, Spring Street Bar & Grill (300 S. Spring Street) serves up wings that truly take flight — batter-free and sizzling with a fair amount of spicy heat and vinegar tang.

Jazz Week

Louisville is a covert jazz town.

Attendance at jazz shows — even major ones — can be sluggish, and there isn't a club in town devoted to jazz. But make no mistake, the players are here, gigging at regular times and places, making national or regional reputations, keeping the faithful supplied with bebop, fusion, vocal and avant garde jazz. A Louisville jazz fan just has to do some investigating to find the who, what and where. But once a year, the riches are embarrassingly abundant and centrally located.

It's called Jazz Week, and it's the University of Louisville's chance to show off their jazz music program via over 40 different performances, lectures and other jazz-oriented events. In the past, the cast of players has included recognizable names such as Wynton Marsalis, Marian McPartland, James Moody and Clark Terry, plus tack-sharp student ensembles from the U of L School of Music including eight different jazz combos, three big bands and a jazz vocal ensemble. For one week, jazz fans can  catch their breath and virtually set up camp at U of L's Belknap Campus (Third Street and Cardinal Boulevard) — most performances are in the North Recital Hall, an acoustically superior room.

U of L's Jazz Week began with a bang in 1993, built on the foundations of a jazz program kicked into high gear the year before by the hiring of instructor John La Barbera, a respected New York state musician who has written charts for Buddy Rich and the Glen Miller Orchestra. La Barbera joins Mike Tracy, Jamey Aebersold and Steve Crews on a faculty that can play as well as it can teach. The school now generally has between 80 and 100 students focusing on jazz music.

— continued on next page

Photo: University of Louisville

Art Farmer on trumpet and Don Braden on sax perform in VOFL's North Recital Hall.

Randy Brecker, a trumpeter who has gained fame playing with his saxophonist brother Michael and with a long list of notables including James Brown, Horace Silver and Billy Cobham, was a featured guest at that inaugural Jazz Week, leading an impressive parade of guest artists who ably represent the jazz tradition and also exhibit considerable teaching chops. These guests don't just play and wave good-bye. When Marsalis visited in 1995, he not only played a dazzling show at the Palace Theatre (in a rare off-campus Jazz Week concert), he also hung out on campus, shot some hoops on an outdoor basketball court and conducted a three-hour master class that included a string of over 50 students working through a B-flat blues on stage with the acclaimed trumpeter. That's the stuff that energizes students for years to come.

Hal Miller's video presentations are another popular feature of Jazz Week. Miller, who is also the percussionist in Carlos Santana's band, is a collector of photo and video footage of jazz performances — some of them quite rare. In the past, Miller has shown footage of performers such as Miles Davis, Charlie Parker, Ella Fitzgerald, Sarah Vaughn, Billie Holliday and many major big bands. One interesting presentation centered on non-American jazz artists.

Everything except the major concerts held on the weekend are free and open to the public. Jazz Week is held the last week of February each year.

---

early and enjoy some fine Ethiopian, Jamaican and Deep South American food from the cafe's intriguing menu.

Utopia International Cafe
3220 Frankfort Ave. • 897-7011

Salsa night on Friday is all the rage at this East End spot, which serves a late-night menu with an international flavor. Utopia has some of the city's best DJs picking out tunes for the dancers, and this often means Afro-pop and world beat sounds. This must be hallowed ground for dancing; the special disco nights held by the business that previously occupied this building were bustling too.

Ermin's
1538 Bardstown Rd. • 485-9755

Disco is the current craze at this Highlands club, which doubles as a good mid-level restaurant. A line of people extends out onto the sidewalk on the weekends, and the booming beats leak out too, advertising the club's wares to passing cars. Dress like the chic person that you are when coming to this club.

Pool

Many bars have pool tables, but they are in a frightening condition. With no human help, the cue ball meanders around the sloping slate surface. Cue sticks are straight as macaroni. There are two three-balls and no 12-ball. If you are a fan of the game of pool, this kind of scene drives you crazy.

A few bar owners understand your pain. For folks like you, they keep their tables well-maintained. They keep a few good cues around. They may even provide chalk for your hands. Here's a list of some of the best places to play pool in Louisville.

Bank Shot Billiards
403 E. Market St. • 587-8260

The Temple of Pool — that's what you could call this Greek Revival building, converted in late '93 to a pocket billiards hall. And it certainly treats Minnesota Fats' favorite game with reverence — it's an attractive place, without any of the picturesque grunge of the classic waste-of-time establishment.

The building was originally German Security Bank, founded in 1867 (the pool hall's pro shop is inside the bank vault). There are 16 Diamond tables on the premises, and you pay by the hour. It's $4 per person per hour, but the lunch special — $5 for an hour of pool, a sandwich and a drink — can't be beat. Beer, but no hard liquor, is served.

Oliver's Billiards
4001 Dupont Circle • 895-6990

Eighteen tables await you at this St. Matthews establishment, located in the heart of Louisville's eastern hub of hospitals and doctor's offices. You can pay by the hour and shoot games until 3 AM every night. You may even see your doctor there after his shift is up. The cost is $3 per person after 6 PM, with a maximum of $8 per hour per table. Tuesday and Thursday are dollar days — $1 per person per hour all day. Afternoons are a bit cheaper: $1.75 per person per hour. Appetizers and a full bar are available.

Barret Bar
1012 Barret Ave. • 458-9640

Hand Walter the bartender your driver's license and play until you're tired on one of the Barret's nine tables. You'll pay $4 an hour for regular tables, $5 an hour for the 9-foot tournament table. Don't forget to use a scratch cloth on your break — the management threatens to revoke pool privileges from anyone who twice fails to do so. The Barret is a no-nonsense place to drink and talk and a surprisingly good place to get a hearty sandwich. It's just south of downtown.

The Back Door
1250 Bardstown Rd. • 451-0659

Usable sticks are a bit too rare at this infamous late-night stop, but the six pool tables are kept in good shape. A game will cost you 50¢.

This bar has the reputation of being a tiny, dark, hole-in-the-wall, but actually, it's a rather large, dark, hole-in-the-wall with the city's best martini and finest club sandwich. It's on the north side of Mid City Mall in the heart of the Highlands.

Cahoots
1047 Bardstown Rd. • 454-6687

This bar only has three 50¢-per-game tables, but a diverse late-night food menu makes all the difference in the world. The clientele is relatively young and mellow; the draft beer selection is generously wide. One never knows whether Cahoots will be crowded —

FYI

Unless otherwise noted, the area code for all phone numbers listed in this chapter is 502.

the people seem to come in unpredictable waves. Perhaps this is a holdover from the building's previous incarnation as Tewligans Tavern, Louisville's grungiest, best home for alternative rock. That very unpredictability of public support closed the club numerous times back when it catered to music fans.

Blues, Jazz and R&B

Air Devil's Inn
2802 Taylorsville Rd. • 454-9911

This unassuming place across from Bowman Field was where folks used to go dancing circa World War II, and it retains a following as a place to grab a pitcher of beer after softball — or as a place to hear blues, from local acts to legends like Muddy Waters' guitarist Jimmy Rogers.

Jerry Green and Friends
Ramada Inn, 4508 Brownsboro Rd. • 897-7753

It's a hotel lounge much like other hotel lounges: patterned wallpaper, bar two steps up from the dance room, mirror ball, PA not quite strong enough for what the vocalist puts it through.

So why does it pack in a crowd that starts in its mid-30s and goes up to people old enough to have heard the phrase "this new singer named James Brown"?

Because of Jerry Green, the singer whose soulful chops tax the sound system and who has given his name to what otherwise would be called something like Smoothie's at the Ramada. Green never has the bored, offhand manner of so many lounge acts. He can cut loose on gritty Stax/Volt material — or make virtually any other song something of his own. And Green's friends are no slouches either: Guitarist Roach Cochrum is a Louisville native who's played with Jackie Wilson, Curtis Mayfield and Marvin Gaye.

Rick's Square Piano Club
20 Theater Square • 583-6090

The clean, sleek atmosphere of Rick

Bartlett's place makes it a nice place to dance in a traditional style or sit and casually listen to Bartlett sing jazzy pop in the Tony Bennett vein. Rick's is located in downtown, across from the Brown Hotel.

Old Seelbach Bar in the Seelbach Hotel
500 S. Fourth St. • 585-3200

Consciously classy, the bar has overtones of a private club: Dick Sisto and his first-rate accompanists (currently bassist Tyrone Wheeler) wear tuxedos, and even the clientele favors coats and ties or fancy sportswear. The jazz Sisto has played in this room for 10 years suits the surroundings but has enough meat on its bones to please demanding fans. Sisto plays a cool piano, but he really cooks on the vibes. He plays happy hour six nights a week.

Stevie Ray's Blues Club
230 E. Main St. • 582-9945

This new blues club in a renovated brick warehouse, which dates back to 1906, is named in tribute to the late Stevie Ray Vaughan. The bands that play here are of a consistently high quality, and the usual blues hounds will have a smile for you when you lean against the bar and listen a bit to the bent notes and mournful words coming from the stage.

Taylor Made Lounge and Grill
2523 W. Broadway • 776-9882

This is a sleek club that's established itself as one of the West End's premier spots to dance and be seen. There's karaoke on Thursday nights, DJs on the weekends and very occasionally a live act playing smooth jazz. (It also has the good fortune to be next door to one of the city's best 24-hour spots, Irma's Cafeteria (see Late-Night Fare in this chapter).

Joe's Palm Room
1821 W. Jefferson St. • 581-1251

One survivor of the glory that was Walnut Street, this club was the center of black nightlife in Louisville for the first half of the century. Joe's soldiers on, a couple of blocks to the north, serving up jazz and rhythm and blues.

Syl's Lounge
2403 W. Broadway • 776-9105

This friendly neighborhood bar usually makes its money from a crowd of regulars. But Thursday nights, Boogie Morton and friends pack the joint with a jazz jam session.

Country

Colonial Gardens
818 Kenwood Dr. • 363-3492

From the outside, with its broad white porch and high columns, this venerable club across from Iroquois Park looks like the setting for an F. Scott Fitzgerald story. But if Scott and Zelda went inside, they'd be tempted to pop a longneck and kick their shoes off — a rotating group of country acts keeps the dance floor

---

INSIDERS' TIP

If there's one drink associated with the city of Louisville, it's the mint julep. The julep — two ounces of bourbon whiskey and a half-jigger of simple syrup that's been infused with mint, poured over shaved ice with a mint sprig strategically jutting up so as to tease the tippler's nose — is widely despised and labeled noxious by the vast majority of Louisvillians. Actually, it's not so bad, when made correctly. Most folks will have a mint julep at Derby time, just to honor tradition.
But here's the tip: Unless you want to advertise your status as a Louisville newbie, don't order a mint julep unless it's early May. Or order a mint julep the way most Louisvillians do: "Gimme a Maker's Mark on the rocks." That way you get the best part of the concoction and save yourself the problem.

moving with some of the best dancers you'll see. Colonial Gardens is one of the most durable nightspots in town and a country boy's (and country girl's) best friend.

Do Drop Inn
1032 Story Ave. • 582-9327

It's as well known in Louisville for its slogan, "Nice People Dancing to Good Country Music," as for the many thousands of nights it's given to Louisville dancers. You walk in along a long hall, one wall of which is filled with plaques honoring winners of its waltz contest, the other with fading promotional pictures that belong in a museum somewhere: Ernest Tubb, Roy Acuff, Del Wood, Jim Ed Brown, Louisville's Pee Wee King.

The dancing in the large, dark room tends to be done by couples, touching each other and standing face to face, as much as line dancing or even two-stepping. There's scarcely a cowboy hat to be seen, either — the Do Drop's middle-age-and-older crowd doesn't seem to need to make that much fuss about who they are.

Rock 'n' Roll

If this selection looks meager, it's partially because the rock pickin's are meager in Louisville, and partially because rock is the musical flavor of choice at most of the megabars.

Sugar Doe Cafe
1605 Story Ave. • 584-8440

If you are familiar with the underground rock scene, then you know how cooler-than-thou it can be. Some of that attitude is present here, but the Sugar Doe is an intimate and pleasing place to see indie rock groups practice their art. Besides, there's no where else in Louisville where one can see bands such as the Rachel's, Shellac and the Shipping News.

Toy Tiger
3300 Bardstown Rd. • 456-1137

Toy Tiger is as close as Louisville nightlife gets to the Vegas archetype. The room has the feel of a '50s lounge (no wonder the Louisville expatriates in suaver-than-suave Love Jones have played several shows here). Bars curve along either side; the stage comes out into the middle of the floor; the bar's namesake reclines against a martini glass on the sign facing onto Bardstown Road.

But the entertainment isn't Tony Bennett or Mr. Wayne Newton; it tends to be heavy metal bands, tribute acts, with the occasional wet T-shirt contest or all-male revue thrown in and visits from time to time from major-label acts on their way up or down.

Neighborhood Bars

Four things define a place as a neighborhood bar. First, live entertainment cannot be part of the offerings. Neighborhood bars rely on their inherent atmosphere and the aura created by its regular patrons to draw people in. Second, draft beer has to be cheap — $1.50 or less is best. Third, when strangers walk in to the bar, all the regulars in the place must stop and give them a thorough looking over.

And most important, the neighborhood bar must be in your neighborhood, filled with people like you from your neighborhood. It is a place where you'll know at least two other people sipping a draft just like you are, a place where you feel comfortable. It's usually dark and full of old beer signs — not vintage ones that cost someone a bundle at an antique store, but signs that have quietly gathered dust on the bar's walls for years.

We don't even pretend to list the best neighborhood bars in Louisville. That would contradict the very idea of the neighborhood bar aesthetic. We simply list a few places that have earned a certain reverence not only among the residents near the bar but among discriminating bargoers from across the city.

Gerstle's Place
3801 Frankfort Ave. • 899-3609

The thirtysomethings that fill this St. Matthews bar may honestly say that this is the bar that their grandfathers frequented. Gerstle's may just be the ultimate neighborhood bar in Louisville. Want proof? As little as two years ago, the building that housed Gerstle's held an impressive restaurant named Avenues. When it closed, a Gerstle's diehard fan, who had purchased the bar's weatherbeaten sign upon Gerstle's sad closing several years earlier, reopened the place and took care to retain the bar's utterly unpretentious demeanor. Now that's the kind of dedication that a good neighborhood bar incites. There's a pool table and a preposterous jukebox that veers from the Bee Gees to Patsy Cline, but the only real reason to come to Gerstle's is because it is Gerstle's.

Shenanigan's Pub
1611 Norris Place • 454-3919

The owners occasionally flirt with illusions of upscale bardom, but the beast that is Shenanigan's will not change. Although the Highlands residents living nearby constitute the bulk of this bar's patrons, one could also make a claim that Shenanigan's is essentially the de facto hangout of Bellarmine College alumni. The school, located just a mile down the road, annually infuses Shenanigan's with fresh blood and "new regulars." The pub food coming from the kitchen shows flashes of bar-fare brilliance, and a big screen TV means good viewing for sports events. Do you want pedigree? Shenanigan's served Guinness Stout way back when most folks considered it something lower than bitter syrup.

Club Cedar
416 S. 26th St. • 772-2081

This dark, attractive bar is sort of a West End Cheers — a popular bar that attracts people not with live music or any kind of gimmick but with good conversation in an emphatically grown-up atmosphere. ("We gear to people over 35," owner Marvin Bass says. "No teenagers — we don't do rap.") They do food, however; the kitchen stays open until 4 AM, specializing in fish from cat to orange roughy and some famous Cajun potato slices.

Kern's Korner
2600 Bardstown Rd. • 456-9726

This tiny place, located just south of the Highlands, is one of the few bars that retains its regulars even if they move to another part of the city. Is it the bartenders? The unbelievably cheap drinks? The bumper-pool table? No, it's the atmosphere, which is homey whether there's two people in it or 30.

Flabby Divine's
1101 Lydia St. • 637-9136

The Germantown neighborhood, located just southwest of downtown, seemingly has the highest number of neighborhood bars per capita of any area in the city. They are each so distinctive and quaint, it's hard to name just one. Check's Cafe, which serves a mean braunschweiger sandwich, has the widest reputation — so much so that it loses its neighborhood bar statu. The Germantown Cafe draws crowds, but — gasp — sometimes books bands into the club. But Flabby Divine's is simply a comfortable Germantown pub, only vaguely noted for its fried chicken. By all means, start an evening at Flabby's, but walk a few blocks in any direction for a handful of more low-key neighborhood bar experiences.

One of a Kind

The Rudyard Kipling
422 W. Oak St. • 636-1311

As admirably eclectic as the restaurant it shares its historic building with, the Rudyard's airy, high-ceilinged nightclub features everything from jazz to theater. One recent success was a play that originated on premises, a captivating evening where four local women with eastern Kentucky roots (including co-owner Sheila Joyce) told stories and sang songs. Local musicians love to play here because of the intimate feel and friendly bar management.

The bar (which is in the other half of the building, in the same room as the restaurant), is one of the city's finest places to sample a variety of opinions — few Louisville nightspots, or spots of any kind, draw such a diverse clientele.

Comedy Caravan
Mid-City Mall, 1250 Bardstown Rd.
• 459-0022
Hurstbourne Hotel, 9700 Bluegrass Pkwy.
• 459-0022

This local operation arrived with the mid-'80s comedy boom and weathered the more recent tightening of the comedy market because the two clubs are only the public face of a Louisville-based comedy empire: Owner Tom Sobel is one of the country's major comedy booking agents. His Comedy Caravan circuit of the Midwest has booked shows in a variety of venues for comedians such as Jerry Seinfeld, Roseanne, Jay Leno, Sinbad, Brett Butler and Tim Allen. Since Sobel settled into the Mid-City Mall in 1987, the likes of Richard Belzer, Paul Reiser and Ellen Degeneres have appeared at the club (formerly known as the Funny Farm).

For the public, this means that Louisville is a more significant stop on the touring comedy circuit than the city's size might otherwise lead you to believe. It also means that Sobel and company know the comedy business inside and out; it makes Tuesday's open-mike evening (Mixed Nuts Nite) more interesting than others of its ilk. Many of the performers who come by are professionals who are, as Sobel puts it, "trolling for dates."

Inside, it's a very well-run version of the standard comedy club schtick: brick-wall backdrop to a single naked microphone; an MC who opens the show hustles drinks and introduces the middle act, a solid pro, and then a headliner. It's worked for seven years, with only a few minor alterations (a bar in the lobby; weeknight music from the Juggernaut Jug Band).

The Hurstbourne club brings the same type of show to a hotel lounge.

Twice Told Coffee House
1604 Bardstown Rd. • 456-0507

Other coffeehouses with a night-time clientele have come and gone, but Twice Told remains — even thrives — because of its prime location in the Highlands and its steady flow of good musical acts. Twice Told was the first Beat-style coffeehouse to open in Louisville during the early '90s java revival, and it will probably be the last to leave.

They haven't forgotten the modus operandi here — the coffee is high grade and the cappuccinos are well-made. Amazingly, this coffeehouse is smoke-free, so one can enjoy the vegeterian-friendly food and the touring folk and rock acts without wading through secondhand smoke. Atmosphere? It's hard to imagine a more laid-back mood than the one cultivated here. This is a good place to kill a rainy afternoon or a lazy winter night.

Roll Out the Barrels

Like any city with a strong German heritage, Louisville was once full of breweries, and it kept loyal to the local Big Three — Oertels, Fehr's and Falls City — into the '50s. A local brewery workers' representative recalls there being an alarm raised when out-of-town beer captured 14 percent of the market.

But Falls City, the last holdout among the breweries that survived Prohibition, closed in 1978, perhaps as divine retribution for being the people who conceived of Billy Beer. (The Falls City beer still sold around town is brewed in Evansville, Indiana.)

With the major local brewers dead, Louisville took its own sweet time hooking onto the trend toward locally made, hand-crafted beer. But today, Louisville is home to one good brewpub — the BBC.

FYI

Unless otherwise noted, the area code for all phone numbers listed in this chapter is 502.

Bluegrass Brewing Company
3929 Shelbyville Rd. • 899-7070

Bluegrass is for the person who takes his or her beer seriously. Brewmaster David Pierce has the ambition of brewing all of the 70-odd beer styles of the world, and he's already made a good start with such rarities as Kolsch (a pale beer from Cologne that BBC may be the only Americans to brew) and an amber-colored alt, a German ale. Special beers have included an exceptional ESB (extra special bitter), a strong pale ale. There's also a mead, Dark Star Porter and an exceptional pilsner (if you like Budweiser, this is what it should taste like).

The best introduction, and an incredible bargain, is a sampler tray that gives you a five-ounce glass of all the brews (except the mead), including all special beers in the house.

BBC has music on a small stage several times a week and has been the occasional host of larger concerts in a tent in the parking lot. There's also a full restaurant menu.

Late-Night Fare

If it's late at night and you're looking for a place to eat, the area has several franchises

Photo: Belle of Louisville

The *Belle of Louisville* hosts a Saturday night dance cruise from June through September.

of the country's reigning after-midnight locale, Denny's, as well as a few Jerry's and the Steak & Egg Kitchens and Louisville's secret passion, the palm-sized burgers of White Castle. But Louisville has a few more distinctive late-night eating spots as well.

La Bamba
1237 Bardstown Rd. • 451-1418

This eatery opened recently and made an instant impression on Louisville's night crawlers. Their motto is "burritos as big as your head," and it's not much of a stretch. The super burritos (around $5) require two hands and good upper body strength to handle. Best of all, the burritos are good. Vegetarians can dodge offerings such as Mexican sausage (chorizo) and choose the yummy bean and avocado burrito. You can drive through or eat in. And no, you haven't had too much to drink — the drive-through window is indeed on the passenger side of the car.

Irma's Cafeteria
2531 W. Broadway • 776-9576

Irma's is one of the city's premier soul food establishments, with everything from well-loved burgers to neck bones, pig feet and yams. Saving room for cobbler or pie is recommended. It also has a great jukebox, featuring everything from Kriss Kross to Bobby "Blue" Bland to Clarence Carter's salacious masterpiece "Strokin'." It's closed Sunday.

The Twig and Leaf
2122 Bardstown Rd. • 451-8944

The Twig and Leaf is a classic diner from the early '40s at the corner of Bardstown Road and Douglass Boulevard — open all night Thursday, Friday and Saturday. It's known for its burgers, claims to have the best breakfast in town and recently installed a new menu of such classic comfort foods as pot roast and meat loaf.

Sportstime Pizza
3312 Plaza Dr., New Albany, Ind.
• (812) 944-2577

Sportstime serves a tasty pizza pie until nearly 4 AM. The decor is nothing special, the plates are made of wood, and the place is hard to find, tucked away in a shopping center off Grant Line Road near I-265. But the beer selection is a heartening sight for import lovers, and Sportstime knows how to bake pizza. Try the Big Ten, a pie burdened with the 10 most popular toppings ordered.

Movie Theaters

First-Run Movies

As any film buff knows, the best stuff sometimes lurks on the fringes. But the blockbuster films usually land first at one of the three big Loew's complexes — the Loew's Corporation dominates Louisville's cinema scene when it comes to first-run movies. Admission at Loew's theaters is $7.50. Matinees (showings before 6 PM) are $4.75 — the same price charged for senior citizens and children at all times.

Showcase Cinemas
3408 Bardstown Rd. • 459-4700

Showcase is the first multi-cinema house in town and the theater that put the Fourth Avenue movie palaces out of business. This Loew's-owned business is still the most centrally located theater for the metro area.

River Falls 10
River Falls Mall, U.S. Hwy. 131, Clarksville, Ind. • (812) 283-3000

The newest facility in the Loew's family is sometimes a more convenient destination for Louisvillians than some of the theaters on the Kentucky side of the water.

Stonybrook 10
Hurstbourne Pkwy. and Taylorsville Rd. • 499-6656

The atmosphere and the equipment are nice at Stonybrook, but if you are coming here on a rainy day, remember that a line to get tickets will probably mean a wet wait in the weather. This Loew's theater took a while to catch on when it first opened, but it's now a Louisville favorite in the East End.

Dixie Dozen
Dixie Manor Shopping Center, 6801 Dixie Hwy. • 935-3771

Which is louder, the carpet or the theater sound systems? Tough call. Additionally, the thermostat at Dixie Dozen seems set the lowest of any theater in town. Let's just call it the most powerful movie experience in Louisville and leave it at that. Matinees before 6 PM are $3.75 — the same price charged at all times for senior citizens and children.

Green Tree 10
Green Tree Mall, U.S. Hwy. 131, Clarksville, Ind. • (812) 284-1603

This Cinemark theater charges $6 for regular admission, $4 for afternoon matinees and for seniors and children at all times.

Oldham 8
Oldham Plaza Shopping Center, 410 S. First St., Exit 22 on I-71, LaGrange, Ky. • 222-8000

The far East End desperately needed a movie theater, and now it has one. Admission is $6.50. Matinees before 6 PM are $3.75

INSIDERS' TIP

More and more people appreciate good microbrewed and imported beers over the domestic brews offered by the likes of Miller and Anheuser-Busch. The folks at Rich O's Public House (3312 Plaza Drive off Grant Line Road, New Albany) take things several steps further, referring to the major American brewers and their slavish followers/drinkers as the "swillocracy," and declaring their friendly and atmospheric pub an LFZ — light-free zone. If you want a light beer, forget the domestics, because they're not even stocked here. Ask for an Amstel Light (from the Netherlands).

And if you insist on ordering a regular domestic beer, get ready to cough up some bills. These people are serious about converting you to splendors like the Czech Republic's Pilsner Urquell, Germany's Celebrator or Boston's Samuel Adams Ale, and they're willing to let push come to shove. Rich O's charges $5.50 for a bottle of domestic beer such as Miller High Life, making it more expensive than most imports. How's that for gentle persuasion?

the same price charged at all times for senior citizens and children.

Other Movies

There are three theaters worth taking further note of — places a little out of the usual run of things that keep alive the idea of moviegoing as an exciting and distinctive experience. And the classics series at a local museum deserves attention as well.

The J.B. Speed Art Museum
2035 S. Third St. • 636-2893

The museum has a free PNC Bank Classic Film Series that shows 25 or so Hollywood classics each year. Every other month, the museum presents a four- or five-week series paying tribute to an individual actor or director or genre, such as film noir. All showings are at 2 PM Sunday in the museum's auditorium.

Georgetown Drive-in
8200 Ind. Hwy. 64 • (812) 951-2616

The drive-in still lives in Louisville and its environs — we have four of them in Jefferson County and Southern Indiana (five, if the one in Salem rebuilds from its 1994 fire).

But the tradition lives most pleasingly in the Georgetown Drive-in, which sits on a grassy hillside that serves as a natural amphitheater (a nice change from the typical flat gravel lot). It also retains some old-fashioned touches — vintage cartoons and intermission reels. There's also a playground in front of the screen. But it gets the latest films. There are few nicer excursions than a trip for ice cream at Polly's Freeze, just down the road, and a drive-in flick. Admission is $6, $2 for children ages 6 to 11.

Vogue Theater
3727 Lexington Rd. • 893-3646

The Vogue, built in St. Matthews in 1939, is the only Louisville movie theater of its era still showing films. But it's more important in Louisville's cultural life than that — it's the city's art house, where films such as Louisville native Gus Van Sant's *My Own Private Idaho*, *Like Water for Chocolate*, *Henry V*, *Cinema Paradiso*, *Passion Fish* and *The Whales of August* have their local premieres.

The fare is a mixture of foreign films (most of which come only to the Vogue), independent releases, classics, animation, second runs of movies that may have played for only a week at the multiplexes and unclassifiably off-the-wall pictures (it's been Louisville's headquarters for *The Rocky Horror Picture Show* midnight showings since the late '70s). It's a good place to see a movie. Renovated in 1992, it has among the largest screens and seating capacities in the city, and it attracts a crowd more passionate about films than the average.

Matinee admission is $3.50; regular admission is $5.

Baxter Avenue Theatres and Filmworks
Mid City Mall, 1250 Bardstown Rd. • 459-2288

The Baxter cinema is noteworthy because it combines part of the Vogue's mission with that of first-run theaters. At any given time, 14 movies may be showing, including two old favorites such as *Willie Wonka and the Chocolate Factory*, *Apocalypse Now*, *Dr. Strangelove* and *Blade Runner*; a foreign or art-house film; and nine recent releases. Baxter Filmworks also has a two-tiered pricing system, with in-demand movies priced at $5.50 and others priced at $1.50. The cinema's location in Mid City Mall in the Highlands makes it a popular neighborhood nightspot.

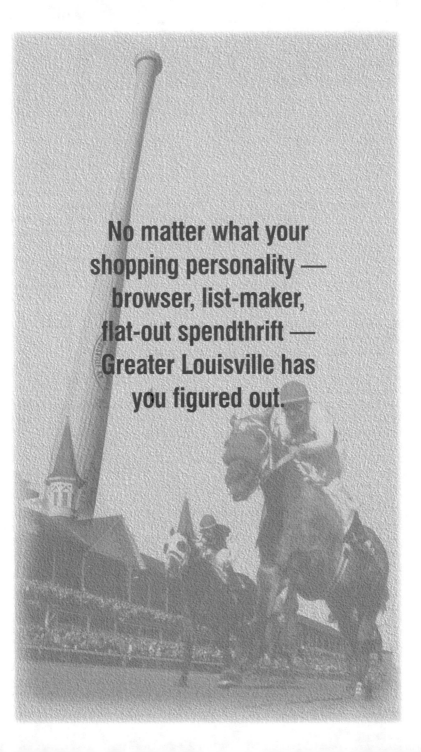

No matter what your shopping personality — browser, list-maker, flat-out spendthrift — Greater Louisville has you figured out.

Shopping

No matter what your shopping personality — browser, list-maker, flat-out spendthrift — Greater Louisville has you figured out.

If you seek the handmade and original, especially the works of Kentucky artists, there are craft shops, potteries and galleries. Museums are also good sources of paintings, textiles, ceramics and such. Our chapter on The Arts describes additional galleries and museum shops.

You can indulge yourself with the tastes — many unique to Louisville — that are available in the area's food and beverage shops. We've suggested some that specialize in fresh-baked breads and pastries, candies, liquor and other goodies. And stop at the dairy case of just about any local supermarket to pick up some Benedictine, a delicacy that originated at Jennie Benedict's restaurant here.

Louisville has its share of antiques. A good place to start your search is in the shops downtown along Bardstown Road and Frankfort Avenue, at the antique malls and at the flea market at the Kentucky Fair and Exposition Center. Even if you have to rent a U-Haul to get that keepsake home, it's worth it.

Bardstown Road, from Baxter and Broadway to Eastern Parkway, is also an enclave of galleries and gift shops. Frankfort Avenue, from Lexington Road to Story Avenue, is dotted with consignment shops, more antique stores and interesting boutiques. Restaurants are sprinkled among the shops.

Greater Louisville's malls are the usual shopping meccas of department stores, specialty shops and eateries. One mall has an amusement park, others have movie theaters, so you can be entertained when you tire of shopping.

Of course, we couldn't tell you about every store in the area, so we've selected some that are representative of Louisville or offer special bargains and products.

The Malls

Like most metropolitan areas, Greater Louisville has been malled by large commercial centers, where you shop in climate-controlled comfort, have plenty of free parking and easy access to a wide variety of shops, restaurants and sometimes movie houses — one even has a fun park. We've listed the major malls, with their anchor stores and special features. All of them have plenty of free parking and are open seven days a week; Sunday hours are usually shortened.

One new development needs mentioning — Springhurst Towne Center. It's not up and running at the time of this book's publication, but slated for opening at Springhurst, which is located on Westport Road at the Gene Snyder Freeway (I-265) are Kohl's, Target, Party Source, Bath & Body Works, TJ Maxx, Books A Million, Kitchen & Company and a 20-screen Cinemark theater complex. Just on the other side of the freeway is a new Wal-Mart that has attracted a few additional retail stores to its site to feed on the inevitable retail traffic. This new mall is an apt indicator of the eastern movement of Louisville's economic development.

Louisville

Bashford Manor Mall
3600 Bardstown Rd. • 459-9600

This mall sits on ground that was once part of an esteemed horse farm, and when it first opened, Bashford Manor had not only the farm's name, but an appropriately horsy decorating theme. That charm is gone, and Bashford Manor looks like any other mall now — but it's still a good place to shop, with Bacons and Target acting as anchors for the Buechel-area (Southeast Jefferson County) mall. Apparel stores run the gamut from T-

Shirt Xpress (featuring while-you-wait airbrushed work) to Sam Meyers Formal Wear. Six jewelry stores, five shoe stores, a photo development place, a cleaners, a bank and a discount grocery are open at Bashford, plus a Walgreen's, Allied Sporting Goods, Musicland and Radio Shack.

Specialty stores include Veeven's, a wonderful, tiny dessert shop; Merle Norman Cosmetics; Aladdin's Castle, a video game parlor; Fashion Shop, a place where good deals on women's clothes and customer mayhem seems to go hand-in-hand; Waldenbooks; K-B Toys and a kiosk called Sweet Tooth Candy Co. that will sell you all kinds of candy by weight. Places to eat include Arby's, Chi-Chi's, Sbarro's, Chick-Fil-A and White Mountain Creamery.

The Galleria
Between Muhammad Ali Blvd. and Liberty St. at Fourth Ave. • 584-7170

Downtown Louisville's three-story mall features Bacons as its largest store. It also has a food court on the third floor, 65 specialty shops, kiosks and restaurants. The concept of downtown shopping is a shaky one in Louisville; call before venturing to The Galleria for evening or weekend shopping, because lack of shoppers has forced early closings in the past.

This center has a number of speciality shops, Schuhmann's Click Clinic, an old Louisville firm that sells photographic equipment and supplies; john conti Gourmet Coffees, which carries 23 fresh-roasted varieties that can also be purchased in decaf (while you're deciding, have an espresso, cappuccino or latté and a fresh pastry); The Candy Emporium — oh, the goodies — for Bauer's Modjeskas (Louisville's famous caramel covered marshmallows), chocolate truffles from Joseph Schmidt Confections in California, gummy fruits, jelly beans and sugar-free candies; and Kites of Kentucky, selling flags, banners and wind socks.

You'll also find mall standards — Radio Shack, The Limited, Shoe Sensation — and the Sales & Rental Gallery of the Louisville

Visual Arts Association (in the hallway to the Starks Building).

The mall parking lot can be accessed from Fifth Street. Some Galleria stores will validate your parking ticket if you make a purchase. Other pay-to-park lots are in the area; their rates vary.

Jefferson Mall
4801 Outer Loop Rd., 1 mile east of I-65 • 968-4101

J-Mall has one of the most inviting interiors of the region's malls; with several seating areas centered around fountains and suspended sculptures, it has the feel of a modern hotel lobby. There are 106 stores, including anchors Sears, Lazarus and JCPenney.

You'll find restaurants and plenty of specialty stores, such as The What Not Shop, A Country Collection, which stocks wall hangings, dolls, toys, pillows, gift items and wooden items with a country motif, and Suncoast Motion Picture Company. You'll also find Family Care Dentists and Monfried Optical.

Other mall standards are Lane Bryant, The Limited, Spencer Gifts and Waldenbooks. Champs Sports carries team wear from basketball, football, hockey and baseball teams. Jefferson Mall has a well-lit spacious parking lot.

The Mall St. Matthews
5000 Shelbyville Rd. • 893-0311

The Mall St. Matthews, Louisville's first mall, and one of its most luxurious, has undergone major renovations and emerged as Louisville's unofficial yet undeniable favorite mall. Anchor stores are Bacons, JCPenney and Dillard's. It's a beautiful, airy place to shop and the only complaint about The Mall would center on the infuriating gridlock that overtakes Shelbyville Road during the holiday season. The Christmastime traffic surrounding The Mall and its neighbor, Oxmoor Center, is nothing but a boon for the other area malls and the specialty stores along Bardstown Road and Frankfort Avenue.

Inside The Mall, a shopper will find the best and finest stores in the Louisville area,

FYI

Unless otherwise noted, the area code for all phone numbers listed in this chapter is 502.

including Brooks Brothers, Abercrombie & Fitch, Dawahares, Guess?, Victoria's Secret, Doubleday Books, Bittner's, Brookstone, The Nature Company and a Franklin planner store. There are also six jewelry stores, eight shoe stores ranging from the Foot Locker to Nine West, an HMV record store and a NRM record store, a Petland, Lerner's New York, Paul Harris, the Body Shop, Lane Bryant, Fashion Shop, Gantos, Structure, Aeropostale and Suncoast Motion Picture Company.

Odd and interesting stores include Taylor Trunk, which seems to stock items useful for a British holiday; the U.S. Cavalry store, where one can buy venison jerky, a sheriff's badge and a full snow-themed camouflage suit; Leather Limited; a terrific toy-and-game store called Imaginarium; and a food court that includes a Tumbleweed, a Hungry Pelican and a McDonald's.

The mall also has a walking club; call 897-8131 for information.

Oxmoor Center
7900 Shelbyville Rd. at I-264 • 426-3000

Oxmoor, another mall situated on land that has an equine history, has long been a staple of Louisville shopping. It's anchored by Jacobson's, Lazarus and Sears but is well known for its upscale specialty stores including Ann Taylor, Yudofsky Furriers, Rodes clothing store and the Baily, Banks & Biddle jewelry store.

Other draws include Victoria's Secret, Eddie Bauer, Banana Republic, American Eagle, Gap, Crabtree & Evelyn, Merle Norman Cosmetics and Florsheim Shoes. There are several stores that are appealing enough to effectively kill your entire Saturday afternoon: These include the Disney Store, the Great Train Store, the Warner Bros. Studio Store, the Museum Company, Natural Wonders and Some-

thing To Do (games, puzzles, models). There's also Radio Shack, Waldenbooks, the San Francisco Music Box Co., Camelot Music, Musicland, Babbage's (a software store) and an extensive food court that includes a Tumbleweed, KFC, Sbarro and a place called Frank & Stein that serves — yep — hot dogs and beer.

The mall has a center-wide gift registry, mall-wide gift certificates, a Mother's Rock and Relax Room, where moms can nurse or rest, the Walker's Club, wheelchairs, a notary public and stroller rental.

Indiana

Greentree Mall
Ind. Hwy. 131 at Greentree Blvd., Clarksville • (812) 283-0741

This mall, located in Southern Indiana less than 10 minutes from downtown Louisville, has just about every shopping need covered, from cowboy boots (Boot Country) to upright pianos (Baldwin Piano), from blush (Merle Norman Cosmetics) to big-screen TVs (Circuit City), from movies you buy on videotape (Suncoast Motion Picture Company) to in-theater flicks (Greentree 10 Theatres).

The big stores include Dillard's, Sears, JCPenney and Target; the speciality stores include Allied Sporting Goods, General Nutrition Center, Fashion Shop, K-B Toys, Musicland, Radio Shack, Babbage's, Pass Pets and Foot Locker. There are nine jewelry stores and seven shoe stores, an Orange Julius, a TCBY outlet, Murphy's Camera Center and Aladdin's Castle — a video game arcade.

Many more restaurants and retail shops are in the parking lots surrounding this mall and its newer neighbor, River Falls Mall.

River Falls Mall
Ind. Hwy. 131 S. at Greentree Blvd.,
Clarksville • (812) 284-6255

It's still a little brother to Greentree Mall in terms of tenants, but River Falls is destined to surpass Greentree in the near future. It's a beautiful mall, with first-run movie cinemas upstairs and Bacons, Toys R Us and Wal-Mart anchoring the downstairs. This is also Greater Louisville's only mall with a family fun park, called RiverFair, which has rides, games, food, movies and miniature golf.

Other attractions include shops such as Casual Corner, Fashion Bug, Paul Harris, Radio Shack, Waldenbooks, Disc Jockey and Grizzly Creek Outfitters. Ten restaurants pack the food court. Perhaps most importantly, a number of stores are moving into River Falls Mall at the time of publication, including Campaigne Internationale Express, Structure and others.

Specialty Shopping

Antiques

Allen House
1419 E. Washington St. • 584-6355

This 4,000-square-foot showroom, located in the oldest standing firehouse in Louisville, specializes in English antiques from the 18th century but also carries older pieces of furniture and items in the French country style. Accessories, porcelain, paintings and rugs are also sold at Allen House, which has been at its present location for almost 30 years. Three interior decorators are on staff. Allen House is open Monday through Friday.

Bittner's
731 E. Market St. • 584-6349

In Bittner's showrooms, the accent is on English, French and continental furniture and accessories from 1690 to 1820. Bittner's also carries an extensive collection of reproduction and contemporary furniture and upholstery created by the country's premier manufacturers, as well as their own Bittner-made reproductions.

Bittner's has been in Louisville since 1854, when Gustav Bittner began his cabinet shop with four furniture artisans; eventually, the business evolved into an interior design firm. Today Bittner's has 10 finishers and cabinet makers and 18 full-time interior designers. The store recently added a commercial development and design division.

The company also runs Bittner's II, which focuses on unusual gifts and accessories, and a small outlet in The Mall St. Matthews. Bittner's downtown is open Monday through Saturday.

Charmar Galleries
2005 Frankfort Ave. • 897-5565

One of the most extraordinary antique resources in the area, Charmar Galleries is for the collector or seller of fine antiques, offering 19th-century French and English furniture, French bronze and ivory sculptures, European collectibles, continental silver, glass, porcelain, oil paintings, prints, Oriental rugs and antique and estate jewelry. Charmar also purchases individual items or entire estate inventories. Services include jewelry designing and special orders, jewelry repair, silver replating and repairs and engraving. Charmar will do appraisals for insurance purposes and has a bridal registry and gift registry. The store is open Tuesday, Wednesday and Friday through Sunday.

Den of Steven
945 Baxter Ave. • 458-9581

English, French and American antique furniture has been sold at this location for almost 20 years. This upper Highlands shop also sells Oriental rugs, paintings and other fine furnishings. It's open seven days a week.

Joe Ley Antiques Inc.
615 E. Market St. • 583-4014

People from all across the country come to Joe Ley Antiques. Its two acres of treasures in the historic Hiram Roberts school building (c. 1890) take you into the past, where you can buy a bit of history to take home. It's a carnival, a museum, a treasure hunt — a trip through time three stories high. Light from yesterday's drawing rooms is here in crystal, bronze, glass and brass: chandeliers and

Photo: Dan Dry and Associates

The Galleria is three floors of specialty shops, kiosks and restaurants.

sconces, table lamps and candlesticks, carriage lamps and coach lights.

For new building projects or restorations, Ley's is a mother lode of architectural details: 5,000 doors; a wide choice of door and plumbing hardware; and hundreds of mantels, balconies, fences, gates, posts, newels, railings, dentils, brackets, shutters and moldings. And if you can't find it, they'll locate it or have it fabricated for you.

Ley's is a place to get in touch with the past, even if you're not shopping. The store is open Tuesday through Saturday.

Louisville Antique Mall
900 Goss Ave. • 635-2852

Located in an impressive old cotton mill (c. 1889), the Louisville Antique Mall has more than 200 choice exhibitors with an astounding selection that encompasses virtually every aspect of household furnishings and collector cessories. He makes two to three an-

nual buying trips to England and provides a shopping service for those wanting something specific.

His wife, Beverly Beaver, a member of the American Society of Interior Designers, provides custom design services for home or office, selecting antiques from the shop to coordinate with fabric, wallpapers and other accents.

The shop covers almost 3,000 square feet, all on one floor. It's open Monday through Saturday.

Swan Street Antique Mall
947 E. Breckinridge St. • 584-MALL

More than 30,000 square feet of antiques and collectibles in 100-plus booths, Swan Street is a showcase for small antiques, jewelry, silver, art deco, '50s items, modern and antique firearms, old toys, vintage photography, glassware and pottery. No crafts or reproductions are allowed here. Swan Street Antique Mall is open seven days a week.

Steve Tipton, Antiquarian
1328 Bardstown Rd. • 451-0115

Steve Tipton carries English, continental and American furniture and accessories made prior to 1820. The owner has 25 years of experience buying and selling antiques. Paintings, engravings, china and crystal, clocks and a few carpets, acquired mostly from estates, are typical of the antiques for sale here. The shop is open Monday through Saturday, but appointmets are suggested.

Apparel

The Clothes Tree
3110 Frankfort Ave. • 895-1391
6921 Southside Dr. • 368-6300

The Clothes Tree, a comfortable place that specializes in gently used adult, teen and children's clothing, opened in 1959 as Louisville's second consignment shop and has grown to become Kentucky's largest. The Clothes Tree's racks have the name brand goods that you'd find in the malls; jewelry, purses and accessories are available, too. (The shops also stock household items such as drapes, sheets and bed and table linens.) Prices are reduced daily on merchandise that has been in the store longer than 30 days; two season-ending half-price sales draw crowds. The quality of the merchandise is why The Clothes Tree has won the Best of Louisville Award from *Louisville* magazine every time consignment shops have been a category. More than 10,000 people have accounts here. Both locations are open Monday through Saturday.

Clodhoppers
1561 Bardstown Rd. • 458-4044

For alternative shoes, accessories and apparel, Clodhoppers is the place. They carry motorcycle boots, utility boots, Naots and Dr. Martens for men and women, platform sneakers by Converse, jumpers, dresses, T-shirts, recycled belts and bags.It's open daily.

Ginna's
4816 Brownsboro Center • 893-2415

Ginna's carries classic styles of ladies' sportswear and dressy fashions in sizes four to 16. The shop also sells handcrafted jewelry by Louisville artist Carlton Ridge. The shop is open Monday through Saturday.

Glasscock Women's Apparel
153 Chenoweth Ln. • 895-0212

Special occasion fashions are emphasized here, as are fine accessories and jewelry for day and evening. Come here to buy a ball gown or a special dress and choose from the works of many different designers. Glasscock also carries some casual wear. Sizes range from two to 24. The shop is open seven days a week.

Karen, Of Course
4903 Old Brownsboro Rd. • 425-1111

"Sophisticated clothing by famous-name designers for the contemporary woman" is how the owner describes her fashions, which come in sizes two through 16. With 4,000 square feet of space, Karen is able to stock everything from the dressiest of dresswear to leggings and jewelry. In January and June, season-ending sales mean 50 to 80 percent off the already below-designer prices. The store, which has been operating for almost 20 years, is open Monday through Saturday.

Lulu's Upscale Resale
1283 Bardstown Rd. • 452-2022

Lulu's carries all-women, all-consignment designer and collection clothes, plus accessories, purses jewelry and hats. Here's a few names to give you a feel for the store's flavor: Donna Karan, Ellen Tracy, Ungaro and Henry Bendel. Lulu's is open Monday through Saturday.

Mary Lou Duke Better Ladies Consignments
2916 Frankfort Ave. • 893-6577

Mary Lou Duke offers a unique alternative for the shopper interested in quality merchandise at a reasonable price. The store sells designer clothing and other fine women's wear and accessories in a former apothecary in the historic Crescent Hill neighborhood. (The apothecary's original cherry cabinetry encircles the main sales floor.) Mary Lou Duke also carries toys, children's clothing, picture frames, jewelry almost everything except men's wear. The shop is a lot of fun and attracts a loyal clientele. It's open Monday through Saturday.

The Leatherhead Shop
1601 Bardstown Rd. • 451-4477

Apparel, jewelry, boots, belts and buckles, leather apparel, saddlery, tack and Western collectibles are for sale here. But this itemized inventory doesn't quite capture the slightly retro/hippy mood of the place. You've just got to be there. They also do custom leatherwork and repairs. The shop is open Monday through Saturday, with extended hours during the pre-Christmas season.

Rodes Men's and Women's Clothing
461 Fourth Ave. • 584-3112
Oxmoor Center, 7900 Shelbyville Rd. at I-264 • 426-2722

Fine quality men's and women's apparel is complemented by great service. Men can buy suits, sportcoats, dress trousers, accessories and shoes. Women's clothing is geared to business and professional wear: suits and separates, some scarves, purses and accessories — and hats, at Derby time. The Oxmoor store is open seven days a week; the downtown store is closed on Sunday. You can park free in the Starks Building and Galleria garages for the downtown store — but just for one hour.

L. Strauss Big & Tall
First and Market Sts. • 582-3737
8003 Shelbyville Rd. • 423-7000

L. Strauss has been in business in Louisville since 1880 selling clothing and accessories for large and tall men. The store stocks a wide range of colors and styles in suits, sport coats, slacks, shirts and activewear for both leisure and dress. Sizes range from 44 to 66 big, 36 to 60 tall and up to 24 in shirts. Both locations are open Monday through Saturday; the Shelbyville Road store is also open Sunday. Parking is free at both stores.

Talbots
194 N. Hurstbourne Ln. • 423-9445

Talbots carries classic (read: conservative) styles in sportswear, special occasion and career apparel in misses and petite sizes, plus shoes and accessories. Services include appointment and personal shopping and in-store catalog ordering. The store is open seven days a week.

Books

Books to Grow On
3636-A Brownsboro Rd. • 893-2507

The city's only children's bookstore is the best place to go if you're trying to find Christopher or Caroline that book you had when you were young but can't remember the title. It also carries books on parenting, audio and videotapes and a few book-connected toys. There are Saturday morning programs and a play area for young children. The store is closed Sunday (except Thanksgiving through Christmas).

Carmichael's Bookstore
1295 Bardstown Rd. • 456-6950

This is the Highlands' home bookstore, and it makes up for having a somewhat smaller stock than the large stores with a willingness (and the knowledge) to talk with and help customers. It's got especially strong collections of mysteries and books about women's issues,

---

INSIDERS' TIP

Some people go into Twice Told Book Store (1578 Bardstown Road) for the books. Some people go for the rare jazz albums on vinyl. We go to listen to Harold, the most interesting and certainly the most droll shop owner in Louisville. Harold talks bluntly about first-edition books, rare Coltrane recordings, politics of the day and virtually anything else under the sun, behind the sun and inside the sun. More than one customer has snapped out of the spell to ask themselves, "What did I come in here for?"

well-chosen fiction and children's books and a standing 15 percent discount on hardcover copies of *New York Times* best-sellers. The magazine rack shows the store's intellectual tenor — it holds more journals and serious periodicals from the alternative press than it does beauty or automotive magazines. There's a Heine Bros. coffee shop attached to the store for the caffeine-inclined. Carmichael's is open seven days a week.

Hawley-Cooke Booksellers
Shelbyville Road Plaza, Shelbyville Rd.
• 893-0133
Gardiner Lane Shopping Center, Bardstown Rd. at Gardiner Ln. • 456-6660
Glenview Pointe, 2400 Lime Kiln Ln.
• 425-9100

The mega-store chans — Barnes & Noble, Books A Million — have invaded Louisville, but the hometown favorite is still this local company. The three stores are as large as supermarkets (the Shelbyville Road approaches superstore size), with restaurants on the premises and software and music sections as well as history, fiction and how-to books. But they're so invitingly decorated and laid out that they have the "browse awhile" demeanor of a small store.

Hawley-Cooke has a standing 25 percent discount on hardcover *New York Times* best-sellers. But it also promotes local and Kentucky authors. They carry a wide selection of out-of-town papers (usually the Sunday editions, which stay on sale all week) and shelf upon shelf of magazines. The stores also serve as great places to buy records; they have no more stock than a small record store, but it's exceptionally well selected. The tables of remaindered books (on the sidewalk at Gardiner Lane, inside at Shelbyville Road and Glenview Pointe) are well-loved sources of bargain books — a small-scale Barnes and Noble. The stores are open seven days a week.

W.K. Stewart Booksellers
Holiday Manor Shopping Center, U.S. Hwy. 42 (Brownsboro Rd.) • 425-5710

Louisville's oldest full-line bookstore (open since 1917) moved, like so much else, from downtown to Brownsboro Road. Half the store is devoted to children's books, book-related items and hands-on learning materials. It's open seven days a week.

Twice Told Used Books & Jazz Records
1578 Bardstown Rd. • 458-7420

This is a classically overstuffed used-book store, well-stocked in most areas, where you might find anything from the junkiest sci-fi paperback to a nice hardbound copy of F.O. Matthiessen's classic *American Renaissance* (it's ours now, and you can't have it). There's also a good collection of modern first editions, Kentucky history and an ardent fan's selection of used jazz records. Twice Told is open seven days a week.

FYI

Unless otherwise noted, the area code for all phone numbers listed in this chapter is 502.

Comics

Book and Music Exchange
5400 Preston Hwy. • 969-4403

Here you'll find an extensive selection of new comics, as well as video and role-playing games, used books and a ton of used albums, tapes and CDs. It's open seven days a week.

Comic Book World
6905 Shepherdsville Rd. • 964-5500

A clean, well-lit shop in a suburban strip center, Comic Book World carries a virtually complete selection of new comics. They also stock role-playing games, miniatures, Japanese videos and collectable card games. The shop is open seven days a week.

The Great Escape
2433 Bardstown Rd. • 456-2216

The Great Escape has the slightly dark, incrementally decorated, head-shoppy air of a business that began in the '70s (as it did). It has the city's best selection of new and used comics and knowledgeable clerks. It also carries games, comic-related T-shirts, posters, toys and trading cards and does a booming business in used CDs, albums, cassettes and videos. The shop's open seven days a week.

Burger's Market: The little neighborhood grocery that could (and does)

For Louisvillians who love to cook, Burger's Market, 1105 Ray Avenue, is an unarguable treasure. This is the ideal grocery — maintaining a neighborhood grocer feel while stocking gourmet and exotic ingredients. It owes much of its character and success to its location: the comfortable, adventurous Cherokee Triangle area in the Highlands. This is a neighborhood that is willing and eager to support a venture like Burger's.

Fresh herbs, fruits and vegetables are displayed in one section. Turn the corner of an aisle and Burger's shows you another one of its faces, from prepared foods such as chicken salad and spinach soufflé to baked goods like German chocolate cake, apple pie and porterhouse rolls. Spend $45 for a delectable balsamic vinegar syrup or $1.25 for a made-to-order braunschweiger sandwich. (Ask for it on rye with mayo and raw onion and watch the man behind the counter smile.) See Ghirardelli hot chocolate mix beside the Ovaltine; note that $45 goose liver pâté is sold in addition to Spam. The short, metal shopping carts look like they came from an antique store — maybe they've been here since Burger's opened in 1958. Have a recipe that calls for sour cherry syrup? Go to Burger's. Morel mushrooms? Pomegranate juice? Grape leaves? Burger's has 'em.

There's plenty of imported and specialty items to spoil yourself with at Burger's, including the European hazelnut spread Nutella, Gethsemani cheese, authentic Kentucky beaten biscuits, galanga root for a unique Thai soup, real country ham (not the interminably salty stuff) and Ed's Bread, a delicious, salt-topped French bread from a secret Louisville baker. Burger's is often ahead of the culinary curve when it comes to stocking trendy ingredients — one reason that local chefs shop at the market for purchases and new ideas. Burger's Market stocked fresh watercress for months before Louisvillians knew that it was a tasty leaf for salads, not a silver flatware pattern.

Burger's is easily accessible to residents from anywhere in Jefferson County. Interstate 64 has an off ramp at Grinstead Drive, and Burger's sits on the corner of Ray Avenue and Grinstead, little more than a mile away. They're open every day except Sunday.

Photo: Courtesy of Burger's Market

The Zone
5005-B Shelbyville Rd., in the same building as Service Merchandise • 893-8654

They call their store an "adventure in pop media." That means they sell comic books, T-shirts, posters and pop culture art prints — more than your typical comic book outlet. If a speciality must be named, it would be Japanimation and other Japanese import videos, models and toys. They buy and sell used CDs and rent digital video discs. The Zone is open seven days a week.

Crafts and Art

Berea College Crafts
The Galt House, 140 N. Fourth Ave. • 589-3707

The hand-crafted items are made by the students and artists at Berea College. Games, coverlets, furniture and more are on display. It's open daily.

Center Shop: Kentucky Center for the Arts
Sixth and Main Sts. • 562-0164

Handmade Kentucky crafts, jewelry, scarves, kaleidoscopes, toys and games and other special items fill the shelves. During the Christmas season, the shop carries holiday items, including a collection of caroler statues. It's open seven days a week.

Discoveries
1315 Bardstown Rd. • 451-5034

Discoveries sells old and new art, antiques and ethnic jewelry, beads, clothing, textiles and accessories from around the world. It's open seven days a week. (See The Arts chapter for more information.)

Edenside Gallery
1422 Bardstown Rd. • 459-2787

Since 1991 this sunny gallery has sold art, fine handcrafted gifts, antiques, ethnic pieces and one of the most extensive art jewelry collections in the area, featuring metalsmiths from across the country. Edenside is open Tuesday through Saturday. (See The Arts chapter for more information.)

Just Creations
2722 Frankfort Ave. • 897-7319

The art of several continents comes together in this unusual shop, a nonprofit venture staffed by volunteers who work with individuals and organizations representing local craft cooperatives in 35 developing countries in Asia, North and South America and Africa. In addition to offering stunning works of art and crafts, both functional and display quality, the store addresses the problems of hunger and poverty by marketing the countries' goods and investigating working conditions, wages and other factors.

You can choose from hand-carved Kissi stone chess sets from Kenya, colorful enamels from El Salvador, Dhurri rugs, wall hangings from Peru, baskets from the Philippines, cotton clothing from Guatemala, unique jewelry and toys. The store is open Monday through Saturday.

Kentucky Art & Craft Gallery & Gift Shop
609 W. Main St. • 589-0102

Discover an outstanding array of Kentucky's finest handmade crafts, including wearable art and jewelry, clothing, toys, pottery, sculpture and folk art. Groups are welcome; free tours can be arranged. Changeable exhibits are also on display. It's open Monday through Saturday. (See The Arts chapter for more information.)

Hadley Pottery
1570 Story Ave. • 584-2171

In the 1940s, Mary Alice Hadley created a set of original stoneware, painted freehand, for a special friend. Today, pottery bearing the inscription, "M.A. Hadley" is highly prized by collectors. Hadley Pottery produces both dinnerware and ornamental pieces. The pottery carries 13 patterns, including the Country Pattern, the Blue Horse, Ship and Whale, Bouquet, Pear and Grape, Christmas Tree and others. Hadley Pottery is sold all over the United States in stores such as Gump's in San Francisco and Port O' Call in Pasadena, California. The display room is open Monday through Saturday.

Louisville Stoneware
731 Brent St. • 582-1900, (800) 626-1800

Louisville Stoneware has a national reputation for fine pottery; the handpainted designs on dinnerware, baking dishes, flower pots and other items are well known. Their nationally known handpainted dinnerware and ovenware come decorated in more than a dozen patterns, including Bachelor Button, Pear, Primrose, Country Flower Blue, Gaggle of Geese, Classy Cats, Precious Pigs and Noah's Ark. The shop will personalize items, including a unique time capsule and a family-tree plaque. Christmas and Derby specialty items are also available year round. You can also find bird feeders and bird baths here. Louisville Stoneware supplies pieces to upscale stores throughout the country and has designed items for the Smithsonian Institution and the White House.

This Louisville institution is also a nice place just to visit. You can see the entire process — from potter's wheel to firing — that has made Louisville Stoneware famous since 1905. The factory showroom outlet is open Monday through Saturday. Have your items packed and shipped anywhere in the United States.

Objects of Desire
3704 Lexington Rd. • 896-2398
The name says it all: 20th-century jewelry, glass and furnishings, including many one-of-a-kind items. This gallery/store, which has an unmistakable glass storefront with a brushed aluminum sign, is closed on Sunday.

Discount Outlets and Department Stores

Enro Shirt Factory Outlet (also known as Apparel Group Ltd.)
4300 Leghorn Dr. (factory store)
• 473-6269
907 Eastern Blvd., Clarksville, Ind.
• (812) 288-9248
11501 Bluegrass Pkwy. • 266-5522
A factory-owned store, Enro offers men's and women's first-quality and irregular merchandise at savings of 25 to 60 percent off the suggested retail price. The store carries 24 sizes, including big and tall. It's open seven days a week.

Fashion Shops of Kentucky
Bashford Manor Mall, 3600 Bardstown Rd.
• 452-9504
Mall St. Matthews, 5000 Shelbyville Rd.
• 895-7467
Dixie Manor, 6801 Dixie Hwy. • 933-1203
4613 Outer Loop • 966-4390
The Galleria, Muhammad Ali Blvd. and Liberty St. at Fourth Ave. • 585-4292
Greentree Mall, Ind. Hwy. 131 at Greentree Blvd., Clarksville, Ind. • (812) 282-8469
336 Pearl St., New Albany, Ind.
• (812) 948-1113
410 New Albany Plaza, New Albany, Ind.
• (812) 944-6495
Fashion Shops is a family-owned chain that sells famous-name apparel at 20 to 70 percent less than at most department and specialty stores. Women's sizes are sold at all locations; petite and plus sizes and children's wear are in some of the stores. Most of the locations are open mall hours, seven days a week.

Grizzly Creek Boot Outlet
3297 Fern Valley Rd. • 964-0684
RiverFalls Mall, Ind. Hwy. 131 S. at Greentree Blvd., Clarksville, Ind.
• (812) 288-4616
Grizzly Creek has discounted work and hunting boots in famous brands, such as Wolverine, Georgia and Carolina, Timberland and Rocky. Western boot makers represented include Justin, Nocona, Tony Lama and Laredo. Both locations are open seven days a week.

Stein Mart
5015 Shelbyville Rd. • 893-6393
Stein Mart carries a full line of discount apparel for men, women and children; ladies accessories; linens; fabric; shoes; housewares; and gifts. It's open seven days a week.

Ethnic

Brother Sam's African Shop
1514 Broadway • 589-7913
Don't blink as you're driving down Broadway or you'll miss this store that specializes in

West African clothes, necklaces, bracelets, hats and scarves. Incense and Afrocentric books are available too. The shop is closed on Sunday and Monday.

Celtic & Heraldic Center
149 Chenoweth Ln. • 897-9050

This unusual shop specializes in coats of arms and Celtic art from Ireland, Scotland and Wales. You can buy jewelry, food, tapes, perfumes, Cladagh rings, china, christening robes, sweaters, books, kilts, woolen Tartan clothing and Galway crystal. The store is closed on Sunday.

The Irish White House
933 Baxter Ave. • 451-7996

Books, tapes and jewelry are for sale here, along with beautiful fisherman's sweaters and even street signs from the Emerald Isle. Don't step foot in this store if you're not willing to chat at length with the staff about your ancestors and the county from which they come. It's open noon to 4 PM Monday through Saturday.

Kente International
1954 Bonnycastle Ave. • 459-4595

Kente specializes in imports from Africa and around the world. Among the selections are African print fabrics, Kente cloth, Guinea brocade fabrics, Indigo mud cloth, African trading beads, natural oils and incense, Moroccan earrings and jewelry, Egyptian jewelry and African drums. It's open seven days a week.

Florists

Aebersold Florist
1217 Silver St., New Albany
• (812) 945-2544

This full-service florist, located 10 minutes from downtown Louisville, features an atrium greenhouse so beautiful that people make appointments to tour the store. Visitors walk on cobblestone floors through the greenhouse that features in-season potted plants from tulips in the spring to tropical species in summer to poinsettias and pines during the holiday season. It's so lovely local companies have staged promotional photos for their products at Aebersold's. And yes, you can also buy a dozen roses — or take advantage of their daily loose flowers special. It's closed on Sundays.

Berry's Flowers
5626 Bardstown Rd. • 239-0343
7710 Fegenbush Ln. • 231-3936

Berry's pretty much has a monopoly on flower sales in the Fern Creek and Highview area and has for 35 years. They handle cut flowers, live funeral arrangements, silk flowers and baskets. The stores are closed on Sunday.

Nanz & Kraft Florists
141 Breckinridge Ln. • 897-6551
4980 U.S. Hwy. 42 • 426-9911
5300 Dixie Hwy. • 447-3641
203 N. Hurstbourne Pkwy. • 426-6030

Voted the Best of Louisville by *Louisville* magazine, Nanz & Kraft has been in business since 1850. It took its current name in the 1950s. This company, Louisville's biggest florist, doesn't charge you for delivering flowers — unless you want them guaranteed to be delivered within three hours of your call. It offers fresh and silk arrangements, plants, planters, decorating for businesses that want a little sprucing up during holidays, home decorating and FTD-wired flowers. Fruit baskets are made on the premises. Nanz & Kraft is open Monday through Saturday, except Christmas. The Breckenridge Lane shop, which has a greenhouse on the premises, is also open Sunday.

Schulz Florist
831 Cherokee Rd. • 459-3666

Schulz isn't as big as other florists, and they aren't as well known. But walking into this small shop is like stepping into a charming garden — albeit one where you pick out your flowers like in an old-time flower market. The people at Schulz also have an artful touch, especially with their tropical arrangements. Schulz has been located next door to Cave Hill Cemetery since 1873; they're open daily.

FYI

Unless otherwise noted, the area code for all phone numbers listed in this chapter is 502.

Food

The Bakery
3100 Bardstown Rd. • 452-1210

The Bakery, one of Louisville's busiest caterers, is both a retail outlet and a training center for students enrolled in bakery and pastry arts at Sullivan College's National Center for Hospitality Studies. As such, The Bakery is a showcase for the skills taught in the college.

In addition to fresh-baked breads and pastries, The Bakery serves and caters daily lunch specials that feature soups, salads, sandwiches and beverages. In addition, they'll prepare baked goods for special events.

Limited seating is available. The Bakery is open Monday through Saturday.

Burger's Market
1105 Ray Ave. • 454-0461

Burger's Market serves double duty as both a neighborhood grocery and a gourmet food shop, and thus, elderly ladies from the Cherokee Triangle area and local chefs rub shoulders over the fresh produce and meats sold at the Highlands store. Shoppers can find a litle bit of everything at Burger's (see our close-up in this chapter). It's closed on Sunday.

Ehrmann's Bakery
Mid City Mall, 1250 Bardstown Rd.
• 451-6720

Opened in 1848 in Louisville by two brothers named Ehrmann, the bakery has been through four locations and several owners since then. Everything is made on the premises from scratch: cookies, pies, breads, pastries and doughnuts, as well as homemade ice cream and a rainbow of sherbets. (According to one of the authors of this guide, the ice cream is the real quality item at Ehrman's.) Ice cream parlor-style tables and chairs provide a pleasant place to stop and enjoy your refreshments. It's open seven days a week.

Ermin's French Bakery and Cafe
1201 S. First St. • 635-6960
455 S. Fourth Ave. • 585-5120

Folks said a bakery was something that the Old Louisville neighborhood needed. Boy, did they ever get one in this attractive and fragrant shop. (The second location on Fourth Avenue serves downtown's business lunchers.) The owner, a refugee from Sarajevo, bakes classic French croissants and breads and sweets made with a less gloppy (but no less satisfying) touch than the Louisville standard. The Old Louisville Ermin's is open seven days a week; the Fourth Avenue location is only open on weekda. .

Great Harvest Bread Co.
12401 Shelbyville Rd. • 244-5231
311 Wallace Ave. • 897-3648
1140 Bardstown Rd. • 473-1872

Baked daily on the premises, huge loaves of sunflower whole wheat, honey whole wheat, old fashioned white, cinnamon raisin walnut, onion dill, nine-grain and sourdough are among the enticing fare. Fruity muffins come in low fat and no fat varieties, and cookies run the full gamut of favorites. The Shelbyville Road and Bardstown Road locations are closed on Monday.

Heine Brothers Coffee
1295 Bardstown Rd. • 456-5108
2714 Frankfort Ave. • 899-5551
11800 Shelbyville Rd. • 244-2064

Heine Brothers is Louisville's first and only micro-roastery. Just coming through the door is an experience. Wide-plank pine floors lend a warehouse feel to the place; customers sit inside or outside the shop sipping coffee, cappuccino, latté or espresso and nibbling on scones and muffins. Coffee is available in whole bean or ground. The gleaming hot-air roaster was custom-made for the store to give a mellow flavor to the coffee. Imported international coffees, mugs, espresso machines and more are sold.

The Shelbyville Road store shares space with Breadworks, creating the perfect way to start your morning — cranberry-walnut scones and a cup of fresh-roasted Kenyan coffee.

The stores are open daily for the caffeine-lover in us all.

International Star Supermarket
9715 Taylorsville Rd. • 261-0707

This new store is a grocery stocked with foods from around the globe, including specialty items from Eastern Europe, India, the Middle East and many points in between. Some items may be familiar to you, others will make you say, "huh?" The next time somebody says they want something different for dinner, visit International Star. It's in Jeffersontown in eastern Jefferson County, and it's open every day except Sunday.

Kingsley Meat & Seafood
2701 Taylorsville Rd. • 459-7585
4919 Brownsboro Rd. • 425-1724

Their specialty is aged prime beef, but some Louisvillians rely on them to smoke turkeys for their Thanksgiving meal. Kingsley's carries all types and varieties of meat, from chicken to pork to seafood such as yellowfin tuna, red snapper, salmon, trout and catfish. Both locations are closed Sunday.

Kizito Cookies
1398 Bardstown Rd. • 456-2891

Originated by The Cookie Lady, Elizabeth Kizito, who started out peddling cookies from an African straw basket atop her head, the company today is housed in a bakery and shop. Her cookies come in nine flavors: chocolate chip, nutty chocolate chip, oatmeal raisin, peanut butter, white chocolate, pumpkin chocolate chip, ginger snap, pumpkin raisin and Lucky in Kentucky pecan chocolate chip. Make your selections (some African crafts are on sale, too) Tuesday through Saturday. You can also buy the cookies at restaurants and health food stores around the city.

Lotsa Pasta
3717 Lexington Rd. • 896-6361

Fresh pasta in a multitude of shapes and flavors is available from this locally owned and operated store that opened in 1982. Consider this sampling: tortellini, ravioli, linguini, fettuccine, spaghetti, lasagne and the flavored varieties (lemon basil, black pepper, sweet red pepper, green chili, spinach, tomato, mushroom and more). Fresh breads — Italian hard-crusted breads, focaccia, ciabatta bread — are baked on the premises. The shop also makes fresh mozzarella, sauces, ices and pizza and has a good deli case. You'll also find Italian, Mexican, Mediterranean and Spanish food products in cans, jars and tubs. It's open daily.

Mike Best Meat Market
4894 Brownsboro Center • 896-2509

This butcher is as well known for its prepared food as it is for its meats. Prepared items include cooked roast beef, smoked ham, double smoked ham and smoked turkey. Mike Best has also gained notoriety for flavored sausages including chorizo, hot, andoullie, duck, turkey, German brautwursts and knockwursts. It's closed on Sunday.

Muth's Candies
630 E. Market St. • 585-2952
Camelot Shopping Center, 8034 New La Grange Rd. • 339-9728

Muth's Candies is an institution in Louisville, opened by Rudy H. Muth and his wife, Isabelle Stengel Muth, at the end of World War I. The shops are filled with tempting homemade confections. Muth's will ship worldwide. The store is open Tuesday through Saturday, but during the holiday seasons, when the kitchens work overtime, you can shop here seven days a week.

Nuts N Stuff
2022 S. Preston St. • 634-0508

Opened in 1985, this wonderful store with all the aromas you can ever want stocks 75 varieties of coffee; 32 kinds of teas; more than 250 herbs and spices; baking and bread-making supplies; beans; home-brew ingredients and supplies; 200 varieties of candy; pastas; dried fruits, jams, jellies and preserves; mixes for muffins, pies and cakes; dried soups; and vinegars and oils. Spices are cheaper than at other stores. Nuts N Stuff is open Monday through Saturday; parking is available across the street.

Rainbow Blossom Natural Foods Stores
106 Fairfax Ave. • 896-0189
12401 Shelbyville Rd. • 244-2022

The largest and oldest natural foods store in the state carries natural foods and deli items, organic fruits and vegetables, personal care items (natural cosmetics, shampoos, toothpaste), vitamins and supplements, sports nutrition, books on nutrition and health, gifts, T-shirts with environmental messages and refrigerated and frozen foods. The store is open daily.

Photo: Louisville Zoological Garden

Teak and Puki are two of the best-known animals at the Louisville Zoo.

A Taste of Kentucky
Middletown Village Square, 11800 Shelbyville Rd., Ste. 104 • 244-3355
The Mall St. Matthews, 5000 Shelbyville Rd. • 895-2733

Gift baskets of Kentucky foods and crafts include Derby Pie, bourbon chocolates, Louisville Stoneware and more. They can be shipped worldwide. Both stores are open daily.

Furniture

Cherry House
200 N. Hurstbourne Pkwy., in the Forum Center • 425-7107
2419 S. U.S. Hwy. 53, La Grange, Ky. • 222-0343

For almost 30 years, Cherry House has sold furniture crafted from cherry, oak, pine, mahogany and other types of wood — usually in traditional styles. The La Grange store has four separate buildings filled with all types of furniture and accessories, including lamps, pictures, mirrors, tables, chairs, living room sets, bedroom furniture, children's furniture, office furniture and entertainment centers. Both locations are closed on Sunday.

Contemporary Galleries
220 N. Hurstbourne Pkwy. • 426-9273

The specialty here is international home furniture, lighting and accessories — think the clean lines of Scandinavian furniture, crafted of wood, metal, leather or upholstery. They're open daily.

Ewald Associates
4868 Brownsboro Center • 896-1479

This is a lushly appointed, stocked-to-the-gills interior design and furniture store focusing on accessories. The emphasis, if there is one clear emphasis, might be the Italian ceramics and pottery bought by owner Giampaolo Bianconcini on one of his excursions to his home country. Ewald is closed on Sunday.

Hubbuch & Co.
324 W. Main St. • 583-2713

This store, a mainstay in Louisville since 1933, carries the total home design catalog in furniture, from dining room tables to mirrors, floral arrangements, picture frames and carpeting. Unique design items and antique reproductions are specialties. There are designers and business system consultants on staff. Hubbuch's is open Monday through Saturday and by appointment.

Scorpio Interiors
1517 Bardstown Rd. • 451-1224

Opened 21 years ago, Scorpio Interiors specializes in contemporary architectural interiors: sofas, chairs, bedroom furnishings, bar stools, desks, shelving, recliners, dining tables and chairs, desk chairs, kids' furniture, lamps and accessories and carpeting and area rugs. If you want someone to talk to, they offer free decorating advice; a design deposit for drawing preparation is rebated when you purchase furniture. Lighting and kitchen and bath design are specialities. The owner, Larry Wolfe, is a registered architect. They're closed Sunday; parking is available behind the store.

Stoess Manor
6541 W. State Hwy. 22, Crestwood, Ky.
• 241-8494

This high-end furniture store does a lot of special ordering, so what you see at their store at any given time is only a part of the Stoess story. Both antiques and antique reproductions are sold here. Their design team will work with you from the ground up if you're building your house, including help with colors, lighting fixtures, wallpaper and all the furnishings. Stoess Manor is closed on Sunday.

Housewares and General Merchandise

Alcott & Bentley
918 Baxter Ave. • 584-8660

It sounds hokey, but this specialty store works a sort of magic on an unsuspecting shopper. The feel is similar to walking into a Maxfield Parrish painting, and the effect is produced by Alcott & Bentley's Victorian Age and turn-of-the-century style goods, from Tiffany lamps to exquisite wall mouldings and ceiling medallions. Sculptures, bird baths and feeders, mirrors and other accessories fill the Highlands store, but ceiling fans constitute half of their business. Of special note is the selection of embossed wallcoverings, which imitate plaster or tin ceilings and can be set off with plaster architectural details.

And from whence comes the name of the store? Owner Don Schagene somewhat sheepishly admits that the Alcott comes from the name of his daughter's favorite author (Louisa May Alcott) at the time of the business's birth, and the Bentley part comes from a previous co-owner's attempt to make the place sound "British." Don't hold these prevarications against them; this store is too fun. Alcott & Bentley is closed on Sunday.

Baer Fabrics
515 E. Market St. • 583-5521,
(800) 769-7776

The quality and quantity will astound even the most seasoned shopper. Baer Fabrics, in business since 1905, is housed in a three-story building packed with yard goods and notions for fashions, home decorating and anything else you can snip and tuck. Baer's is closed Saturday and Sunday. National special orders can be filled by calling the toll-free number above.

Butler's Barrow
3738 Lexington Rd. • 893-5003

This shop has glassware, houseware, dinnerware, kitchen and gourmet cooking supplies and casual accessories for the home. Butler's is open seven days a week.

Campbell's Gourmet Cottage
127 N. Sherrin Ave. • 893-6700

Hard-to-find recipe ingredients, pots and pans, teas and coffees are sold here, but this jam-packed store is best known for being the best place to find odd (and common) kitchen gadgets. People who love to cook can easily kill two hours at Campbell's without knowing it. They're open daily.

Home Textile Outlet
1600 Bardstown Rd. • 451-6510
2724 Frankfort Ave. • 893-6277

Don't let the name fool you; there's more than textiles here. You can buy discounted seconds and irregulars of Fiestaware, Reed & Barton flatware, Hayim rugs, glassware

---

FYI

Unless otherwise noted, the area code for all phone numbers listed in this chapter is 502.

(including occasional Spanish, Italian and Mexican items), casseroles, placemats, napkins and tablecloths, commercial-grade kitchen utensils, pottery bowls, baskets and candles in decorator shapes, such as nutcrackers and pumpkins. The stock is constantly changing as shipments come in from the factories. The Bardstown Road store is open seven days a week; the other site is closed on Sunday.

Jewelry, Silver, Gold and Coins

Buschmeyer Silver Exchange
515 S. Fourth Ave. • 587-0621, (800) 626-4555

Buschmeyer's, across from the Seelbach Hotel, stocks quality flatware and hollowware and offers matching flatware service and theft or loss replacement for 1,600 patterns of sterling, stainless and silverplate in active, inactive and obsolete designs. They sell silver bullion (one to 100 ounces) and U.S. Gold in $5 to $50 pieces. The Exchange is open Monday through Saturday.

Davis Center Jewelers
113 W. Jefferson St. • 587-7707

It's next door to the Davis Center pawn shop, but the atmosphere here is that of elegant jewelry store. Custom jewelry, tennis bracelets, used jewelry, "new" diamonds — Davis Center has it all. The center is closed on Sunday.

S.E. Davis Co.
First and Market Sts. • 585-5818

S.E. Davis is one of the city's largest pawnbrokers; the store has been on this corner, within walking distance of major downtown hotels, for more than 50 years. The store features good buys on new and out-of-pawn diamonds and jewelry and has one of the largest musical instrument and gun departments in the area. Davis is open Monday through Saturday.

Friend's Lapidary and Jewelry Supplies
106 Fairfax Ave. • 893-7855

Baubles, bangles and beads, beads, beads: All the supplies you'll need for making jewelry, including imported beads, gemstones, tools and equipment, gold findings and silver- and gold-filled components are available. Artists, jewelers, craftspeople and hobbyists shop here. It's open Tuesday through Saturday, with extended hours during the Christmas season.

Gumer & Co. Inc.
328 W. Broadway • 583-8070

An established name in Louisville for more than two decades, this locally owned business is the largest jewelry store in Kentucky for buying and selling gold, silver and platinum jewelry and all types of antique and diamond jewelry, as well as rare coins, gold, silver and platinum bullion. Gumer is usually 20 to 40 percent less than other jewelry stores. You can also buy stock silverware sets and tea services, sterling silver flatware and hollowware. Numerous services are available. You can park next door; the store is open Monday through Saturday, with extended hours from Thanksgiving through Christmas.

Imitations
Second Floor, The Galleria • 584-3852

You've seen those dazzling baubles on the stars, now see their faux twins: pieces fashioned after Lady Di's ring, Liz Taylor's 17-carat pear, Chris Evert's tennis bracelet, Rolex and Cartier watches and others. You won't believe your eyes — or that you can afford them! There are rings, necklaces, earrings and watches. Free gift wrapping and worldwide shipping are offered. Imitations is closed on Sunday.

Lemon & Son Jewelers
Providian Center, Fourth and Market Sts., Ste. 100 • 584-6107

This jeweler has made the solid spun gold Derby trophy since 1924. Do you think that constitutes Louisville roots? Ponder this: Lemon & Son is also the oldest continuously operating company in the state of Kentucky (it was founded in 1828).

When they are not making Derby trophies, they simply serve as a high-end jewelry store — arguably the premier jewelry store in Louisville — carrying an assortment of diamond, ruby, emerald, platinum and gold jewelry. They will custom-design pieces, and the store carries a number of unique pieces from national designers. Belleck and Lenox china and an assortment of silver serving pieces are sold at Lemon & Son as well. The store is closed on Sunday.

Seng Jewelers
453 Fourth Ave. • 585-5109

Fine diamonds are here, sure. But Seng is also one of Louisville's best sources for top-quality watches. Aside from being an official Rolex dealer, Seng carries name brands such as Omega, Patek Philippe and Concord. They also sell antique and estate jewelry. The store is in the Starks Building in the heart of downtown, but the people at Seng assure us that no matter where you park in their area, they will validate your parking ticket. Seng is open Monday through Saturday, and they stay open later (until 7 PM) on Thursday.

Liquor and Wines

Cut-Rate Liquors
350 W. Court Ave., Jeffersonville, Ind.
• (812) 288-7283

A decade ago, Louisvillians looking for a big selection or a cheap price on booze had to pass their neighborhood liquor store and drive to this Southern Indiana store. Some things at Cut-Rate were significantly cheaper, some things were not. Now that Liquor Outlet has spread its chains across the metro area and eaten up the discount liquor business of Jefferson County, Cut-Rate has scaled back its specialty beer and wine departments and focused on what it does best: sell liquor, wine and beer to Southern Indiana at a good price. They are closed on Sunday.

End-O-Bin
Corner of Lucia Ave. and 1200 block
Bardstown Rd. • 451-7446

A bargain hunter's paradise for wines and spirits, End-O-Bin is open Thursday through Saturday. The selection of liquor and beer is sometimes scarce, but it's always quite interesting. The selection of wine will make you giddy even before you pop a cork.

Liquor Outlets
1800 Hurstbourne Pkwy. • 491-0753
4048 Dixie Hwy. • 447-6590
3420 Fern Valley Rd. • 968-1666

Your one-stop party shopping store for discount liquor and wines, gourmet foods, party supplies, paper goods and more, it's a veritable warehouse of goodies that will delight your eye and your palate. The beer wall makes a noble effort to be inclusive on a global scale, and you can mix and match a six pack to taste a variety of beers, if you so choose. All locations are open seven days a week.

Old Town Liquors
1529 Bardstown Rd. • 451-8591

Old Town is a great place to find finer potables, especially domestic and imported wines and specialty beers. The prices are reasonable and the location is prime — in the middle of the Highlands. They are closed on Sunday.

Party Mart
4808 Brownsboro Center • 895-4446

This huge liquor store is nearly indistinguishable from a Liquor Outlet, except that maybe Party Mart focuses a bit more on the non-alcoholic items including food, party supplies and paper goods. The name says it all — it's a warehouse full of party goods. The Mart is closed on Sunday.

Musical Instruments

Doo-Wop Shop
1587 Bardstown Rd. • 456-5250

How many Louisville bands *haven't* rented a guitar, a P.A., a four-track recorder or an amp from Doo-Wop? This worn, comfy shop has been defusing emergencies for musicians for years. Not only can you rent, you can buy — everything from a full drum set to a kazoo. The store is locked and quiet on Sundays.

Guitar Emporium
1610 Bardstown Rd. • 459-4153

While Louisville has many fine music shops, only one has Keith Richards, *Saturday Night Live* bandleader G.E. Smith and Billy

Gibbons of Z.Z. Top as regular customers. Don't rush down with your autograph books — they do most of their business over the phone or have the guitars delivered to them backstage at a concert (although Jackson Browne and John Hiatt dropped by for some special midnight shopping one night, and the likes of session star Waddy Wachtel and members of the Counting Crows have wandered in to spend an afternoon).

Why do they shop in Louisville? Guitar Emporium got in on the ground floor, or thereabouts, of the vintage guitar boom when it opened in 1975. Another reason might be the intelligent and friendly service — owner Jimmy Brown would be a strong vote-getter in a poll to pick the nicest guy in Louisville; he also played a mean bass, both electric and stand-up, in the city's raucous blues/rockabilly party band Bodeco.

While it started in a classically cramped storefront farther up Bardstown, the shop is now in more attractive digs — a long, well-lit space with pretty hardwood floors and of course, walls hung with vintage Fenders, Rickenbackers, Gibsons, Martins and National Steels. It's closed Sunday.

MOM's Musicians General Store
2920 Frankfort Ave. • 897-3304

Every music store has musicians who hang out at it, but MOM's has long been a hub of activity around Louisville — perhaps because owner Marvin Maxwell and his two sons are deeply enmeshed in the Louisville music scene. Regardless, MOM's carries instruments suitable for hard rock, jazz, country, pop — you name it. Sound systems, instrument repair and private instruction are also available. MOM's is not open on Sunday.

Novelties and Costumes

Caufield's Novelties Co. Inc.
1001 W. Main St. • 583-0636

Louisville's equivalent of Madame Toussoud's Wax Museum has been supplying costumes, masks, magic tricks, gag gifts,

party supplies and novelties since 1920. Halloween is naturally one of Caufield's biggest seasons, but the shop also stocks party supplies for New Year's, birthdays, Hawaiian luaus, anniversaries and weddings. It's also a source of stork supplies to celebrate births; Fourth of July and other occasion flags from the city, state and most countries; and balloons in all colors and sizes. It's closed on Sunday.

Quartermaster's Depot
1413 Story Ave. • 582-1736

Quartermaster's rents historical period and 20th-century-style costumes. A sampling of eras includes Renaissance, Civil War (other military periods available too), American Colonial, American West, Victorian and the 1940s through the 1970s (should you need a mint green polyester leisure suit and platform shoes). You'll find poodle skirts, flapper dresses, Cleopatra gowns and cave man outfits. You can also rent the required accessories, such as swords, guns and fans.

Records, Tapes and CDs

Better Days Records Tapes & CDs
1591 Bardstown Rd. • 456-2394

Better Days carries a wide variety of new and especially used records (probably the city's largest selection), but it excels most spectacularly in stocking the newest dance music. Owner Ben Jones is a well-respected DJ, and his collection of 12-inch singles and dance music is considered to be the best in town. A few years back, an editor for an audiophile magazine said that it had a better selection of vinyl than any store in New York City.

Blue Moon Records
1832 Bardstown Rd. • 485-9300

Blue Moon owner Mike Bucayu made a locally famous musical 180 when he quit the popular and influential hardcore band Kinghorse and opened this record store, which is a monument to Bucayu's fervent love of

---

FYI

Unless otherwise noted, the area code for all phone numbers listed in this chapter is 502.

bluegrass and old-time country music. Blue Moon also carries some indie rock titles and enough popular albums to help pay the bills, but the Stanley Brothers rule the roost at this Highlands store. The place is named for Bill Monroe's hit "Blue Moon of Kentucky," but it also applies to the special section in the back of the store — the Blues Depot. Run by local blues maven Scott Mullins, it stocks both traditional and contemporary blues titles. You can shop seven days a week. Lately, bluegrass picking has occured at Blue Moon on the weekends as musicians drop in for impromptu jam sessions.

Camelot Records
Hurstbourne Plaza, 263 Whittington Pkwy. • 423-8050

This national chain has stores in local malls, but its superstore is its major presence for serious music fans. It carries an amazing variety of music — an especially large jazz section and a pretty wide selection of world music. Classical music fans love it; it also has a large videotape section. But it possesses some of the impersonality of a chain store. Its selection of local music, in particular, omits some of the city's foremost (and most nationally celebrated) acts. It's open seven days a week.

Disc Jockey Records
Shelbyville Road Plaza • 897-6723

At one point, we might not have listed this store from an Owensboro-based chain — it's not much more than a somewhat larger version of a mall store, although it's nice and spacious. But it added an important new employee a couple of years back — classical record buyer Dave Regneri, whose late, lamented Four Seasons store was the city's preferred shop for the less noisy strains of music. It's open seven days a week.

Double-Time Records
1211 Aebersold Dr., New Albany, Ind. • (812) 945-3142

This New Albany mail-order operation specializes in jazz. Its catalog includes 5,000 jazz titles — everything from a 16-CD set of Art Pepper's recordings for the Galaxy label to Miles Davis' landmark album *Kind of Blue*. Call for a catalog.

ear X-tacy
1140 Bardstown Rd. • 452-1799
12619 Shelbyville Rd. • 245-4980

It's the city's premier independent record store, especially for the alternative/independent rock 'n' roll that sets its prevailing atmosphere. But it's well-stocked in other areas as well. It's the best store for local music, which it displays as prominently as it does R.E.M., or for dropping in to find out what's going on musically in town. Friday and Saturday nights, when the Bardstown Road store stays open until midnight, it's a lively social scene, with young people congregated inside and on the sidewalk out front.

Ear X-tacy is also the source of one of Louisville's great oddball traditions: Folks cut up its enlarged-typewriter bumper stickers to make their own surrealistic slogans: "aX yer cat" was the first one anyone at the store noticed; others include "attack yr eX," "taX year," "da red taXi," "reX ate yr cat," "triX or treat," "redundancy," "eXtra starch" (on a laundry truck) and even one of the store's competitors, "better days." It's open seven days a week.

Ground Zero
1048 Bardstown Rd. • 581-9884

There's pop music, then there's alternative music. And then there's the great underground — the groups that explore the frontiers of music and push forward, the ones that create musical movements that don't surface in the mainstream for three more years. Ground Zero owner Ed Lutz is deeply steeped in the newest groups and well versed in the more obscure and forward-thinking indie bands putting music on wax (and digitally-coded aluminum). Shop here for records by Bad Religion, Snapcase, Stereolab, the Descendents and Double U. The shop is open every day.

Joe's Music Vault
Algonquin Manor, 3501 Cane Run Rd. • 778-6621

West End DJ headquarters — the decorative photos here aren't of bands who've done in-store promotions but Polaroids of local disc jockeys who patronize the store. Owned by musician and disc jockey Joe Crutcher, it's a good place to search out rap, dance music, R&B and gospel. The Vault is open Monday through Saturday.

Ken's Records
109 S. Bayly Ave. • 896-1811

This small but savvy institution is the lengthened shadow of one man, owner Ken Burton, a major fan of British music who opened his shop as an avocation (it's open only evenings and Saturdays). He has a good choice of imports, alternative music and other things you won't see anywhere else and such unique marketing touches as headphone jacks in the front of the store (at its former location) and compilation tapes of new music the musically evangelical Burton rents to interested customers.

Underground Sounds
2003 Highland Ave. • 485-0174

Judging by the name, you may think that this store deals in the undercurrents of alternative rock. Well, there's a smattering of that sort of thing, but owner Craig Rich is actually a guru of blues, jazz and groove-oriented rock. He can talk authoritatively about both an obscure Swedish recording of Miles Davis and the latest release from the Grateful Dead vaults. There's a charming atmosphere at Underground Sounds, and it comes from the fact that the store succeeds on the passion and dedication of its music-loving owner. The store is open seven days a week; Underground Sounds stays open until midnight on the weekends and on Monday for late-night shopping.

Spirituality

Genesis III Booksellers
1589 Bardstown Rd. • 459-8921

If you are seeking the sources of inner peace, scan the shelves here for 12-step recovery books and items, tapes, New Age music, metaphysical books, tarot cards, children's books, meditation items, candles and more. Their bulletin board also contains business cards for therapists, massage therapists, herbalists and other alternative healers. Genesis III is closed on Sunday.

Inspirations
Cathedral of the Assumption, Fifth St. and Muhammad Ali Blvd. • 583-3100

The Cathedral Heritage Foundation sponsors this interfaith gift shop that sells items from around the world. You can find children's books, books for introspection, arts and crafts, spiritual and ceremonial instruments, greeting cards and gifts. Inspirations is open Monday through Friday and Sunday.

Sporting Goods Stores

Greater Louisville has a host of sporting good speciality shops. We've listed a few here.

Allied Sporting Goods
Shelbyville Rd. Plaza • 897-3253
Bashford Manor Mall, 3600 Bardstown Rd. • 456-1505
6609 Preston Hwy. • 968-2226
Jefferson Mall, 4801 Outer Loop Rd. • 968-5300
Dixie Manor Shopping Center, 6801 Dixie Hwy. • 935-5121

Allied is a longtime Louisville business with a team and screen printing division. They carry all kinds of sporting equipment, clothing, shoes and accessories — this is the place to go for sporting goods selection. Most Louisvillians will say that Allied is the nicest and easiest place to find something, but you may very well be able to find it cheaper somewhere else. The stores typically follow mall hours.

Footworks
129 St. Matthews Ave. • 896-6855

Footworks is co-owned by a woman whose father, grandfather, grandmother and uncles are all podiatrists. She knows feet like no one else and will try on every shoe in stock to give you and the kids a proper fit. The store also carries athletic apparel. It's closed on Sunday.

Jumbo Sports
6013 Preston Hwy. • 966-3644
100 Urton Ln., Middletown, Ky. • 254-1800
This business calls itself a sports superstore, offering discounts on name-brand equipment, clothing and shoes. Camping, hunting and fishing gear; equipment for football and other team sports and water sports; running shoes; and in-line skates — you name it, it's here. Both locations are open seven days a week.

Ken Combs Running Store
4137 Shelbyville Rd. • 895-3410
Ken Combs sells running, walking, court, aerobic and fitness shoes and running and exercise apparel. The store is known for its expert fitting of shoes. It's closed on Sunday.

Play It Again Sports
291 N. Hubbards Ln. • 897-3494
4138 Outer Loop • 968-5354
Part of a national chain that buys, sell, trades and consigns used sporting goods equipment and sells new equipment, these stores are good places to get exercise machines such as stair steppers or treadmills. This is not, however, the place for fishing, hunting, camping or similar gear. Both stores are open daily.

Quest Outdoors
128 Breckenridge Ln. • 893-5746
Quest Outdoors sells all kinds of camping equipment, tents, canoes, boots, camping foods and clothing. It's a fun place to go even if you just have the yen to go camping or hiking. It's open daily.

Tobacco

Kremer's Smoke Shop
333 S. Preston St. • 584-3332
Even if you don't smoke, visit Kremer's just to see the tobacco leaves hanging from the ceiling and all the pipes and pipe supplies. It's like going into an old English pipe shop. In addition to pipes and tobacco, Kremer's also sells imported candies, coffees, cigars and accessories, and they repair pipes. Kremer's ships anywhere. They are closed on Sunday.

Oxmoor Smoke Shoppe
Oxmoor Mall, 7900 Shelbyville Rd.
• 426-4706
You can buy a pack of cigarettes or spend several hundred dollars on a hardwood humidor at this shop that specializes in premium cigars. Pipe tobacco and clove cigarettes are also sold at the Oxmoor Smoke Shoppe, which is open daily.

V.I.P. Cigarette Outlet
1270 Bardstown Rd. • 454-0338
A tiny, octagonal building near the Mid City Mall houses this store that deals in very important pathogens: cigars, loose tobacco and cigarettes. Currently, V.I.P. is riding the wave of natural tobaccos with no additives, stocking a variety of upscale brands including American Spirit. Neighborhood kids on skateboards in front of the store might ask you to buy some clove cigarettes for them. Don't do it. The shop is open seven days a week.

The Kentucky Derby is the world's most famous horse race — "the most exciting two minutes in sports" — but its transforming effect on the city begins a good two weeks before the first Saturday in May, the race's annual date.

The Derby and the Downs

At Derby Festival time I act wild — that is a Derby tradition.

— A 6-year-old Louisvillian

For one day a year, Louisville makes a legitimate claim to being the center of the universe, flocked to by celebrities, celebrated in parties across the land, wringing tears worldwide with the first notes of "My Old Kentucky Home."

The Kentucky Derby is the world's most famous horse race — "the most exciting 2 minutes in sports" — but its transforming effect on the city begins a good two weeks before the first Saturday in May, the race's annual date.

Bleachers go up along Broadway in the middle of the night. Otherwise sober and responsible men begin wearing hideous pastel blazers with tiny winged horses — a fashion statement that proclaims their positions as officers of the Derby Festival. Young ladies costumed as Southern belles hand out bourbon-laced chocolates to visitors arriving at the airport. Playing hooky from work becomes a way of life. Folks you never knew cared begin talking about thoroughbreds with the conviction (and accuracy) of a Damon Runyon tout.

The Derby is our version of Mardi Gras, the swallows coming back to Capistrano and the Super Bowl (although there's never been a dull Derby). A measure of how seriously the race is taken here: When I was in seventh grade, in 1968, our teacher announced to the class that Derby winner Dancer's Image had just been disqualified for drug use, the same way our teachers had told us five years earlier President Kennedy had been shot. (In recent years the public schools have closed on Oaks Day, the Friday before the Derby, ostensibly because the traffic around the Downs would disrupt the school buses, but also because so many pupils and teachers would cut classes for the day, anyway.)

The Kentucky Derby is one of America's most successful exercises in hype: promotion so successful that it has shaped reality around it. It began in 1875 at the new Louisville Jockey Club (renamed Churchill Downs a decade or so later, for the owners of the land where the track was located). There was much bold talk in the local press about the Derby becoming "the great race of the country" and Derby Day becoming the city's preeminent holiday.

But by the turn of the century, the Derby was only one of many prominent American stakes, and its reputation was slipping so disastrously that the race almost died (one newspaper called the 1894 running "a contest of dogs"). That decline was arrested by Matt Winn, the leading member of the partnership which took control of the track in 1902. Colonel Winn, once described by the *New York Times* as being so canny he "could give cards and spades to Barnum and beat him," assiduously courted the leading horsemen of the East and the racing press. By 1915, he had turned the Derby into the country's most celebrated race and helped create a tradition around the beauty of Kentucky in the spring that continues to this day.

As a result, the Derby is the one race every horseman wants to win, both for the glory and for the money: The purse is better than $700,000, and it's estimated that winning the

Derby adds $8 million to $10 million to a horse's syndication price for breeding.

Many great horses — Man o' War, Seabiscuit, Kelso, Buckpasser, John Henry, Cigar — never raced in the Derby; others, such as Native Dancer, Nashua, Bold Ruler, Round Table and Alydar, ran and didn't win. But no race anywhere can boast such a roll call of winners: Secretariat, Seattle Slew, Northern Dancer, Spectacular Bid, Citation, Alysheba, Hindoo, Regret, Exterminator, Whirlaway, Count Fleet, Swaps, Needles, Affirmed, Sunday Silence.

The Derby is the first jewel in the Triple Crown classic races (the others are the Preakness and Belmont stakes). Only 11 horses have won all three. For years, the Triple Crown was an honorary title only. Since 1987 Chrysler has sponsored a Triple Crown Challenge that awards $5 million if a horse wins them all (which hasn't happened since Affirmed in 1978).

Unlike comparable sports championships, the Derby comes early in the season, rather than at the end of a grueling series of games and playoffs. Being early means that the Derby brings the news: It is the first time that the best horses in the crop of 3-year-olds meet.

Three-year-old horses are like college basketball players, just coming into their full maturity, but not as strong and fast as they will be at four. Before the first Saturday in May, they have been racing in Florida, California, New York, Arkansas, Louisiana and over at Keeneland in Lexington, many of them studiously avoiding each other before the big race. None of them has ever raced 1¼ miles; the 126 pounds each colt carries is the most weight it's ever raced under (fillies carry 121). And the noise and color of Derby Day creates an unprecedented psychological situation for horse, jockey, trainer and owner alike.

Although 21 horses, from Day Star in 1878 to Winning Colors 110 years later, have led the race wire-to-wire, the Derby is more often won by a horse that lays off the pace. There have been many exciting finishes: Broker's Tip and Head Play heading for the finish line in 1933, their jockeys hitting and grabbing each other; Willie Shoemaker in 1957 mistaking the

16th pole for the finish line and standing up just long enough to let Iron Liege past his mount, Gallant Man; Alysheba stumbling in the stretch and then going on to win in 1987.

And every year brings some drama or controversy: the extraordinary popularity of come-from-way-behind horse Silky Sullivan in 1958; Dancer's Image being disqualified; the hard luck of jockey Pat Day, the Downs' all-time leading rider, who lost 10 Derbies before finally winning on Lil E. Tee in 1992.

But the most noteworthy thing about the Derby is that, for all the sentimentality, greed, corporate aggrandizement and boosterism that get loaded onto the poor horse race, it works: Derby time is Louisville's moment of special grace.

FYI

Unless otherwise noted, the area code for all phone numbers listed in this chapter is 502.

The Social Scene

The racing is, to some extent, just the pretext, or the occasion, for one of the world's most spectacular pageants — raucous and refined, gross and gorgeous, ludicrous and heart wrenching. Many people come for the party, never see a horse and leave happy.

There is a long tradition of wild and strange parties around Derby time, going back at least as far as the days when high rollers from the East would come down in their private railroad cars. In their book *Kentucky Derby: The Chance of a Lifetime*, Joe Hirsch and Jim Bolus tell about one Derby Eve party at the Brown Hotel that included a live pony among its guests. They also mention a custom of the 1950s and '60s: post-midnight hotel parades in which revelers roamed the halls of the city's hotels pounding garbage can lids and other improvised instruments.

Among the hundreds of parties that follow in that tradition, two stand out. The most notorious is Anita Madden's Derby Eve blowout at her family's Hamburg Place farm in Lexington (her husband's grandfather, John E. Madden, bred five Derby winners there). The party, which benefits a Lexington charity called the Bluegrass Boys' Ranch, always has a fanciful theme. A sampling: Rapture of the Deep, complete with mermaids and mermen and a figure of an octopus surrounded by a dry-ice fog; The Ultimate Odyssey, with young people togged out as Greek gods and goddesses while the Trojan War was reenacted under the gaze of a 16-foot statue of Zeus clutching a neon thunderbolt; A Night on Fujiyama; Land of the Midnight Sun; and others in the same vein.

Louisville's brightest bash is the Diamond Derby Celebrity Gala, a fund-raiser for the American Diabetes Association, thrown in a big old house overlooking Cherokee Park in Louisville. The hosts are David Brown and his wife, Patricia Barnstable-Brown (a former Doublemint twin and UK cheerleader). In 1996 the theme was A Nite on the Nile and featured pyramids, live camels and a lounging woman impersonating Cleopatra. So many folks gather outside the Browns' home on Spring Drive in the Highlands to gawk at arrivals such as Rod Stewart and John Goodman that in 1994 two households on the same block unsuccessfully sued to block the gala.

But those are merely the most prominent of a set of formal and informal gatherings throughout the city and state (and even over in Indiana). While the Derby's reputation was made through cultivating those wealthy enough to own thoroughbreds, its appeal cuts across class lines. Even those whose best chance at seeing the race is a black-and-white television set implore out-of-town friends to come down for the excitement.

It's also a big time for music, drawing national acts from George Jones to Veruca Salt and showcasing nearly every local band worth seeing. (In fact, the weekend has become a big one for the alternative music cognoscenti, many of whom are confirmed race fans — most famously Bob Nastanovich of Pavement, who moved into a house across from the Downs and is part-owner of two thoroughbreds.)

And for once in its otherwise star-unstudded life, the city swarms with celebrities. They're not always the brightest lights in the sky — love you, Zsa Zsa! — but they're all recognizable faces, names and reputations. Imagine an episode of "Love Boat" or "Murder, She Wrote" with a racetrack setting.

Here are some recent celebrity guests (a few of whom came for an event during Derby Week but skipped the big race): Patti Davis, Paula Abdul, Walter Cronkite, Stevie Nicks, Mick Fleetwood, George Foreman, Roger Ebert, Jerry Hall, Senate Majority Leader Trent Lott, Don Rickles ("anyone paying $500 to be in the same room with Don Rickles is in need of immediate psychiatric treatment," wrote one local columnist), Geraldo Rivera, Lea Thompson, Barbara Eden, Randy Quaid, Loni Anderson, Bo Derek, Ron Wood, Waylon Jennings, Dennis Hopper, Dwight Yoakam, Susan Lucci, Dixie Carter, Hal Holbrook, James Earl Jones, Tama Janowitz, Ivana Trump, Whoopi Goldberg, Luke Perry, Jason Priestley, Cybill Shepherd, Teri Hatcher, Stefanie Powers, Tony Curtis, Mike Ditka, Gladys Knight, Ed McMahon, Mary Hart, Tanya Tucker, Arte Johnson, Jessica Lange, Sam Shepard, Lloyd Bentsen and Jack Kemp. George Bush came after leaving the presidency, Lyndon Johnson when he was in the Senate, Richard Nixon while he was in office and Gerald Ford many times.

The Festival

The Derby eventually got too big to contain on a single day, or even a single weekend. And so, almost 40 years ago, the festival spirit began annexing more of the calendar.

INSIDERS' TIP

In the Derby, bet against the crowd. The last favorite to win the race was Spectacular Bid in 1979; overall, only 48 favorites have won the 123 Derbies. But don't go overboard — when a horse goes off at 90-to-1, there's usually a reason, and it isn't for the purpose of making you a lot of money. (The famous exception was in 1913, when Donerail, ridden by Roscoe Goose, paid $184.90 on a $2 ticket.)

Photo: Churchill Downs

The Derby is the first time that the best horses in the crop of 3-year-olds meet.

What started as a parade during Derby Week in 1956 is now one of the city's largest undertakings, with a full-time staff of 15, some 4,000 volunteers and 70 official events that begin at the end of March and get going for real two weeks before the race. (A *Courier-Journal* cartoon aptly called it "The most exhausting two weeks in sports.") Those include a spelling bee, a hole-in-one contest and a bass-fishing classic, puppet shows, clogging exhibitions and more kinds of races than you could imagine, including a 13-mile mini-marathon, a steamboat race, bed races, waiters racing with trays of wine glasses (The Run for the Rosé), and rats racing through mazes for a garland of Fruit Loops (Spalding University's Running of the Rodents, not an official Derby Festival event).

For more information call 584-6383. Here are a few of the chief events.

Thunder Over Louisville
Two Saturdays before
Derby Day on the riverfront

Opening ceremonies for the Derby, two Saturdays beforehand, actually outdraw the race itself. An estimated 650,000 people line both sides of the river to watch an afternoon air show and an evening fireworks show billed as the largest show in the country, exploding 44 tons of fireworks in half an hour. While many folks watch the fireworks from hills on either side of the Ohio, Thunder's most exciting moments are best experienced as close to the Fourth Street Wharf (or its counterpart across the river, Clarksville's Ashland Park) as you can get: fireworks streaming down in a "waterfall" from the Clark Memorial Bridge, and the bone-rattling climax which proves the event's name isn't just hype.

The Chow Wagons
Throughout the Derby Festival
at three locations

These aren't roving trucks with a Western-style "Cookie" ladling out slop, but a collection of fair-style, food-and-drink stands, with an entertainment stage thrown into the bargain. The Chow Wagons are meeting places and all-purpose destinations for a night of Derby Week cruising. One is at Waterfront Park and opens the Friday before Thunder Over

Louisville; the others are at an eastern shopping center and the Louisville Motor Speedway. Admission is only with a $2 Pegasus Pin, sales of which provide the Derby Festival with about a third of its revenue.

KyDzFest!
Thursday-Saturday before the Derby at the Kentucky Fair and Exposition Center West Wing

New in 1996, this 200,000-square-foot assemblage of unusual interactive activities, from well-padded jousting to rock-climbing to virtual reality games, has drawn an enthusiastic crowd of 3-to-12-year-olds. As one third-grader wrote in *The Courier-Journal*, "Have you ever had soooooo much fun and laughed soooooo hard that you were crazy with delight? We actually were loud and nobody told us to quiet down!" Admission is $5 in advance, $10 at the door; children 3 and younger are free.

The Great Balloon Race
Saturday before the Derby at Kentucky Fair and Exposition Center parking lot

This is many people's favorite event, just for a chance to see the vivid, gigantic balloons begin inflating in the dawn's light. (Many people come out the night before to see the same thing in the dark at the Balloon Glow.) The place is filled with more than 30,000 folks, but they've often been disappointed — weather forced the race to be canceled in 1991, 1992 and 1993, and the 1994 race was postponed but eventually run on Sunday.

The Great Steamboat Race
Wednesday on the Ohio River

The *Belle of Louisville*, our resident sternwheeler, battles New Orleans' *Delta Queen* for what are referred to as "the coveted Golden Antlers," which symbolize racing supremacy on this stretch of the Ohio. It's a low-speed race, much easier to follow than the lightning-quick Derby, and usually features some form of tongue-in-cheek skullduggery on the part of one or the other rivals (keeping alive a fine old river tradition). Seats aboard both boats will be sold out, but there are good spots to watch all the way from the Clark Memorial Bridge (the start and finish line) up to Six Mile Island, where they turn.

One fine place to stake out a view is The Water Tower, on River Road at Zorn Avenue, which hosts a blowout boat race party every year.

Pegasus Parade
Thursday along Broadway from Campbell to Ninth Sts.

The city's big parade of the year consumes most of Louisville's float-making, marching-band, clowns-in-tiny-automobile energies. There are 10,000 seats (bleachers $7, chairs $9), which sell out quickly. You can pay at the Commonwealth Convention Center or use the mail-order notice which appears in *The Courier-Journal* a week before they go on sale. There are many more viewing spots available from the sidewalks along the route. Parade marshals have ranged from natives Muhammad Ali, Diane Sawyer, Danny Sullivan and Ned Beatty to such outlanders as William Shatner, Gen. Norman Schwarzkopf and John Wayne.

The Kentucky Oaks
Friday at Churchill Downs

Not an official Derby Festival event, Oaks Day is often called Louisville's Day at the Races: more local folks are among the 90,000 or so who show up than will be there on the Derby. Although among American racing days it ranks second in attendance only to the Derby, it's an easier ticket to get your mitts on, it's somewhat less crowded and the air of Derby anticipation gives it a unique feeling of its own. There's advanced wagering on the Derby; the Oaks, in which 3-year-old fillies run one-and-one-eighth mile, is usually a good race in its own right; and enough of the celebrity class shows up on Friday to make it a people-watching day second only to the Derby.

The Derby Eve Jam
Friday at Kentucky Fair and Exposition Center

This annual (but occasionally canceled) concert began as an attempt to make the Derby more rockin'. It's never established a clear identity. Past headliners include Hammer, Dolly Parton, Hall and Oates, Hank Williams Jr. and Bill Cosby. Last year's jam was

Handicapping: Hits and Misses

You can start now and study for the rest of your life and never know enough to predict horse races with accuracy. Even the best handicappers miss more races than they hit. They just know when to get good odds.

But start with at least a modicum of information. There are past performance charts in the Churchill Downs program and in the Racing Form, which is available the evening before the races. The Racing Form's charts are more comprehensive and easier on the eye, but you're going to have to buy a program to know the program numbers, so decide if you can afford both. Either includes a chart that explains how to read their abstracted versions of a race.

The Courier-Journal has a staff handicapper, Rick Cushing, whose analysis includes some information the casual racegoer might not know ("Delightfullyclever led with 100 yards to go last time, goes 100 fewer yards today. Ilk returns to distance and company that suits her, should be a nice price.") His picks every day include a best bet  and several long-shot specials (and he's the only tipper whose record is printed next to his picks every day — lucky for him he does quite well). There are also a number of tipsheets for sale at the track that include intelligence about what's going on backside or reflect MIT-scale number crunching. They're not as baseless as the hot tips that circulate throughout the city, but you won't learn much if you just follow them blindly.

If you're serious about handicapping, Cushing recommends a simple homework exercise: After a race is run, study the performance charts and look for the factors that should explain why the race turned out the way it did.

Churchill Downs publishes an informative pamphlet written by local handicapper and writer Bill Doolittle, *The How to Be a Better Bettor Book*. It includes not only fundamental handicapping principles but some good Churchill-specific dope about trainers, who have predictable behavior that savvy handicappers watch as closely as they watch the race horses.

Doolittle, who teaches a course on handicapping at the University of Louisville, says that the average race fan has one great equalizer:

"A guy walking in off the street cannot compete with a good handicapper. There's just tons of information that you can't possibly sift out. And you can't know who all of these personalities are. . . . "

"The way is to just walk down to the paddock and take a good look at the horses, because these are equine athletes. Horses that are in good form and ready to win — their coats are shiny, just like a person's complexion is healthy. If a horse is on his toes, he's alert and ready to go. If he's walking around with his head down, he's not as interested.

"The body language of the race horse is very ignored by most expert handicappers who take a shower in all their numbers and never look up. The one way you can compete is by looking at horses — and it's pretty. The experience stays with you. You can't go wrong looking at a bunch of race horses getting ready to run in a race."

Head down to the paddock after a race and watch the horses come in for the next race. If a horse is balky and sweating profusely, back off. If it comes out with an attitude that seems to say "Man o' Who?," dig deep.

The people around horses have revealing body language, too. Here's Doolittle again:

— continued on next page

"You look in the paddock and see that Horse No. 1 looks all right, Horse No. 2 looks okay and the jock's a pretty good one — and you get to Horse No. 3 and there's 22 people in the paddock, including the little 8-year-old kid with the coat and tie on. Somebody thinks they're going to win . . . . I think that's probably a pretty good sign. There's one trainer around here I handicap if he's got a coat and tie on and his tie is pulled all the way up tight."

Other clues: Does the horse like the distance? Has it raced against these horses before and won? Is it racing well lately? (Many handicappers look for a horse that finished second but ran well in its last race; others disregard any indications of form that date back more than 30 days.) What are its latest workouts? (A horse working well gallops a furlong, or 1/8 mile, in about 12 seconds.) Do the trainer and jockey know what they're doing?

Any bettor should come to the track knowing how much he or she can afford to lose and bet no more. Doolittle recommends that instead of dribbling out, say, $40 in $4 bets on each of the 10 races, you should put more money on the horse you have the strongest feeling about.

"Make your bet count . . . find your spot and then fire your money in there," he says, putting it in terms that would send chills down spines at Gamblers' Anonymous: "The less you bet, the more you lose when you win."

Picking a Derby winner is even more difficult, since the race takes place under conditions unprecedented in the horse's careers. *The Courier-Journal* and Racing Form's Derby coverage includes stories about something called the Dosage Index, a complicated mathematical formula for expressing the horse's bloodlines. The

Writer and handicapping expert Bill Doolittle urges novice bettors to look at the "equine athletes" and then "fire your money in there."

theory is that only a few horses have the genetic endowment to win at 1¼ mile; the Derby is always run at a fast pace, and the horses are run out after a mile — the last quarter proving who has the stuff of champions. Of the last 65 winners, only Strike the Gold in 1991 fell outside the Dosage guidelines.

Otherwise, look for a horse coming into top form under the tutelage of a top trainer. Some experts think 2-year-old races don't make any difference; others contend just as confidently that wins at 2 lay a winning foundation. Big wins in the major prep races, the Wood Memorial, the Santa Anita Derby and the Bluegrass Stakes, are a good sign, although they've created many unsuccessful favorites over the years.

If you can't pick a Derby winner, don't sulk. It's not easy for the experts, either.

Ordinary bets are made to win, place (second) and show (third). If your horse finishes ahead of the slot you chose, you win your bet, anyway. You can also bet across the board (all three places). Place the bet, naming the amount of money (there's a $2 minimum), the horse's program number and the type of wager ("five dollars on number six to win.")

During the racing day, there are a number of special wagers. In any race, you can

— continued on next page

bet an exacta (first and second in exact order; you can also "box" two or more horses in all possible exacta combinations — the ticket sellers will do this for you). The trifecta, only offered in races with eight or more entrants, and six or more starters, calls on you to pick first, second and third.

To win the Daily Doubles (there are two each day), you must pick winners in two consecutive races. If you have a strong feeling about a horse in one of the races, you can "wheel him," combine him with all the other horses in the next race. Pick-Three and Pick-Six bets are the same principle extended to three and six races, respectively (but don't wheel those — the combinations get so fantastic you'd have to mortgage your house). Because the pot carries over if no one hits a Pick-Six (which often happens), those bets produce the biggest payoffs. Three folks at Churchill in May 1995 won more than $417,000 each. Of course, there's a reason why those pots got so big — a Pick-Six is damnably hard to hit.

If you're confused about any of these procedures, find the beginners' windows; the ticket sellers there will help you.

---

one for the young folk, with alternative rockers Bush and Veruca Salt. The concert never sells out, but it *feels* right — the Derby should call out a major show.

Getting There

Churchill Downs
700 Central Ave. • 636-4400

Churchill Downs is 3 miles south of downtown Louisville. Keep in mind that on Derby Day many streets in the Downs neighborhood are closed, including Central Avenue, the street the Downs faces. The exit ramps from the Watterson Expressway (I-264) to Taylor Boulevard are closed as well. However, Longfield Avenue, which runs along the backside of the Downs, remains open.

One of the best bets is to take one of the TARC buses leaving downtown ($5 each way, in exact change) or the Kentucky Fair and Exposition Center (a $10 round-trip ticket, no one-ways sold).

If you drive, many folks pay to park in the yards near the track (rates vary from $10 to $25: look for small boys carrying cardboard signs). Although it may seem inadvisable to park on the back lawn of someone you've never met, it's a perfectly safe transaction, and you will never know how many vans can be parked in a ¼-acre lot until you see it with your own eyes.

Surviving Derby Day

Getting to the Derby is difficult, in several senses of the word.

Tickets for the race are in high demand; there are 48,500 seats available, but only a few come open every year, and the Downs receives between 8,000 and 10,000 letters every year requesting them (the figure also includes requests from current seat holders to upgrade their seats).

Certain people have priority in Derby requests: season box holders (there are 900), members of the Downs' Turf Club, horsemen and corporate sponsors. Ticket prices range from $42 to $65 for bleacher seats in the grandstand to $3990 for a six-seat table on the Eclipse and Turf Club Terraces (which covers both Oaks and Derby Days and includes a sit-down meal and a champagne toast before the feature race each day).

You never know — seats this good may fall into your lap. A friend may be called to Afghanistan and leave you his box. You may win seats in a contest. You may rescue the governor from drowning. Or you may pay a scalper many times the face value of the ticket; some reports had 1997 boxes going for $3,000-$9,000 (scalping is illegal in Kentucky, by the way).

But even after you have your tickets, reaching your seat is hardly an easy matter. Imagine 130,000 people converging on a facility with 4,500 parking spaces (all of them already spoken for), in a modest neighborhood of narrow streets where some major thoroughfares are closed. D-Day was easier.

And Derby Day weather is good evidence of just how variable Louisville's climate can be. Temperatures have ranged from 43 (in 1989) to 94 degrees (1959); as much as an inch of rain has fallen during the races (1918, when the day's total rainfall was 2.31 inches).

Treat the day like a minor military operation, even if you're dressed in linen and silk: Prepare ahead of time, pack light and stay alert (especially for pickpockets).

Remember one fact: Everything takes more time in a crowd of 140,000, from moving 10 feet to going to the bathroom to placing your bets. You might want to front-load your wagering: The computer system at Churchill Downs allows you to place bets on any of the day's races at any time (although if you're not betting the upcoming race, tell your cashier before you place your wager). Many people bet on the Derby when they arrive and forget about the cashiers for the rest of the afternoon.

If you can't wangle seats to the race, you have two choices: Pay $30 for admission to the Clubhouse Garden, where you will be able to spread a blanket on the bricks, watch the race on a monitor and maybe squeeze through the throng to get a glimpse of the Derby starters in the paddock.

Or you can brave . . .

Infield Madness

The infield on Derby Day is something else — a cross between a company picnic, Woodstock and the infamous Snake Pit at the Indianapolis 500. One young observer looked around at the strutting, swilling, bellowing, lustful display and said, "Mankind at its lowest — by choice!"

A few infield snapshots:

• A man wearing a horse's head and a bright white brassiere sits calmly discussing the Derby contenders.

• A family's quiet meal of fried chicken is interrupted by a water balloon launched from a giant rubber band several hundred yards away.

• A hefty, bare-chested young man runs around the emptying field, bellyflopping on abandoned plastic foam coolers that explode into splinters.

• Two mud-smeared men spot a fellow clad in preppie lime green and plaid, exchange a nod and then snatch and carry him, kicking and screaming, toward a giant mud slick.

It is the sort of place where young men scream to young women, begging them to lift their shirts, and where a few young women comply; where a mud-wrestling man and woman may suddenly break their clinch with a kiss. But it has a softer side (many Derbies are graced by a marriage ceremony performed in the center of the Downs) and it draws many loyal fans who enjoy the raffish atmosphere without violating any of the laws of God or man.

Admission is $30. The preferred entrance is through the gate on Fourth Street; you may also enter through the main entrance to the Downs on Central Avenue. Both open at 8 AM. Glass containers, alcohol, cooking devices, umbrellas (seriously) and weapons are banned; lawns chairs, coolers and PARTY NAKED T-shirts are allowed (lawn chairs may only be brought through the Fourth Street gate).

If you're heading for the infield, bring a blanket (or even better, a tarp), chairs, a cooler (lightweight plastic foam is the best) filled with beverages and food. Pack sunscreen, wear a hat and if there's any chance of rain, bring a poncho (remember, umbrellas are as illegal

---

INSIDERS' TIP

The Derby isn't the only Triple Crown race with a Louisville connection. The winner of each Preakness is awarded the Woodlawn Vase, a Tiffany trophy originally created for Louisville's Woodlawn Race Course, one of several Louisville tracks which existed before Churchill Downs.

as a .22). Veterans suggest wearing layers of clothing, so you can adjust what you're wearing to the climate (there is no indoors to run to, unless you plan to spend all day in a restroom, and believe me, you don't want to). Many people bring a radio or portable television set, so they can actually follow the race: There are few places more remote from the results of the Derby than the infield in the first few minutes after it's been run.

The infield is smaller than it used to be; 5,000 or so spaces were wiped out when the Downs added its turf track in 1985, and infield bleacher seats installed for the 1988 Breeder's Cup have taken away most of the infield spots with a view of the stretch. And recent reports (including arrest records) suggest that it is less wild than during its '70s heyday, if heyday's what you would call it. But the infield will live as long as the Derby; it's now open not only Derby Day but Oaks Day, and the Thursday of Derby Week as well, at a college-oriented event called "Festival in the Field" with a $2 admission.

In a sense, the infield atmosphere starts the evening before the race, with a block party that draws about 30,000 people to Central Avenue, the street that runs in front of the Downs. Vendors line the streets, selling T-shirts, hot dogs and rub-on tattoos. The atmosphere is like spring break at Daytona Beach telescoped into one long night — energy and recklessness overwhelming prudence and purpose. It's even been celebrated in song, by the expatriate Louisvillians in the LA band Love Jones: "Spring nights, knife fights, Central Avenue/ Big hair, everywhere, Central Avenue!"

Like the infield, the Central Avenue party has calmed down in recent years (in 1991 there were more than 100 arrests). But it shows no signs of fading — although the widening of Central Avenue, pending as we write this, may change the street's character.

The Downs

Churchill Downs on Derby and Oaks Days (and the three occasions when the track has hosted the Breeder's Cup races) is one animal; Churchill Downs during the rest of its racing days is another — restful, uncrowded, unhurried, informal. Anyone who has a chance should see the track from both sides.

It used to be that the quality of racing at Churchill dropped off markedly after Derby Day. That's no longer the case. Most observers say that only California has better racing. With daily purses averaging about $370,000, the Downs attracts some of the country's best horses, riders and trainers. The track's proximity to the Bluegrass horse farms means that it's a home track for many of the leading figures in the industry; it also means that there's a strong fan base. The present management is first class, and with the advent of simulcast betting, Churchill Downs has become a popular out-of-town signal, watched from as far away as Trinidad.

FYI

Unless otherwise noted, the area code for all phone numbers listed in this chapter is 502.

As a result, most races at Churchill are very competitive; the favorites don't win as consistently as they do at lesser tracks, and there are full fields of 10 or 12 horses in most races. You have a good chance to hit a long shot, and there's a lot of money floating around: On spring Saturdays there's better than $2 million being bet (although that's only a fraction of what is bet Derby Day).

The chief challenge to Churchill these days comes not from other tracks, but from other forms of gambling. There are already gambling boats on the Indiana side of the Ohio River, and Caesar's World has plans to build a $228-million riverboat casino complex in Harrison County, Ind., just a few miles from Louisville. Churchill has been fortunate so far; in 1996, when statewide wagering on horses fell by 2 percent and shocked the horse industry, Churchill Downs actually increased its handle by $12 million. But the track has been acting like an institution that needs to sell itself: It has a new simulcast betting pavilion on track grounds (following on the success with Sports Spectrum, an offtrack betting parlor located at a former harness track); it added a day of steeplechase races at the end of the spring meet; it reduced prices for food and drink and instituted free parking (after Derby week). And it has begun to lobby the state

Hats: Some revelers let Derby Day go to their heads

Hats are a practical necessity on most Derby Days — the sun can get to you after awhile, and if the sun isn't shining the rain is likely coming down.

They're also a great tradition — every Louisville woman's opportunity to be a lady for the day, every man's opportunity to shade his bald spot with something more elegant than a Rooster Run gimme cap. On Derby Day you'll see hats that seem to

have come straight out of a Dr. Seuss book, hats in tangerine, purple, fuschia and gold, hats that look like trophies, hats with brims that need their own ZIP codes. One man, George Holter of Prairie Village, Kansas, wears a replica of Churchill Downs' twin spires (balsa wood attached to a batting helmet).

Photo: Dan Dry and Associates

They're such a part of tradition that some folks believe they're mandatory. According to *Louisville* magazine, Rod Stewart's manager called the hostess of a Derby party he would be attending and asked if Stewart should wear a hat. His hostess said that Rod could wear whatever he wanted.

"But we want to make sure he follows the rules," the manager said.

Rod wore nothing on his haystack hair, but his wife, model Rachel Hunter, wore a huge lace hat pinned up with a black rose.

---

legislature to allow video lottery terminals inside racetracks.

During the Spring Meet, which runs from the Saturday before Derby until Independence Day or thereabouts, racing begins at 3 PM Wednesday through Friday and 1 PM on Saturday, Sunday and holidays; the track is dark on Monday and Tuesday. In the shorter fall meeting in November, all post times are 1 PM. The day's 10 races go off at roughly half-hour intervals, with the quality of the horses in general ascending until the ninth race, the day's feature.

Churchill Downs is one of the oldest Ameri-

can sporting facilities still in use (the central part of the stands, with the trademark twin spires, was completed in 1895). Because it has grown by additions to that central structure, Churchill Downs is rather labyrinthine; you have to spend a fair amount of time out at the track before you get the hang of it.

The most important distinction to know is between the grandstand, the portion of the track nearest the entrance ($2 admission, enter from Central Avenue) and the clubhouse, which contains the seats with the best view of the finish line (enter either from Central or from the Longfield Avenue parking lot). The grandstand is one of the best cheap outings on earth; the seats aren't the track's best, but every seat at Churchill Downs affords a clear view of the track and the tote board, and the crowd is winningly unpretentious.

Clubhouse admission is $3.50. A number of ground-level boxes are available on a first-come basis, but if you go up the escalator from the Clubhouse Garden and pay $2 to Reserved Seat Sales up at the top, you can sit in a third-floor box under the ancient clubhouse roof, where the occasional bird flies through while you enjoy some of the best seats in the house. (Brash acquaintances say that you don't need to pay $2, that you can walk past the ushers stationed at the clubhouse doors without being challenged, but two bucks seems like a small toll to pay for not having to skulk past an usher.)

The clubhouse offers a greater range of restaurants and bars and more rail space along the paddock to look at the horses before they run. If you can spare the extra cash, it's a bargain.

On Oaks and Derby Days, the Skye Terrace is Millionaires' Row, where the likes of you and I only set foot if we're interviewing celebrities or bringing them a double scotch. But the rest of the year, it's available for groups of 16 or more, at a cost of no more than $9 a seat. If you can get your friends to band together, it's a great way to see how

the other half bets, with a table inside the air-conditioned surroundings, your own balcony to step out onto to watch the race and ticket windows a few yards away. And for an extra $115, you can have one of the day's races named in your honor, with eight members of your party going down onto the track to present an engraved platter to the winning owner.

The Backside

If you have a chance, either through connections or the walking tours offered a few Saturdays during racing meets, visit the Churchill Downs backside. It's a chance to see the working side of the track, a small village focused around a kind of hard, animal-oriented labor that has all but vanished from modern life. Nearly 1,400 horses are bathed, shod, groomed, fed and grazed there during racing season.

On Derby Day, the backside is a peaceful counterpoint to the escalating hoopla everywhere else. It's so quiet that Seattle Slew took a nap an hour before winning the 1977 Derby. On the porch of the racing secretary's office — what Director of Horsemen's Relations J.L. "Buck" Wheat calls backside's "City Hall" — exercise riders, trainers, jockeys, grooms and other horsefolk gather, swapping gossip or waiting in practiced silence. There's also a track kitchen, a recreation building where back-

---

INSIDERS' TIP

The whole city wants to go out to eat Derby Eve and Derby night, so Louisville's best restaurants are usually booked up weeks in advance. A few of them accept small walk-in parties, such as Jack Fry's and Deitrich's, and cancellations open up a few more tables around town. Other restaurants won't accept reservations Derby night except for parties of eight or more — notably Azalea and the three outposts of the Bristol Bar & Grill.

Tables also become more available the further you get from downtown and the "restaurant rows" of Frankfort Avenue and Bardstown Road. They're also easy to find in ethnic eateries; Korean food may not be what you came to Derby to try, but the city has several good Korean places.

The Louisville and Jefferson County Convention and Visitors Bureau will find reservations for visitors who come into its information center at First and Liberty streets. It's open 8:30 AM to 5 PM Derby Eve, 9 AM to 4 PM Derby Day.

side folk place their bets, a print shop and a veterinary barn.

Many of the grooms live in the barns during the racing season. Some barns are fancied up (the quarters where D. Wayne Lukas stables his horses is manicured like a showcase home in the suburbs, complete with a jockey statuette out front) but others are unadorned cinder-block structures, plain as a building can be.

One special view of the backside can be seen from Longfield Avenue the afternoon of the big race: the Derby horses grazing behind Barn 41, the place they're all quartered.

"Around three or four on that afternoon, you can look back there and see $40 million worth of horses out there," says one Downs observer.

If you know a trainer or work on the backside, you can watch the Derby from back there. It may be the most enjoyable way to spend the day.

There's no more view of the Derby finish than there is on the wrong side of the infield, but from the backside you get a good, clear view of the backstretch run. And it's a more civilized, privileged version of what goes on in the center of the track. There's walking room; you can drive your car up to the picnic spot you've chosen and unload your supplies; the Downs even allows you to bring in your own liquor. People are friendlier (many of them know each other from the relatively circumscribed world of the horse business) and the crowd is largely free of the elective, self-promoting degeneracy that gives the infield its special flavor.

It's a light work day. For most of Saturday folks make the rounds of parties, wearing the sort of snappy hats and crass T-shirts that comprise the true meaning of Derby fashion and carrying themselves with the easy but excited air of people on the inside of the world's biggest event.

Kentucky Derby Museum
704 Central Ave. • 637-1111

They only race at Churchill Downs 73 days a year, but the track's history is on view 361 days in the twin-spired building next to the track's main entrance.

The Kentucky Derby Museum devotes its first floor to the world's most famous race, with exhibits that allow you to watch films of great Derbies and view memorabilia of Col. Winn (who took control of the Downs at the turn of the century), the great horses, jockeys and trainers that have made the race what it is.

Its centerpiece is *The Greatest Race*, an award-winning multi-image portrait of the Derby by Louisville's Donna Lawrence Productions. The unique show is projected on a 360-degree screen in the shape of the track. The visual panorama matches an emotional range that covers everything from the quiet of the backside to the exultation of winning the Derby. Although the show is updated yearly, its core is Swale's 1984 victory for the great trainer Woody Stephens.

The movie uses the entire oval of the screen to put viewers inside the tumult of the infield and surround them with roses; it pulls away from the dash out of the starting gate to sketch a quick history of the Derby from Aristides to Go For Gin. The late Derby historian Jim Bolus has said *The Greatest Race* does a better job of capturing the Derby's essence than anything that's been written about the race. The show runs from 9:30 AM to 4:30 PM, every hour on the half-hour.

On the second floor, devoted to thoroughbred racing in general, is an eye-opening exhibit on African Americans in thoroughbred racing; an interactive video where you can try your luck at picking winners; a chance to feel what it's like to get up in the jockey's stirrups; and exhibits on thoroughbred pedigrees and conformation. The museum also contains a restaurant and a gift shop.

Admission is $5 for adults, $4 for senior citizens 55 and older and $2 for children ages 5 to 12. Children younger than 5 are admitted free. The museum is closed for the four major holidays: Thanksgiving, Christmas, Oaks and Derby Days.

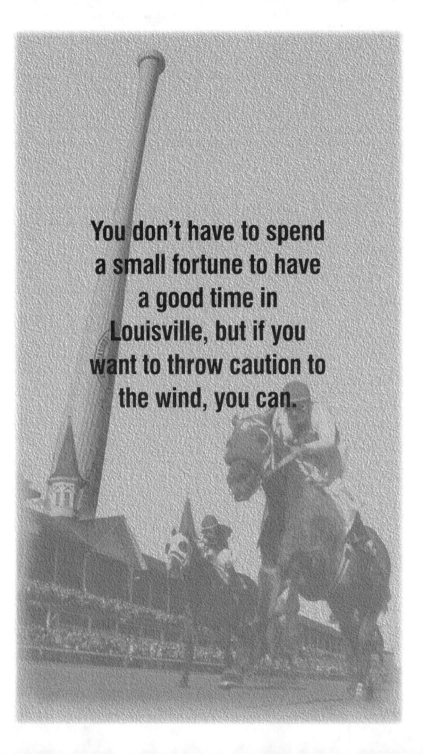

You don't have to spend a small fortune to have a good time in Louisville, but if you want to throw caution to the wind, you can.

Attractions

Louisville attractions? Think "river," think "countryside." Those are two unequivocal assets of this city that any visitor should experience.

To that end, visitors and newcomers would do well to consider a boat ride (the historic *Belle of Louisville* is a good bet) or a journey through the city's suburban scenery (My Old Kentucky Dinner Train is an ideal vehicle for such pursuits). Indoors, we have several fascinating museums, including the fossil-rich Falls of the Ohio Interpretive Center and the history-drenched Filson Club.

Less distinctively Louisvillian but fun nevertheless is Kentucky Kingdom, a theme park that subtitles itself "The Thrill Park" — and doesn't exaggerate. Our zoo does us proud, and the exhibits and IMAX films at the Louisville Science Center mesmerize, educate and entertain visitors of all ages.

Louisville and Jefferson County Convention and Visitors' Bureau, 400 S. First Street, 584-2121 or (800) 626-5646, can provide more information about sites and activities in the city.

Unless we indicate otherwise, parking is free. Attractions near or on the University of Louisville campus offer free parking on the premises. Here's the drill: Enter the campus through the two stone entry columns on Third Street. Ask for a pass from the visitor's center/information booth and park where they stipulate.

Also, you'll find a number of great attractions in some of the other chapters of this guide. Please peruse Historic Preservation and Architecture, Kidstuff and Parks and Recreation to get the full scope of Louisville's attractions.

You don't have to spend a small fortune to have a good time in Louisville — simply strolling through our parks can consume delightful days — but if you want to throw caution to the wind, you can. Our list is by no means exhaustive; it is, however, a good place to begin a lasting friendship with Louisville.

General Attractions

Falls of the Ohio Interpretive Center
201 W. Riverside Dr., Clarksville, Ind.
• **(812) 280-9970**

Fossils are interesting for only about thirty seconds, right? Not at this educational, entertaining museum, which is likely the most surprising and engaging of any Louisville area attraction. The fossils, dating back almost 400 million years to the Devonian period, are outdoors on an expansive shelf of limestone along the river's edge. The story behind these fossilized armored fish, sharks, trilobites and shell fish and the coral reef they inhabited long ago is told inside the Interpretive Center, which also beautifully explores the Ohio River's history, steamboating, area fauna and flora and geology. The $5 million investment that opened this museum in 1994 was money well spent.

The fossil bed, a National Wildlife Conservation Area and an Indiana State Park, is free to explore on your own. The museum is open daily most of the year but closed on Monday from November through March and on major holidays. Admission to the Interpretive Center is $2 for adults and $1 for children ages 2 to 12.

Falls of the Ohio Tours
Falls of the Ohio State Park
201 W. Riverside Dr., Clarksville, Ind.
• **(812) 280-9970**

From Louisville, cross the Ohio River and travel back 390 million years to the Falls of the Ohio Devonian-era fossil beds, once the bottom of an inland sea. American Indian tribes fished there, and settlers navigated their flatboats through its rapids until the Portland Canal was built in 1830. More than 600 species of ancient plants and sea animals are embedded in the rocks, now recognized as the largest exposed fossil bed in the world. Although you'll spend most of your time looking down to see the fossils, take a minute to glance skyward to see the shore birds that nest there and stop to feed on their seasonal migration.

Tours of the fossil beds are conducted from the Falls of the Ohio Interpretive Center Monday, Tuesday and Thursday at 10 AM and 3 PM; Friday, Saturday and Sunday at 10 AM and 3 PM, with a plant hike at 1 PM; and Wednesday at 10 AM in the summer. (During September and October, no public morning hikes are held; that time is reserved for visits by large school groups.) If you want to bring a group, call ahead. Public hikes June 1 through October 31 are free of charge. Visitors stand along the Indiana shoreline to view the birds and the fossils. Schedules of public hikes are printed a month in advance.

The Filson Club
1310 S. Third St. • 635-5083

Everything you ever wanted to know about the history of Kentucky is probably somewhere in this club's vast library of 50,000 research books, genealogies, wills, deeds, marriage records, manuscripts and old photographs.

Especially interesting are the documents from the pioneer, antebellum and Civil War periods and the thousands of early photographs and illustrations. The collections grow every year, making The Filson Club worth more than one visit.

You can also tour a museum that houses art and artifacts, including paintings, firearms, coins, silver objects, ceramics and textiles. One point of interest is the gun of 7-foot-9 "Kentucky Giant" Jim Porter that gives a new meaning to the term "Kentucky long rifle." The club is in the Ferguson Mansion, a Beaux-Arts-style home built in 1905 by industrialist Edwin Hite Ferguson at a cost of $100,000.

The Filson Club was founded in 1884 and named after Kentucky's first historian, John Filson. The club publishes a quarterly journal

and is expanding its collection of World War II documents. You'll pay a $3 research fee to use the materials, but there is no charge to visit the museum. (Also see Historic Preservation and Architecture.)

Kentucky Kingdom:
The Thrill Park at the Kentucky Fair and Exposition Center
Off I-264 (Watterson Expressway) or I-65 at the Crittenden Dr. exit
• 366-2231

Disneyland and Disney World are household words, but the hotbed of amusement/theme parks is the Midwest. And Louisville's entry into the thrills and chills market is gaining national attention.

Louisville's Kentucky Kingdom has roared into the regional consciousness since its opening in 1990 and now draws well over 700,000 people a year. What's the attraction? Four terrifying roller coasters, several other scary rides that push and plummet the rider in unnatural ways and water rides that feature giant waves, giant slides, giant boats and a meandering, Caribbean-themed "river" for tubing.

The architecture, landscaping and color schemes of Kentucky Kingdom have been described as "bold and brilliant" by one magazine writer, and he did not exaggerate. This park is visually striking, although many local thrill-seekers barely notice as they run toward one of the park's trademark coasters. Chang, the newest roller coaster, is the tallest and longest stand-up coaster in the world and also features the largest vertical loop and largest number of inversions (five). T2 (Terror to the Second Power) is a suspended looping coaster that scores a 10 on the fear-o-meter. The Vampire drops you 12 stories, then twists, turns and loops you both forward and backward. A tamer, family-oriented roller coaster called the Roller Skater has cars shaped like — you guessed it — roller skates. And the first of the park's coasters, and still the favorite of many repeat visitors, is Thunder Run, a wooden contraption that gets riders going up to 70 miles an hour via a 10-story drop.

After you have your socks knocked off by one of Kentucky Kingdom's roller coasters,

---

FYI

Unless otherwise noted, the area code for all phone numbers listed in this chapter is 502.

you can sample one of the 105 other rides and attractions — including a whimsical carousel in which kids ride various musical instruments such as tubas, French horns and cellos. The Top Eliminator Dragsters, which cost an additional $10 for two rides, put you in the seat of a simulated dragster as you go from 0 to 75 mph in 2.8 seconds. The Giant Wheel, a 150-foot Ferris wheel offers a good look at the park below and the city skyline beyond. There are numerous food stands with reasonable prices to satisfy the rumblings of your stomach.

The spring season (weekends only) runs April 4 through Memorial Day; the regular season (open daily) is Memorial Day until the beginning of the Kentucky State Fair (mid-August); the fall season (weekends only) runs from the end of the fair through September 28. The park is open and free during the Kentucky State Fair, with each of the rides priced separately. Closing times vary according to the season, size of the crowd and length of the queues. Call to verify park operating hours before you visit.

A season pass is $69.95. General admission is $24.95. Children under 54 inches tall are $14.80, and senior citizens pay $9.95. All admissions include unlimited access to the rides, water attractions at the Hurricane Bay water park area and stage shows throughout the day. Parking is $3 at the KFEC parking lots.

Louisville Science Center
727 W. Main St. • 561-6100

This museum, formerly the Museum of History and Science, has two separate enticements: Its kid-oriented science exhibits and the imposing IMAX film theater.

The focus in the exhibits is on science, math and technology. A space science gallery includes artifacts from Gemini and Apollo space missions; a mummy exhibit includes a 3,400-year-old mummy and other Egyptian items; and "A Show of Hands" is an exhibit exploring the wonder and workings of the human hand. The second floor of the museum was recently converted into a 12,600-square-foot exhibit titled "The World We Create," which explores the mind power behind the material world of manufacturing, transportation, communication and other forms of technology. There's even an educational play room for kids ages 7 and younger; see the Kidstuff chapter for more about this area, dubbed KIDSPACE.

The Louisville Science Center's IMAX theater has a four-story screen with a digital sound system that seems to put you right in the middle of the action, swirling with sights, sounds and motion. The films change throughout the year, so call the museum for the current listings and show times, or check the entertainment page of *The Courier-Journal*.

The museum is open daily. Admission is $7 for adults and $5 for children ages 2 through 12 and seniors. Two different IMAX films run daily, and admission to one IMAX film is included in your museum admission price. To see the museum only, admission is $5.25 for adults and $4.25 for children and seniors. You can see both IMAX film features for $3 extra. Parking is $3.25 at the center's Eighth Street garage.

Louisville Slugger Museum
800 W. Main St. • 588-7228

One's introduction to the Louisville Slugger Museum is not subtle. From blocks away, your kids will erupt in "WOWs" and the like when they see the giant steel replica of a Louisville Slugger baseball bat, more than six stories high, leaning against the Hillerich & Bradsby Co. headquarters at Eighth and Main streets.

Highlights of the museum include a great

INSIDERS' TIP

In the summer of 1997, Louisvillians got a real scare — the *Belle of Louisville* almost sank to the bottom of the Ohio River. The culprit: A freshwater valve left open in the hull. After going into drydock for some cleaning up, *Belle* officials predicted a full recovery for the old sternwheeler.

film about the lure and appeal of the sport of baseball, a replica of a baseball diamond, a machine that fires pitches down a simulated mound-to-plate path at Major League speeds, an announcers' booth with recordings of some legendary game calls, and a large multimedia room that uses films to bring to life great moments and important trends in baseball history.

A tour of the baseball bat factory that traces the process from rough-hewn logs to the trademark burned-in logo is longish but seems to captivate most kids. The factory also makes PowerBilt golf clubs and hockey gear, although the production processes for these aren't as interesting.

It takes between one and two hours to tour the museum. Beware the gift shop — it's many offerings are more than most kids can resist. For admission to the museum, adults pay $5, children ages 6 to 12 pay $3, and seniors must cough up $4.50. It's open 9 AM to 5 PM Monday through Saturday. Metered parking is available on the street, and a parking garage is nearby.

The Louisville Zoological Gardens
1100 Trevilian Way • 459-2181

A visitor can see the usual zoo fare at the Louisville Zoo — lions and tigers and bears, oh snooze — but city residents are currently excited about a new three-acre Islands exhibit, which features the habitat and species of the wilds of Indonesia, the Malay peninsula and the surrounding area. Animals include the black and white Malayan tapir, the Sumatran tiger, orangutans and the Komodo dragon, which grows to be 10 feet long, weigh up to 300 pounds and has breath bad enough to give its presence away in deep brush.

Elsewhere in the Islands Pavilion, the bat exhibit and the Forest Bird Trail have quickly gained a good reputation around town as must-see zoo attractions. The Louisville Zoo introduced a new exhibition method with the Island exhibit: A number of species are moved from one major habitat to another during the day to more closely imitate life in the wild, keeping the animals' instincts sharp and the behavior more natural. In other words, predator smells the lingering scent of departed prey at the water hole, and prey detects signs of predators.

The zoo made a big splash a few years ago with the opening of the HerpAquarium, which showcased reptiles and amphibians. The MetaZoo area offers classes and educational opportunities for children and school groups as well as a look into the microscopic world. The American Wild Cats exhibit hits a little closer to home, and a band shell at one end of the zoo is home to a variety of family-friendly concerts during the year.

Of course, the lions, tigers and polar bears are still thrilling to see, along with the elephants, snow leopards, giraffes, zebras and the always entertaining sea lions. More than 1,200 species of animals are housed in simulated natural habitats at the zoo.

The zoo has a reputation for conservation too. The black-footed ferret propagation program is part of a national effort to repopulate this nearly extinct North American mammal in the wild. The zoo's woolly monkeys aren't just a blast to watch — they're rare. And polar bear triplets are one more achievement on the list of successful breeding programs here. Siberian tigers, maned wolves, white rhinos and golden lion tamarins have all been part of an international species survival plan.

The gift shop stocks environmental T-shirts, jewelry, books and zoo-venirs from around the world. Snack stands and the outdoor LakeSide Cafe sell fast food.

In October kids flock to the zoo for what's billed as "the world's largest Halloween party," which includes trick-or-treating and a "haunted" forest. (If you ride the train, keep an eye out for "attacks" by the headless horseman.) (See our chapter on Kidstuff for this and other kid-friendly events at the zoo.)

You can visit the zoo year round: It's open 10 AM to 4 PM from Labor Day through March

---

INSIDERS' TIP

During the dog days of summer, Kentucky Kingdom usually offers special evening rates of admission in order to boost attendance.

Photo: Kentucky Kingdom

Chang is the tallest and longest stand-up coaster in the world.

31; 10 AM to 5 PM April 1 to Labor Day. Extended hours (enter until 8 PM) are offered on Wednesday, Thursday and Friday June, July and August. The zoo is closed Thanksgiving, Christmas and New Year's Day.

Admission is $7 for ages 12 to 59; $5.50 for individuals 60 and older; $4.50 for children 3 to 11 years old; and free for kids 2 years old and younger. Parking is free. The train ride is $1.75 per person. A tram that makes frequent stops is $1.50 per person, with unlimited off and on privileges.

Patton Museum of Cavalry and Armor
Fayette Ave. (near Chaffee Ave. entrance to Fort Knox), Fort Knox • (502) 624-3812

The relatively innocuous city of Louisville was reputedly a target for Russian ICBMs during the Cold War, and the reason was the gold depository at Fort Knox. The country isn't as dependent on our gold supply now, but the museum at Fort Knox still holds an allure. There's a model of the nearby bullion depository that the villain Goldfinger used to plot his attack on the vault in the James Bond movie at this museum, but the prime attraction here is armory. Depending on the degree of interest you or your kids have in U.S. martial history, the Patton Museum can consume anywhere

from a half-hour to a whole afternoon to explore it. (The museum staff say to budget about an hour and a half to take in the exhibits.)

The collection, which is actually the museum of the Armored Branch of the U.S. Army, earned its name from the many items that came from Gen. George Patton Jr.'s Third Army. In 1949 the museum was dedicated to Gen. Patton and the thousands of cavalry and armored division soldiers who fought in World War II. Galleries display armored equipment and vehicles, weapons, art and other memorabilia that chronicle the development of the armored branch, centering on World Wars I and II. The Patton Gallery also contains many of the general's personal items.

Every Independence Day, some of the historic armored equipment returns to "action" with maneuvers operated by soldiers who re-create the era with authentic uniforms and equipment.

Hours are Monday through Friday, 9 AM to 4:30 PM, Saturday and Sunday 10 AM to 6 PM. Admission is free.

The Photographic Archives
Ekstrom Library, University of Louisville, Belknap Campus, 2301 S. Third St.
• 852-6752

More than an archive, this collection of vintage photographs and historic documents is also displayed in the gallery in rotated exhibits. You'll see Kentucky history and culture through the photographer's eye in this staggering collection of more than 1 million items in antique media and formats: daguerreotypes, ambrotypes, tintypes, cartes de viste, cabinet photographs and stereographs, as well as vintage cameras and other photographic equipment.

Founded in 1962, the University of Louisville Photographic Archives is charged with collecting, organizing and preserving significant documentary and fine art photographs, including negatives and prints from well-known local photographers, a group of historical erotic photographs, fine prints, the K & I Railroad collection and the Macauley Theatre collection. You can browse through photocopies of the originals and order prints for a small fee.

FYI

Unless otherwise noted, the area code for all phone numbers listed in this chapter is 502.

It's open Monday through Friday 10 AM to 4 PM, except on Thursday when it's open from 10 AM to 8 PM.

Joseph Rauch Memorial Planetarium
University of Louisville, Belknap Campus, 2301 S. Third St. • 852-6664

While the presentations at this planetarium allow a close look at the solar system's planets that isn't possible with a telescope, this facility is best thought of as an introduction to astronomy. Using equipment that projects an image of the night sky onto a domed ceiling, the Rauch's program simulates the current evening sky and other visible sky phenomena. See it indoors, then find it outside later that night with your own telescope. On sunny days, programs also include a safe telescopic look at Sol's sunspots and solar flares.

The planetarium, which opened in 1961, hosts shows for the public on Saturday afternoons (call the number above for specific times). During the summer, programs are also held at 11 AM on Tuesday and Thursday. Admission is $3.50 for adults and $2.50 for children age 12 and younger, individuals 60 and older and U of L/Metroversity students. Group rates are available.

You don't even have to attend a program at the Rauch Planetarium to benefit from this resource. The planetarium runs the Sky Hotline, 852-7597, a recording with news on currently visible constellations and planets, plus the odd, delectable tidbit of information.

Multimedia Shows

Kentucky Derby Museum
704 Central Ave. • 637-1111

At the heart of this museum is an award-winning film that the proprietors insist on editing every year.

Actually, it makes sense — *The Greatest Race*, a fifteen-minute film shown on a 360 degree screen that sketches the history and singular experience of the Kentucky Derby, benefits from the addition of the stretch run from the most recent Derby. The movie is shown every hour on the half hour.

Visitors can also view films of every Derby since 1918, including the breathtaking wins of Secretariat in 1973 and Seattle Slew in 1977. Other exhibits include an interactive piece on pari-mutuel wagering, changing exhibits of equine art and history and a permanent exhibit titled "African Americans in Thoroughbred Racing." African American jockeys, including the celebrated Isaac Murphy, won 15 of the first 28 Kentucky Derbys.

The museum is located at Gate One of Churchill Downs, in the famous twin-spired building. Next door is the Derby Cafe, which serves traditional Kentucky food, sandwiches and specials of the day.

It's open seven days a week, 9 AM to 5 PM. Admission is $5 for adults; $2.50 for children ages 5 to 12. Children younger than 5 get in free; admission is $4 for seniors. The museum is closed for Thanksgiving, Christmas, Oaks and Derby Days. (See The Derby and The Downs chapter.)

Floyd County Museum
201 E. Spring St., New Albany, Ind.
• (812) 944-7336

Many types of visual arts are exhibited at this small museum, housed in a historic Carnegie library building in Southern Indiana, but the star of the show is the unique Yenawine

Exhibit, which is both folk art and history. Animated (hooked to electric motors) carved figures act out scenes from life in a turn-of-the-century farm in a diorama created by Georgetown, Indiana, native Merle Yenawine. Scenes depicting a shotgun wedding, farm work at harvest time and lessons at a one-room schoolhouse are enlivened by 475 moving objects made of poplar and pine wood.

Other highlights include an annual juried exhibit and shows featuring contemporary regional artists. The museum is closed on Monday. Admission is free.

Portland Museum
2308 Portland Ave. • 776-7678

The Portland area was important in Louisville's development as a river city, and this museum details the neighborhood's role through exhibits and a light and sound show titled "Portland: The Land, the River, the People." Presented each half-hour between 1 and 4 PM, or as needed, the 23-minute show is a permanently installed exhibit with an automated sound track that guides visitors. Environmental sounds and character voices of historical figures bring the exhibit to life, which is operated in a house built in 1852.

It's open Tuesday through Friday from 10 AM to 4:30 PM. Admission is $3 for adults, $2.50 for senior citizens and Armed services personnel, $1.50 for children younger than 12. Groups rates are also available. (For more information, see our Historic Preservation and Architecture chapter.)

On the Waterfront

Belle of Louisville
Fourth Ave. and River Rd. • 574-2355

Short of perhaps the many hues of green that the summer foliage and rolling hills of Kentucky boast, nothing in Louisville is taken for granted by natives more than the *Belle of Louisville*.

We hear the anachronistic toot of the *Belle's* steam calliope, and a small grin passes over our lips. But visitors are bewitched, and a glimpse at the more than 80-year-old river sternwheeler completely captivates them. A closer look at this red and white, smokestacked riverboat — of all Louisville's National Historic Landmark's the one that seems most comfortable when it doesn't even mark land — is a must for anyone who spends any amount of time in the city.

This 800-passenger pleasure boat has had several incarnations under other names and duties before she began to cruise the Ohio River. Built in Pittsburgh as the *Idlewild*, the vessel served as an excursion boat in the early 1920s and '30s and towed oil barges up and down the Mississippi in the '40s. She was rescued from such drudgery in 1947 and renamed the *Avalon*. Former Jefferson County Judge Marlow Cook bought her at auction in Cincinnati for $34,000 — what a steal! — and brought her to Louisville. Today the *Belle of Louisville* is the oldest operating steamboat on the Mississippi River system.

The Belle cruises past Louisville's Falls Fountain and city skylines on either side, which are especially impressive at night. You can arrange a private charter for conventions, reunions, dances and parties. In addition to catered dinners, the *Belle* has a modest snack bar and a full-service beverage bar (complete with alcoholic drinks).

The *Belle* operates from early June until late October. Afternoon cruises are Tuesday through Sunday, including Memorial and Labor Days; board between 1 and 2 PM and cruise from 2 to 4 PM. Pay as you board (no reservations are required); admission is generally less than $10. Group reservations are accepted; VISA and MasterCard are honored. Tuesday and Thursday sunset cruises board from 6 to 7 PM and cruise from 7 to 9 PM with the same fares as afternoon cruises.

The popular Saturday night dance cruise June through September features a live band. Board from 7:30 to 8:30 PM and cruise from 8:30 to 11:30 PM. Fares are $12.50 for adults. Pay as you board. No coolers are allowed.

Parking is $4 at the lot located at Third Street and River Road.

Call the above number for more information, or for no other reason than to hear the sound of the *Belle's* delightful calliope in the background of the message.

The Spirit of Jefferson
Riverview Park • 574-2355

This boat was built in 1963 to look like an authentic riverboat but with all the modern conveniences the public expects — think air conditioning. *The Spirit* is painted red and white, with black smokestacks like *The Spirit's* older, bigger sister the *Belle of Louisville*. But the *Belle* is an authentic paddlewheeler, while this diesel-powered craft's sternwheel is purely for show.

The Spirit serves a different function: It's a more intimate boat (300-passenger capacity, decks closer to the river's surface, a season that stretches year round), and it also primarily services Southwest Jefferson County, currently docking at the Greenwood Boat Ramp in Riverview Park. This section of the river has much less development, resulting in a river cruise with more lush, green scenery.

County officials purchased the boat from the city of St. Louis in 1996. They plan to dock it at Riverside, The Farnsley-Moreman Landing in 1998. Its hours are roughly the same as the *Belle's*: Afternoon cruises are Tuesday through Sunday, including Memorial and Labor Days; board between 1 and 2 PM and cruise from 2 to 4 PM. Pay as you board (no reservations are required); admission is usually less than $10. Group reservations are ac-

cepted; VISA and MasterCard are honored. Thursday through Saturday and Tuesday, *The Spirit* has sunset cruises that board from 6 to 7 PM and cruise from 7 to 9 PM.

Star of Louisville
151 W. River Rd. • 589-7827

The *Star of Louisville*, a 130-foot-yacht-style boat, offers cruising and dining within fully enclosed dining decks that serve buffets and provide live music and dancing year round. Three outdoor observation decks are good places to view the skylines of Louisville and Southern Indiana as you glide by.

Cruises are available seven days a week; the *Star* plies the river for lunch cruises from noon to 2 PM Monday through Friday, noon to 1:30 PM on Saturday and 1 to 3 PM on Sunday. Dinner cruises run 7 to 10 PM Monday through Thursday and Sunday, 7:30 to 10:30 PM on Friday and Saturday. Fares range from $47 for a weekend dinner cruise to $23.25 for a lunch cruise. Discounted rates are charged for children, approximately half-price for kids ages 3 to 12.

The *Star* regularly schedules cruises with themes such as jazz music, gospel music, bridge (as in whist) cruises, luncheon excursions, comedy cruises and bingo. Parking is $2.

Louisville Falls Fountain
Fourth St. and River Rd. • no phone

The best time to see Louisville's Falls Fountain is after dark, and the Riverfront Plaza Belvedere, adjacent to the Kentucky Center for the Arts, is one good place to view it, although many people say the best vantage point is the Indiana shore. The water sculpture rises to form a fleur-de-lis pattern (that's the symbol on the city's flag), illuminated by 100 colored spotlights that make the 400-foot center plume a spectacular sight. Water patterns change twice every 15 minutes. The fountain is in operation daily from late May through November, 8 AM to midnight — except the last Wednesday of every month, when it is closed for maintenance. Viewing is free.

McAlpine Locks & Dam Front
27th and Canal St. • 774-3514

McAlpine Locks, in the Portland neighborhood, is the only project on the entire 981-mile length of the Ohio River that provides passage around a natural barrier. The Falls of the Ohio rapids, which hindered navigation in the city's early days, are now passable by barges that carry an average of 5 million tons of cargo (mostly coal) through the Portland Canal each month. For a better view of passing vessels, you can take a drawbridge over the canal. (See our Kidstuff chapter.)

Getting Around in Style

Horse and Carriage Rides

For a special event in the evening or afternoon, take a ride in a horse-drawn carriage. Main carriage stops are at The Galt Houses at Fourth and Main and the Old Spaghetti Factory at Third and Market. More than a dozen other pickup points are located throughout the Market, Main Street and Theater Square area; look for the white street signs with the red carriage image on them.

Louisville Horse Trams/Classic Carriages of Kentucky
Various locations • 581-0100

This is the oldest carriage company in Louisville. The carriages, pulled by draft horses, run year round, weather permitting, in the downtown and outlying areas; lap robes are provided for colder temperatures. Minimum fare is $15, with additional charges for additional passengers. Prices vary for trips outside the downtown area, and carriages are available for weddings or other special events.

River City Horse Carriage
Various locations • 895-7268

River City offers horse-drawn rides year round through downtown streets with a running commentary by the driver. Lap blankets (provided) and woolly clothes will insulate you from winter winds. You can reserve a carriage for rides of 30 minutes or more and for weddings in the downtown and outlying areas. River

City's fares are similar — $15 minimum for two people for 15 minutes and $5 extra for each additional person. This company's all-white carriages are popular among city natives.

Train Rides

My Old Kentucky Dinner Train
602 N. Third St., Bardstown, Ky.
• (502) 348-7300

The dinner train is an ideal way to enjoy one of Louisville's greatest attractions: the beautiful green countryside surrounding the metropolitan area. Powered by two early-1940s diesel/electric engines, this train rolls through 35 miles of landscape in the Bardstown, Kentucky, region, including a part of Bernheim Forest and the Jim Beam distillery.

The atmosphere on board the red and silver train is classic 1940s: Elegance was in fashion, traveling by rail was the way to go, and dining cars were the settings for relaxed conversation, fine cuisine and solicitous service, with ever-changing scenery outside your window. Mahogany walls, brass fixtures, air conditioning, tuxedoed servers and fine china plates all scream upscale, but diners are invited to dress as casually as they like. Dinner excursions ($59.95 per person for a five-course meal) last two and a half hours; lunch excursions ($36.95 for a three-course meal) last two hours. Specialties of the train's continental/traditional Kentucky menu include the Angus prime rib and the bread pudding. Cocktails and premium wines are also available at an extra cost.

My Old Kentucky Dinner Train, which will celebrate its 10-year anniversary in 1998, is a popular attraction — the staff recommends making reservations two weeks in advance. Passengers board in downtown Bardstown.

When the whim overtakes them, which is roughly once a year, the Dinner Train staff hosts Murder on the Kentucky Express, a murder mystery excursion in which character actors mingle with passengers who are trying to figure out whodunit to whom before the end of the trip. Call the above number for the next premeditated murder on the rails.

Louisville is a city rich with historic architecture — only Boston and its surrounding Essex County have more properties listed on the National Register of Historic Places.

Historic Preservation and Architecture

Louisville is a city rich with historic architecture — only Boston and its surrounding Essex County have more properties listed on the National Register of Historic Places.

But Louisville's architectural excellence is of a particular kind. This is not a city of monuments or architectural milestones — although it contains one of the world's most attractive post-modern buildings, several extraordinary pieces of industrial design, and one of the few high-rise buildings ever built to a Frank Lloyd Wright design.

Nor is it a city where the historical associations of the site overwhelm you — although you can tour the last home of the man who conquered the Old Northwest, as well as another home with significant links to two of the Mount Rushmore presidents and a third that served as the modest lodgings of the young Thomas Edison.

And yet the city values its past and rewards visitors who enjoy looking at architecture, from the expert on architectural styles to someone who simply enjoys strolling through a historic district. Its greatest pleasures are dispersed widely, especially in the residential architecture of its neighborhoods and what's remaining of the old downtown. The noteworthy architecture is everyday — still used and lived in and walked by and half taken for granted.

When you train your eye to look for details, you begin to see great ones all over the place, starting at the very heart of the city. City Hall, at Sixth and Jefferson streets, built in an elegant, substantial Italianate style in 1866 (with a Second Empire clock tower added in 1876 after a fire) represented the height of respectable fashion when it was built.

But look up at the figures above the second-story windows: Where you might expect to see city fathers, classical statues or even gargoyles, there are the heads of cows, mules, pigs and cattle — playfully reflecting the city's importance as a market town for the outlying countryside. There is also a steaming locomotive coming out of the pediment. Its symbolism was very carefully chosen: The train is heading from the North, designated by deciduous trees, to the South, marked by palm trees — reflecting the city's image as "Gateway to the South."

Likewise, when you look above the wig shops at ground level on Fourth Street, once the city's principal shopping district, your eye discovers a row of wonderfully detailed buildings that many people in Louisville hardly realize exists. Local preservationists wanted to put together a program called Look Up Louisville to inspire people to take more notice of the riches right above their noses.

Louisville has for several decades been in the forefront of historical preservation. It's only fitting, since it's an act of historical preservation that made a city here — the 400-million-year-old Devonian reef, largest of its kind in the world, that creates the Falls of the Ohio. Prosperity in the 19th century built the city up nicely; its slow economic decline meant that the older part of the city grew shabby, rather than decrepit. There was less of an economic engine throbbing to tear down old buildings and create new ones (although there's a lot of money available to anyone who wants to maintain a vacant lot as parking). While urban renewal cleared out great patches of historic buildings — especially along the former center of black Louisville, Walnut Street (now Muhammad Ali Boulevard) — Louisville fared better than some cities. There is still something left to show us what the city looked like 100 or 150 years ago.

And preservation is a widely held value. There are active preservation offices in both the city and county government (although the belief in preservation is not always acted upon, or even treated with respect: The city allowed the demolition of a historic warehouse being cleared for waterfront development to be used as a promotional explosion for the Sylvester Stallone movie *Demolition Man*).

The city hasn't frozen itself architecturally. The Humana Building (see below) was one of the most-discussed buildings of the '80s, and remains one of the most attractive skyscrapers committed in post-modernism's name. The most dramatic building planned since Humana, a swirling, tapering glass tower that Louisville-based healthcare corporation Vencor will build on the riverfront by the turn of the century, bears no visual resemblance to Humana but matches its architectural ambitions and capacity to intrigue from any angle.

Louisville makes use of its historic homes and buildings. Almost all of the house museums are available to be rented, and it's hard to imagine a prettier site for a wedding than the lawn at Locust Grove, by the river at the Farnsley-Moremen Landing or on the oak stairway of the Conrad-Caldwell House. Actors Theatre is located inside what's considered to be the city's best surviving example of Greek Revival architecture. You may have noticed how many times the Water Tower is mentioned in the Festivals and Annual Events chapter; the Louisville Visual Art Association, which occupies it, is not open on Saturday (except for its gift shop) because of the constant demand to use it for various private events. And Churchill Downs has been in the same grandstand (with additions, of course) since 1895.

Many historic homes are still residences or are used as office space. In this chapter, with a single exception for which we got permission, we don't direct you to any addresses that are privately owned. That's for two rea-

sons: First, many of the most significant single dwellings in the area are already open to the public; second, we don't want to send people gawking at folks who are just going about the business of daily life. Although in the neighborhoods to which we'll send you, people are accustomed to having others walk down the sidewalks staring at cornices and leaded glass, and they are neighborhoods where it's possible and pleasant to walk.

For more complete guides to local architecture, look at such valuable books as *Historic Jefferson County*, published by the Jefferson County office of Historic Preservation and Archives; Sam Thomas's two-volume, *Views of Louisville*, as well as his books on Crescent Hill, Cave Hill Cemetery and Churchill Downs; Kenny Karem's unique *Discover Louisville*; and pioneering preservationist John Cullinane's *Walking Thru Louisville*.

We'll start this chapter with a few "mustsee" places: the historic homes and museums that are open to the public and exceptional buildings of more recent vintage. (With a few exceptions, all of them are on the National Register of Historic Places.) Then we'll direct you to significant neighborhoods — they won't exhaust the richness of Louisville architecture and history, but they will give you a good sense of how the city developed and what its chief qualities are. (For more information, see the Neighborhoods and Real Estate chapter.) We'll also mention several churches and synagogues of historical or architectural note.

We'll throw in some oddities (not all of them historic) that you should check out sometime and conclude with a directory of some of the groups that work for historic preservation.

FYI

Unless otherwise noted, the area code for all phone numbers listed in this chapter is 502.

Must-sees

These are the most noteworthy local landmarks, along with some that may not qualify for the list on their merits but have the virtue of being open as well-run museums. The list is a little overloaded with Victorian house museums, but that's true to the city: Louisville was most prosperous and expansive during the

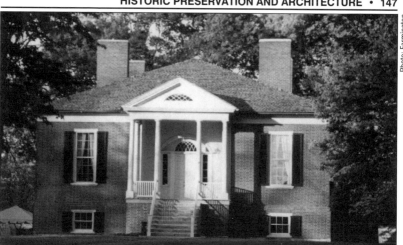

Photo: Farmington

Thomas Jefferson gave the building plans for Farmington to
Lucy Gilmer Fry as a wedding present.

Victorian era, when the idea of the house as a showplace was at its height.

Locust Grove
561 Blankenbaker Ln. • 897-9845

In 1806, on their way back from the historic expedition to explore the Louisiana Purchase, Merriwether Lewis and William Clark stopped at Locust Grove, the home of Clark's sister, Lucy Croghan. Tradition has it that at a party with friends and neighbors, Lewis and Clark set out the trophies of their trip and gave an account of their adventures in the Pacific Northwest. Louisville often seems behind the times, but not that night. Our citizens knew about the pronghorn antelope and Sacajawea before almost any other American did.

That's the sort of history that's taken place at Locust Grove since it was built in 1790. Three U.S. presidents — James Monroe, Andrew Jackson and Zachary Taylor (who lived on the adjoining property, Springfield) — have visited there, as have John James Audubon, Aaron Burr and abolitionist Cassius Marcellus Clay.

A National Historic Landmark, Locust Grove is best known as the last home of George Rogers Clark, the Revolutionary War general who founded Louisville and conquered the Northwest Territory, thereby guaranteeing that

Ohio, Illinois, Indiana and Michigan are in the United States rather than Canada. After his leg was amputated in 1809, Clark came to live with his sister and her husband, William Croghan (pronounced "crawn" rather than "CROW-gan" by his present-day descendants and the Locust Grove staff, although many local historians are dubious). Clark died there in 1818.

While most of the Louisville area's historic homes are opulent-to-garish Victorian mansions, this Georgian home, built from bricks made on the estate and wood hewn there, has a classical simplicity to it, broken occasionally by the sensuality of the serpentine chest of drawers or the French wallpaper in the ballroom.

The grounds contain a number of outbuildings, including the kitchen, ice house and spring house. The estate still comprises 55 of the original 693 acres, enough to give you an idea of what it might have looked like when Clark and the Croghans lived there. It is planted with trees and plants known to have existed in Kentucky before 1818: locusts, Kentucky coffee trees and a giant elm that was probably there before the house was built.

A major event is the Christmas-time candlelight tour, with the house authentically decked out for the holidays (there's no Christmas tree, because the Croghans wouldn't have had one). There's a multi-image show in the modern visitors' center. It's open daily except major holidays (including Derby Day); admission is $4 for adults, $3 for people 60 and older and $2 for children ages 6 to 12. Children 5 and younger get in free.

Farmington
3033 Bardstown Rd. • 452-9920

Thomas Jefferson, enthusiastic amateur architect, often gave building plans as gifts to his friends. Lucy Gilmer Fry, who came from a Virginia family close to Jefferson and became the second wife of Judge John Speed, was one of the lucky recipients. Jefferson's gift, somewhat modified, was built in 1810 as Farmington, a well-proportioned, symmetrical Federal home that was once the center of a 552-acre hemp plantation.

Built a bit later than Locust Grove, Farmington shares some of the same simplicity in a slightly more refined key. Some of its details, such as the fanlights between the front and rear halls and the two octagonal rooms in the center of the house, recall the Adam style popular in the cities along the Eastern seaboard.

The Speeds' son, Joshua, was one of Abraham Lincoln's closest friends; Lincoln spent three weeks at the house when he was courting Mary Todd. (Lincoln later appointed another son, James Speed, as his attorney general.)

Farmington, which opened to the public in 1959, was the city's first historic house museum. It has been restored to the period of 1810-1840 and some of the furnishings, such as flatware and a porcelain doll, belonged to the Speeds. The grounds include a formal garden, a blacksmith shop, a stone springhouse and barn and an apple orchard. It's open daily; admission is $4 for adults 18 and older, $3 for people 60 and older, $2 for students; children 5 and younger are admitted free.

Riverside,
the Farnsley-Moremen Landing
7410 Moorman Rd. (at Lower River Rd.)
• 935-6809

The setting is beautiful, on a tree-dotted riverbank in southwest Jefferson County that gives you a vivid picture of what farm life must have been like in the early days of white settlement. The house faces the river, not the road — the owners knew which was the more important thoroughfare. The boat landing was one of the few ports between the Falls and the Salt River in Bullitt County (after the Civil War, it was known as Soap Landing, for the lye soap produced there). Sand bars allowed you to wade across the Ohio, and animals from the farm were often grazed in the hills on the Indiana shore.

Built around 1837, the house is an I-style structure, a popular Virginia design, with an unusual double portico (essentially, a front porch on both first and second floors). It was once the center of a 400-acre farm (and owner Alanson Moremen had another 1,100 acres east of Dixie Highway). Moremen family tradition has it that the house was known as "The House of Refuge" during the Civil War, and that both Confederate and Union soldiers were allowed to spend the night as long as they left their hostilities outside.

The house tour showcases unusual furnishings that illuminate what life was like on a 19th-century farm: the "mammy bench," a long

INSIDERS' TIP

To an unschooled eye, cast-iron work is almost indistinguishable from masonry. To tell the difference on the 600 and 700 blocks of West Main, use a magnet or rap sharply on the storefront and listen for a metallic "ching!" Or look to the trees and sidewalks: Single ironwood trees are planted in front of the cast-iron buildings, surrounded by iron bands supported by fanciful cast-iron walking sticks; a group of three trees indicates a masonry building. On the sidewalks in front of cast-iron buildings, the bricks are flecked with iron.

bench on rockers that included a short rail on pegs that could hold a baby in place if its mother or nurse had to step away, but which could be removed if the seat was needed when company came; the corn shuck beds; the canvas underneath the dining room table, placed there because it was easy to sweep (crumbs would have stayed in a carpet and attracted vermin).

A modern visitors' center contains an exhibit on archaeological excavations that have unearthed artifacts going back to 1500 B.C. and another about the Farnsley family (owner Gabriel Farnsley was the great-great uncle of former Louisville mayor Charles Farnsley). In 1998 the property is scheduled to become the home of the county cruise ship the *Spirit of Jefferson* (see Attractions chapter).

Riverside is open Wednesday through Sunday; admission is $3 for adults, $2.50 for people 60 and older and $1.50 for children ages 6 to 12.

Jefferson County Courthouse
527 W. Jefferson St. • 574-6161

Built on a grand scale, with hopes of attracting the state capital to Louisville from Frankfort, the present Jefferson County Courthouse was the city's fourth courthouse (one burned, two others came to seem inadequate to the city's size and ambitions). It was designed by Kentucky-born architect Gideon Shryock in the This-Is-How-Democracy-Looks style of the Greek Revival he'd previously employed on the Kentucky Capitol in Frankfort. Work began in 1836; it was occupied in an unfinished state in 1842, the year Shryock quit the project in frustration over frequent setbacks.

A visitor that year wrote: "The Court House is superior to the Illinois State House or any other building in the West. They have been three years upon it, expended already upwards of half a million, and it is not yet half finished. You can hardly imagine any thing more splendid. The stones are not only hewed but polished. No possible expense is spared in its decoration."

But the courthouse sat in the same dishabille for nearly two decades more, mocked as "an almost mouldering ruin," until the city fathers (in particular James Guthrie, who had seen the courthouse called "Guthrie's Folly") engaged bridge designer Albert Fink to complete Shryock's work. Fink scaled it back slightly (using fewer columns across the front and eliminating a towering skylight) and finished the project in 1860. Fink's engineering background is seen in such features as the unique cast-iron floor in the rotunda, supported with bridge-like struts and with inset glass plugs to let light through to the ground level.

There are statues of Louis XVI and Thomas Jefferson outside; Henry Clay's is in the rotunda, as is a rare 1823 engraving of the Declaration of Independence. The courthouse is open Monday through Friday during normal business hours.

John Hay Center
307 E. Market St., Salem, Ind.
• (812) 883-6495

This is a complex of historic buildings in this town 35 miles north of Louisville off I-65. The John Hay House is a house museum, restored as it would have been in the 1840s when Hay — one of the nation's most important diplomats who, as secretary of state to Presidents McKinley and Theodore Roosevelt, was key in creating the Open Door policy toward China and in acquiring the Panama Canal — was born there. Ten other buildings from the pioneer era supplement the house. The Stevens Museum includes old-fashioned dentist and law offices, as well as a collection of historic artifacts and vintage clothing and a genealogical library. The center is closed Sunday, Monday and holidays. Admission is $2 for the Stevens Museum and an additional $2 for the village (which includes the Hay house); children 11 and under are free.

Zachary Taylor National Cemetery
4701 Brownsboro Rd. • 893-3852

Zachary Taylor, America's 12th president, is buried at the cemetery named in his honor in 1928. (His home, Springfield, sits behind the cemetery but is not open to the public.)

Taylor was a general, although not one who stood on ceremony, as his nickname "Old Rough-and-Ready" suggests. He won fame in the war against Mexico, especially in the battle of Buena Vista, where he prevailed despite being outnumbered three-to-one. The Whigs nominated him for president in 1848, and he won without advancing a platform. But he died of cholera 16 months into his term and was succeeded by vice-president Millard Fillmore. In 1991, Taylor's body was exhumed after a historian proposed that the president had died of arsenic poisoning rather than natural causes; no arsenic was found.

Taylor and his wife Margaret are buried in a mausoleum on 16 acres that were once part of the family farm. A 34-foot-high granite shaft next to the mausoleum supports a marble statue of Taylor.

The Water Tower
3005 River Rd. (at Zorn Ave.) • 896-2146

Given the cost-conscious, aesthetics-be-damned design of so many modern industrial buildings, it's astounding to think that some of Louisville's best architecture was created for a pumping station and other buildings for the Louisville Water Company

The clean, upward thrust of the white water tower, finished in 1860 as a wooden structure and then rebuilt in cast iron after the 1890 tornado, is one of the city's most pleasing sights: a 183-foot Doric column ringed by 10 smaller Corinthian columns, each topped by a cast-zinc classical statue — Greek and Roman Gods symbolizing the elements and seasons, with one being a classical rendition of an American Indian and his dog. A National Park Service architect called it "the finest example in the country of the symbolic and monumental function of industrial architecture." Little wonder it's been designated a National Historic Landmark. It was retired from service as a water pump in 1909.

The Water Tower is currently occupied by the Louisville Visual Art Association and hosts a large number of festivals and private events. It's open daily. But it isn't the only significant water company property. All of the buildings the company constructed in the 19th and early 20th century are impressive. Take, for example, the High Gothic gatehouse to the Crescent Hill Reservoir, at Reservoir and Frankfort avenues, which sits at the top of a wide, intricately carved stone stairway. It looks like a limestone chapel or a small chateau. They don't build *mansions* like that anymore, let alone buildings overlooking reservoirs.

Main Street Historical District
100, 300 and 500-900 blocks of W. Main St.
• 562-0723

Cast iron was an early version of prefab architecture — catalogs showed builders and merchants different building forms and a wide variety of ornamentation. It allowed owners and builders to put together a design without an architect's intervention (one such pair came up with a building, since demolished, with its columns installed upside down so that the wide tops tapered to slender bottoms).

Cast iron was lighter, stronger and less expensive than masonry, but once it was painted it was virtually indistinguishable from stone to the untutored eye. The lightness and strength of the iron tend to allow buildings to take slimmer proportions and have larger windows than stone or brick structures.

Louisville had a number of foundries producing cast-iron building fronts — a main reason why, after lower Manhattan, Louisville is thought to have the country's most extensive collection of cast-iron buildings and building fronts. The blocks of Main Street between Fifth and Ninth streets have the largest collection in the city, a largely uninterrupted late 19th-century streetscape of former wholesalers, warehouses, banks and other commercial buildings. The best example is widely considered to be the Hart Block, 726 to 730 Main Street, with a five-story front of subtly differing patterns.

Many of Main Street's cast-iron buildings have been attractively rehabbed, turning what was not long ago an auto parts company, for example, into luxury apartments; other buildings provide office or gallery space. The Louisville Science Center is in the old Carter Dry Goods Building at Eighth and Main streets.

The historic district also contains the site of Fort Nelson, the second permanent garrison on land at the Falls, built in 1782. The Bank of Louisville Building, 320 W. Main Street, now part of Actors Theatre, is a National Historic Landmark long attributed to notable Kentucky architect Gideon Shryock because its perfect Greek Revival proportions were characteristic of his work (such as the Jefferson County Courthouse at Sixth and Jefferson). But Shryock only supervised construction of the building, which was designed by James

Dakin, who also worked in New York and New Orleans. It has been praised by present-day architectural critics as one of the least archaeological buildings ever designed by a Greek Revival architect.

Main Street also contains one of the city's premier tourist attractions, the Louisville Slugger Museum in the 800 block of W. Main Street (see Attractions chapter). And it has a small role in cinematic history — it's where Bill Murray's character lived in the movie *Stripes*.

The Main Street Association at 627 W. Main St. offers tours Monday through Friday 11 AM to 3 PM, weather permitting. For tour information, call 568-2220.

Brennan House
631 S. Fifth St. • 540-5145

Local preservationist Charles Cash calls the Brennan House ". . . almost ghostly. It's as though the family got up and walked out the door one day in 1917 — as if the gloves are still folded on the dining room table."

Built in 1868, the Italianate villa house was purchased in 1884 by Thomas Brennan, an Irish immigrant who made his fortune inventing and manufacturing agricultural implements. Brennan's children lived in the house until 1969 (one carried on a medical practice in an addition built in 1912). They left no heirs.

As a result, the Brennan House is a rarity among historic homes. The furnishings aren't simply from the proper historical era; from curio cabinet to massive beds, everything inside was an actual family possession. It's a marvelous insight into Victorian taste and idiosyncrasies: the grand pieces of ornately carved furniture just a little too large for the rooms in which they're placed; the head of Christopher Columbus on each piece of furniture in the dining room; the many figurines and paintings of Napoleon; the unrelenting Anglophilia of the book collection (the low point may be a biography of Peter Townshend — not the distinguished rock guitarist, but the fellow who almost married Princess Margaret).

And since it is the last house remaining in downtown Louisville not converted to business use (a reminder of the time, only 100 years ago, when large parts of what we now call the central business district were residential neighborhoods) it offers a dramatic insight into how downtown has changed. There is a first-class slide show, a new gift shop, and the guided tours are exceptionally informative. It's open Tuesday through Saturday and by appointment in January and February. Admission is $3 for adults; $2 for people 60 and older, students, military personnel and AAA members; and $1 for children 6 and younger.

Thomas Edison House
729-731 E. Washington St. • 585-5247

In a way, the most moving thing about this four-room museum is its size. This is the only one left standing of the three houses Edison occupied when he lived in Louisville as an impoverished telegraph operator in 1866 and '67 — before he began patenting the inventions that made him famous. His living quarters consisted of one small, sparsely furnished front room in this Butchertown double-shotgun house. (A shotgun house is a single room wide, with no central hall; this house consists of two shotguns with a common center wall.)

After a day at the Western Union office a few blocks west on Main Street, Edison would work on chemical experiments into the night. He was supposedly fired from his job when some sulfuric acid he was experimenting with in a second-story room burned through the floor and onto his boss's desk in the office underneath. He returned to Louisville in 1883, when the Southern Exposition gave his incandescent bulb one of its first major showcases.

In addition to the room that has been redecorated to look as it might have when Edison lived there, the museum has a number of vin-

---

tage Edison machines — several phonographs and dictaphones, a carbon-arc "home kinetoscope" (movie camera), an extensive collection of light bulbs (more interesting than you might think) and memorabilia of early Butchertown.

The site is open Tuesday through Saturday, but hours are short — 10 AM to 2 PM — and by appointment. Admission is $4, $3 for senior citizens, $2 for students; children younger than 6 are admitted free.

Culbertson Mansion
State Historic Site
914 E. Main St., New Albany, Ind.
• **(812) 944-9600**

Mansion Row along New Albany's Main Street between State and 15th streets looks like its citizens spent the city's steamboat era in an architectural game of "Can you top this?"

The clear winner was merchant William Culbertson, once considered to be the richest Hoosier alive and the major backer of the K&I railroad bridge. The 20,000-square-foot mansion he built in 1869, now painted an appealing canary yellow, is an imposing Second Empire structure with such refined appointments as crystal chandeliers, marble fireplaces and hand-painted ceilings, most of which have had to be restored after being painted over by a former tenant, the American Legion.

The first two floors are restored, including the servants' quarters; the third floor, unreconstructed, is a good lesson about how much work goes into a historical renovation.

It's open Tuesday through Sunday, closed January 1 to March 15; admission is free (donations encouraged). A walking-tour map of Mansion Row is available here. The greatest concentration of historic residences is in the blocks around the mansion, roughly from Fifth to 12th streets. Don't miss the next-door neighbor, the Redmen Club, with a great neon sign and a statue of a stag in the yard.

Howard Steamboat Museum
1101 East Market St., Jeffersonville, Ind.
• **(812) 283-3728**

The grandest house in Jeffersonville looks a little bit like one of the "floating palaces" that used to steam up and down the Ohio — not surprisingly, since the Howards who owned it were steamboat builders and used many of the craftsmen from the shipyards across the street to build this massive 22-room mansion built between 1890 and 1894.

The museum contains memorabilia of the steamboat days: 9-foot-high steering wheels, photographs, posters and scale models of famous ships. The shipyards across the street produced such famous boats as *The Glendy Burke*, the second *Robert E. Lee* and the luxurious *J.M. White*. They are now occupied by Jeffboat, which continues the shipbuilding tradition begun in 1834. Open daily except Monday, admission charges are $4 for adults, $3 for people 65 and older, $2 for students age 9 through college and $1 for children ages 6 to 8.

Municipal College
(Simmons University)
Seventh and Kentucky Sts. • **no phone**

Meet an older African-American intellectual or professional in this city and chances are that person was educated or taught on this campus, which for over 70 years had a reputation as one of the country's best liberal arts colleges for blacks.

It opened in 1879 as State University of Louisville, a Baptist school and the only local institution of higher learning open to African Americans during the Jim Crow era. It was renamed after longtime president William J. Simmons. In 1931, the financially strapped institution sold the campus to the University of Louisville. Simmons became Simmons Bible College, located further west; the campus became Louisville Municipal University, U of L's black branch, which stayed open until 1951.

Its chief building, William H. Steward Hall, was designed by Samuel Plato, an alumnus and Kentucky's best-known African-American architect and contractor.

The property is now owned by another prominent Louisville institution, St. Stephen Baptist Church, the largest African-American church in Kentucky. While the buildings are closed at present, visitors are allowed to walk the campus grounds.

Union Station
1000 W. Broadway • **561-5100**

How important was the railroad in the late 19th century? The L&N Railroad's former ter-

Photo: Howard Steamboat Museum

The Howard Steamboat Museum houses 9-foot-high steering
wheels and scale models of ships.

minal, built in 1891, looks from a distance like one of the grandest stone cathedrals in town, with limestone towers and stained-glass windows that would incite most churches to the sin of envy — especially the stained-glass skylight in the vaulted ceiling, which runs most of the building's length, and the large circular windows at either end.

In addition to the soft light those windows provide, the lobby has a colorful ceramic tile floor and walls wainscotted in marble. It also contains a mule-driven trolley car used by the Louisville Railway Company from 1865 to 1901, which is said to be one of only two remaining in the country.

When it was opened, a writer described the $310,000 structure as "the finest station south of the Ohio River . . . which probably has no superior in the United States." General Pershing stopped there; so did presidents Franklin Roosevelt, Harry Truman and Dwight Eisenhower and presidential candidate Thomas Dewey. Train service ended in 1976. Union Station was restored in 1980, at a cost of $2 million, and today serves as the headquarters for TARC, the city bus company. It's open Monday through Friday during business hours; admission is free.

Conrad-Caldwell House Museum
1402 St. James Court • 636-5023

When it was built for tanner Theophilus Conrad in 1895, in the new development called St. James Court, it may have been the grandest house in Louisville and was known as Conrad's Castle or Conrad's Folly. When it was sold in 1940, it was one of the more amazing bargains in local real estate: This massive three-story limestone building, with more than 9,200 feet of usable space, went for $12,500 and was turned into a rooming house.

After another life as the Rose Anna Hughes

Home for retired Presbyterian women, the house was purchased in 1987 by the St. James Neighborhood Association, using proceeds from the annual St. James Art Show as the down payment. In 1992, it was restored to reflect what it would have looked like in 1907, when it was redecorated by its second owners, the family of William Caldwell, a successful millwright and mechanical engineer who started what is now Caldwell Tanks.

Few houses do a better job of recapturing late-Victorian opulence (and the exuberant side of the entrepreneurial spirit). The wood in the front rooms and entry hall alone make it worth a visit; the parlor is carved in the speckled amber of bird's eye maple, while the library is trimmed in exquisitely detailed red cherry. The distinctively patterned parquet floors are slightly different in each room, as are most of the features, from the dense, rectangular radiators to the domed niche underneath the grand stairway from the front hall. Fleurs de lis and other touches throughout testify to Conrad's pride in his French heritage; the scale of things testify to how far he had risen from humble beginnings.

The house is open for afternoon tours Sunday and Tuesday through Thursday; group and school tours are available by appointment at other times. The docents include the Caldwell's grandson, Gordon Caldwell. Admission is $3 for adults, $2.50 for people 60 and older and $1 for students.

Western Branch, Louisville Free Public Library
604 S. 10th St. • 574-1779

The Western Colored Branch of the Louisville Free Public Library, as it was originally called, opened in 1905 in rented quarters and moved into its present building in 1908.

Some sources call it the country's first public library open to members of all races, or the first below the Mason-Dixon line. It was certainly among the first, although libraries for African Americans, under several different institutional arrangements, were created around the same time or earlier in Memphis, Tennessee; Galveston, Texas; and Charlotte, North

Carolina. Louisville's Western branch had national significance because it housed an apprentice program in library science that was for many years the only training available to African-American librarians.

The branch library is one of the city's collection of Carnegie libraries (library buildings funded throughout the country by industrialist Andrew Carnegie). Its handsome, restrained architecture, a classicist version of Beaux-Arts design, now stands out all the more because so few surrounding buildings remain. It's open Monday through Saturday.

Whitehall
3110 Lexington Rd. • 897-2944

The most recently opened of Louisville's historic home museums was originally a modest place — a four-room brick house built around 1855. In 1910, it was transformed into a 15-room mansion in an antebellum style. It's been restored to resemble a proper Victorian home of its original era, using many of the paintings and furniture of its last owners, the Logan family. The two-acre, tri-level Florentine garden has also been renovated. It's open Monday through Friday, 10 AM to 2 PM; admission is $4 for adults, $3 for people 60 and older and $2 for children ages 6 through 12; children younger than 6 get in free.

The Little Loomhouse
328 Kenwood Hill Rd. • 367-4792

These three rustic cabins in the woods of Kenwood Hill — "board-and-batten summer houses, set down in the dignity of nature," as Frank Lloyd Wright approvingly described them in 1940 — have served as a South End cultural center for nearly a century. "Good Morning to You," later "Happy Birthday to You," was first sung in one of these cabins. They are most strongly associated with the late Lou Tate, famous for her work preserving methods and designs of hand-weaving that were threatened to be lost with the development of machine-manufactured textiles.

Eleanor Roosevelt visited the Loomhouse in the '40s. The story has it that as she entered

FYI
Unless otherwise noted, the area code for all phone numbers listed in this chapter is 502.

the oldest of the cabins, called Esta, her foot went through a loose floor board, which she obligingly autographed.

The Loomhouse continues Tate's work under the auspices of the Lou Tate Foundation.

It's open Tuesday through Thursday and by appointment. There's no charge to walk around the site; guided tours are $3, $5 is you care to weave.

Bowman Field
Taylorsville Rd. and Pee Wee Reese Blvd. • no phone

Louisville doesn't have much art deco or Art Moderne architecture, but there are few more appropriate places for the aerodynamic overtones of deco and Moderne than the city's first airfield, the buildings of which were constructed between 1929 and 1937.

The administration building looks like a domesticated Oz, its wings stair-stepping up from one story to two stories and then meeting the three-story central section. The exterior possesses such interesting details as the neon signs above the doorways and propeller-motif plaques accenting the cornice. The atrium is built on a monumental scale, with stylized metal friezes on the capitals of its humongous fluted pilasters. Some of the work was done by the WPA, although it followed the style set by the building's 1929 design.

In the 1920s, the field was a popular spot for plane-watching, an inexpensive family amusement. In 1927, 10,000 people came to see Charles Lindbergh and *The Spirit of St. Louis*, the plane he had flown across the Atlantic. Plane-watching remains a popular pastime from the back deck of Le Relais, a French restaurant in the terminal's east wing that ranks among the city's best and is decorated in a suitably deco style.

Kaden Tower
6100 Dutchmans Ln. • no phone

For years, this was one of the most reviled buildings in town, even though it was based on a Frank Lloyd Wright design adapted by Wright's son-in-law, William Wesley Peters. A pink skyscraper surrounded on three sides with a "solar screen" of white concrete lattice work, Kaden Tower has been called everything from "the doily building" to much worse

(ask a pilot who flies into nearby Bowman Field what the nickname for it is at the airstrip).

Wright sketched the building as a speculative design before his death in 1959. Lincoln Income Life Insurance Company chose it in 1965 when it commissioned the Taliesen firm, headed by Peters, to build a headquarters near Breckenridge Lane in St. Matthews.

According to Andy Blieden, whose family bought the building in 1986 with Jim Karp (hence the combined name Kaden), the building reflects Wright's fascination with things Oriental. It's supposed to resemble a Japanese lantern — an effect that's easier to see at night, when the building's lights are on and it illuminates the surrounding neighborhood. The original plan also included a Japanese-style garden (never built) on the grounds.

Kaden is also structurally unique. It was constructed with a central core, then cantilevered steel beams were laid across it and other floors were suspended from them. In a sense, it was built from the top down, rather than from the foundation up.

Kaden's $2 million renovation in 1986 and '87 brought out the building's qualities and revealed a groundswell of affection for it that no one had foreseen. It also brought a well-loved (now departed) restaurant, The Terrace, to the 15th floor, where a walkway wraps around three sides of the building. Amusingly enough, when the owners decided to renovate it, they considered replacing the much-mocked pink color with a shade of brownish tan closer to what Wright envisioned, but residents in the area protested that it be kept the original color.

Humana Building
500 W. Main St. • 580-1000

Driving in from the west on I-64, Louisville's most striking building — a pink granite skyscraper with a modified ziggurat at the top — appears against the black backdrop of the First National Tower like a balloon in a boardroom.

It's even more unusual when you look at it for a while. Louisville-based Humana Inc. decided in 1982 to make its new headquarters building a work of national importance that would also fit into downtown Louisville. It held a nationwide competition that included the likes of Cesar Pelli and Norman Foster.

Princeton, New Jersey-based architect Michael Graves won it with what the company believed was the one design of the group that could only be built on Louisville's Main Street: an L-shaped building clad in granite that managed to match scale with both the cast-iron store-fronts to its west and the more conventional skyscrapers to the east and south. Its free play of architectural allusion ranges over several thousand years of human history, but it still looks like no other building you've ever seen.

It opened to great publicity and not a little bit of controversy — people either loved or hated Graves' design. The New York Times' architectural critic Paul Goldberger said it was the first American building in years one could imagine people taking their children downtown to see.

It has an incredible richness of materials for a modern building: the polished granite in five colors, decorated in gold leaf; the creamy marble of the lobby; the bird's-eye maple and mahogany in the elevators; and a wealth of references, from Greek and Egyptian elements to a truss intended to reflect the bridges on the nearby Ohio and large slanting shapes rising from the 25th-floor terrace that echo the McAlpine Dam. The last two allusions usually have to be explained to the average person (as opposed to the conical interior lighting fixtures, which look like something Madonna might wear on stage).

Humana employees report that it's a nice place to work. Domestic touches such as chair rails give the offices a comfortable feeling; 17 of the floors have their own sun rooms for meetings and breaks. But Goldberger's prediction of it as an attraction hasn't entirely worked out. Except when there are festivals or other events on Main Street, neither of its public spaces, the outdoor loggia or the lobby, has become the sort of magnet for people that Graves and Humana originally envisioned. Tours of the building are by appointment only.

Nonetheless, the Humana Building is a stop on any tour of the city, if only to look at it

from the steps of the Kentucky Center for the Arts across the street. You can see some of its influence in the major skyscrapers that have been built downtown since, such as the Providian Building. And for all of the fatuous trendiness of much post-modern architecture (how exactly is a 27-story, $60 million building "playful"?), Humana manages to be simultaneously unusual, classical and imaginative. It may yet fulfill the late Humana founder Wendell Cherry's prediction that, in time, it will be one of the country's 10 or 20 most important buildings.

Neighborhoods

Old Louisville

The city's preservation movement began in Old Louisville — indeed, you might say it began with the name Old Louisville, which didn't exist before 1961. Some sticklers started calling downtown Older Louisville, since the city existed for more than three-quarters of a century before any large-scale development went into what was first called the Southern Extension.

The neighborhood has been largely preserved, especially south of Oak Street. Along Third and Fourth streets, it offers something close to a directory of high-end architectural styles, from the Italianate houses built in the 1850s through the 1870s, to Second Empire (French design at a time when Paris was synonymous with urban style) to the rough, massive forms of the Richardsonian Romanesque. And unlike many 19th-century residential areas, the neighborhood was built with a good deal of open space, not only in Central Park and the grassy courts of St. James and Belgravia but also in the way houses are generously set back from the curb.

In the 1830s, the neighborhood was countryside and woods, with a few houses that qualified as country residences. Oakland Race

Course, site of a famous match race between Kentucky-bred Gray Eagle and Louisiana-bred Wagner, was near what's now Ormsby Avenue and Seventh Street Road. Central Park was once owned by the duPont family, who ran it as a profitable amusement park. They later donated the land for part of the Southern Exposition site and eventually sold it to the city.

While the first streetcars and a growing population caused the city to move south of Broadway in the 1860s, full-scale development was spurred by an American version of London's Crystal Palace, the Southern Exposition of 1883, which showcased the technical and industrial advances of the age. Opened by President Chester A. Arthur, occupying 45 acres south of what's now Central Park, the exposition attracted 700,000 spectators in its first months and several million people in the four years it was open. Among its novelties: 4,600 of Thomas Edison's newly invented incandescent bulbs and an electric railroad circling Central Park.

The grandest, most beautiful part of Old Louisville is St. James Court (see the Conrad-Caldwell House, above). It was developed on the site of the Southern Exposition's main building and catered to a taste for things English. Lots languished until the company was renamed the Victoria Land Company and the neighborhood was designed in a fashion that echoed British styles, from the name (after the Court of St. James) to the way the development was arranged, with the houses around a center strip of lawn and trees, decorated with statuary, street lamps and a fountain left over from the exposition. It soon became the most fashionable address in the city and remains one of them almost 100 years later, now that towering trees have grown from the spindly trunks you see in early photographs (giving the neighborhood an encouragingly strong resemblance to the scalped look of modern-day suburban developments).

Less fashionable but equally historical is the Limerick neighborhood to Old Louisville's northwest, bounded roughly by Fifth Street on the east, 10th to the west, Kentucky on the north and Oak on the south. It was occupied by Irish, many of whom worked in the nearby L&N railroad yards and attended St. Louis

Bertrand Church, and by African Americans, who lived along the alleys behind the Irish. The area included two important educational institutions for blacks: Central Colored School at Sixth and Kentucky streets and Simmons University (see above).

While much of the neighborhood consists of shotguns and other modest dwellings, the blocks between Fifth, Seventh, Breckinridge and Oak streets had more substantial homes, similar to Old Louisville's mansions, that were occupied by "lace curtain" Irish and other middle class folk.

The Old Louisville Information Center, 635-5244, at the south end of Central Park, has a brochure of walking tours of Old Louisville and Limerick and other information about the neighborhood. It's open Monday through Thursday.

Cherokee Triangle

"The Highlands" is a vague, amorphous and ubiquitous term that incorporates areas developed over 80 years or more in the corridor on both sides of Baxter Avenue and Bardstown Road. Historians cite the area as a looking glass into the way that America's suburbs developed in the years following the Civil War.

The Highlands was opened up by James Henning and Joshua Speed's Highland Addition, just southeast of Cave Hill in 1870. Henning and Speed were real estate speculators and developers and well-connected members of the Louisville elite. (Speed was the friend of Lincoln we mentioned earlier when discussing Farmington.) At that time, it represented the farthest extent of development along Bardstown Road: The mule-drawn street cars came to Cave Hill and turned around there. Story has it that the housewives of the area protested the idea of trolley tracks going down Cherokee Road by taking chairs and knitting into the road when trolley tracks were going to be laid; the route was changed to Bardstown Road.

Among Highlands neighborhoods, the Cherokee Triangle (its broad outlines lying between Bardstown Road and Cherokee Park from the head of Broadway to Eastern Parkway) makes the most convincing case for the utopian dreams of suburban planners. It is the city's most serious rival to Old Louisville as a place of grand Victorian homes (although the scale is slightly more modest). A walk down Cherokee Road and Cherokee Parkway is one of the city's most salutary strolls. The substantial Gothic, Italianate, Queen Anne and Richardsonian Romanesque houses along the tree-lined streets present such a confident sense of ostentation that their turrets, scrolls and gingerbread shingling seem "almost intoxicating," as a Triangle resident once put it.

The neighborhood was envisioned as a pastoral retreat, and despite the suburban sprawl that has overtaken it, the Triangle continues to have a remarkable peacefulness. Its character is largely dominated by Cherokee Park, second-largest of the city's parks designed by Frederick Law Olmsted (after the city purchased the park property in 1891, land prices in the neighborhood doubled or tripled). The city's best architects did some of their finest work in the area, in styles that range from Victorian Gothic to the prairie houses influenced by Frank Lloyd Wright. It's the profusion of fine homes in such a variety of styles and building materials, rather than three or four notable addresses, that creates the area's unique character. In other words, come on down and bring your walking shoes.

While the area went through a typical decline after World War II, it was almost as early as Old Louisville in developing a strong neighborhood association and was named one of the city's first three preservation districts in 1975.

Butchertown

The name says it all. This working-class neighborhood grew up around the Bourbon and Union Stock Yards east of downtown populated by butchers, tanners, soap makers and others who made use of the animals brought to market, as well as seed companies and other merchants who sold to farmers. It was located along Beargrass Creek, which was used as an early sewer to carry offal into the Ohio (an amateur historian told *The Courier-Journal* that soap and candle makers could scoop fat off the banks of the creek). Ohio Street was at one point known as Pork House

Alley for the businesses along it; Story Avenue was called Butcher Baron Road for the larger homes built by successful meat packers. There was a large German population (one reason why Butchertown used to be the location of the local Oktoberfest).

The neighborhood is marked by a number of small shotguns and other worker houses that are packed in tightly along the streets; there is little of the sense of space of Old Louisville, The Highlands or even Portland. Larger homes and industrial sites are mingled in with the shotguns; the area remains a mix of industrial and residential uses today.

At the center of the neighborhood are two key institutions: St. Joseph's Catholic Church, 1406 E. Washington Street, which sends its pair of Gothic towers 175 feet into the air (the second-most famous twin spires in the community); and Oertel's Brewery, 1332 Story Avenue, one of the city's "big three" brewers and a major employer in the neighborhood until it closed in 1967. There's also the well-regarded Hadley Pottery Company, 1570 Story Avenue, which was a major spur to the renovation of the neighborhood in the 1960s and early '70s when Butchertown was one of the first places where the emergent baby boomers could afford to buy their own homes (an era that also established the Butchertown Pub, 1335 Story Avenue, as one of the city's main nightspots).

Portland

Portland, established in 1814 at the point where the Ohio makes its bend south, was once a city; indeed, it considered itself a rival to Louisville as the principal city at the Falls. Many of the first settlers were French immigrants, some of them probably from the nearby French settlement on Shippingport Island (now vacant and barred to visitors); they were later joined by German and Irish.

The steamboat trade was its making, especially in the years before the Louisville-Portland Canal was built, when ships had to unload their passengers and cargo and move them overland around the Falls. Even after the canal was built, many boats were too large to fit through until after it was widened in 1865. Portland Avenue, which travels through the

Photo: Dan Dry and Associates

The lightness and strength of cast iron allowed buildings to have larger windows than stone or brick structures.

heart of the neighborhood, is the old Portland Turnpike, the portage road to Louisville; the other main drag, Northwestern Parkway, is part of the parkway system designed by Frederick Law Olmsted. The commercial street that faced the wharf, Water Street, was taken away when the flood wall on the Ohio was built.

It is very much a working-class neighborhood, historically and today, with the shotgun house as the predominant architectural type. However, there are many distinctive larger town houses in Italianate and Steamboat Gothic styles, especially on Rudd Avenue by the flood wall (which also includes a set of mooring rings from the old wharf in the yard of the historic Our Lady Church) and along Northwestern Parkway (also the site of one of the city's collection of Carnegie libraries).

The U.S. Marine Hospital, 2215 Portland Avenue, now used as a family-care center and not open to the public, is a striking three-story, H-shaped Greek Revival structure built be-tween 1847 and 1851. It was one of seven hospitals built for the benefit of sick boatmen and other workers on the inland waterways, and it's believed to be the only such hospital still standing. The Portland Museum (see below) gives an excellent overview of Portland's distinctive history.

Corydon, Indiana

This small town 20 miles west of Louisville has an unusual concentration of historic buildings because of its importance in Hoosier history. The city was founded in 1808; in 1813 it became the territorial capital; and in 1816 it became the state capital, which it remained until the seat of government was moved to Indianapolis in 1825.

The capitol building, which still stands on North Capitol Avenue, is another one of those sites that is most impressive for its small size in relationship to its historical importance. The two-story structure, made out of rough blue limestone quarried locally, is only 40 feet square (with walls 2 feet thick or more). The House of Representatives had the downstairs, the Senate and Supreme Court the up.

Corydon's historic buildings also include a Federal-style brick house dating to 1817, which was the headquarters of Indiana governor William Hendricks, at 202 E. Walnut Street; the Posey House, 225 Oak Street, a huge U-shaped brick house also built in 1817, which is now operated as a museum by the Daughters of the American Revolution; and a number of other historical buildings that include cast-iron storefronts, a Carnegie library and other structures. On the hill overlooking the town is the site of the Battle of Corydon, the only Civil War battle to take place in Indiana, fought between Corydon's Home Guard and Gen. John Hunt Morgan's Confederate troops.

Corydon and its vicinity also include a number of attractions unrelated to its constitutional history: There's a scenic railroad that dates back to 1883; a number of shops popular for antiques; the Zimmerman Art Glass Company, 395 Valley Road; and Needmore Buffalo Farm in nearby Elizabeth (see a full listing in Kidstuff). There are also several nearby caves, including Marengo Cave (near Marengo, of course); Wyandotte Cave in Leavenworth, which includes some of the largest rooms and interior mountains of any United States caves; and Squire Boone Caverns, 10 miles south of Corydon off S.R. 135, site of Daniel Boone's brother Squire's gristmill (still standing) and Squire Boone's final resting place, inside the cave that bears his name.

For more information about Corydon, call the Harrison County Chamber of Commerce at (812) 738-2137.

Churches and Synagogues

Quinn Chapel African Methodist Episcopal Church
912 W. Chestnut St. • 583-0324

Quinn Chapel's congregation has been at the forefront of the civil rights struggle from its founding in 1838. There is a story that the Rev. (later Bishop) Paul Quinn stood on the Indiana side of the Ohio, or perhaps Corn Island, and preached to African Americans on the Kentucky side. Quinn was also arrested for preaching in Louisville. But his message of equality — "From one blood God made all nations" — inspired free Negroes to found the city's oldest A.M.E. congregation in a room above a public stable.

The church he inspired was known as "the abolitionists' church." In the late 1840s it opened the first school for black children in Louisville; in 1847 it was the first Negro congregation to use a musical instrument (a violin) in a worship service.

Civil rights protesters marched from the church in every era — in 1870 to desegregate public transportation, in 1961 for open public accommodations and in 1967 in favor of the open housing ordinance (see History). In 1993, Jesse Jackson came to the sanctuary and decried Marge Schott's treatment of black players on the Cincinnati Reds.

After outgrowing a series of locations, the church moved in 1910 into the former Chestnut Street Baptist Church, a Gothic Revival building designed by Henry Wolters, a graduate of the Ecole des Beaux-Arts in Paris and one of the engineers of the Suez Canal.

Another historic church building is one block to the east, Brown Memorial Christian Methodist Episcopal Church, 809 W. Chestnut Street, which is housed in the last building known to have been designed by the prominent local architect Gideon Shryock.

Cathedral of the Assumption
443 S. Fifth St. • 582-2971

The seat of the Louisville Archdiocese (which extends to Nashville) is a Gothic Revival building whose vaulted ceiling, its ribs painted with gold stars on a blue field, inspires the awe to which such cathedrals aspire.

The Cathedral is the fourth-oldest public building in the city and the country's third-oldest cathedral in continuous use. When the spire reached its present height of 287 feet in the late 19th century, it was the tallest in North America.

Dorothy Day and Babe Ruth, Thomas Merton and Al Smith worshipped here. It contains the tomb of Benedict Joseph Flaget, the first Bishop of the West, who transferred the nation's first inland diocese from Bardstown to Louisville in 1841. (He died in 1850, while the Cathedral was under construction.) And its priests have included John Lancaster Spalding, founder of Catholic University of America and an essayist known as "the Catholic Emerson."

The Cathedral, renovated in 1994 at a cost of $9 million, is now the focus of an interfaith spiritual center which plans to open an ecumenical Museum of Faith.

St. Martin of Tours
629 S. Shelby St. • 582-2827

In 1855 a Know-Nothing mob almost destroyed this then-new church in the "Bloody Monday" riot. The parish for German immigrants was only saved when Mayor John Barbee and George Prentice — the journalist whose editorials had helped incite Nativist feelings — intervened.

Today it's among the most impressive Gothic structures in town. It's not as grand as the Cathedral, but sufficiently massive to create what one local writer calls "a church-as-fortress feeling," with stained-glass windows made by the Royal Bavarian Art Institute and a massive pipe organ. It also contains the skeletons of two early-Christian-era martyrs, St. Magnus and St. Bonosa.

The church won an award from the Louisville Preservation Alliance in 1991 for its renovation.

Keneseth Israel Congregation
2351 Taylorsville Rd. • 459-2780

This synagogue, built in 1971, is modernistically plain but pleasing — the sanctuary has a sweeping shape that resembles a baseball park. But the round wall that faces Taylorsville Road contains one of the city's most impressive pieces of religious art: Twelve striking trapezoidal stained glass windows that symbolize the major Jewish holidays. Between the windows, large crevices reflect outdoor light to give the impression of candle flames on the menorah, the traditional Jewish candleholder. At night they're illuminated from the inside.

The windows were designed by artist William Fischer, a member of the congregation, to symbolize the major Jewish holidays. Fischer has been called Louisville's Marc Chagall, in reference to Chagall's famous windows at the Hadassah Hospital in Jerusalem.

Keneseth Israel, the city's largest Orthodox congregation, was founded in 1926 but originated in a pair of local congregations established in 1877 and 1887.

St. Michael the Archangel Orthodox Church
3026 Hikes Ln. • 454-3378

A tour of St Michael's sanctuary is a standard part of this church's wonderful annual festival, and no wonder: Although the church was built in 1972, it is painted in the classical Byzantine style, with a profusion of icons (with traditional gold leaf highlights) representing Christ, the apostles, the evangelists and saints of particular relevance to the congregation, which includes members of Syrian, Lebanese, Jordanian, Egyptian, Palestinian, Greek, Romanian, Serbian, Russian, Armenian, Ukrainian, Indian and Ethiopian descent. There are also magnificently ornate gold-plated chandeliers.

To an outsider, it's an extravagance of art that catches the eye like few other things. But to the faithful, it is, in the words of Father David Alexander Atty, "the heavens come down to earth — not just another auditorium." It's also a carefully organized expression of what the church holds important.

INSIDERS' TIP

Can Paris match this? Louisville has more aesthetically pleasing manhole covers than anywhere else in the world, according to the author of an MIT Press book on the subject. Many of the best examples are preserved on the south side of the 700 block of West Main Street, across from the Louisville Science Center.

The annual fall ethnic fair is one of the city's most enjoyable events. The fair has music, dancing and displays, and the homemade food is amazing. (See our Annual Events and Festivals chapter.)

St. Gabriel Catholic Church
5505 Bardstown Rd. • 239-5481

Few sanctuaries are more brightly lit than this new church, built in 1994 in Fern Creek. It uses many clear-glass windows, including one with an eye-level view of Bardstown Road traffic that has prompted debate about whether it's too similar to the storefronts nearby or represents a commitment to connect with the community. But the most impressive sight is a three-quarter circle stained glass window which frames steel crosses inside and out (it actually resembles a question mark). Its somewhat abstract, spiralling imagery is as profuse in its way as the iconostasis at St. Michael. Its shape can be read several ways: as symbolic of the incompleteness of earthly attempts to create the Kingdom of God, or as an invitation to complete the shape (and the mystery it represents) in our own lives.

Church of the Epiphany
914 Old Harrods Creek Rd. • 245-9733

The modernism and openness heralded by Vatican II are expressed with unusual directness in this church.

Epiphany sits on a 19-acre site of woods, meadows and gardens between Anchorage and Middletown. It is essentially an irregular hexagonal roof with glass walls. There are no permanent fixtures. Flexible platforms can be arranged at different heights, seats in various configurations; worshipers may even face in a different direction one Sunday than they did the previous week. When weather allows, the walls slide back and the congregation sits virtually outside.

St. James Catholic Church
Bardstown Rd. and Edenside Ave.
• 451-1420

We included this church built in 1912 and 1913 for the simplest of reasons — we love the way it looks.

It's built in a beautifully eclectic style: Church literature tentatively describes it as being "Spanish Renaissance, with Roman and Byzantine lines." The orange-yellow glazed brick from which it's made is one of the most beautiful building materials ever invented, and it's set off by regular courses of red brick, by buff and yellow enameled terra cotta and the red tile roofs. The way it's canted onto an otherwise commercial block of Bardstown Road, its belfry tower rising against the mass of the church — it's a lovely thing to contemplate no matter what your religious affiliation.

Inside is a sight we like to think might have struck the young F. Scott Fitzgerald, when he was stationed here at Camp Taylor and squiring around girls from the Cherokee Triangle, and influenced him to create one of the primary symbols in *The Great Gatsby*: The center of the dome contains the single blue Eye of God, a gold burst radiating from it.

Oddities

Charles Heigold House Facade
Thruston Park, River Rd. • no phone

Stonemason Charles Heigold carved out his patriotic feelings toward the United States and Louisville in grand, exuberant fashion right on the facade of his house: "ALL HAIL THE CITY OF LOUISVILLE!" and "THE UNION FOREVER, ALL HAIL TO THIS UNION, LET US NEVER DESOLVE (sic) IT." Next to this outpouring, our enthusiastic mayor Jerry Abramson sounds like Eeyore.

The facade stands by itself in a small park on River Road, one of the few things you'll ever see that could be described as a monument to James Buchanan, the bachelor president who preceded Lincoln and who was in the White House when Heigold took chisel to limestone ("HAIL TO BUCHANAN, NOW AND FOREVER!").

But it isn't silly; it's moving. A German immigrant, Heigold turned his house into a billboard for democracy in the face of the anti-

---

FYI

Unless otherwise noted, the area code for all phone numbers listed in this chapter is 502.

immigrant, anti-Catholic Know-Nothings and at a time when the nation was preparing to dissolve itself over slavery.

When Marion Street, on which the house originally stood, was taken for the city landfill, Mayor Charles Farnsley had the facade saved and moved to Thruston Park, where it remains today (and even appeared in one of the locally famous "There are banks . . . and there is Liberty" commercials).

Gus Ballard's Yard and Shed
The alley behind the 1000 block of Mulberry St. • no phone

In certain circles, this qualifies as a must-see: Ballard, a retiree from American-Standard (a plumbing supplies manufacturer), has decorated the back of his Schnitzelburg house and the shed behind it with an extraordinary variety of bright, mostly plastic, cast-off material: his collection of 2,000 beer caps; carpet samples; a blue rocking horse; hubcaps; scuba flippers; red plastic cups, strung eight or so together; and little colored plastic bowling pins. The main aesthetic is profusion; it makes such memorable jumbles of junk as Watts Tower in Los Angeles look like art school projects.

The Quadrangle
(Jefferson Quartermaster Depot)
10th Street, Jeffersonville, Ind. • no phone

Although it's not up everyone's alley, this isn't very odd; in fact it's considered to be one of the finest pieces of industrial architecture of its time and one of the only two quadrangular military depots still in existence. It's a complex of brick warehouses, the size of four city blocks, built by Quartermaster Gen. Montgomery Meigs in 1874. The arches around the perimeter create a pleasingly regular arcade effect. Inside the square are several buildings from the same era; the grounds were designed by Frederick Law Olmsted, the great landscape architect who designed Louisville's parks. Used through the Korean War and then deactivated, it has most recently been a shopping and industrial complex. A fire in 1992 destroyed its northeastern corner.

Vernon Lanes
1575 Story Ave. • 584-8460

This is what you call adaptive reuse: an 1880s Italianate house in Butchertown turned into a bowling alley. And it has its own hold on history: It is supposed to be the third-oldest bowling alley in the country, operating since 1918. It's open seven days a week.

Portland Cemetery
Bank St. between 18th and 37th Sts.
• no phone

One of the loneliest graves you'll ever see is in this historic cemetery, which includes headstones written in French and German. But its most unusual gravestone has only Chinese characters — no European language of any kind. A University of Louisville professor tentatively translated one of the characters as "terraced mountain," the designation for Taishan district in Guangdong (Canton) province, one of three districts from which most of the first Chinese-Americans came.

Informed speculation has it that the man buried there was a sailor working on the Ohio, and that the inscription on the stone was there on his grave to tell its spirit that Taishan, not Louisville, was its proper home. Also buried in the cemetery is Mary Miller, the country's first female riverboat pilot.

Organizations

Portland Museum
2308 Portland Ave. • 776-7678

This well-designed museum does an excellent job of communicating what the working river was like in the 19th century. Much of the story is told by animated mechanical figures that include Jim Porter, the 7-foot 9-inch "Kentucky Giant"; Mary Miller, the first female riverboat pilot licensed in the United States; naturalist John James Audubon; and Increase Allen Lapham, a 16-year-old boy who helped survey the Portland Canal. A three-dimensional topographic map of the Ohio River at low ebb and a diorama showing the construction of the Portland Canal explain these important facts about the city's history as well as anything you can consult. In a video room you can watch newsreel footage of the 1937 flood.

The historic Skene House, which forms part of the museum, is in the process of being renovated; the museum has also purchased the

Squire Earick House on 34th Street at Rudd Avenue, believed to be the oldest house in Portland. Admission for the museum is $3 for adults; $2.50 for students, senior citizens and armed services personnel; and free for children younger than 5. (Wednesday is Donation Day; there is no admission that day.) Group rates are also available. It's open Tuesday through Friday.

The Filson Club
1310 S. Third St. • 635-5083

The Filson Club, founded in 1884 as the city's first historical society, is one entity that could fit into nearly any category in this chapter, or this book for that matter.

The club is located in one of Old Louisville's noteworthy houses, the Beaux-Arts Ferguson Mansion, which one architectural historian said would not look out of place in Baron Haussman's Paris. It maintains a museum in a back carriage house that contains such curiosities as a "D. Boone Kill a Bar" tree trunk; the gun of 7-foot-9 Jim Porter, which gives a new meaning to the term Kentucky long rifle; a fire engine that dates from before the Civil War; one of the few surviving copper stills (most were destroyed when they were discovered); and a large doll house that is a magnet for children. The club hosts a number of lectures and special events and publishes a scholarly journal.

But its most important function is as the repository of a vast library with two specialties: Louisville and Kentucky history and genealogy. It is the place to go to discover if you're related to Patrick Henry, revolutionary firebrand, or John Henry, steel-drivin' man; to try to reconstruct which maniac it was who built that turret onto the home you now own; to read family histories, 19th-century Louisville newspapers or correspondence from your cousin Herbie about his researches into the family tree, among a multitude of rare and informative documents and books contained in its collections.

It is open Monday through Friday and Saturday mornings. Museum admission is free; nonmembers pay $3 to use the library.

Louisville Landmarks Commission
600 W. Main St. • 574-4140

Created in 1973, the city's preservation office exists as an enforcement agency, regulating any exterior changes to buildings or other features of the city's historic districts and acting as the city's counsel on preservation-related matters and a clearinghouse of information for architects, homeowners, investors and business people. It identifies preservation districts, writes nominations to the National Register of Historic Places and advises how new construction might fit into a historic district. (Other than that, it doesn't do much.)

Landmarks has a hard-working, well-informed staff with a sophisticated sense of preservation. It held a 1992 conference called "Resources of the Recent Past" to begin the consideration of which more modern buildings might be worth preserving. Appropriately enough, it was held at Kaden Tower, with an evening's entertainment at Vernon Lanes.

Jefferson County Historic Preservation and Archives
810 Barret Ave. • 574-5761

This is the county government's equivalent of the city's Landmarks Commission, although it's less powerful because fewer properties in Jefferson County outside the city have been legally designated as landmarks (at this writing, only 15). The office tracks and monitors historical properties in the county, reviewing subdivisions, zoning changes and other actions that might affect them; surveys and inventories historic sites; and writes nominations to the National Register of Historic Places. It also houses the county archives and has published an inventory book, *Historic Jefferson County*, with pictures and brief descriptions of more than 250 sites. The office is open Monday though Friday.

Historic Landmarks Foundation of Indiana, Southern Regional Office
113 W. Chestnut St., Jeffersonville • (812) 284-4534

This statewide private, nonprofit group is the best clearinghouse for preservation information on the northern side of the Ohio. The Jeffersonville office serves 24 counties in Southern Indiana. It gives financial and technical advice to local preservation groups and runs the usual gamut of preservation functions: site visits, National Register nominations and educating the public on preservation issues.

It's especially involved in planning and preservation issues along the Ohio River corridor.

The office is open Monday through Friday.

Louisville Historical League
Peterson-Dumesnil House
301 S. Peterson Ave. • no phone

This all-volunteer historical society exists to promote awareness of local history and to advocate historic preservation. It has produced such valuable resources as Kenny Karem's *Discover Louisville*, slide presentations on Crescent Hill and the 1937 flood, even a midnight vaudeville show in the since-destroyed Savoy Theatre. It publishes a newsletter, primarily focusing on various historic sites in the area. It offers its members monthly tours of the sites it features in its newsletters, many of them not accessible to the general public, or more obscure than the well-publicized historic sites. Tours have included The Water Tower, the Louisville Water Company's filtration plant and reservoir, the Farnsley-Moremen House, the Falls Interpretive Center and the old Louisville Medical College.

Sons of the American Revolution
National Headquarters
1000 S. Fourth St. • 589-1776

This organization for descendants of Revolutionary War soldiers has its national headquarters in Louisville. It contains relics such as a tattered flag from the War of 1812, a clangable replica of the Liberty Bell and muskets from the Revolution. There's also a large genealogical library. It's open Monday through Friday.

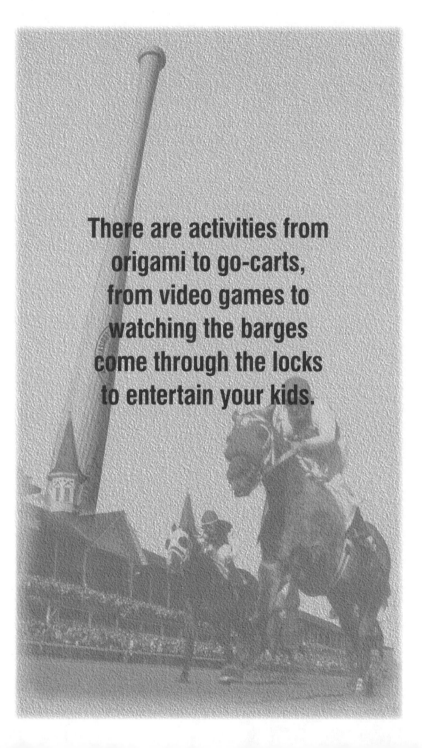

There are activities from origami to go-carts, from video games to watching the barges come through the locks to entertain your kids.

Kidstuff

Louisville is a city that works well for kids. The city's main attractions — the park system, the Redbirds games, Kentucky Kingdom, the Falls Interpretive Center, the Louisville Zoo, the Louisville Slugger Museum (see Attractions) even the track — make splendid outings for children from the preschool years on up. The city's steady diet of festivals (see the Festivals and Annual Events chapter) means that a young person could go through an entire year with some design or another painted on his or her cheek.

Indeed, if you wanted to diversify Louisville's menu of things to do, you might be inclined to start by adding more activities NOT suitable for young children — especially ones aimed at teenagers, who occupy themselves in such time-tested ways as hanging out in a shopping center parking lot after hours or loping up and down Bardstown Road. (Teens — and their parents — should know that there's a curfew: Children under 18 are supposed to be home by 11 PM Sunday through Thursday, 1 AM Friday and Saturday, with exceptions for teens returning from work or religious and school activities. Parents of violators can be fined up to $500; published reports suggest that it's been spottily enforced and widely ignored.)

There's an excellent children's theater company in Stage One: The Louisville Children's Theater (for more information, see The Arts chapter), and several other companies also offer theater or arts for young people. A clutch of commercial playgrounds have opened in the past year, offering tunnels, tubes, pits of balls and the company of scores of screeching peers. There are activities from origami to go-carts, from video games to watching the barges come through the locks.

And of course, like any major city, Louisville has the inevitable accompaniments of American childhood: Chuck E. Cheese's Pizza, 5745 Preston Highway, 966-2550, and four Toys 'R' Us stores (three in Louisville and one in Clarksville's River Falls Mall). There's also a Disney Store, 426-7922, in Oxmoor Mall for all your mouseware needs and a Warner Bros. Studio Store in the same center, 429-6525.

Here are other possibilities for children's activities you may not be familiar with.

Animals

Henry's Ark
7801 Rose Island Rd., Prospect • 228-0746

This is strange enough to appeal to anyone: You're going down a twisty rural road in the far eastern part of Jefferson County, past stables and horse crossing signs, when just beyond a small Baptist church you see a pair of zebras grazing.

This personal menagerie, free and open to the public, contains a host of exotic animals from several continents: American bison; llamas; dromedary (one hump) and Bactrian (two humps) camels; water buffalo; peacocks, Guinea fowl and a pair of rheas, a South American bird similar to the ostrich; and Scottish Highlander cattle, an endangered, shaggy species with blond forelocks tumbling into their eyes.

There are also animals suitable for petting — fainting goats, miniature zebus and such. You're allowed to pet and feed the animals (no junk food), but signs remind you they may butt or bite. Children must be accompanied by an adult.

Owner Henry Wallace is an exotic creature himself — in his younger days a raffish *Life* correspondent in Cuba, later the only person writing letters to the editor from wealthy Prospect to consistently criticize *The Courier-Journal* for taking an insufficiently *leftist* stance.

To get there, turn onto Rose Island Road from U.S. Highway 42 in Prospect. The animals begin to be visible past the third turn in the road. Admission is free (although donations are encouraged).

Huber Orchard and Winery
19816 Huber Rd., Borden, Ind.
• (812) 923-9463
Joe Huber Family Farm, Orchard and Restaurant
2421 Scottsville Rd., Starlight, Ind.
• (812) 923-5255

These adjoining operations, run by several members of the same family, have a number of features kids love. The Huber Orchard has a nice petting zoo with miniature donkeys and horses, llamas, white-tailed deer, potbellied pigs, calves, goats, sheep, peacocks, pheasants and a number of breeds of rabbit. Admission is charged ($2.50 a person; groups of 10 or more, $2 each; pony rides, $3). Joe Huber's farm has a farm-style playground with bales of hay, miniature pedal-driven tractors and a barn with a slide; it's free to restaurant and farm market patrons. There's also a duck pond. Both places are great for a local fall ritual: picking your own pumpkin out in the field (there are also U-pick strawberries and apples during the appropriate seasons). The orchard also has cut-it-yourself Christmas trees.

To get there from Louisville, take I-64 west across the Sherman Minton Bridge. Take I-265 east to State Street. Turn right, go 2.5 miles to Scottsville Road; turn right and go 7 miles. (Don't worry about the different town names — it's a local distinction you can safely ignore. The two operations are right next to each other.)

Iroquois Riding Stable
Southwest corner of Iroquois Park, 5216 New Cut Rd. • 363-9159

In addition to the 24 horses this stable has for riding lessons (for ages 8 and older), there are a number of 37-inch-high ponies. Parents can lead their children younger than 8 around the barn grounds and the small arena while they ride. The barn also houses goats, rabbits, chickens and cats. It's open year round. Horseback rides are $8 for a half-hour, $10 for 50 minutes, $12 for an hour, $18 for an hour-and-a-half; pony rides are $5 per half-hour.

Lessons are $25 an hour.

FYI
Unless otherwise noted, the area code for all phone numbers listed in this chapter is 502.

McNeely Park Riding Stables
6711 Mt. Washington Rd. • 231-9011

This popular fishing lake also has a 17-horse stable and lead-line pony rides. It offers week-long day camps for those 8 and older that cover most equine matters this side of reading the Racing Form: grooming, getting the horse out of the stall, the different colors and breeds, as well as a daily trail ride. Horseback rides are $10 for a 50-minute ride, $15 for an hour and 15 minutes. It's open from March through the late fall.

Louisville Zoological Gardens
1100 Trevillian Way
• 459-2181

It's hard to distinguish the parts of the Louisville Zoo that are especially for kids from the rest of it. Few places in the city are more magnetic for children, whether they're spending a day with the monkeys and elephants or attending the World's Largest Halloween Party, Thursday through Sunday of the last two weekends in October, where kids go trick-or-treating along the zoo's path and a train ride leads you past a headless horseman who rides headlong at the coach.

The zoo also has a number of special programs for children: Two by Twos, a sort of introduction to public life for two-year-olds and their parents; Zooper Kids, a variety of educational programs held throughout the year; and Safari Day Camp, a week-long program during the summer for children age 5 through high school. There's also Night Safari, a program for folks of any age, in which groups of 20 or more can actually spend the night at the zoo, and the daily elephant aerobics and training sessions for the seals.

Admission is $7 for adults, $4.50 for children ages 3 to 11, $5.50 for seniors 60 years and over. A family membership is $49; for $88 you can get a dual membership with the Louisville Science Center. (See Attractions for more information on the Zoo.)

Needmore Buffalo Farm
4100 Buffalo Ln. S.E., Elizabeth, Ind.
• (812) 968-3473, (800) 752-4766

All buffalo, all the time. The Stewart family raises American bison for meat and breeding stock on this 500-acre farm near Corydon. And like some more capitalistic version of the Plains Indians, they have figured out a way to make every bit of the buffalo pay. They run a restaurant with buffalo burgers, buffalo chili and buffalo barbecue. They skin the carcasses to make buffalo robes, bleach the skulls to serve as decorations in that popular Southwestern vein and sell them both in their adjoining Trading Post. They even sweep up the loose buffalo hair and weave it into yarn. (They also run a bed and breakfast on the farm.)

None of this resourcefulness may interest your kids, although it's pretty darn interesting. But on Saturdays and Sundays, the Stewarts offer a 45-minute tour of the farm to show you the 140 head they own of the animal that once dominated the American landscape. (Other days, tours are available by reservation only.) Admission to the farm is free, but a fee is charged for the tour. ($4 for adults, $3 for children 12 and younger.) The farm hosts a fall festival called Rebirth of the Buffalo the second weekend in October, which includes a rodeo, re-enactors (both Native American and Civil War soldiers) setting up villages, displays of antique engines and tractors, apple butter making and other events.

To get there from Louisville, take I-64 west to Exit 113, turn left and drive 3 miles to Ind. 62; turn right, go 3 miles to New Middletown Road; turn left and follow signs to the farm.

The Arts

J.B. Speed Art Museum
2035 S. Third St. • 636-2893

The Speed Museum is the serious face of visual art in Louisville — where the special event is the Ingres exhibit, not an appearance by Lyle the Crocodile; where the main degree of interactivity for children comes from parents and teachers saying, "Remember, don't touch that."

But the museum actually holds a number of items that fascinate young people — a suit of armor; a room from a Tudor manor house that makes you feel as if you're entering a drawing room to plot the return of Bonnie Prince Charlie (and which is supposed to contain a secret panel in one of the walls). A Native American exhibit contains pipes, a rare intact warrior's costume, beaded moccasins and leggings and a marvelous full-length feather headdress. And the one truly interactive exhibit in the place is Vito Acconcini's "The People's Wall," an installation with cutout spaces and mirrors inside them, places for both children and adults to crawl through or sit in. Kids take to it like there's a burger joint next door.

The Speed offers family tours at 11 AM Saturday. They usually follow a theme: "What's My Line?" looked at works of art featuring people at their jobs; "Creepy Crawlies and Scary Monsters" was a Halloween program.

Admission is free.

Stage One: The Louisville Children's Theater
425 W. Market St. • 589-5946, tickets 584-7777, (800)775-7777

The city's children's theater is an especially well-run and adventurous one, from its Participation Plays for younger children at Louisville Gardens to its stage shows at the Kentucky Center for the Arts. The company mixes young actors from the community with professionals and has developed quite a number

---

INSIDERS' TIP

It's hard to go wrong taking the kids to a Louisville park, but Joe Creason Park is a special treasure — there's just enough real wilderness to give kids a taste of what it's like to hike in the woods, with honest-to-goodness birds and animals, without tiring out a child's legs (or dad's shoulders). The playground reigns supreme, and it has one of the city's best sledding hills.

Kids can become a human piston engine at the Louisville Science Center.

of its own plays in addition to such classics as *The Diary of Anne Frank* and *Cinderella*. (It recently sent its musical version of *The Great Gilly Hopkins* to New York.) For more information, see The Arts.

Single tickets are $12.50; tickets for special events may vary.

Walden Theater
1123 Payne St. • 589-0084

Here's another exceptional theater for young people, this one focused on their artistic development. Productions have included a "new wave" version of *The Taming of the Shrew* (Petrucchio bore a certain resemblance to the pre-scandal, Thriller-era Michael Jackson) and a play about the 1937 flood. The troupe has performed at the Kennedy Center, the Edinburgh (Scotland) Festival Fringe and in Actors Theatre's Humana Festival of New American Plays. Six plays written by its young playwrights have been published, and alumni have performed on Broadway, in feature films and in college and regional theaters across the country. (One alumnus, Will Oldham, played the boy preacher in John Sayles' *Matewan*, the father

of baby Jessica McClure — the child who fell down the well — in a TV movie and played the Lollapalooza tour with his band, the Palace Brothers.)

The company performs at the Kentucky Center for the Arts' MeX theater and Actor' Victor Jory Theatre. In addition to its fall and spring academies, it offers a number of summer workshops for aspiring actors.

Adults are $9 for evening performances, $8 for matinees; students and seniors pay $7, $6 for matinees.

Louisville Orchestra OrKIDStra Concerts
Macauley Theatre, 315 W. Broadway • 568-1111

These Saturday concerts for children 4 to 10 years old introduce kids to the orchestra with a lot of sing-alongs and audience participation. The song-heavy repertoire includes tunes from Disney movies, classic folk songs and a few light orchestral pieces. (One memorable program focused on whistling, with music ranging from "The Colonel Bogie March" to the second movement of Beethoven's pastoral Symphony No. 6.) The programs, which last about an hour, have become more visual in recent years — for example, a "Halloween Spooktacular" with both audience and orchestra in costume and a "Barnyard Serenade" which included a petting zoo.

The orchestra also makes inexpensive tickets available to young people through its student rush program, which makes unclaimed seats available prior to performance for $6. Tickets are $14 for adults, $10 for children.

Blue Apple Players
P.O. Box 4261, Louisville KY 40204
• 587-7990

This theater group's accomplishment sounds like an oxymoron — it makes contemporary musical theater out of some of the heaviest issues facing young people: drug abuse, the consequences of teen sexual activity, dealing with cultural diversity, runaway children, sexual abuse and suicide.

But Blue Apple, founded in 1976 by the husband-and-wife team of Paul Lenzi and Geraldine Ann Snyder, has been a signal theatrical success in a city thick with theatrical groups. Pulitzer Prize-winning playwright (and native Louisvillian) Marsha Norman has called them "the finest theater for young people America has to offer." Not everything is heavy — the group also does humorous shows such as *The Three Pigs*.

The company has no permanent stage. Most of its work is done in schools, but Blue Apple has occasional public performances in venues around town, most recently at The Vogue Theatre, (and has performed at such prestigious theaters as Washington, D.C.'s Kennedy Center). Contact the organization for dates, time and place. Appropriate age levels vary with each production, but middle school seems to be the baseline. Tickets are $6.

Derby Dinner Playhouse
525 Marriott Dr., Clarksville, Ind.
• (812) 288-8281

The area's only professional dinner theater puts on about three shows each season for children from preschool through the fourth grade. The participation plays are based on fairy tales or stories that teach morals. The theater also has a student series of its regular productions. Tickets are $10 for breakfast performances, $15 for lunch.

Story Station
6706 Terry Rd. • 937-3900

This brightly, invitingly painted former church features plays for children from ages 3 to 10. Most productions are based on well-known stories and fairy tales such as *The Emperor's New Clothes*, and *Sleeping Beauty*. Tickets are $5, $25 for a six-play season ticket.

Amusements

Baseball Mania
2001 Production Dr. (off Bluegrass Pkwy.)
• 499-7500

This indoor training facility offers batting cages with pitching machines set at speeds from 45 to 70 mph. There are lessons in hitting, fielding, base running and other baseball skills on an artificial turf field. There are also winter indoor leagues for kids 4 through 8 and camps during the summer and school breaks. No wonder the likes of former Dodger manager Tommy Lasorda and slugger Tino Martinez have dropped by.

Baseball Mania is open daily; hours vary according to season

Bicycle Motocross Track
E.P. "Tom" Sawyer State Park, 3000 Freys Hill Rd. between Westport and La Grange Rds. • 426-8950

This large park, named for the late county judge who's Diane Sawyer's dad, has an excellent dirt course for the fast-moving, thrill-packed, jumping two-wheel sport. How good? The sport's Grand Nationals have been held here for 10 years. Admission is free; helmets are required; a long-sleeved shirt and long pants are recommended, and if you can't figure out why you're grounded, young man.

Discovery Zone
4615 Outer Loop • 964-6633
2030 S. Hurstbourne Pkwy. • 491-9695

If you have a young child, you've been to Discovery Zone or another indoor playground like it — a play matrix of tubes, pits of balls, slides, chutes and slopes that's a more elaborate version of what you might find outside a recently-completed McDonald's. There's a snack bar, arcade and video games, a quiet room for parents and a less demanding play area for toddlers. Discovery Zone has one especially nice feature — a layout with a single central exit, which makes it easier to watch your kids. Parents are allowed inside the play land. Admission is $5.99 per child.

Kentucky Kingdom
Kentucky Fair and Exposition Center, 937 Phillips Ln. • 366-2231, (800) 727-3267

Like the zoo, Kentucky Kingdom is on the face of it a perfect place to take the kids, but it has several features aimed especially at them. There's an everyday discount price of $14.80 (as opposed to the regular $24.95) for children under 54 inches tall; children younger than 3 are admitted free. There's also an area especially for young children called King Louie's Playground with rides and games; and an area in the park's Hurricane Bay Waterpark called Barefoot Cove, which is a shallow water play area with slides, a silly sunken sub and a pirate ship, the *Sea Witch*, that has slides, ropes and water cannons. Young children also love the Roller Skater, a junior coaster whose cars are shaped like roller skates.

For teenagers, there's "Day Five Live," a Friday evening outdoor dance with prerecorded dance music and live appearances from local DJs. It's open 8 to 11 PM every Friday from the opening Friday of the park's season in April through the Friday before the State Fair in August.

See our Attractions chapter for more information on Kentucky Kingdom.

KIDSPACE
Louisville Science Center, 727 W. Main St. • 561-6100

Kids love the former Museum of History and Science — especially since the extremely interactive "The World We Create" exhibit opened in 1997, with more cool ways to play with blocks, levers computers and other ways of demonstrating physical forces than you

can shake a Beanie Baby at. (See Attractions.)

But the youngest ones don't always know the difference between a play room and an exhibit. For children 7 and younger, the museum offers 45 minutes of play time in this long room on the west side of the building. There are costumes to try on and a video camera to see how they play word games, computer learning games, water play and a number of books and toys. Admission is free with museum admission — $5.25 for adults, $4.25 for seniors and children; sessions start on the hour and can only accommodate a limited number of children. Parents must stay with their children.

Louisville Redbirds
Cardinal Stadium, Kentucky Fair and Exposition Center, 937 Phillips Ln. • 367-9121

Attending a Redbirds game is generally acknowledged as one of the best things you can do with your kids. The team has a number of promotions aimed at younger customers. Every night there's what's called the Billy Bird Derby in which a young customer gets to chase the Redbirds' mascot. The Knothole Gang is a promotion in which children get free admission to a number of Sunday games.

For a fuller treatment of the Redbirds, see Spectator Sports.

Outer Limits
1900 Outer Loop • 966-4586

Here is the best chance for your budding Danny Sullivan to hone his reflexes without raising your insurance premiums or smashing the Taurus. This deluxe amusement hall across the parking lot from the Louisville Motor Speedway has two go-cart tracks, a junior track for children ages 4 to 10, (you must be at least 40 inches tall), and a larger, "overpass style" figure-8 track. (You must be 10 years old or 58 inches tall, although younger children can ride in a two-seater as a parent's passenger.) It isn't cheap — $3 for 3 minutes — but have you priced body work lately?

There's also a fancy 18-hole miniature golf course, 65 video games and that greatest of all amusement rides, bumper boats — the ac-

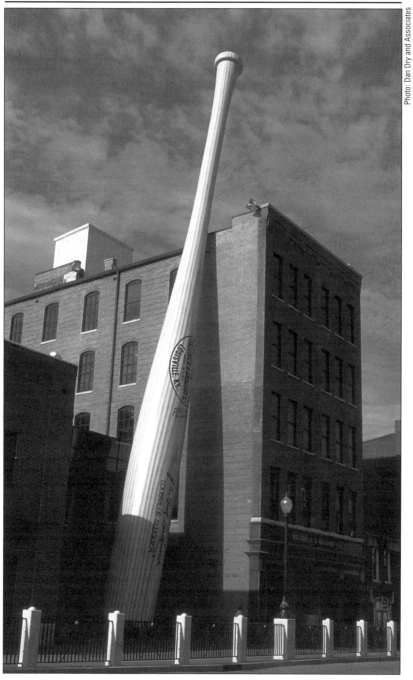

Photo: Dan Dry and Associates

It's hard to miss the Louisville Slugger Museum.

tion of bumper cars but with freedom of movement and a chance to splash your compatriots. On Wednesdays, all rides are $1; any other day, you can purchase a two-hour pass for $20. There is also karaoke Friday and Saturday nights during the summer and teen dances indoors during the winter.

The Park at Middletown
201 Park Place Dr. (off Shelbyville Rd.) • 253-9700

This amusement park has bumper boats, 18 holes of miniature golf, go-carts (if you're 54 inches or taller) and over 50 video and arcade games.

What makes it unique is a mission — it's a Christian-owned and -operated establishment that reviews video games with an eye toward weeding out the goriest and most pro-violence among them. It's open daily; hours vary with the seasons. No admission is charged — you pay by the ride.

Plaster Playground
8706 Bayberry Pl. • 426-8368

It seems weird — a place where children can paint plaster piggy banks, plaques of Batman or Bart Simpson or declarations of affection for parents, friends and Barney. But kids love the solidity of the plaster objects and the chance to mess with paint, glitter and googly-eye buttons. Fees vary, from $4 to $15, according to which things your offspring want to decorate. There are also other crafts, such as wooden birdhouses, wood burning, jewelry- and candle-making.

RiverFair
River Falls Mall, 951 E. Hwy. 131, Clarksville, Ind. • (812) 284-3247

What's it like putting an amusement area inside a mall? Imagine enclosing a state fair midway under a roof — all the noise and frenzy given no room to breathe. It either excites you to paroxysm or makes you want to take a nap. You can bet on which sides of that line most children and parents fall.

RiverFair's attractions include a beautiful old-fashioned carousel, a train, an indoor plane ride, over 200 of the latest video games

FYI

Unless otherwise noted, the area code for all phone numbers listed in this chapter is 502.

and new advances in arcadiana, such as The Thrillrider, a pivoting and thrashing van that puts its riders through something similar to a Hollywood stunt sequence; there's also a balls-and-chutes play area for younger children on the Discovery Zone model. Not to mention two of the most civilized amenities I've ever seen inside a shopping center: miniature golf and bumper cars. (Who hasn't felt like smashing into vehicles after a hard day at the mall?)

It's a major stop on the birthday circuit (watch for the parrots descending from the ceiling when the cake comes). Your hosts are Hooper and Hannabelle Hound. Admission is free; ticket books are $3.95 for 10 tickets, $8.95 for 30; and all-day pass is $6.50.

Southern Sports
6611 Shepherdsville Rd. • 964-GOLF

"Rule 2. Once your opponent has launched a bomb, it is unthinkable to try to avoid being hit. A 'true sport' would stand there and take it with clenched fists and gritted teeth! Any participant found guilty of this evasive action will be subjected to great boos and catcalls from the audience."

This South End multisports facility has a variety of sports games and practice opportunities, from the heated driving range, putting green and sand trap out back, to a batting cage, an 18-hole miniature golf course and a couple of oddball things.

One is Bankshot Basketball, the hoops equivalent of miniature golf. Players shoot at a succession of goals with oddly shaped goals (angled, curved, darn-near occluded), each of which requires a different shooting touch and strategy.

And then there is Water Wars, "a game of the highest integrity and sportsmanship!" (We quoted from its rules at the beginning of this entry.) It's simplicity itself: Players stand in launching stations 45 feet apart and use a pouch attached to elastic springs to lob water balloons at each other. It's amazing there's a dry 13-year-old in the county.

Indoors you'll find a full-line golf shop, pool tables and video and arcade games. No admission is charged — you pay by the activity.

Exploring the City

Downtown Louisville
Broadway to the Belvedere • no phone

It's sad but true — for many youngsters, going to the center of the city isn't a regular experience anymore. But since to a young child any unusual experience can seem like play, the simple things that make up a downtown also make it seem like some sort of eccentric theme park. And while downtown Louisville often has a deserted feel on weekends, it's not scary — the atmosphere is more like having the city to yourself for a day.

Attractions? More fountains per square foot than anywhere else in the city, starting with the giant one floating in the river and going all the way up to Theater Square. The trolley up and down Fourth Street might have been invented for a 5-year-old to ride.

Downtown is also home to the kind of large, rambling store that seems half warehouse, half mad aunt's attic. There's **Caulfield's Novelties**, 1006 W. Main Street, which has amazing Halloween window displays, magic tricks, costumes, (intentionally) ugly wigs and a complete line of plastic vomit. **Joe Ley Antiques**, filled with moose heads and ancient advertising, **Muth's Candies**, **A. Baer** (filled to bursting with varieties of buttons, fabric and rickrack) and **Bunton Seed** — a kid who isn't interested in one of those has problems.

The public sculptures in the lobby of the **Kentucky Center for the Arts** are attractively playful (especially Joan Miro's "Personnage," which has its own bodyguard during Stage One performances to make sure kids don't clamber over its roly-poly ghostliness). A group of little girls was entranced by the central areas of the **Galt House** — the huge chandeliers and the nearly-psychedelic gaudiness that don't look embarrassing to 8-year-old eyes.

And one of downtown's great attractions is a ride in the glassed-in elevator that goes up the 18 floors of the **Hyatt Regency Hotel's** atrium. Even if going downtown to ride the elevators in the Hotel sounds like the set-up for a Minnie Pearl routine, what do kids know from corny? The smooth, swift ride draws the ultimate accolade from kid after kid: "That was cool!"

Another great glassed-in ride is up the outside of the "lacy building," the 15-floor **Kaden Tower** at the corner of Dutchman's and Breckinridge lanes in St. Matthews (see more information in the Historic Preservation and Architecture chapter).

McAlpine Locks and Dam
27th St. and the Portland Canal • no phone

A simple, amazing process — the walls of the lock chamber swinging shut behind a barge, submerged pumps displacing 38 million gallons of water to enable boats to make the 37-foot drop from the upper to the lower pool of the Ohio River — is observable daily during daylight hours, either from a tower that includes an exhibit on the lock system and the river or from top-of-the-lock level down below. It's educational and oddly absorbing.

It's also a neat place to get a glimpse of the working river — a vital but nearly invisible part of the local economy. You will sometimes see a deckhand waiting with his suitcases for his towboat to arrive. The crew at the locks also hands out mail or medical supplies; boats are repaired there; and the Coast Guard makes inspections. More than 60 million tons of coal, rock, grain and chemicals move through the locks each year.

INSIDERS' TIP

The best way to get to the Kentucky Kingdom amusement park at the Kentucky Fair and Exposition Center is to enter the fairgrounds through Gate 2, on Crittenden Drive, and follow the Kentucky Kingdom signs.

Programs

Kentucky Orff-Schulwerk Association

Various locations • (216)543-5366

This is a group of folks who teach music to children from kindergarten through the 6th grade following a method developed by the composer Carl Orff (of "Carmina Burana" fame). The method teaches music through experience, using everything from dance to instrumental practice, singing, improvisation on the recorder and the use of speech patterns as rhythmic ostinatos. For information about a program near you, write the American Orff-Schulwerk Association, P.O. Box 391089, Cleveland, Ohio 44139-8089, or call the number above.

Metro Parks and Recreation

1297 Trevilian Way (in Joe Creason Park) • 456-8100

The parks department runs a number of sports leagues (softball, baseball, flag football, tackle football, basketball, soccer and T-ball) and offers instruction in tennis, golf, swimming and riding. It also runs popular children's day camps during the summer and on school breaks.

And to keep golf course hills from being sledded into mud, it has begun sledding as a program — as much as you can base a program on something as capricious as a Louisville snowfall. Preferred sledding sites are marked with "Open" signs and bonfires (during daylight hours), and park staff are present with first-aid kits. And if the temperature stays below 20 degrees for five consecutive days, ice skating is allowed on some park ponds; call Metro Parks for information.

New Albany-Floyd County Parks and Recreation Department

1721 Ekin Ave. • (812) 948-5360

Children's programs include dance classes, cooking, bumper bowling, karate, gymnastics, art classes and tennis and swimming lessons. Programs for teenagers include basketball leagues and an after-school employment program for teens ages 16 to 18.

Children's Holiday Parade

• 584-6383

This is a parade by and for children ages 5 to 13, who build their own self-propelled floats or march in costumed units. Santa Claus and other local VIPs appear, and there's always a high school marching band. In past years it's been held the Saturday after Thanksgiving at the Mall St. Matthews. Call the Derby Festival at the above number for date and location of this year's parade.

Children's Hour

Indiana University Southeast, University Center Building, 4201 Grant Line Rd. • 941-2316

These Sunday morning programs for children ages 4 to 10 and their parents vary between educational programs (for example, on Japanese culture) to a canine circus. Craft programs are usually things such as papier-mâché and tie-dyeing — some of the messier, more complicated things you might not want to do at home.

It's held every other Sunday during the IUS fall and spring semesters. University students and their children attend free; the public pays a small admission.

Louisville Free Public Library Children's Services

301 York St. • 574-1620

Most of the system's 16 branches have full-time children's librarians and have preschool story hours. The library puts on a host of special events for school-age children that have in the past ranged from puppet shows to flamenco demonstrations. And library branches are regular stops for the Mayor's SummerScene and WinterScene programs (see below).

The Mayor's SummerScene and WinterScene Programs

Various locations • 574-3061

The Mayor's office doesn't entertain in typical mayoral fashion, with slush-fund scandals and the revelations of angry mistresses. It puts on hundreds of performances — music, ethnic dance, magic shows, clowns and jugglers — at libraries, parks, nursing homes, community centers and other venues. (A weekly schedule is printed in *The Courier-Journal's* Neighborhoods section.)

Louisville Visual Art Association
The Water Tower, 3005 Upper River Rd.
• 896-2146

This organization offers a stunning range of art classes (more than 300 a year) at The Water Tower, Tom Sawyer State Park, the Main Library and the Floyd County (Indiana) Museum. The lessons are for 4- and 5-year-olds to adults, and they cover a full range of drawing, painting, pottery, media arts and the like. Instructors rank among the area's better artists. Fees are charged; LVAA members get a discount.

Kindermusik Teachers of Kentuckiana
Various locations • (800) 628-5687

A number of teachers throughout the Louisville area offer this excellent course of music instruction for children from 18 months through age 7. The program progresses from singing, moving and playing percussion instruments through the beginnings of reading and writing musical notation; it emphasizes early learning and creativity. For the teacher closest to you, call Kindermusik International in Greensboro, North Carolina, at the above number.

Little League Baseball
Various locations • 267-7177

For information on Louisville Little League programs, contact district administrator Mike Schaefer at the number listed above. It's for ages 5 and older (the younger ones play T-ball).

Suzuki Program
University of Louisville School of Music, Belknap Campus • 852-5850

This is a major center for the Suzuki method of teaching young children to play instruments, offering instruction in piano and stringed in-struments. Dr. Haruko Kataoka, founder of the Suzuki piano school, comes over from Japan every year for the program's summer institute.

Shopping

Books to Grow On
3636-A Brownsboro Rd. • 893-2507

Madeline and Good Dog, Carl spoken here. This is a small, well-stocked store specializing in children's books (along with books on parenting), audiotapes and videotapes and book-connected toys. The staff is well-informed and helpful, and there are Saturday morning programs and a play area for young children.

Children's Planet
1349 Bardstown Rd. • 458-7018

This store, for children of all ages, specializes in old toys and books — the sort of things today's parents grew up playing with and reading. It's open Tuesday through Saturday.

Hawley-Cooke Booksellers
Shelbyville Road Plaza, 4600 Shelbyville Rd. • 893-0133
Gardiner Lane Shopping Center, 3024 Bardstown Rd. • 456-6660
Glenview Pointe, 2400 Lime Kiln Ln. • 425-9100
Business Office: 895-6789

These are large, attractive bookstores with well-stocked children's sections. Saturday morning children's programs alternate between the three locations every week, except Derby and major holidays. They usually focus around a book theme and include everything from storytelling to jugglers to non-messy craft activities; costumed characters such as the Cat in the Hat or Curious George make appearances about once a month. For

---

INSIDERS' TIP

If you want to get in tune with preschool Louisville, check out Karen Dean, a local performer whose tapes (such as "Out to Lunch" and "Shiver Me Timbers") can be found in car stereos and Fisher-Price tape players across the city.

preschoolers through age 13, the program is free, unless lunch is included.

The Parent Teacher Store of Louisville
3085 Breckenridge Ln. • 451-3774
143 Thierman Ln. • 899-9521

This store specializes in teacher materials and educational games that are actually fun. It also carries an excellent line of sturdy outdoor gyms and swings. Programs vary from art to etiquette classes, all of them conducted at the larger Thierman Lane store; there's also a play area.

Food

Screen Play
6801 Dixie Hwy. in the Dixie Manor shopping center • 933-5437

This locally-owned "pizza fun place" next door to the Dixie Dozen movie theaters is a train-oriented variation on the Chuck E. Cheese model. It's a popular site for birthday parties, with a train ride, a small indoor play land and a glittery array of video and arcade games.

Kids' Night at Shariat's
2901 Bardstown Rd. • 899-7878

In the Restaurants chapter, you'll see Shariat's listed as one of the city's finest and most creative restaurants. It also offers a monthly kids' night in the downstairs private dining room — an on-premises solution to the babysitter dilemma. One Friday a month, it provides dinner, entertainment and custodial services for customers' children. The kids' fare is a little more interesting (and nutritious) than the usual hamburger/hot dog/chicken nuggets routine: Popular entrées have included free-range chicken breast with a honey-orange sauce, linguine with marinara sauce and gourmet pizza. Activities have ranged from a magician to making art from macaroni and vegetables. Reservations are strongly requested.

Ditto's
1114 Bardstown Rd. • 581-9129

Playful decor, bistro cuisine and a choice of nutritious side dishes a kid might actually eat (cheesy broccoli, a fruit plate) make Ditto's a popular compromise between adult and juvenile palates. It's open for lunch and dinner weekly, with morning hours on the weekend.

KT's
2300 Lexington Rd. • 458-8888

It's a large, bustling bistro specializing in burgers and salads. Although they'll gladly tie a balloon to a chair, there's nothing especially child-oriented about KT's — but kids love it for its busyness and the uncomplicated fare.

Lynn's Paradise Cafe
984 Barret Ave. • 583-3447

This wildly popular spot is great for kids (and appeals to the child inside every adult, as well). You'll find wacky decor, the best breakfast and lunch in town and, Thursday through Saturday, dinners that tread a nice line between traditional and contemporary.

Mamma Grisanti
3938 Dupont Cr. • 893-0141

This family-oriented Italian restaurant looks like an Italian farmhouse. "Bambino Night" is Monday and Tuesday, when children 12 and younger eat for free from the children's menu, which features such usual suspects as chicken fingers but also child-sized portions of lasagna, spaghetti marinara and other fare; bambini also get a sundae.

Mike Linnig's
9308 Cane Run Rd. • 937-9888

It's like a gigantic church picnic — lots of outdoor seating, swing sets and walks over the flood wall to look at the river. There's fried seafood in enough varieties (and quantity) to make Captain Ahab blanch.

Old Spaghetti Factory
235 W. Market St. • 581-1070

Located in one of downtown Louisville's most ornate Victorian buildings, the Spaghetti Factory offers simple pasta dishes, great bread and a chance to eat in a trolley car. (Note: While most restaurants in this chain serve only dinner, the Louisville Spaghetti Factory is also open for lunch.)

Rocky's Sub Pub
1207 E. Market St., Jeffersonville, Ind.
• 282-3844

This Hoosier institution may have named itself for its sandwiches, but kids of all ages flock there for superb pizza, especially with whole-wheat crust. Rocky's is open for lunch and dinner.

W.W. Cousins
900 Dupont Rd. • 897-9684

Cousins reigns as Louisville's favorite burger (it always wins the category in *Louisville magazine's* "Best of Louisville" awards), and the reason is that it does everything from scratch: The tasty, big burgers are made from meat ground on the premises; the buns are baked there daily. And Cousins offers a mind-boggling choice of condiments, from relish to coconut, with stops in between that are best not thought about. Best of all, kids 12 and younger eat free with parents after 4 PM Monday and Tuesday.

Dan Dry ∞ Associates

With over 250,000

stock images to

choose from, it's

easy to see why

the editors of this

guide selected

Dan Dry ∞ Associates

as their principal

source of photography.

The Arts

For years, the arts in Louisville had it lucky. Several of the most powerful corporations in the city felt that funding the arts was a great way to both exercise their philanthropic muscles and generate good public relations. Early on, *The Courier-Journal* and Kentucky Fried Chicken made their mark. Later, Humana, Philip Morris, Brown & Williamson and a host of local banks joined in. They also gained the city national attention, such as in the 1955 *Harper's* article "Louisville Cashes in on Culture."

But as out-of-town conglomerates bought up some Louisville companies and '80s downsizing strangled corporate budgets, money became tight at local arts organizations. The arts groups that built strong reputations and followings found new ways to fund their efforts. The others struggled mightily.

As a result, Louisville arts are lean, mean and wholly deserving of national attention. There's Actors Theatre of Louisville, which opened in 1969 and now attracts critics and theater people from around the world to its Humana Festival of New American Plays.

There's the Louisville Orchestra, which has been in the forefront of commissioning and recording works by contemporary American composers. It is the only orchestra in the country that has its own recording company, First Edition Recordings. There's the Kentucky Opera, which has gone from its first budget of $10,000 in 1952 to its current count at close to $2 million.

There's the Louisville Ballet, which has hosted Mikhail Baryshnikov and directors of international reputation and has wowed Louisvillians with its new rehearsal and office space on Main Street.

Shakespeare in the Park continues to bring the Bard into everyone's reach with free performances in summer and school programs in spring, fall and winter. The Louisville Theatrical Association flags down the hottest Broadway shows on the road for its popular Broadway Series. In visual arts, the J.B. Speed Museum has people buzzing about its recent $12 million facelift, and The Water Tower continues to weave art into everyone's lives.

As in cities across the nation, the Louisville arts have felt a financial crunch in the last decade. But unlike some other cities, Louisville has not seen a harrowing drop in the variety or quality of its arts. We can see Tony Award-winning plays and challenging dance pieces. We can watch *The Tempest* work its magic through professional actors. We can hear great jazz, choral pieces and operas, and challenge our minds with new ideas in painting, sculpture and photography.

Make no mistake, Louisville is still an arts town. Just like it has been for more than half a century.

Performing Arts

Dance

Louisville Ballet
1300 Bardstown Rd. • 583-3150,
584-7777, (800) 775-7777

As years pass, Louisville's ballet company gains a higher and higher reputation, bolstered by the tacit endorsement of guest artist Mikhail Baryshnikov and a host of other famed dancers who have performed with the Louisville Ballet, including Margot Fonteyn, Patricia McBride, Galina Samsova and Valery and Galina Panov. Grounded firmly in the classic ballet repertoire, the company has an annual hit with *The Nutcracker*, a holiday favorite and perennial sellout that draws fans from more than a hundred miles away.

Founded in March 1952 as a civic ballet, the company has grown from a small regional ballet to one *The New York Times* has called "theatrical magic." Its repertoire includes full-length ballets by 20th-century choreographers George Balanchine and Antony Tudor. *Swan Lake, Sleeping Beauty, Coppelia, Romeo and Juliet* and *Cinderella* are among audience favorites.

The Louisville Ballet's new home, a one-story building amid the industrial neighborhood of East Main Street, has given the company a new and different kind of visibility; company personnel have noticed that metal workers and other folks working nearby make a lunch-hour habit of catching some of the graceful movements visible through the building's front windows. The structure, which has won awards for its architecture, includes a stage fully the size of the ballet's performance space in nearby Whitney Hall.

Ticket prices range from $25 to close to $100, depending on the location of your seat. Several series subscription packages are also available.

Art! Art! Barking Dog Dance Company
Clifton Center • 254-3713

This new dance group is filling the hole left by the demise of Afterimages, another contemporary/modern dance company. Art! Art! stages original works choreographed by members of the group three or more times a year at a variety of locations. The accompanying music draws from an eclectic mix of styles, from classical to original pieces to the works of Laurie Anderson. A core group of five dancers drives the company and also teach at their school in the Clifton neighborhood. Look for performance information in local newspapers, or call the above phone number.

Theater

Actors Theatre of Louisville
316 W. Main St. • 584-1205, (800) 4ATL-TIX

It's wrong to call Actors Theatre one of Louisville's best kept secrets — the productions get plenty of local press and the company is considered by most to be the premier

FYI

Unless otherwise noted, the area code for all phone numbers listed in this chapter is 502.

drama group in the area. But many Louisvillians may not realize just how good ATL is.

An impressive list of famous actors has graced ATL productions (see the close-up in this chapter), and nearly 200 ATL-premiered scripts are in publication. The annual Humana Festival of New American Plays focuses much attention on Louisville. And the Brown-Forman Classics in Context Festival is a wonderful idea wonderfully executed: A production is surrounded by other events illuminating the play's setting or era — exhibits, lectures, music, workshops. Louisvillians still talk about the lush "commedia dell'arte" Classics in Context that bolstered a 1990 production of *The Three Cuckolds*.

But let's not forget that this is a fairly conservative city. Thus, the enormous success that annual productions of *A Christmas Carol, A Gift of the Magi* and *Dracula* enjoy is not surprising — and it's certainly a welcome boon to the company's bottom line.

Make reservations ahead if you can, but if it's the last minute, try the box office, anyway. Tickets start at $15; subscription rates begin at $64 for seven plays.

Actors has a restaurant where you can dine before and after the play and an art gallery that features the works of local and regional artists.

Kentucky Contemporary Theatre
824 S. Fourth St. • 585-5537

KCT's history is that of the oldest alternative professional theater in the city, but the company is not afraid of moving into the mainstream to pursue a theme. Prime example: A recent season centered on the theme of family, which saw the production of plays by Neil Simon, William Inge and Lanford Wilson. Some other shows from the theater's recent past include Ezra Pound's *Sophokles Elektra*, Ivan Menchell's *The Cemetery Club* and Eugene O'Neill's *The Emperor Jones*.

The theater, which is associated with Spalding University, performs in the university's 900-seat auditorium, but for KCT performances, both set and audience are placed on the stage to create an intimate environment.

KCT uses local actors and directors; volunteers work as ushers, costumers, set-builders, designers and painters, sound and lighting technicians. Ticket prices are kept less than $10.

The Kentucky Shakespeare Festival
1114 S. Third St. • 583-8738

His plays can seem inscrutable on the page, but on stage, the themes are the very definition of accessibility. So, with the philosophy that Shakespeare's timeless texts were written to be performed, not read, this annual festival puts on anywhere from one to three of the bard's plays each summer in Central Park, located in the historic Old Louisville neighborhood.

Often known as Shakespeare in Central Park or Shakespeare in the Park, the festival is the oldest of the four free, professional, independently operated Shakespeare festivals in North America. Louisville summers are hot and humid enough to make the air-conditioned environment of a cinemaplex mighty tempting, but up to 20,000 people each season grab a blanket and a picnic supper to take in some free Shakespeare.

The resulting audience is diverse. That's no accident; the festival goes to great pains to fulfill its charter — providing free professional, accessible, classical theater to everybody. To that end, the stage always includes a shadow-signed performance for the deaf and hearing impaired. Professional actors adept at sign language share the stage and sign the entire show, merging nearly seamlessly into the action of the play. An audio description is also available for blind patrons that same evening.

The Kentucky Shakespeare Festival has an educational program called Shakespeare Alive! that has reached more than 130,000 students in five Indiana counties and 98 Kentucky counties. Performers tour elementary, middle and high schools as well as colleges, community centers and theaters throughout the region. From Page to the Stage: Teaching Shakespeare in the Classroom is another program that involves area teachers.

Stage One: The Louisville Children's Theatre
425 W. Market St. • 589-5946,
for tickets 584-7777, (800)775-7777

The oldest theater company in Louisville and one of the top children's theaters in America, Stage One may sound like it's just for kids, but don't be fooled. Its plays will delight adults as well. Stage One is a developmental theater, which means that productions are geared to the specific stages of a young person's development. When you look at the season brochure or call for ticket reservations, check the recommended ages for each show.

Performances are geared to children age 4 and older. In Participation Plays for the youngest, kids use their voices, bodies and imaginations to become part of the plays. Favorite productions have been of fairy tales, children's classics, folk tales and adaptations of award-winning children's books, including *Sleeping Beauty*, *Cinderella*, *Ananse: The African Spiderman*, *John Lennon & Me* and *The Diary of Anne Frank*.

Tickets are $12.50; a subscription for a three-play season is $27.

Walden Theatre
233 W. Broadway • 589-0084

Walden Theatre brings together young people ages 8 to 18 from all corners of Greater Louisville to immerse them in the arts under the watchful eyes of professionals. Students learn improvisation and take studio classes; they often attract directors from professional theater, television and films. The Young Playwrights Program has produced six published scripts and resulted in more than 40 playwrights receiving royalties.

Tickets are $9 for adults, $7 for seniors

INSIDERS' TIP

If you're a jazz fan, memorize this number: 329-0893. That's the WFPK Jazz Line, which lists concerts and club dates in the area.

Actors' Theatre Brings Out the Best

If you think John Turturro is one of the most interesting and intense actors working in films today . . .

if you think much the same thing about Ned Beatty or Kathy Bates . . .

if *Agnes of God*, *Extremities* or *Getting Out* moved you on the stage or screen . . .

if Timothy Busfield's work on *thirtysomething* had a depth you never expected from television acting . . .

if you'd like to shake the hand of whoever encouraged Louisville journalist Marsha Norman to start writing plays . . .

Close-up

if Michael Gross (the father on *Family Ties*), Max Wright (the dad on *ALF* and the harried station manager on *Buffalo Bill*) or Pamela Reed (the best thing in a number of disappointing projects) ever made you laugh . . .

then you're a fan of Actors Theatre of Louisville whether you knew it or not.

Actors, Kentucky's official state theater, ranks among the most important regional theaters in the country. It's earned a raft of honors, including a special Tony Award in 1980. Its annual Humana Festival of New American Plays has become one of the essential events in the American theatrical year and has introduced some of the best-known and most significant plays of the past two decades.

The roster of actors who have appeared in the festival and other productions glitters with star names — and not only when the actor is starting out, or on the skids: Mercedes Ruehl came to town to star in *Antony and Cleopatra* the month after she received the Oscar for Best Supporting Actress for *The Fisher King*. The company has traveled to foreign countries including Ireland, Finland and Japan.

If one of those proverbial bombs hit the theater at the height of the visitor's weekend at the festival, American theater would be a long time recovering. In Actors' lobby on one of those nights, you might pass an ambitious playwright talking to an up-and-coming director, with a soap opera star preening in the background, on your way in to see a play in which Holly Hunter jumps on stage in leopard-skin underwear (*Eden Court* in 1983).

Turturro appeared in John Patrick Shanley's *Danny and the Deep Blue Sea* in the 1984 festival. The production subsequently went to Broadway and was the making of both the actor and the author's careers (Shanley is most famous for *Moonstruck*). Busfield, an apprentice at Actors who later joined the resident company, has said, "I don't think I'd be anywhere except for Actors."

The resident acting company is excellent. Longtime actors such as William McNulty, Adale O'Brien and Fred Major are respected as teachers by the likes of Busfield. But the main man is producing director Jon Jory (son of actor Victor Jory, who played the overseer in *Gone With the Wind*). Jory, who came to Actors in 1969, is sort of a theatrical equivalent to U of L basketball coach Denny Crum. Both arrived here on what looked like an up-and-out trajectory — young hotshots who'd probably spend a few years, make a reputation and find a better job. Instead, they fell in love with Louisville and stayed to give the city two enduring emblems of excellence. Jory looks as likely to end his career at Actors as Crum does at U of L.

Actors was a good, daring company before Jory came, but its financial status was uncertain. Jory worked hard on a theatrical form of research and development.

— continued on next page

Photo: Richard Trigg

A Christmas Carol is one of the plays in the Actors Theatre repertoire.

"If you're any small company, you find a product opening — you find a niche where it isn't going on, and you play that real hard," he says.

Actors began developing small-scale musicals — *Tricks*, based on Moliere's *Scapan*, went on to Broadway. They began an emphasis on short plays that resulted in a "Shorts" festival and caused the theater to become what Jory calls "kings of the 10-minute play." And most famously, they began what was first called Play Faire and is now the Humana Festival of New American Plays.

The festival's first six seasons each produced a play that went to Hollywood, New York, or both: *The Gin Game*; Louisville native Marsha Norman's *Getting Out*; Beth Henley's *Crimes of the Heart*; *Agnes of God*; *Extremities*; *Talking With*, by the notoriously reclusive Jane Martin, whose identity remains a secret (some people have tabbed Jory, but he denies it). Later seasons added the likes of Martin's *Keely and Du* and Louisville native Jon Klein's *T Bone N Weasel*, which later turned up on Showtime and in your local video store. The 1994 festival included a new work by Tony Kushner, whose Pulitzer Prize-winning *Angels in America* has been one of the few recent dramatic sensations in American theater.

"There is another level of writer whose names won't mean a lot," Jory says. "But I could name maybe 15 of them who are very forward-looking and have moved the profession itself forward, whether or not they're known to the general public."

Hollywood is full of writers who got their first opportunities through Actors.

— continued on next page

In 1994 Actors Theatre unveiled its greatest physical transformation in more than 20 years, a $9.5 million renovation and expansion that affected every aspect of the operation, from sets onstage to the restrooms. Actors added a new mid-size arena, the 336-seat Bingham Theatre, the seats of which encircle the stage (all seats are within seven rows of the stage). There is a new parking garage, a larger lobby, improved restrooms and box office and more seats in the theater's restaurant.

The theater's annual budget has increased 20-fold during the past 25 years, and its physical plant has expanded from the train station's cramped quarters to nearly half a city block. The theater has one of the highest per-capita subscription rates of any American company — annual attendance approaches 200,000 — and it has admirable financial stability.

It has had a dramatic effect on theater in Louisville, with new companies forming at a dizzying rate — paying Actors the sincerest form of flattery and enriching Louisville's cultural life in the process.

Actors Honor Roll
Armand Assante
Kevin Bacon
Kathy Bates
Ned Beatty
Leo Burmeister
Timothy Busfield
Barry Corbin
Harry Groener
Karen Grassle
Michael Gross
Holly Hunter
Ken Jenkins
Will Oldham
Pamela Reed
Mercedes Ruehl
Bill Smitrovitz
Lili Taylor
Patrick Tovatt
John Turturro
Dianne Wiest
Max Wright

and students 18 or younger. Matinee performances are a dollar off the regular admission prices.

Musical Theater

Broadway Series
611 W. Main St. • 584-7469, 584-7777, (800) 294-1849

Arts events with a higher profile than Broad-way Series productions cannot be found in Louisville, where *Cats* mania, *Phantom of the Opera* fever and *Les Miserables* fascination has reigned in the last few years. Since 1980, the 60-year-old Louisville Theatrical Association has strived to bring the best Broadway shows touring at any given time to this series, which spans a wide stylistic spectrum from musicals to dramas, from *A Chorus Line* to *Angels in America*.

Famous Broadway and entertainment-industry names that have appeared in Louisville include Robert Goulet, Carol Channing, Cathy Rigby, Harry Guardino, Tommy Tune, Topol, Mercedes McCambridge, Tom Poston, Joel Grey, Brooke Shields and Davy Jones of The Monkees. Ticket prices vary from $20 to $60; season subscription rates, which include six shows, range from $87 to $480. Performances are generally staged in the KCA's Whitney Hall from October to July.

Derby Dinner Playhouse
525 Marriott Dr., Clarksville, Ind.
• (812) 288-8281

This company does more than just TRY to stage the populace's favorite musicals and comedies; they eliminate all doubt by choosing their repertoire based on audience surveys and information from season-ticket holders. Thus, Derby Dinner has produced all of Broadway's top 50 musicals, including *Oklahoma!*, *Hello, Dolly!*, *My Fair Lady*, *Annie* and *The King and I*.

Productions are mounted year round. This is dinner theater — one of the oldest continually operating dinner theaters in the country — but the draw is more the shows than the food. Dinners feature classic American food, nothing fancy, served buffet style.

Local playwrights have premiered here, too, such as Dudley Saunders with *Charlie Chan and the Phantom of the Opera* and Mary Phyllis Riedley with a musical comedy *And Where Were You, Dr. Spock?* based on her book.

Admission ranges from $21 for the Wednesday dessert matinee to $29 for Saturday night (which includes the buffet, show and coffee or tea).

Music Theatre Louisville
624 W. Main St. • 367-9493

Another dependable summer arts outing is this troupe's annual series of musicals, which have been staged at the Iroquois Amphitheater in the South End for more than sixteen years. Family favorites are the rule, including *Oklahoma!*, *Annie*, *Little Shop of Horrors*, *Peter Pan* and *The Sound of Music*. Fans from across the county fill the outdoor theater's 1,600 seats, each paying $15 or less — the company strives to provide their live entertainment at a price comparable to a night at the movies.

The majority of artists are from the region, mostly from the Louisville area. Ninety-five percent of MTL's employees are local residents, and more than 200 local artists (actors, technicians and designers) are employed each season.

Music

Kentucky Opera
101 S. Eighth St. • 584-4500, 584-7777
(800) 775-7777

This venerable opera company is seeing its audience grow younger with each passing year as the Baby Boomers discover both the elegant and emotional nature of the opera experience and the high quality of the Kentucky Opera Association's productions. The "war horses" (traditional works by Verdi, Puccini, Mozart and other favorites) make frequent appearances in the KOA's seasons, but the association also has a strong history of exploring contemporary works and was the site of a premiere of a piece by Philip Glass.

INSIDERS' TIP

The Lonesome Pine Special series is a concert program held at the Kentucky Center for the Arts featuring music with just one thing in common: It's always good. Klezmer music, North African pop, Lyle Lovett, Buddy Guy and Shawn Colvin have all graced the Lonesome Pine stage. The series has a national following due to its broadcast on public television. Even if you don't look forward to this week's LPS polka band, for example, you're sure to admit that the polka group the LPS people booked is a dang good one.

Founded in 1952 in Louisville by Moritz von Bomhard, the Kentucky Opera has grown to carry an annual budget of around $2 million. The Louisville Orchestra plays for nearly all performances, and the Louisville Ballet has danced with the opera on a number of occasions.

Audiences show a special fondness for two area divas who often grace the KOA's stage: Edith Davis and Marilyn Mims. Their performances have highlighted the best of the KOA's productions in recent years.

Grand operas are generally staged in the KCA's Whitney Hall; other productions are performed in the Macauley Theatre. Tickets range from $18 to $55 for one show or $81 to $120 for a three-performance season subscription.

The Louisville Orchestra
611 W. Main St. • 587-8681, 584-7777, (800) 775-7777

The programs of The Louisville Orchestra are as diverse as its audiences. You can choose from the MasterWorks Series of classical favorites; SuperPops, which features popular entertainers; orKIDStra concerts for youngsters; the New Dimensions Series of 20th-century music; Classical Roots Series, featuring gifted African-American performers; and the Symphonic Specials Series.

The orchestra's history goes back to November 8, 1937, when conductor Robert Whitney and the ensemble that would later be known as The Louisville Orchestra took the stage at Memorial Auditorium for their first public performance. In 1953, a major grant from the Rockefeller Foundation allowed The Louisville Orchestra, as it was known by then, to make recordings.

The group performed at Carnegie Hall in 1989 (the only American orchestra on the Great Ensembles in Concert series) and at the Kennedy Center in Washington, D.C. in 1990. The orchestra has received more American Society of Composers, Authors, and Publishers Awards than any other orchestra.

Performances are held at The Kentucky Center for the Arts, the Macauley Theatre and Louisville Gardens. Ticket costs vary.

Smaller Arts Groups

Greater Louisville's cultural scene is complemented by smaller arts groups that offer specialized music and drama. There are others, of course; this is a sampling of our favorites. Some of these groups are small enough to operate out of a home. Where there is a business address, we've included it. Ticket prices for these groups' performances are usually a bargain — less than $10 in many cases.

FYI

Music

Ars Femina Ensemble
First Unitarian Church, Fourth and York Sts.
• 897-5719

This group, which performs the music of historical women composers, regularly gets glowing reviews from critics and audiences alike. The sextet also makes recordings of music written by women before 1800, including works by Francesca Caccini, Bianca Maria Meda and Elisabeth Olin. The publishing arm of Ars Femina makes available more than 1,500 manuscripts of music by women composers. Watch the newspapers for information on concert times and ticket costs.

University of Louisville School of Music
First St. and Brandeis Ave. • 852-0524

Local musicians speak rapturously about U of L's North Recital Hall, which is considered to be, acoustically, the best room in the city. The university puts some good music into this good room, with faculty, students and guest artists performing in all types of styles including symphonic, choral, ensemble jazz, orchestra, concert band and opera. The performances are usually held during the school year, and they are usually free.

Chamber Music Society of Louisville
U of L School of Music, First St. • 852-6907

This group brings in world-renowned musicians to play music by traditional composers in concerts held during the school year. Season and single tickets are available. Season tickets, which include five performances, start at $70; single performances cost $15.

Louisville Bach Society
4607 Hanford Ln. • 585-2224

Since its formation in 1964, this group has been about more than Johann Sebastian Bach. Yes, the emphasis has been on the great German composer's music, but works by others are included in the group's repertoire as well. And in addition to the roughly 10 annual performances the Bach Society presents, members of the group, which includes as many as 80 people in the chorus and 30 in the orchestra, participate in outreach programs for listeners in the inner city and in children's programs for youngsters discovering classical music.

Their concerts are held in various area churches. Season tickets for four concerts are $39, $29 for seniors and students. Individual shows are $10, $7 for seniors and students.

Southern Baptist Theological Seminary
2825 Lexington Rd. • 897-4115

During the school year (September through May), a mix of contemporary and traditional music, generally sacred, is performed by solo vocalists, instrumental soloists, orchestras and choruses. Students and faculty of the seminary fill most of the musicians' chairs, but an oratorio chorus also features members of the community. The free concerts are held in Heeren Hall or the Alumni Chapel.

The Pride of Kentucky Chorus
Various locations • 368-SONG

This group is a chapter of the Sweet Adelines, an international all-woman barbershop group that was formed in 1983. About 130 women participate. Call for details.

Thoroughbred Chorus
10609 Watterson Tr., Jeffersontown
• 267-SING

This all-male barbershop chorus has won the international championship a multitude of times and has produced several international champion quartets. Membership is open to all men with an interest in singing. The Derby City Chorus, Louisville's other Sweet Adeline affiliate, is also available at the above number.

Jewish Community Center Orchestra
3600 Dutchman's Ln. • 459-0660

The precursor of the famed Louisville Orchestra, this orchestra has several concerts a year. Membership is open to the public. Ticket prices for performances of this traditional orchestra vary widely; some concerts are even free.

Time Change
Various locations • 587-7932

Approximately 10 times a year, this all-vocal group performs sacred music from the late Medieval and early Renaissance period, including some chant repertoire. A mixed-gender group of 10 people, Time Change stages their performances of work from mostly obscure composers in area churches. Performances are often free but occasionally charge a nominal fee. Call for details.

Theater

Bunbury Theatre
112 S. Seventh St. • 585-5306

Professional and nonprofessional actors from the area comprise the Bunbury Theatre, an alternative troupe that performs the gamut from comedies to classics to contemporary pieces and musicals.

INSIDERS' TIP

If you love being around priceless works of art, consider sharing your interest as a docent at the J.B. Speed Art Museum. After an in-depth art history course taught by the museum's education department and practice tours of the galleries, you'll guide visitors and groups around the collections.

Photo: Kentucky Opera

The Kentucky Opera began in 1952.

Since 1985, Bunbury has pulled people to their five-show seasons using plays such as *Godspell*, *The Real Inspector Hound*, *Coffee with Kurt Cobain* and *The Foreigner*. Their intimate performance space is housed in a historic building between Main and Market streets that once held a bank and later a cap factory.

Ticket prices hover around $10; Bunbury's season runs September through June. Seasonal auditions are in August.

Roundtable Theatre
The Rudyard Kipling Restaurant, 422 W. Oak St. • 636-1311

One of the most active, and certainly one of the best publicized theater troupes in the city, the Roundtable Theatre at The Rudyard Kipling is popular not only because the pro-

ductions often feature intriguing works by local playwrights, but also because a home-style dinner is an added option for the theatergoer. Plays begin in early evening; call for information about current productions. Tickets for the play are usually around $8; meals are extra.

Belknap Theatre
The Playhouse, Third St. and Cardinal Blvd. • 852-6814

Run by the University of Louisville's theater department, the company is a combination of community, faculty and students performing plays ranging from Brown & Smalls' *The Wiz* to those of Euripides. Roughly seven plays a year are staged in The Playhouse, a renovated building that was originally a small board-and-batten Gothic Revival chapel. For ticket information and play schedules, call the above number.

Visual Arts

Associations and Museums

J.B. Speed Art Museum
2035 S. Third St. • 636-2893

Works by Rembrandt, Rubens, Tiepolo, Monet and Picasso are highlights in the first and largest art museum in Kentucky and Southern Indiana, established in January 1927.

The Satterwhite Gallery at the Speed houses a distinguished collection of tapestries, textiles and other works from the Renaissance and Baroque periods, while the museum's modern art section continues to grow, anchored by pieces from Constantin Brancusi, Henry Moore, Philip Pearlstein and Sam Gilliam, a Louisville native. Within walking distance of the museum is a reproduction of Rodin's *The Thinker*, which was produced under the sculptor's supervision. In all, more than 6,000 pieces spanning 6,000 years of history are under the care of the Speed Museum, a fine example of neoclassical architecture located adjacent to the University of Louisville campus.

A recent $12 million renovation has touched nearly every inch of the museum's 110,000 square feet of space, improving the lighting and ventilation systems and providing an interactive center that allows hands-on learning via studio workshops, computer stations and other resources.

The Museum Cafe and Museum Shop are open to members and nonmembers. Museum admission is free, unless specified for special exhibitions. Docent-led tours can be arranged for school and community groups, and public tours are held weekly. The museum is closed on Monday.

Louisville Visual Art Association
3005 Upper River Rd. at Zorn Ave.
• 896-2146

The LVAA creates what is arguably the city's best conceived art center at their headquarters on the river adjacent to downtown. More than 300 art and craft classes are offered to adults and children throughout the year; new shows featuring artists ranging from nine-year-old novices to internationally known talents are displayed in six-week runs; and several popular special events put the center prominently in the spotlight each year.

The buildings that house the association are an attraction in themselves — the 183-foot Water Tower and River Pumping Station #1 (put into operation in 1860 by the Louisville Water Company) are on the registry of National Historic Landmarks (see Historic Preservation and Architecture). The setting has helped form the philosophy of the association, which views art as it does water — an important component of human life and rituals that should be accessible to everyone. Few places in the city foster visual arts as dynamically and invigoratingly as The Water Tower does.

The sales and rental gallery and gift shop are open daily, with shorter hours on the weekend. Admission is free.

Galleries

Artswatch
2337 Frankfort Ave. • 893-9661

This gallery, which has been driven by an organization by the same name since 1988, is Louisville's home for the contemporary and cutting edge. Electronic paintings, which combine computer-generated images and traditional painting techniques, have graced the gallery, as has art that utilizes found materials and large format full-color photographs. Performance art, contemporary dance and jazz and music improvisation groups have also staged shows at this small, storefront gallery in the Clifton neighborhood. Artswatch is closed on Sunday and Monday.

Bellarmine College
McGrath Art Gallery
Wyatt Hall, 2000 Norris Pl. • 452-8499

This gallery is notable because it's both a stop for regional and national exhibits and it has a penchant for showing the work of artists bubbling up in the community — art students, faculty and undiscovered talents. A nice space with lots of natural light, the McGrath is open Monday through Saturday.

B. Deemer Gallery
2650 Frankfort Ave. • 896-6687

A roughly 50-50 mix of local and national artists show at this Crescent Hill gallery, which leans toward two-dimensional works in the school of impressionism. Most shows run four to six weeks. Custom framing is available at B. Deemer, which is open Monday through Saturday.

Brownsboro Gallery
4806 Brownsboro Center • 893-5209

This well-established East End gallery takes special pride in showing works by Kentucky and Southern Indiana artists, rotating a new exhibit in every six weeks. Works include paintings, drawings and watercolors. It's open Tuesday through Saturday.

Cathedral Heritage Foundation Spiritual Art Gallery
429 W. Muhammad Ali Blvd. • 583-3100

Although it's housed in the Cathedral of the Assumption, a historic Roman Catholic church, this gallery is an interfaith center that searches for ways to expose people to spiritual art that reflects the artist's personal experience of faith. Various cultural traditions and spiritual perspectives are explored in all media and in both contemporary and traditional styles. Exhibits change throughout the year; the gallery is closed on Saturday.

Discoveries
1315 Bardstown Rd. • 451-5034

Owner Donna Stone travels widely, buying pieces from Thailand to Turkey, from China to Kenya for this gallery, a pleasing mix of old and new art, antiques and ethnic jewelry,

beads, clothing, textiles and accessories from around the world. It's open seven days a week.

Edenside Gallery
1422 Bardstown Rd. • 459-2787

For many, the draw of Edenside is its extensive art jewelry collection, which features work by metalsmiths from across the country. But this local favorite also hosts several shows a year in which textiles and other two-dimensional works take over the gallery for more than a month. Fine crafts and home furnishings are also on sale at this gallery, which is open Tuesday through Saturday.

E & S Gallery
10282 Shelbyville Rd. • 244-7974

Notable for its African-American art, this gallery, housed in an East End shopping plaza, also shows American Indian, Oriental, Southwestern and general art. The gallery is closed Sunday.

Galerie Hertz
636 E. Market St. • 584-3547

Billy Hertz, the owner of this contemporary art gallery and a painter of substantial reputation, looks for works from local, national and international artists who show special skill in handling image and color. A large, charming sculpture garden in the back of the gallery has brought Galerie Hertz national notoriety, and special exhibits such as a recent small show of Matisse works further heighten its profile. Selections range from realism to surrealism. It's open Wednesday through Saturday, or by appointment.

Images Friedman Gallery
833 W. Main St. second floor • 584-7954

The scale of this gallery is mind-boggling, with more than 10,000 square feet of space housing more visual images than one could possibly ingest in anything less than an hour. The works range from glass sculptures to furniture to photos to oil paintings — and beyond. The emphasis is overwhelmingly on contemporary styles and vivid colors — much like the work of the gallery's namesake, Louisville graphic artist and world-renowned designer Julius Friedman. Posters of some of his most famous work, including *Fresh Paint* (colored egg yolks) and a poster for the Louisville Ballet (a ballerina's slippered foot balancing on an egg) are on sale at the gallery, which is open Wednesday through Saturday.

Yvonne Rapp Gallery
2117 Frankfort Ave. • 896-2331

In a brick house dating to 1871, this gallery shows the works of the more than 40 artists it represents from across the nation. Paintings, sculptures and drawings, mostly of a contemporary nature, are available for viewing Monday through Saturday.

Swanson Cralle Gallery
1377 Bardstown Rd. • 452-2904

This gallery enjoys a high profile in the Louisville art scene, in no small part because of its prime location in the Highlands neighborhood and also due to its focus on colorists and other artists with a bracing, contemporary style. Five exhibitions with five-week runs are shown each year featuring paintings, sculptures, contemporary crafts and furniture. It's closed on Sunday.

TriArt Gallery
400 W. Market Street • 585-5550

Part of a nonprofit partnership with three other area agencies, this new gallery has leapt into the city's consciousness with its very eclectic selection of local, national and international artists working in glass, photography, oils and other media. The 2,600-square-foot TriArt Gallery is conspicuous, occupying part of the lobby floor of the Providian Tower, with four large windows to the outside world. It's closed on Sunday.

University of Louisville Photographic Archives
Ekstrom Library, Belknap Campus
• 852-6752

More than an archive, this collection of vintage photographs and historic documents is also displayed in the gallery in rotated exhibits. Copies of many of the photographs, which focus mainly on Louisville and Kentucky, can be purchased for a small fee. It's open Monday through Friday.

Zephyr Gallery
610 E. Main St. • 585-5646

If you want to see what Louisville-area artists are producing, this gallery is a place to begin. Approximately 20 local artists have pooled their efforts, bringing the gallery alternating shows of their works. Consigners throughout the region participate in an annual out-of-towners show. The gallery is open Wednesday through Saturday.

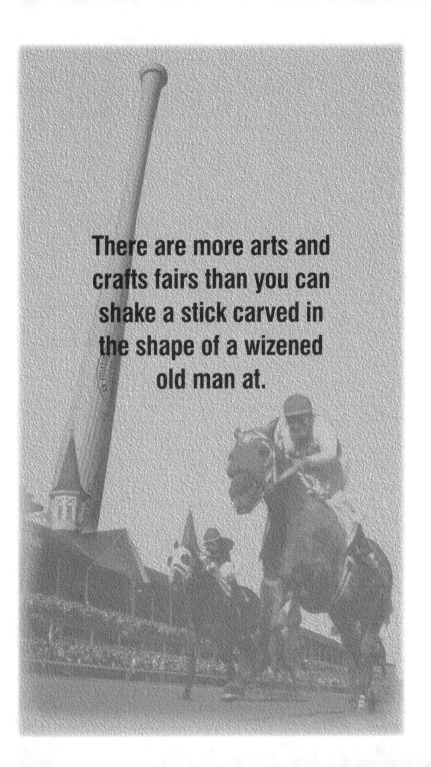

There are more arts and crafts fairs than you can shake a stick carved in the shape of a wizened old man at.

Annual Events and Festivals

Some of Louisville's best moments come once a year, every year:

The car show, where chrome wraps around engines clean enough to eat off, and Trans Ams rotate slowly on mirrored, neon-trimmed pedestals.

The streets of downtown given over for one sweaty, hacking weekend to games of three-on-three basketball.

The State Fair — the world in a corn dog.

There are very few weekends when the Louisville area doesn't host some festival or other public event. The Mayor's Office publishes an annual list of the city's Top 40 Festivals, but it would be just as easy to do a Hot 100, and there would still be omissions from the list. The church picnic, the fish fry, even the ice cream social are still vital institutions in this community, and many people have what you might call "festival friends" — folks they meet every year at the same event and otherwise never see.

Although some of the most successful festivals to come on the scene in recent years charge an admission — anywhere from $2.50 to $11, depending on the event — the majority of Louisville's major festivals are free.

They cover an impressive range of interests. Just look at music — there are festivals devoted to bluegrass, blues, reggae, jazz or oldies rock. (Although you're advised not to hold your breath waiting for a gangsta rap or hardcore punk festival.) There are more arts and crafts fairs than you can shake a stick carved in the shape of a wizened old man at and opportunities to eat some of the finest food served in a city with a pretty decent restaurant scene.

And most of the festivals we've chosen to highlight are in absolutely beautiful settings, from the tree-lined, architectural showpiece that is St. James Court to the city's magnificent park system.

What follows is a selective list of some of the principal dates on the Louisville calendar. (The biggest festival of all — the 70-odd events that make up the Kentucky Derby Festival — is dealt with in the chapter The Derby and The Downs.) The festivals are listed according to their traditional dates, which should be reliable for some years to come — all of these events have their space on the calendar carved out jealously and are just slightly more likely to change their date than the Derby is likely to be moved to July. Unless an entry says otherwise, all events and parking are free.

January

Sport, Boat, RV and Vacation Show
Kentucky Fair and Exposition Center, 937 Phillips Ln. • 244-5660

A chance to dream about summer in the dead of winter: All the outdoor gear a person could ever wish to own, RVs, seminars on hunting and fishing and a chance to see the latest developments in bass-fishing and anti-no-see'um technology. It's held the last week of January; admission is $6.50 for adults, free for children 12 and younger; seniors 60 and older are $5.50, and there's a $3 charge for Fairgrounds parking.

Kentucky Craft Market
Kentucky Fair and Exposition Center, 937 Phillips Ln. • (502) 564-8076

Many people look forward to this all year — craftspeople from throughout the state eager to expose their wares to a wider market, and shoppers eager to buy those wares. In addition to baskets, throw rugs and other traditional crafts, there are free samples of Kentucky food and booths from Kentucky book publishers and the redoubtable Appalshop, a media collective based in Whitesburg, Ky., that is dedicated to preserving Eastern Kentucky's past and exploring the issues of its present. The event draws upwards of 10,000 the last full Friday, Saturday and Sunday in January, but it's only open to the public those last two days (wholesalers have the place to themselves Friday). There are also demonstrations of different traditional pursuits — for example, whittling and marble-making — and other presentations of cultural interest. Admission is $4; children aged 6 to 12 are $1, those 5 and younger are free; there's a $3 charge for Fairgrounds parking.

February

DinnerWorks
The Water Tower, 3005 Upper River Rd.
• 896-2146

This series of four events brings together 30 ceramic artists, half of them local and half national, and local designers to put together some of the most eye-catching dinner tables you've ever seen. One was a beach theme, with a lifeguard's chair as a centerpiece; others have been inspired by everything from a New York subway station to Alice in Wonderland.

It kicks off in late January with a black tie dinner (tickets are $175 each) and then at roughly one-week intervals events around other meals — AfterDinnerWorks (champagne and hors d'oeurves, $25); the DinnerWorks Tea ($15) and the DinnerWorks Luncheon (featuring a guest speaker, $25). It's held in conjunction with CityWorks, a citywide event in which local galleries display ceramic and other interesting kitchen- and dinnerware.

Kentucky Author Dinner
Louisville Free Public Library Main Branch, 301 York St. • 574-1648

The Friends of the Library put on this an-

nual dinner, that rarity among banquets — a truly interesting evening with (more often than not) good food. Modeled on the New York Public Library's "Literary Lions" dinner, it seats a Kentucky author (especially folks who recently published books) at each table; a nationally-known author speaks after dinner. Speakers have included Tony Hillerman, Mary Gordon, Pat Conroy and Wendell Berry. The date moves around between Saturdays in early February. Tickets are $125, and reservations are required. (Free parking can be found on the streets around the library and in the small lot across from the entrance for the party on York Street.)

The Friends of the Library also put on mammoth book sales in spring and fall; their dates and locations vary. And it's worth keeping an eye peeled for other events they sponsor: In recent years they've sponsored speeches by the likes of William Zinsser and Stephen Jay Gould.

Carl Casper's Custom Auto Show
Kentucky Fair and Exposition Center, 937 Phillips Ln. • 267-0077

One of the Midwest's largest car shows is the key date on the local automotive calendar — a chance to show off that '65 Corvette that was mentioned in one count of your divorce decree, an opportunity to inform the world what a low-rider is supposed to look like, a time to let that 4x4 strut. While the acres of immaculately groomed cars are the heart of the event, which claims to be the world's largest indoor custom auto show, they're always combined with hoopla to entertain the less automotively inclined — a battle of the bands, appearances by television characters, bikini-clad calendar girls and celebrity cars (the Batmobile, KITT from "Knight Rider"). It's held the third weekend of the month. Admission is $8 for adults, $3 for children 12 and younger, children 5 and younger are free; there is a $3 charge for Fairgrounds parking.

Louisville is also the occasional host city for the National Street Rod Association's annual August convention, an incredible exhibition of customized pre-1949 automobiles. August 1998 is our next turn. For more information, call the organization's Memphis headquarters, (901) 452-4030.

The Hairball
Various locations • 456-9997

This is wild, in a way Louisville rarely gets, and a great deal of hair-raising fun. It's a benefit for the AIDS support service Heart to Heart. Various organizations — salons, restaurants, galleries — compete to raise the most money for the charity; each of them brings someone in outrageous costume. The grand prize goes to the biggest fundraiser, while the costume contest entertains the crowd. A couple of classics from the past: Ethel Mer-Man, a brawny guy wearing nothing but a mermaid's tail; Cosmic Miranda, a variation on Carmen Miranda in which items from space replaced the fruit the Brazilian singer wore on her head. Someone once wore a hat with such a wide brim it could accommodate a battery-powered train. It's in February, around Mardi Gras, but there's no definite date. Admission is $10.

March

Humana Festival of New American Plays
Actors Theatre of Louisville, 316 W. Main St. • 584-1205

The festival that made Actors' name continues to be one of the most important events of the theatrical year, when between 10 and 12 new plays are given their first major productions. Among the successes the festival spawned are *The Gin Game*; Louisville native Marsha Norman's *Getting Out*; Beth Henley's *Crimes of the Heart*; *Agnes of God*; *Extremities*; *Talking With* and *Keely and Du* by the notoriously reclusive Jane Martin; and *Danny and the Deep Blue Sea*, the first success for playwright John Patrick Shanley and actor John Turturro. For every weak play — we recall only the protagonist's name from one: He was called Gurk — there's an image indelibly printed on the mind, like Holly Hunter's leaping lingerie show in 1983's *Eden Court*.

The festival is held throughout March and into early April. There are two Visitors' Weekends where it's possible to come and see all of the festival's plays; in addition, the ATL box office sets up Humana Festival tour packages that include accommodations at downtown hotels. Admission to the plays ranges from $10 to $33; the average ticket is about $22 weeknights, $27 on the weekends. Parking in the Actors Garage is $3 in advance during performances.

Frankfort Avenue Easter Parade
Frankfort Ave. from Stilz Ave. to State St. • 896-4262

Perhaps the most informal — and in contention for the most enjoyable — event we list here, this event the Saturday before Easter is a spontaneous, homemade parade with a budget in the hundreds of dollars and no requirements to register (although large groups are asked to call ahead). Consequently, you'll see everything from dressed-up dogs to Shriners in little cars and hear anything from bagpipes to the clip-clop of a horsedrawn carriage.

April

Knob Creek Military Gun Show
Knob Creek Gun Range, 690 Ritchey Ln., West Point, Ky. • 922-4457

Hands-down, this is the loudest event we list here: A biannual gathering devoted to showing, selling and most of all shooting some of the most fearsome armaments known to man: machine guns, tanks, howitzers, the kind of gun Arnold Schwarzenegger packed in *Predator*, Civil War canon and the weapon Steven Seagal used to bring down an airplane in *Under Siege*.

If your hobby is collecting automatic and military weapons, Knob Creek is like Derby — an event that attracts an international crowd of impressive size (between 8,000 and 10,000 in attendance) and gathers a growing crowd the entire week leading up to the big weekend. For connoisseurs of the bizarre, it's a chance to see a pack of good old boys shoot up old cars and appliances into so much scrap metal. But recent years have seen some brushes with tragedy — a large gun fell on a teenaged girl, crushing her to death; and videotapes of the 1994 event showed Timothy McVeigh in the crowd. It's held the second Friday, Saturday and Sunday of the month (and the same weekend in October). Admission is $7 a day; a three-day weekend pass is $15; parking is free.

Cherokee Triangle Olde Time Fair
Cherokee Pkwy. at Everett Ave. • 451-3534

The tree-lined heart of one of the city's prettiest neighborhoods fills with a juried arts and crafts show ("juried" means quality-controlled, essentially) and concessions stands. (Drinks are served in sturdy green plastic cups that are almost as ubiquitous in folks' cabinets as Derby julep cups.) It's held the last Saturday and Sunday in April, on perhaps the busiest day of the Derby Festival, but it holds its own in attendance with any of the weekend's events. The day also includes a children's parade, a hefty dose of live music played from a classic gazebo bandstand and a lot of old-fashioned socializing. Saturday night, after most of the booths are closed, the music and refreshments continue in a street party that's become a regular part of the event. Admission is free.

Festival of the Dogwood
City of Audubon Park • 637-5066

This celebration of flowering trees and shrubs is one of the most resolutely uncommercial festivals in the city. There are no concession stands hawking tiger ears and corn dogs, just a booth with homemade cookies, coffee and punch. Some members of the Garden Club and other residents put on antebellum attire; some people entertain by playing music from their front porches. There's an opening ceremony, and an old-fashioned band concert is played Sunday afternoon.

But the key is simply the beauty of dogwoods, azaleas and the like when they reach full flower. The painstakingly tended bushes in the city's central Henderson (formerly Wren) Park have spotlights trained on them; many residents follow suit in their own yards (Audubon Park is not a place to live if you take your lawn lightly). The neighborhood is clogged with foot and auto traffic. The festival is often, but not always, on the Friday through Sunday of the weekend before Derby Week — the date is set early in the year by the true power in this fifth-class city, the Audubon Park Garden Club. Its members try to determine the weekend when the dogwoods are most likely to be at their peak. Admission is free.

Audubon Park runs between Preston Highway and Eagle Pass (a street three blocks west of Poplar Level Road) and from Hess Lane to Cardinal Drive.

May

The amazing thing is that the Derby Festival (see The Derby and the Downs chapter) doesn't turn us into couch potatoes for the rest of the month.

Pitt Academy Barbecue
Location to be announced • 966-6979

The food's the thing — barbecued mutton, chicken and pork prepared by the St. Pius X Catholic Church cooking team from Owensboro, the state's barbecue center, along with fine burgoo and other side dishes. It may be the best barbecue you can get in Louisville

The "Bedlam in the Streets" bed races is one of the zaniest events of the Derby festivals.

(especially Western Kentucky's specialty, the smoked mutton).

It's also a fine, unpretentious social occasion. Folks spend several hours catching up with friends at the long tables set up on the grass. Politicians work the crowd. There are a host of games of the put-your-dime-on-a-number-and-win-a-prize variety, a children's activity center and a shifting roster of entertainment. (Ever seen anyone clog-dance to "Born in the USA"?) It's usually held the third Saturday of the month. Admission (but not barbecue) is free. The event benefits the Pitt Academy (formerly the Ursuline-Pitt School), a local school for special-needs children.

Barbecue organizers are mulling over new spots for the event. Call ahead of time to find out what they've decided on.

Skyline Chili 500
Jefferson Square, Jefferson and Sixth Sts. • 589-3837

It's not the Grand Prix, but it's certainly enjoyable: This event which takes place the third Sunday of the month and benefits the American Diabetes Association pits miniature Indy-style cars (top speed 30 mph) driven on the streets around Jefferson Square by teams from local businesses and other groups (the police department, Hausman Jeep/Eagle,

WQMF-FM and others). There's also a "Kids Korner," concessions and other assorted hoopla. Admission is free.

Kentucky Reggae Festival
The Water Tower, 3005 Upper River Rd. • 583-0333

Kentucky Reggae Festival is a rare opportunity for mostly landlocked Louisville to indulge in Caribbean culture. In addition to music from local and regional reggae bands, there is a limbo contest, a Caribbean Market and food of a more goat-heavy grade than you usually find in these parts. It's held the Saturday and Sunday of Memorial Day weekend. Admission is $5 before 6 PM, $8 after; children 10 and younger are free.

June

Portland Family Reunion
Portland Park, 27th and Montgomery Sts. • 774-2313

Portland was once a city with ambitions to rival Louisville, and even since it was incorporated into the city it has kept a passionate sense of identity. (It recently started its own Hall of Fame for famous natives; the first group included a resident of several other Halls of

Fame, Paul Hornung of the Green Bay Packers, Notre Dame University and Flaget High School). Its homecoming festival has a "Reunion Garden" that features neighborhood talent, along with a register book that helps people track down long-lost friends; another stage has a variety of musical entertainment, from country to the blues. You'll also find a parade, craft booths and rides. The event, formerly called the Portland festival, is alcohol-free. It's the first Saturday of June. Admission is free.

Kentucky Sampler
Infield at Churchill Downs, 700 Central Ave. • 636-4400

A look at some of the best-known Kentucky folkways — the food, the crafts, the horses — is held during two racing afternoons at the Downs. There's bluegrass, barbecue, burgoo, clogging and country ham (clogging in a different sense of the word); a collection of craftspeople from around the state; and an equine section that features 20 different breeds and a blacksmithing demonstration. There's also a chance for anyone, no matter how physically ill-suited, to dress in jockey silks and get a picture taken on top of a horse. It's the first weekend of June; admission is free with track admission.

Equitana USA
Kentucky Fair and Exposition Center, 937 Phillips Ln. • (817) 283-8953

It's not your normal trade show when a quarter horse walks down the center aisle of the exhibit hall and nobody yells for the cops.

They like to call it "the world's fair of equestrian sports" — an international exposition with 600 vendors, 600 horses, 400 different lectures, seminars and demonstrations. If it's about, for, regarding or resembling horses, you can probably find it here, from horseshoe nails to Western apparel to equine-patterned wall-paper.

Daytime is for shopping, meeting and greeting and learning your way from flank to fetlock. At night, the action turns to Freedom Hall, where the Mane Event provides one of the slickest, most showbiz equestrian exhibitions this side of the Little Big Horn (some folks call it the Horsecapades).

Oh, and in case you were wondering — the carpet is one the decorator was going to throw away anyway, and there's a brigade of volunteers on pooper-scooper patrol. It's usually the Thursday through Sunday of the third weekend (although the organizers, the Miller Freeman Group USA, says that could possibly change). Admission is $10 a day or $25 for all four days of the trade show; tickets for the Mane Event require separate admission and range from $18 to $30; parking costs $3.

Winn-Dixie Street Ball Showdown
First and Second Sts. near Broadway and the Jefferson Community College parking lot • 636-1888, (800) 445-0256

This is cool, whether you play or watch — more than 80 basketball courts in a downtown parking lot and streets; more than 1,000 teams, with players ranging in age from 8 to 50-something, all of them playing three-on-three hoops. The action goes on, even in a hard rain — it's street ball, man, not that sissy stuff they play in a gym. There's also a slam dunk contest. If your team didn't sign up in time, there are other games at this basketball festival to show off your shot: A free-throw contest and a game in which you try to make a basket on a rotating goal. There's also a children's area. The Showdown benefits the Cabbage Patch Settlement House (as does a sister event, the Winn-Dixie 3-on-3 Jamboree, held indoors in late winter or early spring at the Kentucky Fair and Exposition Center). The Showdown is held the last weekend of June. Admission is free, but there's an $88 entry fee. Registration ends a week before the event.

Greek Festival
Assumption Greek Orthodox Church, 932 S. Fifth St. (near Cunningham's Restaurant) • 587-6247

The moussaka, souvlaki, dolmathes and pastries galore don't come in bulk from Mike's Make-A-Festival in Chicago — all the Greek dishes in this friendly ethnic festival are made by church members. There's also live Greek music and dancing, Greek jewelry and art, books on Greek history, culture and religion and tours of the church. It's the last Friday, Saturday and Sunday in June; admission is free.

Pride Fair
Willow Park, Cherokee Pkwy. at Willow Ave. • 574-5496

This event is held to promote AIDS awareness and benefit Community Health Trust AIDS and Wellness Services, a nonprofit organization that provides services to people with AIDS as well as addressing health issues in the gay and lesbian community. There's entertainment, information from a wide variety of community-based organizations, a raffle, food, arts and crafts and information on HIV, AIDS and local services for people with HIV-related conditions. It's the last Saturday of the month; admission is free.

July

Waterside
The Water Tower, 3005 Upper River Rd. • 896-2146

A popular event featuring high-quality arts and music in a historic setting on the banks of the Ohio, the Louisville Visual Art Association's Waterside used to be exclusively dedicated to the blues. Last year some Cajun and world music sneaked into the mix, but the core remains the sound that came from the Delta up to Chicago. Artists who've performed have included the cream of local blues talent and Johnny Winter, Albert King, Delbert McClinton, former Rolling Stones guitarist Mick Taylor, Lou Ann Barton, Saffire — The Uppity Blues Women, Zachary Richard, Marcia Ball, Pinetop Perkins and Tinsley Ellis. There are also arts workshops and children's activities. The event is held on the Saturday and Sunday nearest July 4th. Admission is $3 before 6 PM, $6 thereafter. Two-day passes are sold in advance.

Rockin' at Riverpoints
The wharf area of Waterfront Park, between First and Second Sts. • 574-3768

This series of 10 Friday evening concerts was a big success in its first year (1997). It presented national and local acts from .38 Special to Southern Culture on the Skids to the Fixx to Joe Ely to Louisville resident Duke Robillard. The free shows last from 5 to 11 PM. They also include concessions and, on the Fourth of July, a big ole fireworks show.

Crescent Hill Old Fashioned Fourth of July
Peterson-Dumesnil House, 301 S. Peterson Ave. • 895-7975

Crescent Hill throws this old-time celebration kicked off by a parade of antique cars and brought to a rousing conclusion with fireworks in the evening (some of them fired from the roof of the National Register house, built in 1868, the grounds of which are the site of the shindig). There's also a popular children's pet show, arts and crafts and a variety of festival food and drink. It's a neighborhood festival that spills over into nearby streets: Many Crescent Hill residents have their own parties on the Fourth and watch the fireworks from front porches and backyards, while the Peterson-Dumesnil grounds remain crowded with folks who came from more distant climes, like St. Matthews. Admission is free.

Operation Brightside/Coca-Cola Volleyball Classic
Infield at Churchill Downs, 700 Central Ave. • 574-4030

A chance for more sober exertions in the infield than on Derby Day, this classic is one of the country's largest volleyball tournaments, with nearly 500 teams and volleyball nets spreading as far as the eye can see. The event benefits Operation Brightside, the city's donor-supported beautification and environmental program. It's usually held the third weekend of the month. Admission is $1 for adults; children 12 and younger are admitted free; there is a fee to participate (it was $17 a person in 1997).

National City Kentucky Music Weekend
Iroquois Park Amphitheater, Iroquois Park, Taylor Blvd. and Southern Pkwy. • (502) 348-5237, 367-9493

Not all the music in this three-day celebration of acoustic Kentucky sounds is made by Kentucky performers, but the "furriners" belong to the musical streams leading in and out of the state: You might hear an Irish band (precursor) or a bluegrass band from Missouri (diaspora). It's a big event for dulcimer players, acoustic purists and normal folk alike. There are performances in the amphitheater, "close-up" concerts in nearby parts of the park, workshops on topics such as storytelling, harmony singing and banjo, foodstuffs and a concurrent arts and crafts fair. It's the last Friday, Saturday and Sunday of July; admission is free.

August

West Louisville Appreciation Celebration
Shawnee Park, Broadway and Southern Pkwy. • 772-2591

The major festival in the city's African-American community has become so diverse that it resembles a small-scale Derby Festival: It includes a parade honoring civil rights pioneer Lyman Johnson, a hot-air balloon race, a 5K run, a volleyball tournament, booths from area businesses and public service agencies, music from national rhythm and blues artists and a large-scale family reunion for Louisville clans. It also features some games of the Dirt Bowl — Louisville's long-running amateur basketball tournament, which often features future- or past-tense talent from local college and high school teams. It's held the first weekend of the month; admission is free.

St. Joseph Orphans Picnic
2823 Frankfort Ave. • 893-0241

Probably the oldest and largest example of that great Louisville institution, the Catholic picnic, it provides game and crafts booths, a famous chicken dinner and other food and serves as a major reunion spot for folks throughout the city. The picnic has been held every year since 1851 and since 1885 on the present 36 acres of expansive, tree-shaded grounds in Crescent Hill.

It's the main fundraiser for St. Joseph Children's Home, which opened in 1849 to serve German Catholic orphans. It's now non-sectarian and multi-ethnic and tends to serve what director Dennis Davis calls "orphans of the living," children who are victims of abuse and neglect. (St. Joseph's also runs associated foster care and child care programs). It's held the second Saturday in August from noon to midnight.

Strassenfest
The wharf area of Waterfront Park, between First and Second Sts. • 561-3440

It remains an enormously popular beer-and-brats bash, but in recent years the city's celebration of its German heritage has classed itself up considerably. Its Artfest brings together craft demonstrations, performances by regional fine arts groups and a juried arts festival. Strassenfest also purveys more puns on the word "duck" — from the waddling German "duck dance" that is a touchstone for the event — than should be legal, and a "Battle of the Downtown Stars" in which teams from local businesses compete in such events as the Beer Bucket Relay and the Pretzel Pass. And there's continual food and free entertainment.

Now that it's moved to Waterfront Park, Strassenfest is taking full advantage of the water — pleasure boats can dock at the wharf; it has reinstated the "KenDucky Derby" — see what I mean? — in which 20,000 rubber duckies take the plunge off the Clark Memorial Bridge; and a "Tall Stacks" event with as many riverboats as they can lay hands on is being planned for '98.

Strassenfest is held Friday, Saturday and Sunday of the first full weekend of August. Admission is free.

Jazz in Central Park
Central Park, Fourth St. • 562-0175

Jazz on a summer's day, squared: For a Saturday and Sunday, the stage that usually presents Shakespeare devotes itself to a cooler art form. A combination of local and regional jazz acts, spiked with a few national names, draws a crowd that's diverse in age and ethnic background. It's takes place on the third weekend of the month and all performances are free.

Kentucky State Fair
Kentucky Fair and Exposition Center, 937 Phillips Ln. • 367-5000

How can you not love the state fair? Nothing blends the mundane and surreal so effortlessly. (One friend of ours walked into a midway freak show and saw a girl from his 11th-grade algebra class working as the woman with the body of a spider: "Why, it's Barbie Fox!") And few things exert such a gravitational pull on the city: Louisville seems a little different when the fair is in town.

For 11 days starting the second Thursday in August, the fairgrounds hosts competitions you never imagined existed — best beeswax blocks; local qualifying for the national "Best Spam Recipe" contest; oldest family Bible; a costumed poultry competition; racing armadillos. It's one of the best chances for citybound folk to see pigs, goats and polled Herefords. There's always at least one free concert by a genuine legend (Ray Charles, the Everly Brothers, Bill Monroe, the Temptations), or you can catch one of the pricey concerts by hot artists of the moment (lately, the schedule has been leaning heavily toward country). There's enough fudge for sale to veneer Freedom Hall. The World Championship Horse Show offers the richest purses in the saddlebred world. The Midway will fill your stomach, then yank it halfway to Corbin. And the 13-foot-tall figure of Freddy the Farmer sitting on the right side of the Freedom Hall porch will talk to anyone who happens to stroll by, same as he has since 1958. It's also comfortable — it's the largest air-conditioned fair in the country.

Admission in 1997 was $6 for adults, $2 for children 12 and younger and seniors; parking costs $2. There are a variety of special promotions and ticket discounts; check the newspapers for details.

September

Rock the Watertower
The Water Tower, 3005 Upper River Rd.
• 583-0333

What began in the mid '80s as a private party has bloomed into a farewell-to-summer bash that draws between 5,000 and 10,000 to the city's prettiest outdoor venue on the Sunday of Labor Day weekend. Organizers describe it as that apparent oxymoron, a "family-

driven" rock and roll party. But the music comes in the styles of the '50s through the '70s, rather than any more recent, polarizing genre. Children younger than 10 get in free, and there are such un-Jerry Lee events as a 5K run and a hot-air balloon display. Admission is $4 before 6 PM, $8 afterward.

St. Michael Ethnic Fair
St. Michael the Archangel Orthodox
Church, 3026 Hikes Ln. • 454-3378

This church's diverse ethnic makeup — Arabic, Greek, Indian, Slavic and Ethiopian — allows its festival to have one of the most intriguing food lines you'll ever pass through (it's educational, too — everyone provides information on ingredients and how they're prepared). There are tours of the beautifully mosaic-tiled, icon-filled sanctuary; rides; Slavic, Greek and Arabic dancing and entertainment; the carnival versions of ethnic food (gyros, kebab); a bookstore; and a gift shop with clothing, jewelry and ornaments. It's held Friday through Sunday of the first weekend in September; admission is free.

The Strictly Bluegrass Festival
Iroquois Amphitheater, Iroquois Park,
Taylor Blvd. and Southern Pkwy.
• 448-9107, 447-8657

This alcohol-free event celebrates what Bill Monroe wrought — and nothing but — with two days of performances. Past years' performers have included Jimmy Martin, Ralph Stanley, the Osborne Brothers, Del McCoury, J.D. Crowe, Larry Sparks, the Country Gentlemen and the late father of bluegrass himself. It's the second weekend of September; admission is free.

Corn Island Storytelling Festival
E.P. "Tom" Sawyer State Park, 3000
Freys Hill Rd., and Long Run Park, 1607
Flat Rock Rd. • 245-0643

One of the country's major showcases for

INSIDERS' TIP

Look to the river. With the impending completion of the Waterfront Project (scheduled for late 1998), many of the festivals that aren't wed to a certain neighborhood or site (or driven inside by the weather) will be moving down there, following the example — as we all do, every day in every way — of Strassenfest.

the reviving art of storytelling, Corn Island is named after the now-submerged island that saw the first European settlement in the Louisville area. It was at one time a peripatetic event, with sessions all over town, including on the *Belle of Louisville* steamboat. The festival now holds most of its doings at E.P. "Tom" Sawyer State Park (named for the late county judge who was Diane Sawyer's dad) while its incredibly popular night of ghost stories draws between 15,000 and 18,000 to Long Run Park (unless it rains), and a storytelling tour of the city keeps alive its footloose roots.

The roster of storytellers has included, in the words of founder and guiding spirit Lee Pennington, "the people who, if you had a storytelling heaven, they would be the first ones to go in, and they wouldn't have to stop in Atlanta on the way." Their ages have at times spanned nearly a century from the youngest to the oldest. More than 150 storytellers have appeared at Corn Island over the years, including a 110-year-old man who'd been Theodore Roosevelt's bodyguard and a Huli tribesman from the rain forest of Papua, New Guinea.

The International Order of E.A.R.S., the organization that puts on Corn Island, also hosts an evening of ghost stories in May.

It's the third Friday and Saturday of September. Tickets are $10, $5 for children ages 6 to 12, for each of the regular programs (there are four on Friday and five on Saturday) weekend tickets are $50, $90 a couple, $30 for children. Tickets are sold in advance through the International Order of E.A.R.S. (call the number above).

Ursuline Campus Art Fair
3105 Lexington Rd. • 896-3999

At the Ursuline Campus Art Fair you'll find more juried arts and crafts in another beautiful setting — the grassy, tree-lined Ursuline campus. It attracts the sort of artists who harvest their own wood rather than making a trip to the lumber yard every couple of weeks, and it includes other arts as well as the visual ones — in the past, the Louisville Bach Society has played, and the Ursuline School of Music and Drama's students have performed an adaptation of *Charlotte's Web*. There's also a children's art area. It's held the third weekend of the month; admission is free.

Gaslight Festival
Gaslight Square in Jeffersontown (Watterson Trail between Taylorsville and Biltown Rds.) • 267-2070

This is not a week where the residents of a small Jefferson County city attempt to drive each other crazy as their homage to an Ingrid Bergman film. It's a festival that takes place in the middle of the month that celebrates historic Jeffersontown, incorporated in 1797. There's a parade, a firefighters' Olympics, a 5K run, a golf tournament, a balloon race and a weekend full of arts and crafts — and a chance for proud Jeffersontonians (don't call it J-town, if you know what's good for you) to show their community spirit.

Red Crow Inter-Tribal Pow-Wow
Bullitt County Fairgrounds, interchange of I-65 and Kentucky Hwy. 245 • (502) 543-4855

This well-attended annual event presents a more accurate picture of Native Americans than most of us who grew up playing cowboys and Indians knew. This Saturday-through-Sunday event features authentic crafts, food, storytelling and art. Its most spectacular aspect is the dancing in native regalia — a thrilling and moving ritual everyone should see at least once. Admission is $6 for adults; children younger than 12 are $3; children younger than 6 are admitted free; seniors are $5. A two-day pass is $10. The Fairgrounds is at Exit 112 off I-65 (the exit for Clermont and Bernheim Forest).

INSIDERS' TIP

In addition to the Derby Week hoopla, Churchill Downs occasionally becomes the center of the racing world in November as well — it is frequently the site for the annual Breeder's Cup, a day of championship races. The next time Churchill Downs hosts the event is Saturday, November 7, 1998.

St. James Court hosts its own art fair every October.

Irish Family Fest
Bellarmine College, 2001 Newburg Rd.
• 245-6676

The Irish were nearly as major an ethnic group in the growth of Louisville as the Germans, but until 1989 they lacked their own festival. This rapidly growing festival fills the gap, providing salt bread, step dancing, Guinness stout, Irish stew and other elements of Irish culture, from the Book of Kells (in replica) to Irish Dog Breeds to "Irish 101," a lesson in the rudiments of Celtic language. Music acts feature everyone from local bands to the New York band Black 47. The festival does extended duty as a Celt-a-Thon, with a representation of Scots culture as well. It's held the Saturday and Sunday of the next-to-last weekend in September. Admission charge is $5 for adults; children younger than 12 are admitted free.

October

St. James Court Art Show
St. James and Belgravia courts and adjoining blocks of Third and Fourth Sts. and Magnolia Ave. • 635-1842

St. James Court is one of the country's most beautiful residential districts, one of the first stops on any tour of the city. But the normally peaceful surroundings are a bit overwhelmed by the gigantic arts festival on October's first weekend that serves as a sort of kickoff to the Louisville fall.

This baby is huge — there is a total of 700 juried fine arts and fine crafts booths. Savor the full impact of that word "juried": That means that even after they winnowed out the chaff, there were 650 exhibitors judged to be worth including. Exhibitors have come from Canada, Mexico, Guatemala, Russia and Peru (and we don't mean Peru, Indiana). While it's impossible to keep official attendance, the most recent estimates had 350,000 people coming to the event.

There is also a tour of the Conrad-Caldwell House Museum, food, hot cider and beer. Amenities include a first-aid station and the ultimate in convenience, a mobile ATM. The St. James fair spills simultaneously into festivals on adjoining Belgravia Court and nearby blocks of Third and Fourth streets. It's a pet-free event, but admission is free, too, so doesn't that even out?

Minority Consumer Expo
Commonwealth Convention Center, 221 Fourth St. • 772-2591

The Louisville Defender's annual exposition is a blend of booths from businesses and public service agencies; workshops; contests

(The Miss Expo pageant; the Looking Good modeling contest) and shows: a Friday night show featuring R&B acts and a comedian; a Saturday night amateur talent show; and a Sunday gospel concert. Admission is $4.50 for the exhibition hall; there's an additional charge in the $6 range for each of the performances. Parking is $1 an hour up to $6. The event usually takes place at the end of the month, but it varies.

Louisville Jaycees Oktoberfest
The wharf area of Waterfront Park, between First and Second Sts. • 583-0366

Time to celebrate the city's German heritage for the second time in two months, with music, food, dancing and, of course, beer from the land where the lederhosen roam. There's also a wide range of children's activities. It's held the first Friday, Saturday and Sunday of the month. Admission is $2.

Garvin Gate Blues Festival on Theater Square
Theater Square, Fourth St. between Broadway and Chestnut St. • 583-4555

Formerly held in the Old Louisville neighborhood for which it's named, this compact, well-loved blues festival has gone downtown, to Theater Square, and is being run by the Palace Theater. The roster includes local, regional and national acts: Acts in the first relocated festival included Li'l Ed and the Blues Imperials, Mike Henderson and the Bluebloods and the Chicago Rhythm and Blues Kings. It's held the second Friday through Sunday of October; tickets are $2 a day, $5 for all three.

Harvest Homecoming
Downtown New Albany and the riverfront • (812) 944-8572

Harvest Homecoming claims to be Indiana's second largest festival (after the Indy 500 festival) and it has some history to it — the parade that opens it (on the first Saturday in October) has attracted such grand marshals as native son Fuzzy Zoeller; teen idol Bobby Sherman (the story goes that excited fans

ripped off his clothes); and basketball star David Robinson, who somehow squeezed his 7-foot frame into an MG Midget. Nowadays, the emphasis is on do-gooders rather than celebrities, and the grand marshal is the community's person of the year.

And while we all miss the chance to see Bobby Sherman attacked by a crowd, that's probably the appropriate choice: Harvest Homecoming is an old-fashioned small town fair that's too corny for some, winningly nostalgic for others. There are carnival rides by the riverside all week, food and crafts booths Thursday through Sunday and entertainment stages downtown and by the river, a hot air balloon race at Indiana University Southeast, a bicycle tour, a kids' dog show — you get the idea. The food is the most legendary aspect — the kind of old-fashioned fare you don't find widely celebrated anymore, such as grilled chicken dinners; roasted ears of corn; hot ham and cheese sandwiches on homemade bread; giant pork chops; and homemade cider. The chicken and dumplings are so well-loved that when the supply runs out, people stay on line until the next batch arrives.

Harvest Homecoming runs the first through the second weekend; admission to most events is free, but anything that can be penned up requires a lapel pin that costs $2 (similar to the Derby Festival's Pegasus pin).

FYI

Unless otherwise noted, the area code for all phone numbers listed in this chapter is 502.

November

Louisville Film and Video Festival
Baxter Avenue Theatres, 1250 Bardstown Rd. • 893-9661

A showcase of independent film and video work of a national scope that can vary from an evening of lesbian and gay films to local commercial work. The festival has shown premieres of such distinguished documentaries as *Out of Ireland* and *Battle for the Minds* (about the struggles over doctrine and academic freedom at Louisville's Southern Baptist Theological Seminary). Admission to each film (or program of films) is $5.

North American International Livestock Exposition
Kentucky Fair and Exposition Center, 937 Phillips Ln. • 376-5000

This exposition has more animals than the State Fair — in fact, the entire fairgrounds is given over to sheep, beef and dairy cattle, quarter and draft horses, swine and dairy goats from 45 states and several Canadian provinces — more than 19,000 of them (as many as 3,000 sheep alone). It's the occasion for the national competitions for the best of such breeds as Angus cattle and Suffolk and Hampshire sheep. And the exhibit area in the East Wing has a reputation as a great place to shop for authentic Western gear (it's also the location for more agriculturally oriented exhibitors, such as artificial breeding associations). It's held for two weeks ending the Friday before Thanksgiving. Admission is $5 for adults, $3 for children 12 and younger.

Light Up Louisville International Festival
Jefferson Square, Sixth and Jefferson Sts. • 568-7000

The official beginning of the Christmas season: The Mayor flicks the switch to turn on all of downtown's Christmas lights, and there are international booths, vendors and foods. It's the evening after Thanksgiving; admission is free.

December

Children's Holiday Parade
Various locations • 584-6383

This is a parade by and for children ages 5 to 13, who build their own self-propelled floats or march in costumed units. Santa Claus and other local VIPs appear, and there's always a high school marching band. Call the Derby Festival at the above number for date and location of this year's parade.

Old Louisville Holiday House Tour
Various locations throughout the Old Louisville neighborhood • 635-5244

Old Louisville is one of the most interesting neighborhoods in town, whether it's the composition of the population or the (predomi-

nantly Victorian) architecture of the houses. This annual tour for from seven to nine homes gives a look at both, featuring homes furnished in a variety of ways, from the most contemporary to the most hidebound, and decorated for the holidays (or not) by the lights of various traditions. And to show you how it used to be done, it also includes the Conrad-Caldwell House (1402 St. James Court; 636-5023), which serves as headquarters for the tour on the two days it takes place (the first Saturday and Sunday in December). There's also a holiday gift shop there, and transportation circulates between the Conrad-Caldwell house and the homes on the tour.

Tickets are $12 in advance (available at the Old Louisville Information Center in Central Park) and $14 on the day. There's also an afternoon tea that costs $6.

Winterfest
Iroquois Park, Taylor Blvd. and Southern Pkwy. • 456-8100

It's a chance to celebrate the holiday season on the city's best-known and -loved overlook. There's a light display, carolers, games and an appearance by Santa. It's held Friday through Sunday the second weekend of December. Admission and parking are free; there's a shuttle from the parking lot to the top of Iroquois Hill.

Fantasy in Long Run Park
1607 Flat Rock Rd. • 456-8100

This drive through a holiday light display features 25,000 bulbs in nearly 100 scenes of toy soldiers, candy canes, reindeer and the like. It takes place the weekend before Christmas. In 1996 it cost $5 a car; proceeds benefit youth recreation programs.

If you're in the neighborhood, it's worth checking out another holiday light show: The huge homes of the Lake Forest development are lit up like landing strips. You have to see it.

Mayor's Midnight Special
Main St. • 574-3061

Louisville's own equivalent to what goes on in Times Square at the turn of the year — in a G-rated, family-orientated version — with the mayor leading the countdown to midnight. Admission is free.

Kentucky still contains more than its share of idiosyncratic delights lurking just past the next rise.

Daytrips

Louisville, as we've noted elsewhere, is centrally located — most of the eastern part of the United States is within a day's drive. You can get to Cincinnati and Indianapolis in about two hours, Nashville in less than three, St. Louis in a little more than four, Chicago in a little more than five.

But there's no need to leave the region when you long for a change of pace. Kentucky, a state of exceptional natural beauty, was one of the first in the country to develop its park system as a tourist attraction, and the state legislature recently approved funds for much-needed improvements.

The state park system deserves a book of its own. There are 45 state parks and historic sites — lakes, mountain retreats, Abraham Lincoln's birthplace. The 15 resort parks are the jewels of the system, with lodges, cabins and a wide variety of recreational opportunities: hiking, caving, boating, golf, swimming. There are even a number of beaches — not natural creations (they were built by the Army Corps of Engineers) but inexpensive ways to provide swimming opportunities.

Among the resort parks, those surrounding Land Between the Lakes deserve special mention. Land Between the Lakes is a nature preserve, administered by the Tennessee Valley Authority, that lies between the man-made Kentucky Lake and Lake Barkley. In the winter, visitors come for weekend trips to see the eagles that nest in the area; each resort park — Kenlake, Lake Barkley and Kentucky Dam Village — hosts an Eagles Weekend, with trips by van or boat into the nesting area. For more information on the state parks, call (800) 255-PARK, or write the Kentucky Department of Parks, 500 Mero Street, 11th Floor, Frankfort KY 40601-1974.

In this chapter, we've focused on some of the smaller cities and towns in Kentucky and Southern Indiana — unique localities in the vicinity — places that extend the picture of the area we've painted in the rest of the book. At the end, we introduce the reader to some of the more notable metropolitan areas within easy driving distance of Louisville.

But the state of Kentucky is the ideal place for a newcomer to develop what Henry James advocated for visitors to Venice: the habit of getting lost. As much as modernization has brought Wal-Mart and the golden arches to every nook and cranny, Kentucky still contains more than its share of idiosyncratic delights lurking just past the next rise. Take our suggestions, then go explore on your own!

When you're finished with your daytrip, come on back to Louisville. We have it better here.

Lexington

In the heart of the Kentucky's picturesque Bluegrass region lies Lexington, the county seat of Fayette County, about 1½ hours from Louisville.

This scenic area is known for its thoroughbred horses. Keeneland Race Course is located just outside of Lexington — worth visiting not just for the racing but for its natural beauty, distinctive from anything else in the nation. There's no better place to take in the bluegrass hills, picturesque fences and stately farm houses than this part of Kentucky's horse country.

College students come here from across the state to attend the University of Kentucky, known for its undergraduate and professional graduate programs and, not incidentally, great college basketball. UK basketball fans crowd Rupp Arena for games, and tickets are often at a premium (see our Spectator Sports chapter).

Here, we offer our suggestions for places to see to get you started on your visit to Lexington. There are also neighborhoods, antique shops and other attractions that may catch your eye.

If you plan to extend your Lexington daytrip to a weekend or longer, consult a copy of *The Insiders' Guide® to Greater Lexington* for information on overnight accommodations, as well as other attractions that could easily fill your itinerary for an extended stay.

Directions: Lexington is 79 miles east of Louisville via I-64 E.

Attractions

Ashland (Henry Clay Mansion)
Richmond and Sycamore Rds.
• (606) 266-8581

Ashland was the estate of The Great Compromiser, Henry Clay, from 1811 until his death in 1852. Clay, a Lexington lawyer, played a prominent role in U.S. politics throughout his lengthy career, serving as a U.S. senator, speaker of the House, secretary of state and a three-time presidential candidate.

The 20 acres of the estate are filled with ancient and unusual trees, including a ginkgo tree (a species that Clay imported to Kentucky) near the house's entrance. Original outbuildings include a pair of 19th-century round ice houses and a smokehouse.

Ashland is open 10 AM to 4 PM Tuesday through Saturday, 1 to 4 PM Sunday, with tours of the home starting on the hour. Admission is $6 for adults, $3 for students and $2 for children 6 to 12.

Kentucky Horse Park
4089 Iron Works Pike • (606) 233-4303

This is Lexington's tribute to the animal that made Kentucky famous the world over. The only equestrian theme park in the world and built at a cost of $35 million, Kentucky Horse Park opened in 1987. The legendary Man o' War, the thoroughbred that won all but one race in his career, is buried beneath a memorial statue in the park entrance.

Visitors see two wide-screen films — *All the King's Horses* and *Thou Shalt Fly Without Wings* — in the information center before touring the park on foot, aboard a shuttle, horse-drawn carriage or on horseback. On its lush, rolling 1,032 acres, you can see day-to-day operations of a working horse farm, more than 30 breeds of horses in the Breeds Barn and

the Parade of Breeds and learn about racing and show greats in the Hall of Champions.

A 3,500-seat arena hosts world championship equestrian events each year, as well as other horse shows and polo matches. The International Museum of the Horse traces the animal's history and showcases the large Calumet Farm Trophy Collection. A camping resort on the grounds includes a swimming pool and tennis courts.

The Kentucky Horse Park is open from 9 AM to 5 PM daily except from November 1 through mid-March, when it is closed Monday and Tuesday. One-day general admission is $9.95 for adults and $4.95 for children ages 7 through 12. A combination ticket ($12.20 for adults and $6.20 for children) also includes admission to the American Saddle Horse Museum. A one-hour guided trail ride on the outskirts of the park costs $12 a person. Pony rides are also available, as are picnic facilities and an on-site restaurant.

Keeneland Race Course
4201 Versailles Rd. • (606) 254-3412

This is Lexington horse racing for thoroughbreds at its showiest. Keeneland's manicured grounds, tree-shaded paddock and historic setting (Keeneland is a National Historic Landmark) are memorable. For three weeks in April and three weeks in October, Keeneland is the center of attention in the racing world. Queen Elizabeth II has attended races here, but you don't need royal blood to bet on the ponies or observe a favorite horse.

The track's influence is felt even when the races aren't in session. A dozen likely Kentucky Derby winners have been acquired through Keeneland's July and September yearling sales, which recorded a $13.1-million sale in 1985.

The spring racing season typically opens the second Saturday in April and runs six days a week for three weeks, with no racing on Mondays. The fall season opens the second Saturday in October and runs five days a week for three weeks, with no racing on Mondays and Tuesdays. General admission is $2.50; preferred parking is $1 and free parking is available. On weekends and for major stakes races, tickets should be ordered in advance. Reservations for dining in the Keeneland restaurant should be made as far in advance as possible; call (606) 288-4299.

During the race season, you can come early in the mornings, from 8:15 to 9 AM and watch the horses work out. Afterwards, you can have breakfast in the track kitchen with jockeys, trainers and owners. There is no admission charge and reservations are not necessary, but you do have to buy your own breakfast.

Three Chimneys Farm
Old Frankfort Pike • (606) 873-7053

Thousands of people visit Three Chimneys annually to catch a glimpse of the eight stallions who stand stud here, including 1977 Triple Crown winner Seattle Slew and three of his sons: Slew o' Gold, Capote and Fast Play. The farm is generally open year round; tours are by appointment only.

Kentucky Horse Center
3380 Paris Pike • (606) 293-1853

A 1½-hour tour offers a behind-the-scenes look at the horse industry. A 1-mile training track and a 900-seat pavilion are the highlights of this thoroughbred training complex. Tours are offered at 9 AM, 10:30 AM and 1 PM Monday through Friday from April 1 through October 31. Cost is $10, $5 for children younger than 12.

Lexington Children's Museum
Victorian Sq. • (606) 258-3256

Hands-on is the rule here. Children are guided through this two-story, 14,000-square-foot museum that lets them explore a cave, walk on the moon, participate in an archaeological dig, sit in a real flight simulator, wander through a huge model of the human heart and lungs, fight a fire on Main Street, visit foreign countries and travel back in time — and still be home in time for supper.

Kids of all ages will learn about science, history and social studies while they play. Ad-

mission is $3 for adults, free for kids 2 and younger.

University of Kentucky Art Museum
Singletary Center for the Arts, corner of Rose St. and Euclid Ave. • (606) 257-5716

One of the largest in the area, the University of Kentucky Art Museum has two or three special exhibits in addition to its permanent collection, which features European and American paintings, including Francisco Goya's *Portrait of a Bullfighter* and El Greco's *Boy Lighting a Candle*. It's open noon to 4:30 PM Tuesday through Sunday. Admission is free.

Shopping

Boone's Antiques
4996 Old Versailles Rd. • (606) 254-5335

This 27,000-square-foot cinder-block building is a warehouse of 18th- and 19th-century English, French and American antiques. Manager Pete Laughlin will offer insight on the pieces, ranging in price from $5,000 to $13,000. There are chandeliers, Chinese porcelains, Oriental rugs, country French furniture and Louis XV and XVI pieces. They'll ship your purchase. Boone's is not on the regular tourist circuit but probably should be. It's open Monday through Saturday.

Fayette Mall
3199 Nicholasville Rd. • (606) 272-3493

This is a shopaholic's fantasy: The biggest mall in Kentucky, thanks to recent additions and expansion, Fayette has more than 120 department stores, speciality shops, businesses and restaurants. Four large retailers — McAlpin's, JCPenney, Lazarus and Sears — anchor the mall. Apparel shops include Dawahares, New Way Boot Shop, Embry's, Lane Bryant, Victoria's Secret, The Limited and The Gap. You'll also find a cinema complex, a food court (11 fast-food spots with America's versions of international cuisine) and a game room.

Irish Acres Gallery of Antiques
4205 Ford's Mill Rd., Nonesuch
• (606) 873-7235

Irish Acres is just south of Versailles off Ky. 33. More than 50 showrooms of antiques and collectibles are spread throughout this 32,000-square-foot complex. Going to Irish Acres is a daytrip in itself. An on-site restaurant, The Glitz, serves lunch; reservations are strongly recommended. Irish Acres is open Tuesday through Saturday.

The Mall at Lexington Green
3199 Nicholasville Rd. • (606) 245-1513

To find The Mall at Lexington Green, just look for a big bright green roof. A sampling of shops includes Leather Inc. for fine luggage and leather goods; Winterberries Ltd., which features home furnishings, brass, fine art, lamps and unique gifts; Joseph-Beth Booksellers, with a selection of more than 100,000 titles in stock, a coffee shop and Joseph-Beth Kids Club; and Mole Hole, which sells useful and decorative items.

Restaurants

The Atomic Cafe
265 N. Limestone St. • (606) 254-1969

Some Louisvillians make a special trip to Lexington just for this funky spot, which serves Caribbean food in a bright, fun atmosphere. Part bar, part restaurant and part carnival, The Atomic Cafe serves the best conch fritters north of Orlando, coconut shrimp that has earned many a passionate fan and vegetarian dishes that utterly squash the notion that meat-free foods are boring. It's closed on Sunday.

Charlie Brown's
816 Euclid Ave. • (606) 269-5701

Follow the UK students at meal time, and you're sure to find cheap food in comfy confines. Follow them on a given day and you may end up at this eatery that serves good burgers and other sandwiches at student-friendly prices. The decor is the height of comfort: overstuffed easy chairs, fireplaces, bookshelves. The food is predictable yet well executed. Charlie Brown's is open every day.

Joe Bologna's
120 W. Maxwell St. • (606) 252-4933

Joe B's, as it is often called, has pizza in the traditional round, Sicilian pan and specialty versions. You can get meat or vegetable lasagne, manicotti and other pasta dishes, salads and sandwiches. For a great start to your meal here, we recommend Joe B's famous bread sticks (if you're on a diet, you can get the garlic butter on the side). It's open daily from lunch through late night.

Lynagh's Irish Pub & Grill
University Plaza Shopping Center, Woodland Ave. • (606) 255-1292

UK students are also well acquainted with this pub, which serves a mighty fine burger and a nice tall pint of Guiness to go with it for those of proper age. Bring cash — Lynagh's doesn't take plastic. They're open seven days a week.

Merrick Inn
3380 Tates Creek Rd. • (606) 269-5417

The Merrick Inn serves regional cuisine, with a few continental touches, to a loyal clientele made up largely of professionals. The formal dining room has a homey, Colonial inn atmosphere graced by fireplaces and candlelight. Regular entrées include prime rib, Southern fried chicken, seafood and veal, and there

---

INSIDERS' TIP

Like Louisville's I-264, the major cities near Louisville have "ring roads" that make traveling around the perimeter of the city easy. The ring road around Indy is I-465; around Cincinnati, I-275; and around Lexington, the appropriately named New Circle Road. Nashville doesn't have a true ring road.

are nightly specials. Separate menus are available for the more casual bar.

The Inn serves dinner only Monday through Saturday; reservations are recommended.

The Mouse Trap
3323 Tates Creek Rd. • (606) 269-2958

There aren't many tables in this deli, but The Mouse Trap is the ideal first stop when assembling a picnic. Imported cheeses, Greek salad, pâtés, smoked salmon and all types of cookies and crackers are sold daily at this little treasure.

Springs Inn
2020 Harrodsburg Rd. • (606) 277-5751

This is a slightly less expensive place to taste regional specialties, including country ham with red-eye gravy, burgoo, catfish, bread pudding, lamb fries and a Hot Brown sandwich. If breakfast is sacred to you, consider having your day's first meal Kentucky-style, at Springs Inn. They're open seven days a week.

Frankfort

The state's capital from the beginning, Frankfort was laid out by one of the state's most intriguing characters, James Wilkinson, the man who hatched what was known as the Spanish Conspiracy (the notion that Kentucky should declare its independence from the United States and form an alliance with Spain's American possessions).

Shady characters have had an affinity for the city ever since. Given the political scandals that have emerged from state government in recent years, tourists may find that Frankfort has a bit of the odd allure that hangs around crime scenes — although its crime sites are of the suitcase-full-of-dollar-bills-in-a-cheap-motel-room variety, not the sexier that's-where-Vinny-was-eating-clams-when-six-guys-shot-him-up sort of locale.

But Frankfort also has a large historic district (a walking tour from the tourist commission lists 37 stops) that contains a goodly share of antique and craft stores. It's famous for the Corner in Celebrities, a section of Wapping Street that was home to more than 40 celebrated individuals, including justices of the Supreme Court, governors, U.S. senators and cabinet officers (and where Bibb lettuce was developed).

And it has its share of industry, from Union underwear to more tasty manufacturers, including Rebecca-Ruth Candies, 112 E. Second Street, purportedly the originators of the sweet and potent confection known as the bourbon ball (technically, before 1986 it was a federal offense to send one outside Kentucky); and Leestown Company, Wilkinson Boulevard, makers of Ancient Age and our favorite of the new set of small-batch, "single barrel" bourbons, Blanton's.

For more information, write the Frankfort/ Franklin County Tourist and Convention Commission, 100 Capitol Avenue, Frankfort KY 40601; or call (502) 875-8687 or (800) 960-7200.

Directions: Take I-64 E. from Louisville to the Lawrenceburg-Frankfort Exit; take Ky. 127 N. into Frankfort.

Executive Mansion
East of the Capitol • (502) 564-3449

The governor's mansion, a historian friend of ours observes, is not the sort of place you expect to see in Kentucky; more like France, because this Beaux-Arts structure is modeled after the Petit Trianon, Marie Antoinette's summer villa. The native touch is that it was built with Kentucky limestone, in 1914. There are free guided tours of its public rooms Tuesday and Thursday mornings.

Frankfort Cemetery
215 E. Main St. • (502) 227-2403

In 1845 Daniel Boone and his wife Rebecca were disinterred from their ostensible final resting place in Missouri and brought back to Kentucky. They lay in state for six weeks in the Capitol then were reburied here. Neighbors who found a more dignified route to the cemetery include 16 governors and Richard M. Johnson, Martin Van Buren's vice-president. It's open from 7 AM to 8:30 PM in the summer, 8 AM to 5:30 PM in the winter.

Kentucky Vietnam Veteran's Memorial
Coffee Tree Rd. • no phone

As poignant in its way as Washington's famous Wall, the Commonwealth's memorial to the veterans of our most painful-to-remember war is a towering sundial, designed so that its shadow points to the name of each Kentuckian who died in the war on the anniversary of his death. It's open daily until dusk.

Kentucky State Capitol
700 Capital Ave. • (502) 564-3449

The state's fifth capitol (and so still called "the new Capitol" more than 80 years after it was finished) was built from 1905 to 1910, at a cost of $1.75 million. (The old capitol was too small, and for a time the unthinkable was thought: move the state capital from Frankfort.) The French Renaissance-style building with a towering dome bears a strong, imposing resemblance to the U.S. Capitol in Washington.

The famous floral clock behind the Capitol is an oddly working timepiece (it moves not smoothly, but in a quick jerk the last second of every minute) whose 34-foot-diameter face is covered with flowers.

Free tours of the Capitol are conducted daily.

Liberty Hall
218 Wilkinson St. • (502) 227-2560

John Brown sat in the Continental Congress, the House of Representatives (both those posts as a Virginian representing the Kentucky District) and was Kentucky's first U.S. senator. He supervised the building of

---

INSIDERS' TIP

The speed limit on Kentucky's interstates is 65 miles per hour, with 55 mph zones surrounding major cities. This is moderately enforced by the local police and state troopers.

Liberty Hall from 1796 to 1801. It's a classic red-brick Georgian house, with formal gardens extending down toward the Kentucky River. It's also supposed to have served as the first Sunday school this side of the Alleghenies and to be haunted by at least two ghosts.

Even more elegant (and included in the same tour as the one you can take to see Liberty Hall) is the Orlando Brown House, 202 Wilkinson Street, built by Sen. Brown for his son in 1835 and based on plans by the noted Kentucky architect Gideon Shryock. Orlando Brown was a figure of some note himself, a newspaper editor and Kentucky secretary of state whose literary efforts drew praise from Washington Irving.

Tours are given daily; admission is $4.50 for adults, $4 for senior citizens and $1 for children ages 6 through 16.

Old State Capitol and Kentucky History Museum
Broadway at St. Clair Mall • (502) 564-3016

An 1831 Greek Revival structure with a self-supporting staircase, the last capitol before the new one is now maintained by the Kentucky Historical Society. Its museum next door focuses on the state's social history. Admission is free; it's open daily.

Mercer and Boyle Counties

Central Kentucky is one of the most beautiful landscapes on earth. Driving through, you will understand the cliché "rolling hills" and appreciate why it is so evocative to people.

This area is also at the heart of early Kentucky history: site of the first settlement; where the Commonwealth's constitution was ratified; where its first two colleges were founded; where Kentucky's most important Civil War battle was fought; and where its most suc-cessful and unusual utopian community made its home.

Harrodsburg

Harrodsburg is the site of Kentucky's first white settlement. Pennsylvanian James Harrod and his fellow settlers built cabins there in 1774, planted a crop of corn, then left and returned the next year — a month before Daniel Boone founded Boonesborough — to find their cabins had washed away. They started to rebuild on the site, erecting a fort against the threat of Indian attack

Also in the area is one of the state's more offbeat tourist sites: Herrington Lake, said to have the best fishing conditions in the state along with an interesting . . . well, reptile . . . beast . . . creature? One morning in 1972, according to Vince Staten's book *Unauthorized America*, a UK classics professor claimed to see a 15-foot-long monster with a pig snout and a curly tail; there have been numerous sightings since. The lake is near Burgin, just east of Harrodsburg.

For more information, contact the Harrodsburg/Mercer County Tourist Commission, (606) 734-2364,103 S. Main Street, Harrodsburg KY 40330.

Directions: Take I-64 E. from Louisville to the Grafenburg-Lawrenceburg Exit 48, then take Ky. 151 S. to U.S. 127. Follow it south to Harrodsburg, which is about 71 miles from Louisville.

Old Fort Harrod
S. College St. • (606) 734-3314

This reconstruction of the first permanent settlement in the West is tended by costumed townspeople who demonstrate the chores of frontier life: basket making, open-hearth cooking, blacksmithing. The park also includes the Lincoln Marriage Temple, a brick building that surrounds the log cabin where

---

INSIDERS' TIP

For the record, Kentucky's capitol is spelled "Frankfort" and Kentucky's town of Versailles is pronounced "ver-SALES." Don't ask.

Abraham Lincoln's parents were married; a pioneer cemetery; and the Mansion Museum, a Greek Revival home dating from 1830. March 16 through October 31, the fort is open 8:30 AM to 5 PM, the museum 9 AM to 5:30 PM. Admission is $3.50 for those 12 and older and $1 for children ages 6 to 11. Starting November 1, the fort is open from 8 AM to 4:30 PM and the museum from 8:30 AM to 5 PM. The museum is closed from December 1 through March 15.

The Legend of Daniel Boone
James Harrod Amphitheater, 400 W. Lexington St. • (606) 734-3346

Boone's back, and Harrodsburg's got him! More to the point, the amphitheater next to Old Fort Harrod is the home of this long-running musical dramedy, the high point of which is a hair-raising re-creation of an Indian attack. Tickets are $12 for adults, $6 for children younger than 15; there's a 10 percent discount for seniors. For reservations call (800) 852-6663.

The Beaumont Inn
638 Beaumont Dr. • (606) 734-3381

This inn in a former girls' college boasts a restaurant where the traditions of Kentucky cooking stay alive. The country ham is 2 years old, cured by proprietor Charles Dedman (that's good — long curing assures a more mellow taste). The fried chicken is yellow-legged chicken (the yellow cast comes from the corn diet they're fed). The corn pudding is celebrated widely, and Robert E. Lee is honored not only in the collection of photographs but also by the Robert E. Lee cake, a four-layer white cake with orange icing. Lunch seatings are daily at noon and 1:15 PM; dinner seatings at 6 PM and 7:30 PM Monday through Saturday and at 6 PM Sunday.

The Shaker Village at Pleasant Hill
3500 Lexington Rd. • (606) 734-5411

The Shaker Village at Pleasant Hill — known universally as Shakertown — is one of the state's most popular retreats, and it's no wonder: The setting itself, on the top of an especially high central Kentucky hill 7 miles northeast of Harrodsburg on U.S. 68, has an immediately apprehensible spiritual quality.

The 14 exceptional buildings, constructed by the United Society of Believers in Christ's Second Appearing, were restored in the 1960s and now operate as a living museum where you can hear Shaker music (including songs written in unknown tongues) and learn how they made brooms and used herbs. Shakertown is the largest restored Shaker village in the country, and the 2,700 acres of property include beautiful fields for walking.

As you tour Shakertown, you find yourself in a constant dialogue with the Shakers, a utopian Christian sect that believed in direct communication with Christ and the perfectibility of human life on earth. You might find yourselves arguing with their celibacy and segregation of the sexes, their separation from the rest of the world, their cult-like insistence on breaking the bonds of family in favor of a more general loyalty to the community. On the other hand, you'll probably admire their devotion to that community, their industry and economy and their incredible design sense. (This author believes that the Shakers sublimated their sexuality not only into their convulsive worship services that gave them their nickname, from "Shaking Quakers," but into furniture and architecture — there's a spare sensuality in the proportions of their design that could be banned in Boston.)

The Shaker belief in simplicity and economy is shown in their famous lemon pie, made from thin slices of lemon, rind and all, macerated in sugar. But they worked hard, and so they ate heartily, as the abundant repasts at the restaurant in the **Trustees Office Inn** prove daily. Reservations are recommended for breakfast, lunch and dinner. (Dinner seatings in the Trustee's Office are at 5:30 and 8:30 PM daily.) There's also a **Summer Kitchen** offering light lunch fare during the warm months; reservations are not required.

It's also possible to stay overnight at Shakertown, sleeping in the same rooms the Shakers used. They have un-Shaker-like conveniences, such as air conditioning, private baths and television, and neither celibacy nor segregation of the sexes is required.

The other attraction at Pleasant Hill is the *Dixie Belle*, a sternwheeler that takes a one-hour excursion on the Kentucky River, past its

high palisades and underneath High Bridge. It operates from April 29 through Halloween; rates are $6 for adults, $4 for young people ages 12 to 17 and $3 for children ages 6 to 11.

While the tour of the village takes about two hours, a visit to Shakertown can easily occupy an entire day itself. Admission is $9.50 for adults, $5 for young people ages 12 to 17, $3 for children ages 6 to 11 and $25 for a family. There are also tickets that combine admission to the village and the riverboat ride.

The village is open year round except for Christmas Eve and Christmas Day. Hours are 9 AM to 6 PM.

Danville

Danville was the political center of pioneer Kentucky, where the state's constitution was ratified in 1792 on the 10th try. It's also the location of Centre College, the state's premier private college; ironically it's also where Centre's greatest rival, Transylvania University,

was founded (although after a year it moved to Lexington). Its residents have included everyone from Isaac Shelby, Kentucky's first governor, to John Travolta (who performed at Pioneer Playhouse Dinner Theatre).

Travolta and Jim "Hey, Vern!" Varney notwithstanding, Danville has faded slightly from preeminence, but it continues to have a reputation as an especially attractive small town. It's host every June to the Great American Brass Band Festival, a weekend of turn-of-the-century town band music on the campus of Centre College that would make Professor Harold Hill's mouth water.

Contact the Danville-Boyle County Tourist Commission, (800) 755-0076, 300 S. Fourth Street, Suite 201, Danville KY 40422.

Directions: Danville is 9 miles south of Harrodsburg on U.S. 127 (the same road on which we guided you into Harrodsburg).

McDowell House
125 S. Second St. • (606) 236-2804

McDowell House is a landmark for one of

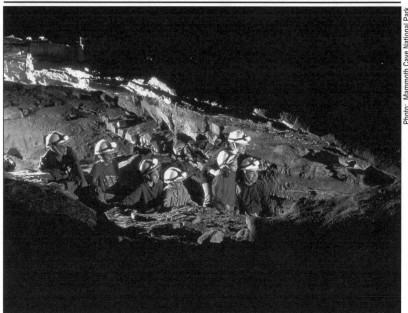

Sections of Mammoth Cave are still being explored.

the events that helped create the modern world — although it's one of those advances in civilization that makes you glad to be an inheritor rather than the pioneer. Upstairs, Dr. Ephraim McDowell performed the world's first successful abdominal surgery, removal of a 22-pound ovarian tumor from Jane Todd Crawford — without benefit of anesthesia or modern antiseptic methods.

The house, built in 1795, has been restored, along with the gardens and adjoining apothecary shop. Admission is $3, $2 for senior citizens older than 62, $1 for students older than 12, 50¢ for younger children. It's open 10 AM to noon and 1 to 4 PM Monday through Saturday, 2 to 4 PM Sundays. It's closed major holidays and Mondays November 1 through March 1.

Centre College
600 W. Walnut St. • (606) 236-5211

While everyone is a little tired of its being the main thing anyone knows about this distinguished small college, the chemical formula C6HO has a special significance in Danville — it was the graffiti written everywhere after Centre's so-called "Praying Colonels" (named for their practice of taking a prayer break in each huddle) beat Harvard, then the top-ranked football power, 6 to 0 in 1921 — the football upset of the century. The college is also alma mater to two U.S. vice presidents and two Supreme Court justices.

Today, Centre is known for academic excellence — magazines rank it one of the nation's 50 best private colleges and one of the top four educational bargains — and an extraordinarily devoted set of alumni (a greater percentage of them donate to the college than at any other institution of higher learning in the country).

The historical showpiece of the campus is Old Centre, the Greek Revival building constructed in 1820.

Norton Centre for the Arts is an excellent 1,500-seat modern auditorium that hosts concerts and other events. Performers have included Rudolf Nuryev, Itzhak Perlman, Hal Holbrook as Mark Twain, the Kronos Quartet and Riders in the Sky.

Perryville

Perryville is an attractive small town with its share of quaint and attractive features — such as the Elmwood Inn, a Greek Revival home that now serves as an inn with a reputation for its afternoon teas, and the 19th-century shopping district of Merchants Row on Old Main Street.

But it's best known for the Civil War battle that occurred in the town.

Directions: Perryville is 12 miles west of Danville on U.S. 150.

Perryville Battlefield State Historic Site
Off Ky. 68 and U.S. 150 • (606) 332-8631

Perryville, October 8, 1862, was the only major Civil War battle fought in Kentucky, but it was a major turning point in the conflict. After a bloody day of fighting with 7,500 casualties on both sides, the Confederates began a retreat to Tennessee that marked the end of their designs on Kentucky (and removed the Confederate threat to Louisville that had existed in the early years of the war).

A federal commission (including film-maker Ken Burns!) recently named the Perryville battlefield — an area of about 3,000 acres that comprises the town and much of the surrounding countryside — as one of the 10 Civil War battlefields most in need of preservation.

The park devoted to the battle takes up only 98 acres of the battlefield. It includes a museum, a gift shop, a burial ground and monuments. The grounds are open year round from roughly 7 AM to 9 PM. The museum and gift shop are open 9 AM to 5 PM daily from April 1 through October 31 and in the off-season by appointment. Admission is $2 for adults and $1 for children ages 6 to 12.

Some 400 people, dressed as soldiers and civilians alike, re-enact the battle annually on the weekend nearest October 8. It's one of the few Civil War re-enactments to take place on a part of the actual terrain where the battle was fought.

Madison, Indiana

A river town in Jefferson County — haven't we spent a whole book talking about one of those?

But few river towns are as pretty or as well-preserved as Madison (seat of Jefferson County, Indiana), which sits on the Ohio 55 miles northeast of Louisville, framed by tall limestone cliffs. The city is an exceptionally well-preserved, preservation-minded place, with 133 blocks, comprising virtually all of its downtown, on the National Register of Historic Places. As the city's promotional materials point out, the concentration of historical structures is nearly unparalleled.

The buildings along Main Street were, for the most part, built before the Civil War (although some received new cast iron fronts and ornamentation in the prosperous 1870s). The broad avenue was built with the proportions to suit a state capital, as Madison once hoped to become; while that didn't come to pass, they remain impressive in a more cramped day. Madison is also noteworthy for its decorative wrought iron. Its manufacture was an important industry in the city; much of the ironwork for which New Orleans is famous was fabricated in Madison.

But Madison is not a museum piece, it's a vital community. The historic district still serves as an active downtown, the center of the city's commerce and business.

Madison's annual blowout is the Madison Regatta, a hydroplane race on the Ohio during Fourth of July weekend, which is one of that 200-mph sport's major events. Much like the Derby, it's preceded by a week of events. The Madison Chautauqua Festival of Art, an arts and crafts festival, draws 50,000 to 70,000 people the fourth weekend in September.

Nearby Hanover College is an excellent private four-year college, Indiana's equivalent of Centre (its most famous alum is Woody Harrelson; you may recall that his bartender character on *Cheers* was always telling tales about the folks back home in Hanover).

Directions: There are two scenic routes and one on the interstate. Take I-65 north from Louisville to Ind. 62 from Jeffersonville, traveling 55 miles to Madison. Or you can take U.S. 42 east from Louisville to U.S. 421 and head north to Madison. Or take I-71 east from Louisville and get off at the Sligo exit; follow S.R. 153 to U.S. 42 and on to U.S. 421. The route you take is mostly a matter of personal preference or convenience — all of them take about an hour.

The Madison Visitors Center is at the corner of Main and Jefferson streets; call (800) 559-2956.

J.F.D. Lanier State Historic Site
511 W. First St. • (812) 265-3526

Madison's showpiece, this mansion facing onto a rich man's view of the Ohio was built in 1844 for financier Lanier, who kept Indiana afloat during the Civil War with loans of $1 million (about a $500-million value today). Admission is not charged, but donations are accepted. It's open Tuesday through Saturday 9 AM to 5 PM, Sunday 1 to 5 PM.

Shrewsbury House
301 W. First St. • (812) 265-4481

Just as Henry Whitestone is Louisville's most name-checked architect, Francis Costigan is Madison's main man, architect of the city's grandest homes. (Costigan's home at 408 W. Third Street, open to group tours by appointment, is a classic architect's home, a mansion's worth of architectural elements packed into a simple townhouse.)

This Greek Revival mansion, built for riverboat entrepreneur Capt. Charles L. Shrewsbury two years after Costigan's Lanier mansion, has one amazing feature: a three-story self-supporting spiral staircase whorled like a corkscrew. Admission is $2. It's open daily April through December, 10 AM to 4:30 PM., but the curator suggests that you call first and make an appointment.

Clifty Falls
Ind. 50/62, 1 mile west of Madison
• (812) 265-1331

Clifty Falls is a nifty little state park near Madison, with hiking through forest and gorge, swimming, tennis, picnic areas and the rest of it.

But its most distinctive features are four different waterfalls ranging from 60 feet to 82 feet high and, in particular, Big Clifty Falls. To get there you walk down a steep set of stairs, then over a creek bed rockier than any quarry, until you come to the base of a marvelous overhang where two shelves come together in a rough right angle. The striated rock shows

you every solution geology ever proposed to the question, "What shall we make in this place, Indiana?"

The waterfall is a natural shower: thin threads of water falling in a mass 30 feet across (but even at its fullest gush, it's no Niagara). Although you're not supposed to do this, many people walk up behind the waterfall, even stand in its path and let the cold water splash down on them. The park is open year round; an admission of $5 for out-of-state vehicles or $2 for Hoosier automobiles is only charged from March through October on the weekend.

The Upper Crust
209 W. Main St. • (812) 265-6727

Many people's favorite restaurant in Madison, this snug continental place is under the direction of Cypriot Nick Izamis, formerly a Louisville restaurateur and a man born to play the host's role. It has an extensive menu for such a small establishment; some of the standouts include saganaki (Greek cheese flamed in ouzo), the best hummus we've ever tasted and Beano's Famous Orange Roughy, a nice big piece of the tasty New Zealand fish, baked in olive oil and lemon sauce.

Dinners come with a copper skillet filled with browned vegetables. It's open for dinner Tuesday through Saturday.

Cave Country

The limestone that creates Central Kentucky's rolling topography does interesting things below the surface of the ground as well — water dissolves limestone, and when that water is underground it creates caves, sinkholes and other dramatic transitions between the earth's interior and its surface. (It also gives a character to the water that makes it perfectly suited for sour-mash whiskey.)

There are so many caves in South Central Kentucky, in fact, that holes in the ground have been a major factor in the local economy, and the enormous cave system called Mammoth Cave has been recognized as one of the rarest and most significant natural sites in the world.

Directions: Take I-65 S. to Exit 53 (Cave City); take Ky. 70 W. 9 miles to the Mammoth

Cave visitor center. Horse Cave is on S.R. 218, to the east of I-65, 6 miles north of the Cave City Exit.

Mammoth Cave National Park
Ky. 70 • (502) 758-2328

Mammoth Cave, 8 miles off I-65, 90 miles south of Louisville, has been called one of the seven natural wonders of the world — a 330-mile-long system of caves, the longest in the world, and still being explored.

In 1981, UNESCO named the cave system a World Heritage site — a designation that applies to such famed locations as the Pyramids of Giza, the Taj Mahal and the Great Barrier Reef. In 1990, UNESCO also named it an International Biosphere Reserve, a designation that means it is a significant or unique ecosystem in need of preservation.

Mammoth Cave has a distinctive ecosystem. The lack of light has led to there being eyeless fish and eyeless species of shrimp, beetles and crayfish.

Tours of the cave system vary in length and arduousness, from a half-tour for the disabled to an extremely strenuous Wild Cave tour (reservations required) that covers 5 miles and takes six hours, including what one source describes as "two hours of crawling and squeezing through small openings." The system includes spectacular cave formations with names straight out of *Tom Sawyer*: Frozen Niagara, the Diamond Grotto, Onyx Colonnade, Moonlight Dome, Bottomless Pit and Fat Man's Misery (an especially narrow passage). There is a dining room 267 feet below the surface, where box lunches are served.

The park also offers hiking trails, fishing and boating opportunities on the Nolin and Green rivers and a number of campgrounds.

Cave trips are available every day of the year except Christmas. The Parks Service recommends you make reservations for cave tours, available through Mistix Corporation at (800) 967-2283. They also suggest visiting Mammoth Cave in early spring, late fall and winter, when tours sell out less often and tour groups are smaller. Cave temperatures are perpetually in the 50s, so a jacket is always advisable. Ticket prices for cave tours vary from $3 to $35. The historic Mammoth Cave tour, a strenuous 2½-hour tour, costs $6 for adults and $3 for children ages 6 to 12. Call Mistix Corp. for more information or to purchase tickets over the phone.

American Cave and Karst Center
131 Main St., Horse Cave • (502) 786-1466

A new attraction in one of the three cities near Mammoth Cave, American Cave and Karst Center opened in 1993 at the entrance to Horse Cave. It includes a mocked-up interior of a cave and exhibits on topics from cave ecology and groundwater to the "cave wars" earlier in the century, when proprietors of local for-profit cave tours participated in cutthroat competition. The most jaw-dropping instance involved the body of Floyd Collins, whose ordeal trapped inside Sand Cave was one of the media sensations of the '20s. After Collins died, his remains were disinterred (against his family's wishes!) and placed in a coffin inside Crystal Cave as a tourist exhibit. Then it was dumped into the Green River by rival cave-owners in 1929. Eventually his remains were reburied in a nearby cemetery in 1989.

The center is open 9 AM to 5 PM daily. Admission is $6 for the museum and cave tour for adults, $3 for kids ages 6 to 12. If you just want to see the museum, you and your kids will each pay $3.

Kentucky Down Under
Exit 58, I-65 • (502) 786-2634

Based on nothing more than a pun — underground caves, Down Under as a nickname

---

INSIDERS' TIP

Bourbon whiskey originated in Bourbon County, Kentucky. A whiskey doesn't have to be made in Bourbon County to be legally called a bourbon, but it's Kentucky's climate (important in aging) and the area's limestone spring water that help give bourbon whiskey its distinctive taste.

for Australia — this has become a popular attraction that combines a tour of small but pretty Mammoth Onyx Cave with a chance to interact with Australian animals (kangaroos, wallabies, emus and the like) and American animals such as the bison, elk and white-tailed deer. There is a flight cage, which people can enter to feed and pet a collection of birds highlighted by lories and lorikeets (small members of the parrot family native to Australia), and a wool shed with hands-on participation in the tasks of an Australian sheep station and a demonstration of the sheep-herding abilities of border collies. It's open 8 AM to 5 PM daily except Christmas and New Year's; hours vary seasonally; animal exhibits are closed November 1 through March 31. Admission is $14 for adults, $7.50 for children age 5 to 14 and free for younger children.

Bardstown

Bardstown, the Bourbon Capital of the World and the seat of Nelson County, once boasted 22 operating distilleries dating back as early as 1776. Today four remain open and two of these offer tours of the distilling process. The Maker's Mark Distillery tour (3350 Burks Spring Road, Loretto, Kentucky, 502-865-2099) is particularly charming; the small operation seems to come straight from the pages of a coffee-table book. A tour of Heaven Hill Distillery (1064 Loretto Road, Bardstown, Kentucky, 502-348-3921) lets visitors see the way the process works at a large distillery. Bardstown is the site of the annual Kentucky Bourbon Festival, the third weekend in September.

Bardstown is Kentucky's second oldest city and the location of My Old Kentucky Home, a popular tourist stop. In 1780 William Bard visited the area as an agent for his brother, David, and John C. Owings. He "laid off" Bardstown in 1785 from an original land grant of 1,000 acres issued from the Virginia General Assembly. The first courthouse, made of hewn logs, was built that same year.

A visit to Spalding Hall, a building of the old St. Joseph College, and the adjacent St. Joseph Proto-Cathedral, the first Catholic Cathedral west of the Allegheny Mountains, will give you insight into the importance that religion and education have played in Bardstown's history.

For further information, call the Bardstown Tourist Commission, (502) 348-4877.

Directions: Take I-65 S. to the Bardstown Exit 112, which leads to Ky. 245. Make a left and travel 17 miles, then turn right at the second red light

My Old Kentucky Home Federal Hill
501 E. Stephen Foster Ave.
• **(800) 323-7803**

The strains of Stephen Foster's ballad "My Old Kentucky Home" before the start of the Kentucky Derby always draw tears.

Federal Hill, the stately mansion on the Rowan estate near Bardstown, was completed in 1818. Built by Judge John Rowan, a distinguished Kentuckian who served on the Kentucky Court of Appeals and in the U.S. Senate, it rests on a sloping 235 acres that are now part of My Old Kentucky Home State Park.

It was here that Judge Rowan entertained such brilliant guests as Henry Clay and Aaron Burr. His home became a landmark for lavish entertaining.

Stephen Foster visited his cousins, the Rowans, in 1852 and wrote the song that is now Kentucky's official state song. When you visit the home you will find rare and beautiful antiques and furnishings that are much the same as when Foster stayed there. Guides in antebellum costumes will lead you on tours through the home. A visit during the Christmas season, when the house is decorated for the holidays, is a special treat; candlelight tours are available.

From June through Labor Day, tours are conducted daily from 8 AM to 7:15 PM; in May, after Labor Day and in October, tours are held from 8 AM to 4:45 PM; the rest of the year tours are held from 9 AM to 4:45 PM. The site is closed Mondays in January and February, as well as Thanksgiving Day, the week of Christmas, New Year's Eve and New Year's Day. There is an admission fee of $4 for adults, $2 for children ages 6 to 12 and $3.50 for senior citizens. Group rates are available.

My Old Kentucky Home State Park features a 39-acre campground. Utility hookups, showers and rest rooms, a grocery store and laundry are nearby.

Photo: Kentucky Department of Parks

Guides in period dress lead tours through Federal Hill at My Old Kentucky Home State Park.

Golfers may take advantage of an 18-hole, regulation golf course. A fully equipped pro shop provides rental clubs, pull carts and riding carts. The course is open year round, weather permitting.

A picnic area is equipped with grills, playground facilities and rest rooms. A picnic shelter can be rented up to one year in advance.

The Stephen Foster Story
My Old Kentucky Home State Park
• **(800) 626-1563**

Kentucky's longest-running outdoor drama is a musical with colorful period costumes, lively choreography and more than 50 Foster songs, including "My Old Kentucky Home." It would be difficult to find a Louisvillian who hasn't seen this production — this musical is a Louisville tradition, and one that generally won't make kids squirm. The show runs from June to September.

The Old Talbott Tavern
107 W. Stephen Foster Ave.
• **(800) 4-TAVERN**

The first permanent building erected in Bardstown was a stone, all-purpose house on the town square, known today as the Talbott Tavern. It is the oldest western stagecoach stop in America, licensed by Virginia Gov. Patrick Henry more than two centuries ago.

The tavern's visitors have included King Louis Phillippe and his two brothers, who were anxious to see the western frontier that in 1797 was Kentucky. It was during their stay that a member of their party painted the murals on the upstairs walls. Legend has it that Jesse James used the murals for target practice, which accounts for the bullet holes.

Washington Irving immortalized a spot just inside the lobby door where, in 1802, the kiss was stolen in his short story, *The Life of Ralph Ringwood*. The Lincoln family, having moved from Pennsylvania, became embroiled in a lawsuit over land, and while the case was being tried, Tom Lincoln, along with his family, including young son, Abraham, stayed in the Talbott's front room. Having lost the suit, the Lincolns moved to Indiana and later to Illinois.

The Tavern serves lunch and dinner and has a gift shop. Entertainment is featured in the pub Friday and Saturday evenings.

Spalding Hall:
The Oscar Getz
Museum of Whiskey History,
The Bardstown Historical Museum,
Bardstown Art Gallery
and Thomas Merton Books
310 Xavier Dr. at N. Fifth St.
• (502) 348-2999

Spalding Hall (c. 1826) first served as St. Joseph's College and Seminary, then as a hospital for the armies of the North and South during the Civil War, and finally as St. Joseph's Preparatory School from 1911 to 1968. Today it is home to the Oscar Getz Museum of Whiskey History and the Bardstown Historical Museum, the Jim Cantrell Pottery and Painting Gallery and La Taberna Restaurant.

This unusual museum contains a collection of rare artifacts and documents concerning the American whiskey industry from pre-Colonial days to post-Prohibition years. The collection includes a copy of Abraham Lincoln's 1833 liquor license for a tavern in New Salem, Illinois, an authentic moonshine still captured in the Kentucky hills and a collection of old copper distilling vessels.

The Container Room displays white oak barrels and 200 antique bottles and jugs. There is an 1854 E.G. Booz bottle from which the word "booze" originated. Another part of the display is about Carrie Nation, the crusader of the Temperance Movement in the early 1900s.

The Bardstown Museum houses artifacts from 200 years of area history, including Indian relics, Lincoln documents, pioneer papers, John Fitch's land grant and a replica of the first steamboat and Stephen Foster memorabilia. Also on exhibit are Jenny Lind's velvet cape and Jesse James' hat.

The gallery and studio of Kentucky artist Jim Cantrell features an extensive collection of his paintings and drawings priced from $200 to $15,000, as well as books by and about monk Thomas Merton. Hours are by chance or by appointment (usually Tuesday through Saturday).

Brown County and Nashville, Indiana

Surrounded by the hills of Brown County, Nashville, Indiana, is an arts and crafts center, with more than 300 specialty shops, antique stores and galleries offering distinctive oil paintings, designer jewelry, candles and more.

The area also attracts theatrical performances and top country and bluegrass entertainment. Artists' studios and galleries are also open to the public. Outdoor recreation includes golf and Indiana's largest state park, Brown County State Park. The restaurants' offerings vary from what is generally called country cooking — fried biscuits with fresh apple butter is one example — to gourmet meals.

For additional information, contact the Brown County Convention and Visitors Bureau, (800) 753-3255, Main and Van Buren Streets, Nashville, IN 47448.

Directions: Take I-65 N. to S.R. 46 W. in Columbus, Indiana. Nashville is about 12 miles straight ahead.

Brown County State Park
Ind. 46 E. or W. • (812) 988-6406

Brown County State Park is the largest state park in Indiana. It has hiking trails, a nature center, horseback riding, dining facilities at the lodge, cabins and other overnight accommodations. Two fishing lakes are located within the park, but you must bring your own boat or canoe. No motor-powered boats are allowed on the lakes.

Columbus, Indiana

Columbus, Indiana, 1½ hours from Louisville, is known for its architectural sights: More than 50 buildings by some of the world's greatest architects — I.M. Pei, the Saarinens, Richard Meier and Robert A.M. Stern — dot the skyline and blend with dozens of renovated historic buildings. Tours are conducted by the Visitor's Center, (812) 372-1954, 506 Fifth Street. A slide show previews Columbus's architectural development. The center has tour maps, a gift shop and tourist information in addition to the guided architectural tours. Reservations are required. For more visitor information, call (800) 468-6564. In this section, we've added highlights of some other attractions.

The Columbus area is also a place for outdoor recreation, including fishing and golf.

Directions: Take I-65 N. about 50 minutes from Louisville, exiting at the first Columbus exit (S.R. 46). Turn right and follow Ky. 46 E. into town.

Bartholomew County Historical Society Museum
524 Third St. • (812) 372-3541

Artifacts, photographs and hands-on activities fill this partially restored Victorian home. The museum is open Tuesday through Friday, 9 AM to 4 PM.

Columbus Public Parks
Various locations • (812) 376-2680

Fifteen city-operated public parks total 479 acres and include nine shelters, 325 picnic tables, playgrounds, baseball and softball diamonds, an indoor ice skating rink and a 50-meter outdoor swimming pool with a 160-foot-long figure-8 slide. Tour Columbus' architectural sites and scenic countryside by bicycle on People Trails, approximately 5-mile-long routes that line the city parks. Maps are available at the Visitors Center.

Lincoln Center, (812) 376-2686, has a regulation hockey rink and a smaller ice-skating rink. Activities include public skating sessions, figure-skating competition, skating lessons and hockey.

There are 26 outdoor tennis courts, 12 with lights; use is free on a first come, first served basis. The parks are open from 8 AM to 11 PM daily.

The Commons
Corner of Third and Washington Sts.
• (812) 376-2535

This downtown public hall, indoor park and playground has been the site of many annual events and special performances. Its centerpiece is a 30-foot-high, seven-ton motion sculpture, *Chaos I*, by Jean Tinguely.

Indianapolis

Louisvillians rarely designate Indianapolis as a general daytrip destination; a trip to Indy is usually goal-specific. A shopping trip to Circle Centre downtown, a cultural event or a Indianapolis Colts football game might be the impetus. Just two hours north via Interstate 65, Indianapolis is close enough to visit just for an afternoon.

Louisvillians once thought of Indy as a city very similar to their own. Then within the last decade, Indianapolis enjoyed a growth spurt and a higher profile through the addition of national sports teams and a revitalized downtown. Now, Louisvillians might go to Indy to see how their northern neighbors took the next step in the growth process of a U.S. city.

This is just a sampling of what 'Naptown has to offer. For more information, check out *The Insiders' Guide® to Greater Indianapolis*.

Shopping

Circle Centre
49 W. Maryland St. • (317) 681-8000

Shopping must be mentioned first when discussing Indianapolis because of one spectacular location: Circle Centre. Located in the heart of downtown, this 800,000 square-foot,

---

INSIDERS' TIP

The interstate system makes getting around Kentucky fast and easy, but the side roads almost always offer beautifully scenic drives. Especially in horse country, in the heart of the state near Lexington, the smaller state highways are a visual treat.

four-story mall is beautiful, upscale, expansive, entertaining and yet somehow cozy. Several open areas in the mall accommodate themed exhibits that give cohesion to the mall's sprawl — on a recent exhibit, the theme was "home," with colorful drawings from school kids in one area, a kid's dream playhouse in another and other touches throughout.

The two anchors of the mall are Nordstrom and Parisian, two monolithic department stores. Abercrombie & Fitch, The Limited, Ann Taylor, bebe, Structure and Lane Bryant are some of the notable clothing stores. There's also Gap, Banana Republic, FAO Schwartz, Warner Brothers, Godiva Chocolatier, Coach and Eddie Bauer stores.

Indianapolis has no trouble pulling people downtown to fill this new mall (dedicated in the Fall of 1995) because Circle Centre offers much more than just shopping. The fourth floor of the mall is dominated by a nine-screen movie theater complex and a huge virtual reality entertainment center, where, for $3.50, you can strap in to a glider and virtually glide through a Southwest desert canyon or the concrete canyons of a futuristic megalopolis. If imaginary battles are more your speed, other games put you behind the controls of giant fighting robots. Also, the dining choices are extensive at Circle Centre, ranging from the Great American Cookie Co. to the upscale eats of Palomino.

Parking is abundant but tricky — with three separate lots devoted to the mall and connected via pedways or elevators. You had better make a note of exactly where you are before leaving the car. Rates are reasonable — just $1 for a three-hour shopping excursion.

The Fashion Mall
Keystone Ave. at 86th St. • no phone

This is the place for designer apparel and other just-out-of-the-mainstream goods. The two anchor stores are Jacobson's and Parisian; specialty stores include The Sharper Image, Crabtree & Evelyn and a bewitching kitchen gadget store named M.G. Tates.

Outside of the malls, there are stretches of specific roads that offer good shopping opportunities. Massachusetts Avenue from New York Street to College Avenue has art galleries, specialty shops and a fine coffeehouse. The Broad Ripple area (Broad Ripple Avenue between College Avenue and Westfield Boulevard) is the heart of Indianapolis's nightlife scene, but during the day, it is also a great place to spend an afternoon shopping. Galleries, consignment shops, home furnishing stores and other specialty shops abound. A warning: Parking is on the street and hard to find.

Attractions

Indianapolis Motor Speedway
4790 W. 16th St. • (317) 481-8500

The premier attraction in Indianapolis is, of course, the Indianapolis 500 auto race. Since 1911, the high-speed race has been held every Memorial Day at the Indianapolis Motor Speedway. If you want to see and hear (and we do mean hear — the roar of the cars gives a decibel meter a workout) the big race, tickets must be purchased via mail for next year's race immediately following the current year's race. Tickets sell out within weeks and cost anywhere from $30 to $140, depending on where you sit. Or, join the beer-soaked carnival in the track's infield; you can purchase the $15 general admission ticket to the infield on race day. Louisvillians have learned what Indianapolis natives have long known — the best way to enjoy the speed and thrill of the Indy 500 is to attend the time trials the week before the race. The cost is about $10, the crowds are thinner, and the general admission seating means you can get close enough to actually see the colorful blurs of cars go past.

INSIDERS' TIP

If you're taking I-64 to Bluegrass Industrial Park or Middletown, Hurstbourne Lane's notoriously nasty traffic can be avoided by using Blankenbaker Road, the next exit to the east.

Also at the Speedway is the Brickyard 400, each August. The stock car race sells out too, and tickets are best ordered by mail through the Speedway's box office. The price range is $18 to $100, with infield admission setting you back $15.

Indianapolis Raceway Park
10267 E. U.S. Hwy. 136 • (317) 291-4090
Beyond the Indianapolis Motor Speedway, there is this complex with a drag strip, oval and road course. The park hosts many races from March to October, call for details.

Indianapolis Zoo
1200 W. Washington St. • (317) 630-2001
The Indianapolis Zoo has long been a beacon to Louisville parents. It has the usual exotics, plus two strong exhibits: the Waters Complex (think polar bears, penguins and the like) and the Deserts Biome (sand, birds, lizards and tortoises). The zoo is easy to find — just outside of downtown on one of the main drags radiating outward from the city. The admission prices are $9 for adults, $5.50 for children ages 3 to 11, $6.50 for seniors; parking is an additional $3.

Children's Museum
3000 N. Meridian St. • (317) 924-5437
Everything in this huge museum is designed for interaction, from the log cabin to the Indy race car to the planetarium. Two favorite attractions are the limestone cave replica and a 2,500-year-old Egyptian mummy. The cost is $6 for adults, $3 for kids 2 to 17 and $5 for seniors. Parking is free.

Indiana Pacers
Market Square Arena, 300 E. Market St.
• (317) 239-5151
The Pacers play basketball at the 16,500-seat Market Square Arena. Tickets range from $9 to $32, call the box office at the number above.

Indianapolis Colts
RCA Dome, 100 S. Capitol Ave.
• (317) 297-7000
The Colts have played football at the 60,500-seat RCA Dome every winter since they moved from Baltimore in 1984. Tickets are $15,

$23, $25 and $29; call the box office at the previously listed number.

Indianapolis Indians
Victory Field, 501 W. Maryland St.
• (317) 269-3545
Indianapolis plays host to the minor league farm team of baseball's Cincinnati Reds, the Indianapolis Indians. Tickets are as cheap as $5.

Cincinnati

If Indianapolis means shopping and sports — daytime events — Cincinnati answers with evening enticements. And the reason for this may be found in two Cincy schools: the Art Academy of Cincinnati and the University of Cincinnati's College Conservatory of Music. Both institutions are more than a century old and enjoy a national reputation. So perhaps it's not so surprising that music and the visual arts are strong in the Ohio city, located just two hours away up I-71. The arts are nurtured there.

Below are just a few of Cincinnati's jewels. For a more complete look at all the city has to offer, peruse a copy of *The Insiders' Guide® to Cincinnati*.

Attractions

Contemporary Arts Center
115 East 5th St. • (513) 721-0390
Ironically, the Contemporary Arts Center is best known for housing a Robert Mapplethorpe exhibit of photographs that spurred the city to charge the center and the curator with pandering obscenity. Look past its past; the CAC hosts some engaging shows of modern visual art. Admission is $3.50 for students, $2 for seniors.

Cincinnati Art Museum
Eden Park • 721-5204
The museum offers works ranging from Picasso to Warhol's depiction of local baseball deity Pete Rose in its 118 galleries. There's also an extensive display of Cincinnati's famous Rookwood pottery, ancient Persian architectural pieces and Jin Dynasty wood carv-

ings. Admission is $5; students and seniors pay $4.

Cincinnati Reds
Cincinnati Bengals
Cinergy Field

Two professional teams — baseballs' **Reds** and football's **Bengals** — call Cincinnati home. They both play at Cinergy Field, a round stadium at the base of downtown and right on the Ohio River. You can't miss it. Reds home games are a bargain — the most expensive ticket is less than $14, and Cincy natives say you can buy a $3 day-of-game nose-bleed-section ticket and easily commandeer a lower seat once the game starts. Call Ticketmaster or the Reds box office at (513) 421-7337 for tickets. Bengals games are pricier — $31 and up. Call (513) 621-3550 to purchase tickets.

Cincinnati Symphony Orchestra
Cincinnati Opera
Music Hall, 1241 Elm St.

For decades, Louisvillians traveled to Cincinnati to hear the Cincinnati Symphony Orchestra (established in 1894) and the Cincinnati Opera (which dates back to 1920). Opera fans might reminisce about hearing the sound of a lion's roar in mid-aria — until 1972, the opera company performed at a shell in the Cincinnati Zoo. Now they join the orchestra in performing at the Music Hall. For tickets to the orchestra, call (513) 381-3300; to attend a production of the Cincinnati Opera company, call (513) 621-1919.

Shopping

Is shopping good in Cincinnati? You betcha — the town is the birthplace of the charge card, in August of 1959. The retail business in the Queen City has slipped a bit, but there remains many good places to drop your dough.

Cincy used to be the destination of choice for discerning Louisville shoppers, and a big reason for it was Sak's Fifth Avenue. That store alone gave Cincinnati shopping more glamour than our local malls could summon. But downtown Cincinnati shopping has dropped off with the rise of nondescript suburban malls.

Two areas still demand your attention (and dollars).

Tower Place
Ground level of Carew Tower at Fifth and Race Sts. • no phone

Tower Place is connected to Sak's by a pedway and holds several other notable stores, including Banana Republic, The Nature Company, The Gap and The Limited.

Fourth Street

One block south on Fourth Street, Closson's offers fine furniture and artful accessories, and a string of specialty shops sell Oriental rugs. There's a Brooks Brothers clothier too.

Main Street

The long strip of Main Street offers an eclectic mix, including several good restaurants and breweries. The area is best known for its galleries, however, ranging from Theresa's Textile Trove, 1327 Main Street, to Only Artists, 1315 Main Street, which specializes in contemporary primitives. There are also bread stores, record stores, coffeehouses and an open-air food market.

Nashville

It's the music city, it's the country music capital, it's the home of the Grand Ole Opry. Thus, when folks go to Nashville, it's most often to hear some tunes.

Attractions

The Grand Ole Opry
2804 Opryland Dr. • (615) 889-6611

The Opry is the grand-daddy of all music attractions and a must-see of Nashville. It's a live radio show that has showcased country music since 1925. It's like a living hall of fame, and it is an unforgettable experience. It's not expensive, either — tickets are $15.50 and $17.50. The Grand Ole Opry runs from May through October. Another live radio show that features good country music and is fun to attend is the Ernest Tubb Midnight Jamboree, 2416 Music Valley Drive, (615) 889-2474.

Country Music Hall of Fame & Historic RCA Studio B
4 Music Square E. • (615) 256-1639

If you're interested in the history of country music, check out the spot. Inside are artifacts, exhibits and the personal treasures of country's biggest stars. A tour of RCA Studio B lets you see where some of country music's legendary albums were recorded. Admission is $9.95 for adults; kids 6 to 11 are $4.95.

Wildhorse Saloon
120 Second Ave. N. • (615) 251-1000

Anyone who watches The Nashville Network (TNN) on cable knows the Wildhorse Saloon. Dancers on the 3,300-square-foot dance floor are showcased regularly on a TV show taped there.

Bluebird Cafe
4104 Hillsboro Rd. • (615) 383-1461

The best songwriters in Nashville show off their stuff in a relaxed, acoustic setting at the Bluebird Cafe.

Station Inn
402 12th Ave. S. • (615) 255-3307

Station Inn is, in the words of one former Nashville resident, "the real deal" — the place where the city's finest pickers show off their chops. Bluegrass is the dominant flavor at Station Inn.

Shopping

Shopping in Nashville is unexceptional, although a few record stores in the downtown area might yield some hard-to-find country music on vinyl to enthusiasts, and western wear shops are abundant for folks trying to achieve the appropriately rustic look of country living. Beyond those two general areas of specialty, the shopping outlook in Nashville can be reduced to two terms: factory outlets and mega-malls.

Bellevue Center
7620 Hwy. 70 S. Bellevue Exit off I-40W • (615) 646-8690

This premier mall is a 200-store extravaganza that features the usual suspects — Eddie Bauer, Ann Taylor, The Disney Store, The Gap, Banana Republic, Victoria's Secret and the like.

Factory Store of America
2434 Music Valley Dr. • (615) 885-5140

The outlet mall concept is nearly perfected at the Factory Store of America, across the street from the Opryland Hotel. Prices are 30 to 70 percent cheaper than retail at this mall's 70 factory stores.

For the nature-minded, Greater Louisville offers proximity to more than a dozen natural areas — forests, preserves, resorts and wildlife refuges, many with recreation areas where you can fish, hunt, hike and camp.

Parks and Recreation

How good is our parks department? You can tell by the nature of the complaints thrown at it. They are generally inconsequential — or, if substantial, the gripes prove foolish over time. Consider the case of the Scenic Loop, a 2.4-mile circuit of road in Cherokee Park that was made one way for motorists in order to accommodate walkers, bicyclists, runners and skaters in the other traffic lane. A howl of protest greeted the proposal to change the park's traffic pattern. Now, you hear only the sighs of pleasure from an appreciative public.

Good leadership at the top and capable people on the front lines of the Louisville & Jefferson County Parks Department (widely known as Metro Parks) make a multitude of programs and services work with nary a hitch. The department also manages to balance preservation of the parks' integrity — particularly the major parks designed by Frederick Law Olmsted — with pragmatic public use. This means that a park like Cherokee can offer breathtaking views of meadows and heavily wooded areas and also offer facilities for golf, basketball, tennis and even concerts.

The Metro Parks and the wide variety of recreational activities available through them constitute a large chunk of Louisville's leisure scene. The private sector ably picks up the slack from there, especially in the sport of golf. Louisville's cycling, volleyball, tennis and running scenes are strong, too.

For the nature-minded, Greater Louisville offers proximity to more than a dozen natural areas — forests, preserves, resorts and wildlife refuges, many with recreation areas where you can fish, hunt, hike and camp. The area's lush forests are also ripe for birding, boating, picnicking and nature study.

Louisville is not a seasonal city. There are events, leagues, programs and competitions year round in a variety of activities. We outline a number amount of them below.

Parks

Metro Parks

The Three Olmsted Parks

The three major parks designed by Frederick Law Olmsted, the father of landscape architecture in America, are a vital part of the lives of many Louisvillians. These three gems — Cherokee, Iroquois and Shawnee Parks — are deservedly beloved. Olmsted wrote that city parks are important because they provide a place for humans to explore their "gregarious" nature. Anyone who has driven through one of these parks on a sunny Sunday knows that Olmsted achieved this goal in his designs — people park their vehicles, congregate, stroll, wax their cars, picnic and generally visit with each other in the meadows and greenspaces of these Louisville treasures. Olmsted's concept of connecting city parks via tree-lined parkways with separate roads for pedestrian and other types of traffic, a concept modeled after boulevards in Brussels and Paris, is well realized in Louisville. Olmsted also designed Boone Square Park, a four-acre space at 20th and Rowan Streets, and his firm designed twelve other playground/park areas in the city after his death.

The parks are generally open from 6 AM to midnight. For more information regarding programs or other specifics, call the Metro Parks office at 456-8100.

Cherokee Park
Between Eastern Pkwy. and Lexington and Cherokee Rds.

It's the most visited of Louisville's parks, and it's no wonder — Cherokee strikes a magical balance between uninterrupted natural beauty and useful facilities. You can fish; ride horseback on a bridle path; play golf, basketball, softball, or tennis; practice archery; watch your kids play on several playgrounds; take your mountain bike on numerous wooded trails; or utilize the Scenic Loop on foot, skates, or bicycles. Hill One offers great kite flying, while structures at Hogan's Fountain and Big Rock are suitable for outdoor meetings, family reunions and big picnics. Even a short visit to Louisville should include a walk or drive through Cherokee.

It's bordered by Lexington Road and Grinstead Drive in the near East End and is connected to the other two major Olmsted parks by Eastern Parkway. The Olmsted firm had a hand in planning the residential neighborhoods near Cherokee Park, and it shows. The area is one of the most desirable places to live in the metro area.

Iroquois Park
New Cut Rd. and Southern Pkwy.

The dominant feature at this 739-acre park is Iroquois Hill, a 260-foot knob accessible by two climbing paths and capped by a circuit path with scenic overlooks — Olmsted's key element for Iroquois Park. Young people love to cruise around the lower circuit drive that meanders around the park's perimeter. Playgrounds, basketball courts, a golf course, tennis courts and walking and bicycle trails are a few of the facilities featured. A 2,200-seat open-air amphitheater, courtesy of the WPA, is the site of professionally staged musicals each summer. (Read more about Iroquois Amphitheater's productions in The Arts chapter.) Iroquois park stretches along New Cut Road and is connected to the other Olmsted parks via Southern Parkway.

Shawnee Park
Broadway and Southwestern Pkwy.

This was the crown jewel of the Olmsted parks in the early part of this century. Low-lying, largely flat, with riverfront on its longest side, Shawnee's 181 acres now hold 10 ball fields, nine tennis courts and five basketball courts. It's sports heaven. In 1891 Olmsted reported to the Louisville Board of Park Commissioners that Shawnee is the right place for "broad and tranquil meadowy spaces . . . offering at once areas of turf to be inexpensively kept in a suitable condition for lawn games." In that regard, our city's leaders have succeeded fully. Broadway ends in the west at the Ohio River, with Shawnee Park lying on the left side of the road. Shawnee is connected to the other Olmsted parks via Southwestern Parkway.

Camps, Leagues and Organized Programs

Metro Parks offers programs in just about every pastime you can think of. Recreation centers and athletic fields provide a lot of activities and programs for all age groups. A short list includes basketball, soccer, fencing, cooking, oil painting and drama. With 112 parks, 10 fishing lakes, nine golf courses, an indoor swimming pool and numerous outdoor pools, there's almost certainly something to interest you. Some of the programs are described below.

Metro Parks' recreation centers throughout the city and county are the neighborhood hubs of organized hobby and sport programs in Louisville. Softball, volleyball and basketball leagues play here, and classes in crafts, yoga, karate, ceramics and computers are only a few of the ones offered through the Parks. Call for the location of the center nearest you, then stop by or call for a schedule of activities and operating hours.

Adapted Leisure Activities
2305 Douglass Blvd. • 456-8148

This division of Metro Parks and Recreation provides athletic and recreational programs for individuals with mental and/or physical disabilities, impaired vision or impaired hearing. They'll also help you locate similar programs elsewhere in the community. Some typical programs and activities include shopping, card games and pot-luck lunches. You get fit and have fun doing it by participating in activities such as wheelchair basketball, horseback riding and walking.

> **FYI**
>
> Unless otherwise noted, the area code for all phone numbers listed in this chapter is 502.

Arts
8360 Dixie Hwy. • 937-2055

The Metro Arts Center offers ongoing classes in a wide variety of arts, including pottery, oil painting, watercolor, photography, topiary, drawing, design, printmaking and more, for adults and teens. As part of the center's programs, the Young Picassos Workshops teach kids aged 10 to 13 a variety of art skills in four one-week programs during the summer. The classes are held at the Douglass Community Center, 2305 Douglass Boulevard.

Athletics
1287 Trevilian Way • 456-8171

The Metro Parks Athletics Department organizes adult and youth sports throughout Louisville and Jefferson County. Basketball and softball leagues for adults and football and baseball camps for youth are among the programs. Independent groups can obtain athletic field permits for softball, soccer and field hockey. Individuals and groups can rent a Metro Parks picnic-and-sports package that includes softball and volleyball equipment, horseshoes, footballs and basketballs.

Muhammad Ali Youth
Sports Program
1297 Trevilian Way • 456-3245

Well-organized, competitive sports camps and leagues are available to children ages 6 to 14 from all points in the county through this program. The focus is on developing skills and knowledge of several sports and building self-esteem. Over 5,000 kids participate in this program, which began in 1992. Soccer is offered in the spring, football in the fall, basketball and cheerleading in winter and sports camps during summer. Registration fees are $25 or less; fee waivers are available. Uniforms are provided in some cases; parents must pay for equipment in some sports.

Summer Camps
1297 Trevilian Way • 456-8100

Children's 1st Summer Camps are designed for youths ages 6 and older. Activities include arts and crafts, volleyball, basketball, swimming, reading, softball, table games and a lot more. All camps offer children an instructional period in addition to recreation.

Sports camps teach basketball, soccer, gymnastics, volleyball, golf, tennis and cheerleading. For a schedule, call the Metro Parks central number listed above.

Metro Parks Track Club
1297 Trevilian Way • 456-8160

Games and People is a once-a-week program that provides activities in track and field, road racing and cross country. It's an informal way to get involved in track and field. Competition covers all age groups. The club holds and manages 25 road races each year that attract from 200 to 5,000 runners for each event, highlighted by the popular "triple crown races," which climax with the Kentucky Derby Mini-Marathon. Distance events vary from 1- to 1.5-mile walks, 2-mile fun runs/walks and 5K runs/walks to a full 26.2-mile marathon. Call for an events schedule.

Forests and Recreational Areas

Kentucky

Bernheim Arboretum
and Research Forest
Ky. Hwy. 245, Clermont • 955-8512

Bernheim was established in 1929 by Isaac W. Bernheim, a German Jewish immigrant who became a successful whiskey distiller. Today this attraction includes a 14,000-acre nature preserve, nearly 2,000 acres of which have been carefully designed, planted and maintained for visitors. Facilities within the arboretum include a nature center, arboretum center, picnic areas, hiking trails and lakes. Many of the trees are labeled with stakes; check out native species such as the Kentucky Coffee Tree and the American chestnut.

Bernheim Forest holds adult and children's classes on the environment, plant identification, photography, cooking with herbs and other topics. Fees vary. The 32-acre Lake Nevin is a good place to fish for bluegill, crappie and bass.

Bernheim is open all year from 7 AM to sunset. Admission is free during the week. On

Photo: Indiana Department of Natural Resources

Tour the fossil beds at the Falls of the Ohio State Park.

weekends, an environmental impact fee of $5 is charged for vehicles carrying up to 10 passengers, $10 for vehicles with up to 20 passengers and $20 for full-size busses with 20 or more passengers.

Jefferson County Memorial Forest
11311 Mitchell Hill Rd., Fairdale
• 368-5404

This forest covers 5,123 acres of land in southwest Jefferson County. You'll find picnic areas and playground equipment, plus campsites and adventure sites (an Alpine tower, rappelling) in the Horine Section, an area used for educational programs. The forest is home to 35 miles of hiking trails — many of them strenuous enough for the experienced hiker, a .25-mile trail accessible to persons with physical disabilities, a fishing pier, horse trails and picnic pavilions. This recreational area keeps a remarkably low profile considering how heavily it is used by organized groups and clubs.

The Horine Section also has an environmental education center, a ranger station and a leadership conference center. This section, the only part of the forest where camping is

available, also rents tents, backpacks and other camping gear.

Fees are $10 per campsite (maximum of 20 people).

The Louisville Nature Center
1297 Trevilian Way • 458-1328

This seven-acre section of the Beargrass Creek State Nature Preserve is an urban oasis for many outdoor programs. You can view 150 species of birds, a plethora of wild animals and 180 species of trees, shrubs and flowering plants along the woodland trails. The center is near the Louisville Zoo southwest of downtown.

Otter Creek Park Resort
Off Ky. Hwy. 1638 • 583-3577

Traveling 30 miles southwest of Louisville, you'll reach Otter Creek, 2,600 forested acres, where recreational choices include mountain biking, hiking, rock climbing, rappelling, canoeing on the Ohio and cave tours. The resort includes a 22-unit lodge, a restaurant, meeting rooms, cabins, pools, a nature center, a boat ramp and trails. Otter Creek hosts a successful Elderhostel program, and many area youngsters attend the park's summer camps. This is a popular place for company picnics and team-building retreats, too.

E.P. "Tom" Sawyer State Park
3000 Freys Hill Rd. • 426-8950
Not far from the bustle of the city is this 377-acre recreational park that serves as a nature retreat for many area residents. Recreation facilities include a 50-meter swimming pool, tennis courts, athletic fields, a BMX bicycle racing track and a mile-long trail. Admission to the park is free. Call for a pool schedule and fees.

Indiana

Clark State Forest
Ind. Hwy. 31, Henryville • (812) 294-4306
Clark is Indiana's first state forest, established in 1903. You can roam scenic roads and hike on paths that wind through 24,000 acres of heavily forested timberland. The forest also has seven fishing lakes, a backpack area and nature preserve, a boat-launch ramp, bridle trails, camping, fishing and ice fishing, hunting, picnicking and shelter houses. There's no admission charge.

Clifty Falls State Park
1501 Green Rd., Madison • (812) 265-4135
The park gets its name from the breathtaking waterfalls and deep-bordered canyon visible from hiking trails through this scenic area. The park has camping, inn and restaurant accommodations, meeting and conference facilities, a nature center, picnicking, swimming pools with a water slide (the pool is open Memorial Day through Labor Day), tennis and other games. It costs $2 per car if you have Indiana license plates, $5 per car for out-of-state visitors.

Deam Lake State Recreation Area
1217 Deam Lake Rd., Borden
• (812) 246-5421
Water-centered activities such as fishing, ice fishing and swimming are plentiful in this 1,300-acre area, established in 1965. The park has a boat-launch ramp and rowboat rentals. You can also camp, hunt and picnic, and it's a

great place for birding. Admission is $2 per car if you have Indiana license plates, $5 per car for out-of-state visitors.

The Falls of the Ohio State Park
201 W. Riverside Dr., Clarksville
• (812) 280-9970
This relatively new park, established in 1990, covers 68 acres along the north shore of the Ohio River, part of the 1,404-acre Falls of the Ohio National Wildlife Conservation Area. The Interpretive Center, which opened in 1994, is a busy place; it houses a research library, theater, gift shop, wildlife observation room, classrooms and a large exhibit gallery. (See our Attractions chapter for more information about the Center.)

The diverse fauna that can be observed at the Falls includes 125 species of fish and more than 265 species of birds, including several that are endangered.

Patoka Reservoir
164 W. State Hwy., Birdseye
• (812) 685-2464
This is a good place to find bald eagles perched along the shoreline in winter — the best view is from the beach area. Other waterfowl, such as mallards, black ducks and bufflehead ducks, are plentiful. Squirrels, deer, foxes, coyotes, rabbits and songbirds also live within the 17,000 acres of land that surround 9,000 acres of reservoir. You can come here 24 hours a day; there is a $2 fee per car for Indiana residents and a $5 fee per car for out-of-state visitors. An additional fee is charged for camping and boat launchings.

Recreational Activities

Bicycling

Louisville Bicycle Club
• 329-1848
This group celebrated their 100th anniversary in 1997, which means they were around when cyclists rode high-wheelers, those dangerous contraptions with one gigantic wheel

Good Louisville Golfers Die and Go to Valhalla

There are other good, extremely exclusive golf courses in the Louisville area — Louisville Country Club, Big Springs and Hunting Creek come to mind. And there are other courses designed by big-time names — Covered Bridge was designed by Fuzzy Zoeller and Lake Forest was drawn up by Arnold Palmer. But Valhalla Golf Club, 15503 Shelbyville Road, 245-4475, is unequivocally the heaven to which all area golfers aspire.

Close-up

Simply, the 18 holes at Valhalla, masterfully designed by Jack Nicklaus, are a premiere test of golf. You'll use every club in your bag to get around this pristine course — and you'll be tempted to use your camera at every hole to capture its natural beauty and breathtaking vistas.

Built in 1986 with the expressed mission of becoming a world-class golfing experience, the course's superiority was publicly recognized when it hosted the 1996 PGA Tournament — to much acclaim from participants and observers alike. Valhalla so impressed PGA officials that they bought part-ownership in the golf course, adding it to their cache of courses that they run across the nation. The PGA tourney is scheduled to return to Valhalla in the year 2000.

It's not a golf course for beginners. Hazards — lots of sand traps, creeks and ponds — make it a nightmare for even an intermediate golfer. One hole in particular has Louisville golfers spellbound. Valhalla's signature hole, No. 13, features an elevated green that is a small island; miss the green, and you're in the drink.

For the vast majority of golfers, navigating that 13th hole is a moot issue. Most will never even lay eyes on Valhalla's fairways — you can't get past the guard gate off Shelbyville Road without a tee time.

And getting a tee time is very difficult. Memberships are limited and expensive. Guest visits are rigidly regulated; even if you know a member, you'll pay a $100 green fee each time and only get to play there a few times a year.

But you can always dream of Valhalla — just like thousands of other links fans across Louisville.

Photo: Bob Bahr

in the front and a tiny stabilizing wheel in the back. More than 600 people are members of this club, with about 150 making up the hardcore group who ride at least once a week. The club distributes a ride schedule at many area cycle shops. Annual dues are less than $20.

Kentucky Mountain Bike Association (KyMBA)
• 569-7676

This group, which is dedicated to off-road cycling, exists to ensure land access for mountain bikers and to educate fans of the sport on the proper times and places to hit the trails. A newsletter, published roughly 10 times a year, helps members keep track of trail conditions in mountain bike hotspots such as Waverly Park (Arnoldtown Road in the far South End), Otter Creek Park (Brandenburg, Kentucky) and the overused trails of Cherokee Park. Dues are $15 a year, rides are scheduled at least twice a week.

Boating

The Ohio River is a great place for small motorboats, houseboats, sailboats and Jet Skis, and a number of lakes offer boat rentals for fishing or canoeing. Free, public docks and boat ramps are available at **Carrie Gaulbert Cox Park** (River Road and Indian Hills Trail in the far East End), **Riverview Park** (Greenwood and Lower River Road in the far South End) and **Otter Creek Park** (Brandenburg, Ky.).

Several marinas in the East End have boat docks and ramps for entry to the river, most for less than $10, including: **Captain's Quarters' Marina**, 5700 Captains Quarters Road, 228-5447; and **Harrods Creek Boat Harbor**, next door to Captains Quarters on Captains Quarters Road, 228-2891.

Climbing

Rocksport
10901 Plantside Dr. • 266-5833

There's really only one game in town for climbing. This facility has three walls, two of them standing 35-feet tall. The fee is $12 for a day of climbing; harnesses and shoes are avail-

able for rental for an additional $5. Introductory lessons are available seven days a week for $8.

Kentucky's landscape provides a lot of opportunities for climbing and rappelling, but some are restricted from the public and others are unsafe. The people at Rocksport can help steer you in the right direction for outdoor climbing.

Dancing

Louisville Country Dancers
St. Andrew's Episcopal Church, 2223 Woodbourne Ave. • 452-9581

This group meets every Monday and the third Saturday of every month at 8 PM for contras, reels, Appalachian squares, English country dances, running sets and circle dances. Live music is provided by local and out-of-town bands with hammered dulcimers, fiddles, tin whistles, lap dulcimers and drums. Beginners are welcome, as callers walk you through each dance, and experienced dancers push and pull you the rest of the way. Partners are not necessary, there are no dues, and walk-ins are welcome.

Coyote's Bar
116 W. Jefferson St. • 589-3866

Coyote's offers free country dancing lessons on Wednesday, Thursday and Friday from 7 to 9 PM.

Churchill Downs VFW
3026 Rodman St. • 637-9658

The VFW has ballroom dancing every Friday starting at 7 PM and '50s and '60s music on Sunday from 6:30 to 10:30 PM. The charge is $1 per person.

Fishing

Here's the bad news: The best fishing by far in the Louisville area is at privately owned farm ponds in the outlying areas. If you want to fish these, start networking with your fellow fishermen and hope to get invited along on an expedition. On the other hand, there are folks who swear by the fishing in the Ohio River. It can certainly be exciting, due to currents, unusual trash and singular species such as gar, sauger and drum. Because of pollution, you don't want to eat anything that comes out of the river.

One popular spot for river fishing is at the **Falls of the Ohio**. It's on the Indiana side of the river in Clarksville, but as long as you're casting into the river, a Kentucky fishing license will work. (Kentucky "owns" the river from bank to bank.) A Kentucky fishing license can be purchased from tackle shops, government centers and from the **Fish and Wildlife Resources Department**, 595-4039, at Bowman Field Airport near the Driver's Testing Station on Dutchmans Lane. (The department is also a good source of information regarding size and bag limits.) If you are 65 or older, your license is free. To fish for trout you have to buy a trout stamp, which costs $5. Licenses are available for residents and nonresidents. Good from March 1 to February 28 each year, licenses cost $12.50. Nonresidents may buy a yearlong license for $30, a 15-day license for $20 or a three-day license for $12.50. Licenses are available at Bowman Field or wherever tackle is sold, including Wal-Mart and Kmart stores.

A handful of pay lakes in the South End keep their waters stocked, but the catch usually consists of channel catfish and bluegill, with a few bass here and there. See the yellow pages for more information.

Ten of the Metro Parks stock their lakes, but our favorites are at **Cherokee Park** (a heavily fished 4.6-acre lake located at Grinstead Drive and Lexington Road) and **Long Run Park** (a 28.7-acre lake, located in the East End of Jefferson County at 1607 Flat Rock Road, that can yield good and tasty dividends to the crafty fisherman).

Most Louisvillians satisfy their craving to wet a line at these metropolitan locations, but plan bigger fishing excursions around trips to Lake Cumberland, Reelfoot Lake, or Lake Barkley, which are all near the Kentucky-Tennessee border.

Fitness

All the YMCAs and the Jewish Community Center have extensive fitness programs and fitness centers. In addition, there are a number of private fitness clubs around the city. Your best bet is to visit the center nearest your home or workplace to see the facilities, a schedule of classes and the fees. We've seen two-for-one membership promotions at some places, so try to negotiate the best terms.

The Young Men's Christian Association has had a strong presence here since 1853, when America's 10th YMCA was established in Louisville. The Downtown Branch opened September 1, 1913, at Fourth and Broadway. (It has since moved to Second Street.) Now, four sites serve Greater Louisville.

Downtown YMCA
555 S. Second St. • 587-6700

This Y is one of the largest indoor fitness and recreation centers in Greater Louisville. Facilities include an indoor, heated swimming pool, a three-lane indoor track, eight handball/racquetball courts and a multiple-activity gym. There is a pro shop; a babysitting service is available. Like many of the private fitness centers, the Y gives you access to all sorts of exercise equipment, plus a sauna and a whirlpool. There is a list of aerobics and fitness classes for all ages.

Northeast Family YMCA
9400 Mill Brook Rd. • 425-1271

The Northeast Y serves all ages, but is especially strong in adult fitness, with a wellness center including free weights, Nautilus machines, personal trainers and fitness evaluations. You can join soccer, softball, volleyball and basketball leagues or take aquatics and swimming instruction, which are available for babies to adults. Water exercise for senior citizens, people with arthritis, multiple sclerosis and other disabilities is offered.

Southeast Family YMCA
5930 Six Mile Ln. • 491-9622

This facility participates in the YMCA/Jefferson County Public School Child Care Enrichment Program, which provides a safe place for kids before and after school; two local churches have cooperative programs with the Y, also. Adults can have a fitness assessment and participate in a number of activities, including arthritis aquatics. Teens play in soccer, flag football, baseball, tee ball and basketball leagues, and the Swordfish Swim Team competes in citywide matches.

Southwest Family YMCA
2800 Fordhaven Rd. • 933-9622

The Southwest Y has a fitness center with the latest equipment; aerobics classes; programs for senior citizens; day care and before- and after-school child care; aquatics programs for all ages; a swim team; first aide and CPR classes; and several sports camps.

YMCA of Southern Indiana
4312 Hamburg Pike, Jeffersonville • (812) 283-9622

This Y boasts two gyms, locker rooms with saunas, a fitness center, a free weight room and an outdoor pool. Programs are available for youth sports and recreation (including in-line hockey and soccer), adult health and fitness and child care. Men and women are welcome; a financial assistance package is available.

Jewish Community Center
3600 Dutchmans Ln. • 459-0660

Louisville's Jewish Community Center, which began as the Young Men's Hebrew Association in 1868 as chiefly a literary and charitable society, is the third oldest in the country in continuous operation. The JCC, a Metro United Way Agency beneficiary, serves Jews and non-Jews with activities, clubs, sports and recreation from preschoolers to senior adults, men and women. The JCC has sports leagues and classes in everything from karate and gymnastics to body mechanics and yoga.

An indoor and outdoor pool, racquetball and tennis courts, fitness equipment, aerobics classes and locker rooms with a sauna, hot tub and massages are available to members and guests. Jewish Hospital, in conjunction with the center, maintains a Preventive Heart Program at the JCC that is open to anyone who suffers from heart disease or who wants a monitored prevention program.

Flying

Devonair
Bowman Field, 2807 Taylorsville Rd. • 459-9637

Devonair instructs students who want to earn their private and instrument pilot's license. Pilots supplies are for sale. Airplane rentals start at $45 an hour; five rental planes are available.

Cardinal Wings
Bowman Field, 2700 Gast Blvd. • 459-6184

Cardinal Wings offers flight instruction, private, instrument, commercial, multi-engine and laser grade instruction. Thirteen planes of seven different kinds are available for rent. They've taught people from nine years old to 77. Airplane rentals start at $46.

Golf

Metro Parks Golf Courses

Metro Park Golf Courses are open from daylight to dark seven days a week, closing only on Christmas and New Year's days. You can rent pull carts, riding carts and clubs. Golf lessons and group outings can be arranged. For information on greens fees (expect to spend about $10), lessons and other needs or to reserve a tee time or equipment, call the course nearest you.

Each Metro Parks golf course has men's, women's and juniors' associations to help individuals attain their U.S. Golf Association handicap. Association membership includes participation in weekly tournaments, cookouts and other leisure events. Clinics and tournaments are held at the public courses. Contact the pro at each course for information.

INSIDERS' TIP

To keep up with the newest in outdoor activities and to read about old treasures, check Linda Stahl's "Getting Out" column in *The Courier Journal's* Weekend EXTRA section every Friday.

Nine-Hole Courses

Bobby Nichols
4301 East Pages Ln. • 937-9051

This hilly, short course is an adequate test of golf. If you're bad with irons, this South End course will give you fits — Nichols Creek comes into play on eight of the nine holes.

Cherokee
2501 Alexander Rd. • 458-9450

This short course is built on a very large hill in Cherokee Park. The unusual layout means a lot of bad lies, and a lot of opportunities to test your short-iron game.

Crescent Hill
3110 Brownsboro Rd.
• 896-9193

A fairly flat, fairly long course in the East End with at least one hole (a par 5, 476-yard challenge dubbed the "quarry hole") that will test experienced golfers.

18-Hole Courses

Charlie Vettiner
10207 Mary Dell Rd., • 267-9958

Fairly hilly and long with a recently added back nine, this course, located near Jeffersontown, offers a lot of variety, with 50 white-sand bunkers, a small creek and three lakes.

Iroquois
1501 Rundill Rd. • 363-9520

Very hilly and long, this golf course and Seneca are the two best public courses in the area. Mature trees, bermudagrass fairways and water hazards on seven of 18 holes make Iroquois a favorite for tournaments. It's located in the South End.

Long Run
1605 Flat Rock Rd. • 245-0702

The name says it all. Long Run is a very long, nice test of golf, with a narrow-fairwayed back nine that was carved out of woods within the last ten years. Two double dogleg par fives will tack some strokes onto your score at this course in the far East End.

Seneca
2300 Pee Wee Reese Dr. • 458-9298

This is the all-around best Metro Park course, and its heavy play and high caliber tournaments attest to this. Hilly, well-kept — Seneca is the default public golf course in Louisville.

Shawnee
460 Northwestern Pkwy. • 776-9389

Flat, short and easy, Shawnee is good for your golf ego and easy on the eyes — it runs along the Ohio River in the West End.

Sun Valley
6505 Bethany Ln. • 937-9228

The notable feature of Sun Valley is its back nine holes, each of which incorporate a water hazard.

FYI

Unless otherwise noted, the area code for all phone numbers listed in this chapter is 502.

Semi-Private Golf Clubs

In addition to the Metro Parks courses, there are several semiprivate golf courses in the area, as well as country clubs with nine- and 18-hole courses for members and their guests. Here are a few of the better semiprivate courses; the country clubs are listed in the yellow pages.

Bellarmine Golf Course
2001 Newburg Rd. • 452-8378

You don't need reservations at this fast-play course. Greens fees are $5 during the week; $6 on weekends and holidays. Bellarmine is a nine-hole par 3 walking course that's extremely hilly and kept in decent shape.

Nevel Meade Golf Course
10509 Covered Bridge Rd., Prospect
• 228-9522

This is a very interesting course — in the Scottish links design — with very few trees, a lot of undulations, rolling fairways and a wide-open feel. The lack of trees can disturb your depth perception, and a plethora of sand bunkers can distress your score. A pro is on staff at this 18-hole course. Reservations are required four days in advance. Greens fees are

$15 on weekdays; $21 on weekends. Riding and pull carts are for rent, and a pro shop is on the premises.

Persimmon Ridge Golf Club
72 Persimmon Ridge Rd. • 241-0819

Next to the hallowed Valhalla course, this is the best test of golf in Louisville. Extremely long and very difficult, with lots of hazards, narrow fairways and hilly terrain, this 18-hole golf course is not for beginners or intermediates. It's tough to get a tee time on the weekends, when members get preference over the public. Expect to pay about $40 in greens fees, with or without a cart.

Quail Chase Golf Course
7000 Cooper Chapel Rd. • 239-2110

Quail Chase is Louisville's only 27-hole golf course; it received a 4-star rating from *Golf Digest* magazine in 1994. This very good, semi-private course is maintained like a country club. Its hilly terrain, excellent maintenance and variety of holes — water hazards, traps, tricky doglegs — make it a favorite among expert golfers. Make reservations two days in advance; call ahead for partners or be paired when you arrive. Greens fees range from $9 to $22, depending on the number of holes and the day of the week. Pull carts and riding carts can be rented, and the course has a snack bar and pro shop.

Hiking

The Sierra Club
Thomas Jefferson Unitarian Church, 4938 Old Brownsboro Rd. • 566-9968

The Sierra Club of Louisville holds programs at the church at 7:30 PM the third Tuesday of every month. A chapter outings schedule for the state of Kentucky can be purchased at the meetings. Anyone can participate in the hikes. The cost, which covers insurance, is $1 for members and $2 for nonmembers.

Louisville Hiking Club
• (812) 945-7264

The Louisville Hiking Club sponsors hikes weekly on Saturdays. The group charters a school bus ($3 per person) that takes hikers to the location of the day. Meet at Central Park at 2 PM. After the hike, participants meet for dinner at a restaurant. Hikes are usually 3 to 6 miles long. Membership dues are $7.50 yearly, and members receive a monthly post card listing the trips. Hikes are in Louisville and Southern Indiana. Members get first consideration for weekend trips.

Quest Outdoors
128 Breckinridge Ln. • 893-5746

Quest Outdoors sells a guidebook titled *Hiking in the Louisville Area* for $12.95. The store carries a variety of hiking gear and clothing. (See our entry in the Shopping chapter.)

(For more information on Hiking, see Forests and Recreational Areas in this chapter.)

Horseback Riding

This being the Bluegrass, horses are naturally going to play a part in the area's avocation: boarding, breeding, training and riding. The yellow pages has four columns devoted to horse breeders, dealers, equipment and supplies, training and stables. With Louisville's winding park trails, there is no shortage of places for a day's outing. We've listed several stables that have public rentals of horses and cater to beginners.

Iroquois Riding Stables
Iroquois Park, New Cut Rd. and Southern Pkwy. • 363-9159

These stables have public horse rentals and offer trail rides through Iroquois Park, with its picturesque lookout. Riding camp and pony rides are also available. Open seven days a week; horses are available on a first-come, first-serve basis. The cost ranges from $8 for a half-hour to $18 for 90 minutes. Lessons are offered for $25 per hour.

McNeely Park Riding Stable
McNeely Park, 6711 Mt. Washington Rd. • 231-9011

Located in southern Jefferson County, this outfit stables eleven horses that can be rented for less than $20. Guided trail rides pass the

46-acre McNeely Lake. You can take lessons for $20 an hour.

Hunting

You will need a Kentucky hunting license ($12.50 for residents, $95 for nonresidents) and a Kentucky Hunting & Trapping Guide, which can be purchased from the Fish and Wildlife Resources Department Office at Bowman Field across from the Driver's Testing Station. Hunting seasons vary according to the game being hunted, so be sure to get up-to-date information and find out about safety regulations. Anyone born on or after January 1, 1975, must take a hunter's safety course before they hunt. Anyone younger than 16 must have a junior hunting license and hunter's safety card to be in the field. For season dates and information, call 595-4039.

Ice Skating

The Alpine Ice Arena
1825 Gardiner Ln. • 459-9500

Alpine is open to the public from October to April. Get a schedule of skating sessions for exact times and fees and plan on spending $6 or less to get in some skates and onto the rink. Adult and youth hockey leagues are available at this almost 40-year-old facility, Louisville's oldest indoor rink.

Iceland
La Grange Rd. and Dorsey Ln. • 327-6613

This relatively new rink is open all year, seven days a week. It's a hotbed for hockey leagues — both adult and youth. You can get on the ice with rented skates for $8 or less, depending on the day and time. In addition to Iceland's two rinks, the facility also has a fully equipped pro shop and laser tag area.

Broadbent Arena
Kentucky Fair and Exposition Center, 437 Phillips Ln. • 367-9121, ext. 665

Kids love to skate in Broadbent Arena because they see the RiverFrogs, Louisville's minor league hockey team, battle it out there during their season, which begins in November. You can skate in Broadbent after RiverFrog games (from 10:30 PM to midnight) or on the weekends, but only during the team's season. Five dollars gets you into some rented skates and on the ice. Call for more information.

In-line Skating

The Louisville MasterBladers
• 625-9684

The MasterBladers is a diverse group of in-line skating enthusiasts. Since 1991, these skaters have embarked on 12 to 25 mile excursions in area parks.

Jogging, Running and Walking

Mall-walking has become a popular indoor pastime year round, and several local malls have walkers' clubs that meet mornings before the stores open. But for those of you who enjoy a little nature with your trek, we offer the following suggestions.

Seneca Park Track off Cannon's Lane is a 1.2-mile oval, popular with local walkers and joggers most hours of the day, and the path is well-lit for evening and winter walking. Come here to see dog-walkers, soccer or softball games, tennis matches, picnickers and kids at the playground while you're walking.

Crescent Hill Reservoir near the Mary T. Meagher Natatorium, between Brownsboro Road and Frankfort Avenue, has a .75-mile-long, wide sidewalk that encircles the duck-filled waters. Lighting makes walking easy any time of the night or in winter. This is your walking spot if you're seeking serenity. The water in the basin smells like a lake or ocean when the breeze blows, the many mallard ducks are always turning their bottoms skyward while they dunk their heads for food and the hilltop view of the train tracks is sensational.

Cherokee Park has the Scenic Loop, which you can jump on at a number of places including the foot of Eastern Parkway. One lane is reserved for walkers, cyclists and in-line skaters. The road winds through the scenic landscape, with hills that will work your

Photo: Metro Parks

Many Louisville parks rent horses.

cardiovascular system. You'll hear birds, walk in and out of patches of sunlight and pass sunbathers, picnickers and readers sprawled on blankets in the fields.

RiverWalk, a roughly 2-mile stretch of asphalt walking path that stretches from the Belvedere riverfront park downtown at Fourth Street to a point past the McAlpine Dam at 27th Street, offers a good view of the river to one side and a good view of factories and river-related commerce to the other side. It's suitable for walking, in-line skating, jogging or cycling. Your best bet for downtown parking is at a meter along Eighth Street or in the Louisville Science Center parking lot at Eighth Street and River Road. Parking will cost you $3.25 at that lot.

Zoolopers Walking Club
Louisville Zoo, 1100 Trevilian Way • 636-7463

Zoolopers is sponsored by the National Association of Senior Friends, a nonprofit organization for adults older than 50 who want to make the most out of life. Members of the association (with dues of $15 a year) and Zoo members 18 and older (dues are $29 for one adult, $39 for couples) are invited to the early-morning walks here. For information about the walking club, call the above number; for Zoo association membership information, call 459-2181.

Martial Arts and Karate

There are numerous karate and martial arts clubs in the city. Some are more credible than others, and one might find a particular form of martial arts more suitable, depending on one's personal goals and temperament. Check the Yellow Pages, then visit and observe classes.

Louisville Karate and Tae Kwon Do School
5075 Preston Hwy. • 964-3800

The school's Master Choi is a seventh-degree black belt whose goal is to teach self-control and self-esteem, coordination and self-defense. This is "not Ninja turtle stuff," Master Choi likes to say with a laugh. His school is the oldest in the area, dating back to 1967. There are ten branches of the school located throughout the metropolitan area that offer classes to men, women and children; call for further information.

Shaolin Kempo Jiu-Jitsu Academy
9614 Taylorsville Rd. • 267-5737

This reputable school in the East End's Jeffersontown area teaches two separate programs: shaolin kempo, a punching, kicking, standing up style of martial art that stresses the art part; and Brazilian jiu-jitsu, which owner/

teacher Allan B. Manganello names as the most practical martial arts for self defense. "It teaches you how to handle anybody no matter what their size," he says. About 350 students attend the academy, which charges anywhere from $40 to $80 a month for classes, depending on the type of class, the type of program and the age of the student. The academy, which has been operating for more than a dozen years, is open Monday through Thursday and on Saturday.

Skiing

Louisville Ski Club
Aero Club at Bowman Field Airport, 2815 Taylorsville Rd. • 499-8228

For a good introduction to Louisville's skiing opportunities, contact the Louisville Ski Club. The club does more than skiing. There are plenty of summertime activities, including sand volleyball, softball and tennis leagues, golf scrambles, a day at the races, hayrides, a trip on the *Belle of Louisville* and water skiing. The club meets the second and fourth Tuesday of the month at 8 PM. Wintertime activities feature ski trips to Colorado and Europe.

Ski Paoli Peaks
2798 W. County Rd. 200 South, Paoli, Ind. • (812) 723-4696

These slopes are located about an hour north of Louisville. The slopes have beginner, intermediate and more challenging runs; a ski school; a NASTAR race course; snow boarding rentals; a ski shop; and man-made snow (as long as the temperature is at least 30 degrees or colder). You hit the slopes with a lift pass and gear for less than $50.

Soccer

The Greater Louisville Soccer League, 634-8292, has men's teams that play at Eva Bandman, South Central, Seneca and George Rogers Clark parks. For more soccer possibilities, see the earlier information in this chapter for Metro Parks, YMCAs and the Jewish Community Center.

Softball

Metro Parks Department has women's, coed and men's leagues for ages 16 and older and a Senior Softball league for people 50 and older. Park leagues play at Camp Taylor Park, Cherokee Park, Churchill Park, Seneca Park and Wyandotte Park.

Summer league signups begin in February, and fall league signups begin in July. Fees vary and are announced prior to registration. To sign up for adult leagues, call the Metro Parks Athletic Office at 456-8100.

Stamp Collecting

Louisville Stamp Society
Crescent Hill Presbyterian Church, 142 Crescent Ave. • 893-5381

The Louisville Stamp Society meets on the first and third Friday of every month at 8 PM for stamp swapping and refreshments. The club has been active since before the turn of the century.

Swimming

Thirteen public pools run by Metro Parks serve neighborhoods around the city, with two — **Central High School** (11th and Chestnut Streets) and **Shawnee** (in Shawnee Park at 41st Street) — boasting Olympic-size pools. The indoor facilities of the Mary T. Meagher Natatorium are closed for major repairs with no scheduled date for reopening. The individual daily fee for public pools is $2 for people 21 and older, $1.50 for people 20 and younger. Season passes start at $55 for one person, with a sliding scale for families. Call 456-8100 for information about the Metro Parks pool nearest you.

In addition to public swimming pools, the YMCAs and the Jewish Community Center (listed under Fitness in this chapter) have swimming facilities, and many condos and subdivisions have private pools. If you love the sun and the water, ask about these facilities if you're house or apartment hunting.

Tennis

Louisville Tennis Center
Joe Creason Park, 1101 Trevilian Way
• 239-6000

The Parks Department maintains 236 tennis courts, but special attention is merited by this one in Joe Creason Park, which used to be the home of ATP tournaments more than a decade ago. The courts at the Louisville Tennis Center are still the only public clay courts in town. Rates are $8 an hour per person, $5 on the weekends. Private lessons, group clinics and classes for adults and youth are available. The center is open May through October. The concrete courts elsewhere in the Metro Park system are free.

Fern Valley Tennis Club
3621 Fern Valley Rd. • 964-3396

This indoor facility has eight rubberized hard courts that can be rented for $12 per court per hour, $24 during peak hours in the morning and evening. Private lessons are available. The public facility is open all year, but during the summer, the courts are closed on weekends.

Other options

A number of private tennis centers have lovely facilities and courts, but you must pay membership fees and dues. Some of these include: Blairwood Racquet Club, 9300 Blairwood Road, 426-8820; Campus Tennis Club, 1900 Norris Place, 452-8312; Dupont Racquet Club, 4014 Dutchmans Lane, 897-7185; Louisville Indoor Racquet Club, 8609 Westport Road, 426-2454; and Mockingbird Valley Racquet Club, 3000 Mellwood Avenue, 897-0673.

Volleyball

The Volleyball Connection
440 Baxter Ave. • 582-3530

The Volleyball Connection sells volleyball apparel and equipment and organizes sand volleyball leagues at The Brewery Bar and Restaurant and Baxter Jack's Bar, the unofficial mecca for serious Louisville volleyball players. The leagues reluctantly stop during the coldest months of the year. Call for specific details.

Ohio Valley Volleyball Center
1820 Taylor Ave. • 473-1200

Ohio Valley sells volleyball apparel, shoes and equipment and organizes a league for indoor play at the center. Adult leagues meet in the evenings, and the center offers clinics and camps for youngsters in the summer months.

Bernie's Volleyball
4028 S. Third St. • 363-3526

Next door to The Stadium Club Bar, Bernie's organizes volleyball leagues for adults in the summer. You have to put together your own team and pay a registration fee, which varies depending on the league. They also sell apparel and equipment.

Other options

Check with the Ys and the Jewish Community Center (listed under Fitness in this chapter) for league information if none of the above meet your needs. Two pubs, O'Shea's Irish Pub, 5000 Poplar Level Rd., 966-9976 and R Place, 9603 Whipps Mill Rd., 425-8516, also have popular leagues but limited facilities.

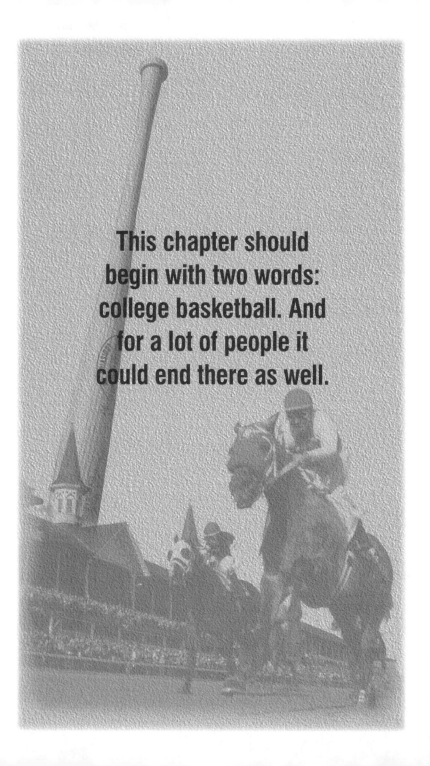

This chapter should begin with two words: college basketball. And for a lot of people it could end there as well.

Spectator Sports

This chapter should begin with two words: college basketball.

And for a lot of people it could end there as well. The University of Louisville Cardinals, the University of Kentucky Wildcats and the Indiana University Hoosiers command such a degree of loyalty that there may be no more crucial badge of identity in the area. The music you listen to, the way you vote — even your religion — to many folks are not as informative about your character as whether you pull for the Cards, Cats or Hoosiers. Only the Duke-Chapel Hill-Raleigh triangle matches the intensity of interest we have in the road to the NCAA's Final Four, and it's the only area of the country that has done better in that annual event than these parts.

And the interest is almost exclusively bound up in college basketball — although hopes for an NBA franchise continue and seem to be a major driving force behind the idea for a downtown arena. While the Kentucky Colonels of the 1970s American Basketball Association were a championship team and a well-run operation, their owners refused to pay the price demanded for entry into the NBA, and so the players dispersed throughout the league. A minor league franchise stocked with local favorites lasted only a few years. And the interest in the college game hurts high school basketball, especially on the Kentucky side of the Ohio — people will stay home to watch U of L or UK on television rather than go out to a high school game during the week.

It takes its toll on all social life: Anyone who doesn't plan parties, weddings or other events with basketball schedule in hand is risking disaster — an empty house or an occasion at which half the guests are going to be sitting in a back room, watching the game on whatever television set is at hand.

Most amazingly, perhaps, college basketball is a year-round topic of conversation. In the middle of a hot baseball pennant race,

folks will call up the sports talk shows to ask "What have you heard about this Jenkins kid in Centralia?" as if there were no other topic worth considering. *The Courier-Journal* runs a weekly College Basketball Notebook year round. Television schedules, injuries in pickup games, events honoring former heroes and all manner of conspiratorial fantasizing keep folks talking 24-7-365 (and 366 in a Leap Year).

Even so, basketball isn't the only spectator sport in the area. The Louisville Redbirds draw more fans than almost any other minor league baseball team, even when they aren't winning. Interest in University of Louisville football has grown incredibly since Howard Schnellenberger arrived in 1985, promising a national championship (although he left early, and we're all still waiting). We see some of the best horse racing in the country (see our chapter on Derby and the Downs), and a number of other equine events, from steeplechase to dressage. There's an active auto-racing community. The RiverFrogs have brought a new level of crazy intensity to local hockey. And Valhalla Golf Club's relationship with the Professional Golfers' Association of America brought the PGA tournament here in 1996 and will bring it back in 2000.

College Basketball

Still, we have to begin in the heart of the obsession. Louisville's border city status extends even to basketball. In the rest of Kentucky, in nearly all of Indiana, there's no question of loyalty — the state university is first in everyone's heart. But in Louisville, while the U of L Cardinals are the favored team, Kentucky runs an uncomfortably close second. And Louisville workplaces are filled with Hoosier commuters who wouldn't turn against IU coach Bobby Knight if he married Boy George.

The rivalry between Louisville and Kentucky is mixed from volatile components, and as a result it is taken more seriously than similar intrastate series. ("I'd root for Iraq against Louisville," a UK fan said on the radio in the middle of the Gulf War.) For a long time, Kentucky took the patronizing attitude that it would play none of the other state universities in basketball, although only Western Kentucky ever played at Kentucky and Louisville's level and then only sporadically. The more established program called Louisville a "little brother," and that attitude rankled.

From Eisenhower's era into Reagan's, the Cards and the Cats met only in the NCAA — in 1959, when Louisville upset the defending champions to advance to the finals; then again in 1983, when the Cardinals won the so-called Dream Game in overtime. Finally, the next season, the schools began playing the annual series that Louisville had been clamoring for (to Louisville's chagrin, Kentucky has a comfortable lead in the series).

The UK-U of L rivalry also plays upon some rather deep divisions in the state. There's the long-standing mutual distrust between the city and the country. And there's a racial strain to it: Kentucky waited a long time before recruiting African-American players, although it caught up fast; in the '70s and early '80s, some UK fans slurred the predominantly African-American Cardinals as "the Blackbirds." (Advance the proposition to a Kentucky fan that there's something discreditable about his basketball opinions, however, and you might as well make a crack about his mama while you're at it.) These matters have cooled off somewhat in recent years, but they're still alive. No wonder some politicians will only discuss basketball off the record.

This fanaticism is not baseless. Among the trio, Louisville has gone the longest without winning an NCAA title, and that's only been since 1986. Kentucky under the recently-departed Rick Pitino was the dominant team of the past several seasons, and Denny Crum and Bobby Knight, with North Carolina's Dean Smith the only active coaches in the Basketball Hall of Fame, dominated the first part of the '80s. They won four titles between them and made as many Final Four appearances

as Michael Jordan, Akeem Olajuwan or Patrick Ewing's teams. And if U.S. Reed hadn't hit that half-court shot against the Cards in '81 . . . .

University of Louisville
Freedom Hall, Kentucky Fair and Exposition Center, 937 Phillips Ln.
• **Ticket information 852-5863, 852-5151**

While Louisville won the 1956 NIT when

that was the post-season tournament of choice and made the NCAA several other times, Louisville basketball history began seriously in the mid-'60s with a great team led by Louisville native Wesley Unseld, the only player ever to be the NBA's rookie of the year and MVP in the same season, and Breckinridge County's Butch Beard. After Denny Crum arrived in 1972 from a job as assistant to UCLA's John Wooden, stars such as Jim Price, Ulysses "Junior" Bridgeman and Wesley Cox kept the tradition alive, and the team made two Final Fours (losing both times to UCLA).

The biggest surprise was that Crum stuck around. Everyone assumed the Louisville job was only a steppingstone for him to take the UCLA position when Wooden retired. He's now stayed in Louisville more than two decades, and his unflappable demeanor has won him the nickname "Cool Hand Luke" (although there are scant resemblances between Crum and the Paul Newman character of that name).

In 1980 Louisville finally won the NCAA. The Doctors of Dunk were led by "Louisville's living legend," guard Darrell Griffith, and a well-loved team composed of Rodney McCray, Derek Smith, one-thumbed Wiley Brown, Jerry Eaves and top reserves Roger Burkman and Poncho Wright. (McCray's brother Scooter, now an assistant coach, sat out the season with an injury.) This was the team that either invented or popularized the high five, the perfect metaphor for their high spirits. The McCrays, joined by the likes of Charles Jones, Lancaster Gordon, Milt Wagner and Billy Thompson, were the nucleus of teams that went to the Final Four again in 1992 and 1993.

U of L has had a rocky decade since winning the 1986 championship behind freshman center Pervis Ellison — hardly terrible, but disappointing to fans who got used to Final Four appearances every couple of years or so. The Cards continue to have their share of talented players like Dwayne Morton, Greg Minor, Cliff Rozier, Samaki Walker and DeJuan Wheat; they go to the NCAA most years, win a game or two, then lose (although in 1997 they made the final eight). Most galling, they rarely beat Kentucky because the game is early in the season, and Crum runs his system so his team peaks at tournament time (not always the case at Kentucky). And the past two seasons — while they've seen the Cards regain much of the spark and grit they showed in the early '80s — have been marked by NCAA rule violations that suggest the program needs to police itself more stringently (or cover its tracks better).

Denny Crum usually recruits a team of excellent athletes — runners and leapers, almost all of them between 6-foot 3-inches and 6-foot 8-inches. He rarely has a good point guard (the recently-departed, sorely-missed DeJuan Wheat, is an exception) and has coached only one 7-footer, Felton Spencer (now with the Utah Jazz). His teams play a switching man-to-man defense and are at their best on a fast break. Crum opposed the three-point goal when it was introduced, and it took years before his teams got comfortable with the outside game, although the past several have been right deadly from outside.

Louisville plays in Conference USA, a league which blends together Louisville's former conference, the Metro, and a number of natural rivals such as Cincinnati and Memphis State (in previous years, second only to Kentucky in fan interest).

Tickets: Season tickets are well-nigh impossible to get. As a first step, you have to have football season tickets; the handful of basketball season tickets that become available each year are assigned according to a priority system that takes into account donations, relationship with the university and so

on. U of L holds 500 or more tickets for each game to be sold to the general public, and they go on sale within three to four weeks of the season's tip-off (watch for announcements in the local media). They're arranged in "mini-packages" of four or more games; those that are unsold go on sale shortly before the game. Tickets are $17; parking is $3. It's abundant (unless there's some event like a flea market at the Fairgrounds) but aggravating; all traffic is routed onto the "Circle of Champions" (a.k.a. Ring Road), a one-way counterclockwise loop around the entire Fairgrounds..

Best bet to see a game: It's possible to pick up a ticket outside the arena for most games except the UK game or something else big, although if security spots a ticket seller they'll run him off. Scalping is illegal in Kentucky, but it's legal to resell a ticket for its face value or less.

The U of L ticket office is in the Student Activities Center on the Belknap campus; there is a branch office in the west wing of the Kentucky Fair and Exposition Center.

University of Kentucky
Rupp Arena, 430 W. Vine St., Lexington
• Ticket information (606) 257-1818,
(800) 928-2287

Kentucky has the richest tradition of any local team, and its present isn't too shabby either.

Under coach Adolph Rupp, the "Baron of the Bluegrass," UK was the UCLA of the late '40s and the '50s, winning four national championships and riding high in the polls most other years. When Rupp retired in 1972, he was the winningest coach in college history, a distinction he still holds. His players and those on succeeding Kentucky teams included Alex Groza, Ralph Beard, Cotton Nash, Louie Dampier, a then-dry-headed Pat Riley, Dan Issel, Kyle Macy, Sam Bowie, Kenny Walker and Rex Chapman.

Under Joe B. Hall and Eddie Sutton, the team continued to win, although often in a

INSIDERS' TIP

If you can't think of anything else to say, you can always talk basketball.

rather joyless fashion: The 1978 team may have taken less pleasure in their NCAA title than any champions ever. In 1989 the team was dealt severe NCAA sanctions for recruiting violations after a package sent by a UK assistant coach to a prize recruit fell open in an Emory Worldwide distribution center, revealing a wad of $50 bills. The school's penalties included reduced scholarships, no postseason play for two years and one year without live television.

Young, dapper head coach Rick Pitino might as well have won the NCAA the way he turned around a Kentucky program marked by that shame. Pitino's first great team, the first one eligible for the NCAA, came in 1991-92. The squad had only one player with top-flight talent (Jamal Mashburn) and was otherwise mostly made up of a group of good old boys from small towns out in the state (Richie Farmer, John Pelphrey, Deron Feldhaus).

After that group went 22 and 6 and missed the Final Four by a single last-second shot, Pitino could have had the deed to Fort Knox. The stigma on the program some observers thought would linger for years had utterly vanished. In the next five seasons UK went to the Final Four three times, winning the 1996 NCAA championship and finishing second in 1997. And Pitino also banished the grimness that surrounded UK basketball, bringing back a sense of fun and unpredictability.

But Pitino's success won him continuing attention from professional teams, and the Boston Celtics finally came up with the $50 million contract that lured Pitino away. HE'S GONE, *The Courier-Journal* headline proclaimed in letters as large as they used when Nixon resigned (the accompanying photograph of a lip-biting Pitino took up half of the front page).

The new coach is Orlando "Tubby" Smith, a former Pitino assistant and head coach at Georgia — and the first African American to hold the job at a school that's often been a symbol of racial insensitivity or worse (Rupp's all-white team losing the 1966 NCAA final to all-black Texas Western has been called basketball's *Brown v. Board of Education*). Folks expect Smith's teams to be like Pitino's, with a fast-paced game that stresses the

three-pointer and a pressing defense but is more disciplined than it appears at first glance.

UK belongs to the Southeastern Conference. For years the SEC was a football conference willing to concede basketball to UK, but in recent years it's become much more competitive.

Tickets: Rupp Arena is a holy shrine to many in the state; consequently, it's extraordinarily difficult to get tickets to UK home games. (Last year, out of Kentucky's 16,000 season ticket holders, fewer than 20 failed to renew.) UK plays at least one game each year in Louisville's Freedom Hall (in addition to the home-and-home series with U of L) and all seats usually go on sale to the general public. Any student tickets unsold before a game go on sale to the general public; the easiest tickets to get are for non-conference games and early-season exhibition games. They're $15. Rupp Arena parking is $5.

Best bet to see a game: Befriend a coal baron.

Indiana University
Assembly Hall, 1001 E. 17th St., Bloomington, Ind. • ticket information (812) 855-4006

IU is dominated by Bobby Knight, whose gift for attracting controversy — throw a chair, make a joke about rape, appear to hit one of his players — almost obscures the fact that he is one of the game's supreme tacticians and that he runs one of the cleanest and most academically successful programs in the country.

Knight has won three championships (1976, 1981, 1987). His teams play a complicated system that requires a great deal of concentration, one reason for his legendary sideline outbursts. But it has the effect of winning with slightly less talented players than the other local schools (although the likes of Isaiah Thomas, Quinn Buckner, Calbert Cheaney and Scott May ain't chopped liver).

Indiana plays in the Big Ten conference.

Tickets: All IU home games are sold out to season ticketholders and students (except for the "mini-season," the several games during Christmas when school is not in session and student tickets are made available to the gen-

Photo: Kurt Vinion

Many Louisvillians think and discuss college basketball year round.

eral public); they go on sale in mid-October and are $12. There is a 2,000-person waiting list for season tickets; to join it, write Athletic Ticket Office, Indiana University, Assembly Hall, 1001 E. 17th St., Bloomington, IN 47408-1590. Parking is $5.

Best bet to see a game: The "miniseason"; the Hoosier Classic, a four-team tournament held each holiday season in Indianapolis' Market Square Arena. One more possibility: Scalping is legal in Indiana, and a good number of second-hand tickets are available for games early in the season, before Big Ten play begins.

Bellarmine College
Knights Hall, 2000 Norris Pl. • 452-8380

The Bellarmine Knights basketball team is one of the best-kept sports secrets in town. They play in NCAA Division II's toughest conference, the Great Lakes Valley. There isn't a bad seat in Knights Hall, and while the players are shorter, the quality of play isn't much different from Division I. In 1994 they hired a new coach, Bob Valvano, brother of the late North Carolina State coach Jim Valvano, a firm believer in the three-point shot. Valvano is as quick with a quip as his brother was — he's even filled in for vacationing radio jester Terry Meiners without a noticeable drop-off.

Season tickets are available at the athletics office in Knights Hall, and range from $40 to $85. Single tickets are available at the door and are $7 for chairbacks, $5 for bleacher seats and $3 for students. There is abundant free parking.

Dirt Bowl
Shawnee Park, Broadway and Southwestern Pkwy. • 456-8100

Darrell Griffith first served notice of what a great player he was in 1973, the summer before his sophomore year in high school, with one shot during a game in Shawnee Park's Dirt Bowl.

The dunk was sensational, but even more sensational was the defender the high school student chose to dunk over — Artis Gilmore, the 7-foot-2 center of the Kentucky Colonels professional team, one of the more intimidating and physical players in basketball history.

That's perhaps the greatest legend of the Dirt Bowl, a summer tournament (June through August) that's over a quarter-century old. But the play continues to be the best loosely organized basketball played in town. Former stars and stars-to-be show their stuff; guys who never made it to college have their chance to show that they can play with the big boys.

There are middle school, high school and super-pro leagues playing various nights and weekend afternoons throughout the summer. For more information, call Metro Parks at the number above. It's free, and there's plenty of free parking in the park.

College Football

University of Louisville
Cardinal Stadium, Kentucky Fair and Exposition Center, 937 Phillips Ln.
• ticket information 852-5863

Other basketball teams may encroach onto our civic pride, but Louisville football is more indisputably the main game in town.

The Cards used to be laughable, although they made bowl trips in 1970 and 1977, and no program that produced Johnny Unitas, Lenny Lyles and Washington Redskins tackle Joe Jacoby is devoid of tradition.

But Louisville only got serious about joining the top ranks of football in 1985, when Louisville native Howard Schnellenberger arrived to take over the program. An All-American end for UK in 1955, former assistant to the likes of Blanton Collier, Bear Bryant, George Allen and Don Shula and coach of Miami's 1983 national champions, he promised to win a national title here.

Never happened. Although Louisville twice cracked the top 20 and won the 1991 Fiesta Bowl and the 1993 Liberty Bowl, Schnellenberger left in 1995 for a disastrous year at Oklahoma.

While he had gone, the interest he kindled in Louisville football remained high, and affable, energetic and up-and-coming new coach Ron Cooper came onto the scene. The Cardinals will have a new stadium in 1998, built with a combination of public and private money (and named — gulp — Papa John's Cardinal Stadium). Louisville now rivals Kentucky as school of choice for the state's talented high school football players. And the

---

INSIDERS' TIP

Many fans who can't afford the cost — in money or effort — of seeing a UK, IU or U of L game can catch a preview glimpse in one of the preseason scrimmages the teams play in various locations around Indiana and Kentucky. Watch the papers in October and November for announcements. UK also hosts Midnight Madness, a yearly basketball practice held in its old arena, Memorial Coliseum, starting the first minute past midnight when practice is legal. There's no deceptive advertising here: It's insane.

school's schedule now includes such heavy-weights as Penn State, Oklahoma and Utah. (Louisville plays in Conference USA.)

But Cooper hasn't won a national champi-onship, either, and there's a certain impatience growing that he hasn't seen more success with the talent he's had.

Tickets: While the Cardinals have sold out most of their home football games in recent seasons, it's much easier to get your hands on football tickets than it is for basketball. (See ticket information under U of L basketball.) Tickets range from $13 to $23. Parking is $3.

Best bet to see a game: Know someone who bought season tickets just to hold onto his basketball seats.

Unity Classic
Cardinal Stadium, Kentucky Fair and Exposition Center, 937 Phillips Ln.
• 584-4466

Every September the city hosts this foot-ball contest between two historically African-American schools. The event also includes an incredible half-time battle of marching bands, and usually an evening concert follows the game. Proceeds benefit Clothe-a-Child. Tick-ets range from $12 to $22 and are available from Ticketmaster outlets and local Kroger stores.

Baseball

Louisville Redbirds
Cardinal Stadium, Kentucky Fair and Exposition Center, 937 Phillips Ln.
• 367-9121

Louisville was a major league city in the 19th century; the team even went to the 1890 World Series against the Brooklyn Bride-grooms — the only World Series ever can-celed because of snow — and the previous year entered the record books in more dubi-ous fashion: On an early-season road trip they lost 26 consecutive games, a record for futility that still stands, and were at one point be-lieved to have perished in the Johnstown flood.

In succeeding years the club saw such greats as charter Hall of Fame shortstop Honus Wagner, pitcher Rube Waddell and (after the team became a minor league franchise) home-town boy Pee Wee Reese. Eventually, the fran-chise left twice, the second time for Pawtucket, Rhode Island, in 1972.

The Louisville Redbirds became succes-sors to that history when they moved here from Tulsa in 1982. They're also a true phe-nomenon, one of the institutions Louisville's fondest of and one of its most successful re-cent enterprises.

In recent years, winning has not exactly been the club's forte. Although they won the American Association pennant in 1995, the Redbirds have made the playoffs only one other time in the last decade. Even so, the Redbirds continue to draw over 500,000 fans a year, off a bit from their 1983 draw of over a million but good enough to rank among the best-attended minor league teams.

The reason for such fan devotion is that the Redbirds run a superb operation. Original owner A. Ray Smith's entrepreneurial and management skills were so pronounced the Redbirds were profiled in one of management guru Tom Peters' *In Search of Excellence* vid-eotapes. In 1986 Smith sold the team to a group of nine local "movers and shakers" who have continued his approach. Cardinal Sta-dium is a large, clean, well-maintained ballpark. Tickets are inexpensive, concessions are plen-tiful and parking is easy — if you have $2.

The team has also served as a significant incubator of major league talent. If you follow baseball, you know these former Redbirds: Willie McGee, Vince Coleman, Terry Pendleton, Andy Van Slyke, Bob Tewksbury, Todd Worrell, Andres Galarraga, Jeff Fassero, Ken Hill and Mark Clark, Todd Zeile and Alan Benes (no relation to Elaine).

In 1997 the Redbirds ended their affiliation with the St. Louis' Cardinals and became the top farm team for the Milwaukee Brewers, in a new set-up called the Inernational League. And the team is supposed to be in a spanking new stadium on East Main Street, near the Water-front Development, by Opening Day 1999.

The Redbirds' season is from early April through early September. Almost all Redbirds games are in the evenings (except for Sun-days, Tuesdays and Memorial and Labor Days). Box seats for games Sunday through Thursday are $5 ($3 for children 17 and younger); for Friday and Saturday games they're $7 ($4 for children). General admission for all games is $3.50, $1 for children 17 and younger. Seniors 62 and older pay $3 for any seat on any day.

A full season ticket is $290. A weekend package for all Friday and Saturday games is $99; a Saturday package is $79; a big-game package that includes all the team's major promotions — concerts, fireworks, appearances by the Famous Chicken — costs $49.

Hockey

Louisville RiverFrogs
Broadbent Arena, Kentucky Fair and Exposition Center, 937 Phillips Ln.
• **367-9121**

Louisville is no kind of hockey hotbed, but the RiverFrogs have brought the right kind of off-the-wall showmanship and attitude to get the city excited about what a friend of ours calls "the gladiator sport of the modern era."

While the 'Frogs haven't exactly burned up the East Coast Hockey League (the 1996-97 record was 29-31-10), the atmosphere in "The Swamp" — a.k.a. Broadbent Arena — attracts the crowds anyway, to see the laser light show as players are introduced and the 25-foot-long frog balloon ("Airship Froggie") that flies over the arena between periods, and to enjoy such amenities as a rink-side hot tub and a section with couches and recliner chairs ("The Pad"). It may come as no surprise that the folks behind the 'Frogs are the marketing whizzes at the Redbirds.

The same friend who saw the "Spartacus" factor on the ice says "It's not the best hockey, but it's all we have." Where else are you going to see brawl-blood on the ice while the house organist plays the Blue Danube waltz? And then skate on that same ice after the game is over?

The season is from October through March. Tickets are $5 to $12 for adults, $3 to $9 for children and seniors 62 and older. Season tickets are $269, $349 for VIP seats at rinkside, for 35 home games. Parking is $3 and is usually plentiful unless there are other events going on at the Fairgrounds.

High School Sports

High school sports in Jefferson County draw only a fraction of the interest college sports do. The structure of the school system — with many students attending school out of their home districts — has educational and social advantages, but it doesn't do much toward building fan connection to the fortunes of a neighborhood school. And the universities have captured the minds of fans — high school students as much as anyone — in a uniquely powerful way.

That doesn't mean Jefferson County teams don't do well in sports: With the state's largest population, we have half the teams that play 4A football (the state's highest level), and one of our teams usually wins the state championship. Local high schools have produced their share of famous players, from Paul Hornung (who starred at Flaget before winning a Heisman Trophy at Notre Dame and setting scoring records with the Green Bay Packers) to Super Bowl-winning quarterback Phil Simms, who threw passes for Southern High.

Jefferson County teams also do well in the boy's basketball tournament and have produced stars from Wesley Unseld to Alan Houston.

The biggest Louisville football game — some would say including U of L's schedule — is between parochial powers St. Xavier and Trinity, who often find themselves rematched in the playoffs farther down the line (each school has won a number of state championships). Held toward the end of September, it draws more than 30,000 spectators to Cardinal Stadium. The game is as much a social event as a football game (if the teams meet in the playoffs, they usually draw half as many spectators as they do for the regular-season game).

Louisville hosts two high school basketball tournaments that attract teams from the rest of the state and, occasionally, the country: the King of the Bluegrass, at Fairdale High School in December, and the Louisville Invitational Tournament, in mid-January at Louisville Gardens. There's also a major high school all-star game in the McDonald's Derby Festival Basketball Classic, the Saturday before the Derby, and the annual pair of summer games between the Kentucky and Indiana all-stars.

Unfortunately, a lack of fan support caused the city to lose the biggest tournament: the Sweet Sixteen, the finals of the boys' basketball tournament, which has settled permanently (for the foreseeable future, at any rate) into Lexington's Rupp Arena.

Indiana is something different, especially where basketball is concerned. No state goes crazier over high school hoops. The game between Jeffersonville and New Albany (usually the first Friday in January) attracts an intense 5,000 or so spectators. Almost as intense are New Albany's game with Floyd Central and Jeffersonville's cross-river series with Ballard.

Golf

Louisville loves to play golf and develop golf courses — in recent years, they've proliferated like kudzu. It seems as if Louisville always has a favorite-son golfer or two, from Bobby Nichols and Frank Beard in earlier generations to Jodie Mudd, Ted Schulz and New Albany's Fuzzy Zoeller today.

Watching golf is a little more difficult. There are two pro-celebrity tournaments held annually, detailed below, and every presidential year, apparently, we'll have a chance to see the best golfers in the world: In 1996 Valhalla Golf Club, 15503 Shelbyville Road, hosted one of the four major tournaments, the PGA (Mark

Brooks won). The PGA will return to Valhalla in 2000. The Professional Golfers Association owns 50 percent of the operation and has an option to buy the rest of it in 2001.

Ned Beatty Hope for Children Classic
Oxmoor Country Club, 9000 Limerick Ln.
• 584-9781

Memorial Day brings the Ned Beatty Hope for Children Classic, a benefit for Easter Seals hosted by the veteran character actor and Louisville native. (Beatty took the event over from fellow Louisville native Foster Brooks.) Celebrity participants in 1997's first installment included actors Hal Linden, Clint Howard, Dick O'Neill and Conrad Bachmann, musician Johnny Mann, U of L football coach Ron Cooper and golfers Kenny Perry, Brad Fabel, Larry Gilbert, Bobby Nichols and Russ Cochrane. Tickets in 1997 were $10 in advance, $12 at the gate.

Fuzzy Zoeller's Coca-Cola Wolf Challenge
Covered Bridge Golf Club, 12510 Covered Bridge Rd., Sellersburg, Ind.
• (812) 949-6219

Fuzzy Zoeller — now unfortunately famous for ill-advised remarks he made about Tiger Woods — invites a group of golfers (in 1997 they included Arnold Palmer, Chi Chi Rodriguez, Jim Furyk and David Duvall) and celebrities (Amy Grant, Donny Most, Mike Ditka) to compete in a format sometimes called "Captain's Choice." It's a classic golf betting game: Each hole has a "captain," who chooses

INSIDERS' TIP

Design by Dante: Traffic at U of L basketball games has always been difficult, if somewhat thrilling. It was rationalized, to a certain extent, when the Fairgrounds built what's technically called the Circle of Champions but is usually referred to as Ring Road, a single counterclockwise circuit of the Fairgrounds's perimeter. That means on the one hand that all traffic is moving in a single direction, and there are a number of exits and entrances off the road. On the other hand, it means that you are in a single traffic stream with everyone who attended the game, and people are trying to get across multiple lanes to make the most convenient exit.

Come out to Louisville Motor Speedway Friday or Saturday, April through September.

a partner after the other players tee off, or cries "wolf" and challenges the other three himself. It will be held Labor Day and the preceding Sunday 1998, and it's likely to keep that spot in the calendar.

Horse Racing

This is horse country, and that isn't limited to what happens at Churchill Downs; events from team penning to steeplechase command local attention.

Oxmoor Steeplechase
Oxmoor Golf and Steeplechase Course
• 491-7877

This annual event is a major one on many people's social calendars. Just like the Derby, the races over hedge and fence serve as a pretext for some high-quality carousing.

Oxmoor, now moved from late April to the last Saturday in September, takes place on the historic Bullitt family farm, which dates back to 1784. Its new course can accommodate better than 30,000 spectators.

The day includes at least four steeplechases and other events such as donkey races, a polo match and a performance by the Louisville Orchestra. It's also accompanied by a fair that features arts and crafts, entertainment, raptor shows and the sport of kings, terrier races. The event benefits the Louisville Orchestra.

General admission is $5; children younger than 10 are free. Grandstand tickets are $25. Box seats area as high as $120 and are available from the Orchestra office, 587-8681.

Spring Run Horse Trials
Spring Run Farm, 10200 Ky. 329, Prospect
• 228-3456

This two-day horse trial — dressage, stadium jumping and cross country — takes place the second weekend in June on the only preliminary-class cross-country course in the area.

Rock Creek Horse Show
3114 Rock Creek Dr. (by Seneca Park)
• 893-7792

This outdoor show the first week of June forms part of the so-called Triple Crown of Kentucky saddlebred horse shows, with the Lexington Junior League Horse Show and the World Championship Horse Show the second week of the Kentucky State Fair (see Annual Events). 1998 marks the 61st annual installment. It's $5 general admission every night; boxes (which contain six seats) are $300 for all six days.

Sports Spectrum
4520 Poplar Level Rd. • 962-2200

It's the closest legal thing in Louisville to a Las Vegas casino. It may not surprise you to learn that it's built entirely around horse racing.

Sports Spectrum is an off-track betting facility open on those days Churchill Downs (which owns it) does not have live racing and Derby Day. In 1994 Kentucky law changed to allow whole-card simulcasting — in other words, to allow Sports Spectrum and similar places to broadcast the entire day's races from several different tracks. You can bet on as many as 50 races in five hours. There's a confusing profusion of monitors showing races from all over, and you can bet on any track at any betting window (so have your bets clear in your head).

Hours vary according to post times at the tracks simulcasting to Sports Spectrum; admission is charged.

Auto Racing

Louisville Motor Speedway
1900 Outer Loop • 966-2277

A well-run but rather short track, Louisville Motor Speedway draws consistent crowds on both Friday night (when sportsmen and three classes of figure eights race) and Saturday (the night for late models, thunder trucks and street stocks). Promoter Andy Vertrees was named national promoter of the year in 1995, and he mixes up the fare: There are races featuring touring groups such as the NASCAR Craftsmen Truck Series; a monster truck challenge; several demolition derbies; and other attractions such as free country music concerts that have featured the likes of Garth Brooks (just before he became a superstar), Brooks and Dunn, Alan Jackson and Clint Black. The track is open Friday and Saturday, April through September. Tickets are $8 for adults, $5 for seniors and teenagers, $2 for children ages 6 to 12.

Jeffersonville Sportsdrome
1207 U.S. Hwy. 31 E. • (812) 282-7551

This quarter-mile asphalt track has races every Saturday night, April through September. It's known for figure-eight racing — there

are two different figure-eight championships in October — street stocks and drummers. It also hosts vintage car and pro truck races and the MMRA Mini-Cup series (scale model lookalikes of NASCAR-type stock cars). Two Sundays a month it puts on the Falls City Kart Club go-cart races. Unless there's a special event, tickets are $8 for adults, $4 for teenagers and $2 for children 12 and younger.

Salem Speedway
Ind. 56 W., Salem, Ind. • (812) 883-6504

Salem Speedway's half-mile, high-banked asphalt track has been a racing fans destination since 1947. It has races several times a month from April through October, usually on Sunday afternoons, and hosts a number of touring sprint and stock-car circuits.

The track has a lot of tradition, having seen the likes of A.J. Foyt, Parnelli Jones, Mario Andretti, Bobby and Al Unser, Darrell Waltrip and Bobby Allison race. The 33-degree turns are something of a throwback to the tracks of yesteryear. The infield is open to spectators. The big race of the season, the Joe James-Pat O'Connor Memorial USAC Sprint classic in August, honors two popular drivers who died in races in the 1950s. Admission varies from $5 to $20.

To get there, take I-65 north to the Scottsburg exit and follow the signs to Salem.

Ohio Valley Raceway
Katherine Station Rd. (off Dixie Hwy. near the county line) • 922-4152

The local drag-racing track attracts speed enthusiasts — doers and watchers alike — from miles around to its Wednesday night test-and-tune program and Saturday races. (If you've never gone to a drag strip, look into ear plugs.) The track's big event is the Doorslammer Nationals, a three-day weekend in September. Admission is usually $8 for adults; children 12 and younger are free. Doorslammer Nationals tickets are $10 on the spectator side, $15 by the pits; children 12 and younger are free.

Good neighborhoods are
as plentiful as hats on
Derby Day.

Neighborhoods and Real Estate

"Neighborhood" is a freighted word in Louisville. It commands a great deal of loyalty, no small bit of identity and sometimes a little defensiveness. As it is almost anyplace, where you live signifies your social and economic status, but in Louisville it sometimes seems more personal, an aesthetic and almost philosophical statement: Where you live says something not only about your station in life but your values as well.

This is ludicrous on one level, because there are few bum choices in the lot. In a city that is most comfortable at the family and neighborhood level, where good housing and friendly people are resources that the city relies on for economic development, good neighborhoods are as plentiful as hats on Derby Day.

Many neighborhoods in Louisville have developed a healthy (or better) sense of pride, with active neighborhood associations, a neighborhood festival and even banners to let people driving through know what part of town they've entered.

In the late 1960s and early '70s, residents of different neighborhoods began to band together against certain threats they perceived — development, deteriorating buildings, crime. Their movement was further encouraged by the growing interest in historic preservation and by a number of federal programs that targeted neighborhoods for funds (the still-operative map of Louisville's neighborhoods was developed to meet the requirements of a federal grant). When political neophyte Harvey Sloane became mayor in 1973, neighborhood associations and the preservation movement formed a good part of his power base.

Not every Louisville neighborhood has a high profile. While everyone knows Old Louisville, Portland, Crescent Hill and Audubon Park, there are others, such as Edgewood (south of Standiford Field) and Rock Creek-Lexington Road (between I-64 and Lexington Road near Seneca Park), with names that might not even be known by everyone who lives inside their boundaries. The term neighborhood has no legal status in any local ordinance, and neighborhood names are used with great imprecision — the only neighborhood officially called The Highlands is the so-called Original Highlands, about three blocks by eight blocks just south of the head of Broadway, but what most people mean when they use the name is an area at least 20 times as large. In Jefferson County the term has more force, since many neighborhoods are actually small incorporated cities; in Southern Indiana, it barely exists, and the operative distinction is between the different school districts.

As we mentioned in the Area Overview, when people in Louisville talk about the various ends of town, they're talking as much about who you are as where you are (and lumping together extremely disparate people in the process). Local real estate parlance essentially follows the same geographical scheme, although it adds one term to the vernacular: Southeast, describing the area roughly between Bardstown Road and Preston Highway — perhaps to give it a bit of that cachet the East End is thought to possess.

The East End has the reputation of Moneyland — where you go to show you've arrived. But while you'd have to be blind to think that the East has lost its mysterious allure, one of the most interesting developments in recent years is the desire of successful professionals, white and black, to stay in the 'hood. In the past, people who'd reached a certain level of success used to be forced to move east to get what real estate people call "executive homes."

But in recent years — especially after the Gene Snyder Freeway made the outer edge of the county more accessible to downtown and other areas where employment's concentrated — developers in the South End have begun building equivalents to the East End's Plainview and Hurstbourne. At the same time, black professionals have engaged in a kind of soul-searching about whether they should stay in the predominantly black sections of town, serving the same function as role models that black professionals did perforce under segregation. As a result, there is significant rehab action and even some new construction going on in the West End, especially in the Russell neighborhood, which has been targeted for such efforts.

Both Southern Indiana and Oldham County have been experiencing major housing booms, due in large part to folks commuting from Louisville (or fleeing its perceived problems). At present, Floyd Knobs is a quicker commute than the farther reaches of eastern Jefferson; I-71 makes La Grange not too much more of a drive from downtown than Lake Forest.

As we've already mentioned several times in this book, Louisville is a city with a high quality of residential architecture: Some economists rate our housing stock as the city's single greatest economic asset. And while it's true they don't build them like the old days — lacking the inexpensive labor of well-trained craftsmen and cheap, high-quality materials — new construction in the city hews to a high standard, as standards go in contemporary building.

The houses are not only well built, they're also inexpensive. In the late 1980s, Louisville was the cheapest major housing market in the nation. Prices have risen, but Louisville remains a great place to buy and own a home.

The median price of a home has increased from $78,500 in 1993 to $95,000 in 1996 — about 89 percent of the national median. And the house you get for your money, especially among older homes, will make your friend from New York, Chicago or Los Angeles get wistful at what your $150,000 was able to buy (new construction is closer to regional standards).

The Louisville market has never seen the booms and busts that cities such as Houston saw in the '80s. "We don't have the highs and the lows that other metropolitan areas have, but we still have good steady growth in all parts of the area," says appraiser Linda English. For decades, prices have increased at a steady 6.3 percent nearly every year — nothing to retire to Florida on, but a perfectly Louisvillian rate of steady, unspectacular growth and a much better deal than having to take a $50,000 hit on something you bought in a fit of Reagan-era enthusiasm.

And there's a lot of choice here. The city's prosperity in the 19th century has left a heritage of older homes in a wide variety of styles. There is more new development right now than a non-Realtor's mind can comprehend, and the surrounding area becomes rural quickly enough that there are small farms within a half-hour's commute of downtown (although it probably won't be in Jefferson County — development has reduced the number of large, unimproved and privately held tracts to a literal handful).

You can live on a bluff overlooking the Ohio in Glenview or have the river be your backyard on 47th Street south of Shawnee Park. You can live in the hills of Southern Indiana or those of southwestern Jefferson County. You can be alongside a golf course just about anywhere. One aspect that may be lacking is the availability of homes for less than $100,000; the condemnations that went along with the airport expansion took out 1,000 homes in that bracket (although 79 of them were literally moved a bit to the west to make a new subdivision, Nichols Meadow), and it's only recently that developers have begun building in that more moderate price range.

We've tried to provide a look at Louisville-area neighborhoods and real estate that's informative whether or not you're buying a home. You may not be able to afford a house in Glenview, but you should be aware of what Glenview is like, to know the role it plays in Louisville's conversation about itself. And we've tried to list a number of different neighborhoods and developments to reflect a range of geography, price and housing type. Given that the city of Louisville alone has 69 different neighborhoods, we've had to be somewhat selective. No judgments are implied, no warranties given.

All numbers in this section (except for rentals) are estimates, prepared with the help of real estate professionals, and may have changed by the time you read them.

Neighborhoods

The East End

The East End is many things to many people — curse, bragging point, a place to hurry through on their way out to Oldham County. But more than anything else, it has been the suburbs: As you travel away from town along Bardstown Road, Brownsboro Road or the interlocking system that is Frankfort Avenue and Lexington Road and Shelbyville roads, you see a number of different conceptions of how this thing called a suburb might be created.

The Highlands, as people usually use the term, refers to the corridor along both sides of Baxter Avenue and then Bardstown Road between Cave Hill Cemetery at the head of Broadway and past Taylorsville Road, almost to the Watterson Expressway. A few key traits of the neighborhood:

• A diversity of fine older homes. They're as architecturally interesting as you'd find in any part of Louisville. The Highlands' primary years of development were from about 1870 through the 1940s (see the discussion of its showpiece, the Cherokee Triangle, in the Historic Preservation and Architecture chapter). Sixty percent of the houses were built before World War II.

• The pervasive influence of Cherokee Park and, to a lesser extent, Tyler Park. The tree-lined streets tie the entire neighborhood together. "You live in a park!" visitors tell Highlands residents (although the park and neighborhood trees sustained a good deal of damage in the 1974 tornado).

• Bardstown Road. The area's commercial strip — originally an important 19th-century turnpike — is known as Restaurant Row for the many eateries lining it. It's also a major antique-boutique strip. And since the 1960s, it has been local headquarters for whatever counterculture is in session. It currently has as many long-haired, baggy-pantsed teenagers loping down its sidewalks as any place east of Seattle, the majority of the city's independently-owned record stores and a healthy dose of coffee shops. The neighborhood octoplex, the Baxter Avenue Theatres, mixes second-run features with art-house fare.

But the Highlands is solidly bourgeois. It is one of the few neighborhoods in Louisville (Old Louisville and Crescent Hill are others) that works as a walking neighborhood, and people walk through the parks and along Bardstown all the time. Indeed, it's one of the few places in Louisville where you can live fairly conveniently without a car, thanks to the good bus service.

The streetscapes range from the charm of the **Cherokee Triangle** to **Tyler Park**, where the closely packed, well-tended large houses on sloping streets give the neighborhood an oddly European tone, to the more modest bungalows of Deer Park.

The diversity of housing types brings an equivalent mix of people into the neighborhood. This writer recalls living on Speed Avenue, the boundary between the Bonnycastle and Highlands-Douglass neighborhoods, in the early 1980s. People up the block were on food stamps; three blocks the other way lived the late Wendell Cherry, the Humana founder who owned a Picasso self-portrait eventually sold for $47 million.

Cherokee Triangle houses sell for anywhere from $120,000 to $700,000; houses in Tyler Park go for $90,000 to $300,000.

The more modest houses in **Deer Park**, shotguns mixed with bungalows, have risen dramatically in price in recent years: As the desirability of The Highlands has grown, it's been one of the few neighborhoods where young couples starting out could find a place. Houses go from $80,000 for a (rare) fixer-upper to $110-120,000 for some of the larger two-story frame houses.

Houses in **Strathmoor** (developed from 1920 to 1940), a neighborhood off Bardstown past Taylorsville Road in what's sometimes called the Outer Highlands, are anywhere from $100,000 to $200,000.

In some ways, **Crescent Hill** is a twin to The Highlands — or better, a cousin who bears a striking family resemblance. Frankfort Avenue, its principal business street, is Bardstown's only rival as a restaurant district, and it also contains a burgeoning number of art stores and other interesting shops. Frankfort is not quite such a major thoroughfare, and the railroad tracks on the north side limit businesses to one side of the street for most of the neighborhood. (They've also inhibited some of the fast-food development that's taken out historic stretches of Bardstown.)

Crescent Hill was another early suburb. Its valleys and hills caused its streets to be laid out in a less regular pattern than the usual grid. The yards tend to be larger, and the houses somewhat simpler, with more frame houses and bungalows — although there are some fancy Victorian homes.

The 1974 tornado devastated Crescent Hill, but it had a happily ironic result: It rejuvenated the neighborhood's spirit. After the proposed library-taxing district was defeated in 1991, the Crescent Hill Friends of the Library group mobilized itself to raise funds for improving the neighborhood branch. The annual Old-Fashioned Fourth of July celebration at the Peterson-Dumesnil House is a major event (see Annual Events and Festivals). While it lacks parks, large institutions such as the reservoir, the Masonic Widows and Orphans Home, Southern Baptist Theological Seminary and St. Joseph's Children's Home serve a similar function of open space and places for people to walk.

For many years, **Clifton**, an older neighborhood closer to town, was considered to be little more than a district of Crescent Hill. But about 15 years ago it essentially seceded from Crescent Hill, forming its own neighborhood organization and establishing its own identity. Its community spirit has been held up as exemplary — a U of L professor called it "a political scientist's dream." Clifton is where much of the commercial development has been happening on Frankfort Avenue, giving it one of the most interesting streetscapes and social scenes in the city.

It also has one of the city's most interesting institutional clusters: the American Printing House for the Blind, the nation's largest Braille publisher; Industries for the Blind; and the Kentucky School for the Blind, the country's first school for the visually impaired. The neighborhood has loud buzzers at crossings and variously textured sidewalks so blind people can know where they are.

Clifton was developed a little earlier than Crescent Hill, and it tends to have smaller homes, including a number of shotgun houses (one of the distinctive housing styles found along the Ohio and Mississippi waterways: a single room wide, with no central hall; with a second story in back, they're called camelbacks). Realtors tell us that lately it's been hotter than a two-dollar pistol. Homes in Clifton sell for $70,000 to $140,000; prices in Crescent Hill, which has a wider variety of housing, go from $85,000 to $350,000.

When people said "the suburbs" in the 1950s and '60s, they meant some place very much like **St. Matthews**, which begins east of Crescent Hill on Frankfort Avenue. You can find the kind of doorway the Beaver walked out of all through this small city.

It actually began with Floyd's Station, a small fort on the middle fork of Beargrass Creek; then it was known as Gilman's Point and developed a commercial district where Westport Road, Breckenridge Lane and Frankfort Avenue intersect. It was renamed in 1851 for an Episcopal church. At one point it was surrounded by farms and served as the second-largest potato shipper in the world. It fought a long, hard and ultimately successful battle to resist annexation by Louisville, becoming a fourth-class city in the process.

It's one of the few neighborhoods left with a neighborhood movie theater (which just happens to be the Vogue, the longtime local outlet for foreign films, art movies and the occasional underground flick) and a variety of shopping, including Hawley-Cooke Booksellers, the home furnishings of Dolfinger's and Butler's Barrow, the great foodstuffs at Lotsa Pasta and the multiple stores of the Mall St. Matthews. There's also a growing set of first-class restaurants, including Equus and Asiatique.

It's another neighborhood with a great variety of housing, although houses tend to be clustered by type a little more than in The High-lands and Crescent Hill. Houses range from $90,000 (though there are few less than $100,000) to $375,000, with higher prices for some of the larger brick homes in **Norbourne Estates** (actually a small sixth-class city com-pletely surrounded by St. Matthews and orga-nized St. James Court-style around a central boulevard) and some of the surrounding neigh-borhoods.

Shelbyville Road is the most prosperous and upscale of the city's commercial strips. The community's first mall (called, with typical Louisville bluntness, The Mall) opened on Shelbyville Road at the Watterson Express-way in 1960; by 1971 it was joined by a ritzier counterpart, Oxmoor Center, developed from part of the historic Bullitt Estate, on the other side of the Watterson (the two have in recent years switched status after the Mall St. Matthews, as it's now called, underwent a dra-matic makeover).

The real transformation of this part of Jefferson County — flatter and thus more amenable to development than the hilly pre-cincts off Brownsboro Road (U.S. 42) — be-gan with the development of **Hurstbourne**, an old estate east of Oxmoor. Hurstbourne, built along with a country club headquartered in the old Hurst house, was the sleekest of modern subdivisions at the time it began to be developed in the early '70s (the city of Hurstbourne incorporated in 1982). Now it's begun taking on the settled characteristics that cause people to stop referring to it as a development and begin using the term "neighborhood." Realtor Harrell Tague, who lives and works in the area, calls it "The High-lands of the near future." And like The High-lands or St. Matthews or the neighborhoods around Iroquois Park, it's a place where it's possible to move up greatly in the price of your home and not leave the general neigh-borhood.

Plainview, built on the site of a former dairy farm across Hurstbourne Lane to the east, was the area's first planned community, designed to be almost totally self-contained. It was sty-listically conservative; the homes were Colo-nial Revival, the office buildings modern glass-and-steel, the shopping center New England quaint. But it was radical in its dependence on the automobile — there are sidewalks in the neighborhoods, but Hurstbourne Lane vies with Dixie Highway as the most pedestrian-unfriendly major thoroughfare in the area — and radical as well in its independence from the center of the city.

The area is a prototypical "edge city." It's a major center of employment, having three of the area's largest office complexes and major headquarters, including the UPS air group and Blue Cross/Blue Shield. In terms of people fed, Hurstbourne might be the real Restaurant Row: While Bardstown and Frankfort both trounce it in terms of quality, its string of ware-house-like franchised restaurants probably moves more people in and out than the other two strips combined. Hurstbourne's conges-tion has been major enough to spur concerns about air pollution, but there are no signs that it has hampered development, and there are plans in the works to improve the traffic flow.

Of the two principal developments, Plainview is a bit more moderately priced, with a younger population and more turnover. Con-dominium prices begin around $80,000; houses go from about $125,000 to $250,000. Hurstbourne, a bit more settled, has house prices that range from $140,000 to $1.5 mil-lion (with one $3 million home built in there); the average house sells for about $250,000.

Lake Forest, begun in 1983 off Shelbyville Road east of the Gene Snyder Freeway and

---

INSIDERS' TIP

The Sunday *Courier-Journal* prints real estate transactions by ZIP code — the best guide to what's happening in the Louisville market (and a gossip's treasure trove, since the names of both parties to the sale are included). *Business First* publishes the same information every six months in its "At Home" supplement, but it's only listed by address.

still growing (only 942 homes of the nearly 1800 in its master plan have been developed), is probably the hottest of the planned communities. It was developed by NTS, the giant company that also put together Plainview. Residents include a large number of transferred-in executives and enough doctors and lawyers to start an on-site health care crisis.

Homearama after Homearama has put its mark on Lake Forest, leaving it with an abundance of bells-and-whistles homes. Houses range from two-story ranches that might begin at $200,000 all the way up to sky's-the-limit contract homes (the development works with more than 60 custom builders). There are also a few "patio homes" requiring minimal external maintenance. There's an Arnold Palmer-designed golf course, as well as a swimming pool, tennis and volleyball courts, the namesake lake (formerly a commercial fishing hole) and a clubhouse that serves as a sort of social center.

For a long time, the corridor along Brownsboro Road (U.S. 42) has been considered the prime area of local real estate. Local Realtor Ken Jones says many real estate agents have had tunnel vision about it — telling people who move into town, for example, that the area's Ballard High is the only school worth sending your children to (although in a time when students are free to attend any Jefferson County school of their choosing, a school district is a somewhat less urgent consideration, and many of the most attractive school programs are in magnet schools designed to draw students from throughout the system).

Certainly the east county in general has a similar population — predominantly white, upper-middle class and up — whether you're off Shelbyville or Brownsboro or La Grange Road; and as we said before, there are great neighborhoods throughout the area. Nonetheless, a little bit more of an "old money" feeling is attached to the Brownsboro corridor, and it is closer to the river, which has its own cachet.

Realtor David Bell notes that many Louisville natives look for houses off Brownsboro inside the Watterson Expressway because they're closer to downtown. **Indian Hills** is an incorporated city that begins where Chenoweth Lane intersects Brownsboro and

extends on down to the Louisville Boat Club. It's noteworthy in particular for the pleasantness of the gently rolling area, with curving streets that follow the natural curve of the land (it was designed by — who else? — the Olmsted firm, beginning in 1925) and large lots with venerable trees. Prices for the solid two- and three-story brick houses run from $350,000 to $900,000. Also desirable to those who can afford them are the large homes (up to estate-size) in the woody defiles of Mockingbird Valley (prices ranging from $350,000 to $2 million) and on the other side of the Louisville Country Club, Rolling Fields, with houses comparable to those of Indian Hills and prices ranging from $250,000 to $500,000. And throughout the area there are small, select and often elevated neighborhoods — Box Hill, River Hill and, further toward the Oldham County Line, Nitta Yuma — where values can be in the millions.

The Woods of St. Thomas, off U.S. 22 a little east of its intersection with Brownsboro, was a popular new development of the early '80s, with its own pool and clubhouse and houses of at least 2,400 square feet. They sell for about $200,000 to $400,000.

Glenview, off River Road near Lime Kiln Lane, is a few hundred houses, most of them built in the early part of this century, on a bluff overlooking the Ohio. Glenview claims to be the first suburb outside the Louisville city limits; it's more famous as the home of the Bingham family, former owners of *The Courier-Journal* and other media companies, and a number of other wealthy industrialists. It has no shopping district, of course, although there is a well-regarded private school, the Chance School, for children age 2 through the 3rd grade.

Houses that range from works of modern art to mid-19th century Italianate mansions sit on large to estate-size lots, many of them hidden from roadway view. They sell for $600,000 up to $3 million.

A little farther down River Road, lying between U.S. 42 and the river on either side of Wolf Pen Branch Road, is the community of **Harrods Creek**, which is as exclusive as Glenview (at one time it was the second-wealthiest ZIP code in the country). Harrods Creek has come under scrutiny in recent years because it's the most likely spot at which an east-county bridge would make landfall. Many contend that a prime reason it's not been built is the clout of the wealthy people whose estates would be taken or irrevocably altered by a bridge.

Farther out U.S. 42, past the small business district of **Prospect** — stop as you're going through for some of Vince Staten's barbecue — are two newer subdivisions that seem intent on showing that the Brownsboro area is not likely to be scrounging for dimes and cigarette butts anytime soon.

Sutherland sits behind a lake facing the highway, with a floating fountain in the center that looks like a miniature version of the Falls Fountain. It has a large number of contract homes on sites varying from a quarter-acre to an acre. And of course there's a clubhouse, tennis courts and pool. Houses are 3,000 square feet and way up, and run from $350,000 to $800,000.

Estates of Hunting Creek, an addition to the well-established Hunting Creek subdivision, borders what's considered to be one of the toughest golf courses in the area (course record set by Ken Venturi in 1964). Houses go from $275,000 to $1 million.

"Every Republican's dreamscape," *Louisville* magazine once called Anchorage — a bucolic, slightly insular and very pretty village off La Grange Road where Victorian homes sit on large lots and residents present a solid front against incursions of the outside world.

Anchorage, named after a steamboat captain who put an anchor in his yard and proclaimed it his final guess-what, was originally a summer retreat for wealthy Louisvillians; later it was one of the farthest points of the Interurban railroad line. Parts of it were laid out according to a landscape plan drawn up by Louisville's favorite landscapists, the Olmsted firm, and the rest would hardly have Frederick Law turning in his grave.

It has a small business district consisting primarily of a few shops, a fire station, a good restaurant called The Train Station and not much else. Its greatest attraction is not the shopping, its architecture or the flora, but the Anchorage Public School (kindergarten through grade 8), which consistently ranks among the state's top schools.

There's enough heterogeneity in the neighborhood's housing to have one of the widest price ranges in the area — anywhere from $165,000 up to $1.5 million.

Off Dorsey Lane, just east of Anchorage (but not in its all-important school district) is **Owl Creek**, a newer development (most of it was developed in the last 10 years or so) where homes go from $200,000 to 400,000.

Further east from Anchorage, near the formerly rural fastness of Eastwood and almost to the Shelby County line, are a brace of new developments that have been hot the last couple of years — Ashmoor Woods, Curry Crossings and The Polo Fields (you just know that's not going to be the name of a public housing project, don't you?) — where prices range from $250,000 to $800,000.

The South End

Louisville's South End is another "vernacular region," in the phrase of U of L geographer Bill Dakan: It exists in people's minds rather than on a map. (The map in most people's minds would extend from Preston Highway west to the river and from U of L south to Bullitt County.)

An area of modest, affordable housing traditionally occupied by blue-collar workers, the South End has usually felt excluded from power in the city, although many of its residents have a fierce independence that makes them treat any suggestion of being disenfranchised with a scornful snort.

Like most generalizations, the idea of South Enders as "a forgotten people," as one activist put it in the early '70s, can be exceptioned to death. South End representatives have frequently been the leaders of the Jefferson County legislative delegation. A state law requires the county judge/executive to geographically distribute his or her appointments to county boards and commissions.

Nonetheless, in 1991 a U of L professor studying the local power structure found that among the folks who appeared most often on the boards of major local institutions, only one or two were from the South End; 53 of the 67 whose addresses could be determined were from the East End. Some areas of the South End lack sewers, often at the residents' behest, although the Metropolitan Sewer District is working hard in the area. (When you drive out of town on Dixie Highway, notice when you stop seeing nationally franchised businesses. You've passed the end of the sewer lines as well.)

Between its older neighborhoods and a flurry of new development, the South End has some of the most interesting neighborhoods in the area. Frederick Law Olmsted named Southern Parkway Grand Boulevard, and it's easy to see why: The width of the street, the handsome frame houses along either side, the stately procession of it all toward Iroquois Park make up a prospect that is minuscule in no regard.

Beechmont, the neighborhood Southern Parkway slants through, is another former streetcar suburb and another great Louisville neighborhood built around an Olmsted Park. (Its neighborhood theater is the Iroquois Amphitheatre, an open-air venue for musicals, festivals such as Kentucky Music Weekend and other events.) There's a strong neighborhood association that was very active in the struggle over airport expansion.

The housing stock includes small brick cottages built after World War II and more impressive two- and three-story frame houses that went up around the turn of the century; the neighborhood likewise contains a wide spread of individuals. In addition to the working-class folk suggested by the South End's unfair redneck image, Beechmont and nearby **Kenwood Hill** have a long-standing reputation as areas that attract a number of artists, such as the Little Loomhouse's Lou Tate, and freethinkers of many stripes.

Houses on Southern Parkway come up for sale rarely and generally sell for $125,000 and up. Some of the smaller homes in Beechmont go for $55,000 to $75,000; typical prices are more in the $65,000 to $80,000 range.

There has been a great deal of development on the other side of Iroquois Park, with Parkridge off Manslick Road and the adjoining Parkridge Place and Parkridge Woods. When Parkridge opened, there was so much demand for it — much of it from people who grew up in the area and wanted to stay — that lots were sold by means of a lottery. Houses start at $170,000.

Shively, which lies along Dixie Highway (mostly to the west) from Millers Lane south to Rockford Lane, was incorporated as a city in 1938, largely as a way for the distilleries in the area to avoid paying Louisville taxes (although it dates back to the 1780s and was originally called St. Helens). Its nickname, "Lively Shively," comes from the adults-only businesses on Seventh Street Road and its rough politics (a former police chief went to jail in 1985 for accepting bribes). Most of the city is considerably more staid. Shively is also where Dixie Highway begins its zoning-be-damned, autos-be-praised commercial development, which continues out to the county line. Most houses in the area are in the $70,000 and $80,000s; the Cloverleaf neighborhood, east of Dixie just south of the Watterson, is solidly in the $90,000s to low 100,000s.

South of Shively is **Pleasure Ridge Park**, an unincorporated neighborhood that dates back to a 19th-century railroad stop that featured a hotel, a popular dance hall and a distillery that gave away free samples at noon. PRP, as it's universally known, fought off annexation by Shively in 1984. Its volunteer fire department is the perennial top fund-raiser for the WHAS Crusade for Children; the boys' basketball team at the high school was state champ in 1989. It's also the site of the belatedly bustling Riverport Industrial Park and the eternally-packed Mike Linnig's, a tribute to golden-fried fish. Topographically, it has some of the greatest variation in the county — some of the area on the west side of Dixie Highway is built in the flood plain, with drainage a perpetual problem; other parts of PRP are as high as the Indiana Knobs.

Developer W.L. Peterson built two signal developments in the 1960s that continue to be popular. Windsor Forest, off Arnoldtown Road, is on a set of especially high and rolling hills (up to 700 feet above sea level). For a suburb of its vintage, it has comparatively large lots, and few trees were cut in its development; nearly a fifth of it is given over to such common amenities as playing fields, hiking trails and a well-stocked fish-and-duck pond. Prices range from $120,000 to $200,000.

Peterson's earlier development was Prairie Village, on Old Third Street Road near Page Lane, a large development that shows staying

Old Louisville was developed with many open spaces.

power of several kinds — some of its original homeowners are still there, while property values have nearly doubled in recent years: They now range from $85,000, for story-and-a-half homes with a detached garage, up to $140,000 or so. In the same neighborhood, the new development of Bridgegate, which some people consider to be in Valley Station, has houses from $200,000 (for an approximately 1,700-square-foot, two-story brick home) to $800,000 (for showplaces that may top 8,000 square feet). On the west side of Dixie, Hunters Point, off Upper Hunters Trace, has grown quickly in the past few years — many of its buyers, a Realtor tells us, coming from PRP residents not interested in crossing to the other side of the highway. Its ranch houses go for anywhere from $140,000 to $220,000.

The next community going out Dixie Highway is **Valley Station**, which was first settled at the beginning of the 19th century (its early structures include one of the county's historic home museums, Riverside). Like PRP, it was named for its railroad station; like PRP, much of it lies in the flood plain; also like PRP, it grew rapidly in the 1950s and '60s and attracted folks who worked in Fort Knox as well as Louisvillians looking for a more suburban home. Among newer subdivisions, the ranch houses of Grafton Place go for between $85,000 and $124,000; nearby Pine Trace has homes from $80,000 to $95,000. Stoneridge Landing, a growing development on East Pages Lane near the Southwest Medical Center, has condominiums going for between $105,000 and $125,000 and homes between $135,000 and $225,000.

As far south as Valley Station, but considerably to the east, is another significant neighborhood, **Okolona**, the largest unincorporated community in the county. It has resisted creating itself as a city to keep from bringing in another level of taxation (although the community built its own water and sewer systems, since taken over by Louisville Water Co. and MSD).

The fake Indian name comes from a massive oak tree that stood for years at the corner of Preston Highway and Okolona Terrace (it was felled after it was struck by lightning 20 years ago). It has a rough background, as a swampy place called "the Wet Woods" that was a haunt for robbers and other blackguard who congregated at the (this is not made up) Black Jack Tavern. It also has prouder points of history: Preston Highway, the main thoroughfare, at some points follows the path of the last leg of the Wilderness Trail; it remained a corduroy road (logs laid over swampy ground) into the 20th century. Nowadays, the Wilderness Trail is lined with businesses, serving as a tribute to the automobile and the strip style of development.

Okolona is accessible to the main operations of the area's three largest private employers (UPS, Ford and GE); Jefferson Mall is the area's largest shopping center. And right now, with the opening of the Snyder Freeway, the area — where land prices still lag behind other parts of the county — is one of the most active sites for residential construction. Some observers predict this trend will increase dramatically. The Apple Valley subdivision off the Outer Loop, begun in the 1960s, is still adding new homes; they go for $120,000 to $170,000. Autumn Woods, begun in fall 1993 off Blue Lick Road, has homes from $79,000 to $90,000. New, smaller developments in the area include Adams Run, off Beulah Church Road south of the Snyder, where homes go for $135,000 to $180,000; Charleswood Forest, off Cooper Chapel Road ($110,000 to $135,000); Cooper Farms, off Mt Washington Road close to the Bullitt county line ($125,000 to $165,000); and in Cooper Farms' vicinity, our favorite recent neighborhood name, Enclave ($95,000 to 120,000).

The West End

Louisville's West End, much more level than the land to the east but not as blessed with streams, developed fitfully over more than a century. The early river towns of Portland and Shippingport sprung up not long after Louisville itself was founded; other tracts of the area remained as farmland into the 1920s. The West End was the site of much of Louisville's industrial expansion during the last half of the 19th century. It suffered worse from the 1937 flood than any other part of town; nearly all its population was evacuated.

The West End is now predominantly African American, although that predominance has come fairly recently. Soon after their emancipation, blacks began moving west of the center city. The first black residential neighborhood was Downtown, west of Seventh Street between Market Street and Broadway, which eventually became known as Russell. Little Africa, begun in 1891 in an area adjacent to Parkland, was what historian Marcia Dalton calls the city's first successful example of African-American suburban "pioneering" (much of it was later replaced by the Southwick Urban Renewal development). Although the Russell neighborhood has been a center of Black Louisville since the early part of this century, under segregation it had a western boundary firmly marked at 30th Street, where most of the majors streets changed names (and some still do — for example, Chestnut becomes River Park Drive). It was not until the 1960s and open housing laws that the entire area west of Ninth Street (except for the white enclave of Portland) became a mostly black neighborhood, as African Americans moved into the neighborhood's best homes around Shawnee and whites moved to other parts of the county.

The West End contains some of the city's deepest poverty and some of its finest homes. Developments such as the Lyles Mall at 28th and Broadway have brought a new level of shopping to the area. It has a number of good soul-food restaurants, from Irma's Cafeteria, 2531 W. Broadway, to the venerable Jay's Cafeteria, 1812 W. Muhammad Ali Boulevard, one of the genuine crossroads of the entire community.

Many black professionals have stayed in the area, where housing bargains abound — one young community leader told the *Courier* he bought a house for a price in five figures that would cost more than $150,000 in the eastern part of the county.

West End Realtor Frank Clay thinks **Russell** may be "the next Old Louisville" — that is, a revitalized historic district within easy range of downtown. It certainly holds a unique position in Louisville's African-American history. The Western Branch of the Louisville Free Public Library, still open at 10th and Chestnut, was among the country's first public libraries for blacks. Walnut Street in Russell was for many years the center of black nightlife in Louisville, with clubs such as the Top Hat, The Idle Hour and Joe's Palm Room (still open at a different location). It was the sort of neighborhood where that distinguished-looking man walking down the sidewalk might turn out to be Duke Ellington.

And it certainly is the focus of an extraordinary amount of attention these days. The neighborhood between Market and Broadway, Ninth and I-264 (called the Shawnee Expressway rather than the Watterson for the stretch through West Louisville, because of namesake Henry Watterson's paternalistic racial views) has everyone including Habitat for Humanity, the University of Louisville and the federal government pouring money and effort into rehabilitation and such developments as Hampton Place in the blocks around 15th and Madison. New houses go from $55,000 to $80,000; structures to be rehabilitated in this National Register district can be bought for less than $20,000.

As those low prices suggest, Russell isn't entirely out of the woods yet — it continues to experience some of the problems common to all inner cities. But people are beginning to talk about "the Russell miracle," and there are a lot of indications that it may be more than a sleight of hand.

Shawnee and **Chickasaw**, the neighborhoods on either side of Broadway at the western edge of the city, were the latest of the park neighborhoods to develop. They have many brick bungalows, some with tile roofs, and a number of large houses with four or more bedrooms, 2½ baths and distinctive construction. Forty-Seventh Street, which only runs for a few blocks on the south side of Broadway, is one of the most enviable streets in the city — especially on the west side of the street, where the homes literally have the Ohio River at the end of their backyards (and yet sit so high they haven't been flooded, even in 1937). And the entire neighborhood has access to Shawnee and Chickasaw, the only two of the major parks to face the river. Houses go for as low as $40,000 in the neighborhood, which runs east as far as 39th Street or so; but the best homes are a steal in the $110,000 to $115,000 range. And the new Fountain Estates development, at the foot of Market Street abutting the Shawnee golf course, has homes selling in the $250,000 range.

The Central Area

Old Louisville, the grandest of the city's historical districts (see Historical Preservation and Architecture), has not made the full move into stylishness that its architecture would seem to require. While it has a full contingent of boosters, its real estate is not quite as sought after as The Highlands' or Crescent Hill's — a good measure of how suburbanized Louisville's taste is, even in older neighborhoods.

But where 20 years ago Old Louisville was primarily composed of rooming houses and apartments, it's now primarily owner-occupied (whether in single-family houses or owner-occupied apartments) and is able to boast a diverse population that includes people of almost every ethnic or economic stripe, students and professors for U of L and those guarantors of middle-class desirability, professionals and families. Its central location means it has unique amenities: free Shakespeare in the neighborhood park, the city's largest festival in the St. James Court Art Show and the city's two best-stocked libraries, the public library's main branch and U of L's Ekstrom, at either end (not to mention the unique historical-genealogical resource of the Filson Club in the middle). And as the district in which Louisville's neighborhood and preservation movements began, it has a uniquely active neighborhood association — which other one has its own building?

Old Louisville is a neighborhood into which many people move when they come from larger cities. The density and the proximity to downtown are similar to what they knew, while the housing values are refreshing: Prices vary anywhere from $85,000 or so for renovated shotguns to about $300,000 for some of the 5,000- to 6,000-square-foot mansions on Third and Fourth streets.

Germantown and **Schnitzelburg** are adjoining neighborhoods to the southwest of The Highlands, which most people except the residents tend to lump together under the single name Germantown; technically, Schnitzelburg is the section south of Goss Avenue. As the names suggest, they were settled by German Catholics (although Germantown also absorbed a French Huguenot settlement called Paristown).

Some combination of luck and Teutonic temperament has kept them remarkably stable for such a modest urban enclave. Most houses stay in the same family over generations, and the people who move into the neighborhood aren't radically different from the ones who moved out. For all the social and political changes over the past several decades, it remains largely Catholic and Democratic. The neighborhood nurtures eccentrics, like scavenger artist Gus Ballard (see the Historic Preservation and Architecture chapter); it keeps alive such seemingly anachronistic institutions as the All Wool and a Yard Wide Democratic Club and the obscure game of dainty, which is like stick ball played with a wooden peg, with rules even weirder than that might suggest. (It's an annual feature of the neighborhood festival, when white-haired men show how you take stick to peg. Writer John Filiatreau, who grew up in Germantown, is dubious that any child ever really played the game.)

The neighborhood is also home to a number of restaurants where the plate lunch tradition is alive and well, and frying remains the cooking method of choice. Check's Cafe, at the corner of Burnett Avenue and Hickory Street, is the best known outside the neighborhood, but there are a half-dozen others that require an electron microscope to distinguish from each other yet remain a touchstone of a kind of Louisville cuisine more basic than Hot Browns and Benedictine spread.

Two-bedroom shotguns go for between $60,000 and $80,000 (less, if your Uncle Gunther will cut you a deal).

Audubon Park, between Poplar Level Road and Preston Highway near the fairgrounds, bears the name of the great naturalist not because of any associations with his stay in Louisville, but because this densely wooded neighborhood near Standiford Field is a bird sanctuary (not to mention a National Register Historical District), one of the most verdant and pleasant little enclaves in the city.

The neighborhood has a variety of architectural styles because it was built piecemeal between 1917 and 1951 (every major event of those decades, including World War I, the Great Depression and World War II, interrupted development). As a result, no two houses are built on exactly the same pattern. It is one of the earliest golf communities, dating to Audubon Country Club's 1921 founding, back when an amenities package was something your Greek neighbors brought over at Christmas. There are two garden clubs working daytime and evening shifts, and the annual Festival of the Dogwood, featuring folks done up in antebellum costumes, is one of the city's more distinctive festivals. Houses range from $100,000 to $290,000, with most selling between $145,000 and $175,000.

The Southeast

The Southeast lacks the strong local profile of other sections of town — it isn't the subject of pride, pejoratives or any kind of stereotype. People tend to be loyal to their particular neighborhood, which is more often than not a small town that has been absorbed by the community's outward sprawl.

Jeffersontown, for example, has a long history. It was incorporated as a town in 1797, named for then Vice President Thomas Jefferson (although for years German-American settlers called it Brunerstown). It was first settled by the Tyler family, some of whose holdings continue as a 600-acre rural historical district, which includes the Blackacre Nature Preserve, an estate used as a nature center for the Jefferson County Public Schools.

It has grown exponentially since World War II. There were fewer than 1,000 residents in the 1940s; now there are nearly 26,000, making it the second-largest city in the county and 11th-largest in the state. The explosive growth along Hurstbourne Lane (property on the east side of Hurstbourne is in Jeffersontown) has brought a great deal of prosperity to the city. It's one of the only neighborhoods with two movie theaters — Loew's Stony Brook 10, which brings in first-run films, and the J-town

4 Theaters, $1 at all times. Its annual Gaslight Festival is one of the community's largest events. J-town has a wide range of housing types, from suburban to rural, selling for anything from $32,000 to $265,000 (although the average house is in the high $80,000s).

Don't look for new construction in Jeffersontown proper — there are no more large tracts to be developed. But south of what residents would just as soon you didn't call J-town, things are booming. Saratoga Woods, off Taylorsville Road near Chenoweth Run Road, has been one of the county's hottest developments lately. One site of the 1994 Homearama, Saratoga Woods is a club community, with a pool and clubhouse, in a somewhat more moderate price range than others of the ilk: about $175,000 to 225,000.

Fern Creek, to the southwest of Jeffersontown, was once known as Stringtown because it was strung out along the Louisville-Bardstown Pike. Rural for years, it began to grow with the arrival of General Electric's Appliance Park in nearby Buechel. It seems to have an attraction for developments with foreign pretensions: The Tudor storefronts of Piccadilly Square are within sight of the Spanish Cove strip center; behind Piccadilly is the Oxford apartment complex, whose promotional materials at one time included the words, "Sir Walter Raleigh gave us the idea . . . ."

One of its most interesting areas is the deeply wooded stretch of Watterson Trail that runs between Bardstown Road and Glaser Road. Its showpieces are homes in the wooded valley near the point where Fern Creek crosses the road, an area that reminds some folks of the Smoky Mountains. There are still silos visible and other evidence of a lingering farm presence; there are also classic tract subdivisions such as Cedar Creek and Hollow Creek. Estates with five acres or more go for anywhere from $150,000 to $500,000, depending on the condition of the houses; those in the more conventional subdivisions run from $90,000 to $135,000.

But the biggest news in Fern Creek of late is Glenmary, south of the Gene Snyder freeway, the first major development to open up the county outside the Snyder. Many in the local real estate market thought developer HFH was taking a major risk in developing so far out; the development now has more than 500 homes and is a long way from seeing its last piece of construction equipment. More modest and affordable than Lake Forest — with prices for low-maintenance patio homes starting around $135,000 and others from $175,000 to $300,000 — it nonetheless offers many of the same features, including that all-important golf course. (At the moment, Glenmary residents are up in arms because the planned widening of Bardstown Road will come quite close to the houses in Glenmary that front Bardstown.)

There are likely to be more Glenmarys in the future by that name and others (in fact there's a Glenmary East, and a Glenmary West is planned), because the Gene Snyder isn't the only vital service extended to the area. In 1995 the Metropolitan Sewer District finished its Cedar Creek waste-water treatment plant west of Bardstown Road.

Indiana

Southern Indiana does not have the same degree of neighborhood-consciousness that

Two words to the wise: Flood plain. A lot of Jefferson County, especially the southwestern part of the county, was built in areas susceptible to flooding, and when the Ohio feels like wandering, it can be an imposing guest. That's especially true for homes that went up before 1978, when a new ordinance required structures to be built a foot above flood level. Many people complained about it up until March 1997 but see the sense of it now. Ask how a house you're interested in buying did in that '97 flood, one of the worst in local history.

Louisville does, especially when you get outside the established cities of Jeffersonville, Clarksville, New Albany and some of the other townships. The counties across from Louisville were predominantly rural until just recently, and large portions of the area continue to be (the area around Borden and Starlight in Clark County is home to a number of U-pick farms).

The key dividing lines are the school districts (even those, many Hoosiers will say, are loyalties that matter more to natives than they would to a newcomer) and the river: Southern Indiana's greatest selling point is as a cheaper, more convenient alternative to the Louisville suburbs. In the past, a home in Southern Indiana might cost 15 percent less than a comparable home in Louisville; the gap is closing, but Southern Indiana real estate remains less expensive.

The Southern Indiana cities — **New Albany**, **Clarksville** and **Jeffersonville** — began as river towns. While they never matched Louisville's size, they were major centers: In 1850, New Albany was the largest city in Indiana (and it remains the largest city in Southern Indiana, with more than 36,000 residents). New Albany and Jeffersonville in particular were major shipbuilding centers, a tradition that continues in diminished form at Jeffersonville's Jeffboat, the lineal descendant of the Howard Ship Yards and the country's largest inland boat builder. While Southern Indiana has only one company large enough to rank among the area's top 25 employers, it has seen significant job growth among small manufacturing firms. The longtime "Big Three" — Pillsbury, Colgate-Palmolive and Jeffboat — remain the largest private employers, but new companies, such as New Albany's Beach Mold and Conway Enterprises, are closing the gap. (The U.S. Census Processing Center in Jeffersonville is the largest employer of any kind, with 1,600 employees — more than Pillsbury and Colgate combined.)

Their age means that both New Albany and Jeffersonville have historic downtowns and surrounding residential districts — New Albany's so-called Mansion Row and Riverside Drive in Jeffersonville are among the most attractive streets in the area. Clarksville has less of a historical district, but more history: It was the first Anglo-American town in the Northwest Territory and home to George Rogers Clark after the Revolutionary War. It's also the point on shore closest to the 400-million-year-old fossil bed that is the entire reason we're not writing this book about Pittsburgh or Cairo, Illinois.

For most of the years of white settlement, Clarksville has been overshadowed by more commercially minded Jeffersonville and New Albany, but in recent years it has gained some of the most important sites in the area: Colgate-Palmolive and its giant illuminated clock, larger than Big Ben; Southern Indiana's only two malls, Green Tree and RiverFalls; and the new Falls of the Ohio Interpretive Center.

In Floyd County, only New Albany and Georgetown have public sewers, although some subdivisions have private sewer systems; most townships in Clark have their own systems.

Silver Hills is a well-wooded neighborhood built during the postwar years in the hills west of downtown New Albany. It has a secluded, suburban feel, like St. Matthews in Louisville, but set up high — the large yards of the era in front of a variety of homes: brick ranch, stone, two-story frame and shingle houses. Houses are priced from $110,000 to $600,000, and those two may be sitting next to each other.

The hills to the north of New Albany are **Floyds** — or Floyd, for stickling longtime residents — **Knobs**. Until the 1960s the Knobs was an extremely homogeneous area, made up of a few handfuls of extended families. Suburban development has changed it dramatically, turning it from a rural area into a bedroom community for Louisville (with a shopping center) — a bedroom community with incredible views and a number of houses that strive to be as breathtaking as the scenery. One of the glitziest developments is Plum Hill, where square footages start in the vicinity of 4,000, and prices average around $395,000 and go up to the higher end of the local market. In a more moderate vein, houses in Wymberly Woods, a subdivision begun in the '70s off Buck Creek Road, go from $80,000 to $110,000 (although a few exceed that average); a little newer is 10-year-old Countryview off Ind. Highway 150; its prices range from $100,000 to $130,000.

A recent success in Southern Indiana is Chapel Creek, outside New Albany between

Charlestown and Grant Line roads, 2 miles from I-265. It has two-story brick homes, many with features of local high-end building, such as arched windows and multiple roof lines; they're 2,500 square feet or more and sell for between $170,000 and $300,000. While most of its trees are saplings, a few taller ones give the area less of a scalped look than many new developments.

In the fast-growing area along County Line Road in Clark County near Sellersburg, Deer Run Park, a site of the 1996 Southern Indiana Homearama, has homes selling from $120,000 to $175,000; the same area also includes Dovir Woods, where prices are from $95,000 to $145,000.

Elke Pointe, off the Jeffersonville-Charlestown Pike, across from the Elks Golf Course, is just over the line between Jeffersonville and Clarksville and as a result is convenient to the malls as well as the interstate. Houses there are in the $150,000 to $250,000 range. Mallard Run, begun in 1994 off the Jeffersonville-Charlestown Pike, is a popular new location in a (by contemporary standards) more moderate range: $95,000 to $140,000.

Plum Run is a popular, expanding neighborhood of modest one- and two-story brick homes at the present edge of the suburbs, just outside Hamburg in northern Clark County. Although it's hidden behind some woods, and a moment's drive north will find you in farmland, it's right off the Sellersburg Exit of I-65. Its contemporary brick houses go for $110,000 to $150,000; there's an estate section where prices go as high as $175,000. The only development further north is Covered Bridge, on Perry Crossing Road in Sellersburg, a development built around a golf course designed and developed by local golf hero and ethnic food expert Fuzzy Zoeller and opened by long-ball hitter John Daly. Houses are $190,000 and up.

Oldham County

Oldham County has been growing at an explosive rate — the population has increased 23 percent just since 1990. In one sense, Oldham can be seen as the easternmost extension of Jefferson County's fast-developing East End; it was also a classic locus of white flight after the 1975 court order that Jefferson County desegregate its school system. The appeal can also be attributed to what people describe as an easier-going, more laid-back lifestyle (which, given that it's easygoing Louisville that's the hectic big city in this equation, suggests a Buddha-like degree of calm). Not to mention that its schools are generally considered to be among the best in the state. It's also a dry county — decide for yourself whether that's an advantage.

The county is largely rural, with a typically pretty, rolling Kentucky countryside interrupted by a few small towns; in 1990 more than two-thirds of the county was farmland (although subsequent development has surely eaten into that percentage). Sewers are virtually nonexistent, which means that most new houses have septic systems and so are legally required to have lots of an acre or more (although Louisville's Metropolitan Sewer District is extending service into the county's major towns). Natural gas is available only in limited parts of the county, which makes its availability an important selling point (although most subdivisions built since 1992 have gas, and a number of older subdivisions have added it as well).

La Grange, with the hospital and courthouse, is the county seat. It's also the county's real boom town, where the super Kroger, Wal-Mart, Luxbury Hotel, the Oldham 8 movie theaters and other commercial enterprises have sprung up since I-71 came through in 1970. Main Street has set itself up as an antique-and-tea-room district. Three TARC buses a day come to carry commuters into Louisville.

Among many developments going up in La Grange, Gleneagles Estates on Ky. 53 has proven a popular location, with new homes selling for $200,000 and more. The more moderately-priced Fox Trail, off Old Moody Lane toward Buckner, has homes that start in the $100,000s and edge into the $180,000 range.

The hot area for new construction in the past several years has been in the vicinity of Ky. 393 where it intersects I-71 near Buckner. Hottest of the hot have been Westwood and Westwood East, on Ky. 22 east of Crestwood which opened in 1994 and 1995 and sold out almost immediately. The houses are in the $160,000 to $220,000 range.

Sixty percent of houses in the Highlands were built before World War II.

Pewee Valley, just over the county line from Jefferson County along La Grange Road, is a historic community built along the railroad track, with much more architectural distinction than that might suggest. It's famous for its Confederate cemetery and for showcasing two different conceptions of femininity: It's the home of both Annie Fellows Johnston, who set her Little Colonel books in the small town, and the Kentucky Correctional Institute for Women.

Because of its proximity to Louisville, Pewee Valley has been one of the most densely-developed locations in Oldham. Ashebrooke "90," south of town on Ash Avenue, has newer homes from $86,000; across the street, the homes in Village Green sell in the $60,000s.

In the past, people have wanted their telephone numbers to have the 241 prefix that means **Crestwood**, which has generally been considered Oldham County's most prestigious address. This may no longer be true, as La Grange has matured. There has been less new building in Crestwood recently than around La Grange and the Ky. 393 corridor. Starter homes in the Orchard Grass subdivision go from $65,000 to $100,000. Briar Hill Estates is an older subdivision (although a newer section shares a sewer system with Orchard Grass). Houses go for as low as $140,000 up to $350,000 in the newer section.

The pent-up demand in Oldham has been for neighborhoods priced in the first-time buyer's range (roughly $60,000 to $80,000) but the likes of Village Green in Pewee Valley, Country Village in Crestwood and in the La Grange area, Lakewood Valley, Pear Orchard and Greenwood Commons, have been picking up the slack.

Shelby County

Shelbyville calls itself "the gateway to the Bluegrass," and it certainly seems to be a point balanced between Louisville's influence (literature boosting Shelby County schools mentions the many attractions in the area, every one of them in Jefferson County) and a small-town gentility that recalls the more prosperous areas around Lexington. (Little wonder the UK-U of L basketball game was brokered at a Shelbyville restaurant.)

Its prosperity is attested to by such businesses as the Wakefield-Scearce Galleries in Shelbyville, where you can find that $42,000 satinwood bookcase you've been looking for, and the exemplary Science Hill Inn, one of the area's best restaurants. **Simpsonville**, the county's second-largest city, is no slouch when it comes to dining: It has Claudia Sanders, the Colonel's Lady (we trust we don't need to tell you which chicken-frying Colonel that is) and the Old Stone Inn. (The county is dry, except for Shelbyville.)

Like the area around Lexington, Shelby County is horse country, although the steed of choice is National Velvet, not Man o' War — it is known as the Saddlebred Horse Capital of the World, and its annual horse show is a major event. But even more, Shelby has been a strong dairy and tobacco county. It also has a bit of manufacturing, with plants such as Budd Co., Purnell Sausage and several spin-off plants manufacturing parts for the Toyota plant in Scott County (perhaps coincidentally, the Toyota deal was struck by Shelby County native Martha Layne Collins, the state's first female governor). The county was runner-up for the Saturn Plant built in Spring Hill, Tennessee — and quite a few Shelby Countians are glad the plant didn't come and transform a place they're well-pleased with.

Like Bullitt and Oldham, Shelby has benefited from Louisville's sprawl (and white flight), although the growth has been steadier and more controlled than Oldham's; there has been very little "hopscotch development," with housing springing up in the middle of nowhere, and fewer large-scale subdivisions. Most new building has been around Shelbyville, with a few speculative developments around Simpsonville. Houses in those two cities are on sewer lines; the rest of the county is on septic systems.

Brentwood, on Ky. 53 N. adjacent to the Shelbyville Country Club, was built in the early '80s and sat for a few years until the economy got rolling. It's Shelby County's version of Louisville subdivisions such as Lake Forest — it has that Homearama look, with plenty of extras; it was the first place in Shelby County to show such trendy features as arched windows and vivid colors in the decor. Homes go for $220,000 to $295,000. Other Shelbyville developments of recent note include Weissinger Estates ($185,000 to $250,000) and Charleston Estates ($125,000 to $150,000), a pair of developments with lots of an acre-plus, both off Ky. 53 south of Shelbyville, and the new and very hot High Point Village on Boone Station Road ($125,000 to $145,000).

The large, almost outsized houses you see along U.S. 60 between Simpsonville and Shelbyville aren't just a coincidence of likeminded property owners. It's actually a development called Canterfield Way, an old farm split up into five-acre lots (although some homeowners combined parcels of land to give themselves spreads as large as 30 acres). Houses range from $250,000 up at least as high as $750,000.

Bullitt County

The tornado of May 1996 was a terrible blow for Bullitt County, but it served as a kind of public relations stroke for the area — as news helicopters showed the devastation the storm had wrought in Brooks, Pioneer Village, Hillview and Mount Washington, folks in Jefferson County were amazed to see how much new construction there was in an area with a previously rural image.

Bullitt County was the site of some of the most important sites in the area's early history — Bullitt's Lick Salt Works near what's now Shepherdsville; there were also iron furnaces. But the area's rugged terrain limited growth: Population grew by fewer than 2,000 in the first 50 years of this century, and the county was predominantly rural and wooded (Bernheim Forest, the state's official arboretum south of Shepherdsville, is more than 60 years old).

Bullitt County's growth began to take off in the 1950s with the arrival in nearby parts of Jefferson County of General Electric's Appliance Park and Ford's Fern Valley plant. For the first time, the county began to function as part of the Louisville metropolitan area. In the past 40 years, Bullitt's population has more than quadrupled. Improved highways have played a large part: There are now five interchanges off I-65 when there was once only one complete one, in Shepherdsville; I-65 is a six-lane road through the county, and many Louisville places of employment are now within a decent commuting time. The 1970s saw what the county planning and zoning commissioner called "the big boom" in the wake of court-ordered busing in Jefferson County; development has approached that level over the past several years, until Bullitt rivals Oldham as the state's fastest-growing county.

The county's rural character remains a selling point, however much it may be changing as more people come out in search of it. Bullitt real estate agents say they're always dealing with Louisville suburbanites with visions of acquiring five acres and a house for a fraction of what they paid in Jefferson County.

The county's largest city, **Hillview**, grew from a number of subdivisions built in the 1950s just across the county line from Jefferson; it was only incorporated in 1974, and it continues to be the center of a growing northern Bullitt area that also includes **Zoneton**, **Brooks** and **Pioneer Village**. It's seen recent building in such developments as Meadowbrook (home costs range from $110,000 to $185,000) and Tanyard Springs, developed from a farm that had been cultivated for about 200 years ($110,000 to $160,000). Deer Run is a new, upscale subdivision south of Meadowbrook off Hebron Lane. Houses there are priced from $150,000 to $250,000.

Mount Washington, the second largest city, is just down Bardstown Road from Fern Creek (and it looks forward gleefully to the widened Bardstown Road causing such consternation in Glenmary). Twelve Oaks represents a change — the beginning of developments aimed primarily at white-collar folk. Homes are from $175,000 to more than $300,000 (a few are as large as 5,000 square feet).

Shepherdsville is the county seat and home to such large employers as Publishers Printing. Lazy River Estates and Lazy River North, on Ky. 44 between Mount Washington and Shepherdsville, are new subdivisions with houses between $110,000 and $280,000. A little closer to Shepherdsville, Sycamore Bend has a wider price range, from $80,000 to $275,000.

One new focus of development has been Beech Grove Road, a mile and a half west of downtown Shepherdsville (and recently annexed into the city). Houses in the subdivisions River Valley, Kate's Landing and Dogwood Run go from $70,000 to $95,000.

FYI

Unless otherwise noted, the area code for all phone numbers listed in this chapter is 502.

Neighborhood Associations

Most neighborhood associations don't have a permanent home — the address is usually in care of whomever happens to be president at the time.

The best source for neighborhood associations in the city of Louisville is the Neighborhoods Programs office in the city's Department of Community Services, 574-3380. Its county-level equivalent is the Jefferson County Community Outreach, 574-6720.

Apartments

Instead of listing a large number of apartment complexes, we're listing a few that everyone should be aware of, because they have a presence on the landscape; and we've listed several property management companies that control a large number of apartments.

Some of the nicest apartments in the city are in converted homes, especially in The Highlands and Old Louisville. Some of these are controlled by property management companies, but many more are owned by people whose marketing expertise involves nothing more complicated than buying an "Apartment for Rent" sign at Kmart.

The best guide to apartment complexes — and one of the few clear and easy-to-use real-estate publications we've ever seen — is the *Greater Louisville Apartment Guide*, published monthly and widely available at grocery stores and other high-traffic locations. Or you can pick up a video version at local video stores. About as good is the rival *Apartment Blue Book,* available in the same sorts of locations; there's also a *Louisville, Surrounding Counties and Southern Indiana Apartments Magazine* published by the same people who put out *Homes* magazine.

While we've listed rents, these may change at any time — their purpose is to let you know whether you're looking in the right price range. For more up-to-date figures, check out the most recent editions of the apartment guides.

Management Companies

Camden
9100 Shelbyville Rd. • 426-6110

Camden, a Houston-based firm, manages six newer apartment complexes in the East End (Hurstbourne, the oldest, is 28 years old) and is soon to break ground on a seventh. All of them have pools, clubhouses, tennis courts and the like. They range from Sundance, self-described as "festive," on La Grange Road around the corner from Oxmoor Mall, where rents go from $445 to $600, to more traditional Hurstbourne, where rents go from $570 to $895 and some units are as large as 1,700 square feet. The newest is Glenridge, at U.S. 42 and Lime Kiln Lane, done in an updated version of New England clapboard architecture ($650-$810).

Insignia Residential Group
1014 Whetstone Way • 244-7194

This local arm of the country's largest property management company manages four East End apartment complexes. It's headquartered in the Plainview Apartments, at the corner of Hurstbourne Parkway and Linn Station Road, and offers loft homes, garden apartments and townhouses in one of the city's best-recognized communities (rents range from $440 to $885). Nearly as well known is La Fontenay (the name is said to mean "the fountain," but look that up in your French dictionary; it's actually named after a French town, to match the quasi-French architecture).

A little further east than Plainview, off Shelbyville Road, it has large floor plans and a rather quiet feel (it's been around long enough for the trees to get fairly tall). Breckenridge Square, off Breckenridge Lane near I-264, offers large floor plans in its one-, two- and three-bedroom apartments; the rent ($489-$789) includes gas heat and hot water. Churchill Park, a little further south on Breckenridge ($479-$739), pays residents' heat and air-conditioning.

All four complexes are pet-friendly (which means they're more receptive than many of their peers to larger pets).

Medford Property Co. Inc.
7505 New La Grange Rd. • 423-8800

This company manages just fewer than 4,000 apartment units throughout the city and Southern Indiana, from Millwood off Poplar Level Road (one-bedrooms from $399, two-bedrooms from $516) to Coppershire, a complex off Zorn Avenue that has won architectural design awards for such features as spiral oak staircases ($535 to $780). Some of its properties have concierge service, in-house pubs and a variety of unique athletic features (including the world's only Tudor-motif parquet basketball floor at the Villages of Oxford in Fern Creek). Its new showplace is Fenwick Place, off Hurstbourne Parkway near the Stony Brook shopping center. It features concierge service, washers and dryers (or connections for same) in every unit, high ceilings, French doors and a variety of floor plans, including town homes and one-bedroom lofts. Rents range from $509 to $907.

Underhill Associates
100 Kentucky Towers • 581-8800

This company, which manages Kentucky Towers (see below), also manages a number of historic homes in Old Louisville split up into three- and four-plex apartment buildings (a total of 800 apartments). All of them have been renovated, with updated utilities; rents range from $350 to $800.

Apartment Complexes

Crescent Centre
657 S. Third St. • 589-2828

This stylish red-brick development just south of Broadway got off to a slightly rocky start when it opened in 1989, and it has yet to attract any of the ground-level shops originally envisioned as part of the project (it's now marketing those spaces to the medical industry). But occupancy is way up, and most observers say Crescent Centre has become a vital downtown community. It has both one- and two-bedroom apartments and distinctive two-bedroom townhouses on the second level of the crescents that scoop dramatically away from the street front. There's a private fitness club and club and social rooms. All access is by programmed code only; reserved parking under cover is available. Rents run from $485 to $760.

The 800
800 S. Fourth St. • 583-9800

This 29-story blue-and-white modern building — which looks like someone got a pastel Leggo set for Christmas — went up in 1963 and was the city's tallest building until it was overtaken by the Citizens and First National towers. There are penthouse apartments with skyline terraces, a doorman on 24-hour duty, valet parking, an in-house delicatessen and beauty salons and a rooftop solarium. Rents range from $465 to $1,500.

The Harbours at Riverpointe
1 Riverpointe Plaza, Jeffersonville, Ind. • (812) 288-1100

"The perfect setting for those who prefer to live on the edge," its first ads said. It looks like a Miami Beach hotel: two slanting bays of high-rises right on the water. But it's an apartment building on the Ohio in Jeffersonville (the Hoosierbleu?) that's an initial step in the city's plans to develop its riverfront. All units have a river view.

The high-rise runs a bit like a hotel: concierge service, continental breakfast two mornings a week, dry-cleaning pickup and delivery. Rents were scaled back when early occupancy didn't meet expectations; they range from $545 to $1,160; penthouses are $1,750 to $2,000.

Kentucky Towers
Muhammad Ali Blvd. at Fifth St. • 581-8800

Downtown's largest residential property has 285 apartments in its 19 stories; 75 of them are furnished as corporate suites for relocating professionals. There are also executive suites set up as office space with a common secretary and fax machines, etc.

The apartments have a 24-hour doorman and the state's highest outdoor swimming pool, on the seventh floor roof. Rents are $375 to $800 for unfurnished apartments, $495 to $1,400 furnished.

The Woodlands on Harrods Creek
5630 Timber Creek Ct. • 228-3300

"Why buy a quarter-million-dollar view when you can rent one?" its ads ask. The only Louisville apartments where rents start at $1,100, this Prospect development of rental homes is like a pay-by-the-month Lake Forest, with 9- and 12-foot ceilings, golf privileges at a nearby club, swimming and tennis and views of Harrods Creek and the surrounding woods.

Organizations

Louisville Tenants Association
425 W. Muhammad Ali Blvd. • 587-0287

The Tenants Association is an advocacy group for the rights of low- and middle-income tenant families in Louisville and Jefferson County. It works to improve living conditions, understanding of tenant rights and responsibilities and tenant-landlord relationships. It also provides counseling, crisis intervention and dispute mediation. It publishes a *Tenants Rights Handbook* and makes other information available to the public.

Louisville Apartment Association
7400 South Park Pl., Ste. 1 • 426-6140

The local organization of apartment owners — its members and landlords must meet the association's standards of professionalism and ethics. It also investigates tenant complaints against its members.

Real Estate Agencies

This listing emphasizes some of the larger players in the Louisville market, along with some agencies that specialize in particular parts of town.

We list only a single office number and address for each firm, but many of the ones we list have several offices and can refer you to the one nearest you.

Bauer Blake Biery Inc., Realtors
2627 Charlestown Rd., New Albany, Ind. • (812) 945-2356

One of Southern Indiana's largest agencies, with offices in New Albany, Louisville and Corydon, Ind., Bauer Blake Biery specializes in real estate on the sunny side of the river (although several agents have Kentucky licenses) and has recently begun developing subdivisions, such as the popular Plum Run in Clark County and Quail Chase in Floyd County.

It's the area's only affiliate of the Better Homes and Gardens Real Estate Service. Agent Bob Taylor was the Southern Indiana Realtor of the Year in 1993.

Century 21
Joe Guy Hagan Realtors
119 Hurstbourne Pkwy. • 426-3600

This large company — by some measures the second-largest in town — was formed in 1965 and joined the Century 21 family in 1977. It has five Jefferson County offices, arranged strategically around the county, and one in Bardstown, which does a major part of its business in auctioning farmland. The company was early in using computer software and continues upgrading to stay on the cutting edge.

Century 21
Reisert, Baker, Walker
& Associates
1302 10th St., Jeffersonville, Ind.
• (812) 285-5000

This Southern Indiana affiliate of the gold-coated folk is more than 50 years old; founder Jane Reisert's son is CEO. Its 57 agents focus primarily on Southern Indiana real estate. They have development, relocation, commercial and property management departments.

Two· of its principals, Jim Baker and Charles Reisert, have been president of the Southern Indiana Realtors Association; Baker was 1994 Realtor of the Year and Win Walker Jr. held the title in 1995. They maintain offices in Clarksville, Jeffersonville and New Albany.

Frank Clay Realty
2301 W. Broadway • 774-8794

The company Clay founded in 1978 is the West End's leading real estate firm and one of the city's largest African American-owned businesses, employing 10 agents. The company does some development, renovation and new construction, but its primary focus is sales. It works in a number of ways to help first-time home buyers: home ownership counseling for banks and the housing authority and free how-to-buy-a-house classes. Clay is a member of the state Real Estate Commission, the Board of Realtors and has also been president of the National Association of Real Estate Brokers.

Coldwell Banker Action Realtors
5908 Bardstown Rd. • 239-2100

This independently owned agency in Fern Creek is among the largest of Coldwell Banker's Kentucky franchises and among the top 100 in the Midwest (it led the region in units of sales in 1995 and '96). It does a good deal of relocation and networking work, especially with some of the major corporations with which Coldwell Banker has a national relationship. Of 35 agents in the firm, all but two are full time.

Edelen and Edelen Realtors
2721 Taylorsville Rd. • 456-1817

This 22-year-old company has 25 agents working out of its headquarters near Bowman Field. While several agents specialize in eastern parts of the county, the agency has a particular reputation as one of the largest Realtors in The Highlands. It also manages rental property in Crescent Hill and The Highlands.

Edelen is affiliated with the RELO national relocation network and has an in-house mortgage company. Founder Louise Edelen was the 1994 Realtor of the Year for both Louisville and Kentucky; Glenn Edelen is current vice-president of the Board of Realtors.

Inno-Max Realty/Fisbo Magazine
4900 Brownsboro Center • 895-4900

This aggressive and innovative small company began in 1987 publishing a magazine to advertise houses for sale by their owners. Four years later, they were also in the real estate business, either taking a low 3 percent com-

---

INSIDERS' TIP

Lake Forest, out Shelbyville Road, is a showplace for Christmas lights, attracting bumper-to-bumper crowds throughout much of the Christmas season.

mission if the client showed the house or a 5 percent commission if they acted as a conventional agent. In two years the company grew from three to 26 agents and began selling in Southern Indiana. It's now a force to be reckoned with on the local scene.

Inno-Max was the first local company to have a home-line telephone system (899-5656). It also continues to provide, through its widely distributed *Fisbo Magazine*, a way for people to advertise homes they're selling themselves.

The Prudential Parks and Weisberg
6040 Dutchmans Ln. • 458-1988

This second-generation firm, in business 46 years, has three offices in Jefferson County and two across the river. With 120 agents, it ranks among the area's largest agencies. While most of its business is in the East End, it sells throughout the seven-county area. The company has had its own mortgage company for nine years and is HUD approved in both Kentucky and Indiana. It offers a full set of relocation services: spouse counseling, a job bank and rentals (the company's property management division can set up a new arrival in an apartment within 24 hours). It is an independently owned affiliate of Prudential.

Rainey, Jones & Associates
6520 Glenridge Park Pl. • 327-1000, (800) 999-0151

This full-service company with more than 170 agents and five local offices does a little bit of everything in commercial and residential real estate; it has an active relocation division, a mortgage division and a site development division. It has the highest average sale price of any of the large local companies ($157,600 in fall 1997). While it sells throughout the area, if it has any focus, it's on more expensive properties in the East End (and on into Oldham and Shelby counties).

RE/MAX Properties East
10503 Timberwood Cr., Ste. 100 • 425-6000

Like all RE/MAX franchises, this one has a staff of full-time, experienced agents who pay a fee to be in the office instead of sharing their commissions. (RE/MAX stands for "real estate maximums.")

This has been one of the most successful franchises in a fast-growing company — among the 10 largest in the country, and its 1996 dollar volume lagged only behind local giant Paul Semonin. Owner/broker Harrell Tague was the company's Owner/Broker of the Year in 1991, and a number of other agents have served as officers or members of the Board of Realtors. Annell Kuelpman was the company's broker/manager of the year in 1995. There is an in-house mortgage company, and relocations are handled through RE/MAX Relocation Services.

RE/MAX Professionals
420 Hurstbourne Ln., Ste. 104 • 423-1331

This RE/MAX franchise is strongest in eastern Jefferson County, but it works throughout the area. Several agents specialize in working with large corporations' transferees. Several Realtors in the office have been Realtor of the Year.

Schuler Realty
2867 Charlestown Rd., New Albany, Ind. • (812) 948-2888

The largest Realtor in Southern Indiana with more than 90 active agents, 17-year-old Schuler has three offices in New Albany, Jeff and Knobs. The locally-owned company works closely with builders. New construction and relocation are their specialties.

Paul Semonin Realtors
4967 U.S. Hwy. 42, Ste. 200 • 425-4760

The monster: Semonin is not only the largest real estate company in Louisville and the state of Kentucky, it's the 52nd largest real estate company in the country. In 1997 its sales were $924 million. Semonin has 677 sales associates and six Louisville offices, one in Oldham County, two in Southern Indiana and one in Lexington.

While it's been in business since 1915, Semonin stays abreast of current technology: Its Semonin Hotline, 584-HOME or (800) 442-7335, is a computerized phone system that allows customers to call up for listings a bit more extensive than the standard classified ad and to find out about properties in neighborhoods and the price range they're looking for. There is also a *Semonin Homes* magazine, with all the company's current listings. It also airs a showcase for Sunday home-shoppers, *The Semonin Home Show* (Sunday morning on WAVE-3).

Semonin has its own mortgage company and is associated with Reliance Relocation, a network of 449 firms (including 26 of the top 50 real estate firms in the nation).

Wakefield, Reutlinger and Co. Realtors
6511 Glenridge Pl., Ste. 10 • 425-0225

With 23 agents, Wakefield Reutlinger is a medium-sized agency by national standards, a small one in the Louisville market. It makes the most of its size — it boasts that all of its agents will have been inside every house it lists; its relocation work is handled not by a relocation department but by the owners of the firm. These methods seem to pay off: It has the highest median sale price of any of the area's 25 largest firms.

It focuses on Louisville and Jefferson County east of I-65, although it also does some work with farms in the outlying counties to the east. Principal broker Tom Wakefield is 1998 treasurer of the Board of Realtors.

Walton Jones Realtors
2518 Frankfort Ave. • 896-4262

This small but savvy company specializes in historical and other older properties in Clifton, Crescent Hill and The Highlands; it handles both residential and commercial work.

Publications

Fisbo Magazine
4900 Brownsboro Center • 895-4900

This innovative publication provides a place to advertise homes and property for sale by owner (FSBO). (See the previous entry for Inno-Max Realty.)

Homes Magazine
2100 Gardiner Ln., Ste. 101 • 458-1515

This 400-page magazine consisting of ad-vertisements from local real estate companies, published by Arkansas-based J.V. Rockwell Publishing, lists homes, apartments, condominiums, farms and commercial properties on the market in Louisville and most of the surrounding counties. It's distributed free in a number of locations, including banks and grocery stores.

Builders

There is no single large builder or group of them that dominates the Louisville market. Instead, the vast majority of them belong to the Louisville Home Builders Association, which represents the 71st-largest market in the country but has its fourth-largest membership.

This results in competition, and as you may recall from Econ 101, it also results in competition in both price and quality. When Louisville builders go into the Lexington market, for example, they find themselves making much higher profit margins; they are forced by the competition here to put more extras into their homes, elevating costs and reducing profits.

The local **Home Builders Association**, 429-6000, runs a tight and professional ship: Its Registered Builder program is a regional model that puts all members through a credit check, solicits references from subcontractors and customers and requires continuing education of its builders. In the past, members who haven't met its requirements have been expelled from the association. Its builders are required to give a one-year warranty, and the association also conciliates complaints between builders and dissatisfied customers (and will submit them to arbitration if conciliation is impossible).

The Home Builders Association has a weekly television show, *Louisville's Best Homes*, broadcast Sunday at 1 PM on WHAS-11. And the Homearama it sponsors is a big affair, drawing 40,000 spectators to three locations; in recent years the Homearama has included one moderately priced site in the $45,000 to $60,000 range.

The Aging Resource Center is the best friend a Louisville senior ever had. If you have a question about senior activities or opportunities, they have the answer or can steer you in the right direction.

Retirement

When we talked about this chapter of the book with Al Allen, the affable writer of the "seniors" column in the daily newspaper, he paused for a moment, considering the concept. "Seniors are interested in everything from archery to zoology," he said. "They're not sitting around on the back porch knitting and playing checkers all day. They are lifting weights, bird-watching. Seniors do everything that anybody else would do."

Allen made a very good point. Seniors have never been more active than they are today; it's as if Americans' middle-age is widening and their old age shrinking.

Nancy Lacewell, the president of Louisville's Aging Resource Center, said she doesn't consider someone aged unless they are a minimum of 85 years old. Thus, this entire book is relevant to retirees — even the Kidstuff chapter is valuable to seniors who are on the constant lookout for things to do with their grandchildren.

Still, there are several agencies, services and features of this city that are geared directly toward retirees. We outline them below this introduction.

For a metropolitan area, the cost of living remains reasonable for retirees. Also, nature's scenery in this part of Kentucky is breathtaking in the spring, when the city's parks and neighborhoods are resplendent with dogwoods, azaleas, redbuds and lilacs and tulips and daffodils blanket yards and hillsides. Fall foliage beckons you to put on a sweater and take paints and canvas outdoors. The climate is generally mild, but there are some cold winter days and occasional snow, and late summer can get pretty muggy. All things considered, however, the moderate weather results in many picture-perfect days for outdoor leisure.

The arts are rich here, and recreation is easy to find too on the public and private golf courses, at indoor and outdoor tennis courts and on fishing lakes a short drive away. The public park system offers bicycle routes, jogging paths, horseback riding trails and scenic picnic vistas.

Medical services and hospitals emphasize preventive care and specialties at heart-lung centers, cancer and geriatric institutes, a world-renowned hand center, women's treatment centers, adult day care and nursing homes.

A city-wide bus system serves those living downtown or in the suburbs. Senior citizens ride free with an ID card during off-peak hours. And those who have reached their 100th birthday can a free bus pass. Some buses, as part of the TARC3 program, have been equipped with wheelchair and kneeling lifts, and special van pickups can be arranged. An expressway system speeds up travel to every part of the city — 30 minutes to the most distant point.

There are travel clubs, free tuition at the University of Louisville and a popular Meals on Wheels program. The Louisville Free Public Library has books on tape and large-print books at no charge.

If you like to volunteer, the Kentucky Center for the Arts, Actors Theatre of Louisville, the Iroquois Amphitheater, the Macauley Theatre and the Kentucky Shakespeare Festival can use you as an usher — and you get to see the performances for free. Hospitals and shelters are always looking for another pair of hands (Home of the Innocents volunteers hold and cuddle the babies and play with older children at the home).

Information and guidance for any of the above is available at one number: 589-4941. The Aging Resource Center is the best friend a Louisville senior ever had. If you have a question about senior activities or opportunities, they have the answer or can steer you in the right direction.

Agencies

Aging Resource Center
900 S. Fourth St. • 589-4941

This center, which has a knowledgable, helpful staff and an excellent resource library specializing in publications dealing with the social and psychological aspects of aging, also houses a namesake organization that acts as an umbrella for over 40 local organizations serving the aged. A phone call to the Aging Resource Center will allow you to get in touch with groups ranging from the Alzheimer's Association to the local Veterans Association medical center. In addition to serving as a clearinghouse for information, the center also hosts a speakers network and explores relevant community issues. One recent target was the new problems and opportunities presented by the aging of the Baby Boomers' parents.

Twenty programs are underway at any given time through the center, utilizing over 400 volunteers. Some of the most popular of these focus on intergenerational activities.

A free quarterly newsletter from the Aging Resource Center is available to help individuals stay informed about the various activities and offerings.

Kentucky Association of Homes for the Aging
1244 S. Fourth St. • 635-6468

KAHA is an association of not-for-profit homes and services, the members of which share a commitment to provide services to older persons and act as advocates for them. KAHA provides lists of retirement communities, retirement housing available on a sliding scale financial basis and family-care homes where small groups of elderly persons are cared for in private dwellings.

Nutrition Programs for Senior Citizens
• 574-6325, TDD 574-6013

Community centers serve hot, noontime meals to people 60 and older and coordinate daily activities and programs for them.

Homebound individuals older than 60 are also eligible for home-delivered meals (widely known as Meals on Wheels). There is no set fee for the lunches, but contributions of up to the full cost of $2.10 are encouraged. Many centers, however, charge $1 to $1.50 or do not charge at all if the situation warrants.

South Central Indiana Council for the Aging
426 Bank St., New Albany, Ind.
• (812) 948-8330

This group provides a truly comprehensive network of services for the people of Scott, Clark, Floyd and Harrison counties in Southern Indiana. Call the above number to get information on adult day care, legal services, transportation, nutrition programs, health services, outreach and counseling, in-home services, case management, advocacy or to speak to confidential nursing home ombudsman.

The council also oversees senior centers in Jeffersonville, New Albany, Corydon, Charlestown, Scottsburg and Austin that provide educational and recreational programs.

FYI

Unless otherwise noted, the area code for all phone numbers listed in this chapter is 502.

Residences and Communities

An excellent guide to senior housing opportunities, titled *Choices*, is published by the Aging Resource Center. We have used this 70-page booklet as a primary source for the list of communities below. Many more communities than these are listed in *Choices*; we have included the facilities that come recommended by local experts on housing for the aging and disabled. Please pose a plethora of questions to any facility you are considering for yourself or a loved one.

A word about the terms we use here: In this context, "subsidized" apartments mean the rent is determined in part by the resident's income. "Long-term care facilities" provide 24-hour assistance on a long-term basis ranging from general medical assistance and housecleaning to critical-care nursing. "Retirement community" is a catch-all phrase for facilities that provide the flexibility for everything from totally independent living to critical-care nursing.

Baptist Towers
1014 S. Second St. • 587-6632

This 17-story building stands on a patch of land in between the Old Louisville neighborhood and downtown. Almost 200 subsidized efficiency and one-bedroom apartments are available in this centrally located high rise, which was renovated in 1996. Amenities include an exercise room, laundry, community room, van outings and an activities building across the street with indoor recreation such as bingo, pot-luck dinners, games and crafts.

Episcopal Church Home
1201 Lyndon Ln. • 425-8840

Located off Westport Road in the East End of Louisville, this Christian community sits on 15 acres of land. For independent living, there are town houses and laundromats. For others, there are nonsubsidized apartments and a long-term care facility at this retirement community. There's usually a waiting list, and Episcopalians are given preference.

The Forum at Brookside
200 Brookside Dr. • 245-3048

Located in the deep East End, this retirement community does not hesitate to use the term "luxury" to describe its amenities. They include an indoor heated swimming pool, exercise room, nature trail, shuffleboard court and a pavilion that includes a beauty shop, restaurants, a library and a branch of a local bank. Nonsubsidized apartments and a long-term care are available.

Winner of a Jefferson County Beautification Award for landscaping, the facility's 38-acre grounds include formal rose gardens, walking paths, gazebos and bountiful flora, The Forum is near St. Matthews' shopping, dining and entertainment establishments.

Four Courts Senior Center
2100 Millvale Rd. • 451-0990

The setting for this retirement community is truly beautiful — and safe. To one side is Cherokee Park, to the other, a police substa-

tion. The nonsubsidized apartments are efficiency- and studio-sized, and long-term care is available. All the food is Kosher and prepared on site.

Hillebrand House
1235 S. Third St. • 636-1453

This 16-story high rise, located in Old Louisville, has subsidized efficiency and one-bedroom apartments. The Hillebrand House encourages its residents to grow flowers and vegetables in an assigned garden plot. In-house groceries, van outings, a lunch nutrition program and a beauty shop are added pluses, and the Hillebrand House sponsors many activities, including birthday parties, cookouts and pancake breakfasts.

Lourdes Hall
735 Eastern Pkwy. • 574-2626

Mature trees and pleasant walking paths beautify the green space surrounding this five-story facility of subsidized apartments, which is within walking distance of a grocery and other businesses. A residents' council plans many activities, including bingo, holiday dinners and day outings. Efficiency and one-bedroom units are available for 30 percent of your yearly income. It's located near the University of Louisville on the edge of downtown and the beginning of the city's South End.

Puritan Apartments
1244 S. Fourth St. • 634-4731

This Old Louisville building was once the Puritan Hotel, a distinguished stop in the city. Now, residents of its efficiency and one-bedroom units enjoy paid utilities and appliances at this subsidized facility. Residents enjoy a secure courtyard, a billiards room/recreational area with exercise machines, a nondenominational chapel, a laundromat, a lunch restaurant and a small, in-house grocery store.

Shalom Towers
3650 Dutchmans Ln. • 454-7795

There's a waiting list to get into this East End community, which features one- and two-bedroom units. The cost is 30 percent of your adjusted income; amenities include trash chutes on every floor, a craft room, a small chapel, a commissary and a small grocery.

Shalom Towers is very close to several shopping centers, restaurants, hospitals, doctors' offices and even an eight-screen movie house, and the public bus line stops right at the front door. Planned activities at the facility include van outings, movies and ceramics. All denominations are welcome.

Treyton Oak Towers
211 W. Oak St. • 589-3211

This retirement community is plush, with flexible care to meet a variety of needs including long-term care and amenities that include an exercise room, whirlpool, game room, library and green house. Nonsubsidized units have one, two or three bedrooms. It's located in Old Louisville.

Trinity Towers
537 S. Third St. • 584-4124

This 17-story, brick high rise has nonsubsidized efficiency and one-bedroom units both furnished and unfurnished. The location is prime: walking distance to the Galleria shopping mall in the heart of downtown. A roof garden, laundromat, 24-hour security, grocery and the nondenominational, rooftop "chapel in the sky" are additional features. Trinity Towers attracts a mix of people — roughly half are seniors and the rest include doctors, students and married couples. Parking is a problem — a lot across the street charges up to $80 a month.

Wesley Manor Retirement Center
5012 E. Manslick Rd. • 969-3277

Nestled off Preston Highway in the South End, this retirement community has a rural, park-like atmosphere and a wide variety of nonsubsidized living units. An early-stage Alzheimer's Disease care unit and other long-term medical care is available. Amenities include a beauty shop, laundromat, restaurant/dining room, nondenominational chapel and a full-time activities director who plans crafts workshops, tours, bingo and card games, visits from various entertainers and movies.

Westminster Terrace/Rose Anna Hughes Presbyterian Home
2116 Buechel Bank Rd. • 499-9383

These two buildings, which face Bardstown Road in an area southeast of downtown called Buechel, is one of the more popular retirement communities in the city. That means a waiting list — and some of the best living arrangements of any community. Nonsubsidized small studios, large studios, one-bedroom units and one-bedroom suites are available. Established in 1966, this complex has enjoyed a good reputation for years. Long-term medical care is available.

Westminster Village Kentuckiana
2200 Greentree N., Clarksville, Ind.
• (812) 282-9691

Westminster Village occupies 40 acres 20 minutes from downtown Louisville. It is owned and managed by Retirement Housing Foundation, a nonprofit organization affiliated with the United Church of Christ, which owns and manages more than 100 U.S. retirement communities. Nonsubsidized studio, one- and two-bedroom units are available, with optional carports. Westminster Village has a woodworking shop; a social center that offers lectures, films and concerts; and a park next to the complex. Long-term medical care is available.

Organizations

Service Corps of Retired Executives
• 582-5976

SCORE is a national network of volunteer business executives and professionals (mostly retired but some still active) that provides small businesses with technical and managerial training in addition to counseling. To volunteer as an advisor or to obtain information about starting your own small business, call SCORE at the Small Business Administration office number (above) between 9 AM and 2 PM weekdays.

American Association of Retired Persons
• 426-0540

AARP is a nonprofit, nonpartisan national organization that helps older Americans gain independence, dignity and purpose in their retirement years. Kentucky has 400,000 members in 63 chapters statewide. Kentucky's

AARP promotes improvements in insurance rates, health services and other quality-of-life areas. It has programs dealing with tax assistance, retirement planning, preventing discrimination and women's issues. Part of the organization's initiative is legislative lobbying.

PRO-POWER
Urban County Government Center, 810 Barret Ave. • 574-6439

More than 200 retired professionals and executives volunteer their expertise to help nonprofit agencies in this program. These skilled volunteers are ready to offer free consultation in 35 areas including administration, engineering, budgeting, marketing, public relations, systems analysis and many others. Any nonprofit human-services organization, governmental department or educational institution can receive free services from PRO-POWER.

Senior Citizens Centers

Senior Citizens East
Jeffersontown Center
10617 Taylorsville Rd. • 267-9101
Buechel/Southeast Center
3907 Bardstown Rd. • 451-0741
St. Matthews Center
311 Browns Ln. • 896-2316

These busy nonprofit centers serve the East End of the county from Jeffersontown to St. Matthews. They specialize in providing services to home-based seniors, operating programs such as Meals on Wheels (hot lunches delivered on weekdays) and a bevy of recreational programs.

The Desk Mates program features volunteers who help with insurance and personal finance problems, and with tasks like reconciling bank statements. Life Line Kentucky is an emergency monitoring system featuring a trigger button that you wear on your wrist or around your neck that is connected to a central computer. There's also a transportation program in which volunteer drivers drive seniors on their errands for a suggested dona-

tion and a companion program in which a volunteer visits a senior a few times a month to be a friend and help with small chores.

Senior Citizens East publishes a monthly newspaper with a readership of more than 25,000 people called *The Leisure Scene* that lists classes and activities offered at the three centers. Some of these include low-impact exercises, arts and crafts, games, discussion groups, classes, bridge, travel clubs and other special interest clubs.

Jewish Community Center Senior Adults Program
3600 Dutchmans Ln. • 459-0660

Kosher in-house and Meals on Wheels lunches are served Monday through Friday. Activities include excursions to arts and cultural activities; games and recreation, including billiards and table tennis; films; discussion groups; gourmet dining and walking clubs; and arts and crafts.

Publications

Senior Citizens Services Guide
810 Barret Ave. • 574-8232

The Office of the Jefferson County Judge Executive and a local hospital publish an excellent 110-page guide about books and educational opportunities, care for physically and mentally impaired adults, clothing, companionship and numerous other topics. You can pick up a free copy at Room 128 of the Urban Government Center, at the address above.

Kentucky Home Care
RAM Publishing, 3418 Frankfort Ave., Ste. 345 • 893-2610

The subtitle of this bimonthly magazine says it best: "Your Guide to Modern Caregiving." Straightforward, information-packed articles help older people and especially their caregivers understand and keep informed on issues such as Medicaid, hospice services, health conditions that particularly affect the aged, and, of course, home care providers. Call for subscription information.

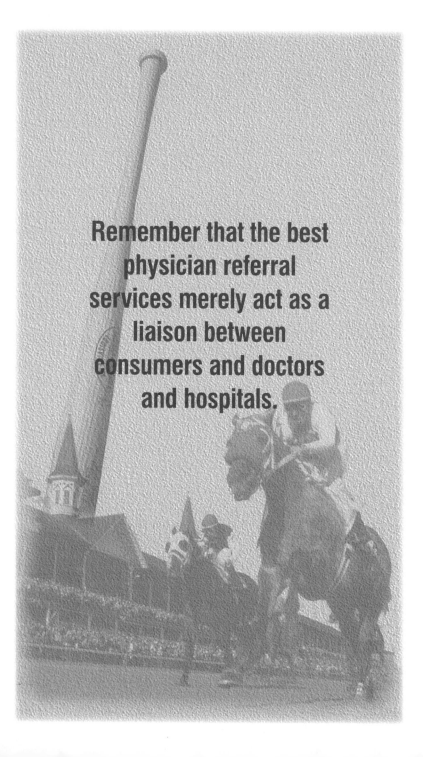

Remember that the best
physician referral
services merely act as a
liaison between
consumers and doctors
and hospitals.

Healthcare

Louisvillians care about healthcare. Sure, everybody cares about their personal health, but this is a city with an economy that is driven in no small amount by healthcare dollars.

Thus, most everyone forms pseudo-wise opinions about which hospital is the best, which doctor is good at hand surgery, or who the best neurologist is. They form these positions because their sister, their mom, or their best friend works in healthcare and knows the straight story, the real deal. These convictions are so rampant they go completely unnoticed. In this chapter, we hit you with some of our own opinions. Please make calls to find the best hospital or treatment center for you. Of course, we're sure you'll end up agreeing with us in the end, because we know the real deal, the straight story. We heard it from our big brother.

Whatever ails you can probably be treated at one of Louisville's medical facilities — even if what you need is a new heart.

Thanks to the early work of heart transplants and artificial hearts that occurred at Audubon Hospital, Louisville's reputation for heart surgery is a national one. But we have other strengths. There are clinics dedicated to women's health problems, inpatient and outpatient psychiatric care, a children's hospital and rehabilitation centers. The University of Louisville School of Medicine contributes immensely to the high quality of care and services, complemented by the city's physicians and support practitioners.

In the early 1800s, when Louisville was a mere settlement at the Falls of the Ohio, physicians were already part of the community. Stagnant ponds and low river levels in summer created a breeding ground for mosquitoes. Malaria, called "the Fever," became the first real public health problem, along with diseases transmitted by dirty well water. During the 1822 epidemic, physicians came to Louisville to treat the sick. Only the fall frosts killed the mosquitoes, and the Fever returned every summer. Smallpox and measles killed many others. The first public health officer, appointed in 1814, recommended draining the ponds and urged the creation of the first public water supplies.

In 1823 the first public medical facility, Louisville Marine Hospital, was established to care for transient mariners. Some doctors trained apprentices; medical education was formalized in 1838 with the opening of the Louisville Medical Institute, which trained Southerners in hopes that they would stay to practice medicine in the South. More than 50 percent of the Institute's students were from Kentucky.

In response to the influx of population during the Civil War, enrollment in the medical schools increased, and Louisville assumed importance as a medical teaching center. The Kentucky School of Medicine was founded in Louisville in 1850. There were numerous military hospitals here during the Civil War, some in barns and warehouses — wherever patients could be housed.

During the 1870s and '80s, hospitals were organized to serve the religious communities, and the presence of a medical school greatly improved the quality of medical care in the community. This upward trend continued into the late 19th century with better techniques for fighting contagious illnesses.

Louisville's hospitals became even more important after World War II as doctors came for training through supervision of the American College of Surgeons, the American Medical Association and the American Hospital Association. An expanding base of knowledge and the development of technology contributed to the growth of many specialties in medicine.

Today, hospital "chains" dominate the medical landscape in Louisville. The metamorphosis to this state of affairs was not painless; Columbia moved its headquarters to Nashville under rather tense circumstances, and the Louisville public seems to be holding a solid grudge against the hospital system giant. Kentucky's insurance laws have made it increasingly difficult to understand where to go for covered healthcare, and the HMO system has only exacerbated the confusion. Check with your insurance provider to sort out the particulars of your coverage.

Luckily, healthcare from top to bottom is pretty good in the river city — no matter where you end up.

Physician Referral Services

Many of the numbers below are associated with a hospital or healthcare provider. They are naturally going to try for your business. Remember that the best physician referral services merely act as a liaison between consumers and doctors and hospitals.

These numbers are good to call if you have a medical problem or need and don't know what kind of doctor would treat it, or you need to find out data on types of insurance accepted by a given doctor's office, hours of operation or basic fees. But remember that just because a physician is mentioned doesn't necessarily mean that the physician was screened or is recommended by the service. It simply means that the physician asked to be on the list or is otherwise affiliated with the service.

Also, if you have an urgent need for medical care and it is after business hours, go to an emergency room or an immediate care center.

Baptist Hospital East • 897-8131
Humana On-Call Physician Information Service • 580-5000
Jefferson Co. Medical Society • 589-2001
Kentucky Academy of Physicians • 451-0370
Kentucky Podiatric Medicine Association • 425-1333
M.D. Connection • 361-6363
Physician Finder • 629-7300
Physician Referral Service • 587-4912

St. Anthony Medical Center • 627-1450
DRCALL (Jewish Hospital) • 587-4912, (800) 333-2230

Hospitals

Louisville

Alliant Medical Pavilion

315 E. Broadway • 629-2000, Emergencies 629-7200

The Alliant Medical Pavilion opened in 1960, the result of a shared venture of the United Methodist Church and the United Church of Christ.

Its outpatient orthopedic services are widely recognized for detecting and treating acute and chronic joint problems and arthritis. The Diabetes and Endocrine Center, the first local program recognized by the American Diabetes Association, attracts patients from across the region.

The Decontamination Center is nationally and internationally recognized as a leader in the handling of victims exposed to toxic chemicals. This facility also gives special care to the worker — Health at Work, an Alliant occupational medicine program, provides pre-employment screenings, physicals and emergency care as well as ongoing health promotion services to help local business and industry control healthcare expenditures while providing health services to their employees. The Progressive Care Unit eases the transition for patients moving from full-scale hospital care to life at home.

Additionally, the Alliant Medical Pavilion is known for its outpatient cancer treatment and surgical oncology programs, and it houses the resource center for Alliant's The Women's Pavilion (a respected medical center that covers obstetrical care, breast care, osteoporosis and a host of other women's health needs).

Columbia Audubon Regional Hospital

1 Audubon Plaza Dr. • 636-7111

This 480-bed acute-care hospital, part of

the Columbia chain, is noted for cardiovascular medicine (Audubon Heart Institute), neurological diagnosis and treatment (Neuroscience Center of Excellence) and a full range of women's and children's services. The Emergency Department offers 24-hour emergency care, including a dedicated Chest Pain Center staffed by a team of physician and nursing specialists certified in Advanced Cardiac Life Support.

Audubon's Advanced Cardiovascular Institute's treatments include a number of innovative ones, such as the Palmaz-Schatz balloon-expandable stent, open heart surgery (with or without the use of blood products) and heart transplants.

Other treatments are available through Audubon's Sleep Disorders Center, Non-Invasive Vascular Lab, Fetal Diagnostics Center, Neonatal Intensive Care Nursery, day surgery program and breast diagnostic services.

Baptist Hospital East
4000 Kresge Way • 897-8100

Baptist Hospital East, a 407-bed acute care hospital in suburban St. Matthews, is 9 miles east of downtown Louisville. It's one of the region's top 10 employers, it's known for general medical and surgical care, and it sits in the center of a 52-acre park-like campus that also includes three physician office buildings, a day care center and a parking garage.

Baptist Hospital also has full maternity care, a cardiac rehabilitation center, multiple sclerosis and muscular dystrophy clinics, a sleep disorders lab and cancer treatment center. Five satellite facilities offer a variety of services ranging from family counseling to occupational health and wellness.

Jewish Hospital
217 E. Chestnut St. • 587-4011, (800) 333-2230

Jewish Hospital HealthCare Services developed from a single facility — Jewish Hospital — that opened its doors in 1905. Today Jewish Hospital is a 442-bed regional referral center that has a formal relationship with the University of Louisville School of Medicine involving training and research projects.

The skinny: Jewish Hospital is arguably the best place for heart and lung treatment in Louisville, and quite possibly one of the best in the nation. In addition to their expertise in these areas, the hospital's staff also focuses on neuroscience, occupational medicine, organ transplant, outpatient care, plastic/aesthetic surgery, primary care and rehab medicine.

The Transplant Center, in partnership with the U of L School of Medicine, performed Kentucky's first heart/lung, pancreas and liver transplants. The Center is approved to perform all five solid organ transplants (heart, kidney, liver, lung and pancreas).

JHHS opened Kentucky's first freestanding outpatient care facility in 1986, adjacent to Jewish Hospital. Emergency and urgent support are available at a moment's notice.

The Plastic and Aesthetic Surgery Center was the first in the region dedicated to the plastic surgery patient. The hotel-like atmosphere and specially trained staff offer unique and personal care for plastic, cosmetic and reconstructive procedures.

Since 1954, rehab services for Jewish Hospital are provided through Frazier Rehab Center, a 95-bed regional healthcare system dedicated entirely to rehabilitation. Frazier has nine branches beyond its main facility on Abraham Flexner Way.

Kosair Children's Hospital
231 E. Chestnut St. • 629-6000, Emergencies 629-7225

Kosair Children's Hospital is Kentucky's only full-service hospital for children, and its care is sufficient to be named one of the nation's 10 best by *Child* magazine. Patients come from all 50 states and other countries, but its primary mission is to serve the children of Kentucky and Southern Indiana.

INSIDERS' TIP

Some pediatricians in the Louisville area now have separate waiting rooms for contagious and noncontagious children.

The hospital was founded in 1892; its first location was a three-story house at 220 E. Chestnut Street, with 25 beds. It consolidated with Norton Hospital in 1969 and with Kosair Crippled Children's Hospital in 1981. In 1986 the facility opened at its current location.

Say "Kosair," and Louisvillians will immediately think of this hospital's reputation for two things: cancer and severe burn treatment. The oncology department is considered a national leader in cancer treatment and has received national acclaim for its high survival rate of patients with certain leukemias. Kosair's burn unit is Kentucky's first and only burn unit for kids.

The hospital's Center for Children with Diabetes is strong in education and emotional support, and it has a complete medical facility for treatment and care. Kosair's neonatal intensive care unit and pediatric intensive care unit have phone numbers that many Louisville parents keep close by. Their reputations are sterling. In 1985 the hospital began using a heart/lung bypass procedure that allows a child's lungs to rest, changing the odds from an 80 percent chance of dying to a 94 percent chance of living.

Other areas of care at Kosair include allergy, poison control/toxicology, psychiatry, craniofacial disorders, neurodiagnostics/neurosurgery, cardiovascular surgery, radiology and rehabilitation.

The Louisville Veterans Administration Medical Center
800 Zorn Ave. • 895-3401

In 1952 The Louisville Veteran's Administration Medical Center opened to care for the burgeoning patient population after World War II and, later, the Korean Conflict and Vietnam Era veterans. Today the hospital is a 310-bed acute-care facility serving nearly 180,000 veterans in Kentuckiana. The Louisville VAMC handles more than 166,000 visits annually for a variety of services, including ophthalmology, substance abuse treatment, Post Traumatic Stress Disorder, infectious disease treatment, cardiac rehabilitation and wellness programs.

Norton Hospital
200 E. Chestnut St. • 629-8000, Emergency 629-7200

Norton Hospital was founded by the women of St. Paul's Episcopal Church in 1886. It's now a major component of the University of Louisville School of Medicine's residency and medical education programs. But it's beloved in this community for The Women's Pavilion, an area of Norton's that is breathtaking in its inclusive, patient-friendly treatment of female patients. The Pavilion enjoys a good reputation for its general and high-risk obstetrics, breast care, fertility center, cosmetic and reconstructive surgery, woman's heart center, gynecological surgery and mid-life care center. Its prenatal and postnatal care for mother and child alike are highly touted. And a pedway connects The Women's Pavilion to Kosair Children's Hospital, in case more intensive care is needed.

Norton's spine and neuroscience treatment is well-respected as well. The Kenton D. Leatherman Spine Center offers medical and surgical options for spinal injuries and pain, and the hospital's Brain Institute is noted for its special emphasis on strokes and their immediate treatment.

For more than four decades, the Norton Psychiatric Clinic has provided psychiatric care in a medical setting. It introduced a cognitive behavioral therapy program to combat depression and was one of the first facilities to offer an adolescent treatment program. Norton's also has dedicated departments for heart disease, cancer treatment and bone and joint disorders.

CARITAS Medical Center
1850 Bluegrass Ave. • 361-6000

Formerly Saints Mary & Elizabeth Hospital, a 331-bed facility run by the Sisters of

---

INSIDERS' TIP

Midwifery is enjoying a newfound respectability in the Louisville obstetrical world.

Louisville-based Humana, a large medical insurance company, built this skyscraper to serve as its headquarters.

Charity of Nazareth, this entity now encompasses the previous hospital plus the CARITAS Peace Center (formerly Our Lady Of Peace), one of the largest private psychiatric hospitals in the country (see our later entry in this chapter). CARITAS also has a number of smaller treatment centers/clinics in the area treating both physical and mental health.

CARITAS's strengths include cancer treatment, pain management, diabetes treatment, cardiopulmonary services, cardiac rehabilitation, sports medicine, occupational health and holistic medicine/wellness programs. The company retains its links to the Catholic archdiocese.

Columbia Southwest Hospital
9820 Old Third St. • 933-8100

Since 1978 Columbia Southwest Hospital, a 150-bed acute medical/surgical hospital, has provided diagnostic, therapeutic and surgical services, including a 24-hour emergency department, to the residents of southwest Jefferson County.

The hospital has an eight-bed intensive/coronary care unit and a 20-bed transitional care unit.

The Diagnostic/Outpatient and Educational Services include day surgery and a monitored cardiac rehabilitation program. The occupational medical program serves local businesses.

Inpatient and outpatient services include

cardiology testing, cardiac catheterization lab, physical therapy, respiratory therapy and diagnostic imaging services. Columbia Southwest Hospital has a dedicated endoscopy suite and a surgical suite with four operating rooms.

Columbia Suburban Hospital
4001 Dutchmans Ln. • 893-1000, Emergencies 893-1083

Columbia Suburban Hospital in St. Matthews opened in 1972 to meet the needs of people living in eastern Jefferson County and surrounding areas. Its location, smack dab in the middle of the largest medical hub outside of downtown Louisville, makes it convenient for most Louisvillians. Suburban's specialties include the Advanced Orthopedic Center for treatment of arthritic and other bone and joint disorders; The Birthing Center, including a special care nursery and private rooms; a urological center, including lithotripsy services for advanced treatment of kidney stones; The Advanced Surgical Care Center, which utilizes lasers and other innovative technology for advanced surgical procedures; and the Wound Care Center, which treats wounds that won't heal.

Outpatient services include day surgery, diagnostic imaging, cardiac and pulmonary rehabilitation, physical therapy and respiratory therapy. In addition, the 380-bed hospital has a 24-hour physician-staffed emergency department.

University of Louisville Hospital
539 S. Jackson St. • 562-3000, Emergencies 562-3015

This hospital, which recently regained its independence after a rather acrimonious split with the Columbia system, is known for its excellent emergency room treatment. Louisvillians up on the area's medical facilities could very well have another preference for

general hospital care, but if you are seriously injured in an accident, University Hospital's ER is where you want to go.

The 404-bed acute, tertiary facility is affiliated with the University of Louisville School of Medicine and has 24-hour, in-house specialty coverage and up-to-date diagnostic and clinical protocols. The facility houses Kentucky's only adult Level I Trauma Center, and the STAT Flight emergency helicopter services makes treatment accessible to the western half of Kentucky and Southern Indiana.

FYI

Unless otherwise noted, the area code for all phone numbers listed in this chapter is 502.

Southern Indiana

Clark Memorial Hospital
1220 Missouri Ave. at I-65, Jeffersonville, Ind. • (812) 282-6631, (800) 866-4415

Clark Memorial Hospital has been providing healthcare services to Southern Indiana residents for three-quarters of a century. In 1992 it affiliated with Jewish Hospital HealthCare Services. The 285-bed system focuses on advanced care with a hometown touch. Among its services are emergency care, maternal-child health, inpatient psychiatric care, occupational health, home health and cardiology. Clark Memorial and Jewish Hospital have teamed up in a nursing-education program, a cardiac-catheterization lab and the Health and Information Center at River Falls Mall in Clarksville that provides health screenings, physician referrals and a resource library.

Floyd Memorial Hospital
1850 State St., New Albany, Ind. • (812) 944-7701

The Joslin Center for Diabetes makes a strong claim as being the area's best treatment center for diabetes — for adults, expectant mothers and children. Affiliated with the Joslin Diabetes Center in Boston, Floyd

Memorial's program keeps close ties to the Boston staff, and the American Diabetes Association has officially recognized the center's work.

Beyond the Joslin Center, this hospital is home to a large staff covering a variety of medical specialties. The radiology and cardiology departments have up-to-date equipment; the emergency room is ready with 24-hour service. A sleep disorder lab and a bevy of wellness programs also serve the Southern Indiana community.

Floyd Memorial has grown from a small community hospital into a 266-bed healthcare center. A study of the nation's 5,600 acute-care hospitals, conducted by Health Care Investments Analysis and an independent consultants firm, recently determined that Floyd Memorial is among the top 100 in offering cost-effective care.

Psychiatric and Mental Health Facilities

Louisville

Brooklawn Youth Services
2125 Goldsmith Ln. • 451-5177

Brooklawn Youth Services, a nonprofit ministry that focuses on boys ages 8 to 17 who suffer from severe emotional and behavioral problems, traces its origins back to 1851. In 1991 it became the first psychiatric residential treatment facility in Kentucky. Of particular concern are youth who have had numerous placements or who have suffered physical, sexual or emotional abuse, abandonment and adoption failure. Brooklawn's 25-acre campus houses two programs — one designed for group living and the development of self control and the other focusing on the building of healthy relationships with peers, adults and society.

Charter Louisville Behavioral Health System
1405 Browns Ln. • 896-0495, (800) 292-2747

Established in 1979, Charter is one of many psychiatric facilities owned by Charter Medical Corporation, the largest private behavioral-health system in America. Charter Hospital of Louisville, a 66-bed facility, provides care for adolescents and adults with emotional, behavioral or related substance-abuse problems. Inpatient, partial hospitalization, intensive outpatient programs and outpatient counseling are the core of Charter Louisville's care. In addition, the Charter Diagnostic Center provides a battery of tests used to help diagnose individuals who have attention deficit disorder, maladaptive behaviors, learning deficits and other problems. Free confidential assessments are available 24 hours a day by calling the telephone numbers above.

CARITAS Peace Center
2020 Newburg Rd. • 451-3330, Emergencies 451-3333

The foundation was laid nearly 180 years ago for what was called Our Lady of Peace Hospital, one of the largest nonprofit psychiatric facilities in the United States. In 1812 The Sisters of Charity of Nazareth began caring for frontier families in Bardstown. The Sisters' numbers grew, as did the extent of their charity.

Through the years the Sisters provided medical services to Civil War casualties, operated a girls boarding house and opened a Louisville home for patients with psychiatric and nervous disorders. In the late 1940s, the Sisters raised funds to build a new hospital, known as Our Lady of Peace, which opened February 1, 1951.

The hospital has since become part of the CARITAS system, but it still stresses healing the whole person — body, mind and spirit— through programs for children, adolescents and adults suffering from addictions, emotional, behavioral and psychiatric disorders.

The hospital has a network of neighborhood centers for outpatient care and counseling throughout Greater Louisville. It offers programs for children ages 3 through 18 as well as geriatric patients and those with addictions.

Ten Broeck Hospital
**8521 La Grange Rd. • 426-6380,
(800) 866-TURN**

Ten Broeck Hospital is a 94-bed private psychiatric and substance abuse hospital that treats adults (including geriatric patients), adolescents and children. The hospital, with 97 acres of landscaped grounds in eastern Jefferson County (the former site of Kentucky Military Institute), provides full psychiatric services. Mental health and addiction treatment is available as inpatient care, partial hospitalization, or outpatient programs. Free assessments are available 24 hours a day at Ten Broeck Hospital or at a pre-approved site.

Seven Counties Services Inc.
101 W. Muhammad Ali Blvd. • 589-8600

Seven Counties Services is the largest of Kentucky's comprehensive community mental-health centers and one of the largest centers in the United States. The private, nonprofit corporation has a staff of 1,000 employees working in psychiatry, social work, nursing, counseling, rehabilitation and other related fields, supplemented by more than 400 volunteers. The agency targets care for mental health, mental retardation and chemical dependency and provides counseling services in Bullitt, Henry, Jefferson, Oldham, Shelby, Spencer and Trimble counties.

The Jefferson Alcohol and Drug Abuse Center offers inpatient and outpatient chemical-dependency treatment services, and the Developmental Services Division specializes in services for people with mental retardation. Seven Counties Services serves patients all along the mental healthcare continuum, from emergencies to halfway houses, from addiction treatment to family counseling, from occupational stress management programs to school-based initiatives.

There is also a 24-hour telephone crisis hotline, which handles about 100,000 calls a year, and 24-hour, 7-day a week psychiatric services for children in acute psychiatric or emotional distress.

Hospice Services

Hospice of Louisville
3532 Ephraim McDowell Dr. • 456-6200

This nonprofit, nondenominational agency, founded in 1978, was the first hospice in Kentucky. It provides support services for terminally ill patients and their families through physical, emotional and spiritual care. This agency serves residents of seven counties, regardless of ability to pay. Care is primarily provided in the home but can also be administered in a hospital or nursing home.

Emergencies

Below are a list of walk-in clinics and emergency numbers if you or a child needs medical care.

Walk-In Clinics

These walk-in clinics expect to get paid at the time of your visit, but they will bill your insurance company afterward. Use your common sense — if someone is seriously injured, the emergency room of a hospital is where they belong. But for smaller injuries, these neighborhood clinics are just the thing.

Alliant Immediate Care Centers
**7926 Preston Hwy. • 964-4357
1102 Lyndon Ln. • 423-7911
10284 Shelbyville Rd. • 244-5827
9409 Cedarlook Dr. • 239-8431
610 Eastern Blvd., Clarksville, Ind.
• (812) 284-5014**

These clinics are open every day from 9 AM to 9 PM. A basic visit starts at $65.

Columbia Primary Care Centers
Hikes Point Family Healthcare Center, 3606 Klondike Ln., Ste. A • 451-4322

It's open 9 AM to 4:30 PM Monday through Friday, 8:30 to 11:30 AM on Saturday and is closed on Sunday. A basic visit starts at $86. The clinic is staffed with general practitioners.

Fairdale Family Healthcare Center
189 Outer Loop • 361-0159

Open from 9 AM to 5 PM Monday through Friday, the clinic is staffed with general practitioners. A basic visit costs $50.

The Family Healthcare Center in Fern Creek
9131 Fern Creek Rd. • 239-3228

It's open from 9 AM to 5 PM Monday through Friday, 9 AM to noon on Saturday and closed on Sunday. A basic visit costs $65. The clinic is staffed with general practitioners.

Floyd Memorial Hospital Urgent Care Center
800 Highlander Point Landmark Bldg., Floyds Knobs, Ind. • (812) 923-6336

This clinic operates as more of an extension of the hospital than a neighborhood clinic, but it can take a look at that weird insect bite too. It's open 10 AM to 9 PM Monday through Friday and 10 AM to 6 PM on Saturday and Sunday. A visit costs $50 and up.

Southside Primary Care Center
5334 South Third St. • 367-2288

This clinic is equipped to do a little more than a GP's office. It's open from 9 AM to 4 PM Monday through Friday, and a basic visit starts at $45.

Emergency Numbers

Police/Fire/Medical Emergency • 911
Crisis and Information Hotline
• 589-4313
Poison Control Center • 589-8222
Crimes Against Children Unit • 574-2465
Legal Aid Society • 584-1254
Public Defender • 574-3800
Hazardous Wastes • 595-4254

Crisis Intervention and Social Services

Metro United Way InfoLine • 589-4770
Adult Protective Services • 595-4803
Child Protective Services • 595-4550
Rape and Sexual Assault Hotline
• 581-7273
Spouse Abuse Center • 581-7222

Jefferson County's
public schools have won
national recognition for
pioneering moves in
education.

Schools and Child Care

Public schooling has been among the hottest topics in Kentucky in recent years, and there's little chance it will cool off any time soon, thanks to four letters: KERA.

That's the acronym for the 1990 Kentucky Education Reform Act, which came about when a group of property-poor school districts sued the state school system, charging that Kentucky schools were inadequately and inequitably funded. In 1989 the state Supreme Court ruled the school system unconstitutional. Instead of simply reapportioning the money, the General Assembly did something more drastic: It completely remade the state's schools, not only their financing but their governance, the way they're assessed and held accountable — the entire system. All of a sudden, Kentucky, where the educational mantra had been "Thank God for Mississippi," was the nation's leader in education reform.

The complicated law — more than 1000 pages — creates a set of learning goals the thrust of which is the application of knowledge rather than its acquisition, as well as improving drop-out rates, attendance and the percentage of graduates who make a successful transition to college, work or the military.

Students are tested in grades 4, 8 and 11. The assessments combine short essay and multiple-choice tests, performance tests in which groups of students demonstrate their ability to transpose what they've learned into new situations and examinations of student portfolios. Schools are expected to show progress against a baseline set in the 1991-92 school year (so they're measured against themselves rather than better-advantaged schools). The schools that improve are finan-cially rewarded; those that fail to improve face a number of possible sanctions, including dismissal of educators and takeover by the state Department of Education. The department publishes yearly results, school by school and county by county, that show their progress. KERA also increased (and evened out) school funding, via an income tax increase, and required a major investment in technology.

KERA doesn't mandate any particular classroom strategies, except the primary program, which replaces the normal structure of kindergarten and the first three grades with multi-age, multi-ability classrooms. (Everyone still refers to children's status by the traditional "1st-grader," etc., rather than "Primary 2" and the like.)

But to meet KERA's goals, most schools are employing a number of reform ideas, such as so-called "whole language instruction" (which uses real literature rather than readers and involves much more writing than former methods of teaching literacy); and cooperative learning in small groups as well as individual work. (Teachers assure parents that competition has not vanished from the classroom.)

KERA has attracted a good deal of criticism. There are those who believe that its learning goals include attempts to inculcate values that should be taught in the home. (Especially this mystifyingly controversial one: "Schools shall develop their students' ability to become responsible members of a family, work group or community." Not with my kid you don't.) Others believe "the basics" are being neglected, although KERA's intention is to teach basic skills along with higher-order skills, such as fluent writing. The method of assessing school performance has been attacked as too subjective, and after some tests for the '96-97 school year were graded too low, the state fired the consultant that designed the test. Even supporters of reform say that educators have not done a good job of explaining KERA to the community.

It will take years before KERA's results are clear — some key parts of the reform (such as school-based decision-making councils of teachers, parents and principals, which will actually determine the course the school is to take) have only been in place a year at this writing. The first students to have had their entire education under KERA's provisions will graduate in 2008, a long time to wait for a question of politics and public policy to resolve itself.

But some changes are already visible: The average teacher salary increased 18 percent, lifting Kentucky from 38th to 29th nationally; per-pupil expenditures increased 35 percent, a shift from 42nd to 29th nationally; and the disparity between the richest and poorest school districts was cut in half between 1990 and 1993. There is a feeling of energy and excitement in the schools — as well as stress from changing long-established ways of doing things.

KERA is only one aspect of a diverse, competitive school scene in the metropolitan Louisville area. Jefferson County's public schools have won national recognition for pioneering moves in education. The school systems outside Jefferson County often sell themselves as alternatives to Jefferson — partly because of the very real instances of excellence they've achieved, partly because Jefferson County continues to have busing for desegregation (although the busing system has changed radically in recent years).

The reform act only applies to Kentucky's public schools, and many private schools are seen by parents as a refuge from the uncertainties of a changing school system — although many others were using education reform methods years before KERA. In short, a parent in this area doesn't lack for choices in education.

Here's a directory of the public school systems and some of the leading private schools in the area, as well as several important childcare services.

Public Schools

Kentucky

Jefferson County Public Schools
VanHoose Education Center, 3332 Newburg Rd. • 485-3011

FYI

Unless otherwise noted, the area code for all phone numbers listed in this chapter is 502.

The Jefferson County system — merged by court order in 1975, although city and county governments remain distinct — is one of the country's 24 largest school districts, with more than 96,000 students in 87 elementary schools, 23 middle schools, 20 high schools and 20 other learning centers that offer alternative and special education programs. Sixty-seven percent of JCPS graduates go on to college or other post-secondary schooling, a good percentage for a school system that includes many impoverished inner-city areas in its boundaries (and whose area has a number of alternatives for more affluent families to opt out of the Jefferson County system).

Because it's so large, JCPS offers a greater range of educational options than any other local education system. There are more than 90 different options and magnet programs, from elementary through high school, including the Youth Performing Arts School, traditional programs and magnet career academies — a national trend in which Jefferson County has been a leader — in subjects from aviation to public safety technologies. One caveat: a parent has to take the initiative to ask the district what these choices are (JCPS has a yearly magnet fair, and printed information about its programs is readily available).

The system received national attention in the 1980s for rebounding from the problems caused by its 1975 desegregation. The most important of its innovations was the 1983 New Kid in School program that put computers in every classroom at a time when they were rare; it's been continued as New Kid Moves Ahead. The national average for school technology is one computer for every 50 students; JCPS has one for every eight. The system has also been a leader in forging school/business partnerships (in 1990 it won the National Alliance of Business Distinguished Performance Award for such partnerships). It has sometimes seemed to take the attitude that KERA was more necessary for the rest of the state than it was for Jefferson County — which reformers on the state level will tell you is assuredly not the case — but that's only a reflection of how far ahead of the reform game JCPS (or parts of it) was before KERA was passed.

The system won the National Alliance of Business 1993 Scholastic Community Award for excellence in education; the organization called JCPS "one of the country's true trailblazers in the area of education reform." Teachers from this system have been named National Teacher of the Year (in 1984), Kentucky Teacher of the Year (in 1984, 1989 and 1993) and have won Presidential Awards for Excellence in teaching math, among many awards. Two schools, Manual High School and Wheeler Elementary, were named Blue Ribbon Schools by the U.S Department of Education; Fairdale High School and its former principal, Marilyn Hohmann, have been among the most studied and emulated schools and educators of recent years. The former superintendent, the PR-savvy (to a fault, some would say) Donald Ingwerson, was National Superintendent of the Year in 1992.

In 1992 the school district revamped its system of busing for elementary schools. Project Renaissance relies on a mix of magnet schools and special programs to desegregate the system by choice rather than forced assignments. Middle school students are assigned to schools in geographic attendance zones drawn to ensure racial balance; so are high school students, although all 9th graders have the option of choosing a school under an Open Enrollment Policy (about 80 percent of requests are approved). The various magnet schools have different requirements for enrollment.

The Advance Program is for students judged to have exceptional academic abilities; it culminates in a number of Advanced Placement high school classes. Some educational experts believe this sort of tracking is incompatible with education reform, but the Advance Program — which has grown dramatically in number of students during the past 20 years — has strong advocates among parents, and it won't go without a major fight (although it's likely to change to a more informal classroom identification, rather than the old pattern of separate Advance classes, especially in the primary grades.)

The JCPS food service was recently recognized by a nutrition-advocacy group for improving its meals to include less fat — only 32 percent of calories came from fat, as compared to 38 percent nationally (nutritionists recommend 30 percent or less of our calories come from fat). Students participate in tastings to choose much of the menu, and schools have included a variety of educational efforts related to nutrition.

A number of schools have Family Resource Centers that assist families with any problem presenting a barrier to learning and serve as a sort of clearinghouse for social services information.

Information is available from the school district's FACTLINE at 473-3228; a relocation package is available for newcomers.

Anchorage Independent School District
11400 Ridge Rd. • 245-8927

One of this affluent, bucolic community's

great sources of pride is its excellent school system for children in kindergarten through grade 8, the other public system in Jefferson County. Fourth and 8th graders consistently score at the top of statewide tests, and it's no wonder: With 420 pupils and 38 teachers, it has a low teacher-student ratio that allows for a good deal of individualized attention; the high tax rate in the district (91.7¢ per $100) pours lots of resources into the school (75 percent of the school's $3.5 million budget comes from Anchorage taxes).

It's located in an attractive building — white stucco with a red tile roof, begun in 1912 and added onto through 1990. It looks more like a mansion than a schoolhouse, although few mansions have two gyms and a 400-seat auditorium.

The school offers Special Education, Extended School Services and a Gifted and Talented program. Kindergartners in the "Lunch Bunch" can stay until the upper school dismisses; there is no after-school care. Anchorage competes in soccer, basketball and track and field.

Because the school district basically conforms to the boundaries of Anchorage, the school offers no transportation. Parents in the process of building a home in Anchorage can pay tuition for their children to attend the school; likewise, families who move out of the district when school is in session can pay tuition to finish out the year.

Bullitt County Schools
1040 Ky. Hwy. 44 E., Shepherdsville
• (502) 543-2271, Louisville 955-6269

Compared to Jefferson County, it's a small district — 10,000 students, 18 schools, an annual budget of $44,702,000 — but it still ranks as one of the state's larger systems. In 1994

Bullitt County invested $4.5 million in technology, putting four computers into each elementary classroom, hooked into a central file server. A system-wide network comes online during the '97-98 school year. A program for gifted students called I-Leap or GT (depending on grade level) is available, not as a separate track but as a resource to qualifying students within a class and as a separate class in the upper levels.

Oldham County Schools
2510 S. Ky. Hwy. 292, LaGrange
• 222-8880

The highly regarded system has doubled in size in the past 20 years, in keeping with Oldham County's population growth. OCS is the 14th-largest school district in the state, with 7,800 students in its 12 schools; the system has an average 18-to-1 student-teacher ratio.

It boasts one of the state's lowest drop-out rates — 97 percent of its students graduate; 70 percent of graduates go on to college (another 3 percent pursue other post-secondary education). *Money* magazine selected Oldham County's schools in 1996 as one of its "100 Top Schools in Towns You Can Afford." In the state assessment tests results released in 1996, Oldham County was the highest-ranking county district (although a few independent school districts did better).

The system was a leader in implementing KERA: Centerfield Elementary was one of six state model schools for the primary program.

Six of its schools (including four of the six elementary schools) have been recognized as National Schools of Excellence by the U.S. Department of Education. Teachers have been named Kentucky Teacher of the Year (and others have been finalists for the honor), earned

---

INSIDERS' TIP

Jefferson County Schools desegregate by means of Project Renaissance, which uses magnet schools and other programs to attract white students to minority neighborhoods. These are often some of the most sought-after schools in the district. Parents should be aware that there's a November showcase of the various "options and magnets," as the term goes, and a deadline in January or February to apply.

Kids are all smiles at Metro Parks' summer camps.

Presidential Awards for Excellence and a number of other honors.

Population pressures put strains on the system's physical capacity earlier in the decade — in some schools, classes were forced to meet in cafeterias and on auditorium stages. But after the county school board passed a tax increase, the system's been building new facilities like gangbusters — a new middle school in 1996, a major addition to La Grange Elementary in 1997 and a new elementary school scheduled for 1998 and other construction is almost certainly in the works.

Shelby County Public Schools
403 Washington St., Shelbyville
• (502) 633-2375

Like Oldham, Shelby County has been a leader in implementing KERA.

It's the state's pilot district for the Kentucky Education Technology System (KETS). All of the schools have their computers linked into a network that is further linked, through the central office, with the state Department of Education (this also means that all computer stations have the capacity to access the Internet). Library catalogs and checkout are computerized, and the system has widespread E-mail capability. The system was also a pilot for the

primary program and for the fashion in which districts might design their KERA-mandated plans for transforming themselves.

Its gifted and talented program works on an informal, in-classroom basis in the early grades and moves on to honors and advanced placement classes; a number of different programs serve students with disabilities (including some technological applications).

Shelby County Technical School teaches a variety of vocational subjects, from automotive technology to health services, and also offers entry-level skill training to adults from Shelby and six neighboring counties. The system consists of 10 schools with about 4,600 students and 300 teachers (among them, a state secondary Teacher of the Year, along with other honors) and other certified staff. The annual budget is $19.6 million.

Indiana

Clarksville Community School Corporation
200 Ettels Ln., Clarksville • (812) 282-7753

This small system for the city of Clarksville (a total of 1,423 students) consists of two elementary schools, a middle school and a high school. Elementary class sizes range from 18

Photo: Metro Parks

in the primary grades to 23 in fourth and fifth grades.

Fifth graders go on an annual camping trip to a nearby park, and some members of the class produce news, weather and sports programs broadcast to the rest of the school. Middle school students receive at least six weeks of computer instruction. In 1997 the system completed a major computer upgrade that put computers in each classroom; all schools are linked and have Internet access, and all teachers have laptops that can dial in (allowing, for example, a teacher at home sick to communicate with students and substitute).

Clarksville High School's graduating classes average 100, and the average classroom has fewer than 20 students. The high school completed a $15.9 million renovation (including a new gym) in 1996.

Greater Clark County Schools
2710 E. Ind. Hwy. 62, Jeffersonville
• (812) 283-0701

The largest of the three Clark County school systems — 18th-largest in Indiana — serves Jeffersonville, Charlestown, New Washington, Nabb and Utica, among other communities on the east side of the county. It has nearly 10,000 students in 18 schools.

All schools have their own Internet access and are designing their own web pages. Spring Hill Elementary offers the only Montessori program in Southern Indiana. And the system has a national reputation for including special education students — the NEA recognized Clark County Co-Op as one of the nation's top two sites for inclusion.

The system includes educators who have been recognized as the state Teacher of the Year in art, conservation and physical education and state Counselor of the Year. Utica Elementary, which has a 4-to-1 student-computer ratio, has a MIDI computer/synthesizer for composing music electronically.

New Albany-Floyd County Consolidated Schools
2813 Grant Line Rd. • (812) 949-4200

As the ninth-largest system in Indiana, New Albany-Floyd schools have won recognition for everything from the student symphony to organizational restructuring. And it's been a leader for years — New Albany High School was the first public high school in Indiana, opening in 1853.

The system has 13 elementary schools, three junior highs, two high schools and a vocational school serving five neighboring counties. There are 12,000 pupils and 700 teachers; the staff includes the 1992 Indiana Teacher of the Year and a number of finalists for that honor. The budget is $43.7 million.

The school corporation was one of five school districts to win the Saturn/UAW-NEA Partnership Award for the smooth relations between administrators. The system's literacy programs have also received national recognition. Its summer school, which includes enrichment as well as remedial programs, is the largest in the state.

The Floyd County Youth Symphony (an after-school program administered by the consolidated schools but available to all young people in the metro Louisville area) has performed in Rumania and went to the Vienna Music Festival in 1995; it usually returns from national and international competition with highest honors.

Its students have a television show on Marcus Media Cable Channel 2 and broadcast throughout the school year on the delightful WNAS, 88.1-FM, where the DJs always play their favorite song, no matter who played it 15 minutes ago.

West Clark Community School District
601 Renz Ave., Sellersburg
• (812) 246-3375

This is a small system consisting of eight schools in Sellersburg, Henryville and Borden in the western part of Clark County. More than 90 percent of its students graduate (98.7 in 1996). One of its elementary teachers was a semifinalist for 1994 Indiana Teacher of the Year; a teacher at Silver Creek High School was named state teacher of the year in journalism; a business teacher was named "Entrepreneur of the Year" for Kentucky and Indiana.

Class sizes average between 15 and 20 (although in actual practice they vary from 12 to 30). The system recently sunk $1 million into computer technology and has at least one computer in each classroom. The schools are networked with fiber optic lines. The system offers "tech prep" classes; there is also a gifted and talented program in grades 6 through 12.

Private Schools

Louisville

Archdiocese of Louisville
Office of Lifelong Formation & Education 1935 Lewiston Dr. • 448-8581, Catholic school information line 634-1315

The third-largest school system in the state, with 53 schools in Jefferson County and 16 others in other parts of central Kentucky, it sends a phenomenal 96 percent of its graduates on to college or other post-secondary education and has a 98 percent graduation rate among high-school seniors.

More than 20,000 students attend the Catholic schools in Jefferson County; more than 3,500 are in the rural schools. A number of students have been National Merit finalists and Governor's Scholars. Three of the high schools — Assumption (twice), St. Xavier (three times) and Trinity — have been recognized as National Schools of Excellence, as has St. Raphael Elementary. Trinity and St. X are also dominating teams in local sports, especially football.

While the Catholic schools are not governed by KERA, they have adopted many of the same learning goals, adding a religious component; the system uses an outcome-based approach to designing its curriculum and incorporates performance assessments as a way of measuring student progress.

The system offers gifted and accelerated programs for the academically gifted; thematic programs; both graded and ungraded schools; and cooperative learning and independent study. Several of the parishes offer before-school, after-school and preschool programs. All elementary schools are coeducational; of the nine high schools, Holy Cross is coed, while the others are single-sex schools. The system's drug-prevention effort has been recognized as one of the nation's 20 best and serves as a benchmark for other systems.

Financial aid is available.

The Chance School
4200 Lime Kiln Ln. • 425-6904

This excellent school for children age 2 through the fifth grade has 74 students in its elementary program.

Located in an historic building, the former Rogers Clark Ballard School, Chance has been practicing the ungraded method of teaching for 20 years (in fact, Jefferson County teachers trained there after KERA was passed). The school believes in a developmentally sensitive, experience-based approach to education.

Named after founder Virginia Chance, the school has been accredited by the National Academy of Early Childhood Programs, a division of the National Association for the Education of Young Children.

Some financial aid is available.

Christian Academy of Louisville
3110 Rock Creek Dr. • 897-3372

Christian Academy is a traditional Christian school, supported by local independent Christian churches, and an incredibly fast-growing institution: Its enrollment has grown by nearly 50 percent over the past three years. In 1998 it moves into a new campus on South English Station Road with 100 classrooms, an auditorium, a media center, cafeteria and a pair of gymnasiums. There are 980 pupils in grades K through 12; average class size is 20.

The school describes its mission as providing "a Christ-centered environment where students are challenged to achieve academic and spiritual excellence. The academy is committed to traditional values and service, with an emphasis on integrating Christian principles into the lives of its students." It has not embraced the techniques or philosophy of education reform.

Several students have been recognized as National Merit Semifinalists and Scholars; the graduating class of 1997 received over $1 million in college scholarships. All teachers are certified.

Executive director William McKinley, formerly of the Whittier Christian High School, is coeditor of the book *Critical Issues Facing Christian Schools* and a founding member of Christian Schools International, the largest organization accrediting Christian schools.

Friends School
Douglass Boulevard Christian Church, 2005 Douglass Blvd. • 899-1822

This small parent cooperative school has one of the city's better quality preschools. Its foundation is a strong belief in each child's uniqueness (and a well-deserved reputation for accommodating children with special needs). Its elementary program is a nongraded, academically challenging program in its fifth year.

The school, nondenominational but originally sponsored by the Friends Meeting, has a noncompetitive, nonviolent philosophy and directs a good deal of attention to the child's social development. There are 45 students in kindergarten through fifth grade. Some financial aid is available.

Kentucky Country Day School
4100 Springdale Rd. • 423-0440

This college-preparatory school on an 80-acre campus in eastern Jefferson County gets the job done — all of its graduates go on to college, and it claims three-quarters or more of them are accepted at their first-choice school.

KCD has 725 students in kindergarten through 12th grade and 82 faculty members, of whom 62 have advanced degrees; three of them have been awarded Klingenstein Foundation Fellowships. Class sizes average 15 in the upper school. It offers Advance Placement in 14 subjects; art opportunities include kilns for student pottery and three schoolwide dramas every year, including a spring musical. Nearly 90 percent of high school students participate in at least one sport.

In educational practice, the school strikes its own path between tradition and innovations: For example, KCD has been using literature-based reading instruction for nearly two decades, but it eschews the multi-age primary program.

Financial aid is available.

Louisville Collegiate School
2427 Glenmary Ave. • 451-5330

This college-prep school opened in 1915 and has been in its handsome Cherokee Triangle building since the Coolidge administration (although the structure has been added to since Silent Cal's day). Its philosophy attempts to combine "the best of the old and the new" — its small size ensures individual attention, but the curriculum is a traditional one. You're not likely to hear the buzz-phrases of education reform.

Collegiate enrolls about 600 students in grades K though 12. Class sizes are small (the student-to-teacher ratio is 13-to-1, and no class is larger than 18 students). Teachers have received the Presidential Award for Excellence in Teaching, National Endowment for the Humanities grants and fellowships from the Klingenstein Foundation.

Collegiate offers a number of Advance Placement courses and a midwinter week of special classes and activities called Interim. Collegiate has a 1-to-1 computer-to-student ratio, with computers in all classrooms. All computers have Internet access, and the school's web page was designed by students.

Financial aid is available.

Sacred Heart Model School
3121 Lexington Rd. • 896-3959

This small Catholic school for children in kindergarten through 8th grade dates back to 1876, when it was part of the Academy of the Sacred Heart, and took its present name in the 1920s when it became the laboratory school for teaching students at Ursuline College (since joined with Bellarmine). It shares the pretty Ursuline campus with several other schools, including Sacred Heart Academy, a Catholic girls' high school and, like the upper school, draws students from throughout the metropolitan area. The school has 350 students and 30 teachers; class sizes vary from eight to 15, and there are 20 students in each homeroom.

The model school's philosophy is to develop a student's academic ability, personal spirituality and sense of social justice. Its curriculum has a heavy emphasis on writing and includes foreign language instruction starting in the first grade. Computers are integrated into classwork at all levels, as are art and music instruction; physical education in kindergarten through 4th grade incorporates both standard PE and movement classes.

FYI

Unless otherwise noted, the area code for all phone numbers listed in this chapter is 502.

St. Francis School — Goshen
11000 W. U.S. Hwy. 42, Goshen • 228-1197

This independent school for kindergarten through 8th grade students takes a developmental approach to education that recognizes different individual rhythms of intellectual growth (one of its mottos is "We give the gift of time") and hands-on learning. Students in grades 1 through 4 are placed in multi-age "family groups."

It's located in a contemporary school building on a 74-acre campus that includes woods and an environmental land lab. It was founded in 1965 as an offshoot of St. Francis in the Fields Church and continues to be affiliated with the Episcopal Diocese of Kentucky. There are 311 students (500 including the preschool) and 75 teachers. The preschool operates an after-school program for students through grade 5.

Financial aid is available.

St. Francis High School
233 W. Broadway • 585-2057

While many local private schools sell parents on their secluded, verdant campuses, St. Francis is an urban school that takes advantage of its downtown setting for everything from resource materials — it views the main branch of the Louisville Free Public Library, across the street, as its school library — to opportunities for community involvement (twice a month the entire school closes down for a morning while students and faculty leave the building to perform community service).

St. Francis was started in 1977 by parents whose children had attended St. Francis in Goshen, but the schools are otherwise connected only by being affiliated with the Episcopal archdiocese and sharing educational philosophy. St. Francis calls itself a "classic progressive school," self-affirming and intellectually stimulating. There are no bells, dress codes or hall monitors; student discipline is by a jury system. There are 138 students in grades 9 through 12; the student/teacher ratio is 8-to-1. Two-thirds of them participate in competitive sports; teams have a no-cut policy: If you show up for practice, you're on the team.

Thirty percent of the students receive financial aid.

Walden School
4238 Westport Rd. • 893-0433

A small school for kindergarten through 12th grade (about 215 students, 32 teachers), Walden is independent, nonsectarian and coeducational. Its philosophy is to meet students where they are developmentally, and its small class size — all classes are limited to 15 students — allows for a great deal of individualized instruction.

Walden employs an integrated approach to learning that cuts across disciplines. Student preferences play a large part in determining the course of study. But while the school honors its students' individuality, it also provides a rigorous college prep education: 100 percent of Walden students go on to further education, nearly all of them at four-year colleges and universities.

Students have been Governor's Scholars and have been tabbed by the Duke University Talent Identification Program. There's a full sports program, and the school's soccer team is a local power.

Financial aid is available.

Waldorf School of Louisville
8005 New Lagrange Rd. • 327-0122

This growing school (founded in 1992) currently has 50 students, from preschool through the third grade, and intends to grow by adding a grade each year through the eighth grade. Its 10 teachers include instructors in German and Japanese.

Part of a network of 130 Waldorf schools in the United States, the school follows the educational philosophy of philosopher Rudolf Steiner, which teaches to all aspects of a child — the mind, the body and the feelings, using a great deal of physical education, movement and dance and also emphasizing the arts. Oral storytelling is the basis of the curriculum. To quote from the school's brochure: "From the Waldorf perspective, a premature focus on intellectual pursuits dulls a child's ability to act in the world."

Seasonal celebrations draw the entire school community for festivals. There's an after-school program, a morning play group for parents and children three and younger and adult education classes in such subjects as painting, drawing and handicrafts.

Financial aid is available.

Indiana

Our Lady of Providence Junior/Senior High School

707 W. Ind. Hwy. 131, Clarksville
• (812) 945-2538

Southern Indiana's only Catholic upper school is a coeducational junior and senior high with 720 students and an average classroom ratio of 14-to-1. It's renovating the original part of the school, which dates to 1951 and makes up two-thirds of the plant. It should be completed in the fall of 1999.

Providence has well-regarded art and theater programs and a full complement of extracurricular activities. While the school does not discriminate on the basis of ethnic origin, creed or ability, attendance at the worship service is mandatory, and the dress code is nonnegotiable.

Financial aid is available.

Child Care

For a city its size, Louisville has a large number of child-care options — about 500 licensed operators in Jefferson County alone.

Many are commercial operations, franchises of national chains; others are locally owned and run centers with large student populations; and there are family child-care centers that amount to one or two people taking care of several children in a home. Some are nonprofits, run by the community ministries in different areas or administered by community agencies such as the United Way. The public schools also offer day-care options. A few large companies — among them Providian, The Courier-Journal, Alliant Medical Group, Baptist East Hospital and the Federal Building — have child care for their employees, but that's a trend that hasn't yet reached Louisville in any major way.

Plenty of them are good, but some are not, and the best ones often have waiting lists. And in some special situations — day care for infants, evening child care — you don't have a multitude of choices.

How does a parent go about the process of finding good child care?

A day-care owner of our acquaintance says that parents usually ask questions that beg for standard answers, such as ratio of teachers to children or method of discipline. ("No one's going to tell you they're out of compliance [with state laws that limit teacher-student ratios], no one's going to tell you they hit kids.") The training of staff is an important issue, but he warns that in most cases you won't find staff with degrees.

But he recommends two lines of inquiry that may produce useful information: Ask about the longevity of the staff (staff turnover is the greatest complaint about day care, he says); and ask the director for parent references (other parents are usually quite frank with their opinions about day care).

The best source of child-care referrals comes from the following agency. We've also included information about several children's services available in Louisville.

Community Coordinated Child Care

1215 S. Third St. • 636-1358

Four-Cs, as it's called, does not recommend individual institutions, but it can provide a list of regulated day cares in a particular area — even along a particular route — along with costs and the ages of children they serve. The organization also serves as an advocacy group for children, consults with businesses on child-care

---

INSIDERS' TIP

The most comprehensive collection of Louisville-area community services ever put together is the 578-page *Guide to Community Services*. It's available for $30 plus $5 shipping and handling from the Community Resource Network, 334 E. Broadway, P.O. Box 4488, Louisville KY 40204, or at the receptionist's desk at the Metro United Way office (same address). It's also available in an electronic version.

issues, trains people who work with children and administers a number of programs.

The best way to find out about day care is to ask acquaintances about their arrangements, and really listen — gauge their level of enthusiasm. Consult 4-Cs and work up a list of prospective day cares. Then start visiting them.

In a brochure available from 4-Cs, parents are encouraged to spend a fair amount of time observing a prospective day-care center, looking for adults who are nurturing and warm; children being given choices and encouraged to be independent; play being valued as a way to learn; opportunities for art, music and dramatic play; clear, simple and consistent rules; adults speaking frequently to children and encouraging children to talk.

The Nanny Program at Sullivan College
3101 Bardstown Rd. • (800) 844-1354

Since 1988 Sullivan has been placing a number of full-time, in-home care givers throughout the country. Its students learn infant, child and adult CPR, first aid and water rescue; their course work includes etiquette, child development and nutritional cooking, among other subjects. Participants must also be nonsmokers and undergo crime and driving-record checks, have a health test and provide work and personal references.

The program is one of only a few accredited by the American Council of Nanny Schools; Sullivan says it places 98 percent or better of its graduates.

Angel Care at Vencor Hospital-Louisville
1313 St. Anthony Pl. off Barret Ave.
• 627-1170

Every parent has faced this situation at one time or another — your child is ill, AND you absolutely need to be at work, in court or somewhere else that can't be postponed. You can't use your regular day care — it wouldn't be fair to your child, the day-care center or the other children.

The best solution this side of a helpful grandparent is Angel Care, a program that looks after mildly ill children from 6 weeks through 14 years old. Parents need to call at least an hour in advance to make sure there's room (the program has a limit of 25 children). The nurses who run the program will administer prescriptions, take temperatures and provide the parent with a copy of notes on the child. They will dispense Tylenol to children with a temperature more than 100 degrees. Breakfast, lunch and a snack are provided for older children. Parents must supply diapers, formula or baby food for young ones.

Angel Care is open from 6:30 AM to 6:30 PM, Monday through Friday; cost is $7.50 an hour, to a maximum of $50 a day; discounts are available for frequent customers.

The program can't look after children with highly infectious diseases, for example measles, mumps or chicken pox; children with a temperature greater than 103 degrees, unless the child has been seen by a doctor; or a child with an undiagnosed rash.

Kids Fun Connection
7400 LaGrange Rd., Ste. 212 • 327-8099

This company provides on-site child care at events from weddings to trade shows. They come up with activities for the kids ranging from pizza parties to educational looks at Kentucky history and culture. Staff at each site includes at least one person trained in first aid and CPR. Fees change from event to event.

The cost begins at $3 per child per hour and increases inversely with the age of the children (since young ones require more people to look after them) and in an otherwise straightforward manner depending on such factors as type of service, the length of the activity (there's a four-hour minimum) and the number of staff Kids Connection needs to supply.

La Leche League International
Various locations • (800) 525-3243

This mother-to-mother group provides full support for breast-feeding mothers: It provides information on breast-feeding's advantages, helps in overcoming problems and also provides information on how a new baby affects a family. Group leaders are trained and accredited by the organization. At present there are six groups in the Louisville area and others in outlying cities; to find the group nearest you, call the toll-free number listed above.

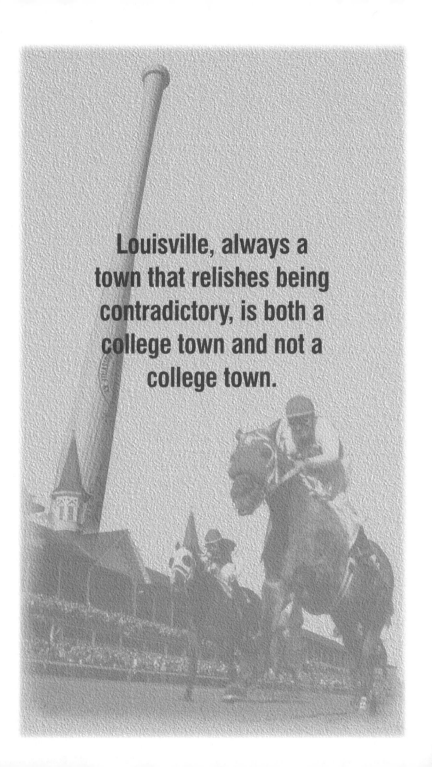

Louisville, always a town that relishes being contradictory, is both a college town and not a college town.

Colleges, Universities and Trade Schools

Louisville, always a town that relishes being contradictory, is both a college town and not a college town. We have several colleges here, most notably the University of Louisville, Bellarmine College, Sullivan College, Spalding University and Jefferson Community College. But the students are largely of the commuter nature, not the throw-down-and-party, go-to-clubs-and-enliven-the-economy type. It surely doesn't SEEM like a college town.

Perhaps the more important point is that you don't have to leave Louisville to get a really good education. Baptist, Catholic, liberal arts, vocational, law school, engineering — Louisville's education spectrum is wide.

Most of Louisville's schools offer evening and weekend classes as well as continuing education programs for professional education or personal enrichment. Make a few phone calls and find the program that suits your needs.

It's hard to talk about local colleges without mentioning sports — especially basketball. For many Louisvillians, the words "U of L" evoke images of Felton Spencer standing in the paint rather than academic symbols such as the university's Ekstrom Library or the replica of Rodin's *The Thinker* in front of campus. When U of L plays the University of Kentucky in basketball, the world stops. Even football, baseball and soccer games between these in-state rivals get the passion pumping for local fans. You'll also find good basketball at Bellarmine College and Sullivan College. For more information, contact the athletic offices of the university or college team you'd like to support. (See our Spectator Sports chapter.)

Louisville Colleges, Universities and Seminaries

Kentuckiana Metroversity is a consortium of colleges and universities in Kentucky and Southern Indiana that includes Bellarmine College, Indiana University Southeast, Jefferson Community College, Louisville Presbyterian Theological Seminary, Southern Baptist Seminary, Spalding University and the University of Louisville. Students enrolled at any of the participating schools may take courses at the other institutions, borrow books from the schools' libraries and take part in special student activities.

Bellarmine College
2001 Newburg Rd. • 452-8000, (800) 274-4723

It used to be referred to derisively as "the high school on the hill," and Bellarmine did indeed have a small-school feel at one time. But that began to change in the 1980s, and it is total fiction now that BC opened a new $10 million, 72,000-square-foot library, which features state-of-the-art computer labs and bays and sleek study and meeting facilities. The liberal arts education (philosophy and theology courses are requisites, among others) offered at Bellarmine aims at producing a well-rounded graduate.

Named for St. Robert Bellarmine (1542-1621), the college was founded in 1950 as a private undergraduate school. Over the years, several graduate programs have been added.

The school's first catalog made it clear that Bellarmine was to be more than a place to amass knowledge: "The College does not accept the notion that a school's responsibility is to teach students simply to fit into the society in which they live. It submits that students must be taught to evaluate this society and to exercise their trained human powers to change it whenever necessary."

Bellarmine has Catholic roots — it was sponsored by the Roman Catholic Archdiocese of Louisville, with special assistance from the Conventual Franciscan Fathers — and is deeply influenced by the Second Vatican Council. It is a center for ecumenical research and exchange among faculty and students of many religious and philosophic positions. It was one of the first colleges in Kentucky to be open to all races.

In 1955 the college began presenting the Bellarmine Medal, based on "civic and moral excellence," to individuals from America and abroad. Recipients have included Henry Cabot Lodge, Mother Teresa of Calcutta, Walter Cronkite, Lech Walesa and Arthur Ashe. In 1963 the college opened the Thomas Merton Center devoted to the works of Thomas Merton, nearby resident at the Abbey of Gethsemani and friend of the college. In its archives are more than 40,000 items; more than 100 doctoral dissertations and master's theses have been written from materials at the Center.

The first graduate program, the Masters in Business Administration, began in 1975. Graduate programs have been added in education, nursing, social administration and liberal arts.

More than 1,200 students study full time in the undergraduate program, with 400 of them living on campus. Several hundred more attend graduate school at BC, primarily for business degrees.

Academic scholarships, student loans and work-study programs are available, and students may study abroad.

Jefferson Community College
Downtown Campus, 109 E. Broadway
• 584-0181
Southwest Campus, 1000 Community College Dr. • 935-9804

In some circles JCC's reputation isn't as good as some other area colleges, perhaps because it is a community college instead of a primary university. The irony is that hundreds of students go to the University of Louisville and the University of Kentucky because their parents want them to go to college, while those who attend JCC are going there to LEARN. JCC attracts dedicated, smart students who see college as more of a learning opportunity than a four-year keg party.

A multi-campus school with primary facilities in downtown Louisville and southwestern Jefferson County, JCC is the largest, more than 9,500 students, of the 14 institutions that comprise the University of Kentucky's statewide system of community colleges. JCC opened its doors in the spring of 1968 in a Gothic building that once housed the Presbyterian Theological Seminary. As the student body increased, the physical facilities were expanded. In 1972 JCC opened a suburban campus at Jesse Stuart High School to serve southwest Jefferson County, and in 1980 a complex of five new buildings was constructed. Additional buildings have been added since. In the spring of 1990, JCC began offering classes in Carrollton.

Students may attend full or part time during the day, evenings and weekends. The class offerings are varied; students can fill their sched-

INSIDERS' TIP

Spalding University's Running of the Rodents is a fun and frivolous addition to Derby Week hysteria. Spalding students pit their mice against all others in a race for the garland of Fruit Loops.

ules with everything from accounting and astronomy to trigonometry and women's studies.

Louisville Presbyterian Theological Seminary
1044 Alta Vista Rd. • 895-3411

This 100-year-old campus is set against a tree-lined vista that encompasses two architectural gems — one old, one modern.

Completed in 1906, Gardencourt, with grounds designed by the firm of Frederick Law Olmsted, was the home of the daughters of financier George W. Norton II (it more recently housed the U of L School of Music). The seminary purchased the house, and citizens from all denominations rallied to raise restoration funds. Today, Gardencourt is a popular site for weddings, private parties and corporate events. For information about rental fees, call 895-3411. The Louisville Institute for Protestantism and American Culture, a research center, is also housed here, along with offices and classrooms.

Across the lawn, the contemporary Caldwell Chapel reaches skyward. The chapel's interior is decorated with signs and symbols, both ancient and modern, that focus on Jesus and His followers and people from different parts of the world and other times in history. When you visit, stop by the seminary's office and pick up a booklet that explains the symbols. Worship services, open to the public, are held at 10 AM Tuesday through Friday. The building was the site of several interfaith services during the Persian Gulf War.

The library holds a collection of rare Judaic and ancient art, including scrolls and pottery. Free lectures and occasional organ recitals are open to the community.

The school's mission is to prepare ministers, and it offers master's and doctoral degrees in divinity, along with degrees in Christian education, marriage and family therapy, counseling and religious thought.

Simmons Bible College
1811 Dumesnil St. • 776-5549

Simmons Bible College opened in 1879, one of the first institutions in Kentucky to offer a college education to blacks. From 1889 to 1918, Simmons awarded degrees in medicine, law, theology and other academic areas.

Simmons, an undergraduate college, is owned and operated by the General Association of Black Baptists.

Students come primarily from Greater Louisville and outlying Kentucky counties. International students are frequently spouses of those attending other seminaries in the area. Local clergy makes up the bulk of the faculty, and an average of 12 men and women graduate each year.

In 1951 a son of a former Simmons president became the first African American named to the faculty of the University of Louisville.

Housed in a historic building, the school has a library of 10,000-plus volumes. Worship services, open to the public, feature music by the college's ensemble.

Southern Baptist Theological Seminary
2825 Lexington Rd. • 897-4011

Founded in 1877, this is the second-largest seminary in the world and one of the largest private educational institutions in the nation, with a student body of 3,000. Professional, master's and doctoral degrees are offered in theology, church music, Christian education and church social work. The Billy Graham School of Missions, Evangelism and Church Growth, the only school bearing the name of the famous evangelist, opened in 1994.

The seminary came to Louisville in 1877 and moved to its location in the 1920s. Men and women from across the United States and from foreign countries, including many present and future leaders of the national Baptist Conventions, study here. Courses are also offered in Moscow, Nigeria and Eastern Europe.

The arrival of Albert Mohler in 1993 resulted in a major shake-up on the seminary grounds — the faculty and administration found themselves split on ideological grounds, with the more fundamentalist, conservative side (Mohler's side) gaining the firm upper hand. Long-tenured professors quit or were fired. Some students reportedly felt betrayed; others felt that the seminary was righting itself after listing into a less faithful position. This transformation was quite public and rather ugly, with recriminations coming from deposed professors and steadfast administrators alike.

The Georgian Colonial buildings are near

Seneca Park. An archaeological museum with relics (including a mummy) and displays of ancient Near Eastern Biblical sites, as well as an art gallery with rotating exhibitions of a religious nature, are open to the public at no charge.

The James P. Boyce Centennial Library, one of the world's largest with 750,000 cataloged items, attracts scholars from all continents. Private citizens can also use the materials but may not check them out. The rare Bible collection includes a third-century papyrus fragment and a limited-edition Guttenberg Bible facsimile. The music collection totals 45,000 scores, 20,000 books and 17,000 recordings.

Year-round lectures, recitals, concerts, church music and drama programs and weekly chapel services are also open to the public. While there, take note of the chapel's 113 Rank Aeolian-Skinner organ, a magnificent instrument with more than 6,000 pipes ranging in size from 32 feet high to smaller than a pencil.

Spalding University
851 S. Fourth St. • 585-9911

Spalding's strengths are its 16 to 1 student to teacher ratio, its international studies programs and the fact that 62 percent of its faculty have earned a Ph.D. or the highest degree available in their field. The coeducational Catholic university is located on an attractive urban campus on the edge of historic Old Louisville.

Founded by the Sisters of Charity of Nazareth, the school is dedicated to value-oriented education. Spalding offers the following degrees: Bachelor of Arts, Bachelor of Science, Associate of Arts, Doctor of Education, Doctor of Psychology, Master of Science and Master of Arts. The university also offers a bachelor's degree in social work and bachelor's and master's degrees in library/information services.

More than 1,100 students seek undergraduate degrees at this private college, and more than 400 enroll in the graduate programs. It's a commuter campus.

University of Louisville
Belknap Campus, 2301 S. Third St.
• 852-5555
Shelby Campus, 9001 Shelbyville Rd.
• 852-8700

The University of Louisville was a municipally supported institution before joining the state university system in 1970. It has three campuses: the 177-acre Belknap Campus, 3 miles from downtown Louisville, housing seven of the University's 11 colleges, schools and divisions; the Health Sciences Center, in downtown Louisville's medical complex and the University of Louisville Hospital; the 243-acre Shelby Campus, in eastern Jefferson County, which has the National Crime Prevention Institute and the Office of Continuing Studies and External Programs. Courses have also been offered at Fort Knox.

The University of Louisville resulted from a merger between the Louisville Medical Institute and the Louisville Collegiate Institute in 1846. The school's history is punctuated by the addition of professional schools for law, arts and sciences, dentistry, music, social work, business and allied health.

In the fall of 1996, U of L had 21,020 students enrolled, 63.4 percent full time. Women comprise 53 percent of the enrollment, and the average age of the student body is 27.

U of L awards associate, bachelor's and master's degrees. It gives doctoral degrees in education and philosophy and professional degrees in law, medicine and dentistry. The library contains nearly 1.4 million volumes and 13,139 periodicals.

Established in 1846, the U of L School of Law is Kentucky's oldest law school and America's fifth-oldest in continuous operation. In 1950 the School of Law merged with the Jefferson School of Law that created a part-time night division. The School of Law is the

INSIDERS' TIP

Although it's categorized as a junior college, Sullivan upholds the Kentucky tradition of assembling excellent basketball teams. The Sullivan College Executives are a regular fixture in the NJCAA Top 20, and the 1994-95 team enjoyed a 28-4 record.

repository of the papers of former Supreme Court Justices John Marshall Harlan and Louis Brandeis. The remains of Justice Brandeis and his wife lie beneath the classical portico of the Law School building. In 1990 the School of Law became one of America's first to make donated service (pro bono) a mandatory part of each student's legal education.

Speed Scientific School, U of L's engineering school, has an excellent reputation and offers six degrees: chemical, civil, electrical, industrial and mechanical engineering, engineering mathematics and computer science. Named for industrialist James Breckinridge Speed, the school became part of U of L in 1925.

The university also has a nationally ranked program in English rhetoric and composition. And recently, *Success* magazine mentioned U of L as one of the 25 best schools for entrepreneurship, along with Harvard and Northwestern.

U of L is the default school of choice for Louisville high school seniors, and like any educational experience (but perhaps more so for U of L students), it can be as challenging or as irrelevant as you choose to make it.

Southern Indiana Universities

Indiana University Southeast
4201 Grant Line Rd., New Albany
• (812) 941-2000

Indiana University Southeast was established as the IU Falls City Area Center in 1941. Classes were offered in local high schools until 1945, when the center moved to Warder Park in downtown Jeffersonville. It awarded its first baccalaureate degrees in 1968 and has graduated almost 12,000 students. In 1973 the new 177-acre Grant Line Road campus was opened in New Albany. The campus includes the library, University Center (housing meeting rooms, food service, student offices, conference facilities, game room and cafeteria), Activities Building (for intercollegiate and intramural sports) and five academic buildings. The Paul W. Ogle Cultural and Community Center, a $10.5 million building that has earned raves as host of various arts events, opened in the spring of 1996.

Indiana University Southeast, one of the eight campuses of Indiana University, serves the Greater Louisville metropolitan region, including the Indiana counties of Clark, Crawford, Floyd, Harrison, Jackson, Jefferson, Orange, Scott and Washington. In the 1993 fall semester, nearly 5,400 students were enrolled. Approximately 85 percent of the students take advantage of the school's flexible scheduling and work full or part time, and the median age of IUS students is 26. Roughly half of the student body is composed of nontraditional students.

Students may select from five master's degree programs, 25 bachelor's degree programs and nine associate and certificate programs. Through the Division of Continuing Studies, the campus provides noncredit personal and professional development classes as well as individualized training for business and industry.

Kentucky residents may attend master's and associate degree classes and pay in-state Hoosier rates, which can save students more than 50 percent off tuition.

Webster University
Jeffersonville Metropolitan Campus, 319 E. Court Ave., Jeffersonville
• (812) 283-1000

The Jeffersonville campus of this Missouri-based university opened 17 years ago; it offers strictly master's degrees — in the arts and business administration. Webster University, founded as a Catholic women's college in 1915, has 57 campuses worldwide. The median age of students is 30.

Most of the 250 students enrolled in the fall of 1997 were part-time. All classes are taught in the evenings by adjunct faculty members. Webster prides itself on hiring faculty members with Ph.D.s and, more importantly, practical experience in their field.

Trade Schools

Kentucky Tech-Jefferson State Vocational/Technical School
727 W. Chestnut St. • 595-4221

The Kentucky Tech system is made up of 87 schools that provide vocational training in areas such as automotive technology, cos-

Kentuckiana Metroversity is a consortium of colleges and universities in Kentucky and Southern Indiana.

metology, horticulture, food service, graphic arts and air conditioning. The school is operated by Kentucky's Department for Technical Education, Cabinet for Workforce.

The programs are for adults, high school graduates and GED recipients. Kentucky Tech also offers customized training for business and industry in many of its subject areas. In 1996 the school had 370 full-time and 570 part-time students.

Louisville Technical Institute
Watterson Expressway at Newburg Rd.
• 456-6509, (800) 844-6528

Founded in 1961, Louisville Technical Institute is part of the Sullivan Colleges System. Associate degrees are offered in drafting, computer engineering technology, mechanical engineering (with emphasis on robotics) and computer aided design and drafting (CADD) technology. Certificates and diplomas are granted in marine mechanics, drafting and interior design. As with all of Sullivan's schools, the emphasis is on practical courses and job placement.

The College of Merchandising and Design is a division of the Louisville Technical Institute. Its graduates work as buyers, bridal consultants, store managers, illustrators and in

related vocations. It's located just south of Louisville in a light industrial area.

Enrollment is around 500 students.

RETS Electronic Institute
4146 Outer Loop • 968-7191

Louisville's RETS school opened in 1972, a branch of the original school founded in 1935 in Detroit as a response to the rapid growth of radio broadcasting. Today "radio" has grown to encompass broader electronics fields — television, microwaves and especially computer technology. The school's library has resources for a wide range of technologies.

Spencerian College
4627 Dixie Hwy. • 447-1000,
(800) 264-1799

This college has long had a reputation for producing graduates in the business field — since 1892 to be exact. The school of business administration is still thriving, but the school of allied health sciences has blossomed too. The school, part of the Sullivan Colleges System, offers certificates and diplomas in business administration and allied health sciences. Among careers targeted by the school are business office management, executive assistant, accounting specialist, practical nurse, medical office assistant and medical transcriber.

Sullivan College
3101 Bardstown Rd. • 456-6504

Sullivan College, founded as primarily a business school in 1962, is now accredited to award bachelor's degrees in addition to its one- and two-year certificates and associate degrees. And it has become the second largest private college or university in Kentucky.

Sullivan's strengths include business administration, paralegal training and computer education, but the crown jewel of the college's schools is the National Center for Hospitality Studies. Aspiring chefs no longer need travel to attend Johnson & Wales or the Culinary Institute of America to earn a respected degree in culinary arts — they now have the viable, reputable option of Sullivan College. The culinary arts program has gained national recognition, and the school successfully operates an outside bakery, catering operation and fine dining restaurant in which students sharpen their skills (see the Winston's Restaurant listing in the Restaurants chapter). One can earn a degree in hotel and restaurant management too.

Sullivan now has branches in Fort Knox and Lexington, giving them a total enrollment of more than 1,800.

Continuing Education Programs

University of Louisville Center for Continuing and Professional Education
2301 S. Third St. • 852-6600
Bellarmine College
Office of Continuing Studies
2001 Newburg Rd. • 452-8131
Indiana University Southeast
Division of Continuing Studies
4201 Grant Line Rd., New Albany, Ind.
• (812) 941-2315

Spalding University
Egan Leadership Center
851 S. Fourth St. • 585-7135

Do you now have the time or money to work past your GED? Are you retired and want to get the formal education in philosophy that you always wanted? Want to learn photography? You can continue your studies full or part time in Louisville colleges. You can pursue knowledge via credit or noncredit courses (credit courses cost more and add up to a degree; noncredit courses are cheaper and are strictly for your own edification). You can go to day classes, weekend classes or evening classes. Area colleges participating in the Metroversity program allow full-time students to take up to two courses at other institutions at no penalty. The options are many. Call the institution of your choice for more information.

Jefferson County Public Schools Adult and Continuing Education
• 485-3400

This nonprofit entity offers classes ranging from six weeks to one day in length on a variety of vocational and special interest topics, everything from computer use, foreign languages and personal fitness to plumbing, mathematics and HVAC technology. Course fees run from $99 to $150.

The Learning Network
3900B Dupont Square • 893-9182

Founded in 1991, this for-profit company calls itself a "general, eclectic, leisure adult learning program. The curriculum is indeed eclectic, ranging from classes on partners massage, introduction to Japanese, day at the Downs, golf and tennis to successful juggling. As of late, the emphasis has been on one-day computer classes, especially those that are an introduction to applications handling word processing and spreadsheets.

The Courier-Journal has consistently ranked as one of the nation's best papers, and (with its deceased sibling, *The Louisville Times*) it has won nine Pulitzer Prizes — six of them since 1967.

Media

The organs of the Louisville media, low and high, have for years received recognition for their quality and accomplishments.

Louisville papers have been important editorial voices for almost the entire period of the city's history. Except at the beginning and, some would say, in more recent years, *The Courier-Journal* has consistently ranked as one of the nation's best papers, and (with its deceased sibling, *The Louisville Times*) it has won nine Pulitzer Prizes — six of them since 1967.

WHAS Radio, a pioneer in broadcasting, has a clear-channel signal that allows it to be heard at night throughout much of the continental United States.

Louisville used to be a one-horse — or, more accurately, a one-stable — media town. That stable was owned by the Binghams, the family which owned *The Courier-Journal*; WHAS; a country radio station, WAMZ; and a television station, also called WHAS. These outlets dominated the market.

The Binghams sold their properties in 1986 after a well-publicized family dispute (see our close-up in this chapter). But their paper and broadcast stations, now owned by out-of-town companies Gannett, Clear Channel Communications and A.H. Belo, continue as the leaders in their fields, although the television market is entering a "news war" that could shake up the status quo.

However, in the last few years, cheap printing, gaps in the market and the exodus of fed-up *Courier* employees have brought Louisville quite a number of new papers and magazines that have shown unusual staying power. The weekly *Business First* recently celebrated its 10th anniversary; the alternative newspaper *LEO* is in its seventh year.

Louisville radio is conservative, but quite diverse: There are three 24-hour gospel stations (two black, one country), all the major national talk shows (except Don Imus) and public radio of genuine distinction.

Television is much like it is anywhere else. The stations brag about helicopters more than about their reporters' experience or abilities. Bad weather — the 1994 blizzard, the tornado of 1996, the flood of 1997 — brings out their best and most valuable reporting. Still, the local television news is, according to those familiar with other markets, less sensationalistic and more serious than in many other places. Wow.

Publications

Daily Newspapers

The Courier-Journal
525 W. Broadway • 582-4011
Despite everything — the decline of the newspaper industry and reading in general, the paper's purchase by Gannett after an emotionally wrenching sale by the Bingham family — *The Courier-Journal* continues to be the strongest media presence in the Louisville market, and its reporting and writing continue to set high standards (see our close-up in this chapter). When you travel to a city of a similar size — Tulsa, say — the *Courier's* quality, no matter how vestigial, hits you with a wallop.

The paper's editorial voice is liberal, although it's come rightward a bit since the days when it urged readers to march in protest of Richard Nixon's second inauguration.

It covers the high arts carefully (the Binghams were great patrons of Actors Theatre, the Louisville Orchestra and others). The food section, traditionally a strong point in the hands of Cissy Gregg and Lillian Marshall, is well-written and informative on a number of issues. The "Weekend" section provides a full almanac of events in the city and the region and a listing of performers at local nightspots.

The *Courier's* circulation is 234,742 daily and 321,449 on Sunday.

The Evening News
221 Spring St., Jeffersonville, Ind.
• (812) 283-6636

Each of Southern Indiana's two daily papers focuses on its home county (in the *Evening News's* case, that means Clark) with occasional "raids" into the other's territory. *The Evening News* takes a harder approach than the *New Albany Tribune* and often beats other papers (including *The Courier-Journal's* Indiana bureau) to local stories, such as Jeffersonville's delay in making curb cuts required by the Americans with Disabilities Act. It's also known for its outdoors writer, Marty Kime, and his column "Lures Truly."

Published six days a week, never on Sunday, *The Evening News* is owned by Community Newspaper Holdings, Inc. of Lexington, Kentucky. Daily circulation is 11,000.

The Tribune
303 Scribner Dr., New Albany, Ind.
• (812) 944-6481

Published weekdays and Sunday, this daily owned by American Publishing, a subsidiary of the Canada-based Hollinger International, has shown signs of improvement in recent years, especially in an attractive redesign. It covers Floyd County news, as well as the Clark County border town of Sellersburg. It tends to take a "good news" approach unlikely to raise any local hackles. The sports pages focus on area high school teams. Columnists include Dave Barry, Andy Rooney, Linda Ellerbee and local generalist Scott Wilson. Daily circulation is about 10,000.

Weekly Papers

Business First
111 W. Washington St. • 583-1731

Even though it's a weekly, published on Fridays, *Business First* often beats *The Courier-Journal* to business stories — most famously, a story about the *Courier* itself: Sallie

Bingham's decision to sell her stock in the family company, the move which ultimately led to the newspaper's sale. That's partly because over the years the *Courier* has hacked off a number of local movers and shakers who have business scoops to relay; because, with a few signal exceptions, the Courier has never covered business especially well; because *Business First* rarely takes an adversarial role toward its subjects; and because *Business First's* reporters have cultivated their sources and worked doggedly to get the scoops.

It's one of 35 subsidiaries of American City Business Journals, a company based in Charlotte, North Carolina. Its first president and publisher was Mike Kallay, a native Louisvillian and a former editor at *The Louisville Times*; he's been succeeded by Tom Monahan, another longtime local journalist.

Business First knows and serves its market well — don't look for it to be advocating civil disobedience or a guaranteed annual income anytime soon — but neither does it take the kind of reactionary positions that make *The Wall Street Journal's* editorial page so scary to many.

Its yearly compilation of lists is a unique resource, a guide to the Louisville-area economy that gives the largest employers, highest paid executives of publicly held companies, largest travel agencies, florists, conventions and trade shows, stockbrokers and so on. *Business First* also publishes *Call to the Post*, a slick, full-color magazine about the Derby; a twice-yearly real estate section called "At Home"; and other special projects. It's sold at newsstands, street boxes and by subscription.

LEO
St. Matthews Station, 3900 Shelbyville Rd., Ste. 14A • 895-9770

It's a measure of something about Louisville that its most successful alternative paper was founded by a group of retirees from *The Courier-Journal*, the basketball coach at the university and the baby-boomer heir to a local fortune. (One of the *Courier* alums and coach Denny Crum have since dropped active participation; the remnant has been joined by a group of younger contributors.) It's an alternative with connections — something that's often true in other cities but rarely in so obvious or so un-Bohemian a fashion.

And that bluntness is part of the charm of *LEO* (the initials stand for *Louisville Eccentric Observer*). The other part is an almost programmatic irreverence: It doesn't take itself seriously, which makes it a nice foil to *The Courier-Journal*. ("You believe this crap?" was the cover line for its astrology column one week.) *LEO* can be tasteless, and frequently illogical, but it's hard to hold that against something published by SAYWHAT! Corporation.

Published on Wednesday, distributed in bookstores, restaurants, colleges, libraries, shops and other locations through the area, it's a good free read, with an excellent selection of syndicated features (Dave Barry, News of the Weird, Molly Ivins and some longer stories from alternative weeklies in other parts of the country) and locally written pieces that range from provocative to provoking. It also publishes extensive entertainment listings and reviews, and occasional experiments, such as a serial novel called *Naked Came the Longshot* (a tip of the hat to the '70s success de scandale *Naked Came the Stranger*).

While *LEO* is generally liberal, differing with *The Courier-Journal* point by point rather than in any more overall fashion, it's the one general-interest publication with an avowedly conservative local columnist, managing editor Joseph Grove. It also publishes personal ads a bit more, you know, . . . interesting than the *Courier's* prim "Meeting Place." ("Bi-curious witch, 25....")

Henry Watterson, who edited the *Courier-Journal* from Reconstruction through World War I, was "the most widely quoted editor since Horace Greeley."

writes literate and informative food pieces. Syndicated features include Robert Novak, investment columnist Andrew Leckey, Dear Abby and a week's worth of "Dick Tracy" comic strips.

Published Wednesdays, it's available by subscription and in street boxes throughout the eastern part of the county.

The Voice-Tribune
3818 Shelbyville Rd. • 897-8900

The former *Voice of St. Matthews*, now approaching its 50th anniversary, is one of the state's largest paid weeklies. It covers the East End from the river all the way south to Jeffersontown. It's very much a community paper, with extensive obituaries and page upon page of society news and photos: There are two society columnists, Carla Sue Broecker and unintentional prose surrealist Lucie Blodgett. Former *Courier* sports editor Earl Cox covers sports. Former chef Steve Coomes

The Louisville Defender
1720 Dixie Hwy. • 772-2591

The longtime voice of the city's black community, The Louisville Defender was founded in 1933. Along with locally produced stories, it runs Associated Press reports pegged to African-American issues that often get missed by other media outlets. It runs a number of comics, including "Henry" and "Bringing Up Father." The paper sponsors two major annual events, August's West Louisville Appreciation Celebration and October's Minority Consumer Expo (see our Annual Events and Festivals chapter).

The Defender, published every Thursday,

is sold at local retail outlets and by subscription.

Kentucky Jewish Post & Opinion
1551 Bardstown Rd. • 459-1914

This is the local edition of a national weekly published in Indianapolis. It contains three or four pages of news of the local Jewish community with national and international news. Its coverage also includes sports, recipes and a media column assessing the portrayal of Jews in the media.

The paper is published every Wednesday. It is available at its office or by subscription.

Magazines

Louisville Magazine
137 W. Muhammad Ali Blvd. • 625-0100

Begun in 1950 by the Louisville Chamber of Commerce, *Louisville Magazine* grew over the decades into an interesting magazine well beyond the dimensions of the usual chamber production. It grew so interesting, in fact, that it sometimes found itself caught in the contradictions of journalistic independence and its ownership — most notably in 1988, when a rather mild article by local writer Dan Crutcher about changes at *The Courier-Journal* was killed, on the grounds that the magazine's policy was not to run critical articles about Chamber members such as the *Courier*. (The article later ran in *Business First*.)

That's unlikely to happen again. Crutcher bought the magazine in 1993, and he's been taking the magazine in a more hard-hitting, independent direction: It ran its first story on the AIDS epidemic, took an in-depth look at the strike at Fischer Packing Co. and profiled controversial Afrocentric minister Kevin Cosby. Editor Ronni Lundy, former Courier-Journal music critic and restaurant reviewer, has brought the magazine a liveliness that recalls the glory days of the *Louisville Times'* SCENE.

The magazine gives yearly Best of Louisville awards, voted on by readers and displayed throughout the city; it also provides extensive dining and calendar listings.

The Ragged Edge
PO Box 145, Louisville KY 40201
• fax 899-9562

Formerly *The Disability Rag*, this feisty, in-your-face alternative bimonthly magazine about issues of disability rights is published in Louisville, but it has a national circulation and scope. It has published strong work on actor Christopher Reeve, the FDR memorial and extensive coverage of assisted suicide.

Other Publications

Louisville Music News
P.O. Box 148, Pewee Valley KY 40056
• 241-2699

This free monthly publication covers the Louisville music scene exhaustively. It's strongest in its coverage of local songwriters (it grew out of the newsletter for the Louisville Area Songwriters Cooperative). But it writes about a wide swath of music, from bluegrass to all-ages punk, and boosts all scenes. It's known for lengthy cover interviews with local bands, which are sometimes informative and sometimes you-had-to-be-there.

Louisville Computer News
3900B Dupont Square South • 893-9147

A lively monthly publication, the *Louisville Computer News* was founded in November 1996 to cover the local computing scene — not so much about hardware and software but about the ways in which local businesses and individuals are using hardware and software. Features have included a look at buying a car on the Internet, a review of a local hospital web page paired with a look at how computers were being used in two local medical

---

INSIDERS' TIP

Well-informed slugabeds know that WFPL-FM plays NPR's *Morning Edition* for 4 hours weekday mornings, from 6 to 11 AM (playing the 2-hour newscast twice).

The Courier-Journal: A Glorious Past, An Uncertain Future

In 1986 newsman John Chancellor observed, "Louisville is not a large city, but *The Courier-Journal* behaves as though it were." That distinction has made this newspaper (and its ancestors) a point of local pride for a century and a half.

Few papers have a more distinguished history than *The Courier-Journal*. *The Louisville Journal* was the most widely circulated paper in the West from 1830 through the Civil War, mainly due to the editorials of George D. Prentice, a writer of unusual insight (although his legacy is darkened by the role his anti-immigrant editorials played in the "Bloody Monday" riot). In 1868, the Journal was merged with *The Louisville Courier* (its main rival, a secessionist paper that had spent much of the war behind Confederate lines). The new owners, the Haldeman family, hired *Journal* editor Henry Watterson, a Tennessean who had served reluctantly in the Confederate Army.

Close-up

History has betrayed Watterson. He was a man of his time in his patronizing attitudes toward African Americans (he was known as "Marse Henry," slave patois for Master Henry), but he was also an important spokesman for the idea that the New South should accept the post-bellum amendments to the Constitution and rebuild itself industrially. His advocacy of what appears to contemporary eyes as a more humane brand of racism was on the liberal side for his day; some credit him for preventing the Ku Klux Klan from having influence in Kentucky. A vivid writer published in magazines such as *Harper's* and *The Saturday Evening Post* and the author of bestselling books, the *Kentucky Encyclopedia* calls Watterson "the most widely quoted editor since Horace Greeley." He was also a national figure sometimes mentioned as a possible Democratic presidential candidate; in 1918 he won the Pulitzer Prize for editorials advocating the United States enter into World War I.

In 1918 the Haldemans sold the paper (and the afternoon *Louisville Times*) to the rising young politician Robert Worth Bingham, who had inherited $5 million after the death of his second wife, Mary Lily Flagler, the widow of multimillionaire Henry Flagler. Watterson left soon after when he and Bingham disagreed over the League of Nations. In 1933 Bingham became U.S. ambassador to the Court of St. James.

Bingham's son Barry Bingham Sr. took over the papers upon his father's death in 1937. Under his control — and especially under the editorship of Mark Ethridge — the *Courier* was the model of a newspaper operating in the public's interest. It became axiomatic that everything progressive that happened in Kentucky came about through the Binghams' influence. The papers also set important milestones in the newspaper business, hiring the first ombudsman in the country and the nation's first woman managing editor at a major metropolitan daily.

The Binghams were Louisville's, and Kentucky's, closest equivalent to the Kennedys — wealthy, powerful, liberal, blessed with fortune but cursed by fate: Worth Bingham, designated heir to his father as the papers' publisher, died in a freak 1966 accident, and a reluctant Barry Bingham Jr. (originally interested in the family's broadcast stations, WHAS radio and television) became editor and publisher in 1971. Barry Jr. believed in high ethical standards; he wielded the power of the *Courier* in a much less free-handed

— continued on next page

Photo: The Courier-Journal

Barry Bingham Sr., publisher of the *Courier-Journal* and patriarch of Kentucky's equivalent to the Kennedy clan.

fashion than his father had. He was criticized, especially after the sale of the papers, for an excessively rigid, distant and high-minded style; but three of the paper's Pulitzers were won on his watch, and his ideas about ethics were in the forefront of the news business.

The *Courier's* reputation has meant a slew of famous journalistic careers have included a stop there, from such venerable names as the *New York Times'* Arthur Krock to contemporary worthies such as Joel Brinkley, Howard Fineman and William Greider. (The most influential journalist Louisville ever spawned, Hunter S. Thompson, wrote a few freelance pieces for the paper at the start of his career.)

Rifts in the family, compounded by the difficulties of handing a family-owned corporation between generations, caused Barry Sr. to put all the family's media properties up for sale in January 1986. The announcement of the sale stunned the state: Some people in Louisville not intimately involved in the papers nonetheless acted as if their sale to Gannett was the end of their dearest dreams.

Louisville thought the Bingham tragedy resembled *King Lear*, but to the rest of the country it played like the plot line on *Dallas* in which Miss Ellie told Bobby and J.R. she was going to sell Ewing Oil if they didn't learn to cooperate. The family struggles made such an irresistible story of that type that an entire Bingham lit has sprung up; its volumes fill a small bookshelf (the best of the lot is *The Patriarch*, by Susan Tifft and Alex Jones, who won a Pulitzer for his coverage of the sale in *The New York Times*).

Complaining about the *Courier* is such a venerable tradition that you will still find people who hold grudges against the paper for something it did two owners ago. (Some older Louisvillians of German descent still resent Watterson's fierce editorials saying "To hell with the Hapsburg and the Hohenzollern!")

Many of the present-day complaints have a kill-the-messenger quality; others are ideological, or based in a perception that the paper favors either U of L or UK in its basketball coverage. If the words "the dominant liberal media culture" send you into a righteous rage, you will not like the *Courier*, even though its liberalism is moderated from the early '70s, when it was one of the few papers to endorse George McGovern's presidential candidacy (it viciously attacked the very idea of McGovern's brief candidacy for the 1992 nomination and took a rather hawkish attitude toward Central America in the 1980s). It was a lightning rod for community discontent when busing for school desegregation began in 1975 because it had editorially endorsed the court order that mandated the plan.

The sale to Gannett created a different kind of complaint: The fear that the *Courier* would change into an imitation of that company's flagship paper, the lightweight *USA Today*. As if to confirm these fears, shortly after Gannett took over, it closed *The Louisville Times* (a move the Binghams had been contemplating).

— continued on next page

These days, most observers would say that the *Courier* is clearly less than it was. The type and headline sizes are bigger, the stories shorter, the staff somewhat smaller (not through firings, but by attrition and early retirement deals) and the average day's paper seemingly thinner — although a master's candidate who studied the newspaper before and after its sale to Gannett said that budgeted new space increased by 41 percent between 1985 and 1991.

Gannett has largely kept Bingham-era personnel (not always to a happy effect). The fortunate holdovers include such astute political writers as Bob Garrett and Al Cross, big compassionate columnist Bob Hill (Louisville's closest equivalent to Mike Royko or Jimmy Breslin, but much less abrasive than either) and many talented reporters and feature writers. Some of the additions during the Gannett era, such as sports columnist Pat Forde, have been as good as any of the writers they joined.

In the first years after the *Courier* was sold, its editors and managers largely consisted of people who had come up under the Binghams. George Gill was tapped by Gannett as publisher after a career in which he'd been the *Courier's* managing editor and president of the Bingham companies. Gannett's first appointment as editor, Michael Gartner, was a respected journalist known for his work at *The Des Moines Register* and *The Wall Street Journal*; his next major post was as president of NBC News (although that didn't work out too well). But Gartner was only here briefly, as a transitional figure, and he was succeeded by longtime Bingham employee David Hawpe.

But Gill resigned the position in 1993 and was replaced by Edward Manassah, formerly of *The Desert Sun* in Palm Springs, California. Hawpe was replaced as editor in 1996 by Gannett employee Mark Silverman, and began writing an op-ed column. Silverman left in 1997 to become publisher and editor of the Detroit News and was replaced by Bennie Ivory, the first African American to serve as the paper's top news executive.

The *Courier* still has the talent pool and the inclination to free up reporters for major projects, and those often hit pay dirt; it just happens less often. It won a Pulitzer under Gannett for its coverage of the 1988 Carrollton bus crash. The *Courier* was one of the first newspapers to carefully examine the claims in political advertisements, in an easy-to-read format on the op-ed page that runs an image from the commercial, its script and an analysis of the ad's assertions. A week-long 1995 series about a year inside Highland Middle School was one of the most compelling pieces of journalism the *Courier* has ever printed — some of us woke up in the morning awaiting the next installment as eagerly as the crowds on the New York docks used to wait for the next number of Dickens' *The Old Curiosity Shop*.

The paper continues to cover the entire state and Southern Indiana, with regional bureaus in Lexington, Frankfort, Hazard, Elizabethtown, Bowling Green, Somerset, Paducah, Indianapolis and New Albany. It remains Kentucky's leading paper, although *The Lexington Herald-Leader* has pushed it hard in recent years.

The Courier-Journal largely continues the Bingham tradition of being averse to tabloid-style sensationalism. The local television news led two nights running with a "devil worship" story that amounted to nothing more than a few sallow dweebs vandalizing a park with occult graffiti. The *Courier* handled the incident in two paragraphs, in the "Regional Round-Up" column. Readers expect such restraint. When the *Courier* led one morning with the bizarre story of a Paducah man who killed his family and committed suicide with a hammer, outrage at such a trashy approach filled the paper's letter columns.

It remains a rather solemn paper — the major holdout being the Saturday SCENE section, formerly part of *The Louisville Times*, which will have readers submit David Letterman-style Top 10 lists or run stories judging whether Cole Porter or UK basketball player Kyle Macy is the more typical product of Peru, Indiana.

practices and a two-part examination of the high-tech job market in Louisville. It prints an annual roundtable on the state of the Internet and publishes a variety of useful charts. It's distributed free in bookstores, computer stores and other retail outlets and libraries.

Burt!
P.O. Box 4504, Louisville KY 40204
• 584-6241

This more-or-less monthly paper, which changes its name slightly with every issue, purports to be "The Official Burt the Cat Fan Club Newsletter." It often prints its feline namesake's "interviews" with celebrities, and Burt receives more fan mail than Randy Travis. But the paper is actually a wise-guy's take on local alternative culture: Comics, music shows, internet sites, restaurant reviews (by "Harry Roach") and a ton of record reviews by, as one issue put it, "a bunch of people with nothing better to do."

Its heart is probably editor (and Burt's owner) Paul Curry's continuing nightlife journal, which records one schlub's journey through the local music scene. The tone is reminiscent of the autobiographical comic-book authors (Joe Matt, Chester Brown, Harvey Pekar) that Curry loves — recording the petty particularity of life as it's led moment-to-moment. There's a lot of immature sniping at enemies, but also a surprising sense of drama.

And *Burt!* runs some fine writing — most notably Curry's piece on Hunter S. Thompson's homecoming appearance in Louisville, a clear-eyed report that was the only local article about the event that didn't get sucked into imitating Thompson's style — and lots of big pictures, many of them of semi-or-more-naked women (one issue that caused an uproar contained pictures of chest-baring women taken at Mardi Gras alongside excerpts from the *Norton Anthology of English Literature*).

Whatever the name is this month, *Burt!* is never dull, and it has the courage of its (occasionally misbegotten) convictions.

FYI

Unless otherwise noted, the area code for all phone numbers listed in this chapter is 502.

Television

Local television is much like it is anywhere: Network or cable-channel programming, local news that takes its lead from the police scanner and a few other locally produced shows. The stations are capable of doing good work — their tireless coverage of the 1997 floods vindicated all the money (and some of the promotional time) they sunk into helicopters — but in less urgent times they use some pretty weak excuses to draw an audience. (One recent low point: An "Ooh, cooties!" report on the beds at local hotels.)

WAVE Channel 3
725 S. Floyd St. • 585-2201

The local NBC affiliate and the first television station in Louisville, WAVE is now owned by Cosmos Broadcasting of Greenville, South Carolina. WAVE has one of the two most valuable sports franchises in town: It broadcasts University of Kentucky football and basketball games.

By most accounts, WAVE did the best job of covering the 1996 tornadoes which devastated parts of Bullitt County. Ever since, it's seriously challenged longtime leader WHAS as the place people turn during a weather emergency.

WHAS Channel 11
520 W. Chestnut St. • 582-7840

Formerly the Bingham family's television station, WHAS is now owned by A.H. Belo Corp. of Dallas. It is the local ABC affiliate (switching over from longtime network CBS a few seasons ago).

WHAS calls itself "Kentuckiana's News Channel," and it has led the way toward the present plethora of local news. WHAS was the first major station in the country to devote most of Saturday morning (7 to 11 AM) to a newscast that recaps the week's events. It provides local newsbreaks on CNN Headline News and produces *Louisville Tonight*, a nightly local feature magazine. Its technological point of pride is PowerCam, a helicopter-borne infrared camera.

In addition to ABC sports, WHAS carries

all-day coverage of the Kentucky Derby and the Kentucky Oaks.

WBNA Channel 21
3701 Fern Valley Rd. • 964-2121
An independent station owned by a local ministry, WBNA is also the local affiliate of the WB network, which means on Monday nights it segues from *Buffy the Vampire Slayer* to *Word Alive*. At other times it shows a mixture of religious programs, shopping shows, cartoons, pro wrestling, old movies and family-safe reruns. It also runs the weekly talk show of Dr. Frank Simon, an ultra-conservative allergist who is the bogeyman of local liberals.

WLKY Channel 32
1918 Mellwood Ave. • 893-3671
The local CBS affiliate, owned by Pulitzer Broadcasting, has long been the whipping-boy of the local media, regarded as the least stringent and most sensationalistic local news. But Pulitzer has been pouring resources into an effort to make WLKY the top station in town: a bunch of new hires (which promise to give it a larger staff than its competitors) and a $4 million expansion of its studios. It now broadcasts more hours of news than any other local station.

WDRB Channel 41
624 W. Muhammad Ali Blvd. • 584-6441
Originally an independent station, Channel 41 affiliated with FOX when that network started up. Its one-hour newscast at 10 PM is the most sober television news in town, despite some silly syndicated features. It also broadcasts U of L basketball, football, the coaches' shows and a weekly half-hour magazine devoted to the university's other sports teams. And it generally outbids the competition for the best sitcom reruns: It's where you'll see repeats of *Seinfeld*, *The Simpsons* and the like.

WTFE Channel 58
624 W. Muhammad Ali Blvd. • 584-6441
WDRB's sister station, affiliated with the fledgling UPN network, also carries a good selection of movies and syndicated series such as *Xena: Warrior Princess* and *Star Trek: Deep Space Nine*.

WKPC Channel 15
KET2 Channel 68
4309 Bishop Ln. • 459-9572
These two stations used to be a prime example of the unnecessary duplications caused by Louisville's bolixed relationship with the rest of Kentucky: The city had its own independent PBS affiliate, along with a translator for the statewide public network, KET. So often the stations duplicated programming ("Will I watch Masterpiece Theater on 15 or 68?") and the only advantage was a choice of different days and/or times for, say, *Frontline* or *Sesame Street*.

But when management and revenue problems forced WKPC to close and absorb into KET, it meant that the two stations became complementary, with Channel 15 serving as a classic public station, while KET2 runs PBS programming aimed at a baby-boomer-and-younger demographic (*P.O.V.*, *Sessions at West 54th*, *Charlie Rose*).

TKR Cable of Greater Louisville
1536 Story Ave. • 448-7750
The cable system for Louisville and Jefferson County supplies the channels familiar from systems throughout the country. But while most of the unincorporated part of Jefferson County has been wired with fiber-optic lines that bring an expanded roster of 80-plus channels, including many previously unavailable here — Comedy Central, Bravo, ESPN2, Court TV, VH-1, the Cartoon Channel, the Food Channel and E! — a face-off between TKR and the Board of Alderman has

INSIDERS' TIP

Louisville's unofficial class clown is Terry Meiners of WHAS-AM. When he brought a zany-morning-nutball approach to the city's most mainstream station, it was a small sign the world had changed.

kept city residents to about half as many. One optional tier, which corresponds to what used to be standard service, is "Plus 4," which, in addition to American Movie Classics, WGN of Chicago and Ted Turner's WTBS, offers the Disney Channel, usually a premium channel.

WYCS Channel 24
4421 Bishop Ln., Ste. 600 • 451-9000

Kentucky's first television station with African-American ownership, WYCS serves the African-American community with nationally-syndicated programs and a locally-produced talk show featuring *Courier-Journal* columnist Betty Baye. During the day it features movies of impressive vintage, health programs and reruns. Broadcast as UHF Channel 24, it's carried on TKR Channel 70 in Jefferson County; in Louisville, it airs from 11 AM to 5 PM weekdays, 9 AM to noon on Saturday and 7 to 10 AM Sunday on TKR Channel 8.

Radio

Louisville radio goes through the same format changes, ownership amalgamation and personnel shuffles as any other radio market.

And yet it's surprisingly stable.

WAMZ, a country FM station, holds the top spot with all listeners, as it has for years (Louisville is country when country isn't cool and when it is). Its program director, Coyote Calhoun — namesake of the city's biggest bar — is a major figure in the country business: He's been Billboard's On-Air Personality of the Year seven times, Program Director of the Year five (for mid-sized markets) and has won two Marconi Awards (the first non-syndicated personality to win twice). WAMZ was the Association of Country Music's Station of the Year in 1992.

It occasionally swaps off the top spot with

its AM sister, WHAS Radio, the first station in the market and a former Bingham property. (It's a bit of a rarity, another sign of Louisville's intense traditionalism, that this old-line, full-service AM station remains a major presence in the market.)

To our ears, the most exciting recent change in Louisville radio has been the Public Radio Partnership, which brought the city's three public stations under a common management. We used to have two classical stations and an NPR news/jazz/folk one. We now have all-news WFPL; all-classical WUOL; and WFPK, which plays the music you won't find anywhere else on the radio: A weekday afternoon jazz show; blues, bluegrass and worldbeat shows; and eclectic drive-time shows that fit into that fuzziest of radio concepts, "Triple A," or Adult Album Alternative.

The city still lacks a college station that really rocks (the biggest criticism of WFPK might be that it stresses the first A of its format a little too much) and there is no foreign community large enough to warrant its own station. Otherwise, the city runs the gamut, from stations that say "Rush" and mean the Canadian trio fronted by Geddy Lee, to stations that say "Rush" and mean the king of talk radio.

Metro Louisville Radio Stations

Adult Alternative
WFPL 91.9 FM (public-supported adult alternative, jazz, folk, blues and bluegrass)

Adult Contemporary
WDJX 99.7 FM (contemporary hits)
WVEZ 106.9 FM (soft adult rock)

INSIDERS' TIP

It's far away from the city, and its signal is such that it's hard to pull in until you reach the far eastern reaches of Jefferson County. But WKX-AM (1600) in Eminence, Kentucky, is a treat for the ears when you can pick it up. The station plays only bluegrass and traditional country: You're more likely to hear Hank Williams Sr. than Garth Brooks.

WKJK 1080 AM
WAVG 1450 AM (adult standards, big band)
WSJW 103.9 FM (smooth jazz)

Christian
WFIA 900 AM (Christian talk)
WXLN 1570 AM (southern country gospel)
WJIE 88.5 FM (contemporary Christian music)
WLLV 1240 AM (Black gospel)
WLOU 1350 AM (Black gospel)

Classical
WUOL 90.5 FM

Country
WAMZ 97.5 FM
WHKW 98.9 FM
WMPI 105.3 FM

News/Talk
WFPL 89.3 FM (NPR news, talk and public affairs)
WNAI 680 AM (CNN Headline News, news and sports talk)
WWKY 790 AM (news talk)
WHAS 840 AM (full service; local and syndicated talk shows; U of L and UK sports)
WLKY 970 AM (Associated Press news; simulcasts of WLKY-TV newscasts)

Oldies
WSFR 107.7 FM ('70s and '80s rock)
WRKA 103.1 FM ('50s, '60s, '70s hits)
WLSY 94.7 FM (R&B oldies)

Rock
WNAS 88.1 FM (student-selected rock from New Albany High School during the school year, 6 AM to 9 PM)
WTFX 100.5 FM (album rock)
WLRS 102.3 FM (alternative rock)
WQMF 95.7 FM (classic rock)
WRVI 105.9 FM (adult rock)

Sports
WTMT 620 AM (sports; races from Churchill Downs)

Urban
WGZB 96.5 FM
WMJM 101.3 FM (urban adult contemporary)

Louisville is a model
among U.S. cities for
interfaith cooperation.

Worship

Hollywood has taught us where the Old West was, but history books tell us that the Old, Old West was the wilds of Kentucky, the first frontier. It was a dangerous land, and the pioneers who settled here lived a rough life. They came to seek their fortune — or at least a decent living. Make no mistake, the settlement of Louisville was driven and marked by commerce, not religion. But once the land was "settled," the spiritual needs of the people needed attention.

A Baptist church was established in Bardstown, Kentucky, in 1781, and Squire Boone, Daniel's brother, reportedly traveled to Louisville to preach the city's first Baptist Sermon. The Rev. John Whitaker founded the Baptist Church of Beargrass here in 1784, and that faith has remained the dominant religion of the river city to this day.

Roman Catholics established a parish in Bardstown one year later, and branched up to Louisville in the following decades. Louisville remained enmeshed in tobacco, whiskey distilling and other forms of, shall we say, sinful business. Episcopalian settlers and ministers arrived around 1800, when Louisville's reputation remained rough — one Episcopalian minister was quoted in 1820 as saying that Louisville was a city where "much caprice and indifference toward religion prevailed."

The Presbyterian faithful welcomed their first minister in Louisville in 1800, and a Presbyterian clergyman presided over the funeral of city founder George Rogers Clark in 1818. Today, the Presbyterian Church U.S.A. has a strong presence. In fact, its national headquarters are in a large renovated building on Louisville's riverfront, the church's home since 1988.

In 1806, an itinerant Methodist preacher named Asa Shinn arrived in Louisville and pursued a different mission: converting the area's American Indians, sometimes with the help of tribal chiefs. The Methodists were fairly successful in this endeavor; the faith also proved popular among African Americans, perhaps due to the faith's intriguing mix of discipline and spirituality. Methodists still constitute a large part of Louisville's population. In contrast, their fellow Protestants the Lutherans didn't establish a church here until after the Civil War. The Lutheran church gained a foothold in Louisville, but it is still one of the lesser branches of Protestantism in the city.

Hard times in other parts of the world in the mid-1800s resulted in an influx of immigrants to the area, and with them came religious orders, especially Roman Catholic ones. Trappist monks from France established Gethsemani, their new abbey, in 1848. The locale became famous worldwide a century later when one of its monks, Thomas Merton, became one of the most widely read religious writers of the modern age. The Cathedral of the Assumption, a neo-Gothic structure on South Fifth Street, was built in 1852 and was believed to have been the tallest cathedral of its time in America. Catholics were a small minority in Louisville, but they counted among their number most of the Irish and German immigrants who were tightening up the city's job market and stirring ire among nationalistic Louisvillians. The low-paying jobs were going to the immigrants who were desperate to work.

Tensions worsened. When a papal delegate visited in 1853, he was burned in effigy. When the mayor of Louisville, a member of the prestigious Speed family, converted to Roman Catholicism during this era, his political career was nearly ruined. The Know-Nothing political party was a temporary but strong presence in American politics at this time, and Louisville was ripe for such demagoguery.

The anti-Catholic fervor boiled over one election day, Bloody Monday, August 6, 1855, when at least 22 Irish and German immigrants were shot in their neighborhoods, on the city streets and even on the courthouse lawn. At issue was the right to vote, which the Know-Nothings were denying to naturalized immigrants. *Louisville Journal* editor George Prentice did his part with editorials naming the Vatican "the prostitute of Satan," and calling for action. The new cathedral and St. Martin's Church would have been burned by angry mobs had Know-Nothing Mayor John Barbee not physically searched them with a group of men and announced the churches free of munitions. Ironically, the bloodshed helped Roman Catholics in the long run — by provoking sympathy and thus creating an atmosphere of tolerance that continues to this day.

During the Civil War, area churches felt the divisiveness that swept the nation. Denominations split along Northern and Southern lines, and groups such as the Southern Baptists were born. In one congregation, the organist played "Dixie" during the recessional and afterwards received a good talkin' to from the minister. Still, Louisvillians gathered in the Catholic Cathedral to mourn the dead from both sides of the conflict.

Catholics and Jews both pop up regularly in newspaper accounts of the last 100 years — not because their numbers were great, but because they weren't. It simply wasn't news when an Episcopalian man became mayor, but a Catholic one was another story. This notoriety has lessened; Louisville recently thrived under several terms of Mayor Jerry Abramson, and his Jewishness was hardly mentioned in news accounts.

The Jewish faith touched the city of Louisville long before Mayor Abramson — since the very beginning. George Rogers Clark's party that traveled down the Ohio River and founded Louisville was outfitted by Jews, Bernard and Michael Gratz of Philadelphia. However, the first synagogue wasn't built in Louisville, on Market Street, until 1843.

But by the 1880s, Jews had become a presence in Louisville, as Eastern Europeans migrated to the shores of the Ohio. It is said that at one point, Yiddish was heard more than English on Preston Street in downtown, and one Butchertown neighborhood was dubbed Jerusalem for a while.

The Jewish Community Center, a facility that welcomed Reformed and traditional Jews and non-Jews alike, traces its roots to 1862. Today, the Dutchmans Lane center provides activities raging from sports, arts, worship and day care to kosher lunches. It still maintains a vital library for Jewish studies. (See our Retirement or Parks and Recreation chapters.) In 1905 Jewish Hospital opened — as a necessity at first, as Jewish doctors weren't allowed full staff privileges at other local hospitals, and Jewish patients were inconvenienced by hospitals that didn't speak Yiddish and didn't honor kosher dietary laws. Jewish Hospital is now considered one of the nation's finest heart and lung treatment centers. (See our chapter on Healthcare.)

One of the nation's finest theological studies centers now resides at 2825 Lexington Road: the Southern Baptist Theological Seminary. In 1877 the seminary, now the second-largest in the world, opened its doors (at a another location). Today, a student body of almost 3,000 earn professional, master's and doctoral degrees in theology, church music, Christian education and church social work. In the last decade, ideological shake-ups among the faculty and administration of the seminary — mirroring the conflicts within the denomination — have shoved the institution considerably toward a conservative, fundamentalist stance. This transformation was quite public and rather ugly, with recriminations coming from deposed professors and steadfast administrators alike.

The Jewish Community Federation of Louisville opens two interfaith programs to the community annually: Yom HaShoah (Day of Remembrance), which usually falls in April and features a solemn program memorializing six million Jews and others who perished in the Nazi Holocaust; and Passover Seder, led in several Kentuckiana churches by Jewish congregation members to commemorate the Jews' exodus from slavery in Egypt.

The headquarters of Presbyterian Church U.S.A. is in Louisville.

In the late 19th century, Catholics and Protestants began to erect massive buildings that looked like cathedrals and reflected the region's ethnic heritage. St. John's Evangelical, at 637 E. Market Street, is a good example, with its ornate interior of fine German woodcarving. In contrast the Church of the Epiphany, a Roman Catholic parish founded 25 years ago in the northeast part of Jefferson County, meets in a church of modern, irregular hexagonal shape with large glass panels, and its politics in the past has mirrored this liberal style of architecture. But Louisville religion, as ably reflected in its church architecture, has always been conservative.

The town remains overwhelmingly Protestant. Church leaders often prove to be civic leaders as well, influencing public policy from the pulpit. This once capricious and religiously indifferent town has come to integrate religious ideas into its social and political fabric. Southeast Christian Church, a mega-church located in the far East County, has more than 10,000 members and facilities that rival a major university. Its conservative brand of Protestantism plays a significant role in local politics. Protestant African-American pastors in the city's West End often serve as a needed voice for the city's people, airing grievances to the government and corporations. Catholic grade schools, high schools and colleges are known for their quality education, with some schools perennially boasting a long waiting list.

Louisville is a model among U.S. cities for interfaith cooperation. Membership in Kentuckiana Interfaith Community includes churches, synagogues, the Board of Rabbis and Catholic Archdiocese, Presbyterian Church U.S.A., the African Methodist Episcopal Church, Indiana-Kentucky Synod/Evangelical Lutheran Church and others. It's a far cry from Bloody Monday.

Enough of the historical — what's happening this week in Louisville? For information about special events and news in local churches, check the *Courier-Journal's* regular religion column, located on the second page of the Metro section each Saturday.

Index of Advertisers

Index

Going Somewhere?

Insiders' Publishing Inc. presents 48 current and upcoming titles to popular destinations all over the country (including the titles below) — and we're planning on adding many more. To order a title, go to your local bookstore or call (800) 765-2665 ext. 238 and we'll direct you to one.

Adirondacks	Minneapolis/St. Paul, MN
Atlanta, GA	Mississippi
Bermuda	Myrtle Beach, SC
Boca Raton and the Palm Beaches, FL	Nashville, TN
Boulder, CO, and Rocky Mountain National Park	New Hampshire
Bradenton/Sarasota, FL	North Carolina's Central Coast and New Bern
Branson, MO, and the Ozark Mountains	North Carolina's Mountains
California's Wine Country	Outer Banks of North Carolina
Cape Cod, Nantucket and Martha's Vineyard, MA	The Pocono Mountains
Charleston, SC	Relocation
Cincinnati, OH	Richmond, VA
Civil War Sites in the Eastern Theater	Salt Lake City
Colorado's Mountains	Santa Fe
Denver, CO	Savannah
Florida Keys and Key West	Southwestern Utah
Florida's Great Northwest	Tampa/St. Petersburg, FL
Golf in the Carolinas	Tuscon
Indianapolis, IN	Virginia's Blue Ridge
The Lake Superior Region	Virginia's Chesapeake Bay
Las Vegas	Washington, D.C.
Lexington, KY	Wichita, KS
Louisville, KY	Williamsburg, VA
Madison, WI	Wilmington, NC
Maine's Mid-Coast	Yellowstone

THE INSIDERS' GUIDE ®

Insiders' Publishing Inc. • P.O. Box 2057 • Manteo, NC 27954
Phone (919) 473-6100 • Fax (919) 473-5869 • INTERNET address: *http://www.insiders.com*